# MANUFACTURERS AND PROCESSORS

UTILITIES

CONSTRUCTION

MANUFACTURERS

Food products
Wood products
Paper products
Printing and publishing
Chemicals
Petroleum and coal products
Rubber products
Leather products
Stone, glass and clay products
Metal industries
Machinery
Transportation equipment

# The Wiley Marketing Series

# SECOND EDITION
# MARKETING IN A CHANGING ENVIRONMENT

**Robert J. Holloway and Robert S. Hancock**

*University of Minnesota*        *University of Arizona*

John Wiley & Sons, Inc.   New York / London / Sydney / Toronto

This book was set in Melior by York Graphic
Services, and printed and bound by Vail-Ballou, Inc.
The text and cover were designed by Nancy Gruber.
The drawings were designed by John Balbalis and
executed by the Wiley Illustration Department. The
editor was Ronald Nelson. Dennis Hudson super-
vised production.

*Library of Congress Cataloging in Publication Data:*

Holloway, Robert J
  Marketing in a changing environment.

  (The Wiley marketing series)
  Includes bibliographies.
  1. Marketing, I. Hancock, Robert Spencer, joint au-
thor. II. Title.
HF5415.H7425 1972             380.1           72-7489
ISBN 0-471-40709-7

Printed in the United States of America

10-9 8 7 6 5 4 3 2 1

This book is dedicated to:

The late Roland S. Vaile
*Emeritus Professor of Economics and Marketing*
*University of Minnesota*

Harvey W. Huegy
*Emeritus Professor of Marketing*
*University of Illinois*

Who shaped the thinking and intellectual curiosity of a multitude of marketing students and who shared their time, abundant knowledge, and wisdom so generously with the authors.

# Preface

Our first effort, in 1968, to deal with *Marketing in a Changing Environment* was a logical evolution of the traditional approaches to marketing and a blending of environmental forces that were then just beginning to be recognized. Since our original volume, the adaptations of the environmental approach made by our colleagues and the increasing emphasis given to environmental constructs have been most encouraging. Our basic theme can be stated this way: "just as man is conditioned by and responsive to his environment, so our marketing system, its activities, and the marketing plans of firms must also be responsive to the environment." This revised edition builds upon that environmental approach. Through the addition of eight new chapters and the substantial revision of all the original chapters, we have strengthened our discussions of marketing institutions, their managerial phases, and the many social concerns facing marketers in a changing environment. The result is an expanded text which offers an environmental construct that is, we feel, more complete and integrative—and more teachable in the classroom.

How does this revised book fit into marketing curricula? It is intended for any introductory course in marketing, at either the undergraduate or the graduate level. It is designed to provide students with understanding of the many diverse and important principles of marketing. And it is devised both to serve their interests as potential business managers in the operational and managerial phases of marketing and to deal with their concerns as citizens in present and future social issues.

The organization of the volume in the following divisions indicates the general nature and major emphases of our approach to the study of marketing:

Part I     The Nature of Marketing in a Changing Environment
Part II    The Marketing Environment and Buyer Behavior
Part III   Marketing Management in a Changing Environment
Part IV   Social Issues in a Marketing Environment
Part V    Market Performance and the Future Environment

Part I, "The Nature of Marketing in a Changing Environment," first provides the student with a clear understanding of the origin and value of marketing in an advanced economic system. Chapter 2 then presents the essential idea of the firm as a subsystem of the marketing system. In addition to knowing about the role of the firm, at the introductory phase of study the reader needs to appreciate the vast complex of markets and market institutions that function in a changing environmental structure; this is the focus of Chapter 3. Because marketers' horizons today are worldwide there is an early exposure to other national environments in Chapter 4. A shrinking world and an expanding understanding of other social and economic systems promote an increasing appreciation of the universal application of contemporary marketing concepts and their impact on different life styles and cultures. This chapter permits us throughout the book—and an instructor throughout the course—to refer meaningfully to other marketing systems.

The core of this book is Part II, "The Marketing Environment and Buyer Behavior." Here we examine the several and diverse environmental influences and consider in detail both household buyer behavior and nonhousehold buyer behavior. A new chapter (5) in this section, "The Natural Environment and Marketing," introduces the concept that marketing managements can no longer avoid the impacts of their decisions on the natural habitat. The geography of marketing is also discussed in this chapter because the geographical character of a country influences many marketing decisions and practices. The economic, legal, and technological environments are presented in Chapters 6, 7, and 8. These chapters deal with the major environmental influences and constraints that affect the marketing activities of the firm, the nature of the forces in the marketplace, and the impacts they have on buyer behavior. "The Economics of Demand" (Chapter 9) provides the student with the basic economic considerations affecting buyer behavior and consumption. But buyer behavior and purchase decisions are also importantly influenced by noneconomic factors, and these are developed in the next four chapters (Chapters 10, 11, 12, and 13). Three of these chapters are concerned with the aspects of household buyer behavior and consumption, demographic variables, life-cycle and life-style influences, and relevant sociological and psychological forces. The many variables affecting buyer behavior are treated as internal and external forces and several models of buyer behavior are presented. Concluding this section is an examination of nonhousehold buyer behavior (Chapter 13), an area of marketing activity where many students may find their careers.

With an understanding of the diverse environmental forces acting on marketing, the reader will be prepared to study in Part III the actual marketing activities carried out by firms. This section, "Marketing Management in a Changing Environment," blends environmental concerns and influences with the practical aspects of the marketing manager's job. This part of the book has been substantially expanded to give additional emphasis to marketing channels, logistics, and pricing.

For many students and instructors the most provocative and stimulating section of this revision may well be the four new chapters in

Part IV, "Social Issues in a Marketing Environment." The extensively developed chapters on "Ethical Issues and Marketing," "Consumerism," "Marketing to the Disadvantaged," and "Turning Points for Marketing" offer one of the first major opportunities to integrate a consideration of the social issues related to marketing into the introductory course. This section should provide many opportunities for stimulating class discussion and debate, and it may suggest numerous study areas for worthwhile student projects. It was our aim in presenting these materials to provide a complete treatment of the discipline in an introductory course. We hope thereby to make the study of marketing more integrative, interesting, and challenging, and to leave the reader not only with many facts and principles to remember but also with many unresolved problems to reflect upon.

Finally, Part V, "Market Performance and the Future Environment," evaluates marketing from the viewpoint of society as well as that of the firm. The book closes with a lengthy and, we trust, stimulating presentation of numerous contemporary trends that may well shape the marketing system that the readers will experience at the height of their business careers.

To illuminate concepts and to clarify important principles, we have made a liberal use of illustrations and quotations that are closely integrated into the text. In many instances these materials have been reproduced from works of other authors. In addition to enriching our approach to the study of the discipline, the illustrations also expose the reader to viewpoints and approaches taken by other marketing academicians.

We are greatly indebted to many people for their generous insights and contributions. The manuscript was reviewed by Professor Donald Shawver, University of Missouri, Professor Eberhard E. Scheuing, Hofstra University, and Professor John Wish, University of Oregon. For their thoughtful suggestions and their help in shaping our insights we indeed express our appreciation. Robert A. Peterson, University of Texas, made many helpful suggestions in addition to handling most of the development of the Instructor's Manual. We are grateful for the tireless efforts of our secretaries—Mary Jo Loso, University of Minnesota, and Bernice Grenier, The University of Arizona—who greatly assisted in the preparation of the manuscript and other materials. Without their loyal and high-quality assistance, the task of revising the book would have been immeasurably greater. Finally we are indebted to Ronald Nelson, of John Wiley & Sons, for his editorial guidance and many excellent suggestions. No book is a product of a few people, and our many colleagues, graduate students, and students in introductory classes have, through their comments and suggestions, substantially enhanced the quality of our approach. We are most grateful for their continuing interest and the strength they have brought to bear in advancing the marketing discipline.

Robert J. Holloway

Robert S. Hancock

# CONTENTS

# THE ENVIRONMENT

**NATURAL**

**HUMAN**

Ch. 1. Marketing and society
Ch. 2. The firm and its marketing environment
Ch. 3. Markets and marketing institutions
Ch. 4. Marketing in different environments

# PART I

# THE NATURE OF MARKETING IN A CHANGING ENVIRONMENT

*Separation of the producer from the consumer sector of the economy results in specialization, which is the basis of trade, or marketing. The marketing system and the firm are devices that man has designed to serve his needs and wants. Both man and marketing are constantly adapting to the ever-changing total environment.*

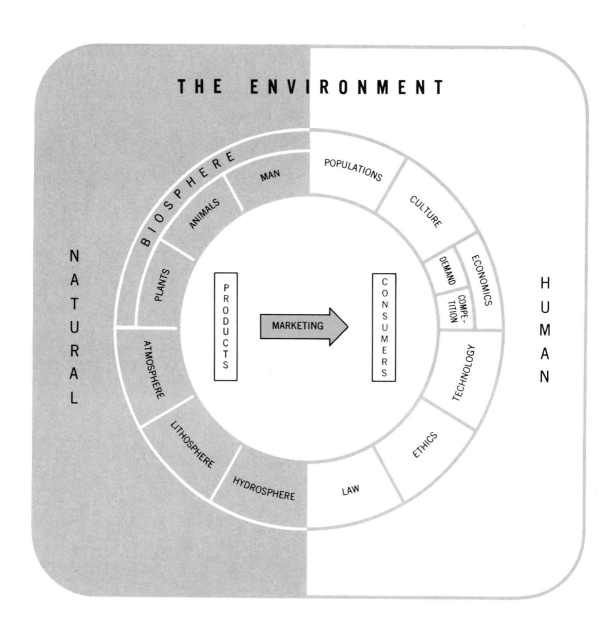

# CHAPTER 1
# MARKETING
# AND SOCIETY

*Marketing, which originates in human adaptation to the environment, has its foundations in money, marketplaces, and specialization. Marketing creates particular values for society as it links producers and consumers.*

If we lived in a simple, small, and isolated society we would have little trouble in explaining, analyzing, and evaluating marketing. Our answers to questions about our society, the economic behavior of individuals, the institutions that make up our marketing system, and the consumption of goods and services would be relatively simple. But our society is highly complex, large, and at the center of the world stage. It is made up of millions of diverse interdependent units, and no easy answers present themselves to queries about our society and marketing.

As a social science, marketing is concerned with individuals' behavior as consumers, with the behavior of the institutions engaged in marketing, and with the consumption of goods and services. As a first step in investigating the field, it will be helpful to know something about the origin of marketing. This knowledge will help us to develop our definition of marketing with more clarity.

## THE ORIGIN OF MARKETING

The human being, a highly ingenious creature, has always devised and invented things to serve his well-being. Our present society, culture, and economic development evolved through human ingenuity over a long period of time. In primitive societies each family unit supplied most material needs by itself, producing its own food, building its own shelter, and making its own garments. Needs were few and the material goods available were scarce. Even a person in a primitive society associated with others in that society, of course, and if his needs could not be met by his work, he might find someone with whom he could engage in barter trade. But barter is an inefficient method of acquiring goods and services. Imagine the time and effort necessary to acquire your needs if you had to run from person to person asking whether he or she would agree to barter trade. Imagine also the preposterous situation if your available assets were nine camels of various ages and questionable health and what you wanted was a color television set.

The operation of barter trade, which is still carried on to a limited extent, is shown in 1-1. As a society advances from the level of self-sufficiency, this method of acquiring goods and services would not serve the economy and society very well. As an economy develops, many forces come into play and people respond by creating many forms of social and economic organizations. In adapting to a changing environment, people have devised three basic ingredients to serve their demand for goods and services. These are money, specialization, and markets in which to carry on exchange, and they are the foundations on which our modern industrialized society, our economy, and our marketing rest.

## Money

Money permits a society to evaluate all goods and services in terms of a standard unit. When all goods and services are taken to be "worth" some amount of money, it becomes easy to compare values. Money, then, serves as a common medium of exchange and as a common denominator for expressing all exchange rates. Because of its great utility practically all societies use some form of money. Certainly a monetary system is essential to a modern industrialized society. For businesses the system makes the pricing of its goods and services easy—and in addition it makes the purchase decisions of consumers easy to evaluate and contemplate. Anyone who has money (or credit) is in a position of equality in relation to a person who has goods and services. It becomes a simple matter to switch money for goods. In contrast, imagine the great costs, wastes of time and energy, and difficulties of trying to operate by barter trade. The role of money as a facilitator of exchange is often overlooked. But because of money, rather than spend time engaging in barter, people can specialize in the production of goods and services.

## Specialization

Few of us produce any of the numerous goods and services we consume. Rather than devote our time to the many tasks needed to meet our needs, we find great social and economic advantage in performing a single task. Society learned long ago that self-sufficiency is inefficient, time-consuming, and wasteful of human resources. Even primitive societies acknowledge that individuals possess unique skills. Some might be skilled in fishing, others in hut construction, and still others in weaving. Thus a division of labor enhances productive efficiency

**1-1** Operation of Barter Trade

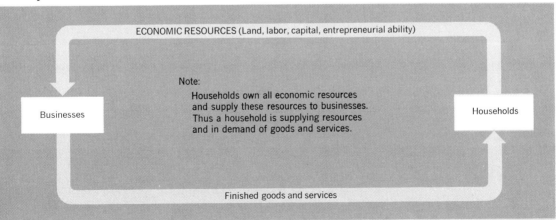

ECONOMIC RESOURCES (Land, labor, capital, entrepreneurial ability)

Businesses

Households

Note:
Households own all economic resources and supply these resources to businesses. Thus a household is supplying resources and in demand of goods and services.

Finished goods and services

in several ways. First, it takes advantage of individual differences in abilities and skills. Second, specialization saves and makes the best use of a worker's time, for through it the loss of time entailed in shifting from one task to another is avoided. Finally, specialization improves the general quality of the productive outputs enjoyed by society. For the most part, goods and services improve in quality when they are produced by specialists as contrasted with jacks-of-all-trades.

In a complex and economically advanced society the occupations (that is, skills) become very numerous. There are thousands of specialized tasks to perform. In the United States, for example, there are approximately 78 million workers. More than 70 million of them are either full- or part-time nonagricultural employees in the several industrial groupings shown in 1-2. Only 3.5 million are employed in agriculture and the remainder are unemployed. As an economy advances and becomes more and more industrialized and as scientific and technological discoveries are applied to the production of man's needs, the number of workers declines in agriculture. As recently as 1950 the United States had more than 7 million people employed in agriculture, but with vast scientific, technological, and ownership changes in this segment of the economy, the number of employees declined 50 percent by 1971. Other changes in the specialized work of our society can be observed in 1-2. What accounts for the decline in employees in manufacturing and the marked increase in employment in government and service industries between 1950 and 1970?

Our society and economy are so highly geared to the principle of specialization that every facet of our lives is influenced by it. We specialize because we can better serve ourselves and society by working for salaries and wages and in turn exchanging our money for the goods and services we need and desire. Most of us are neither capable nor desirous of being self-sufficient. And even if we were, we would be very poor indeed. It is precisely because of our complex system of specialization and our ability to exchange money for things that we enjoy the abundances and luxuries of a modern-day economic system.

By the same token specialization is desirable for countries and geographical regions. California, for example, produces more oranges than the residents could possibly ever need; Oregon and Washington have enough trees to rebuild every house in the United States; and the harvest of lobsters in Maine is much in excess of the needs and tastes of the local population. Each region finds it economically desirable to specialize, producing a product greatly in excess of regional needs, and to trade one with another. Specialization and exchange permit each region to make the best use of its economic resources. In this way each region enjoys both more of its own products and more of the products of other regions.

In short, geographic and human specialization are both prerequisite to the efficient use of economic resources. Even though the concept of specialization is almost self-explanatory, it is essential to an understanding of production and marketing in a modern society.

## Markets

The third ingredient essential to the origin of marketing is a market. How would an individual, country, or region engage in trade without a marketplace? A market, defined more precisely in Chapter 3, is any place or institution in which exchange can be negotiated. Usually markets are concentrated in some well-defined geographical area—a town, a city, or at least a group of people living near one another. Marketing communications about buying or selling are registered in

**1-2** Distribution of Nonagricultural Employees, 1970 (Exclusive of Alaska and Hawaii)

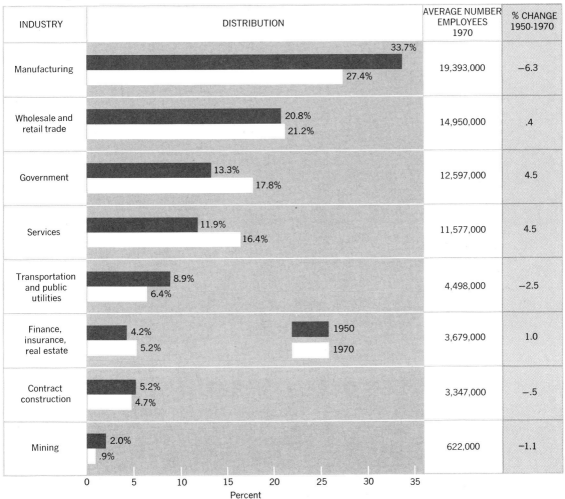

| INDUSTRY | DISTRIBUTION | AVERAGE NUMBER EMPLOYEES 1970 | % CHANGE 1950-1970 |
|---|---|---|---|
| Manufacturing | 33.7% / 27.4% | 19,393,000 | −6.3 |
| Wholesale and retail trade | 20.8% / 21.2% | 14,950,000 | .4 |
| Government | 13.3% / 17.8% | 12,597,000 | 4.5 |
| Services | 11.9% / 16.4% | 11,577,000 | 4.5 |
| Transportation and public utilities | 8.9% / 6.4% | 4,498,000 | −2.5 |
| Finance, insurance, real estate | 4.2% / 5.2%   ■ 1950  □ 1970 | 3,679,000 | 1.0 |
| Contract construction | 5.2% / 4.7% | 3,347,000 | −.5 |
| Mining | 2.0% / .9% | 622,000 | −1.1 |

Percent

SOURCE: U.S. Department of Commerce, Bureau of the Census, *Statistical Abstract of the United States, 1971* (Washington, D.C.: GPO, 1971).

a market. If a student, for example, wants to buy or sell a used car there is a market where he can get the greatest amount of information about possible exchange opportunities. The market system for buying and selling and getting information has proved to be an efficient way to acquire goods and services.

Another characteristic of markets is the presence of specialized agents, brokers, retailers, wholesalers, and establishments such as mill supply houses and bulk plants that provide a place or a method for potential buyers and sellers to meet. Thereby, through communication devices, all consumers and all institutions can get information about products and services and exert their choices.

Markets are a basic organizing force for all societies. In a capitalistic system the preferences of all buyers and sellers are registered on either the supply or demand side of the various markets. The outcome of these preferences is a system of pricing made possible by the use of money in the exchange process. The prices in the market are the device with which consumers, businesses, and all owners of resources register their choices so as to further their own welfare and self-interests. Through the system of markets and prices society makes decisions on what the economy should produce, how production is to be organized, and how the rewards of productive endeavor are distributed to the economic units that make up capitalistic society.

Now that money, specialization, and markets have been discussed as the essential ingredients of economic activity, we can show the general operation of a capitalistic economy. In 1-3 the counterclockwise flow is of economic resources that create goods and services, and the clockwise flow is of money. Households supply land, labor, capital, and entrepreneurial ability to the resource markets from which businesses produce goods and services. In turn, goods and services flow to the product markets and are consumed by households. Households receive money income for supplying the resource markets. Money income then becomes consumption expenditures for the purchase of goods and services. Consumption expenditures flowing through the product markets become receipts for businesses from which they meet their costs, and so on to complete the flow of money. The demand and supply functions of the households, businesses, and markets are shown for the inner loop. These functions obviously are reversed for the outer loop flow of money.

Observe that 1-3 is devoid of certain facts and implications on the workings of the economy. Government, for example, plays no role in this flow process. Actually, the American economy is not purely capitalistic and government plays a role in regulating the economic system. It is often referred to as "mixed capitalism," for government sets up rules and policies, and it influences the decisions made in each sector of the economy. Be that as it may, the circular flow is a generalized look at the economy, and it is helpful in understanding marketing.

### Marketing—A Subset of the Economic System

We have shown that money, specialization, and markets are essential to the operation of our economy. Each of these elements is essential

**1-3** Operation of Markets in a Monetary Economy

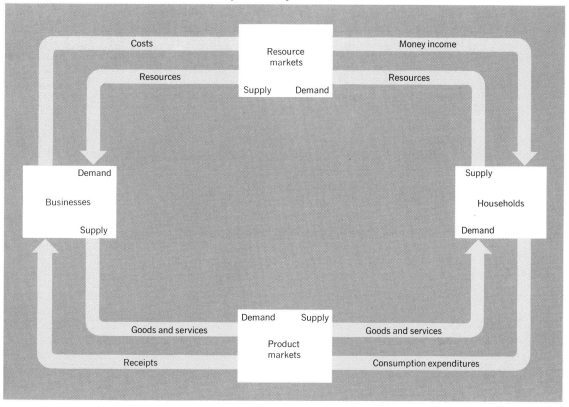

to exchange, by means of which people acquire goods and services. How do the three essential ingredients of the economic system relate to marketing? The answer is that a *marketing system is a subset of the economic system*. The goal of marketing activities, and the goal of our complex marketing system, is the exchange of goods and services. The same basic elements that are supportive and essential to the economy are also necessary to the marketing system.*

The size and importance of marketing vary from one society to another. In a society at an advanced stage of development such as the United States, marketing constitutes a major segment of the economy. In an economically poor society the extent of marketing, in general, will be limited and consonant with a depressed economic system. But in each instance marketing is still a subset of the total economic system and thus relative to its size and complexity.

*The term *marketing system* refers to all the interrelated components of marketing designed to accomplish a common goal. Throughout the course of study of marketing, analysis of the system is a frequent exercise. Analysis of a system, while appraising the performance and adequacy of each component individually, focuses on the interrelationships among the components. The marketing system and marketing activities are discussed in more detail in Chapter 2.

# MARKETING DEFINED

The focus of marketing is the exchange of goods and services. It requires a party of a sale and a party of a purchase. In a modern economy with a monetary system and prices, goods or services are exchanged for money. Marketing takes place in the circular flow of goods and services and money, as shown in 1-3 at several places. To simplify the process we can visualize marketing in the following sequential process.

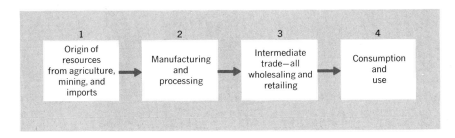

Marketing takes place as resources are sold to industrial institutions; it takes place as fabricated goods move to intermediate trade; and it takes place as goods are consumed and/or used by households, industrial firms, institutions of all kinds, and governments. This process is explained in detail in Chapter 2, but at this point it is important to recognize the flow of goods and services through the major sectors of the economy. As one sector markets to another sector, and that one to the next, exchange takes place. Our definition, then, is: *Marketing is a set of activities necessary and incidental to bringing about exchange relationships in our economic system.*

This definition emphasizes that a set of activities is needed to bring about exchange. What are these activities? Clearly products must be designed and developed, branded, packed, shipped, and distributed to buyers. Goods also have to be stored at strategic geographical points; information about the products must be communicated to the market and prospective buyers; and of course a price must be established at which the product can be purchased. Often research is employed concerning products, markets, and many other facets of the marketing process. Services, although intangible, involve most of these same marketing activities. We, therefore, can organize all marketing activities under the following headings:

1. Marketing research.
2. Product—including product development.
3. Distribution—including marketing channels and marketing logistics.
4. Pricing—including price policies and price practices.
5. Marketing communications—including advertising, personal selling, and other communicative devices.

A major portion of this text (Part III) explores these several marketing activities. They are treated there within the context of a changing environment, the central theme of this text.

Because of the complexity of marketing, its dynamic character, its economic importance, and its management implications, perhaps no single definition of marketing can serve the student. Marketing has certainly been defined in many different ways, and each definition serves to convey a particular point of view or a particular approach. An idea of the diversity is revealed in the following statement.

> Marketing has been described by one person or another as a business activity; as a group of related business activities; as a trade phenomenon; as a frame of mind; as a coordinative, integrative function in policy-making; as a sense of business purpose; as an economic process; as a structure of institutions; as the process of exchanging or transferring ownership of products; as a process of concentration, equalization, and dispersion; as the creation of time, place, and possession utilities; as a process of demand and supply adjustment; and many other things. (Marketing Staff, The Ohio State University, 1965.)

A number of selected definitions are shown in 1-4. They reveal various frames of reference. Marketing is all the things stated and implied in these definitions. It involves business activities, it relates to the flow of goods and services, it affects the transfer of ownership, it creates utilities for society, it deals with potential market relationships, it is part of the productive process, and it is a management function.

We suggest that more than one definition be applied in the study of marketing. Throughout most of this text we adhere to our definition that *marketing is a set of activities necessary and incidental to bringing about exchange relationships in our economic system.* It serves well in characterizing marketing as a subset of the economic system; it characterizes the flow processes leading to exchange; it supports the values created by marketing for society; and it implies that marketing is needed to influence and actuate consumption and the use of goods and services.

But there is a point at which we would like to interject a managerial emphasis into the study of this subject. In Part III we deal with the activities of marketing under the title "Marketing Management in a Changing Environment." For this section we need a descriptive definition that conveys the interrelationship of management and marketing activities. Thus: *Marketing management analyzes, plans, organizes, implements, and controls marketing activities. Its goal is to bring about mutually beneficial exchange with customers in the market. Marketing management adapts and coordinates research, products and services distribution systems, prices, and market communications for achieving its goal(s).*

## 1-4

The performance of business activities that direct the flow of goods and services from producer to consumer or user. (American Marketing Association, 1960.)

Marketing covers all business activities necessary to effect transfers in the ownership of goods and to provide for their physical distribution. (Beckman and Davidson, 1967.)

Marketing includes all the activities involved in the creation of place, time, and possession utilities. (Converse, Huegy, and Mitchell, 1965.)

Marketing is the analyzing, organizing, planning, and controlling of a firm's customer-impinging resources, policies, and activities with a view to satisfying the needs and wants of chosen customer groups at a profit. (Kotler, 1967.)

Marketing is the performance of business activities which direct the flow of goods and services from producer to consumer or user in order to satisfy customers and accomplish the company's objectives. (McCarthy, 1971.)

Marketing, in the full sense of the word, must involve change in ownership: physical movements merely facilitate this change or make possible the use of the commodity by the new owner. All the rights, privileges, and responsibilities, either of use or of further sale, attach to ownership and are passed on with change in ownership. (Vaile, Grether, and Cox, 1952.)

Marketing . . . any activity which actualizes the potential market relationship between the makers and users of economic goods and services. (Cox, Alderson, and Shapiro, 1964.)

Marketing is part and parcel of the modern productive process, the part at the end that gives point and purpose to all that has gone before. Marketing is getting the product to the consumer. (U.S. Department of Agriculture, 1954.)

Marketing includes all those operations of a business system that are involved in determining and influencing existing and potential demand in the marketplace. (Lipson and Darling, 1971.)

---

In recent years the term *social marketing* has come into use among marketers. This term is used to describe the use of marketing techniques, practices, and concepts by nonbusiness institutions such as fund-raising agencies, churches, hospitals, symphony societies, art museums, and even governments. Philip Kotler and Gerald Zaltman define social marketing in the following way:

> Social marketing is the design, implementation, and control of programs calculated to influence the acceptability of social ideas and involving considerations of product planning, pricing, communi-

cation, distribution, and marketing research. (Kotler and Zaltman, 1971.)

They continue by saying, "It is the explicit use of marketing skills to help translate present social action efforts into more effectively designed and communicated programs that elicit desired audience response." In other words, marketing techniques can be the bridging mechanisms between the possession of knowledge and the socially useful implementation of what knowledge allows.

Most of us have witnessed marketing being applied for a social cause. The Peace Corps, Vista, safety campaigns by the National Safety Council, and Amtrak are only a few of the numerous examples of social marketing. The authors believe there are rapidly expanding opportunities to apply marketing analysis and marketing know-how to many of our national issues. Deficiencies in medical care, inadequate mass transportation, ecological crises, and products harmful to society are possible problem areas in need of good marketing to draw public attention and support for solutions. Marketing techniques may be used to deal with social issues in much the same way as they are applied to goods and services. The potential for application of the concept of social marketing is great. Appropriately, then, the concept of social marketing and the way it is defined will find their way into a portion of this study of marketing.

## THE VALUES OF MARKETING

As a subset of the economic system marketing contributes certain specific values to society:

1. The creation of time, place, and possession utilities.
2. The serving of the material and service needs of society.
3. The provision of a communications network for the functioning of the economic system.
4. The advancement of economic welfare.
5. The fostering of social and economic change.

### Time, Place, and Possession Utilities

In the common view our economic system is a process of *production* and *consumption*. The production phase of the process results in the creation of *form* utility, which is the difference between the value of raw materials and the value of objects shaped from them. For example, a quantity of wood is more valuable when it is fabricated into the shape of a chair. But the chair, even though it is a finished article, cannot as yet satisfy a human want. For it to be of value to a buyer it must be available in the market, it must be purchased by a buyer at a money price, and it must be put to use in home, factory, office, school, or elsewhere. Thus the concept of the economy as only a process of production and consumption is incomplete. In a broader perspective, the system is *the allocation of needed resources through production and marketing to the consumption and use sector of the economy.**

In order to have value and in order to satisfy a human want a product must have more than form utility. It also must have time, place, and possession utilities. These are values of great importance to all buyers in a market, and they are created by our marketing system. Time utility must be planned by manufacturers in the production and subsequent physical distribution of goods. Storage, for example, is a direct result of providing a time value to goods. Transportation and the location of goods at places where they are demanded create place utility. Possession utility is created by transfers of ownership through the exchange mechanism of the economy; it is simply a matter of getting goods into the hands of processors, merchants, consumers, or any other economic unit that needs or desires them. Selling, establishing credit terms, and transferring title are some of the activities that facilitate possession utility.

A physical good with mere form utility has no value *per se*. It has value only when a marketing system exists to create the other necessary utilities. Milk on the farm, automobiles at the factory, lumber at the mill, and beer at the brewery are not the same commodities as milk in the supermarket, automobiles in the parking lot, lumber at the construction site, and beer in the refrigerator. To each of the latter have been added time, place, and possession utilities. These utilities make it possible to acquire goods and thus satisfy human needs. Indeed, the value of any commodity is enhanced by the values created by the marketing system. If our economic process was only one of *production* and *consumption,* there would be a vast gap between the physical output of firms and the eventual satisfaction of human wants.

## Serving Our Needs

Everyone relies on marketing to acquire goods and services; indeed, our involvement with marketing is so extensive that lives, life styles, societies, and even cultures are directly influenced by it. As consumers we are all familiar with those markets in which we customarily shop and purchase. Because of our familiarity with retail markets it may appear that the marketing of goods and services for an entire economy is a simple matter. But retail markets constitute only a part of an elaborate marketing system. Not only do we as consumers acquire goods and services through markets, but so do governments, industries, and many other institutions.

In an economy of abundance, such as that of the United States, huge quantities of goods and services are needed. The task of supplying them

---

*In many instances consumers do not actually consume a product, rather they "use" it and then discard it. The authors suggest that *consumers are the temporary users of fabricated materials.*

is accomplished through two general categories of markets: household and nonhousehold. Household markets serve the needs of all families and all other individuals. Nonhousehold markets serve the needs of industries, institutions, and governments. This classification is shown in 1-5.

**1-5** Classification of Markets

| HOUSEHOLD MARKETS | NONHOUSEHOLD MARKETS | | |
|---|---|---|---|
| | Industrial | Institutional | Governmental |
| All families—People tied by kinship residing in a common domicile.<br><br>All individuals—Single or grouped together in a common domicile. | All manufacturing, fabricating, milling, processing, and other industrialized enterprises. | All institutions such as hospitals, churches, colleges, and universities. (Usually nonprofit.) | All political subdivisions—federal, state, regional, local, and municipal political bodies. |
| Serviced by: the reselling by wholesalers; retailers; and other, nonstore, dealers. | Serviced by: Merchant wholesalers, manufacturers' sales outlets, merchandise agents, petroleum bulk plants and terminals, and assemblers of farm products. (*Note:* Industrial terminology often makes reference to wholesalers as "industrial distributors.") | | |

The many business institutions needed to accomplish the huge task of these markets are known as "marketing intermediaries" or "marketing middlemen." Some of the more common marketing institutions serving the markets of our economy are also shown in 1-5.

## Fostering Communications

When considering the purchase of a product, where is the best place to get full information about it? If you want to buy or sell a used bicycle, for example, you can get information about possible exchange opportunities with little cost and effort in the market. Information is obviously one of the services that markets provide to buyers and sellers. You might advertise, and thus publicly inform other people of your desire to buy or sell a bicycle. Advertising is oftentimes the lowest-cost method of locating potential buyers and sellers.

Through marketing the function of communicating information about the market and its available goods and services is performed. Sellers pass information to markets through promotion and receive information in return as feedback of their promotion efforts. Marketing communication is accomplished by means of advertising and personal selling. The seller may use radio, television, newspapers, magazines, or salesmen. Customers receive information from the market with little effort, their search time is reduced, and their knowledge about possible market offers is enhanced.

Marketing provides a communications network that can be used by all sellers and resellers in the marketplace. The goal of information conveyance is most often the stimulation of a purchase. A simplified flow of information from a consumer-goods manufacturer can be characterized as shown at left.

To each audience different kinds of information flow. To other manufacturers salesmen with technical backgrounds carry the message. To wholesalers and retailers salesmen and media emphasize gross margins, turnover, and profit potentials. To the consumer the mass media encourage purchase at a retail store.

## Advancing Economic Welfare

An important consequence of exchange is that the parties to a transaction are better off. Earlier we stressed that specialization gives rise to exchange. If there were no exchange each specialist in producing something would have large quantities of his specialty on hand. Markets and marketing activities permit us to engage in exchange and acquire other things that we cannot produce. Specialization permits us to produce some things beyond our own immediate needs, but at the same time we cannot efficiently devote our time to producing the other things we need. Because specialization is an efficient producer of goods and services, we are eager to exchange and acquire the things we lack. An actual purchase means we value the object or service purchased more than the money price we pay. Correspondingly, whoever sells the object or service values the money paid as being equivalent to (or worth even more than) the thing sold. In this way we satisfy our personal needs for goods and services and the merchant has traded for money income. Each member of an exchange transaction is better off, in terms of either money acquired or goods and services acquired. Extend this simple explanation to an entire economy and you can better understand how our marketing system delivers the necessities, conveniences, and luxuries of modern life. Not all marketing enhances social and economic welfare, of course, but more often than not it does.

## Fostering Social and Economic Change

In a profound way social and economic change depends on values. The values of a society dominated by religious and mystical beliefs will be reflected in life styles, products, and even the general characteristics of the market. Such a society is likely to place emphasis more on spiritual traditions than on material comforts. In contrast, the United States and other industrialized nations evaluate material things in terms of convenience, comfort, and improved life style, as we conceive it. What measure of influence does marketing have in shaping society and changing cultural traditions? There is no straightforward answer to this question. But it is known that the abundance of material goods and mass communications media affect our basic values. Marketing as an instrument of social and economic change plays a pivotal role in changing individual and family life. The automobile, television, processed foods, wearing apparel, birth control pills, and a host of other products have facilitated changing tastes and changing cultural patterns. As you progress in your study of marketing you will have many opportunities to evaluate the impact of marketing on society and how marketing affects change in the economy. If, as we believe, marketing has the power to influence our value system, then marketing people have responsibilities that are complex and yet apparent.

## THE COST OF MARKETING

Although marketing provides society with a number of indispensable values and advantages, it levels costs on each and every user of the system. Everything acquired costs money, but only a portion of the value is attributable to the cost of production. Another portion can be charged to marketing. It is not an easy matter, however, to define the output of marketing. Product costs can be clearly isolated because they are tangible, but much of marketing results in intangible values, such as time, place, and possession utilities. Whether marketing is viewed as creating intangible values or as delivering a bundle of satisfactions, the measurement of marketing costs is difficult.

There have undoubtedly been advances in marketing productivity. Over time there has been and continues to be an increasing quantity of goods and services distributed to society; more goods are moved by the marketing mechanism over greater distances; and more people enjoy more products and services provided with convenience and improved economies of scale. Yet there are no precise measures of such advances. In those studies that have been undertaken, the estimated marketing costs are separated from the formative (production, processing, and any form of fabrication) costs in the whole economy. Yet there have been a few attempts to separate marketing costs and formative costs for selected industries and individual firms.

In separating approximate expenditures for the production of goods and costs for the marketing of goods several investigators have come close to a 50–50 division. Reavis Cox estimated that, overall, marketing costs in the mid-1960s represented 41.7 percent of the final buyers' dollars (Cox, 1965). Another study dating back to 1948 attributed 51.9 percent to production and 48.1 percent to marketing.

If marketing costs can be reduced by increased efficiency and if this saving is passed on to purchasers in lower prices, then society will be well served by the increased productivity of the marketing system.

## THE ENVIRONMENTAL APPROACH TO MARKETING

At the outset of this chapter we described marketing as a social science concerned with the behavior of consumers, with the behavior of institutions engaged in marketing, and with society's purchase and use of goods and services. Our discussion has shown how marketing evolves, how it benefits society, and how difficult it is to define in precise terms. As a social science it is a broad and complex discipline; to deal with the elements noted, marketing scholars draw from other disciplines to sharpen their analysis and understanding. Thus marketing is an eclectic discipline that recognizes and synthesizes all doctrines, methods, and principles that contribute to an understanding of marketing phenomena. Scholars from many fields—economics, sociology, psychology, anthropology, law, philosophy, history, and ecology—have made significant contributions to marketing thought. And marketing scholars have been adaptive in applying selected doctrines to improve and formulate marketing thought.

By its very nature marketing will be influenced by the environment in which it is carried on. The environment of marketing also harbors a number of forces that generate change in a marketing structure. If these forces and the environment of marketing explain its existence, character, and dimensions, then it is desirable to study marketing within an environmental framework.

## The Global Environment

The global, or total, *environment* is an enormously complicated, dynamic, changing system. It is the sum total of all forces and conditions that act on an organism or communities of organisms, including man. Marketing, as a work of man, is a part of this global environment, and as such it is constantly influenced by the various forces that operate in our "web of life." *The response by marketing people to the dynamic environment determines how successful a business firm will be in serving its customers and ultimately in making profits.*

One part of this global environment is the natural system, which in the past few years has become increasingly taken into account by business. The interrelationships among the components of the natural system are shown below.

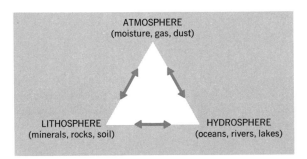

Each of these components has resources—such as coal from the ground, fish from the lakes, or crops from the soil—that are utilized economically and ultimately marketed in some form. Note that these examples are all organic. In fact, the organic component is so distinctive that it can be conveniently separated out. The living organisms in these three spheres are collectively called the *biosphere*—the sum total of life on earth. The major categories in the biosphere are plants, animals, and man.

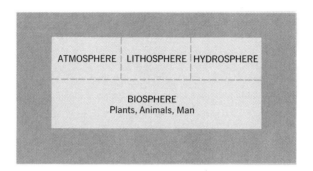

Marketing relates directly to this natural environmental system in many ways: climate, rivers, lakes, soil, topography, altitude, oceans, energy, mineral resources, plants, animals, and other resources are all factors that marketers must take into account. Thus the environmental approach helps us to understand, for instance, the needs of consumers, transportation capabilities, and pollution.

## The Human Environmental System

In addition to the strictly natural environment there is the human system, which includes the "accomplishments" of man in his global environment. The human system consists of:

Human beings
- Communities of populations
- Culture
- Economic systems
- Technology
- Ethics
- Law (including political systems)

Together, then, we have all living organisms and the natural and human systems interacting with one another in the global environment. The global scheme is illustrated in 1-6. While our schematic diagram attempts to show the natural and human environments in their true relationship, our emphasis throughout this study will be on the human environment.

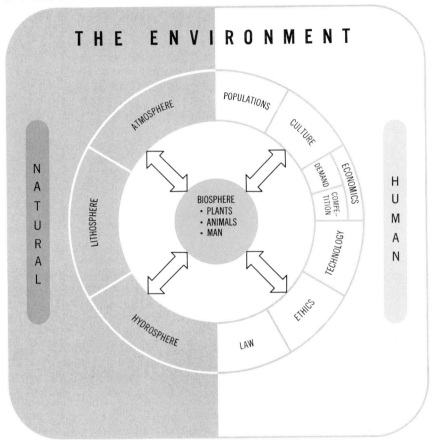

## The Business Firm in the Environment

Where in all this are the business firm, its marketing activities, and consumers? As the schematic diagram shown in 1-7 suggests, they are under the influence of all these factors. The business network evolves from the economic sector to serve society's needs. Marketing in the aggregate functions between producers of goods and services with their eventual consumption and use by consumers of all kinds. By the positioning shown in 1-7 the role of marketing within the global environment is portrayed.

Realistically marketing must be viewed within the total environment. Marketing after all does not occur in a vacuum. Nor does it relate only to consumers. By recognizing that marketing is indeed operating within a dynamic environment which influences business firms and populations of human beings alike, we can gain a more complete understanding of the role of marketing in today's society. As we proceed through the book, note these two things:

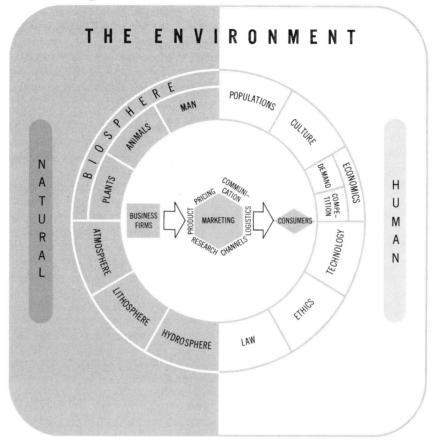

The text is organized so as to develop the interrelationships of marketing and the environment.

Our environmental schematic diagram is adjusted to adapt to the specific subject matter under study.

Although it would be appropriate to study all relationships and all marketing in a composite way, it becomes necessary to compartmentalize the study and progress a step at a time.

In the next chapter we take a first step by examining in some detail the activities of the firm in its environment.

## STATEMENTS TO CONSIDER

*Note: At the end of each chapter we have placed several statements to consider. You may or may not agree with them, but we hope that they stimulate your thinking about marketing.*

Marketing is any activity that actualizes the potential market relationship among the market users of economic goods and services.

The final objective of marketing is to make goods and services available for use.

In marketing terms, it is somewhat more precise to say that exchange takes place in order to increase the utility of the assortments held by each party to the transaction.

It follows, then, that the two principal or most basic tasks of marketing are (1) to direct the use of resources and allocate scarce supplies in conformity with existing demand, and (2) to aid in making consumption dynamic in conformity with changes in our ability to cater to human wants.

The market provides society with a communication network. This operates to the advantage of both sellers and buyers.

Time, place, and possession utilities are outweighed in value by form utility.

The natural and man-made environments are inseparable insofar as contributing to the resources made available to a society.

As a society advances man devises many institutions to serve his welfare.

Man's response to his environment helps to explain the basic reasons for much social and economic development.

The observation that goods are produced by horsepower and distributed by manpower is still basically valid. (Teele)

## QUESTIONS FOR REVIEW

**1.** Explain the limitations of barter trade. Can an economy grow and prosper with barter trade alone?

**2.** How does the use of money equalize the positions of the buyer and the seller?

**3.** Can marketing be carried on in a society without specialization? Explain the relationship of specialization to the exchange of goods and services.

**4.** What accounts for the steady decline in the number of workers employed in agriculture?

**5.** It is said "that markets are a basic organizing force for societies." Explain the meaning of this statement.

**6.** Why is it desirable to utilize more than a single definition of marketing? What are three useful but different definitions that characterize the breadth of marketing?

**7.** Show how time, place, and possession utilities add to the value of manufactured goods.

**8.** A rough estimate of the cost of marketing is that it takes about 50 percent of the consumer's dollar and production takes the other half. Can improved efficiency in marketing be passed on to the consumer in the form of lower prices? Explain.

**9.** "The response by marketing people to the dynamic environment determines how successful the business firm will be in serving its customers and utimately in making profits." Is this a valid statement?

**10.** Marketing is an eclectic discipline. Does this complicate the study and analysis of marketing phenomena?

## Further Readings

Marcus Alexis, Robert J. Holloway, and Robert S. Hancock (eds.), *Empirical Foundations of Marketing* (Chicago: Markham Publishing Co., 1969).

Victor P. Buell (ed.), *Handbook of Modern Marketing* (New York: McGraw Hill, 1970).

Philip Kotler, *Marketing Management* (Englewood Cliffs, N.J.: Prentice-Hall, 1972).

William Lazer, *Marketing Management* (New York: John Wiley, 1971).

E. Jerome McCarthy, *Basic Marketing: A Managerial Approach* (Homewood, Ill.: Richard D. Irwin, 1971).

*Note: All chapter references are cited at the end of the book, pp. 693–704.*

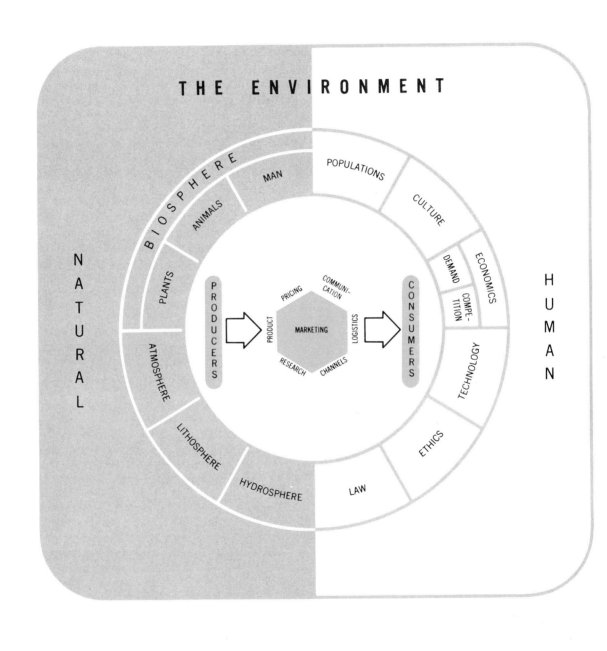

THE ENVIRONMENT

NATURAL

HUMAN

BIOSPHERE

MAN
ANIMALS
PLANTS
ATMOSPHERE
LITHOSPHERE
HYDROSPHERE

POPULATIONS
CULTURE
ECONOMICS
DEMAND
COMPE-TITION
TECHNOLOGY
ETHICS
LAW

PRODUCERS

CONSUMERS

PRICING
COMMUNI-CATION
PRODUCT
MARKETING
LOGISTICS
RESEARCH
CHANNELS

# CHAPTER 2
# THE FIRM
# AND ITS MARKETING
# ENVIRONMENT

**The Setting of the Firm and Marketing Management**

**The Firm—A Subsystem**

*Marketing Philosophy*
*Management of the Marketing Function*
*Marketing within a Natural and Social Environment*

**The Marketing System**

*Marketing Functions*
*Dimensions of the Marketing System*

**A Rationale for the Environmental Approach**

**The Plan To Accomplish the Study**

*Marketing is a subsystem of the economic or business system, and
a firm's marketing organization is a subsystem of the marketing system.
The firm's marketing program is its response to all the environmental
forces as it attempts to make profits by providing goods to the various
kinds of markets.*

In the previous chapter we described the origin of marketing, explained it as a subset of the economic system, and examined it as a socio-economic process. Finally we introduced our environmental approach to the study of marketing. We now turn from the macro perspective of marketing to a micro perspective, giving emphasis to the firm and its administration of marketing. In so doing, we extend the idea of the environment in which a firm operates and executes its marketing activities.

## THE SETTING OF THE FIRM
## AND MARKETING MANAGEMENT

Throughout most of Parts II and III of this text our frame of reference will be either the firm and its marketing management or individual segments thereof. For the fact is that the firm is the crux of marketing, the place in which *activities necessary and incidental to bringing about exchange relationships* originate. These activities, as noted earlier, are marketing research, product development, distribution, pricing, and market communications.

At the heart of a firm's marketing, of course, is the marketing manager, an executive who is subject to a bewildering and often conflicting array of pressures. From within the firm originate the company's objectives and the decisions of other executives that help to shape the marketing manager's activities and plans. From outside the company come the stimulation and constraints of the environment in which all business operations take place. It is the marketing manager who has responsibility for the direction of all the firm's marketing activities.

As our study of marketing proceeds we will need to examine each of the firm's activities in detail. In doing so we want to keep the responsibilities of marketing administrators constantly in mind. But first it will be useful to explain the marketing network in which the marketing manager operates with his firm's resources.

## THE MARKETING SYSTEM

The colossal task of distributing goods and services in a multibillion-dollar economy, as in the United States, is depicted in 2-1. At first glance the schematic diagram may appear bewildering and complex, but on examination it turns out to be condensed and yet comprehensive. It

**2-1** The Flow of Goods and Services

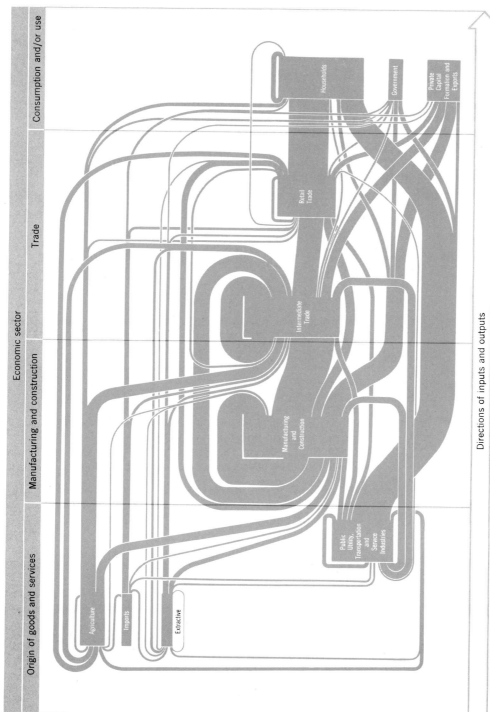

*SOURCE*: Adapted from Reavis Cox, *Distribution in a High-Level Economy* (Englewood Cliffs, N.J.: Prentice-Hall, 1965). Reprinted by permission.

shows in a generalized way the inputs and outputs of goods and
services by the several sectors of the system as well as the interconnec-
tions of the several sectors, and thus it represents a self-contained and
highly dynamic system.

From the *origin* sector goods and services flow either directly or
indirectly to all other sectors of the system. Most tangible things originate in agriculture, imports, or the extractive industries; intangibles in
this sector include public utility services, transportation services, indeed, all other services. The *manufacturing and construction* sector
includes all processes that change the form of the inflowing material.
Most goods produced by this sector then flow to the *trade* sector, which
includes all wholesale and retail enterprises. The flow of goods termi-
nates in the *consumption and use* sector, which includes the households, institutions, and governments that ultimately utilize the goods
and services coming through the system. Of course, to complete the
entire picture this sector accounts for private capital formation, which
originates from the profitable operation of business enterprises in all
the other sectors of the economic system, along with exports (which
enter the origin sector as imports in another country).

A few other observations about 2-1 are essential to understanding
the complete portrayal of our system. Contrary to popular belief, a large
amount of trade (or marketing) occurs between the business units in
the same sector—for example, trade among manufacturers or among
intermediaries. This kind of marketing—depicted in 2-1 by the loops,
or backflows, in the upper portions of the blocks—is referred to as
*industrial marketing.*

As shown in 2-2 merchant wholesalers in 1967 shipped 37.0 percent
of their goods to industrial users and another 14.5 percent to other
wholesalers. Only 39.4 percent of the goods were shipped in the retail
channel. The figures in 2-2 are percentages of *total* shipments: flow
of goods do vary considerably by product. For example, 88 percent of
construction and mining machinery were shipped to industrial users
and 41.3 percent of piece goods were shipped to other wholesalers in
1967.

The outflows in 2-1 are of greater magnitude than the inflows. This
difference is roughly equivalent to the value added by the several
sectors. Each sector, that is, adds value to the things it purchases and
in turn sells. You will often be confronted with the term "value added,"
which is an approximate measure of the additional worth created by
the productive and distributive processes. The value-added concept
avoids double counting since it signifies the difference between shipments (or sales) and the cost of materials, supplies, utilities, and containers purchased. Thus in each block in 2-1 the difference between
the outflows (sales) and inflows (purchases) represents a rough measure
of the value added by that block.

Numerous markets appear implicitly in 2-1. In Chapter 1 we said that
a market is any place or institution in which exchange is negotiated.
The flows in 2-1, including the backflows as well as the direct movements of goods and services, tell us that business units are exchanging

with one another in the nonhousehold markets. It also shows the exchange processes of businesses with households. All of this is traceable in this diagram.

Another way of visualizing our marketing system is shown in 2-3. This diagram is based on many of the same flow concepts as 2-1, except that it shows wholesale enterprises more explicitly and is less complex in detail. However, this diagram shows more clearly the alternative marketing channels that are available to the domestic business units of the system. The flow of goods and services may involve few intermediate stages or many; the precise character and kind of institutions involved is determined by the nature of the product, its market characteristics, and the marketing activities needed to gain customer acceptance. Marketing activities may be carried on by any unit within the system. Some are performed by manufacturers and processors, some by the marketing intermediaries (wholesalers and retailers), and some even by the final customer.

Marketing activities are thus located within the aggregation of business firms as shown in 2-1, 2-2, and 2-3. Marketing managers may direct their marketing operations at any of the stages shown or in any of the economic sectors. At whatever point, we find ourselves in a complex, interrelated system that serves all of society with its abundance of needs and wants.

**2-2** Wholesale (Merchant) Shipments, 1967 (Percentages of Total Shipments)

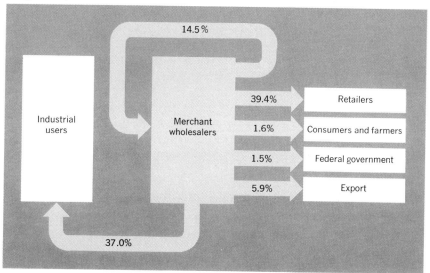

SOURCE: Adapted from U.S. Department of Commerce, Bureau of the Census, *Wholesale Trade, 1967* (Washington, D.C.: GPO, 1967).

**2-3** Alternative Marketing Channels and Flows—Goods and Services

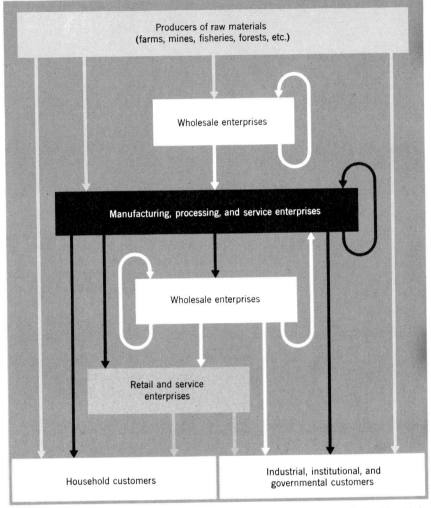

SOURCE: Adapted from Harry A. Lipson and John R. Darling, *Introduction to Marketing* (New York: John Wiley, 1971), p. 686.

## Marketing Functions

A number of marketing functions are performed by the thousands of marketing institutions that constitute the system for distribution. A farmer who has a roadside stand performs the complete array of marketing functions, from the producer to the consumer. But because of the spatial separation between most producers and consumers, much of the marketing operation is carried on by wholesalers and retailers who perform vital marketing functions.

The functions, or tasks, of marketing are those jobs performed by marketing specialists. They gather information, finance purchases, promote sales, and ship the goods to various destinations. A list of these functions follows:

Buying

Gathering information

Selling

Storing

Distributing

Transporting

Advertising

Pricing

Financing

Some of the tasks relate directly to the ultimate transfer of title from the seller to the buyer; some to the physical handling of the goods; and some to the facilitation of the process, as in the case of granting credit and bearing the financial risk. Functions of marketing are performed by manufacturers, wholesalers, retailers, and specialists such as marketing research firms and advertising agencies.

## Dimensions of the Marketing System

Some idea of the dimensions of the marketing task is gained from 2-4, which shows aggregate data about the business units in our economic system. All business units accounted for in 2-4 are not exclusively engaged in marketing, but many of them are. It is important to recognize that the production, financing, and raw material functions

**2-4** United States Establishments, Employment, and Receipts, 1971

| Industrial divisions | Number of establishments (in thousands) | Number of employees (in thousands)* | Total receipts (in billions) |
|---|---|---|---|
| Agriculture, forestry, and fisheries | 3,210 | 3,262 | $ 53.9 |
| Mining | 76 | 615 | 29.5 |
| Service industries | 2,711 | 11,791 | 105.2 |
| Retailers | 2,030 | 11,395 | 364.6 |
| Wholesalers | 480 | 3,866 | 221.6† |
| Finance, insurance, and real estate | 1,326 | 3,764 | 146.9 |
| Contract construction | 861 | 3,301 | 67.9† |
| Manufacturing | 366 | 18,591 | 693.5† |
| Transportation, communications, electricity, and gas | 377 | 4,445 | 116.5 |
| TOTAL | 11,437 | 61,030 | 1,799.6 |

*Nov. '71 data
†Oct. '71 data

SOURCES: U.S. Department of Commerce, *Survey of Current Business* (December 1971); and U.S. Department of Commerce, Bureau of the Census, 1971, *Statistical Abstract of the United States* (Washington, D.C.: GPO, 1971).

are included in this data and that marketing, while of importance, may not be the principal activity of each unit.

The data in 2-4 suggest the magnitude, complexity, and interrelated flow of goods and services that result in billions of transactions for more than a trillion dollar volume of sales. Each of the units in this table function within one or more of the sectors identified in our earlier schematic diagram, 2-1. With a national population of 205 million, more than 60 million households, and millions of business units to accommodate, you can visualize the magnitude of the marketing task. It is within this gigantic system that the firm and its marketing administration operate.

## THE FIRM—A SUBSYSTEM

Within a firm the same circulatory processes are evident as in a total system. The firm is thus a subsystem of the total marketing system. As such the marketing activities provide for the flow of products and services into the firm for processing and/or resale. The firm is thus a market supplier. Through its resale of things it contributes to the revenue-circulating process. Revenues flow in exchange for needed goods and services from the markets served by the firm. The entire process for a firm may be very complex or quite simple. It is easy to visualize the input and output of shoes by a shoe store and its gain of revenue, but it is more difficult to imagine the process for milk, when the flow of the product and the return flow of revenue pass through numerous intermediate stages between farmer and household consumer. The flow process occurs, however, for each transaction entered into by any firm in the system.

The work of marketing by the many business units in the system is organized to accomplish each firm's goals. In manufacturing firms

**2-5** **A Marketing Organization**

marketing is organized under specialists, whose responsibilities include sales, advertising, market research, product management or product planning, physical distribution, and other related and necessary functions. A marketing organization structure for a modern company with several divisional units might appear as in 2-5. This organization would be typical of a large consumer-oriented manufacturing firm.

In contrast, your favorite shoe store, an individual enterprise, may have sales, advertising, store layout, inventory management, and the host of other incidental activities centered in the owner himself. The way in which the work of marketing is organized is dependent on the size of a firm, its range of products, the markets it sells in, and the magnitude of its marketing task. No one organizational arrangement has universal application.

### Marketing Philosophy

If the marketing task is to be effectively executed, marketing administration must be an integral part of a business. Marketing managers—concerned with establishing objectives, implementing marketing programs, and evaluating the marketing performance—attempt to translate customer needs and wants into company action in the marketplace. In other words, they are bringing the resources of their companies into correspondence with the needs and wants of the marketplace.

Although marketing has many specialized activities it cannot be limited by a narrow or specialized philosophy. Within the management team marketing should be recognized as an inseparable business function, along with manufacturing, personnel management, and finance. Marketing is no more important than the other functional divisions of a business, but it does establish the parameters of the other business functions. If marketing falls short of the established goals or if it exceeds them, the impact on financial, personnel, and manufacturing managers is obvious. Every firm, then, needs to develop a viable marketing orientation.

### Management of the Marketing Function

The philosophy of a firm will permeate down through the ranks of those in marketing. Those firms that have developed a strong marketing orientation will make their marketing decisions with the consumer in mind as they integrate their marketing activities for profit. This is known as the "marketing concept." The principal decision-making areas have to do with the product, distribution of the product, pricing the product, and persuading people in the marketplace to buy it (see 2-6).

Essential to the management of the marketing tasks is information. Marketers rely on *marketing research* departments to furnish information to help them plan various marketing activities. Information comes from accounting records, reports, salesmen, periodicals, government data, and people in the marketplace. It is used to solve many kinds of marketing problems. What product should the firm offer? What colors? Sizes? Prices? What kinds of advertising should be used? How

**2-6** The Marketing Job

much should be produced? Who will buy? The research, or information, function is clearly basic to the marketing operation.

The *product* receives the attention of almost everyone in marketing: the design, price, package, distribution, and promotion decisions are all product-related. After all, it is the product that the firm is selling and that the customer is buying. Marketing strategies are, therefore, related to the product. A firm may attempt to differentiate its product through design work, produce a product for each identifiable market segment as an automobile manufacturer does, develop a full line as in the case of a book publisher, or set up a unique distribution system.

The product is handled through marketing institutions that make up a *channel of distribution,* as suggested earlier: manufacturer $\longrightarrow$ wholesaler $\longrightarrow$ household buyer. Business firms have a wide variety of channel alternatives to choose from in order to attain narrow or wide distribution of their products. Another part of the distribution function has to do with *logistics.* Marketing managers must plan for transportation and inventory as they handle the physical aspects of distributing their products.

*Price* is a key marketing variable. Internally it helps determine a firm's revenue, assuming it does not hamper sales goals. Externally it is influenced by general business conditions, the activities of competitors, and customers' responses. Price must be set with knowledge of sociopsychological variables that influence customer behavior.

Through *marketing communications* a firm informs a buyer in the marketplace about the product. Communications can be through advertising, public relations, sales promotion, or personal selling. The idea is to stimulate the buyer and encourage him to buy a particular product, perhaps from a certain retailer or manufacturer. No other marketing activity so obviously plays on our psychological desires and motives, and no other task of the marketer receives so much attention from those outside of marketing.

The marketing management decision areas discussed above—research, product, channels of distribution, logistics, price, and communications—encompass the marketing activities of a firm that directly influence the acceptance or rejection of a product or service by a buyer. Through the management of the marketing operation a firm makes an *offer* in the marketplace and buyers purchase the market offer. A buyer purchases more than a tangible product or a useful service since products are distinguished by their design, brand name, package, and place of sale. The buyer sees *all* the ingredients of the product when he or she buys, and the term "offer" suggests the total product as opposed to a more restricted meaning of the word "product" itself.

## Marketing within a Natural and Social Environment

We have already suggested that it is important for marketers to have a good understanding of the environment in which they operate. We have for purposes of presentation arbitrarily suggested two environ-

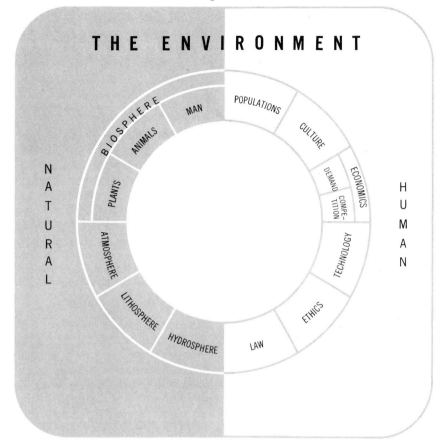

# THE ENVIRONMENT

ments—the natural and the human. This distinction is used in order to develop the necessary material in an organized way.

Each and every marketing function is affected by one or more environmental forces. The natural environment affects and is affected by products that in some way relate to the air, land, or water. The social environment must be considered by marketers since laws, ethics, technology, income, the business system as a whole, and people in their cultures determine much of the direction of marketing.

## A RATIONALE FOR THE ENVIRONMENTAL APPROACH

In recent years there has been a growing interest in both the natural environment and the environment created by human beings. Since the early 1960s we have witnessed more and more business research directed to the environment. People now recognize that the environmental forces interact with one another, and our focus in this volume is to emphasize how *marketing* interacts with all those forces.

The natural environment in some ways is delicate and destroyable. Marketers should understand this fact. Further, the end of the marketing cycle for many products is trash, and marketers need to be more aware of the impact of spent products than they have been in the past.

The marketing manager's decision-making is more a function of the environment than of his subjective ideas about what consumers want. A good deal of the marketing research effort is directed toward environmental concerns as the researcher gathers information about people's wants, to be sure, but also about their culture and their incomes, the legality of the marketing operation, the ethics of it, and the way it interacts with the natural environment. A good job of marketing is a good job of adapting to the total environment, each and every part of it. These points have been articulated by an executive of Procter & Gamble, a firm that has its share of environmental problems.

> *First,* is our commitment to broad research and development activities. *Second,* is the development of an organization geared for growth. And, *third,* is our responsiveness to the economic and social forces shaping our society.
>
> To realize the full potential of the future, our efforts will be directed, as in the past, toward improving and broadening our service to the consumer through the development of products that set new standards of performance, products that will immediately be recognized as superior by consumers.
>
> From our research laboratories has come a steady stream of new and improved products. The names of these products are familiar ones, familiar because they established themselves quickly in the face of stiff competition by bringing consumers a new dimension in performance. . . .
>
> Other products represent significant contributions to the health and well-being of the public. Crisco shortening has been completely reformulated to make it highly unsaturated—without sacrifice of any of the qualities so popular with consumers. Head & Shoulders, a dandruff-control shampoo, Safeguard, an antibacterial toilet soap, and, of course, Crest, the first stannous fluoride toothpaste, continue to compile impressive clinical evidence of their effectiveness.
>
> In every one of our product fields, there is no let-up in our efforts to keep abreast of changes in consumer tastes, needs and preferences. (Fite, 1970.)

Another reason for an increased emphasis on the marketing environment is the need for firms and their products to adapt to the larger changing environment. New technology, changes in politics and governments, and new data on resources all have their impact on what we market. Companies can react to auto pollution by building nonpolluting engines; they can silence many consumer complaints by selling safe products; and they can improve the situation in the Third World by helping rather than exploiting the population. Business has traditionally adapted well to changes in tastes, and it now has to learn how to adapt to the more fundamental changes in the environment.

## THE PLAN TO ACCOMPLISH THE STUDY

This volume has been planned so as to present the study of marketing within the total environment as shown in 2-8. In Part I we are building a foundation of broad societal needs as they relate to marketing (Chapter 1), the firm and its marketing system (Chapter 2), the structure through which marketing operates (Chapter 3), and the manner in which the environment influences marketing in various parts of the world (Chapter 4).

**2-8** Interrelationship of Environment and Marketing

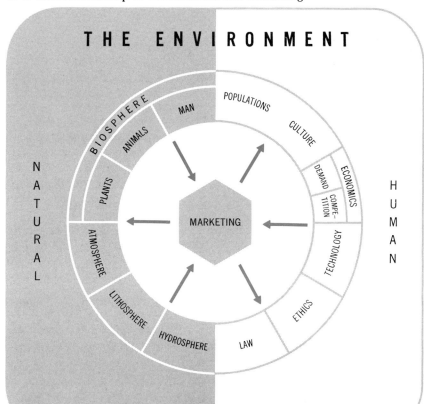

In Part II the various segments of the environment are discussed as they relate to marketing. The organization of Part II is shown on the schematic diagram in 2-9.

The marketing manager's job is developed throughout Part III as shown in 2-10. The final chapter of Part III focuses on marketing in the international environment.

**2-9** Organization of Part II

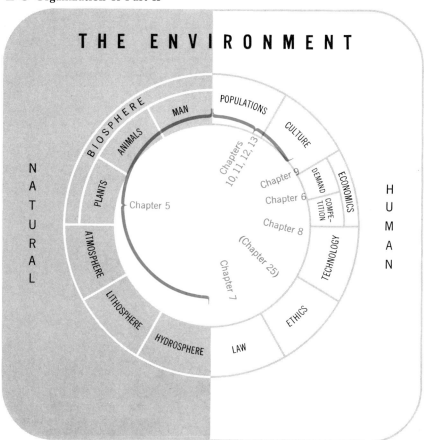

**2-10** Organization of Part III

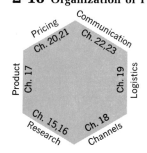

In Part IV the reader is given the opportunity to take a good look at marketing in today's world. A number of criticisms of marketing are made as we examine problems relating to ethics (Chapter 25), consumerism (Chapter 26), the disadvantaged (Chapter 27), and environmental considerations (Chapter 28).

The final Part of the book has two chapters: Chapter 29 evaluates marketing from the standpoint of its efficiency in the economic system and Chapter 30 looks to the future—what will marketing be like in the decades to come? Indeed, what will the future be?

This, then, is the plan for the book. It is meant to be an organized approach to the study of basic marketing in a dynamic environment, and its stress is the adaptation of marketing to a changing environment.

## STATEMENTS TO CONSIDER

Distribution by one means or another is an essential intermediate step between production and consumption in all economies beyond the subsistence household stage of development. (Preston)

The raison d'être of marketing in a private-property economy is the effecting of transactions, for thereby suppliers and demanders—all types: firms, noncommercial units, and individuals—satisfy some of their goals. (Narver/Savitt)

A theory of marketing can be valid for only one mix of social and natural environmental factors.

All middlemen have one thing in common—they are too often looked upon by the general public as anachronistic appendages, useless leeches on the economy, adding cost but no value to the goods they handle. (Courtney)

Approximately two-thirds of the U.S. economy can be classified as in the area of free competitive enterprise.

The great advantage of our basic marketing mechanism—which is essentially a vast network of transportation and communication—is that it permits people living in one part of the country to enjoy products grown or produced hundreds or thousands of miles away. (Alderson/Halbert)

Marketing has a threefold mission—to find the shortest route to market for existing products, to bring new products to market, and to bring more people more fully into the market economy. (Alderson/Halbert)

The management of a market-oriented firm is largely dependent on the use of information about channels, competitors, and people.

What is ordinarily said about the American consumer by marketing men might lead one to believe that he is a child upon whom the sun of fortune has shone so benignly that he has no problems at all. (R. Cox)

The central problem of the marketing manager is how to combine the ingredients of the marketing mix—product, price, channels, logistics, and communications—in such a way as to ensure the highest amount of profit for the firm.

## QUESTIONS FOR REVIEW

**1.** What are the major flows of goods in the U. S. marketing system?

**2.** What is the significance of loops and backflows as shown in 2-1?

**3.** Do you agree that there can be a "value added by marketing"? Why?

**4.** Merchant wholesalers ship approximately 40 percent of their goods to retailers. Where does the remainder of their goods go?

**5.** Marketing people perform a variety of tasks or jobs: What are they?

**6.** What is meant by the term "marketing system"? "marketing subsystem"?

**7.** If there is such a thing as a marketing philosophy, how would it differ from financial, production, and technological philosophies?

**8.** Do you see any conflicts between marketing goals for society versus marketing goals for the firm?

**9.** Suggest specific ways in which marketing activities are influenced by the total environment.

**10.** In what ways does marketing influence the environment?

## Further Readings

Wroe Alderson and Michael H. Halbert, *Men, Motives, and Markets* (Englewood Cliffs, N.J.: Prentice-Hall, 1968).

Ben M. Enis and Keith K. Cox, *Marketing Classics* (Boston: Allyn & Bacon, 1969).

Ronald R. Gist, *Marketing and Society* (New York: Holt, Rinehart and Winston, 1971).

John C. Narver and Ronald Savitt, *The Marketing Economy* (New York: Holt, Rinehart and Winston, 1971).

Lee E. Preston, *Markets and Marketing, An Orientation* (Glenview, Ill.: Scott, Foresman, 1970).

Richard A. Scott and Norton E. Marks, *Marketing and Its Environment* (Belmont, Cal.: Wadsworth, 1968).

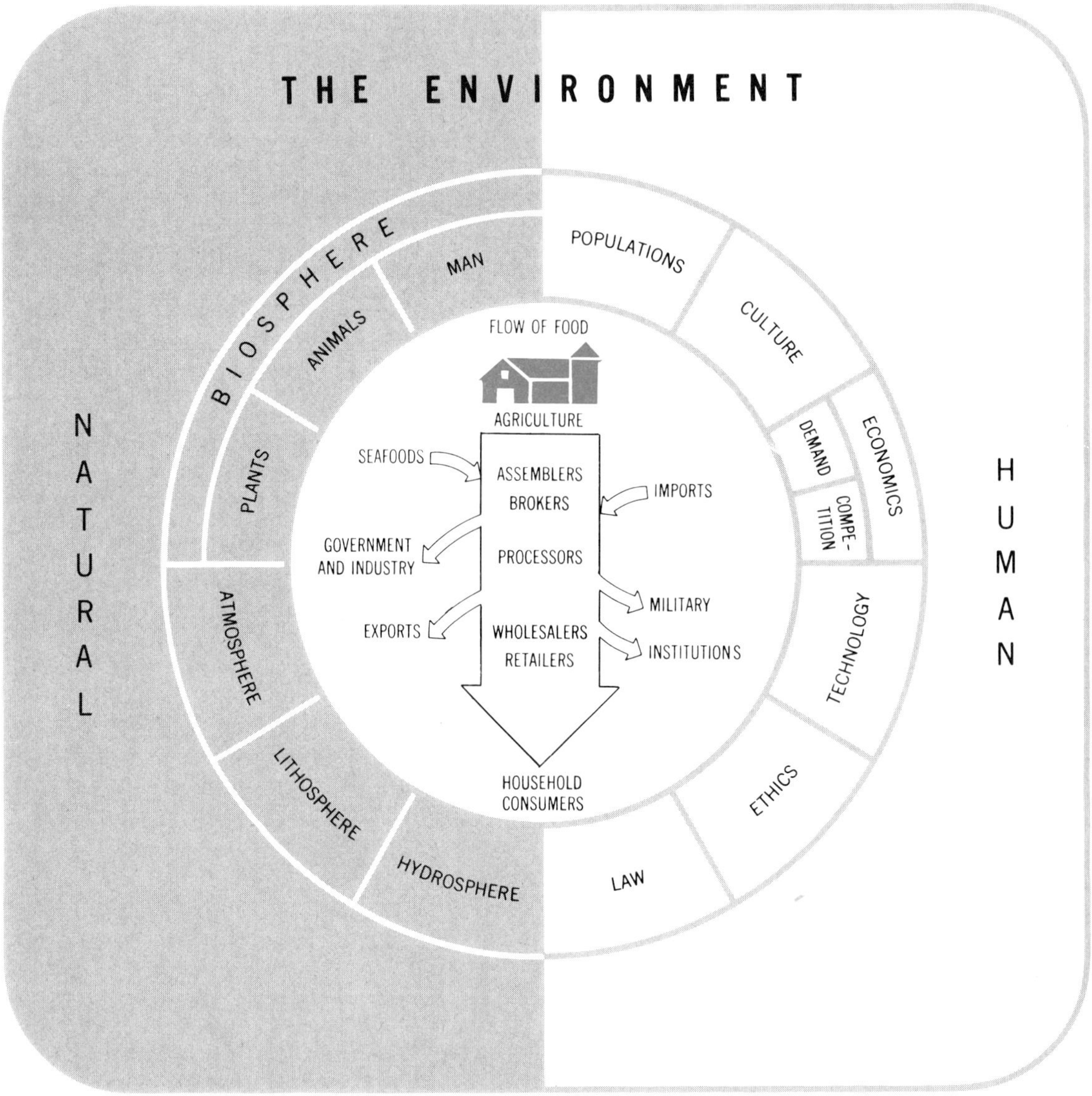

THE ENVIRONMENT

NATURAL

HUMAN

BIOSPHERE

MAN
ANIMALS
PLANTS
ATMOSPHERE
LITHOSPHERE
HYDROSPHERE

POPULATIONS
CULTURE
DEMAND
ECONOMICS
COMPE-TITION
TECHNOLOGY
ETHICS
LAW

FLOW OF FOOD

AGRICULTURE

SEAFOODS
ASSEMBLERS
BROKERS
IMPORTS

GOVERNMENT
AND INDUSTRY
PROCESSORS

EXPORTS
WHOLESALERS
RETAILERS
MILITARY
INSTITUTIONS

HOUSEHOLD
CONSUMERS

# CHAPTER 3
# MARKETS AND MARKETING INSTITUTIONS

*There are many kinds of markets that are served by a complex struc-
ture of marketing institutions—processors, wholesalers, retailers, and
facilitating agencies. The structure has dynamic characteristics as it
adapts to the changing environment.*

We have explained the general role of marketing in the distribution
of goods and services and we have presented our rationale for the
environmental approach to marketing. In the following chapters we
will examine particular segments of the environment and market behavior. First, however, we need to examine the structure of the marketing system, and to do that we want to consider what a market is.

## THE MARKET

One problem for any student of marketing is the exact meaning of the
term "market." It has many definitions:

> The market is the stage on which economic actors—firms, house-
> holds, and unions—meet and make key economic decisions for soci-
> ety. Out of the process of market exchange come the prices, wages,
> and profits that serve to determine the allocation of the economy's
> resources and the distribution of the national income. (Steiner, 1968.)
>
> A market is the aggregate of forces or conditions within which
> buyers and sellers make decisions that result in the transfer of goods
> and services. (American Marketing Association, 1960.)
>
> A market is the aggregate demand of the potential buyers of a
> commodity or service. (American Marketing Association, 1960.)
>
> A market is a group of buyers and sellers within a geographical
> area: (a) for a product or reasonable substitute; (b) at a particular
> stage in the trade channel, such as manufacturers selling to retailers,
> or consumers buying from retailers; and (c) at a particular time.
> (Converse, Huegy and Mitchell, 1965.)
>
> A market is an exchange relationship among buyers and sellers.
> (Preston, 1970.)

Thus a market can be the downtown area or the West Coast. A market
can also be the total potential buying power for a given commodity
(all possible automobile buyers) or the actual sales recorded (such as
the $4 billion annual television market). The term is used in the aggre-
gate sense (the market for housing in the United States) and more
restrictedly in terms of firms, brands, and even individual sellers. In
the automobile market, for instance, the total market may be 9 million
autos, the compact market may be 1.5 million, and the Maverick market
0.5 million. For one dealer the figure could be in the dozens. One
subdivides the total market in going from general product class to firm
to brand.

There are "class" markets—low-income, middle-income, and high-income; "people" markets—youth, college students, blacks, females, and the aged; "thing" markets—cigarettes, autos, houses, books, and television repair; "area" markets—United States, metropolitan, rural, southern, European, and Japanese. A market may be bounded by religious dictates or by climatic conditions. It may be stable, declining, or growing. It may be monopolistic or very competitive. It may be tangible or intangible, as in the grain exchanges where there are both a market dealing with the actual physical commodity and a market dealing only in contracts for futures. The term "market" is broad, complex, and elusive. It can refer to a structure or to behavior. It can mean the entire marketing system or a subsystem of marketing.

In 3-1 you can see some of the different characteristics of markets and their populations. These classifications of markets are useful for the marketer in focusing on a segment of the total market. *Market segmentation* is of little concern in economies that have a homogeneous demand, that is, where most of the population demands identical things. In an abundant economy, as in the United States and other highly developed economies where there is heterogeneous demand, many opportunities exist for a firm to segment the market. Market segmentation presents the opportunity for a manufacturer to obtain a strong hold on a portion of the market by means of product differentiation. Why is it that markets can be segmented? One reason resides in diverse demographic characteristics—differences in age, sex, geography, money available for spending, occupation, education, and ethnic group. Another and somewhat subtler reason for this phenomenon may be found in buyer attitudes. The attitudes of buyers are influenced by their motivations, cultural patterns, esthetic preferences, and values.

In Chapters 10 to 13 we will discuss the buying behaviors of the major kinds of markets—household, institutional, industrial, and governmental. In this chapter, however, we want to concentrate on the marketing structure that serves the many markets.

## THE INSTITUTIONAL FRAMEWORK

The following quotation sets the stage for the discussion of marketing institutions:

> Marketing, then, must be thought of as a set of continuous flows through an intricate network of facilities. The flows alternately run into and out of large and small pools. They start at countless points of production and end at numberless points of consumption. Between the extremes is a complex of storage and mixing tanks, pipes, junctions, elbows, reducing nipples, valves, single or multiple outlets, and propelling equipment. Acting in combination, these instruments sort and re-sort materials into new combinations, hold them for a time, change the direction of their flow, build them into larger flows or reduce them into smaller ones, and eventually disperse them to final consumers.

These fittings are the institutions and agencies of marketing. Where a change in direction, size, or rate of flow is necessary, an entity must step in. (Vaile, Grether, and Cox, 1952.)

**3-1** A Graphic Picture of a Market

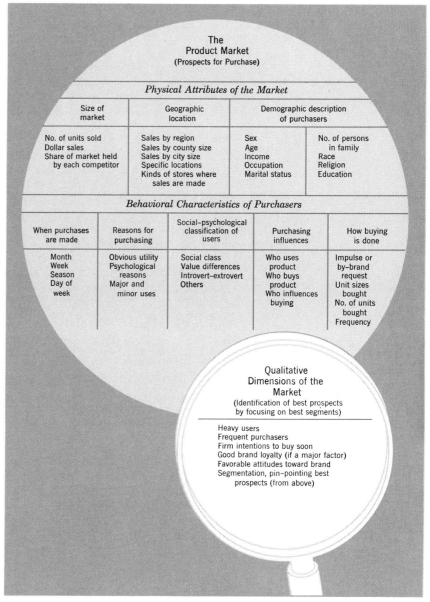

The
Product Market
(Prospects for Purchase)

*Physical Attributes of the Market*

| Size of market | Geographic location | Demographic description of purchasers | |
|---|---|---|---|
| No. of units sold<br>Dollar sales<br>Share of market held<br>by each competitor | Sales by region<br>Sales by county size<br>Sales by city size<br>Specific locations<br>Kinds of stores where<br>sales are made | Sex<br>Age<br>Income<br>Occupation<br>Marital status | No. of persons<br>in family<br>Race<br>Religion<br>Education |

*Behavioral Characteristics of Purchasers*

| When purchases are made | Reasons for purchasing | Social–psychological classification of users | Purchasing influences | How buying is done |
|---|---|---|---|---|
| Month<br>Week<br>Season<br>Day of<br>week | Obvious utility<br>Psychological<br>reasons<br>Major and<br>minor uses | Social class<br>Value differences<br>Introvert-extrovert<br>Others | Who uses<br>product<br>Who buys<br>product<br>Who influences<br>buying | Impulse or<br>by–brand<br>request<br>Unit sizes<br>bought<br>No. of units<br>bought<br>Frequency |

Qualitative
Dimensions of the
Market
(Identification of best prospects
by focusing on best segments)

Heavy users
Frequent purchasers
Firm intentions to buy soon
Good brand loyalty (if a major factor)
Favorable attitudes toward brand
Segmentation, pin-pointing best
prospects (from above)

SOURCE: Jack Z. Sissors, "What Is a Market?" *Journal of Marketing*, Vol. 30, No. 3 (July 1966), p. 21.

A distinct sequence of marketing institutions forms for almost every commodity and service or for every group of buyers. This sequence of institutions is known as a marketing channel and will be discussed in detail in Chapter 18. Most goods destined for the household market flow in a channel from producer to consumer in the following way.

Manufacturer $\longrightarrow$ Wholesaler $\longrightarrow$ Retailer $\longrightarrow$ Household

Marketing functions are performed by each institution in the channel. This is only a general picture, however, for a business institution may integrate its activities forward or backward, thus eliminating the need for some of the other marketing institutions. For example, a large food chain may do its own baking, thus eliminating the need for an outside source for its bakery products. The chain not only performs its own manufacturing as in this case, but it also performs the marketing formerly done by an outside bakery. A wholesaler may establish its own retail chain, and vice versa. Despite the integration and the subsequent elimination of institutions, the marketing functions remain. The intermediaries can be eliminated but not the tasks they perform.

Nonhousehold buyers in the institutional, industrial, and government markets typically buy in large quantities from wholesalers and manufacturers (retailing is mostly confined to the household market), thus necessitating a special structure of wholesalers, advertisers, salesmen, financial establishments, and so on. Special wholesalers handle the needs of hospitals, for example; other companies specialize in educational products.

In addition to the marketing institutions involved directly in the sale of merchandise, there are facilitating and supportive institutions —advertising agencies, marketing research firms, credit companies, transportation and storage firms. These firms supplement the marketing work carried on by the regular wholesalers and retailers.

The marketing system was shown in the aggregate in 2-1, page 27. Though this flow diagram may well look confusing, it is a vast oversimplification of the marketing system. For a simpler schematic presentation of a marketing channel, see 3-2. The flow concept, the value added by marketing, and the positioning of institutions in the channel system are all shown. Let us look at each of the major groups of marketing institutions.

## Producer Types

Although primary producers (such as farmers, mining companies, and foresters), utilities, and manufacturers are not considered marketing institutions, we want to include them as institutions that do perform marketing tasks. Their primary tasks are some kind of processing, but they do sell their products and in so doing perform many of the marketing functions previously enumerated in Chapter 2. Thus the producer types are part of the marketing chain, they perform marketing functions, but they are primarily manufacturing firms or other kinds of business enterprises.

## 3-2 The Channels of Distribution

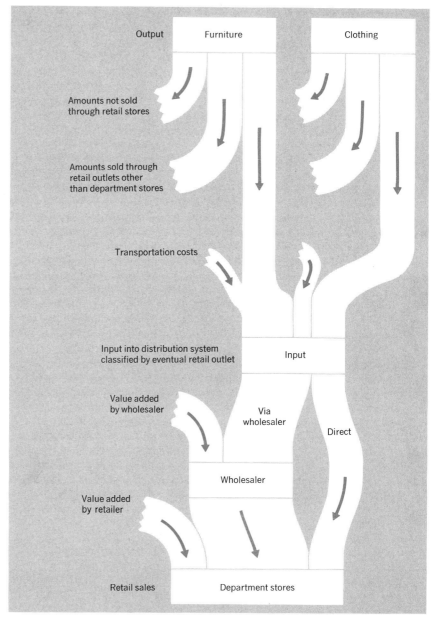

SOURCE: Adapted from Harold Barger, *Distribution's Place in the American Economy Since 1869* (Princeton, N.J.: Princeton University Press, 1955), p. 68.

## Wholesalers

Wholesalers are "business units that buy and resell merchandise to retailers and other merchants and/or to industrial, institutional, and commercial users but do not sell in significant amounts to ultimate consumers" (American Marketing Association, 1960). This is shown in the figure in 3-3. Therefore, if a wholesaler sells to a household buyer, he is actually performing a retail service. According to the latest count by the Census Bureau, 311,464 wholesaling establishments were operating in 1967, sales amounted to $459 billion, paid employees numbered 3.5 million, and the payroll was $24 billion. As noted below, whole-

**3-3** Percentage Distribution of Sales by Type of Operation and Class of Customer, 1967

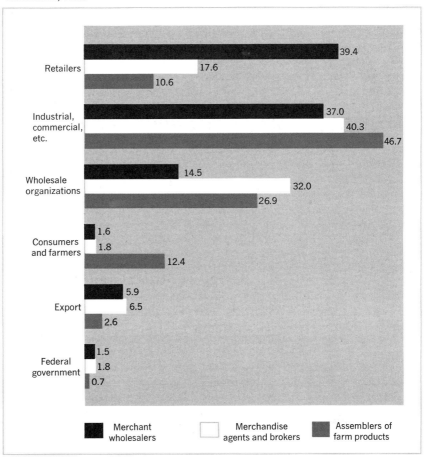

SOURCE: U.S. Department of Commerce, Bureau of the Census, *1967 Census of Business* (Washington, D.C.: GPO, 1967).

saling data include establishments that do not actually take title to the goods but do perform marketing functions of a wholesaling nature. The Census Bureau classifies wholesaling activities into five main types of operation as follows:

*Merchant Wholesalers*—Establishments primarily engaged in buying and selling merchandise on their own account. They take title to the goods.

*Merchandise Agents and Brokers*—Establishments whose operators are in business for themselves and are primarily engaged in selling or buying goods for others. They do not take title to the goods.

*Manufacturers' Sales Branches and Sales Offices*—Establishments maintained by manufacturing and mining companies apart from their plants or mines for marketing their products at wholesale.

*Petroleum Bulk Stations, Terminals, LP Gas Facilities*—Establishments primarily engaged in the wholesale marketing of gasoline, kerosene, distillate and residual fuel oils, liquefied petroleum gases, and other bulk petroleum products.

*Farm Products Assemblers*—Country grain elevators, cream and produce stations, fruit and vegetable packing houses, and other

**3-4** Wholesaling in the United States, 1967

| Number of establishments | Types of establishments | Sales (in billions) |
|---|---|---|
| 41,330 | Petroleum bulk stations and farm assemblers | 35 |
| 30,679 | Manufacturers' sales branches and sales offices | 157 |
| 26,462 | Merchandise agents | |
| | | 61 |
| 212,993 | Merchant wholesalers | |
| | | 206 |
| 311,464 | Total U.S. wholesaling establishments | $459 |

SOURCE: U.S. Department of Commerce, Bureau of the Census, *1967 Census of Business, Wholesale Trade, United States* (Washington, D.C.: GPO, 1967).

establishments primarily engaged in purchasing from farmers and assembling and marketing farm products.

Wholesalers differ in many respects. The ownership of the firms may be private (individual, partnership, or corporate), cooperative, or even governmental in the case of public warehouses. Some take possession of merchandise but others do not. Some take title, others do not. Some represent the seller, others the buyer. The total wholesaling picture is shown in 3-4, with the total number of establishments and their sales and also establishments and sales of each of the five main groups. In order to give you a better idea of the wholesaling structure, we will examine the principal wholesaling institutions in each of the five categories.

The first group is *merchant wholesalers* who take title to the goods they handle, that is, they buy and sell as merchants. There are over 200,000 wholesale merchants in the United States and they perform in a wide variety of merchandise lines, as the following Census Bureau data for 1967 show.

| Number | Types | Sales (in millions) |
| --- | --- | --- |
| 212,993 | Total merchant wholesalers | $206,055 |
| 4,783 | Motor vehicles and auto equipment | 31,329 |
| 7,742 | Electrical goods | 17,701 |
| 2,543 | Groceries and related products | 15,547 |
| 3,475 | Piece goods, notions, apparel | 9,596 |
| 3,760 | Drugs, chemicals, and allied products | 9,233 |
| 9,619 | Machinery, equipment, and supplies | 8,410 |
| 2,515 | Tobacco and tobacco products | 5,315 |
| 4,438 | Hardware, plumbing, heating | 4,439 |
| 680 | Farm products—raw materials | 3,169 |
| 4,865 | Amusement and sporting goods | 3,001 |
| 2,089 | Books, periodicals, and newspapers | 1,403 |

SOURCE: U.S. Department of Commerce, Bureau of the Census, *U.S. Census of Business: 1967* (Washington, D.C.: GPO, 1967).

Closely allied to the merchant wholesalers are those *agents* who do not take title to the goods but who nevertheless perform many of the other marketing functions. They may act as the sales force for a manufacturer, or may function as a contact person (broker), or may furnish a selling area (auction house) for many products. The following types of agents together handle over $60 billion of wholesale business annually.

*Auction Companies*—Primarily engage in selling merchandise on an agency basis by the auction method.

*Merchandise Brokers*—Primarily engage in selling or buying merchandise in the domestic market on a brokerage basis, but do not receive the goods on consignment. They can represent either buyer or seller in negotiating purchases or sales.

*Commission Merchants*—Operate in the domestic market receiving goods for sale on consignment. Generally arrange credit, delivery, collect payments, deduct fees, and remit the balance to the principal.

*Manufacturers' Agents*—Wholesale establishments in the domestic market selling for a limited number of manufacturers on a continuing agency basis. Handle noncompeting but related lines of goods.

*Selling Agents*—Wholesale establishments primarily engaged in selling, on an agency basis in the domestic market, *all* or the major portion of the output of clients.

*Purchasing Agents, Resident Buyers*—Wholesale establishments primarily engaged in buying merchandise on an agency basis, in the domestic market, for a limited number of customers on a continuing basis.

*Export Agents*—Merchandise agents and brokers in the domestic market selling to or buying for foreign customers.

*Import Agents*—Merchandise agents and brokers in the domestic market buying merchandise from or selling merchandise for foreign firms.

The relative importance (1967 data) of each of these types of agents is shown in the accompanying table.

| Number | Types | Sales (in millions) |
|---|---|---|
| 26,462 | Total agents | $61,343 |
| 12,106 | Manufacturers' agents | 15,256 |
| 5,425 | Commission merchants | 14,068 |
| 4,373 | Merchandise brokers | 14,030 |
| 1,891 | Selling agents | 6,889 |
| 1,594 | Auction companies | 4,792 |
| 548 | Export agents | 3,372 |
| 270 | Import agents | 1,790 |
| 255 | Resident buyers, purchasing agents | 1,146 |

SOURCE: U.S. Department of Commerce, Bureau of the Census, *U.S. Census of Business: 1967* (Washington, D.C.: GPO, 1967).

The *manufacturers' sales branches and sales offices* may stock merchandise and handle sales operations on a decentralized basis or they may handle only the administrative details of the sales.

| Number | Types | Sales (in millions) |
|---|---|---|
| 30,679 | Total manufacturers' sales branches and sales offices | $157,095 |
| 13,970 | Sales offices—without stock | 89,921 |
| 16,709 | Sales offices—with stock | 67,174 |

SOURCE: U.S. Department of Commerce, Bureau of the Census, *U.S. Census of Business: 1967* (Washington, D.C.: GPO, 1967).

The number and sales volumes of the *petroleum bulk stations and terminals* and the *assemblers of farm products* are as follows:

| Number | Types | Sales (in millions) |
|--------|-------|---------------------|
| 30,229 | Petroleum bulk stations, terminals | $24,821 |
| 11,101 | Assemblers of farm products | 10,155 |

SOURCE: U.S. Department of Commerce, Bureau of the Census, *U.S. Census of Business: 1967* (Washington, D.C.: GPO, 1967).

In total, the wholesaling structure stores, provides credit, breaks bulk, buys, sells, promotes, prices, and delivers products to their customers, who may be retailers, manufacturers, producers of primary products, or other wholesalers. Integration from above or below can squeeze out the wholesaler, but the wholesaling institution continues to provide useful marketing functions as indicated by the increase in the total number of wholesalers from 1963 to 1967 by 3,290. Merchant wholesalers increased by the largest number, followed by manufacturers' sales branches (vertical integration), and merchandise agents. Petroleum bulk dealers and farm product assemblers, however, showed decreases in the number of establishments during the same period.

## Retailing Establishments

The third component of the marketing structure is retailing. A retailer is a merchant, occasionally an agent, whose main business is selling directly to the household buyer. The 1967 Census reported 1,763,324 retail establishments in the United States. They accounted for $310 billion of sales, employed 9,380,616 persons, and had a payroll of $8,811 million. Retailers differ radically in size, type of ownership, kinds of goods handled, location, and even the functions they perform. Not all have stores, as in the case of mail order firms, for instance, and companies that sell primarily through vending machines located on the premises of other businesses. Some are highly specialized and others handle a wide assortment of goods. There are individual proprietorships, partnerships, corporations, and cooperatives. There are individual units and large chain operations. The relative importance of each of the major categories is shown in 3-5.

Stores vary greatly in volume of sales: general merchandise stores are on the average almost ten times the size of eating and drinking establishments. Other larger-than-average retailers are automotive dealers, food stores, drug stores, and building material establishments. There were, in 1967, 1,201,179 small retailers—gasoline service stations, apparel and furniture stores, eating and drinking places, and nonstore and miscellaneous retailers—that averaged only $93,000 each in annual sales. (Nonstore retailing includes mail-order, vending-machine, and direct selling operations. This miscellaneous category includes vendors of liquor, antiques, sporting goods, jewelry, fuel and ice, flowers, cigars, books, hay, garden supplies, newspapers and magazines, hobbies, toys, cameras, gifts, and optical goods.)

**3-5** Retailing in the United States, 1967

| Number of establishments | Types of establishments | Total sales (millions) | Sales per establishment (thousands) |
|---|---|---|---|
| 86,373 | Building materials | 17,200 | 200 |
| 67,307 | General merchandise | 43,537 | 647 |
| 294,243 | Food stores | | |
| 105,500 | Automotive dealers | 70,251 | 239 |
| 216,059 | Gasoline service stations | | |
| 110,164 | Apparel | 55,631 | 527 |
| 98,826 | Furniture | | |
| 347,890 | Eating and drinking | 22,709 | 105 |
| | | 16,672 | 151 |
| | | 14,542 | 147 |
| 53,722 | Drug stores | 23,843 | 68 |
| 288,772 | Miscellaneous | 10,930 | 204 |
| | | 27,274 | 95 |
| 94,468 | Nonstore retailers | 7,623 | 80 |
| 1,763,324 | Total U.S. | $310,214* | $176 |

*Due to rounding detail will not add to total.

SOURCE: U.S. Department of Commerce, Bureau of the Census, *1967 Census of Business, Retail Trade, United States* (Washington, D.C.: GPO, 1967).

## Services

A fourth major category of marketing institutions comprises the services industries, which also serve all the major markets—households, businesses and institutions of all kinds, primary producers, and government agencies. Unfortunately we do not have a precise count of all service establishments, only those counted by the Bureau of Census, which leaves out, to name a few, medical centers, banks, and transportation companies. A more complete picture of the services industries is needed because we are moving toward a services-oriented economy in terms of employment and it will be increasingly important for us to study it. Selected services are shown in the accompanying table.

| Number | Types | Sales (in millions) |
|---|---|---|
| 211,835 | Business services | $22,595 |
| 498,935 | Personal services | 11,750 |
| 87,006 | Hotels, motels, tourist courts and camps | 7,038 |
| 139,243 | Automobile repair | 7,028 |
| 96,029 | Amusement and recreation services | 4,826 |
| 138,014 | Miscellaneous repair services | 3,826 |
| 16,752 | Motion pictures | 3,476 |

SOURCE: U.S. Department of Commerce, Bureau of the Census, *U.S. Census of Business: 1967* (Washington, D.C.: GPO, 1967).

To give you a better picture of the range of services, here is the Census breakdown of personal services.

Laundry, cleaning, other garment services
Coin-operated laundries and dry cleaning
Power laundries
Industrial launderers
Linen supply
Diaper service
Dry cleaning
Rug cleaning
Garment pressing
Beauty shops
Barber shops
Photographic studies
Shoe repair, shoe shine, hat cleaning
Funeral service and crematories

Marketing has not yet become an important function for most service institutions. Banks have perhaps made the greatest advances as they have begun to advertise and to provide more services for their customers than they did years ago. Services have a considerable personal element in their relationships with the public, more so than do the other marketing establishments. Perhaps we will see the services industries become more marketing-conscious in the decade ahead.

Quite a number of the business services can be thought of as *supportive* or *facilitating marketing services*, including:

Advertising
 Advertising agencies
 Outdoor advertising services
 Radio and television representatives
 Publishers' representatives
 Miscellaneous advertising
Business and consulting services
 Business management, consulting
 Statistical and computer services
 Interior decorators
Adjustment and collection agencies
Mercantile reporting agencies
Consumer credit reporting agencies
Duplicating, mailing, stenographic services

**3-6** The Marketing Structure

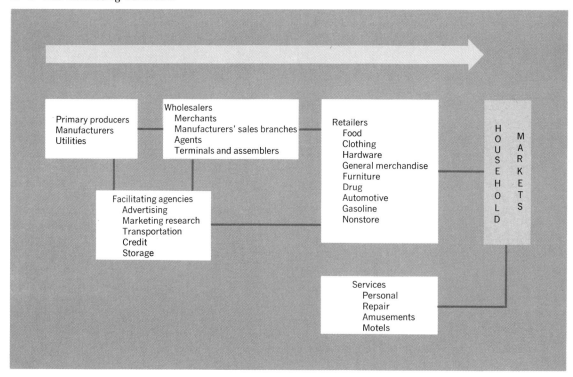

*The Nature of Marketing in a Changing Environment*

Commercial research

Armored car services

Leasing, rental of equipment

Trading stamp services

Sign painting shops

Telephone answering services

Packaging, labeling services

These businesses play large roles in our economic life. The 1967 Census revealed that 20,124 advertising agencies had, for example, receipts of $8,341 million and that they had a payroll of $983 million for 109,118 employees. These figures do not include the many people in advertising who are employed by manufacturing, service, or retailing firms.

We have examined a number of marketing institutions that perform all the marketing functions. A graphic summary of the main categories of the marketing structure is shown in 3-6.

## INSTITUTIONS AND THE ENVIRONMENT

A few years ago one of the authors noticed a sign along a highway in the Midwest:

> The Market system
> Is out of date.
> Join NFO*
> Before it is too late.

Actually the marketing system, if permitted to operate freely, stays *in* date by continually adapting to the environmental pressures of the day. Everyone is dependent on the system and has certain expectations of its performance, as a buyer or seller or both. The desires of buyers and sellers are reflected in the marketplace and thus the system is characterized by its dynamics as well as its adaptive capacities.

The retailing structure is an excellent example of the adaptive marketing institution. Its location is determined by the distribution of the population, highways, and the presence or lack of other retailers. The building itself is influenced by the merchandise handled and the needed flow of traffic through the store. The merchandise reflects the needs of the local population, and these in turn are determined by natural conditions such as climate, by income, and by fashion. The prices charged provide some indication of the kind of clientele served, and the hours clearly relate to the available time of the buyers. Retailing tends to be "consumption bound," that is, the stores are dependent on

*National Farm Organization.

those people who live within the trading area. A wholesaler, by contrast, ships merchandise hundreds or thousands of miles to retailers in other trading areas.

Retailers adapt to laws—hours, prices, packaging, and building codes, for example. A change in a law is promptly reflected by the retailers, as when the ban on the sale of colored margarine was lifted in dairy-producing states.

The competitive pressures, sometimes caused by changes in the environment, are strong and can be seen especially on downtown merchants who strive to remain profitable as the move to the suburbs makes downtown less important relative to a total metropolitan area. Merchants band together in these cases and struggle to maintain attractive offerings for buyers. They build shopping malls and parking ramps, modernize their stores, and offer fashion shows. They may invest in the construction of office buildings and encourage the development of new civic centers in order to keep the downtown population large and to provide people with many reasons to go there.

Retailers in recent years have also adapted to the social forces of the environment. They have hired minorities and have become conspicuously involved in various kinds of civic endeavors—orchestras, youth groups, and civic celebrations. Their need is to maintain a strong community, for from a strong and dynamic community comes their business.

# CONCLUDING COMMENTS

This chapter has focused on the institutional structure of the marketing system, the markets served by the system, and the flow of goods through it. The structure bridges the gaps between producers and consumers as it makes the multitude of goods available to buyers. The structure includes virtually every business establishment in the country, though the mainstays are those firms that have been organized especially to handle the various marketing needs of buyers and sellers—wholesalers, retailers, and facilitating agencies.

There is nothing permanent about the marketing structure. It exhibits an ebb and flow of establishments, both in number and in kind, as it continually adapts to the total and changing environment of laws, technology, population, economics, life styles, and forces of the natural environment. The structure includes generalists and specialists, privately owned and publicly owned firms, single and multiple units.

The adaptation of marketing and its structure to the environment is easily seen when marketing in various countries is examined and compared, as will be done in Chapter 4.

# STATEMENTS TO CONSIDER

Marketing institutions are primarily the effects, rather than the causes, of marketing functions. (McInnes)

On balance, cost is the most important consideration in determining any middleman's place in the channel of distribution. (Tousley)

Retailing institutions enter as innovators in low-status, low-margin, and low-price beginnings and mature as relatively high status, high costs and high prices and with a top-heavy vulnerability. (McNair's "wheel of retailing")

Retailing serves the functions of aiding people to match, conveniently, their wants with available goods and services. (Baranoff)

Marketing channels are social systems, organized behavior systems, which have technological, economic, sociological, and psychological features. (Alderson)

The low-income women go mainly to the broad-appeal and the price-appeal stores, although some patronize the fashion-appeal stores. (Britt)

Retailers are highly adaptive to the social and economic changes of our society.

Although there are economies of scale in retailing, in many lines the most efficient size is not the largest. (Douglas)

Population and distance account for almost all the variation in sales between cities. (Reilly)

. . . as long as the economies of intermediate sorting are great, there will be substantial opportunities for nonintegrated intermediate agencies. (Vaile)

# QUESTIONS FOR REVIEW

**1.** What do you understand by the term "market"?

**2.** Take any product and classify the markets it might be sold in.

**3.** What are the principal distinguishing features among the five major types of wholesalers?

**4.** How can you account for the differences in distribution by wholesalers as shown in 3-3?

**5.** Why would a manufacturer use the services of an agent middleman instead of organizing his own marketing department?

**6.** There were 261,059 gasoline stations in operation in 1967. How many do you think were actually necessary?

**7.** How would you characterize the marketing by those in personal services?

**8.** What is a facilitating service?

**9.** There are a number of new cities being planned for the United States. If you had the task of planning the retail sector, what would you include?

**10.** How many of each retail establishment would be needed for a new city of 100,000 people?

## Further Readings

Reavis Cox, *Distribution in a High-Level Economy* (Englewood Cliffs, N.J.: Prentice-Hall, 1965).

Douglas J. Dalrymple, *Retailing* (New York: Free Press, 1969).

Victor R. Fuchs, "The Growing Importance of the Service Industries," *Journal of Business,* Vol. XXXVII (October 1965), pp. 344–374.

Rom J. Markin, Jr., *Retailing Management* (New York: Macmillan, 1971).

David A. Revzan, *Wholesaling* (New York: John Wiley, 1971).

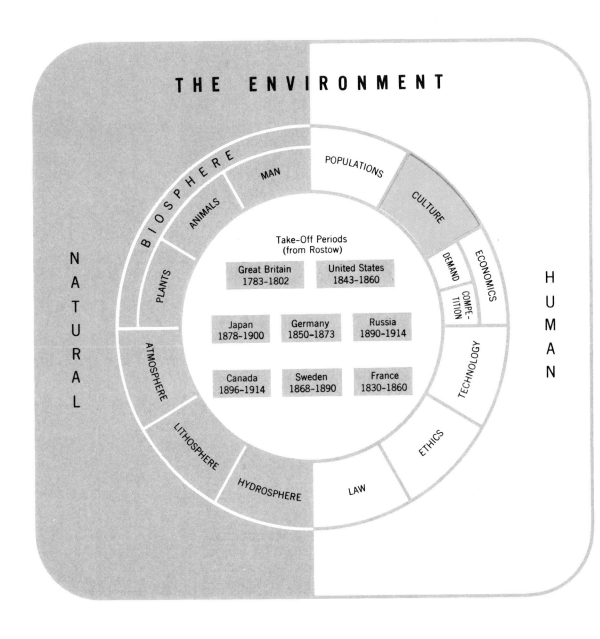

# THE ENVIRONMENT

**NATURAL**

**HUMAN**

BIOSPHERE

MAN

POPULATIONS

ANIMALS

CULTURE

PLANTS

DEMAND

ECONOMICS

COMPE-TITION

ATMOSPHERE

TECHNOLOGY

LITHOSPHERE

ETHICS

HYDROSPHERE

LAW

Take-Off Periods
(from Rostow)

Great Britain
1783–1802

United States
1843–1860

Japan
1878–1900

Germany
1850–1873

Russia
1890–1914

Canada
1896–1914

Sweden
1868–1890

France
1830–1860

# CHAPTER 4
# MARKETING IN DIFFERENT ENVIRONMENTS

**The Nature of
Comparative Marketing**

**The Study of
Comparative Marketing**

*Purpose
Limitations*

**Approaches to the Study
of Comparative Marketing**

*Boddewyn's Conceptual Framework
Rostow's Stages of Development
An Outline for Comparative
   Marketing Analysis*

**The Interrelationship of
Marketing and Environment**

**Selected Country Comparisons**

*The study of various marketing systems around the world reveals the important cause-and-effect relationships between environmental forces and marketing. Planned economies reflect the strong governmental influence.*

Every society, with few exceptions, in one way or another engages in marketing. The exceptions are those few remaining primitive societies with wholly subsistence economies. In the crudest form, indeed, a subsistence economy need not even involve markets and money, inasmuch as each person (or each grouping of people) is his own consumer, and thus the market is himself. In a subsistence economy there is little or no *organized* specialization of economic activities.

In most other societies of the world, however, marketing is an important subset of the economic system. As noted in Chapter 1, the size and relative importance of marketing varies from one society to another, depending on the stage of a society's economic and social development. Some nations may be characterized as "modern market economies," such as the Western European nations; others as "developing economies," such as some of the countries in the Middle East, the South American nations, and the recently franchised African nations; and others as "economically depressed," such as India and its neighboring countries. Whatever the stage of development, each society is influenced by the same environmental factors, but here again, by varying dimensions of influence.

One cannot expect, nor should he, that the environmental factors influencing marketing in the United States will have the same measure of influence elsewhere. As a nation develops economically and socially, its priorities change and adjust. The present-day emphasis on consumer affairs in this country could not be duplicated in a country that is economically stagnant. Rather, a stagnant economy may have priorities such as better health care, improved foreign trade relations, and the alleviation of poverty for the vast majority of its populace. Briefly, then, the environment of a society helps to determine its priorities, and in turn the priorities determine the nature of the market. Thus the task of marketing and the way it serves society are different in the Soviet Union, in Japan, in Peru, and elsewhere.

The study of marketing in different environments, known as "comparative marketing," can help us to increase our understanding of our own system and the environmental influences that shape all marketing—wherever it may occur.

## THE NATURE OF COMPARATIVE MARKETING

We should clarify what we mean by the term "comparative marketing." According to Robert Bartels, one of the few academicians who has studied the subject in depth, *"comparative marketing is concerned with different marketing systems of mankind, with the interpretation of different yet comparable elements"* (Bartels, 1964).

The development and evolution of a nation's marketing system is the result of many complex factors. A traveler going from one country to another can superficially observe striking differences in marketplaces and in marketing activities and contrast them with what he knows of his native country. He may notice, for example, that bulk products such as fuel oil are sold, not by the standard gallon, but by the variable quantity of an old wine bottle or more commonly the ubiquitous Coca-Cola bottle. Sometimes a container of this kind becomes a standard measure by virtue of its wide usage. This may be a sign, as is true in some underdeveloped economies, of a lack of standard weights and measures as they are understood in the economically advanced countries.

The marketing institutions in the underdeveloped nations may also differ greatly from those of technically and economically advanced countries. In many tribal communities and small villages of the Middle East and southern Asia, people market their products and acquire their needs through an intermediary who represents an entire village group. For example, a geographer reports about some villagers in North Vietnam:

> There is considerable trade among the tribal groups and between them and the Lao and Vietnamese. A peculiar feature of this trade is an institution and practice known as *Lam*. This means, briefly, that a person known as a Lam acts as an intermediary between the parties concerned. Usually the Lam is a Lao who comes from a village located so as to be accessible to both the tribal settlements and the outside markets. He is frequently a village or district headman. The tribal people come to the Lam whenever they have some items to trade or sell and procure from him the items they need. These are salt, clothing . . . cloth . . . soap, nails, flashlights and batteries, and such rare luxury items as kerosene and powdered coffee. (Thoman, 1962.)

Developments in rural China provide convincing evidence that marketing interacts closely with its environment. C. William Skinner, an anthropologist, has described how the traditional marketing structure shaped the local social organization in rural China. Skinner comments: "Basic alterations in the distribution of markets and the patterning of marketing behavior provide a sensitive index of progress in modernization . . . an adequate interpretation of developments since 1949 in the Chinese countryside must rest on a prior analysis of premodern peasant marketing." But while peasant marketing traditions shaped the Communists' instruments for rural transformation, Skinner concludes that the transformation "inevitably and quite literally reshaped them [marketing communities] in turn" (Skinner, 1965). Thus marketing affects and is affected by environmental forces.

Transportation differs from place to place too. In European countries a traveler can hardly fail to notice the extensive use of rivers and canals in the distribution of products. The Rhine, Danube, and Elbe rivers, interconnected by other rivers and canals, carry a vast tonnage of industrial and consumer products. This single natural resource has provided a low-cost, efficient means of distribution serving millions of people. Although Europe also enjoys overland and air transportation, the rivers have dominated trade for centuries. Additionally, these rivers have influenced the location of major cities and the concentration of population in those cities.

In some areas, after becoming familiar with the business community and its history, a visitor will learn of the "dominant family" and the power it exerts over the marketplace. In some Near Eastern countries and most Latin American nations, importing, exporting, wholesaling, retailing, and even manufacturing are dominated by wealthy "controlling class" families. For centuries these families have (through closed corporations and inherited wealth) shaped the economic and marketing practices of their countries. Not only is the family name dominant in the country, but the practices of the firms have been passed from father to son so rigidly that the procedures today differ little from what they were a century ago. The influence of the closely held family marketing firm (usually in importing, exporting, and domestic wholesaling) can be so powerful that the "system" tends to determine consumer choices. In Lebanon, for example, three large family-owned firms dominate the marketing scene. The impact of such closely held control is a restraint of marketing activities. One writer commenting on the market power of the "Big Three" in Lebanon says:

> The resulting drag on the competitive process has tended to minimize choices available to the consumer, reduce price rivalry, diminish the need and opportunity for advertising and promotion, and give unfair advantage to the large firms. A further concomitant of this situation is to render the market less accessible to new items which might be produced by local manufacturers. Even though it might be possible for new industry to be established in Lebanon. . .unless the manufacturer assumes the distribution function it might be difficult if not impossible to secure an effective channel of distribution for its products. The [existing] channels members may not be willing to handle the product if it competes with a foreign import controlled by one of the dominant firms. (Call, 1965.)

These examples illustrate some isolated differences in marketing from our usual frame of reference, twentieth-century U.S.A. A further careful examination of other countries could reveal both marked differences and marked similarities of the entire marketing system. These similarities and differences are necessarily linked to the environment, and in trying to explain them we need to dig out the relevant physical, social, economic, political, and cultural factors. But we must not become bemused by environmental studies *per se*. The focus of marketing comparisons should be on the marketing systems within their environments.

We stressed in Chapters 1 and 2 that knowledge of environmental influences on marketing assists our understanding of the *why* of marketing. Conversely, as marketing systems are compared we often learn that the major differences and similarities rest on environmental factors. For example, advertising as we know it is absent in some countries, and in others it is fundamentally different from ours in appeal; the explanation of these various advertising practices resides in economic, social, and cultural differences. Similarly, the restraints imposed on the market in Lebanon, as described above, are the result of cultural, legal, and economic forces.

# THE STUDY OF COMPARATIVE MARKETING

## Purpose

Our accustomed frame of reference, the twentieth-century United States, is very useful in understanding American marketing, but it does little to give us a perspective on the rest of the world. Yet business administration—marketing in particular—is not an isolated field of study. Marketing as an economic function, as a social function, and as an activity of the firm is worldwide. What you learn from comparative marketing will aid in understanding other marketing systems; it will sharpen your knowledge about our own marketing system; and it may even provide an insight into environmental differences.

Some students of marketing will have career opportunities with multinational corporations. Clearly, for them a study of marketing with a single-country focus is too limited. But a comparative emphasis and a stress on environmental influences will provide a background for appreciating different marketing systems. Marketing as a field to study is growing in many universities abroad. For students in foreign countries and foreign students studying in this country, comparative marketing can be enlightening.

Finally, comparative marketing can be of considerable value to the student of economic development. In most of the economically depressed nations marketing is inefficient, low in productivity, and wasteful. And it exacts a cost from society that society can ill afford. Such a marketing system functions against the improved welfare of the people. If change is to occur, a reformed marketing system must be planned as part of a general program of economic development. Of course, environmental adjustments will stimulate marketing changes as economic development gets under way.

## Limitations

If you were to travel abroad and describe the marketing operations of a foreign country, would your approach be much different from the following?

What might [a casual tourist] see as he travels about a country and looks about him? Such a traveler tends to emphasize the picturesque.

He is interested especially in remnants of simpler times that have managed a precarious survival into the twentieth century because they have had some degree of isolation from the rest of the world or because they have been preserved deliberately by governmental or other agencies. He sees "mammy traders" in West Africa, open-air markets in Latin American and West Indian towns, dark shops lining the alleys of Moslem cities, itinerant merchants in Italian hill towns, stalls along the sidewalks in front of some of the world's most famous department stores in Paris itself. What he looks for is conversation pieces with which to regale the folks back home. He seeks color— both in the figurative sense and in the literal sense that gives him something to record on transparencies or motion picture film. (Cox, 1965.)

Underlying the colorful surface, however, there may be a substantial and intricate organization to a foreign marketing system. The basic purpose of the system, indeed, is the same as that of our own. Unfortunately, most studies of comparative marketing are as superficial as tourists' reports, concentrating on easily observed differences and ignoring more elusive structural similarities. Another drawback is that basic quantitative data about other marketing methods and other marketing systems is either unorganized or even nonexistent. For the most part, marketing academicians have gathered much useful data, but the surface has only been scratched.

One of the problems is assembling really significant data. Although it may be of interest to know the number of department stores in India as contrasted with the United States, it is much more useful to know the character of the Indian retail structure and why it developed as it did. For example, the peddler and stall-keeper in peasant markets are picturesque, but from a marketing standpoint it is more useful to know that many peasant markets are controlled by the government. Control of market sites by the government had its origin many centuries ago, and license fees, taxes, legal regulations, and legal protection of trade are a few of the consequences. The particulars vary, but how different is the Indian system from the controls exerted by political agencies on our own retail centers?

## APPROACHES TO THE STUDY OF COMPARATIVE MARKETING

In recent years marketing scholars in growing numbers have turned their attention to the study of comparative marketing. The impetus for this new interest has come from several sources: the much greater involvement of American business with other nations, the decline of isolationism, the federal government's numerous assistance programs to other nations, and the need to comprehend the development and behavior of our own marketing structure. A number of approaches to marketing comparisons has resulted. Each approach has its own scheme and each has considerable merit. We will briefly discuss three of the leading ones.

## Boddewyn's Conceptual Framework

J. Boddewyn asks: "When comparing marketing systems, what should be compared?" In answering his own question he has developed a conceptual framework ". . . concerned with the systematic detection, identification, classification, measurement, and interpretation of similarities and differences among [marketing] phenomena." An abbreviation of Boddewyn's framework is shown in 4-1. Of particular interest is the precision possible in this plan. By isolating problems as shown in 4-1, this approach emphasizes the marketing elements to be studied. This framework is obviously not an environmental approach to the subject. Rather it centers on the ". . . *relationships* among function, structure, process, actors, and environment" (Boddewyn, 1966). Is it possible that in-depth research into the environment may not provide all the answers? Certainly the Boddewyn approach would produce a valuable store of systematically organized comparative knowledge.

An example of a comparison of marketing activities possible under this approach is shown in 4-2. This is a comparison between two Eastern Bloc countries that at one time may have had more similarities than differences. Yugoslavia, with a politically liberalized economy, has made great strides in recent years. Romania, on the other hand, has more politically centralized decisions. Marketing in each country is of major importance, but Yugoslavia uses it to develop its international trade, whereas Romania sees it as an accelerator of the economy.

## **4-1** Construct for Comparative Marketing Research

| Problem | Aspects to be studied comparatively |
|---|---|
| Who are the marketers? | The actors' characteristics:<br>    Physical, economical, political, social, cultural |
| What do marketers do? | The actors' activities and interactions:<br>    Activities: assembling, transporting, etc.<br>    Initiatives: (who initiates the contacts?)<br>    Techniques: competition, cooperation, etc. |
| How are marketers related to each other? | The actors' relationships:<br>    Membership, arena<br>    Scope (over what matters?)<br>    Nature (in what types of relationships?) |
| What do marketers contribute? | The actors' contributions:<br>    Nature: psychological, economic, etc.<br>    Recipients: society, consumers<br>    Size: quality and efficiency |
| How are marketers affected by their environment? | The interdependence between environmental factors and the actors' characteristics, activities, interactions, relationships, and contributions. |

SOURCE: Modified from J. Boddewyn, "A Construct for Comparative Marketing Research," *Journal of Marketing Research*, Vol. III (May 1966), p. 151.

**4-2** Comparison between Yugoslavian and Romanian Marketing Systems

| Activity | Yugoslavian | Romanian |
|---|---|---|
| General | Relatively decentralized with some incentive and competition at the enterprise level. | Relatively centralized. |
| Product research | More emphasis on the prevailing consumption patterns as guidelines for national plans. | Product research to prevent accumulation of unwanted goods or excessive supplies. |
| Assortment | Decentralized and more consumer-oriented, especially at the foreign-trade level. | More production-efficiency–oriented with some recent tendencies to decentralize. |
| Price | Partial central control, with increasing proportions being liberalized. | Primarily centrally administered; one price policy nationally. |
| Promotion | Basically to inform the consumer and somewhat to stimulate demand in cases of international trade and at the point of purchase. | Primarily to eliminate bottlenecks in distribution as well as some consumer information. |
| Location | Decentralized, decisions are made at regional and local levels. | Centralized, based on established population-trade space ratios. |

SOURCE: A Coskin Samli, "A Comparative Analysis of Marketing in Romania and Yugoslavia," *Southern Journal of Business*, Vol. 5 (July 1970), p. 112.

## Rostow's Stages of Development

Another of the better-known approaches to the problem of developing economies is Walt Rostow's theory of five stages of economic growth. According to Rostow's hypothesis, all economies would fit into one of the five stages, which are:

1st—traditional society, essentially poor and stagnant.

2nd—transitional society, preconditions for take-off are being established.

3rd—take-off, resistances to steady growth are finally overcome and the economy takes off as growth becomes the normal condition.

4th—drive to maturity, modern technology extended over the economic front.

5th—age of high mass-consumption, or the affluent society. (Rostow, 1960.)*

*For a complete discussion see W. W. Rostow, *The Stages of Economic Growth* (Cambridge, England: Cambridge University Press, 1960).

**4-3** The Rostow Timetable—Tentative, Approximate Take-off Periods and Maturity Dates

| Nation | Take-off period | Maturity |
|---|---|---|
| Great Britain | 1783–1802 | 1850 |
| France | 1830–1860 | 1910 |
| United States | 1843–1860 | 1900 |
| Germany | 1850–1873 | 1910 |
| Sweden | 1868–1890 | 1930 |
| Japan | 1878–1900 | 1940 |
| Russia | 1890–1914 | 1950 |
| Canada | 1896–1914 | 1950 |
| Argentina | 1935– | not yet |
| Turkey | 1937– | not yet |
| India | 1952– | not yet |
| China | 1952– | not yet |

SOURCE: "Take-off, Catch-up, Satiety," *Business Week*, April 9, 1960, p. 100. Copyright held by McGraw-Hill Book Company, Inc.

There are aspects of Rostow's stages of development that are applicable to marketing institutions and activities, for as a society's economy develops so does its marketing system. If marketing bridges the gap between production and consumption, then it will adapt as a society evolves through the several stages of development. Product, price, promotion, and distribution, all will be affected by any change in the stage of development. Of course consumption and use patterns of society will undergo change and thus add increased impetus for marketing to develop as the evolutionary process moves a country from one stage to another.

Depicted in 4-3 is Rostow's timetable for the take-off period and the dates of reaching maturity for selected nations. A somewhat different, but related, example is given in 4-4, which shows the evolution of the marketing process through various stages of an economy, as developed by John M. Hess and Philip R. Cateora. The important point here is that marketing functions, marketing institutions, and marketing channels are affected by the successive stages of development. In both schemes of development, the patterns of marketing change and the resultant mass distribution process are common to the evolutionary process.

Systematic categorization of development into stages permits us to make a logical explanation of the development of marketing. It also clarifies our understanding of the interdependence among all economic segments of a nation. Production, marketing, and consumption—indeed, all facets of an economic system are inseparable parts of the total network. This kind of analysis also gives us insight into the *why* of marketing phenomena.

## An Outline for Comparative Marketing Analysis

Some of the most extensive work in comparative marketing has been done by Robert Bartels. Under the sponsorship of the American Mar-

## 4-4 Evolution of the Marketing Process

| Stage | Substage | Examples | Marketing functions | Marketing institutions | Channel control | Primary orientation | Resources employed | Comments |
|---|---|---|---|---|---|---|---|---|
| Agricultural and raw materials (Mk.(f) = Prod.) | Self-sufficient | Nomadic or hunting tribes | None | None | Traditional authority | Subsistence | Labor, Land | Labor-intensive, No organized markets |
| | Surplus commodity producer | Agricultural economy —i.e., coffee, bananas | Exchange | Small-scale merchants, traders, fairs | Traditional authority | Entrepreneurial Commercial | Labor, Land | Labor- and land-intensive, Product specialization, Local markets |
| Manufacturing (Mk.(f) = Prod.) | Small-scale | Cottage industry | Exchange, Physical distribution | Merchants, wholesalers, export-import | Middlemen | Entrepreneurial Financial | Labor, Land, Technology, Transportation | Labor-intensive, Product standardization and grading, Regional and export markets |
| | Mass production | US economy from 1885–1914 | Demand creation, Physical distribution | Merchants, wholesalers, traders, and specialized institutions | Producer | Production and finance | Labor, Land, Technology, Transportation, Capital | Capital-intensive, Product differentiation, National, regional and export markets |
| Marketing (Prod.(f) = Mk.) | Commercial— Transition | US economy from 1915–1929 | Demand creation, Physical distribution, Market information | Large-scale and chain retailers increase in specialized middlemen | Producer | Entrepreneurial Commercial | Labor, Land, Technology, Transportation, Capital, Communication | Capital-intensive, Changes in structure of distribution, National, regional, and export markets |
| | Mass distribution | US economy from 1950 to present | Demand creation, Physical distribution, Market information, Market and product planning, development | Integrated channels of distribution, Increase in specialized middlemen | Producer, Retailer | Marketing | Labor, Land, Technology, Transportation, Capital, Communication | Capital- and land-intensive, Rapid product innovation, National, regional, and export markets |

SOURCE: Philip R. Cateora and John M. Hess, International Marketing. (Homewood, Ill.: Richard D. Irwin, 1971), p. 202. Reprinted with permission from the authors.

keting Association, he initiated an organized effort to pioneer interest in marketing abroad. One result was a multi-author volume entitled *Comparative Marketing: Wholesaling in Fifteen Countries,* which adhered to the following criteria: "(1) descriptions or discussions of the respective national wholesaling practice should emphasize contrasts between those of that country and those of another country; and (2) the practices of . . . [the] country [under study] should be interpreted in terms of the prevailing socioeconomic conditions" (Bartels, 1963). The articles in the book provided a store of quantitative data about different countries and insight into the economic and noneconomic elements affecting marketing.

In conjunction with that project Bartels developed an outline for making marketing comparisons. His outline, modified in 4-5, can serve as a guide to a systematic approach to marketing comparisons. Note that his approach reflects the social characteristics of marketing as well

---

**4-5** Outline for Comparative Marketing Analysis

Introductory Characterization
  General analysis of marketing including any significant findings which explain the marketing operation. For example, the role of marketing, stage of development, principal marketing problems, level of technical efficiency, etc. would be included in this introductory part.
Society Depicted
  Nature of society in terms of sociological concepts
  Distinctive features of each of the major social institutions
  Depict the means by which the basic needs and wants of society are supplied (mostly nonmaterial wants)
The Economy
  Means by which society provides for its material needs
  Production, distribution, standard of living, security, status in world
The Marketing System
  The Market
    Buyers and sellers
    Satisfaction of the market
    Physical—number of consumers, purchasing power, location, patronage habits, etc.
  Conceptual aspects
    Occurrence of a transaction
    Supply and demand
  Types of separation in the market
    Functional—leads to merchandising and store keeping
    Informational—gives rise to buying, selling, advertising, etc.
    Spatial—gives rise to transportation
    Temporal—gives rise to storage
    Financial—gives rise to credit and marketing finance (*cont.*)

---

**4-5** Outline for Comparative Marketing Analysis, *Cont.*

Marketing Behavior
    The behavior of individuals performing the marketing functions
    The action and interaction of people in the process of a certain type of
       want fulfillment
    State vs. private agencies; profit vs. nonprofit agencies; producers vs. dis-
       tributors; wholesalers vs. retailers; business vs. consumers

The Marketing Structure
    Various combinations of economic units—labor, capital, facilities, etc.
    Combinations of factors in marketing management—the marketing mix
    Direct marketing
    Retailing system
    Scale of operation
    Services rendered
    Multi- and single-lined stores
    Nonstore retailing
    Wholesaling system
    Manufacturers' sales organizations
    Competition
    Distributors
    Channels
    Facilitating marketing institutions—warehouses, credit services, advertising
       agencies, standards associations, financing agencies, etc.

Control of Marketing
    Checks and balances of the society
    Preplanning
    Automaticity of the market mechanism
    Countervailing powers
    Cost data
    Voluntary restraint
    Government regulation
    Social ethics
    Consumer resistance

SOURCE: Modified and abbreviated from Robert Bartels (ed.), *Comparative Marketing: Whole-saling in Fifteen Countries*, (Homewood, Ill.: Richard D. Irwin, 1963), pp. 299–308.

as the mechanics. Marketing is thus viewed as the action and interaction of many people to satisfy the goals of the marketing system.

Only a few approaches for making marketing comparisons have been discussed, but these, and all others, aim to uncover the same dynamics and interrelationships about marketing. As a consequence the goal of *understanding* marketing can be accomplished in several ways.

# THE INTERRELATIONSHIP
# OF MARKETING AND ENVIRONMENT

The central purpose of comparative marketing is to understand the similarities and differences in marketing in various countries. Bodde- wyn stresses the need to focus on the marketing system *per se,* rather than on the environment. Other approaches have tended to analyze the environment as well as the marketing system and its elements. Boddewyn, although distinguishing between the two, points out that the independent variables are to be found in the environment and that the marketing system in effect becomes a consequence, or a dependent variable. The authors of this text stress the relationship between the environment and marketing and believe that bare comparisons of marketing yield only "technical" information. It is the "social" aspects that help explain the marketing comparisons. In 4-6, taken from Bartels, there is a clear picture of these different aspects. Using Bartels's scheme, it is easy to point out the relationship between comparative marketing and comparative study of environments (see 4-7).

Comparative analyses encompassing the marketing process and the environment have practical managerial implications. Certainly a for-

**4-6** Relations of Environmental Factors to Dependent Elements of Marketing

| NATIONAL ENVIRONMENTS | ELEMENTS OF MARKETING | |
|---|---|---|
| | Technical | Social |
| Physical and economic<br>Size of:<br>   Country<br>   Population<br>   GNP<br>Level of living<br>Transportation system<br>Etc. | Products<br>Price<br>Profits<br>Costs<br>Brands<br>Differentiation<br>Layouts<br>Scales<br>Channels<br>Markets<br>Institutions<br>Flows<br>Processes | |
| Societal and social<br>Family<br>School<br>Church<br>Economy<br>Government<br>Military<br>Leisure | | Social systems<br>Roles<br>Behavior<br>Interaction<br>Management |

SOURCE: Robert Bartels, "Are Domestic and International Marketing Dissimilar?" *Journal of Marketing*, Vol. 32 (July 1968), p. 58.

**4-7** Model for Comparative Analysis

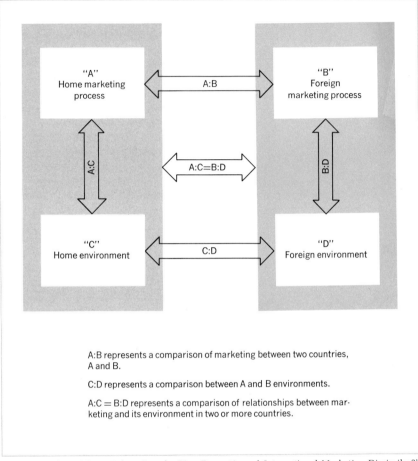

A:B represents a comparison of marketing between two countries, A and B.

C:D represents a comparison between A and B environments.

A:C = B:D represents a comparison of relationships between marketing and its environment in two or more countries.

SOURCE: Adapted from Robert Bartels, "Are Domestic and International Marketing Dissimilar?" *Journal of Marketing*, Vol. 32 (July 1968), p. 59.

eign-marketing strategy can be better conceived with an understanding of the foreign environment. The dual approach also enhances a manager's perception of what can and what cannot be done as a firm develops a multinational thrust.

## SELECTED COUNTRY COMPARISONS

We've been discussing comparative marketing systems in general, even in abstract terms. The point has been made that the environment is the basis for the marketing system and the changing environment influences the nature of marketing operations. For one example, the concentration of people and industries in urban centers has the consequence of concentrated retailing and wholesaling centers; for another, the measure of government control determines the prerogatives of management in the marketplace. Some additional examples are given in the list below; obviously the list makes no attempt to develop complete comparisons; rather, it illustrates different kinds of comparative marketing research (Sommers and Kernan, 1968).

| Environmental Causal Factors | Marketing Consequences |
|---|---|
| **INDIA** | |
| People place low value on material things | |
| Inefficient transportation system | → High cost of marketing goods (physical) |
| Adverse attitudes toward advertising, illiteracy, scarce TV coverage | → Little demand creation on all levels |
| **NIGERIA** | |
| Lack of know-how of indigenous population | → Distribution carried out in part by foreign countries |
| High degree of illiteracy | → Visual display of goods and easy price comparisons |
| Emphasis on interaction | → Personal selling and bargaining |
| **FRANCE** | |
| Emphasis on personal contact | → Small retailer in large numbers |
| Adverse attitude against mass-produced goods | → Retail trade fragmented; small retailers with personal services |
| **EGYPT** | |
| Inadequate storage facilities | → Buyers obtain goods in small quantities on everyday basis |
| Government intervention | → Pricing limited by government regulations |
| Lack of newspapers outside large cities | → Limited advertising |
| **CHILE** | |
| Government intervention | → Regulation of product line Price intervention to prevent inflation |
| Low state of marketing technology | → Slow development of supermarkets |
| **JAPAN** | |
| Large merchant houses of the past | → Strong wholesaler influence in marketing |
| Shortage of space | → Sales space increased at expense of storage facilities |
| **TURKEY** | |
| Economy of scarcity | → Little promotional activity, supply orientation |

USSR

Scarcity of consumption goods ———▶ Relatively little promotion
Apartment type of living ———▶ Stores in or near apartments
Historically heavy emphasis ———▶ Continued use of markets for food
   on public markets             and other items
Centralized, planned economy ———▶ Fixed prices by government
                                  Controlled production of goods
                                  Controlled advertising
                                  Little competition
                                  Few innovations in marketing

Let us elaborate briefly on the situation in the Soviet Union. There are retail establishments and other forms of marketing familiar to the Westerner. But stores are stocked with fewer varieties of products, although the assortment is improving as the USSR increases production. Buying is very time-consuming—it has been estimated that Soviet citizens waste about 30 billion hours a year in shopping, the equivalent of a year's work for 15 million men (Gwertzman, 1969). The society does not permit competition except as it may occur on a small scale between retailers. Even if the planners catch up with the demand for refrigerators, for example, they would not permit competition at the manufacturers' level but would simply convert a refrigerator plant over to, say, vacuum sweeper production. Soviet managers perform some marketing research but get extremely little market information because they lack a price-feedback system based on supply and demand.

One Novosibirsk manager of a textile store wrote that "We should spare no effort in the organization of good advertising. Neither should we economize on advertising, because expenditures for it are repaid a hundredfold" (Argunov, 1966). However, one of the authors visited Novosibirsk and found that the store's advertising was limited to a few spot TV announcements and a little space in newspapers. What the manager referred to as advertising was mostly in-store displays.

Historically, the Soviets have downgraded marketing and made it out to be a parasitic function of some kind. Recently, as consumer-goods production has become respectable, there has been a change in attitude. People have been encouraged to enter marketing, and ideology has been "developed" to rationalize this change. Further, Schools of Distribution have been organized where students take essentially the same kinds of courses as do business school students in the United States. There seems to be a heavier emphasis on the physical aspects of distribution in these schools and also a rather heavy emphasis on learning about the products themselves.

Basically, the centralized planning system controlled by the government is probably the most important factor affecting marketing in the USSR. Decisions that are made in the West by consumers and businessmen are typically made by the central planning agencies. Most of the marketing mechanism found in the United States is to be found in the USSR, but its control is far different. In the agricultural sector private products and an actual market exchange exist, but this is an exception to the overall policy.

# CONCLUDING COMMENTS

Comparative marketing gives us a perspective about marketing throughout the world. Although differences and similarities between any two marketing systems can be highlighted, our main question is *why?* By comparative study our data can be reduced to comparability and the processes can be traced to their foundations in the environments. Through studying the interrelationships of marketing and environment we can improve our level of knowledge about other societies and about our own marketing network.

As this study of the environment of marketing continues, many opportunities will present themselves for comparisons of one country with another, especially if marketing is conceived as both a social and an economic process.

# STATEMENTS TO CONSIDER

By viewing marketing as a social process we better understand the role of individuals in the marketing system.

Marketing is critical to economic development.

The Soviet Union by controlling price can also achieve proportionality between supply and demand.

The role of advertising in a centrally planned society is relative to the planned goals of the market.

As a society develops and the economic welfare of the populace advances, one expects that the society's priorities will adjust and change.

The understanding of culture can help the marketing manager cope with his problems of nonrational consumer behavior in other countries.

The geographic distance between countries can easily be overemphasized. The really crucial factor in developing international markets is the socioeconomic environment.

If people place a low value on material things, as is the case in some Far Eastern and Middle Eastern countries, then marketing functions are likely to be viewed adversely.

There is more to marketing than its functions and activities. These applied to a developing economy must be supported by physical systems such as transportation, storage, and business enterprises.

A country experiencing a change in the educational level of its populace will also experience a change in products demanded.

1. What is meant by the term "comparative marketing"?

2. If a society is dominated by political authority, what would you expect with regard to marketing activity?

3. Comment on the statement, "Every society gets the marketing job done in one way or another."

4. How might wealthy "controlling class" families control marketing in some countries?

5. "Our marketing system and the attendant functions are a reflection of our culture." Comment on the validity of this statement.

6. Enumerate the basic reasons for the study of marketing in different environments.

7. In what ways can the study of marketing similarities and differences help a manager in a multinational firm.

8. Describe the kind of marketing you would expect and the changes that most likely would occur as an economy progresses through Rostow's stages of development.

9. Explain how the relative importance of labor and land changes with the evolution of marketing processes.

10. In those economies where Rostow's "age of high mass-consumption" has been reached, we find great similarity of products. Comment.

## Further Readings

Cyril S. Belshaw, *Traditional Exchange of Modern Markets* (Englewood Cliffs, N.J.: Prentice-Hall, 1965).

Paul Bohannan and George Dalton, *Markets in Africa* (Garden City, New York: Doubleday, 1965).

Bertil Liander, *Comparative Analysis For International Marketing* (Boston: Allyn & Bacon, 1967).

Karl Polanyi, Conrad M. Arensburg, and Harry W. Pearson, *Trade and Market in the Early Empires* (Glencoe, Ill.: Free Press, 1957).

Stanley J. Shapiro, "Comparative Marketing and Economic Development," chapter in George Schwartz (ed.), *Science in Marketing* (New York: John Wiley, 1965), pp. 398–429.

# THE ENVIRONMENT

NATURAL

HUMAN

Ch. 5. The natural environment and marketing
Ch. 6. The economic environment and competition
Ch. 7. Marketing and the law
Ch. 8. The force of technology
Ch. 9. The economics of demand
Ch. 10, 11, 12. Household buyer behavior
Ch. 13. Nonhousehold buyer behavior

# PART II
# THE MARKETING ENVIRONMENT AND BUYER BEHAVIOR

*Marketing is the result of the total forces of the environment—natural, competition, legal, technological, demand, and populations. Each force interacts with the efforts of marketing managers in the thousands of firms that constitute the business system.*

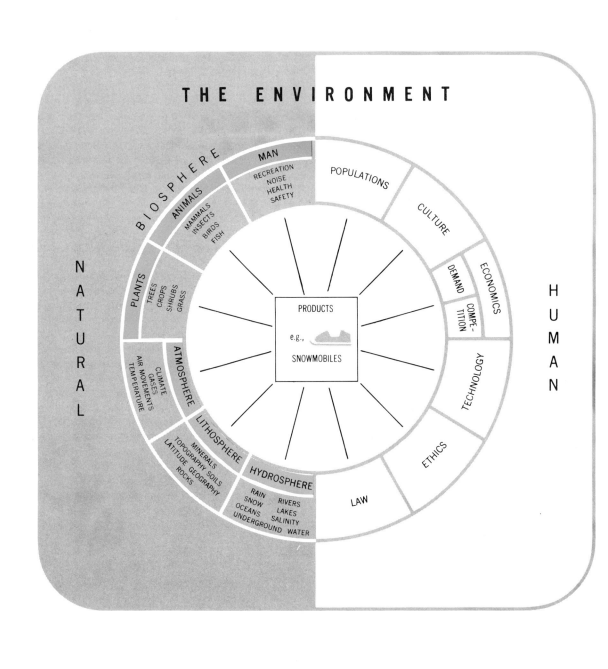

# THE ENVIRONMENT

NATURAL

HUMAN

BIOSPHERE

MAN
RECREATION
NOISE
HEALTH
SAFETY

ANIMALS
MAMMALS
INSECTS
BIRDS
FISH

PLANTS
TREES
CROPS
SHRUBS
GRASS

ATMOSPHERE
CLIMATE
GASES
AIR MOVEMENTS
TEMPERATURE

LITHOSPHERE
MINERALS
TOPOGRAPHY SOILS
LATITUDE GEOGRAPHY
ROCKS

HYDROSPHERE
RAIN     RIVERS
SNOW     LAKES
OCEANS   SALINITY
UNDERGROUND WATER

PRODUCTS
e.g.,
SNOWMOBILES

POPULATIONS

CULTURE

DEMAND

ECONOMICS

COMPE-
TITION

TECHNOLOGY

ETHICS

LAW

# CHAPTER 5
# THE NATURAL ENVIRONMENT AND MARKETING

*The challenge of man is no longer the mastery of his environment, but rather the mastery of his desires, judgment, and actions with respect to his natural environment. The geographical environment is highly relevant to marketing because of the space intervening between producer and consumer.*

The public concern over environmental matters that began in the 1960s was long overdue. Marketers like others had ignored the needs of nature while they worked to satisfy the needs of man. Increases in population meant only larger markets and new technology meant new products for these markets. But finally we recognized that increasing population and diminishing resources are twin forces with which we must reckon. Finally we saw the need for marketers to develop an awareness of their relationship to the natural environment.

Although this chapter emphasizes the man-marketing-nature relationship, a number of other chapters clearly relate to the topic. In the first chapter marketing was placed in a total context that includes natural as well as man-made components. The marketing institutions described in Chapter 3 are influenced in their locations by geographic considerations. Chapter 4 pointed out how marketing differs from nation to nation partly as a result of different natural environments. Chapter 8 raises a number of issues about technology and its impact on the natural environment. Consumer behavior (Chapters 10, 11, 12) reflects man's adaption to the natural environment. All of Part III deals with the management of the marketing function and presupposes throughout an appreciation of the natural environment. Finally Chapter 28 is devoted to a number of concerns that relate to man and nature: the indiscriminate use of resources—air, water, and land. While this chapter is devoted to the natural environment and its interaction with marketing, an awareness of the relationship is carried throughout the text.

## THE NATURAL ENVIRONMENT

The diagram at the beginning of this chapter suggests many of the features of the natural environment that we usually take for granted or even ignore when we study marketing. Yet any one of these natural features could dominate a marketing decision. Take the snowmobile and its relationship to nature. Nature acts as an enabling force (snow, terrain, and temperature) for a product, but at the same time the product can have negative effects on nature, such as plant life, animals, and wilderness setting. (Perhaps an offsetting advantage is that snowmobiles attract people out of the city into the wilderness where the spirit can be renewed.) Marketing research uncovered people's desires for snowmobiles, advertising helped influence them to buy, and retailers made the machines available for the buyers.

There are four principal points developed in this section on the natural environment. First, man is a part of the natural environment and as such he is dependent on nature for his livelihood. Second, man and nature interact as man produces goods from natural resources and then consumes or uses these products in adapting to his natural surroundings. Third, the relationship between man and nature is a dynamic one. Fourth, marketing as a part of the total environment is both affected by and affects nature.

## Man and Nature

We have many wants and needs that are both caused and satisfied by nature. Our food, plain or fancy, comes from nature: we hunt, fish, and raise crops. Our housing needs are satisfied with wood from the forests and materials from the ground. Our clothing comes primarily from plants and animals. Nature provides us the energy we need whether we dig coal, harness water, tap natural gas supplies, or process uranium. Our recreation is based in large part on what nature offers: we buy skis, boots, and clothing; stay in a chalet; eat in a restaurant; and then ski down nature's hill. Thus man the producer reaches out for resources that can be used to satisfy his desires as consumer. His "cycle"

natural resources $\longrightarrow$ producer $\longrightarrow$ consumer $\longrightarrow$ disposal

is incomplete as far as nature is concerned, for nature provides for decomposers that prepare for the succeeding production in a never-ending cycle. As man learns more about producing and consuming with nature in mind he will more closely approach nature's complete cycle.

## Man the Adapter

Many of the things that people buy reflect the ways in which they adapt to the environment. Some of these have already been suggested but there are hundreds of others. We wear raincoats when it rains and heavy coats when it is cold; turn on air conditioners when it is hot and furnaces when the temperature drops; bulldoze the land to build homes and fill basins for the same reason; keep dogs for pets and kill horses to feed them; ski down hills and ride motorcycles up hills; buy snowmobiles in order to traverse snow-covered areas and to make the winter bearable; spray insects and bugs in order to combat nature and save our crops; place houses on stilts in rain-drenched areas and on firm foundations in colder climates; build elaborate devices to facilitate the landing of aircraft when visibility is near zero; and equip our cars with heaters, defrosters, nonskid transmissions, antifreeze, thermostats, snow tires, engine heaters, and winter oil in order to adapt the machine to the cold.

Man clearly is an adapter. His technology permits him to go so far as to modify nature in his adaptation process. Where there is no snow he puts down layers of artificial snow; replaces grass with synthetic turf and his worn-out body organs with "new" ones; seeds the clouds when it does not rain; builds superhighways where there are no paths; constructs dams and reservoirs where there are no lakes; irrigates land that receives inadequate rainfall; develops new strains of wheat and new breeds of hogs that have little fat; and makes clothing and shoes from chemicals. Thus man goes to great lengths to adapt to his natural environment, to conquer nature, but he always remains dependent on it. Even when man spans a river with a bridge or splits an atom he ultimately is dependent on nature, for natural conditions determine how long the bridge will remain and how long the uranium deposits will last. "Man *adapts* continually and progressively; but he *controls* neither nature nor her rewards" (Parson, 1964).

## The Dynamic Relationship

Our wants and needs continually change as we proceed through our life cycles and sustain changes in our occupations, incomes, and places of residence. Technology adds new dimensions to our lives and other components of our man-made society change from day to day. Like man, nature is also ever-changing—through winds, erosion, and recycling. Nature causes man to change his ways, and in return man changes some of nature.

Marketers have listened carefully to the desires of consumers and have encouraged manufacturers to produce items to match consumer desires. We lived with the Myth of Superabundance (Udall, 1963) and in an affluent society. If women wanted feathers for their hats (or could be persuaded to wear feathers), egrets were killed; if householders liked black walnut furniture, there were those willing to cut down the trees; if consumers liked the succulent meat of the passenger pigeon, hunters shot them by the millions. But we have learned that natural resources are finite and that we could exterminate species. Today there are no passenger pigeons and the few remaining black walnut trees are being sold for as much as $20,000 apiece. The beaver was almost exterminated because it was fashionable for men to wear tall beaver hats. Ironically it was also fashion that saved the beaver, for the tall fur hat went out of fashion.

Historically, as we expended the resources in one area, we simply moved to another location or substituted one resource for another. When coal petered out we shifted to water power for the production of electricity, and when the dams silted up we harnessed nuclear energy. We seem now to be moving away from the philosophy of superabundance, however, and toward one of finite resources. Accordingly, marketing is going to develop a new posture if it serves the needs of consumers in the future as it has in the past. "The times they are a'changin'."

## Marketing and the Natural Environment

The above three points may seem like digressions from marketing, but not if you look at marketing as part of the total environment. Marketing in fact plays an important role in the interaction between man and his natural environment. *Marketing research* is used to learn what consumers want and need, and in this way the research results become an important input to decisions relating to production and the use of resources. The *products* that are manufactured draw down our stockpiles of resources; they may pollute the air and water during use and they may cause disposal problems when the users discard them. People are persuaded to buy these products through *advertising* and *personal selling*. *Marketing institutions* make the products available to the consumers, and the facilitating institutions provide the *credit* and *transportation* necessary for the distribution and sale of the goods. *Prices* reflect the marketing costs involved in bringing a natural resource to the manufacturer and on to the wholesaler, retailer, and consumer.

Thus marketing relates man in many ways to the natural environment, and the relationship extends all the way from natural resources to disposal. A few years ago this chapter would not have been concerned with such issues, but hopefully people in our society now have a better understanding of their relationship to nature and some of the environmental consequences of marketing.

One aspect of the natural environment that marketers have always been aware of is geography. Markets have spatial connotations, and people in almost all phases of marketing could hardly avoid learning of the impact of geography on their market areas, delivery times and costs, and concentrations of customers in different geographic regions. Because of the relevance of geographic considerations to marketing, we will examine them in some detail in the next section.

## THE GEOGRAPHY OF MARKETING

The geographical environment relates to just about every aspect of marketing. Goods and services must be physically moved from one place to another; marketing institutions must be strategically located to facilitate the movement of goods; retailers, wholesalers, and industrial sellers must be located so as to serve the markets; and the market system as a whole is spread out over a relatively large area with many diverse geographical influences. The geographical environment is relevant to marketing because of the spaces between where goods are produced and where they are sold and where they are consumed. Marketers have location decisions to make that relate to where markets are and how channels of distribution can be designed to reach them. Geography also affects costs and prices (e.g., distances covered), market behavior (e.g., concentration of buyers or sellers), and sometimes even variations in a product itself (e.g., winterproofing).

Several areas of marketing geography are particularly significant. These are (1) locational factors, (2) urbanization, (3) the geographical structure of wholesale and retail trade, and (4) the effect on international trade. A study of these geographical influences helps to explain the structure of marketing as we know it today. Knowing how geographical problems have been dealt with in the past may help in overcoming space problems in current decisions. The natural character of the landscape is a major factor in explaining where industrialization took place. Geography also helps to explain the development of particular industries, through the bringing together of natural resources, sources of energy, and transportation. Closely associated with industrialization are concentration of people, concentration of markets, and location of wholesale and retail trade.

## Locational Factors

The primary influencing factors to be examined are sources of supply, markets, labor, transportation, technology, and energy. Following are some examples of these locational factors at work.

Some of today's major industrial areas are not located conveniently in terms of present markets, technology, and transportation. They reflect the patterns of distribution and technology that prevailed when they developed. During the early industrialization of the United States and Western Europe, the location of natural resources—such as basic raw materials, sources of energy, and the labor market—determined the location of industrial plants. Today, technology in particular can overcome the strong locational influence once dictated by natural characteristics. (See Alexandersson, 1967.)

Water power, coal, and charcoal were at one time the principal sources of energy and they were not easily movable. Many Midwestern and Eastern towns were created because of a local source of energy. To this day many plants are strung along rivers and streams. Even though other forms of energy are today almost universally available, changes in location to serve a market better are impeded by the financial investment in the current plant.

The iron and steel industry is well worth examining because of its special locational patterns. Iron and steel production in this country is for the most part neither at the source of raw material (principally the iron ore ranges of Minnesota) nor at the source of energy. What happened was that the Great Lakes and the railroads tied the source of coal and the source of iron ore together by providing low-cost transportation, enabling the steel-producing plants to be located in Chicago, Gary, Detroit, Trenton, Cleveland, Erie, and Buffalo. This is shown in 5-1. In Pennsylvania production *was* located close to the coal reserves, and the area had the added advantage of the upper Ohio River and nearby Great Lakes ports. Thus the Great Lakes fostered the development of a large iron and steel industry, which, combined with related industries, forms a gigantic industrial complex that stretches from Milwaukee and Chicago eastward to New York City. Iron and steel production was fundamental to the formation of many of the cities and towns in this manufacturing belt. Steel-using industries subsequently located in this same area, thus placing the markets near the production.

Modern technology and transportation efficiency have decreased the importance of locating plants at the source of raw materials. Some heavy industries now locate near their markets or at least at a water

**5-1** Iron Ore Movement and Blast Furnace Locations

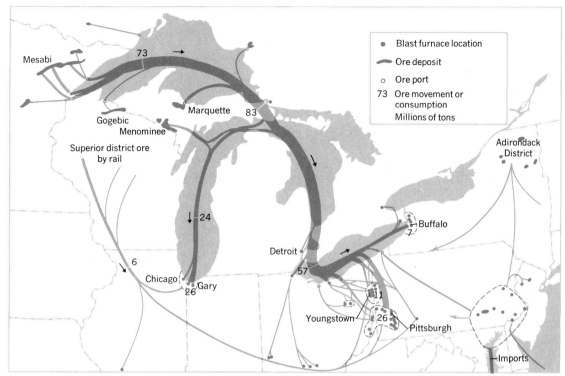

Blast furnace location
Ore deposit
Ore port
73 Ore movement or
consumption
Millions of tons

Mesabi
73
Gogebic
Menominee
Marquette 83
Superior district ore
by rail
Adirondack
District
↓24
Detroit
6
Chicago
26 Gary
57
Buffalo
7
11
Youngstown 26
Pittsburgh
Imports

SOURCE: Adapted from J. Russell Smith, M. Phillips, and T. Smith, *Industrial and Commercial Geography* (London: Constable, 1955), p. 358.

port from which bulky and heavy items can be shifted to the markets at an attractively low cost. Grain mills and sugar refineries are particularly suitable for location at water ports because of the low-cost transportation the water affords.

There are two principles of plant location that geographers cite in explaining the relationship between raw materials and plant location. First, "if the raw material loses much bulk or weight in the manufacturing process, the factory location may still [despite efficiencies in transportation] be tied to the sources of raw materials (sawmills, pulp mills, brickyards and packing plants). This principle is stressed if the product can be sent in bulk (as, for example, cement)" (Alexandersson, 1967). Of course, perishable goods leave no alternative. Thus, milk, products of the sea, fruit, and vegetables are processed very near their source. Second, "if a product gains in bulk or weight, production will be located near the market" (Alexandersson). The production of automobile parts is centered in Michigan and Wisconsin, but cars are assembled in other locations close to market areas: Los Angeles, for instance, has seven auto assembly plants and two are located in the San Francisco Bay area; as market development warranted it, assembly

**5-2** Motor Vehicles and Equipment (Value Added by Manufacture, by State, 1963)

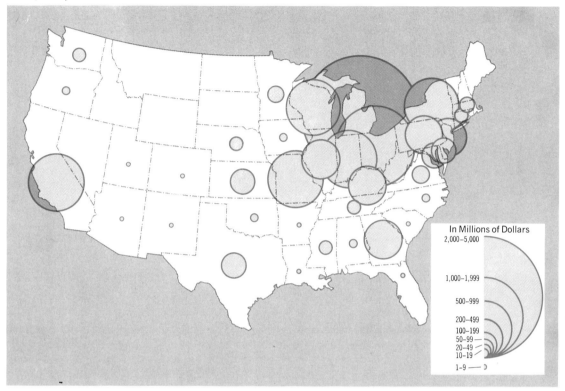

In Millions of Dollars
2,000–5,000

1,000–1,999

500–999

200–499
100–199
50–99
20–49
10–19

1–9

SOURCE: U.S. Department of Commerce, Bureau of the Census, 1963. Data for 1967 census are not provided in sufficient detail to use.

plants were located in Missouri, Illinois, Texas, and elsewhere. The dispersion of motor vehicles and equipment is shown in 5-2. Soft drinks are another excellent example of a product whose manufacture is located near the point of sale because of its increased weight after processing.

As we noted earlier, energy at one time exerted a major influence in plant location, when industries relied principally on water and coal. Electricity, petroleum, and natural gas, however, can be transported (or transmitted) with relative ease. Regional cost differences for energy are now of little importance in locating a plant. Of course, if energy needs are substantial, as for aluminum plants, it may still be advantageous to locate near the source of supply to avoid high transportation costs. The decision will depend on the trade-off with other factors, such as costs of serving the market.

Labor costs have always been a major locational factor. If a manufacturing facility produces a labor-intensive product the wage differences between one region and another will play an important role in plant location. The postwar expansion of Japan, Hong Kong, and Taiwan has been explained by the international migration of industry to low-wage countries where it became economically advantageous to produce labor-intensive goods (Alexandersson). In the United States, labor, in general, has always been mobile, hence the migration of workers and their families from rural areas to cities and from rural southern states to the industrialized northern states. This migration of workers was greatest during and immediately following World War II, although there has been a migratory tendency from the farm to the city since the late 1800s.

Entire industries have been affected by a combination of changes in labor costs and expanded sources of energy. A case in point is the movement of the textile industry during the 1920s and 1930s. This industry was once located along waterways of New England, but it was faced with high-cost labor, old and outmoded plants, and outmoded sources of energy. Gradually it relocated in the South, which had experienced a rapid growth in the availability of electric power and was also favored by a large low-cost labor pool. In 5-3 you can see the very high concentration of textile employees in the Southeast. The garment industry remains concentrated elsewhere in a few centers—

**5-3** Percentage of Employment in Textiles, by State, 1967

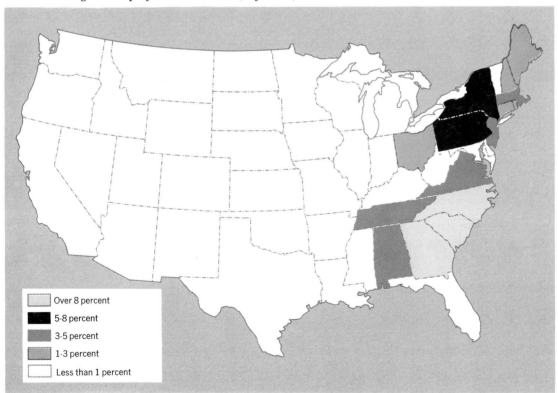

SOURCE: U.S. Department of Commerce, Bureau of the Census, *Census of Manufacturers,* 1967 (Washington, D.C.: GPO, 1967).

New York, Chicago, Los Angeles, and Houston—the same cities where the major wholesaling takes place. Thus the textile industry is located in response to energy and labor factors, whereas the garment industry, its principal customer, is located to serve the garment markets.

## The Phenomenon of Urbanization

The location of American industry spurred the development and influenced the location of our major wholesaling centers. Concurrently, the rapid growth of our metropolitan areas occurred at the same places. The resulting concentration of people and industries reflects the process known as *urbanization*, a development that is basic to an understanding of the scale and operating practices of our marketing system.

When a society and its industries are nonurban the task of marketing is diffused among small social and economic units. Clearly such a marketing system, serving a very large number of small communities, would differ from one serving relatively few very large urban areas. In the United States our large metropolitan areas have brought about not only a concentration of industries but also a concentration of industrial markets, wholesale markets, and retail markets.

Within the United States two patterns of population movements are in process. One is the movement of people from nonmetropolitan areas to the metropolitan areas (cities plus their suburbs). The other is the movement of people away from the central cities to the suburban areas. Between 1950 and 1970 the population increased by about 53 million people. Of this number, cities gained only 6 million, the suburban fringes more than 36 million, and nonmetropolitan areas 11 million. The move to the suburbs has many attributes of interest to marketers, for the suburban population (in contrast with city population) is characterized by more families with children, more families with high incomes, and higher levels of educational attainment. The distribution of families by income in 1970 was as follows:

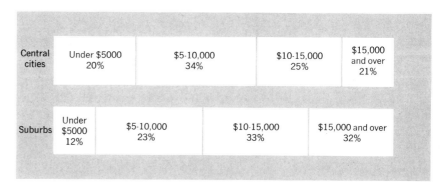

| Central cities | Under $5000 20% | $5-10,000 34% | $10-15,000 25% | $15,000 and over 21% |
| Suburbs | Under $5000 12% | $5-10,000 23% | $10-15,000 33% | $15,000 and over 32% |

With such differences in income and family characteristics, there are marked differences in spending patterns and, of course, life styles.

In order to deal systematically with urbanization, the Bureau of Census developed Standard Metropolitan Statistical Areas (SMSAs); 5-4 shows the 230 SMSAs delineated in 1970. An SMSA is defined as a county or group of counties containing at least one major city (or twin cities) with a population of 50,000 persons or more, plus adjacent counties that are economically and socially integrated with the central city. Urbanization is a worldwide phenomenon that accompanies industrialization. For industrialization and the mushrooming of cities mean jobs and higher incomes to rural immigrants. As the agricultural areas become more efficient with the use of machines, fewer agricultural workers are required to feed the population. Thus the migration to the cities has been brought about by technological advance and the changes in the locations of economic opportunity.

The SMSAs shown in 5-4 are where industry, wholesaling, retailing, and population are all concentrated. Although not all marketing is carried on within the SMSAs, they definitely dominate the marketing of goods and services. A manufacturer marketing his products in the United States gains economies in the deployment of his marketing resources in SMSAs. He need not reach every hamlet to gain market acceptance, but he can concentrate his marketing effort in relatively few places and yet tap the major portion of effective demand. Other facilities concentrated in the SMSAs of importance to marketers include promotional media and other facilitating institutions such as banks and credit companies.

## The Geographical Structures of Wholesale and Retail Trade

Wholesale and retail trade are concentrated in the SMSAs. Though groceries constitute the leading wholesale line for many of the SMSAs, farm products lead in several Midwestern SMSAs, lumber in one in the Northwest, petroleum in several, motor vehicles in Detroit, and metals and machinery in several Ohio SMSAs.

This descriptive view of the geography of wholesaling has a rich history that has evolved over time. The pattern of wholesaling had its origin with the first cities of a region, and it was from the cities that wholesale trade opened the development of smaller communities. As one authority says ". . . trade did not grow OUT of American economic development, rather it induced that development" (Vance, 1970). In other words, trade spreading outward from the cities permitted the development of new regions and new towns. This process, multiplied over and over again, helps to explain the early economic development of the United States. The wholesaling pattern of today is in part the result of the historical development of the nation, in part the response to national and regional tastes, and in part the result of the technology of transportation. Perhaps the most constant operating force shaping the location of wholesale trade is regionalization, since wholesaling serves a large area in contrast to retailing, which serves consumers

**5-4** Standard Metropolitan Statistical Areas

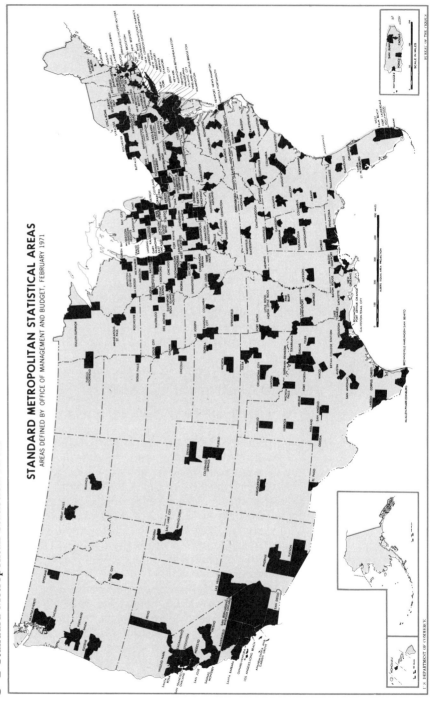

STANDARD METROPOLITAN STATISTICAL AREAS
AREAS DEFINED BY OFFICE OF MANAGEMENT AND BUDGET, FEBRUARY 1971

*SOURCE:* U.S. Department of Commerce, Bureau of the Census, 1971.

located nearby. Such geographic features as mountains, rivers, and distances help shape wholesale areas.

As might be expected, retailing in the United States is highly concentrated in populated areas. As noted in an earlier chapter the retail structure has always adapted quickly to the changing character of an area, for population attracts retail institutions. As a general proposition, there is a parallelism of population, disposable income, retail establishments, and retail sales. If you were to examine the relationship of these factors (available in issues of the *Survey of Current Business*), you would find that as population grows in an area, personal income grows, and retail sales expand. In short, retail sales are a function of population and purchasing power.

The 1970 Census of Population recorded more than 205 million people in the United States. This census, even more dramatically than past ones, shows the very high concentration of population in the SMSAs, for more than 73 percent of the people now reside in the metropolitan zones. Retail trade, shifting along with the population, accounts for about 72 percent of its total volume in the 230 SMSAs.

Although the metropolitan areas have consistently accounted for an increasing proportion of retail sales, the movement of population within the urban areas has caused further changes in marketing. The 1970 census confirms that for the first time the number of people residing in suburbs exceeds the number in cities. Some cities actually experienced an absolute loss in population. St. Louis, Missouri, for example, lost nearly one of every five inhabitants. The surrounding area, or suburbs, however, increased in population by more than 34 percent from 1960 to 1970.

The changing geography of retail trade coincides with the declining importance of central cities and the increasing importance of the suburbs. In a study of SMSAs published by the Columbia Broadcasting System, it is reported that:

> On the basis of the 28 sample areas studied in this report, suburban communities in 1967 . . . accounted for 53 percent of total metropolitan area business, while the central cities accounted for 47 percent. In 1958—after making the necessary adjustments for geographic comparability—stores located in the suburbs of the identical areas accounted for only 42 percent of the total sample area sales, while those doing business in the cities accounted for 58 percent. (CBS, 1970.)

Thus in the course of a decade the suburban shopping centers have overcome the retail sales dominance of central cities. The 28 areas studied in the sample and the percentage of retail sales in suburbs is shown in 5-5. A number of factors may account for the differences among suburban areas shown in the figure. The level of suburbanization, the boundaries of the central city, and the relative ease or difficulty of access to the city are a few reasons why some SMSAs are still

**5-5** Suburban Retail Sales in Selected SMSAs as Percentages of Total SMSA Sales, 1967

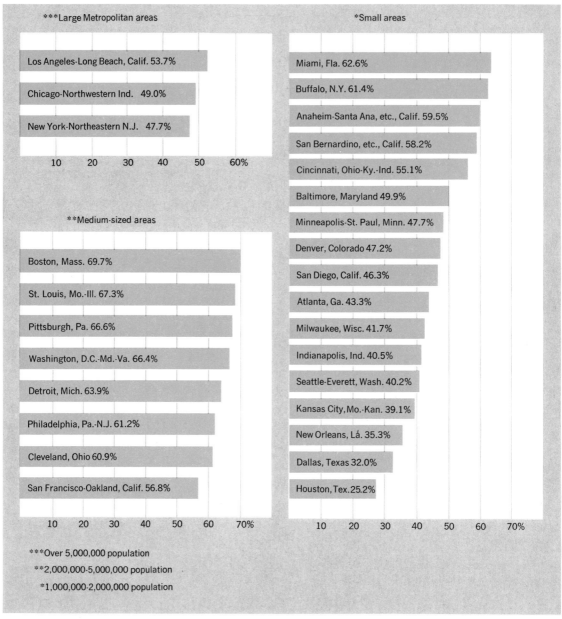

***Large Metropolitan areas

Los Angeles-Long Beach, Calif. 53.7%
Chicago-Northwestern Ind. 49.0%
New York-Northeastern N.J. 47.7%

10  20  30  40  50  60%

**Medium-sized areas

Boston, Mass. 69.7%
St. Louis, Mo.-Ill. 67.3%
Pittsburgh, Pa. 66.6%
Washington, D.C.-Md.-Va. 66.4%
Detroit, Mich. 63.9%
Philadelphia, Pa.-N.J. 61.2%
Cleveland, Ohio 60.9%
San Francisco-Oakland, Calif. 56.8%

10  20  30  40  50  60  70%

*Small areas

Miami, Fla. 62.6%
Buffalo, N.Y. 61.4%
Anaheim-Santa Ana, etc., Calif. 59.5%
San Bernardino, etc., Calif. 58.2%
Cincinnati, Ohio-Ky.-Ind. 55.1%
Baltimore, Maryland 49.9%
Minneapolis-St. Paul, Minn. 47.7%
Denver, Colorado 47.2%
San Diego, Calif. 46.3%
Atlanta, Ga. 43.3%
Milwaukee, Wisc. 41.7%
Indianapolis, Ind. 40.5%
Seattle-Everett, Wash. 40.2%
Kansas City, Mo.-Kan. 39.1%
New Orleans, Lá. 35.3%
Dallas, Texas 32.0%
Houston, Tex. 25.2%

10  20  30  40  50  60  70%

***Over 5,000,000 population
**2,000,000-5,000,000 population
*1,000,000-2,000,000 population

SOURCE: *The Suburbanization of Retail Trade* (New York: Columbia Broadcasting System, 1970), pp. 67, 72, 74.

dominated by a central-city retail structure. In some newer communities the boundaries reach out over great distances and some areas have grown in their suburban developments at a faster pace. These too may be explanations for the differences shown.

## Geography and International Trade

Geographic influences are also important to firms engaged in international trade, in fact they may be more crucial than in domestic marketing. The same problems of development face the exporter, foreign subsidiary, and joint-venture operation as face a domestic firm, and thus the geography of the country of operation will shape the distribution of goods and affect marketing practices. The American businessman is often well advised to have some reasonable knowledge of a nation's geography so as to appreciate trade patterns, the availability of natural resources, the different customs influenced by natural factors, and the transportation network. Along with knowledge of the natural resources of a country, its people, and its history, he will need to know what is now manufactured and marketed. A marketing manager functioning in a foreign country has the same tasks as the manager in a domestic situation. He will evaluate markets, gather data about markets, select channels of distribution and modes of transportation, and identify the trade areas for wholesale and retail centers. The geography of the country and the geography of the marketing institutions will of course enter into his decision. (International trade will be further discussed in Chapter 24.)

Gulf Oil Corporation is a good example of a multinational firm (i.e., it has direct financial holdings in several countries) that faces change and contends with geographical factors as an everyday occurrence. This company has oil holdings in the United States, the Middle East, and Venezuela. The crude oil produced by its foreign operations is shipped on tankers to refineries in Europe and the United States. The gasoline and other refined products are transported by pipelines to United States and European wholesaling centers. From the wholesaling point the oil products are shipped by truck to retail outlets. In planning for the future Gulf explores new oil fields, modifies the refining and transportation processes, and researches potential markets and market changes. The planning gives the company versatility in its operations and helps it to maximize the geographic features relevant to its operations. A company of this size is geared to operating at many geographical locations throughout the world and thus accepts geographical changes in markets and production locations as an unavoidable factor of its operations.

## Geography and Marketing Management

The primary purpose of calling attention to the geographical environment is to focus on a part of the natural environment that affects marketing decisions. The spatial aspects of any marketing system relate to inequalities of natural resources, differences in the location of human populations, and the ever-present problem of locating and moving things over the landscape. The design of a firm's marketing system is generally related to an optimization of the spatial variable to the time and quantity variations of the market. Therefore, location, transportation, and the quantities involved must be coordinated to the best market opportunity.

## CONCLUDING COMMENTS

In this chapter we have attempted to provide some understanding of how marketing relates to the natural environment of which we all are a part. Goods we purchase are produced from natural resources. Our recreation and our energy are resource-based. Things that we buy affect the air, land, and water when we use them and frequently cause problems when we dispose of them. Marketers have a role in helping man adapt to his environment and they have a responsibility in protecting nature in the process. Everything in the environment is interrelated and marketers need to develop and maintain an awareness of this truth.

## STATEMENTS TO CONSIDER

Man-made features of environment almost universally mediate the relation between individual humans and the rest of nature. (P. Wagner)

A clear stream, a long horizon, a forest wilderness, and open sky—these are man's most ancient possessions. In a modern society, they are his most priceless. (Lyndon Johnson)

The relationships between man and the earth which result from his efforts to get a living are in general the most direct and intimate. (Barrows)

The Corps is now working toward the maximum development of our rivers. (U.S. Army Corps of Engineers)

Man's rampant technology has placed him, once again, under the direct selective influence of an environment of his own making: the city. (P. Wagner)

The artificial environment, created and continued by the efforts of the whole society, is the new harvesting ground of consumers, who stalk through its shopping districts gathering manufactured and transported products as the nomad Semang prowl the forest in quest of natural products. (P. Wagner)

Man is everywhere a disturbing agent, wherever he plants his foot, the harmonies of nature are turned to discords. (Marsh)

We do not own the earth, not even our own acre of it, but only walk here at this instant which will become history. (Laycock)

Increasing artificiality favors intense regional specialization of production, and at the same time a widening generalization of consumption patterns. (P. Wagner)

No satisfactory industrial location theory has been formulated . . . spatial variations in demand and costs make the formulation of a practical industrial location theory extremely complex. (Miller)

We live because we adapt, and we live only if we adapt. (Potter)

Complete adaptation to environment means death. The essential point in all response is the desire to control environment. (J. Dewey)

# QUESTIONS FOR REVIEW

1. Select any product and trace the environmental impact it may have (e.g., outboard motor, dune buggy, mini bike, etc.).

2. Does man control the natural environment?

3. What is the proper role of marketing in terms of the natural environment?

4. Do marketers have any responsibility for protecting the natural resources?

5. Do any of the natural environmental forces have greater impact on marketing than does geography?

6. What really determines the location of industry—resources or markets?

7. Are geographic considerations dynamic in nature? Think in terms of specific industries.

8. How does the concentration of employment in the textile industry (5-3) influence marketing of textile products?

9. Would you expect the SMSAs to have the same percentage of retail trade of the U.S. total that they do population? Explain.

10. How would your answer to question 9 differ with respect to wholesale trade?

## Further Readings

Gunnar Alexandersson, *Geography of Manufacturing* (Foundations of Economic Geography Series) (Englewood Cliffs, N.J.: Prentice-Hall, 1967).

William Applebaum, "Consumption and the Geography of Retail Distribution in the United States," *Business Topics,* Vol. 15 (Summer 1967), pp. 25–41.

Brian J. L. Berry, *Geography of Market Centers and Retail Distribution* (Foundations of Economic Geography Series) (Englewood Cliffs, N.J.: Prentice-Hall, 1967).

David A. Revzan, *A Geography of Marketing: Integrative Statement* (Berkeley, Cal.: The Graduate School of Business Administration, University of California, 1968).

Richard S. Thoman and Edgar C. Conkling, *Geography of International Trade* (Foundations of Economic Geography Series) (Englewood Cliffs, N.J.: Prentice-Hall, 1967).

Philip L. Wagner, *The Human Use of the Earth* (London: Collier-Macmillan Limited, 1964).

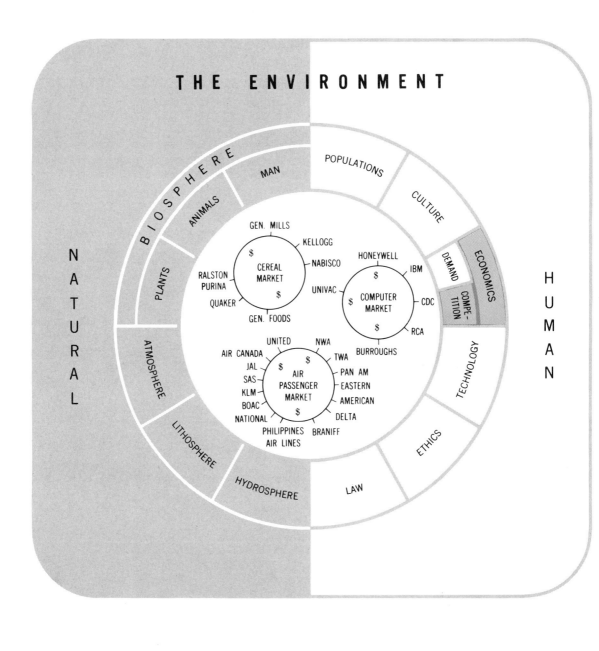

# CHAPTER 6
# THE ECONOMIC
# ENVIRONMENT
# AND COMPETITION

*The competitive framework of the firm is a force that importantly influences marketing strategy. . . . Differentiation of the market offer is widely practiced so as to create a protected competitive edge. . . . Marketing managers plan their market strategy so as to steepen the demand curve.*

Competition is a powerful influence in determining the extent and nature of a firm's marketing activities. Competition broadly interacts with the other environmental forces such as law and ethics, technology, the marketing structure, buyer behavior, and even the spatial aspects of the natural environment. Almost no marketing action is free of competitive pressures, except for a legalized monopoly. But even some legal monopolies, because of modern technology, face the threat of actual or potential product competition.

Competition, moreover, is uncontrollable. Although a firm may exert some control in an actual market situation, its dominance is precarious and most often subject to change. By virtue of size and kinds of strategy, a large firm is sometimes regarded as having a secure market position, but competition can humble even the most complacent giant. Consider these notable examples: the market penetration of small foreign cars, which inspired the development of the so-called "compact" cars; the demise of a major market supplier in the refrigerated-food field, leaving the market to a few large-scale companies and numerous small regional food processors; and the inroads made by Pepsi-Cola, Royal Crown Cola, and other soft-beverage firms against a once-impregnable Coca-Cola. Thus if a firm seems to dominate competition, it is perhaps well to view the situation as subject to erosion, or at best temporary.

A theoretical and practical knowledge of competition, its variables, and their probable influences is vital to a marketer. The basic concepts and theoretical descriptions of competition provided by economists are highly useful as a frame of reference and guide to orderly thinking. Economists simplify the problem of competition and price determination by limiting the assumptions necessary for their theoretical descriptions of market structures. The table in 6-1 indicates the market-structure models within which prices are determined. Pure competition and pure monopoly are the extreme conditions, whereas monopolistic competition and oligopoly are intermediate, representing a mixture of the elements of the extremes. The essential features embracing each market structure are of particular importance, and these also are shown in the table.

Any discussion of competition and market structure must of necessity be limited to the purpose at hand. In surveying the theoretical models of competition, you should recognize that the real world is so complex that no brief discussion can do justice to the subject. The material that follows may fall short of giving a complete portrait of competition, but you can amplify the basic points from other sources (see Further Readings).

## 6-1 Market Structures and Their Features

| Features | Pure competition | Monopolistic competition | Oligopoly | Pure monopoly |
|---|---|---|---|---|
| Number of sellers | Very large number | Substantial number | Few | One |
| Product | Undifferentiated perfect substitutes | Differentiated products with close substitutes* | | No close substitute for unique good |
| Price | No control over price—seller must accept market price | Administered prices | | Much control over price—but can sell only what market will take at his price |
| | | Some price competition can prevail; price control depends much on degree of differentiation | Pricing in concert is strong tendency; firms mutually interdependent | |
| Entry of new firms | Easy | Somewhat easy—but depends on technology and size of firms | Usually difficult because of size of firms and high costs | No entry as resource access is blocked |
| Marketing effort | None | Very large amount of nonprice competition with heavy emphasis on brands and product differentiation; wide use of advertising and any marketing activity to build market share | | Little, but can enjoy benefits if less product elasticity is created |

*Except for undifferentiated oligopoly which is not common in actual market situations.

## PURE COMPETITION AND PURE MONOPOLY

### Pure Competition

The essence of *pure competition* is that no one seller has an appreciable influence on the market price. All participants sell an identical product, so that the buyer is indifferent about whose output he buys. When there are many sellers vending identical products a producer must adapt his activities to market conditions. He has no distinct advantages over all the other producers as he has no product or price appeal to change market conditions, and therefore he must accept the competitive conditions of the purely competitive market. He will thus determine his quantity to produce on the basis of his costs relative to the market price. The individual producer will expand output so long as the additional cost (marginal cost) is less than the price he can charge for the additional unit. Of course, when marginal cost surpasses price, he will contract his output.

Even though an individual seller acts as though he has no influence on the market price, the aggregate actions of all sellers exert a great influence on price. If costs are high relative to market price, all producers will restrict their output, thereby reducing supply, and other things remaining equal, market price will rise. Conversely, if costs are low relative to market price, producers will increase output and the price will fall. Thus the quantity produced and sold, together with the market price, is automatically determined by impersonal forces of the market.

If any firm were operating under conditions of pure competition, marketing activities would be restrained. There would be no promotion, no incentive to improve a market offering, and no distinguishing characteristics of a sale. All such activities would only increase the firm's costs, placing it at a competitive disadvantage because no seller can command a price higher than the market price.

Pure competition is virtually nonexistent, however. Agriculture —barring government controls, exchange regulations (that is, cotton, wheat, and other commodity exchange regulations), and grading —closely approximates the competitive model that has been an effective tool for analyzing the allocation of resources in a market-price system. Agriculture is often used as the norm against which competitive problems are measured, but this practice stirs controversy—particularly when public regulation of competition is at stake. From a marketing standpoint, the case of agriculture is a helpful aid in studying the behavior of firms in certain other sectors of the economy.

In some minor respects, retailing, wholesaling, service industries, and agricultural marketing institutions perform as though competition were pure. Certainly the offerings of competitors are not identical, and most sellers can exert control over price. Competitive pressures are very strong, however, and if the price of any seller is at all out of line, he feels the loss of patronage and reacts as if the market were purely competitive.

Some observers, notably politicians, occasionally imply that pure competition is the ideal for American business. Perhaps they do so without considering the long-run social impact. For essentially pure competition means the survival of the most efficient; you can question for yourself the desirability of a competitive system governed solely by costs and market prices.

### Monopoly

The other extreme market structure in 6-1 is monopoly, and it too is rare, except for monopolies sanctioned by public policy. The essential characteristic of a monopolist is that he is the sole seller of a product that does not have a close substitute. Local public utilities, the aluminum industry prior to the Second World War, the manufacture of shoe machinery, and a few other industries are approximations of pure monopoly. But notwithstanding such instances of complete control of an economic good, almost everything has a substitute. Gas and electricity are becoming more closely substitutable than before, and certainly aluminum now has several substitutes, such as plastics, processed wood, and specially produced steel products. Whether pure monopoly exists is not of prime importance. The value of monopoly theory rests in its usefulness in analyzing real problems of pricing, output, and resource allocation, and in providing a clearer understanding of monopolistic competition and oligopolistic market structures.

In a purely monopolistic market a seller can set the price as he pleases and sell what the market will take *at that price*. Since he has complete control over price, the market demand will determine the number of units he sells. This contrasts with the seller in pure competition, who can sell any quantity, but at the market price. How then would a monopolist set price? Knowing that the number of units to be sold depends on the price, he would compare total costs and total revenues at each level of output and select whatever output maximizes his profit. An alternate method involves the use of marginal analysis, which shows that maximum total profit increases as long as the marginal revenue from producing each additional unit exceeds the marginal cost of producing it. Both methods are shown in 6-2. The most profitable position is that output at which marginal cost equals marginal revenue.

Any monopolist can enjoy the rewards of marketing activities, whereas under pure competition there is nothing to be gained by marketing efforts. Any device that encourages the public to regard his product as highly desirable tends to reduce the elasticity of demand and also to shift the demand curve to the right. In real-life competitive situations, much marketing effort is designed to accomplish these ends. Of course, the use of marketing efforts (advertising and others) complicates the pricing process, and it then becomes necessary to estimate the additional revenue generated by the marketing effort.

## MONOPOLISTIC COMPETITION AND OLIGOPOLY

Somewhere between pure competition and pure monopoly is where most real-world activity lies. Nobody in the United States has a pure monopoly; nobody operates in a purely competitive market. Almost all industries exhibit a mixture of the two. Some are in markets heavily

**6-2** Hypothetical Revenue and Cost Data—Pure Monopoly

| Output | Price | Total revenue | Total cost | Net profit | Marginal revenue | Marginal cost | MR−MC (marginal profit or loss) |
|--------|-------|---------------|------------|------------|------------------|---------------|----------------------------------|
| 10 | 24 | 240 | 35 | 205 | 240 | 35 | +205 |
| 20 | 23 | 460 | 70 | 390 | 220 | 35 | +185 |
| 30 | 22 | 660 | 156 | 504 | 200 | 86 | +114 |
| 40 | 21 | 840 | 265 | 575 | 180 | 109 | + 71 |
| 50 | 20 | 1000 | 405 | 595 | 160 | 140 | + 20* |
| 60 | 19 | 1140 | 583 | 557 | 140 | 178 | − 38 |
| 70 | 18 | 1260 | 816 | 444 | 120 | 233 | −113 |

*Most profitable output.

populated by competitors with very close substitutes or in markets with weak partial monopolies. These fall toward the left in 6-1. An industry with a strong monopolistic element(s), such as few sellers, fall toward the right. Economists have identified these intermediate markets respectively as *monopolistic competition* and, if there are few sellers, *oligopoly.**

The question of the number of sellers in a given market causes some confusion. How *many* sellers must there be for monopolistic competition? How *few* sellers are required for oligopoly? There are no precise answers to these questions, but in general we can say that monopolistic competition prevails ". . . when the number of sellers is large enough so that the actions of any one have no perceptible effect upon the other sellers and their actions have no perceptible effect upon him. . . ." (Leftwich, 1966). An oligopoly, on the other hand, has so few participants that the actions of one of them do have an effect on the others, who in turn react so as to offset repercussions. In other words, the individual oligopolistic seller is aware that his actions have repercussions—and when changing his price, output, product quality, sales promotion, and other marketing variables, he must take the probable reactions of the other few sellers into consideration.

Before discussing pricing under both monopolistic competition and oligopoly, we want to introduce the concept of "differentiation," for it is the essence of both monopolistic competition and differentiated oligopoly.

## The Concept of Differentiation

As a practical matter all sellers' offerings are differentiated from those of their competition. Two little-understood aspects of differentiation have limited the appreciation of the theory of monopolistic competition. One is the view that *product* differentiation *per se* is the full extent of the concept, the other is a failure to comprehend the basis of differentiation. An understanding of both points is essential to a clear conception of competition within a firm's environment.

Perhaps it would have been well for economists to have adopted the term *offering differentiation,* for this is what Edward Hastings Chamberlin meant when he explored the concept in his classic volume, *The Theory of Monopolistic Competition.* He wrote:

> Differentiation may be based upon certain characteristics of the product itself, such as exclusive patented features; trade names; peculiarities of the package or container, if any; or singularly in quality, design, color, or style. It may also exist with respect to the conditions surrounding its sale. In retail trade to take only one instance, these conditions include such factors as the convenience of the seller's location, the general tone and character of his establishment, his way of doing business, his reputation for fair dealing,

*Economists further distinguish between *pure oligopoly* and *differentiated oligopoly.* As a practical matter most sellers in oligopolistic industries differentiate their products.

courtesy, efficiency, and all personal links which attach his customers either to himself or to those employed by him. In so far as these and other intangible factors vary from seller to seller, the "product" in each case is different, for buyers take them into account, more or less, and may be regarded as purchasing them along with the commodity itself. When these two aspects of differentiation are held in mind, it is evident that virtually all product offerings are differentiated, at least slightly, and that over a wide range of economic activity differentiation is of considerable importance. (Chamberlin, 1947.)

Any differentiation by a firm, then, gives it a partial monopoly and hence can influence its price. For example, Coca-Cola and Bayer Aspirin have partial monopolies because of their strong brand recognition; a Safeway or an A & P supermarket is convenient to the people in its vicinity and therefore enjoys a measure of monopoly; a small neighborhood dairy store can charge more for milk and ice cream by virtue of a locational monopoly, an hours-of-operation monopoly, or both.

## The Basis of Differentiation

There is more to the concept of differentiation than the differences in quality, design, patents, trade names, and other features that often distinguish one similar product from another. Such differences are planned by manufacturers and have their source in the production function even though they are planned to establish some level of market superiority. Differentiation of product *per se* is often used to build superiority in the market, but all firms recognize the differences which they can exploit that have their sources in the tastes and preferences of consumers. In other words, what we know about the economic and noneconomic aspects of buyer behavior gives a firm an opportunity to strengthen its market advantage by developing real or fictional distinctions about its market offer. Chamberlin recognized the broader concept of differentiation when he wrote:

A general class of product is differentiated if any significant basis exists for distinguishing the goods [or services] of one seller from those of another. Such a basis may be real or fancied, so long as it is of any importance whatever to buyers, and leads to a preference for one variety of the product over another. Where such differentiation exists, even though it be slight, buyers will be paired with sellers, not by chance and at random (as in pure competition), but according to their preferences. (Chamberlin, 1947.)

The foundation of competition for American industry rests, then, on differences in consumer tastes and preferences. This latter feature of differentiation explains much of the nature and character of marketing activity, because most of it is planned to create a distinct preference for a firm's market offer. A seller can pair his market offering to correspond to buyer tastes and preferences. Product services, image, status connotations, quality, and any economic or noneconomic factor are all illustrations of the firm's attempt to create and foster the concept of differentiation. Consumer differences also help to explain the constant development of new and improved products and new and improved marketing techniques. The basis for differentiation is the same whether the markets are characterized by monopolistic competition or oligopoly.

## Pricing under Monopolistic Competition

Of particular interest to students of marketing is the price-making process under conditions of monopolistic competition. Because the partial monopolist does not have to accept the market price, he does not have to produce at minimum possible cost. Although he is not entirely free from competitive pressures, he has considerably more pricing freedom when competition is less active. Returning to 6-1, therefore, we can note that monopolistic competition is characterized by administered prices. Pricing, then, is very likely subject to management decisions. The prices set by managements blend some aspects of pure competition with some aspects of monopoly.

How does a manager set prices? First, he has a differentiated product, and every effort is made to convince buyers that it is really different and that nothing else serves as a satisfactory substitute. The more successful he is in differentiating his product, the less elastic the demand curve will be. If the demand becomes relatively inelastic, a higher price may be commanded from the market without deterring trade. He thus sets himself apart from competition in a protected position.

Second, the manager has a pretty good idea of how his competition will behave. Under most circumstances he does not have perfect knowledge about his rivals. But the more the firm knows about its competition, the more likely it is that a reasonable prediction of rival prices and retaliation can be made.

Third, the manager knows that if price is set high, and in turn high profits are forthcoming, new entrants into the field are likely to upset existing price policies. In general, economic theory tells us that the larger the number of sellers competing, the more intense the competition, particularly if competition is on a price basis. But market entry is a much more complex problem today than in the past. Advances in technology and the tendency for firms to grow to great size make entry more difficult. For these reasons, the withdrawal of a single firm from the market may have a marked effect on prices. Furthermore, the widespread use of nonprice competition to build market share is often so costly as to preclude market entry for some prospective rivals.

The main difficulty with maximizing revenue by pricing at the point where marginal cost equals marginal revenue is that even if the manager knew unit marginal cost and unit marginal revenue, he would not necessarily know where the most profitable output was. Most businessmen have never heard of these terms, though they may act in a way that makes it seem as if they engaged in marginal analysis, equating marginal cost with marginal revenue.

A reasonable and realistic alternative to marginal analysis is maximization of the difference between *total revenue* and *total cost*. Although total costs are seldom accurately stated for any product, many business firms can reasonably approximate them. Under this method, also known as "break-even analysis," a schedule of fixed costs and variable costs at varied levels of sales is prepared. From the schedule a manager can construct a graphic representation of the break-even point and the point of maximum distance between total costs and total revenue, once the break-even point has been passed. The manager also knows that the demand for his product is a function of both the total consumer demand for all similar but differentiated products and the firm's share of the total demand.

The success of a market entry will hinge on the firm's ability either to increase total demand for the product, to take customers away from competition, or both. Dial soap, for example, was introduced into the market at a price higher than most of the well-established brands, among them Lux, Palmolive, and Ivory. Yet Dial captured and has been able to retain a respectable market share. Did costs dictate a higher price for Dial? Was management trying to create the impression that Dial was a more highly differentiated soap and hence worthy of a higher price? In other words, does Dial have less price elasticity than its competition? Apparently so. Because of the strong brand identity created for Dial, the appeal of substitutes was diminished and the demand curve for Dial steepened. As this example shows, under monopolistic competition the relative elasticity, or relative inelasticity, of a firm's demand curve depends on how successful it is in creating a distinct differentiation and on what all other firms in the industry do.

In the long run, in any situation of monopolistic competition new firms enter the field and old ones leave. Theory—and common sense—tells us that economic profits will attract new rivals and losses will cause firms to depart. But to describe real economic life these concepts need to be recast as statements of tendency. For example, a firm may have created such a measure of differentiation that new rivals do not enter, knowing that to penetrate the market would be either too costly or virtually impossible. Perhaps alternatives elsewhere are more attractive than meeting established firms in an industry head-on. Then there are always those in real life who accept less from their business than they could earn elsewhere, particularly owners of small individual enterprises.

## Pricing under Oligopoly

Oligopolistic market structure characterizes several important industries in the United States. As 6-3 shows, some important markets are dominated by as few as four firms. It goes without saying that vast size characterizes the firms in the oligopolistic industries listed in the table. It should also be noted that small firms in local markets dominated by two, three, or even four suppliers have strong oligopolistic tendencies—for instance, building supply companies, drug stores, and department stores.

**6-3** Market Domination by Leading Firms

| Industry | PERCENTAGE OF VALUE OF SHIPMENTS ACCOUNTED FOR BY | |
|---|---|---|
| | 4 largest firms | 8 largest firms |
| Aluminum | * | 100 |
| Electric lamps (bulbs) | 91 | 95 |
| Soap and other detergents | 70 | 78 |
| Chewing gum | 86 | 96 |
| Cereal breakfast foods | 82 | 94 |
| Tin cans and other tinware | 73 | 84 |
| Cigarettes | 81 | 100 |
| Typewriters | 81 | 99 |
| Computing and related machines | 66 | 83 |
| Flour mixes and refrigerated doughs | 70 | 93 |
| Motor vehicles and parts | 76 | 81 |
| Tires and inner tubes | 70 | 88 |
| Household laundry equipment | 78 | 95 |
| Storage batteries | 61 | 83 |
| Photographic equipment and supplies | 69 | 81 |

*Withheld to avoid disclosure.

SOURCE: U.S. Department of Commerce, Bureau of the Census, *Concentration Ratios of Manufacturing, Part I, 1967 Census of Manufacturers* (Washington, D.C., GPO, 1967).

One paramount principle should guide any analysis of oligopoly: *when a market is dominated by few sellers it is both critical and imperative for each participating firm to weigh the reactions of the other firms in planning competitive and production policies.* Prices under oligopoly are administered. The price, or cluster of prices, established thus must be fairly satisfactory to all sellers. In several oligopolistic industries a price leader can be identified, especially in industries populated by one or two large firms and several small firms, and in markets entirely dominated by large-scale enterprises. In these situations the price set by the leader permits the other firms to achieve a tolerable profit.

Prices set by oligopolists are generally rigid, and a persistent threat exists that disastrous price wars will erupt if one oligopolist in an industry lowers his price. A live-and-let-live policy must prevail; otherwise the industry or some of its members might face antitrust action if price decreases threaten the existence of weaker sellers. Hence nonprice competition is likely to be the principal form of competition among oligopolists. Another interesting aspect of oligopoly is that the market share of each seller is a critical measure of performance, for a few percentage points increase or decrease in market share can readily be converted into revenue gained or lost.

The kinked demand curve in 6-4 is a simplified graphic explanation of these aspects of oligopoly. The curve helps us to visualize what may happen if one of the few sellers contemplates raising or lowering price.

If one firm raises price within the range of DP, his sales will fall off and those maintaining price at P will gain in market share. Note that this portion of the demand curve is relatively elastic, which means that sales will decline by a greater proportion than the proportional increase in price—assuming that the other sellers will not follow the newly established higher price. If, however, the industry is led to a higher level by a price leader, a new price is established almost in concert. No seller loses share of market, for the industry merely reestablishes the kink at a point in some range above P. Clearly, if the new higher price takes some customers out of the market the new kink will be above and slightly to the left of point P. You can easily redraw a number of possibilities of industry behavior as price moves upward.

On the other hand, if one firm lowers price along the range of PD', the market shares of those retaining price P will decline and be distributed to the lower-priced rival. This portion of the demand curve is relatively inelastic. The lower-priced rival will thus increase his business, but relatively less than the proportional change in price. What is gained comes from the other firms in the industry. Chances are that the rest of the industry will not stand idly by and let its market shares erode.

There is no sense in pricing below the industry maverick. Rivals have only to lower price to the same level and the market shares will be redistributed essentially as they were before. It will not be long before

**6-4** The Kinked Demand Curve

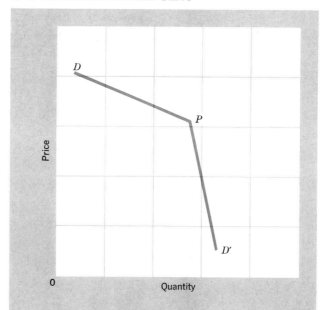

all participants in the oligopoly recognize the futility of price cutting. No one gains anything except the short spurts of sales volume achieved by the firm originating the price cut. Rather than risk these measures, the industry is likely to be most content at the higher price. Common sense will tell any participant that his price increases can be ignored by the other oligopolists and his price decreases met. The use of price as a competitive weapon goes far to explain why price changes are infrequent and why firms avoid ruinous price wars. When and if price changes occur, they are likely to be industry-wide and based on general cost adjustments.

### Limitations of Theory

Economic theory is often charged with falling short of analyzing real-life competition. It is true that theory leaves unexplained some of the practical and subtle aspects of actual competitive behavior. But an economist has a different purpose from that of market rivals. For he makes certain assumptions—one product, knowledge of its marginal cost and marginal revenue, and the decline or absence of competition as the number of sellers diminishes—in order to analyze the behavior and performance of the whole economic system.

Despite its pragmatic shortcomings, economic theory serves the marketer by providing order and precision for his thinking. For example, the discussion of oligopoly did not explain how $P$ was originally arrived at in 6-4. The price $P$ is theoretically found by the equation of marginal cost and marginal revenue. This fact was not important to the discussion, but the oligopolist's view of the reaction of his rivals to price increases and decreases is most important. Certainly cigarette pricing, the clustering of auto prices (that is, model for model), the pricing of tires and gasoline, and pricing in a number of other basic industries—all reflect the behavior described by portions of oligopoly theory. Although not all economic theory is of practical use to a marketer, still certain aspects of it can lead him to a clearer understanding of the basis of competitive behavior and of rivals' reactions he is likely to encounter.

Despite its wide acceptance and usage, economic theory falls short in explaining real-life competitive behavior. Joel Dean, a well-known managerial economist, has taken a strong position in contrasting the economist's views of competition with those of businessmen. His hallmarks of an intensely competitive situation in 6-5 have been held by theorists to be symptomatic of monopoly or at least strong monopolistic tendencies. Yet from a practical market point of view, they imply aggressive competitive activities.

Throughout this discussion of monopolistic competition and oligopoly we have implied that price *per se* is not the sole competitive variable in real-life rivalry. Some price competition is observable, of course, but by and large American businessmen are very adept at nonprice competition. It is to this kind of competition that we now turn.

## 6-5

**Hallmarks of Competition**

1. *Price uniformity.* Close similarity of quoted prices of rivals, usually accompanied by undercover price shading.

2. *Price differentiation.* A structure of price discounts characterized by wide spreads between the lowest and the highest net price, e.g., the discount structure that is usual for suppliers of fairly standardized products to the automobile industry.

3. *Selling activities.* Substantial promotional outlays, i.e., much advertising, point-of-sale merchandising, and direct personal salesmanship.

4. *Product differentiation.* Preoccupation with the modernity, quality, and style of the company's products as compared with rivals' products and with "good service."

5. *Product research.* Large outlays on product research that is focused on creation of new products and continuous improvement in the firm's existing products.

6. *Selective distribution.* A strong dealer organization, i.e., rivalry through and for sponsored, franchised (and often exclusive) distributors.

7. *Market share.* Acute consciousness of the activities and position of competitors, and preoccupation with the company's market share and with the market occupancy of individual rivals.

8. *Market raiding.* Uninhibited efforts to detach big customers from rivals, often by price shading, or special concessions, business patronage, and "services." Sporadic penetration of the market by distant rivals, who frequently dump, so that their net-back is much lower than from sales in their own backyard territory. The converse is customer-freezing, i.e., the use of sewing-up devices such as requirements contracts, reciprocity, and lavish gifts, which make good customers hard to alienate.

9. *Customer sharing.* Widespread acceptance of the strike-born doctrine that for each important material or component the buyer needs the protection of having at least two suppliers.

SOURCE: Joel Dean, "Competition as Seen by the Businessman and by the Economist," in Harvey W. Huegy (ed.), *The Role and Nature of Competition in Our Marketing Economy* (Urbana, Ill.: Bureau of Economic and Business Research, College of Commerce and Business Administration, University of Illinois, 1954), pp. 8–15.

## NONPRICE COMPETITION

Nonprice competition refers to all those marketing activities, except price, designed to build sales volume. Indeed, most commonly observed marketing techniques and practices are instances of nonprice competition, such as the following:

| | |
|---|---|
| Credit cards | Trading stamps |
| Premiums | Contests |
| Customer services | Location of seller |
| Dealer or store image | Advertising |
| Public relations | Brands and trade marks |
| Guarantees and warranties | Packaging |
| Styling and product design | Channels of distribution |
| Point of sale aids | Sales activities |

The basic reason for the heavy emphasis on nonprice competition is found in the complexity of markets and the character of demand. For example, the abundance of products and their increasing complexity tend to make comparisons difficult, and price differences are sometimes not a useful yardstick. As one writer contends, "Our knowledge of machinery . . . is so limited that most of us cannot compare directly the relative merits of different refrigerators and of different automobiles. Our decisions to buy such products are more significantly influenced by the reputation of the seller or the effectiveness of his advertising rather than by differences in price" (Backman, 1953).

Any monopolistically competitive firm or oligopolist can gain a market edge through nonprice marketing efforts. These firms often use product differentiation, in the broad sense as explained by theory, to adapt an offering to consumer demand. As a counterpart to this effort, they use advertising and other promotional means to generate consumer demand for their output. Competing on this basis, rivals avoid destructive price wars and concentrate on building proficiency and expertise in the nonprice areas. This advantage is not trivial when we consider the social and economic costs of cutthroat or ruinous competition.

Nonprice competition coupled with the ever-stimulated drive toward differentiation serves the American consumer well. It may be, as so often argued, that we pay more because of the absence of the purely competitive model in real life. As a practical matter most of us would not want to live in an economy based on pure competition. Monopolistic competition and oligopoly provide a vastly wider range of free choice to the consumer. Our tastes, whatever they may be, are most fully and satisfactorily met by *actual* competition rather than by the advantages claimed for the competitive model. If price, rather than nonprice factors, were the only variable we would base all buying decisions on price alone.

## THE FIRM'S MARKETING COSTS

Sometimes a firm is driven by competition to expand its marketing costs beyond the point of profitable market potential. When increased sales volume goals are heavily supported by increased marketing expenditures in advertising, personal selling, and other marketing techniques, there is the danger that additional marketing expenditures will not produce revenues of sufficient magnitude to cover the costs. In other words, too much marketing effort is deployed for the remaining amount of the market and thus costs accrue at a rate in excess of revenue.

To avoid this problem most businessmen recognize the value of planning marketing operations in terms of fixed costs and variable costs and their relationship to total revenue. Break-even analysis is a useful tool for measuring marketing expenditures relative to total revenue at various sales volume levels. As sales expand, marketing costs increase, since each additional increment of volume necessitates expenditures for market development. Assuming a given price per unit, the total-revenue curve is linear and slopes upward starting at point O, as in 6-6. The total-cost curve originates at a point above O because some fixed costs arise even without output and at zero sales. Maximum profits are gained where the total-revenue curve is farthest removed from the total-cost curve. This occurs at sales volume Y, which is also the point where marginal cost equals marginal revenue. Most firms do not possess marginal-cost and marginal-revenue data, however, whereas they often have total-cost and total-revenue information.

If market development activities carry the firm beyond point Y, total costs will mount at a more rapid rate than revenue. The chart also suggests that if the firm is not careful it can make sales but lose money as it passes P′—the second break-even point where total costs for each increment of volume become greater than total revenue. Within a substantial range marketing costs are variable. Thus when market expansion efforts are not deployed with some awareness of their results, a firm could conceivably be better off to retrench and move back to the area closest to point Y. The curves in 6-6 provide a lesson for those who try to expand sales at *all costs*.

## 6-6 Break-even Chart

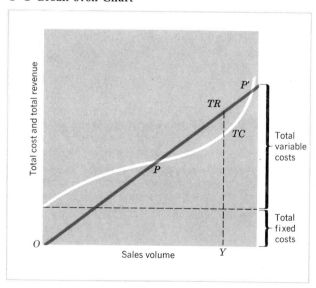

## 6-7

**"Year-end Results: Earnings Up; Sales Down"**

General Mills expects net profits for the fiscal year ended May 29, 1966, to reach a new high of $23.3 million. This represents earnings per share of $3.07, also an improvement over last year.

While earnings figures rose, total sales figures recorded a decline as the result of the closing of nine of the company's 17 flour mills. Total sales of $524.7 million were about six percent less than last year's $559 million. However, sales of all products exclusive of bakery flour increased about nine percent. Profits per sales dollar represented an increase over the 3.6 cents earned last year.

Chairman Charles H. Bell and President Edwin W. Rawlings attributed the improving earnings picture primarily to a continuing strong demand for the company's established brands, a high level of consumer acceptance of some of its newer products and streamlining of the company's milling operations in low profit areas.

In releasing the preliminary figures, the company emphasized that they are subject to adjustments after the public accountants have finished their review. The company's annual report will be mailed to reach stockholders by August 1, 1966.

SOURCE: General Mills, Inc., *The Modern Millwheel*, Vol. 30, No. 7 (Minneapolis: 1966).

Retrenchment by a well-known firm is illustrated in 6-7. This exemplifies the principal features of break-even analysis. This famous company recorded a sales decrease while earning more profits. Thus, it enjoyed more profit by doing less in a very competitive field.

## STATEMENTS TO CONSIDER

Product innovation is largely an outgrowth of instability and uncertainty: instability of competitive position and instability—also, perhaps, unpredictability—of consumer needs and desires.

In marketing the excesses of competition are to be found primarily in the performance of the selling function; at least this is the area that is customarily criticized.

The severity of competition usually gives distributors strong incentive to stress selling, regardless of the presence of economies of scale.

Product competition supplements rather than supplants price competition.

There is probably no concept in all of economics that is at once more fundamental and pervasive, yet less satisfactorily developed, than the concept of competition. (McNulty)

How we ought to make competitive decisions is reflected in the contributions of economic theory.

Consumer tastes and preferences give the marketing manager strong clues about product differentiation.

There is a prevalent use of marginal analysis in making decisions about output relative to market potential.

Present-day business practice can be traced to the concepts of microeconomics.

If an industry is highly concentrated, it is likely that nonprice competition will play a dominant role in market strategy.

# QUESTIONS FOR REVIEW

**1.** Can we rely on competition to shape the marketing processes as we would like to have it do?

**2.** Assume that you are the marketing manager of a commercial bank. One of your competitors increases the interest rate on savings by one percentage point. What are your alternatives?

**3.** How do you compete when prices are regulated by the government? (Airlines, for example, have their fares regulated.)

**4.** As a businessman, would you prefer to compete on a price basis or on a nonprice basis? Why?

**5.** Explain the concept of differentiation. Is this concept helpful in characterizing competitive strategy of American industry?

**6.** What actually is competition? Define in your own words.

**7.** Is the airline industry more competitive than the auto industry? What criteria do you use to answer this kind of question?

**8.** Concentration of industries (6-3) was higher for 1967 than for 1963. Has competition been reduced by this higher concentration?

**9.** What do you conclude after reading Dean's comments in 6-5?

**10.** You have had courses in economics. Do you know how to compete on the basis of price and nonprice competition now?

## Further Readings

Joel Dean, "Competition as Seen by the Businessman and by the Economist," in Harvey W. Huegy (ed.), *The Role and Nature of Competition in Our Marketing Economy* (Urbana, Ill.: College of Commerce and Business Administration, University of Illinois, 1954), pp. 8–15.

Richard H. Leftwich, *The Price System and Resource Allocation* (New York: Holt, Rinehart and Winston, 1966).

Campbell R. McConnell, *Economics: Principles, Problems and Policies*, 5th ed. (New York: McGraw-Hill, 1972).

R. S. Meriam, "Bigness and the Economic Analysis of Competition," *Harvard Business Review*, Vol. 28 (March 1950), pp. 109–126.

Paul A. Samuelson, *Economics: An Introductory Analysis*, 8th ed. (New York: McGraw-Hill, 1970).

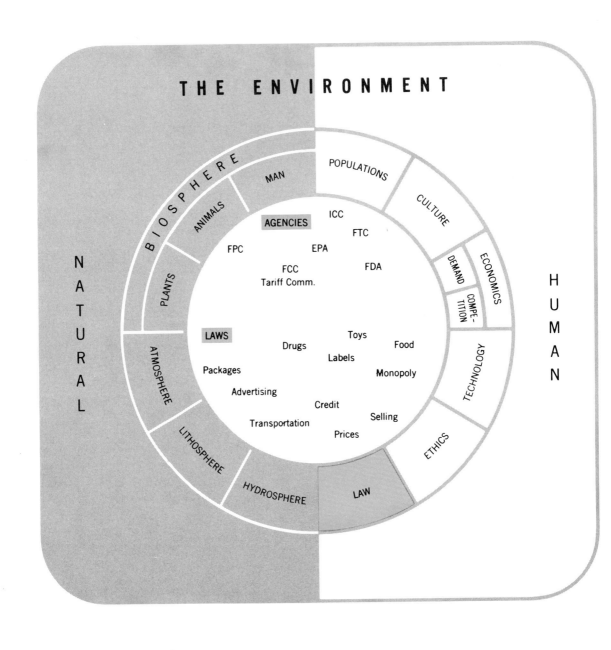

# CHAPTER 7
# MARKETING AND THE LAW

*Our society has not left business to its own devices—rather, business operates within the constraint of law. The legal environment of business has as its basic purpose the equalization of market opportunity. In recent years consumer protection has become a priority issue.*

Theoretically, a free and open competitive system unencumbered by government interference and legal restraint would assure the best allocation of resources. Thus, if self-interest of individuals were given free play, the only curb on their actions would be rival competition and the most desirable social ends would follow. In general, this theory favors the efficient and powerful firm at the expense of the inefficient and less powerful, which would tend to disappear from the market. It not only forces businessmen to compete with their rivals but also encourages them to restrain competition so as to ensure profits and their own survival.

Restraint of trade can be accomplished by several devices: price-fixing schemes, the division of markets among conspiring competitors, discriminatory pricing practices, and vertical restraints on institutions within a channel of distribution. Such practices deny firms equal opportunity to compete and also diminish the freedom of entry of potential competitors. For these reasons antitrust laws are designed to check those who would attempt to monopolize an already imperfect market condition. In a basic sense, the intent of antitrust laws is to perpetuate a free and open competitive system, protect all businesses from acts that would destroy their ability to compete, and provide freedom of entry to markets.

Not only is business conduct restrained and in turn protected, but consumers are also protected against false and deceptive practices. Consumers are not always well informed, and it is possible for a business to capitalize on their ignorance. False and deceptive advertising and mislabeling; the unrevealed presence of used, reprocessed, and substitute materials; the use of impure materials and substances harmful to the human body; and the practice of misleading the public about the true retail price of an item (automobiles, in particular) represent the bases for some laws enacted to protect the public. False and deceptive practices do not tend to create monopolistic conditions, but they are regarded as unfair to competitors and detrimental to public welfare. Hence the intent of consumer-protection laws is to keep competition on a fair basis and thus protect the ethical seller while guarding consumer interests.

## ANTITRUST LAWS

### The Demand for Legislation

The public demand for control of American business enterprise has its roots in the industrial revolution. Whereas industrialization began to evolve early in the nineteenth century, it was not until the end of the Civil War that rapid economic growth and expansion occurred. From the end of the Civil War to the turn of the century, the social and economic structure of the nation underwent rapid change. Large-scale business enterprises and the concentration of economic power became realities of the era. These important developments were paralleled by the following:

1. The growing demand for capital created by the higher investment requirements of specialization. This demand was being met by the corporate device for raising capital that was widely adopted.

2. Pressures for larger and larger volumes of sales to compensate for the high costs of industrialization, which meant that firms could no longer survive on local product demand.

3. The expanding network of railroads providing the means of market expansion. The railroads stood out as the corporate giants of the day.

4. The opportunities for skilled and unskilled labor in the cities, especially northern cities, precipitated a migration from rural areas to the industrial centers.

As market opportunities grew, enterprises that had once enjoyed a virtual local monopoly were threatened by competition. The widely separated business rivals became intense and even bitter competitors. Vast personal fortunes were to be made, and this prospect encouraged numerous new businesses to engage in an even more competitive search for customers. Cutthroat tactics and business failures characterized the marketplace. Under such conditions a natural tendency is to attempt to reduce the rivalry. Hence, monopolistic devices that insulated a firm from the inroads of competition were common. Businesses that failed to enter into monopolistic agreements and combinations were at the mercy of the ruthless, underhanded power of the giant trusts.

The corporate form of business and the problems of the era leading to combinations have been concisely presented by Clair Wilcox.

The corporate form of organization, in turn, facilitated industrial consolidation and made for increasing concentration of control. In this situation the growth of monopoly was stimulated by a steady decline in the general level of prices, accompanied by recurring periods of business depression. Concerns with large investments, entailing heavy fixed charges were impelled successively to slash their prices in an effort to cover some portion of their costs. Competition, on this basis, threatened to become mutually destructive, and business sought refuge in monopolistic agreements and in the combination of competing firms. This movement was stimulated, too, by the prospect of profits that were to be obtained in the process of promoting corporate reorganizations and those that were to be realized through the exercise of monopoly power. In consequence, during the 1880s, many of the country's major industries were brought under some form of concentrated control. In petroleum, cottonseed oil, linseed oil, meat packing, cordage, sugar, lead, coal, whiskey, tobacco, matches, gunpowder, and elsewhere, power over markets was attained through the devices of monopoly. (Wilcox, 1960.)

A case in point was the vast productive and market power of the Standard Oil Company. Through acquisition of competitors, pricing policies that destroyed the competitively weak, and other practices, which included a system of railroad rebates, the company had amassed control of about 90 percent of the country's refining capacity and almost as much control over the oil pipelines. This phenomenal degree of domination was accomplished in the brief period from 1870 to 1882.

It became evident that the public and the economy would have to be protected from the growth of corporate concentration and its resulting threats to the competitive system. Discontent with "trusts" and combinations rapidly became widespread. Farmers who were subjected to a decline in farm prices, but high prices for manufactured goods; small businessmen and others who were threatened with extinction if the competitive system of the time prevailed; raw-material suppliers who found themselves competitively weak against one or a few giant buyers in monopolized industries; and labor that relied on industrial jobs—all gave strong support to the antitrust movement. This organized discontent was instrumental in fostering the development of state and national third-party reform platforms. As the antitrust movement spread, all political parties professed opposition to monopoly. By 1888 each of the nation's four principal political parties included an antitrust plank in its platform. The issue had thus become central in the political arena and the movement soon achieved its goals.

Commencing with the movement just described and the subsequent demands by business and other interests, a body of federal laws known as the antitrust laws were enacted. In 1890 the Sherman Act was enacted at the federal level, and states enacted antitrust laws between 1889 and 1891 (Wilcox, 1960). During the 60 years from 1890 to 1950 the following federal acts became law:

Sherman Act—1890
Federal Trade Commission Act—1914
Clayton Act—1914
Robinson-Patman Act—1936
Wheeler-Lea Act—1938
Celler Antimerger Act—1950

## The Sherman Act

The Sherman Antitrust Act of 1890 is the hallmark of public policy toward restraint of trade and monopoly. Though brief, it is a general statement of intent to preserve freedom of entry and the maintenance of competition. Section 1 declares that "every contract, combination in the form of a trust or otherwise, or conspiracy, in restraint of trade or commerce among the several states, or with foreign nations, is hereby declared to be illegal. . . ." Section 2 declares that "every person who shall monopolize, or attempt to monopolize, or combine or conspire with any other person or persons, to monopolize any part of the trade or commerce among the several states, or with foreign nations, shall be guilty of a misdemeanor. . . ." Thus Section 1 of the Act applies to agreements of two or more persons that restrain trade. The second section has broader application and applies also to individual activities that monopolize.

Many years of judicial interpretation of the Sherman Act have set forth a number of business practices as illegal *per se*. All vertical and horizontal price agreements,* restriction of production as a device of price fixing, division of markets by competitors and group boycotts are illegal *per se*. Such practices violate Section 1 of the Act, and the law has generally been enforced against them without investigation or regard for their effects.

Section 2 of the Sherman Act establishes no illegality *per se*. Cases brought under Section 2 require that all circumstances be examined and in particular that their effect on competition always be part of the inquiry.

The use of the word *every* in the Sherman Act implies that all contracts and agreements among firms are illegal. This was not the intent of Congress, but not until 1911 was the famous "rule of reason" applied. Two historically important cases decided by the United States Supreme Court—*Standard Oil Co.* vs. *United States* and *American Tobacco Company* vs. *United States*—gave rise to the rule of reason with respect to restraint of trade.† As a result every contract or agreement among businesses is *not* automatically illegal. Only unreasonable agreements that restrain trade are now held illegal; reasonable agreements do not involve restraint. The acceptance of the rule-of-reason doctrine has compounded much of the confusion and controversy that have characterized the Act since its inception.

Examples of recent violations of the Sherman Act are summarized in 7-1 and 7-2. Perhaps the most shocking recent violation of Section 1 of the Sherman Act is what has become known as the "electrical conspiracy." American industry was apprised of one of the most clandestine antitrust violations as the facts and devices of the conspiracy were exposed in the press. The essential aspects of the case are summarized in 7-1 (Smith, 1961).

A conspiracy of a different nature is revealed in 7-2. This case arose from one of the more complex and subtle problems in marketing—manufacturer-distributor relations. Because of the value of good relations with distributors, manufacturers are strongly tempted to go to their aid when they request help. Yet a manufacturing firm often places itself in legal jeopardy by doing so. This was the result in *United*

*Except vertical price agreements permitted by the Miller-Tydings Act and McGuire Act in those states with resale-price maintenance laws. These agreements are commonly referred to as "fair trade" agreements.
†*Standard Oil Company of New Jersey* vs. *United States* (1911) and *American Tobacco Company* vs. *United States* 221 U.S. 106, (1911).

## 7-1

**The Electrical Conspiracy, a Violation of Section 1, Sherman Act**

In February 1960 a federal grand jury in Philadelphia indicted 14 electrical equipment manufacturers and 18 individuals on charges of price fixing. Later in the year additional indictments brought the total number of companies charged to 29 firms and 53 individuals. In effect, this represented virtually the entire electrical equipment industry.

Among the indicted companies were: Westinghouse Electric Corp., General Electric Co., Allis-Chalmers Manufacturing Co., I-T-E Circuit Breaker Co., Ohio Brass Co., McGraw-Edison Co., and other firms representing every type of power generation and distribution equipment. The indictments grew out of government charges that the industry rigged prices and doled out market shares among the 29 companies involved. General Electric, Westinghouse and Allis-Chalmers Manufacturing Corp. had by far the largest at stake in settlement of the government's charges. They along with others agreed to either plead guilty or nolo contendere (no contest) to almost all of the Justice Department's charges.[a]

The cost of being guilty of conspiracy charges can be high. Fines totaling about $2 million were imposed on the 29 companies and 45 of the individuals originally indicted. Individual executives paid fines of $2000 to $3000, but one defendant was fined $12,500. Judge Ganey, for the first time in the history of the Sherman Act, imposed prison sentences of thirty days on seven corporate officials. Additionally, the defendant companies faced more than 1800 damage suits brought by customers. The guilty pleas by defendants opened the way for damages three times the value of the overcharge. It was estimated that for General Electric alone the settlements with customers would exceed $160 million.[b]

[a] SOURCE: *Business Week,* December 3, 1960, pp. 32–34, and January 28, 1961, p. 35. Copyright held by McGraw-Hill Book Company, Inc.
[b] SOURCE: Reprinted with permission of *The Wall Street Journal,* April 30, 1964, p. 4.

---

*States* vs. *General Motors,* in which the Supreme Court found a *per se* violation of the Sherman Act where General Motors cooperated with three Chevrolet dealer associations in stopping discount houses from selling new Chevrolets in the Los Angeles area. The Court referred to this case as a "classic conspiracy" and called their activities a group boycott to protect GM franchised dealers from apparent price competition.

### The Federal Trade Commission Act

Passage of the Sherman Act did not end dissatisfaction with trusts, discriminatory practices, and other devices of monopolistic character. By 1914 it had become evident that the Sherman Act greatly needed strengthening and improved enforcement. Powerful new combinations arose in steel, farm machinery, tin containers, and several other indus-

## 7-2

*United States* vs. *General Motors Corporation et al.,* a **Violation of Sec. 1, Sherman Act**

*Boycott—Manufacturer and Dealer Cooperation—Automobile Sales Through Discount Houses*

An automobile manufacturer and three dealer associations unlawfully conspired to eliminate sales of cars through discount houses in the Los Angeles area and thereby eliminate discount houses as a class of competitors, in view of evidence that one association complained to the manufacturer about sales through discount houses, the manufacturer discussed the matter with every dealer and obtained from each a promise not to do business with discounters, the three associations created a joint investigating committee and jointly policed such promises, the associations supplied information to the manufacturer at its request so that it could bring dealers into line, and several dealers were induced to repurchase cars they had sold through discount houses and promised not to sell cars through discounters in the future. The elimination, by joint collaborative action, of the discount houses from access to the car market was a *per se* violation of the Sherman Act.

*Findings of Conspiracy*

These findings include the essentials of a conspiracy within § 1 of the Sherman Act: That in the summer of 1960 the Losor Chevrolet Dealers Association, "through some of its members," complained to General Motors personnel about sales through discounters (Finding 34); that at a Losor meeting in November 1960 the dealers there present agreed to embark on a letter-writing campaign directed at enlisting the aid of General Motors (Finding 35); that in December and January General Motors personnel discussed the matter with every Chevrolet dealer in the Los Angeles area and elicited from each a promise not to do business with the discounters (Finding 39); that representatives of the three associations of Chevrolet dealers met on December 15, 1960, and created a joint investigating committee (Finding 40); that the three associations then undertook jointly to police the agreements obtained from each of the dealers by General Motors; that the associations supplied information to General Motors for use by it in bringing wayward dealers into line, and that Chevrolet's O'Connor asked the associations to do so (Findings 41 and 42); that as a result of this collaborative effort, a number of Chevrolet dealers were induced to repurchase cars they had sold through discounters and to promise to abjure such sales in [the] future.

These findings by the trial judge compel the conclusion that a conspiracy to restrain trade was proved.

SOURCE: Commerce Clearing House, Inc., Trade Regulation Reporter, 1966, p. 82,470, par. 71,750. Reproduced by permission.

tries. In the national political campaign of 1912 trusts and monopoly again became a central issue. It was recognized that some agency would have to be established to strengthen enforcement of the law and adherence to it. In 1914 the Federal Trade Commission Act established a specialized administrative agency known as the Federal Trade Commission (FTC). The Commission was given broad powers over the enforcement of Section 5 of the Act, which declared "unfair methods of competition" illegal. Since its establishment the duties of the Commission have been broadened by amendments and subsequent legislation.

An important amendment to the Federal Trade Commission Act came in 1938 with passage of the Wheeler-Lea Act. Before, Section 5 of the FTC Act was concerned with the somewhat limiting and ambiguous phrase "unfair methods of competition." Adverse court rulings made it apparent that this phrase needed broader and more inclusive language to deal with the problem. The Wheeler-Lea Act thus amended Section 5, which now outlaws "unfair or deceptive acts or practices in commerce." The Commission was also given jurisdiction over false advertising of foods, drugs, cosmetics, and curative devices. The Wheeler-Lea Act further provides the Commission with power to restrain the dissemination of false advertising by means of injunctive proceedings.

Today the duties of the FTC are:

1. To promote free and fair competition in interstate commerce in the interest of the public through prevention of price-fixing agreements, boycotts, combinations in restraint of trade, other unfair methods of competition, and unfair or deceptive acts or practices (Federal Trade Commission Act, Section 5).

2. To safeguard the consuming public by preventing the dissemination of false or deceptive advertisements of food, drugs, cosmetics, and devices (Federal Trade Commission Act, Sections 12 to 15).

3. To prevent certain unlawful price and other discriminations, exclusive-dealing and tying contracts and arrangements, acquisitions of the stock of competitors, and interlocking directorates (Clayton Act, Sections 2, 3, 7, and 8).

4. To protect producers, manufacturers, distributors, and consumers from the unrevealed presence of substitutes and mixtures in manufactured wool products (Wool Products Labeling Act of 1939).

5. To supervise the registration and operation of associations of American exporters engaged solely in export trade (Export Trade Act).

6. To petition for the cancellation of the registrations of trademarks which were illegally registered or which have been used for purposes contrary to the intent of the Trade-Mark Act of 1946 (Lanham Trade-Mark Act).

7. To gather and make available to the Congress, the President, and the public, factual data concerning economic and business conditions as a basis for remedial legislation where needed, and for guidance and protection of the public (Federal Trade Commission Act, Section 6).

From the above it should be noted that the Commission is concerned not only with restraints of trade but also with deceptive practices that may injure competitors and mislead consumers. Insofar as marketing is concerned, the first four duties noted are of major significance.

## The Clayton Act

To strengthen the Sherman Act further and strike down certain restraints of trade that persisted, the Clayton Act was passed in 1914. This Act attempted to make the law more specific with respect to restraints of trade and also sought to bar incipient trusts, conspiracies, and monopolies. The original Act outlawed price discrimination (Section 2), agreements by buyers not to deal in goods of other sellers (Section 3), intercorporate stockholdings (Section 7), and interlocking directorates. None of these provisions of the law were absolute, but they were forbidden where the effect "may be to substantially lessen competition or tend to create a monopoly in any line of commerce."

Section 2 of the original Act (later amended by the Robinson-Patman Act in 1936) forbade sellers to discriminate in price between different purchasers of commodities . . . where the effect of such discrimination may be to substantially lessen competition or tend to create a monopoly in any line of commerce: *Provided,* That nothing herein . . . shall prevent discrimination in price . . . on account of differences in the grade, quality, or quantity of the commodity sold, or that makes only due allowance for difference in the cost of selling or transportation, or discrimination in price in the same or different communities made in good faith to meet competition (38 Stat. 730).

Section 3 stands unamended and declares that "it shall be unlawful . . . to lease or make for sale or contract for sale of goods, wares, . . . supplies or other commodities . . . on the condition, agreement or understanding that the lessee or purchaser thereof shall not use or deal in the goods . . . of a competitor. . . ."

Section 7 (later amended by the Celler-Kefauver Act of 1950) originally declared "that no corporation . . . shall acquire . . . the whole or any part of the stock or other share capital of another corporation . . . where the effect of such acquisition may be to substantially lessen competition . . . or tend to create a monopoly in any line of commerce."

With passage of the Clayton Act the more general foundation established by the Sherman Act was supplemented and some of its shortcomings were overcome. The general terms of the Sherman Act led to problems of interpretation and dealt with monopoly after the fact. The more explicit Clayton Act was concerned with the *methods* through which monopoly was reached. Hence, the latter Act and its subsequent amendments, which will be seen in the discussion of the Robinson-Patman Act and the Celler-Kefauver Act, are designed to curb those activities that may tend to restrain trade, create monopoly, or both.

It should be noted that tying contracts and exclusive dealer arrangements, dealt with in Section 3, may enhance competition but may also be harmful to it. The reasoning behind this contention takes the following form:

> Modern production may necessitate the use of certain commodities in conjunction with others and may, as a means of protecting the manufacturer, justify the imposition of restrictions or conditions upon sale. As a consequence, tying contracts may even enhance competition. Similarly, exclusive-dealer arrangements may lead to economies of production or marketing, when they bring about a concentration of distribution that results in greater marketing efficiency. On the other hand, both devices may be used effectively to restrain competition or maintain monopoly. The purpose of the law was not to outlaw these business practices but only to prevent their use when the result would be substantially to lessen competition or to tend to create a monopoly in any line of commerce. It is the difficulty of drawing the line between the desirable and undesirable aspects that has rendered the enforcement of the law halting and uncertain. (Pegrum, 1965.)

## The Robinson-Patman Act

The Robinson-Patman Act completely revised Section 2 of the Clayton Act. The original section was intended to curb large manufacturers from price-cutting in selected areas while leaving other market prices unaffected. This was a notorious practice of some of the early trusts and often resulted in elimination of smaller competitors. The attempts of the Clayton Act to deal adequately with this problem were disappointing. The courts had ruled against the Federal Trade Commission in a number of price-discrimination cases, and clarification of the law was needed.

Perhaps more influential in generating the need for additional antitrust legislation was the rapid growth of the corporate chain during the era from the end of the First World War to the mid-1930s. Wholesalers and retailers across the nation faced powerful competition and lower prices. The lower prices of the mass distributors were in part attributed to the lower prices paid to manufacturers and other market suppliers. The power of the large chains further enabled them to bargain for and receive concessions not usually granted to smaller independent buyers. Brokerage allowances, even where a broker was not employed, were demanded, and bargaining for advertising and other concessions was out of proportion to the quantities purchased. Because of the substantial proportion of a manufacturer's output sold by chain stores, manufacturers were placed in a vulnerable position if they refused to yield to these demands.

The Robinson-Patman Act was designed to provide equality of opportunity for buyers. In attempting to accomplish this end, Section 2 of the Act amended Section 2 of the Clayton Act. It now reads in part "that it shall be unlawful for any person engaged in commerce . . . to discriminate in price between different purchasers of commodities of like grade and quality . . . where the effect of such discrimination may be substantially to lessen competition or tend to create a monopoly in any line of commerce, or to injure, destroy, or prevent competition with any person who either grants or knowingly receives the benefit of such discrimination, or with customers of either of them. . . ." The broadening of the Act was achieved by inclusion of the words "prevent competition with any person."

The same section permits price differentials, as did the Clayton Act, provided the differences are made for "only due allowance in the cost of manufacture, sale or delivery resulting from differing methods or quantities." The Federal Trade Commission is empowered to fix and establish quantity limits, and to adjust them where purchasers of greater quantities are so few as to discriminate unjustly or promote monopoly. In other words, quantity discounts, even though allowable by the seller's cost savings, could be limited if large-scale marketers were given an undue advantage. Section 2 further provides for "price changes from time to time . . . in response to changing conditions affecting the market" (49 Stat. 1526).

The amount of leeway a seller has to adapt prices to changing market conditions is most difficult to determine. The burden of proof that there has been no discrimination rests with the seller charged with violating the Act. Of course, a seller may argue that a price was lowered in good faith to meet competition. Whether this is an adequate defense remains for the FTC and the courts to decide. Much controversy about the Act revolves around this unsettled issue.

The law also forbids other concessions that often have been used to cloak price discrimination. It outlaws brokerage and other compensations by stating, "It shall be unlawful . . . to pay or grant, or to receive or accept, anything of value as a commission, brokerage, or other compensation . . . except for services rendered in connection with the sale or purchase of goods, wares, or merchandise." If a seller offers anything of value to a customer, such payment or compensation must be "available on proportionally equal terms to all other customers competing in the distribution of such products or commodities."

Section 3 of the Robinson-Patman Act forbids any transaction which discriminates against the buyer's competitors by means of any discount, rebate, allowance, or advertising benefit which is greater than that available to them. This section also forbids sales in one locality at prices lower than those in other localities when the purpose is to destroy competition. Finally, it forbids prices at unreasonably low levels for the purpose of ending competition or eliminating a competitor.

From a marketing standpoint the Robinson-Patman Act is perhaps the most important single piece of legislation. It should be noted that it endeavors only to establish standards of competition. Any attempt to measure discrimination or the lack of it by cost standards is extremely difficult. The Act has been criticized for failing to do so, since it can be argued that it imposes restrictions on large-scale producers at the expense of consumers. This, of course, assumes that economies of scale which produce lower costs are passed on to the consumer through the distributive process.

Of interest is a ruling of the Supreme Court of the United States in

## 7-3

*Federal Trade Commission* vs. *The Borden Company*, a Violation of
Section 2, Robinson-Patman Act

The United States Supreme Court has reversed a 5th Circuit Court
of Appeals decision (which, in turn, had reversed a Federal Trade
Commission ruling) to the effect that a product marketed under an
extensively advertised and well-known brand of its manufacturer is
not "of like grade and quality" with a physically identical commodity
when packaged under a private brand.

In this case, involving national and private brands of evaporated
milk, Borden was charged under section 2(a) of the Robinson-Patman
Act with unlawfully discriminating in price between customers of its
house brand and customers of its private label goods. In defense of
the difference in price between the two classes of goods, Borden
asserted that they were not "of like grade and quality" (a requirement under section 2(a) before discrimination can be found) because
of the greater consumer demand that had been created for the house
brand by extensive advertising. This argument was rejected by the
Supreme Court on the ground that Congress intended that only
chemical and physical properties of products be taken into consideration in determining "like grade and quality."

Unanswered by the decision is whether the difference in prices
between the national and private brands was justified by cost differentials, and whether the price difference was potentially injurious to
competition. These questions were referred back to the Court of
Appeals for decision. In a dissenting opinion, two of the Supreme
Court Justices stated that they thought it unlikely that economic differences could reasonably be taken into account in answering the
remaining questions. Assuming that the cost justification and "injury
to competition" questions would be answered unfavorably to The
Borden Company, the dissenting Justices said that the result of the
decision would be that: ". . . Borden must now make private label
milk available to all customers of its premium brand [or to] avoid
supplying a private label brand to a premium brand customer, Borden
need only forego further sales of its premium brand to that customer."

SOURCE: Legal Bulletin, Association of National Advertisers, Inc., New York, April 1966.

the case of the *Federal Trade Commission* vs. *The Borden Company*.
The decision summarized in 7-3 was originally brought by the FTC on
a charge of price discrimination between customers of the Borden
national brand and the company's private brand.

## The Celler-Kefauver Act

Section 7 of the Clayton Act was amended in 1950 by the Celler-
Kefauver Act (64 Stat. 1125). The inability of the original law to meet
competitive problems stemming from mergers and acquisitions led to
its passage. The now broader Section 7 reads in part: "That no corporation engaged in commerce shall acquire, directly or indirectly, the
whole or any part of the stock or other share capital and no corporation

subject to the jurisdiction of the Federal Trade Commission shall acquire the whole or any part of the assets of another corporation engaged also in commerce, where in any line of commerce in any section of the country, the effect of such acquisition may be substantially to lessen competition, or to tend to create a monopoly."

This legislation is much more restrictive than the original Section 7. It has a wider objective in that it applies to the lessening of competition in *any* line of commerce in *any* section of the country as well as between a corporation acquiring the stock and one whose stock is acquired. It also was intended that mergers tending to lessen competition would be halted at the outset.

Companies often seek to merge with other companies or acquire them outright for sound marketing reasons. The most common reason for merging appears to be for the purpose of diversifying product line or expanding existing lines with compatible products. The much discussed attempt of Procter & Gamble to acquire the Clorox Chemical Company (maker of Clorox bleach) is related in 7-4. This case is unusual in that the merger was illegal by virtue of Procter & Gamble's market power and the efficiency with which it develops markets.

The *Journal of Marketing* for many years has carried a legal section that reviews marketing cases handled by the courts. The classification of the cases and recent examples of each are shown below. Although the comments are inadequate for full understanding of the cases, they do provide a good idea of the impact of the legal segment of the environment on marketing.

### I. REGULATION OF MONOPOLISTIC METHODS

A. *Market Control (OKC Corp., et al.)*—This case is the most recent one in the Federal Trade Commission's continuing campaign against vertical integration in the cement industry. Between May and December, 1969, OKC Corporation, a producer of cement and petroleum products, acquired 88 percent of Jahncke Service, Inc. Jahncke produces ready-mixed concrete cement and other building and industrial materials. The Commission ordered OKC to divest itself of Jahncke. (Vol. 35 (April 1971), p. 69.)

B. *Collusive Practices (Tropic Film Corporation vs. Paramount Pictures Corporation, Paramount Film Distributing Corporation and Motion Picture Association of America, Inc.)*—Is the movie trade association engaged in a group boycott violative of the antitrust laws by refusing to distribute the film "Tropic of Cancer" without an "X" rating? The district court stated that a group boycott does not automatically constitute a *per se* violation. (Vol. 35 (January 1971), p. 76.)

C. *Market-Exclusion Tactics (Curtis C. Flood vs. Bowie K. Kuhn, et al.)*— Because of Mr. Flood's inability under the contract to negotiate with any other professional baseball team, he brought this action against the 24 major league ball clubs comprising the National and American Leagues, their respective presidents, and the Commissioner of Baseball, asserting that baseball's "reserve system" is unlawful. Although on all causes of action brought by Flood, the court found in favor of the leagues, it stated that it

## 7-4

*Federal Trade Commission* vs. *Procter & Gamble Company,*
a Violation of Section 7, Clayton Act and the Celler-Kefauver Act

For the second time, a Commission hearing examiner has ruled that the acquisition of The Clorox Chemical Co., Oakland, Calif., by The Procter & Gamble Co., Cincinnati, Ohio, is illegal, and issued an order which would require P & G to sell Clorox so as to restore it as a going concern.

P & G, the nation's leading producer of soap and detergent products, acquired Clorox, maker of "Clorox," the dominant brand of household liquid bleach, on August 1, 1957 through an exchange of stock valued at approximately $30 million. The FTC's complaint challenging the acquisition was filed on September 30 of that year. In an initial decision of June 17, 1960, the examiner had held the acquisition violates Section 7 of the Clayton Act, the Celler-Kefauver antimerger law, and issued an order of divestiture. The Commission subsequently remanded the case to the examiner for receipt of further evidence concerning the competitive impact of the acquisition, and further hearings were held before him last December 1 and 12 in Washington, D.C.

In this decision, the examiner again found that the acquisition is unlawful because its result "probably will be the substantial lessening of competition between the respondent-owned Clorox and the smaller manufacturers and distributors of household liquid bleach, in the United States, and the definite tendency to create a monopoly in" P & G in this industry.

This finding was based on the following factors, among others:

Clorox's dominant market position was increased as a result of the acquisition and the various advertising campaigns, sales promotion programs and devices subsequently employed by P & G;

P & G's financial and economic strength and advertising and promotional experience as compared with its competitors in the liquid bleach industry;

Its ability to command consumer acceptance of its products and to acquire and retain valuable shelf space in grocery stores because of its advertising and promotional experience and financial resources;

The increasing tendency of concentration of competitors in the industry;

Clorox's ability, through aggressive P & G-inspired advertising and promotional methods, to prevent the entry of additional competitors into the industry, and to prevent existing competitors from expanding by normal methods of competition.

In addition, the examiner pointed out, according to the testimony of competitors, "there is an apparently well-founded fear on their

was not without hope that an amicable change in the reserve system might be forthcoming. (Vol. 34 (January 1971), p. 76.)

II. REGULATION OF PRODUCT CHARACTERISTICS

A. *Product Standards* (Federal Trade Commission Advisory Opinion, Edward S. Jones)—In this advisory opinion, the Federal Trade Commission part that the aggressive advertising and sales promotion methods of respondent P & G used by Clorox in the household liquid bleach industry will result in serious injury to their business. The evidence introduced at the recent hearings showing a decline in the market share of some of Clorox's smaller competitors, since the acquisition, indicates that such fear expressed by at least some of these competitors was, in fact, well-founded. . . . [T]he record indicates that it was not the policy of the Clorox Chemical Company, the acquired corporation, to meet the sales promotions or test marketing of its smaller competitors with aggressive counter-promotions and retaliatory tactics. It had attained its leading position in the household liquid bleach industry mainly by national advertising. However, the evidence indicates that it has been the policy of Clorox, since its acquisition by P & G, to meet, and meet vigorously, the promotions and test marketing of its competitors. . . . [T]hese retaliatory tactics have been used especially against Purex and Roman Cleanser, the second and third largest household liquid bleach manufacturers in the industry."

The deciding factor in concluding that the acquisition may substantially lessen competition and tend toward monopoly, the examiner said, is the ability of P & G's "conglomerate organization to shift financial resources and competitive strength through a broad front of different products and markets and its ability to strategically alter the selected point of greatest impact as time, place and market conditions require. It is not necessary that the conglomerate enjoy a predominate position in any industry or market, although in this particular case Procter & Gamble does enjoy such a position in the soap and detergent industry. The test of conglomerate power is whether a corporation is able to concentrate its competitive efforts at one point by shifting its financial resources and competitive strength from one industry or market to another. Procter & Gamble possesses this power and ability."

After additional hearings the acquisition was held unlawful and divestiture was again ordered. The Court of Appeals for the Sixth Circuit reversed this decision and directed the FTC's complaint dismissed.

This case was finally decided by the Supreme Court of the United States during its October 1966 term. The Supreme Court reversed the decision of the Court of Appeals and ordered the enforcement of the FTC order (i.e., divestiture).

SOURCE: Commerce Clearing House, Inc., Trade Regulation Reporter, 1962, p. 20,582, par. 15,773; U.S. Supreme Court Bulletin, No. 342, October Term, 1966.

refused to sanction the use of the terms "gold finish," "gold brushes," and "gold manner" as descriptive of costume jewelry containing a gold coating of ten-carat fineness and 3/1,000,000 to 5/1,000,000 of an inch thick. (Vol. 36 (January 1972), p. 76.)

B. *Product Quality* (*United States* vs. *American Angus Association*)—The Justice Department has proposed a consent decree prohibiting an association of purebred Angus cattle breeders from restricting the sale of Angus semen for eight years. (Vol. 35 (January 1971), p. 78.)

C. *Packaging and Conditions of Sale* (Phosphate Content of Detergents, Minnesota Attorney General's Opinion)—A proposed ordinance of the City of Duluth would require among other things the affixing of labels to boxes of detergent giving the phosphate content thereof. The attorney general has ruled that the Fair Packaging and Labeling Act expressly preempts local labeling of consumer products which move in interstate commerce. Hence, the states and political subdivisions may not locally regulate this labeling. It is arguable that this opinion is in error, as a close reading of the preemption language merely applies to state laws which "require information *different from* the requirements" of the FPLA. (Vol. 35 (April 1971), p. 73.)

## III. REGULATION OF PRICE COMPETITION

A. *Price Discrimination* (*Bardahl Lubricants, Inc.* vs. *Bardahl Oil Company*)—The plaintiff, Bardahl Lubricants, is in Massachusetts. It complained that its competitor Bardahl Oil (located in Missouri) violated the Robinson-Patman Act and the Massachusetts Unfair Sales Act by its pricing practices. Both firms have approximately the same manufacturing costs, and both employ similar systems of distribution. The district court concluded that the defendant consummated many sales below cost with the probable effect of lessening competition to a substantial degree. In addition, the court concluded that as a consequence of sales below cost and discriminatory sales, plaintiff lost goodwill, customers, distributors, employees, and potential sales. (Vol. 35 (July 1971), p. 80.)

B. *Resale Price Maintenance* (*Norman's On the Waterfront, Inc.* vs. *Wheatley*)—Norman's, a retailer of alcoholic beverages using a discount coupon plan, brought an action to challenge a law of the Virgin Islands which compelled each producer, importer, or wholesaler of alcoholic beverages to file a wholesale price schedule which would fix a minimum resale price. Using a combined interpretation of the Organic Act which limits the legislative power to acts "not inconsistent with the laws of the United States," the Sherman Act, and the McGuire Act, the district court found the statute invalid. (Vol. 35 (July 1971), p. 81.)

C. *Price Control* (*Minimum and Maximum*) (*Catalina, Inc., et al.* vs. *P. Zwetchkenbaum & Sons, Inc.*)—In this decision, the Rhode Island Supreme Court overruled the lower state court and said that it is within the right of a manufacturer to go to court to seek an injuction against retailers who are selling below cost in violation of the state's Unfair Sales Practices Act. (Vol. 35 (January 1971), p. 81.)

## IV. REGULATION OF CHANNELS OF DISTRIBUTION

A. *Operating Features of Marketing Institutions* (*Semmes Motors, Inc.,* suing on behalf of itself and together with Ford Dealers Alliance, Inc., *et al.* vs. *Ford Motor Co.*)—The lower court had granted a preliminary injunction against the auto manufacturer's termination of a dealership. The action was under the Automobile Dealers Franchise Act of 1956. (Vol. 35 (January 1971), p. 81.)

B. *Relations Between Buyers and Sellers, Exclusive Dealing Arrangements, etc.*—(Fontana Aviation, Inc. vs. Beech Aircraft Corp. and Hartzog-Schneck Aviation, Inc.)—In this decision the termination of a retail dealership by a distributor was found to be in conflict with the antitrust laws. The granting of treble damages was, therefore, in order. (Vol. 35 (April 1971), p. 75.)

## V. REGULATION OF UNFAIR COMPETITION

A. *Advertising* (Arthur Murray Studio of Washington, Inc., *et al.*)—The examiner ruled that the studios' advertised contests were not bona fide, but were lures to get prospects into studios and to subject them to sales talks designed to get them to sign up for long-term and expensive contracts. (Vol. 35 (January 1971), p. 83.)

B. *Nonadvertising Promotional Methods* (Coca-Cola, *et al*)—A Federal Trade Commission hearing examiner has refused to dismiss a Commission complaint against a soft drink company and the creator of its "Big Name Bingo" contest. (Vol. 36 (January 1971), p. 83.)

C. *Trademarks and Trade Names* (J. B. Williams Co., *et al.; in re* Coca-Cola Co., *et al*)—The Commission has announced that the proposed order against the Coca-Cola Company has been modified to no longer require the banning of the trade name "Hi-C." The newly proposed order, instead of requiring a disclosure in future ads that the use of the name "Hi-C" deceptively indicated that the drink was high in vitamin C, would compel the company to disclose in its ads that the Commission has found that "Hi-C" has been falsely advertised in the past in that the advertisements gave the false impression that the nutritive value of the drink was the equivalent of orange juice or other citrus juices. (Vol. 35 (October 1971), p.77.)

## VI. PROCEDURAL AND MISCELLANEOUS DEVELOPMENTS

(*United States* vs. *National Dairy Products and Raymond J. Wise*)—Wise, a corporate officer, was named as a codefendant with his corporation in a government criminal antitrust suit. Both the corporation and Wise were found guilty. Wise was fined $52,500 and put on probation. The court set aside the fine and the probation. The corporation appealed the case, had the charges against it dismissed, and won a retrial. Wise failed to appeal his case, because he had been relieved of the obligation to pay the fine and his probation had been terminated. The problem arose when Wise was named as a codefendant in a private civil treble damage antitrust suit. The court stated that justice required that Wise be permitted a new trial and that his previous conviction be abrogated. (Vol. 35 (January 1971), p. 84.)

# FEDERAL LAWS AGAINST DECEPTIVE PRACTICES

Antitrust laws serve the public interest by maintaining competition. If competition is maintained, access to markets is open to all, prices reflect more closely the actual competitive and demand conditions of the market, and consumer welfare is indirectly served. It is not enough for the government to preclude restraints on competition, price fixing, and other unfair market practices. It must do more. Fraud and deception in the marketplace have always been practiced by the unscrupulous few to the disadvantage of consumers. Business and industrial buyers are in a much better position than consumers to avoid deception: skilled purchasing agents who have objective information set specifications on quality and performance, and tests conducted in a firm's laboratories can insure that a product it is buying meets the business or industrial need. Consumers, on the other hand, do not have the skills of purchasing agents and more often than not cannot develop them in view of the variety, complexity, and abundance of things on the market. It is only the rare individual who feels that he can judge quality and performance, to say nothing of meeting his sociopsychological needs with the purchase of a product. Hence it is up to the government to protect the consumer against deception.

The purpose of the federal laws designed to prevent fraud and deception is twofold. First, the laws protect the scrupulous businessman from unscrupulous rivals. Fraud and deception do not usually create monopolistic conditions, but they are dangerous in that an entire industry may be forced into the worst forms of competition rather than being able to attain the most ethical. Second, the laws protect consumers from the unscrupulous behavior of businessmen. They offer protection in part from the following practices.

1. False and deceptive advertising.
2. Unfair methods of competition.
3. Deceptive product contents in alcohol, fur, wool, and textile products.
4. Contaminated, unclean, and injurious products produced for human consumption.
5. Hazardous substances which without warning may cause personal injury or death.

In addition, standard weights and measures and standardized container sizes serve the public interest. In some instances standard grades of products have been established by law. Whereas the Constitution gives Congress the power to establish standard weights and measures, the Congress has not taken full responsibility for them. The states have been active in enacting and enforcing laws and in supervising established specifications. For example, gasoline pumps, scales, and dispensers of food and drink are usually inspected by state agencies.

## The Demand for Consumer Protection

For almost a century the federal government has undertaken laws to protect consumers. Since 1872 the use of the mails to defraud has been unlawful. The need for laws stemmed originally from the development of canned foods, the growth of patent medicines, and the lack of standards in the processing of meat products and other consumable items.

By 1880 it became apparent that some laws would have to be enacted to guard the public against harmful substances used to preserve canned food, habit-forming and dangerous drugs used in medicines, and the filth found in meat-packing plants. The public became aroused in 1906 by Upton Sinclair's book *The Jungle,* which described the conditions and diseased meat products in Chicago packing plants. Government scientists took the initiative in uncovering contaminated food and harmful substances used in products. A series of articles in *Collier's* magazine exposed the drug business. Women's clubs, political groups, and others became aroused and organized drives for legislation. As a result the Pure Food and Drug Act of 1906 was passed. In 1927, much impetus for additional and stronger legislation came from the publication of *Your Money's Worth* by Stuart Chase and F. J. Schlink. During this century numerous bills have been proposed calling for regulation. Among those which have been passed are the following.

1. The Pure Food and Drug Act, 1906, which outlawed adulterated and misbranded foods and drugs sold in interstate commerce.

2. The Federal Trade Commission Act of 1914, amended and strengthened by the Wheeler-Lea Act in 1938 which outlawed unfair methods of competition and unfair or deceptive practices. The latter Act also forbids the dissemination of false advertising of foods, drugs, cosmetics, and devices.

3. The Tariff Act of 1930, required that imported articles or their containers clearly indicate the country of origin.

4. The Federal Alcohol Administration Act of 1935, which forbids commercial bribery, misleading advertising, and deceptive labeling of alcoholic beverages.

5. The Food, Drug, and Cosmetic Act of 1938, which strengthened and broadened the Pure Food and Drug Act of 1906. This Act gave the Food and Drug Administration authority over problems of contamination, filth, and those compounds and preparatory substances which might be injurious to health. The Administration was empowered to set standards for canned foods in respect to quality, conditions of the contents, and fill. The law extended the scope of products to include cosmetics and therapeutic devices. It forbade cosmetics that may be injurious, false and misleading labels, and deceptive containers. It also provided that labels of such products must give adequate warnings of irritation and injury.

6. The Wool Products Labeling Act of 1939, required full disclosure of the percentages of new wool, reprocessed wool, and other fibers or fillers used. Such information must be shown on the labels of products containing wool, except carpets, rugs, and some other textile items.

7. The Fur Products Labeling Act of 1951, required labels that fully disclose whether the fur is new or used, from what part of the animal the fur derives, and whether the fur is bleached or dyed. The FTC, after hearings concerning the confusion and problems of the trade, issued a Fur Products Name Guide.

8. The Federal Aviation Act of 1958, which forbids carriers to enter into unfair or deceptive practices including misleading advertising.

9. The Automobile Information Disclosure Act of 1958, which requires auto manufacturers to post the suggested retail price, detailing the price of all extra equipment and transportation charges on all new passenger vehicles.

This law was designed to stop dealers from inflating the price of a new auto so as to misrepresent the true value of the customer's trade-in. (Few people had any idea of the suggested retail price of new autos prior to the passage of this law.)

10. The Hazardous Substances Labeling Act of 1960, which empowered the Food and Drug Administration to require all household products which contain hazardous substances to give warnings on the labels. Products such as household cleaning agents, paint and varnish removers, and pressurized containers are a few of the products which may cause injury because of toxic, corrosive, or highly flammable substances.

11. The Drug Amendments Act of 1962, which amended the Federal Food and Drug Commission Act to assure that drugs are manufactured in accordance with accepted standards of safety and purity. The Act requires the Secretary of Health, Education and Welfare to refuse to approve, or to withdraw approval, of a new drug if there is a lack of substantial evidence of effectiveness or if the labeling is false or misleading.

12. The Federal Fair Packaging and Labeling Act of 1966 (known as Truth-in-Packaging), which insures that the labels of packaged consumer commodities adequately inform consumers of the quantity and composition of their contents and promotes packaging practices that facilitate price comparisons by consumers.

13. The Wholesome Meat Act of 1967, which gives the Secretary of Agriculture specific authority to require inspection and authorizes the Secretary to require denaturing and identification of meat not suitable for human consumption.

14. The Truth-in-Lending Act of 1968, which requires all persons extending credit to another to make full disclosure in writing of all finance charges prior to consummation of the transaction.

15. The Toy Safety and Child Protection Act of 1969, which provides for labeling under the Federal Hazardous Substance Act of toys intended for use by children that are dangerous because of the presence of electrical, mechanical, or thermal hazards.

From the listing it is apparent that several government agencies are assigned the task of protecting the consumer. The Food and Drug Administration has been empowered with a comprehensive set of responsibilities ranging from problems of mislabeling to the use of chemical agents that may cause injury or even death. The FDA cooperates with the Department of Agriculture, the Public Health Service, and any other agency that can be of assistance in examining business claims, product composition, and any additives which might be harmful to the user. In recent years the use of pesticides has come under attack, especially after the publication of the late Rachel Carson's *Silent Spring*. The FDA and the Department of Agriculture have been criticized for not taking a strong and an early position against the wide use of pesticides and herbicides. Unquestionably there will be tighter controls on their use in the future. Fish kills and the loss of wildlife by mass spraying is of major concern to the Public Health Service, the

Department of Interior, the Department of Agriculture, and the FDA.

With few exceptions public health and safety are the direct responsibility of the agencies noted and in particular the Food and Drug Administration. On the other hand, the Federal Trade Commission concerns itself with protecting the public and business firms from false and deceptive practices and unfair methods of competition. Some idea of the breadth and nature of FTC activities is shown in 7-5. In recent years the FTC has stepped up its activities on behalf of the consumer. This thrust was imposed on the FTC by the activities of consumer advocates and the claim that the FTC did not well serve the interests of the American consumer. Since 1968 the FTC has taken a much more aggressive posture in citing business firms for alleged false and deceptive practices.

## LEGISLATION IN THE STATES

In conjunction with the antitrust movement that brought about federal legislation, about one half of the states enacted their own laws against monopolies and trusts. These statutes vary in detail, but in general they outlaw price discrimination, price fixing, division of markets, and other devices that may restrain trade. Although some states have enforced their antitrust laws, the overall assessment is that states have not engaged actively in attempting to prevent monopolistic practices. For all practical purposes antitrust has been a federal concern.

Some legislation, rather than being primarily directed toward maintaining competition, has often had the effect of limiting it. At one time most states legalized resale price maintenance, and more than half of them have statutes prohibiting sales below cost, thus assuring wholesalers and retailers a margin of profit. Certain products such as milk (especially in dairy states), gasoline, cigarettes, and alcoholic beverages are sold at prices regulated by some states. The purpose of this legislation has been the protection of the small independent retailer from the pricing tactics of the large integrated chain. Some products are also singled out and their sale is forbidden because of some special-interest group. The once widespread ban in the midwestern states on the sale of yellow oleomargarine is a case in point. Wisconsin until 1967 discriminated against the sale of yellow oleomargarine by outright prohibition; Minnesota still levies a per-pound tax that is earmarked for enhancement of the dairy industry. When states regulate the resale price of selected products (by restricting the number and specifying the location of establishments), a true geographical monopoly exists. As a result of this practice consumers pay artifically high prices and their real income is diminished.

### Resale-price Maintenance

Perhaps the most widespread and controversial kind of legislation adopted by the states is resale-price maintenance, or so-called fair trade.

## 7-5 Selected FTC Proceedings, 1971 and 1972

1. Sixteen manufacturers of cold and cough remedies have been ordered by the FTC to furnish it within 60 days documentation for designated advertising claims.

Following are typical claims for which substantiation is demanded:

Dristan Tablets effectively relieve the body aches which may accompany a cold or the flu.

Listerine Antiseptic Throat Lozenges can relieve a sore throat so effectively that only minutes after taking them one who has a sore throat is no longer bothered by it.

2. The FTC announced that it has provisionally accepted consent orders requiring six major cigarette manufacturers to include in all cigarette advertisements a clear and conspicuous disclosure of the statement: "Warning: The Surgeon General Has Determined That Cigarette Smoking Is Dangerous to Your Health." The six firms manufacture approximately 99 percent of all cigarettes sold in the United States.

3. The FTC announced its intention to issue a complaint alleging that the four largest manufacturers of ready-to-eat (RTE) cereals have illegally monopolized the industry. The proposed complaint alleges that for at least the past 30 years their actions or inactions have resulted in maintenance of a highly concentrated, noncompetitive market structure in the production and sale of RTE cereals.

The four firms and their approximate market shares in 1969 or 1970 are:

Kellogg Co., Battle Creek, Mich.—45 percent

General Mills, Inc., Minneapolis, Minn.—21 percent

General Foods Corp., White Plains, N.Y.—16 percent

The Quaker Oats Co., Chicago, Ill.—9 percent

4. The FTC announced that it supports the concept of "counter-advertising," *i.e.,* the right of access to the broadcast media for the purpose of expressing views and positions on controversial issues that are raised by commercial advertising. Identifiable categories and examples are as follows:

*Advertising asserting claims of product performance or characteristics that explicitly raise controversial issues of current public importance.*—Claims that products contribute to solving ecological problems, or that the advertiser is making special efforts to improve the environment generally.

*Advertising stressing broad recurrent themes, affecting the purchase decision in a manner that implicitly raises controversial issues of current public importance.*—Food ads which may be viewed as encouraging poor nutritional habits, or detergent ads, which may be viewed as contributing to water pollution.

*Advertising claims that rest upon or rely upon scientific premises which are currently subject to controversy within the scientific community.*—Test-supported claims based on the opinions of some scientists but not others whose opposing views are based on different theories, different tests or studies, or doubts as to the validity of the tests used to support the opinions involved in the ad claims.

*Advertising that is silent about negative aspects of the advertised product.*—Ad claims that a particular drug product cures various ailments when competing products with equivalent efficacy are available at substantially lower prices.

5. The FTC announced it has set up a special Flammable Fabrics Information Center designed to provide consumers with information about Commis-

sion action involving enforcement of the Flammable Fabrics Act.

6. The FTC has issued a trade regulation rule requiring that articles of wearing apparel bear permanent labels clearly disclosing instructions for their care and maintenance.

Also required by the rule is that piece goods sold to consumers for the purpose of making wearing apparel must be accompanied by care labels which home sewers can affix permanently to the goods by normal household methods—sewing, ironing, and the like.

7. The Federal Trade Commission on December 9 announced a revision of its Trade Regulation Rule relating to the posting of minimum octane numbers on gasoline pumps. The revised Rule continues the requirement that marketers of gasoline post minimum octane numbers on the gasoline dispensing pumps. The Rule as revised substitutes the use of the minimum octane number derived from the sum of Research (R) and Motor (M) octane numbers divided by two; i.e. $(R + M)/2$, in place of the minimum research octane number originally included in the Rule as the benchmark for posting.

8. A proposed FTC complaint challenges weight reduction claims made for sugar by two trade associations composed of growers, refiners and processors of the product.

The Commission announced on December 2 its intention to issue a complaint against Sugar Association, Inc., and Sugar Information, Inc., and Leo Burnett Co., Inc., the advertising agency that prepared the questioned advertisements.

9. A consent order provisionally accepted by the Federal Trade Commission prohibits Ted Arnold Used Cars, from violating the Truth in Lending Act. The complaint alleges that in its Motor Vehicle Purchase Orders used in credit transactions, the firm does not:

   Furnish in writing all required credit cost disclosures before consummation of the credit transaction.

   Exclude state license, registration, and certificate of title fees in computing the "cash price."

   Use the required descriptive terms "cash downpayment," "unpaid balance of cash price" and "amount financed."

   In some instances, disclose the "annual percentage rate," "total of payments," and "deferred payment price."

10. The FTC announced its intention to issue a complaint alleging that Chock Full O' Nuts Corporation, New York City has illegally restrained competition by fixing the resale prices of food in its franchised restaurants and by requiring franchisees to purchase food and restaurant supplies from Chock.

The proposed complaint alleges that since at least 1963 the firm has fixed its franchisees' resale prices by the following means, among others:

   Furnishing printed price inserts to be placed on menus, specifying prices;

   Requesting that old price inserts be removed and returned to Chock;

   Instructing franchisees by means of letters and bulletins as to the prices they are to charge for food;

   Telling franchisees that Chock will set the pricing policy for all restaurants bearing the Chock name, and that all will serve the same food at the same prices;

   Threatening franchisees with termination of their franchise agreements and loss of the right to operate under the Chock name if they sell food at other than Chock's specified prices.

SOURCES: FTC, News Summary and Consumer Alert, various issues, 1971, 1972.

These laws permit manufacturers to set the resale price of branded products throughout their channels of distribution. Obviously, this is a vertical pricing arrangement and a circumvention of the Sherman Antitrust Act. To legalize such activities, a federal statute amending the Sherman Act was enacted. The Miller-Tydings Act of 1937 was the first Act to amend the antitrust law directly so as to permit vertical price agreements. The Act simply legalized resale-price maintenance in interstate commerce and hence permitted manufacturers to enter into such agreements.

Resale-price maintenance had its origin during the Great Depression of the 1930s. Manufacturers sought to maintain their resale prices because some retailers were using well-known branded products as "price leaders" to build customer traffic. Manufacturers feared that many retailers would fail to push their products or that the distribution of their goods would become unprofitable if something was not done to stem the "price leader" tide. Some branded goods, particularly dentifrices, were commonly used in this way; as a result retailer loyalty was destroyed and retailers were even encouraged to drop such items from their stocks. Manufacturers of well-known brands along with small independent retailers vigorously supported fair-trade legislation. To this day retail druggists through their association (National Association of Retail Druggists) are perhaps the most adamant in support of such legislation.

The first of the resale-price-maintenance laws was passed in California in 1931. It soon became apparent that some device to bind all resellers to the stipulated price was necessary because those who did not sign price agreements undercut the price of those who had signed. Hence, the nonsigner clause was incorporated into state fair-trade statutes. This stipulation bound those not party to a contract to the contract price. As a result a manufacturer would need only the signature of one retailer and one distributor in any state with a price-maintenance statute in order to fix the resale price, which would then be binding on all resellers.

The need for amendment to the Sherman Act arose because most manufacturers do not sell their products solely in intrastate commerce. Because of the interstate implications and the fact that such agreements violated the Sherman Act, Congress enacted the Miller-Tydings Act, which, as noted, provides for resale-price maintenance to be an exception to the antitrust law. As the states enacted their own fair-trade laws, they copied a model statute drafted by the National Association of Retail Druggists. In all, 46 states adopted the essentials of the NARD model statute.

The nonsigner provision of the statutes ran into trouble in 1951 when the Supreme Court ruled in the cases of *Schwegmann Brothers* vs. *Calvert Corporation* and *Schwegmann Brothers* vs. *Seagram Distillers Corporation*. Schwegmann, a price-cutting nonsigner to a fair-trade contract in Louisiana, had been sued by Calvert and Seagram. The case went to the Supreme Court, which ruled in favor of Schwegmann. The response to this decision was dramatic, as nonsigners reduced prices on many branded goods in fair-trade states. A result was the enactment of the McGuire Act in 1952, which extended the basic antitrust exemption and went further to sanction nonsigner's clauses. The Federal Trade Commission, the Department of Justice, the American Bar Association, and organizations of labor and agriculture opposed the bill. It was enacted, however, with the help of the NARD and the American Fair Trade Council. Since passage of the McGuire Act the Supreme Court has either refused to review lower court decisions or has found the nonsigner clause in conformity with the Act.

Fair Trade has nevertheless been dealt some death blows in state courts. In many states resale-price maintenance has been nullified either by rulings of unconstitutionality or by ruling the nonsigner's clause null and void. The fair-trade issue is not dead, but it is quite dormant at the present time.

## AN EVALUATION OF THE LEGAL FRAMEWORK

The federal and state laws pose a complex and often bewildering environment in which marketing operates. Some of the laws, it should be noted, came into being by virtue of either an assumed or a real impact of marketing behavior. That is, the antitrust laws resulted from observable competition and the injurious long-run effects of particular kinds of competitive behavior. Other laws, particularly those concerned with public health and safety, are the result of carelessness and disregard by some businesses for the welfare of the consuming public.

Most economists agree that the antitrust laws have made important contributions to the maintenance of competition. Simon N. Whitney has stated that the laws have prevented cartelization of American industry along European lines; they have barred consolidations intended to enable firms to dominate their industries; and they have helped preserve freedom of entry and equality of opportunity (Whitney, 1958).

Edward S. Mason, another authority, views the antitrust laws as affecting business decisions; he states that "the consideration of whether a particular course of business action may or may not be in violation of the antitrust laws is a persistent factor affecting business judgment" (Mason, 1949).

Criticism of the antitrust laws does not usually ignore the laws as a positive force for maintaining competition; rather, it is directed at problems of interpretation, the apparent view of the courts that bigness is evil *per se*, and the inability of the laws to reflect adequately a changing competitive structure and the attendant competitive devices.

Consumer-protection laws continue to be passed, since fraud, deception, and misrepresentation are still live issues. Federal legislation on consumer matters has been supplemented by state laws and departments—and even city laws in some instances. The period since 1965 has been an era of consumer legislation.

# STATEMENTS TO CONSIDER

Trade regulation is a necessary concomitant of the free-enterprise system, to assure the maintenance of free and effective competition.

Where certain conditions of demand and supply are present, business firms realize that unless they act to try to control prices, their profits are likely to suffer.

The fact that prices are identical in itself proves nothing about price-fixing.

In general, law remains a secondary consideration as compared with demand, competition, cost, and the structure of distribution.

The large body of law affecting marketing decisions has been enacted to insure that company behavior is consistent with the "public interest," which is identified as protecting the buyer from the seller, the seller from the buyer, and one competitor from another.

Too much competition may not be good for the consumer.

What is good for the American consumer must be the joint responsibility of business and government.

What is new about government constraints on the functioning of the market economy is the greatly intensified vigor with which old constraints have been administered.

The potential illegality of business activities today will become the actual illegalities of tomorrow.

Even if it were possible it would not be worth the price to eliminate all the uncertainty in antitrust areas for business.

# QUESTIONS FOR REVIEW

**1.** Discuss the relationship between operation of the marketing system and some laws that are essentially nonmarketing laws.

**2.** How far should government go in regulating marketing? Who should decide? Who does decide?

**3.** What kinds of legal issues can you visualize that will become important issues in the next decade? Can these be detected ahead of time? What should marketing do about legal trends?

**4.** What kind of competition is government trying to preserve?

**5.** Does Adam Smith's "invisible hand" no longer function in the United States?

**6.** Is the market force dead?

**7.** How effective has the government been in maintaining competition?

**8.** What are the forces behind laws regulating competition?

**9.** Is there more or less competition among heavily regulated industries than among less heavily regulated ones?

**10.** Draft a statement of your own in which you describe your own personal philosophy of the role of government regulation.

## Further Readings

John Kenneth Galbraith, Walter Adams, Willard F. Mueller, and Donald F. Turner, "Are Planning and Regulation Replacing Competition in the New Industrial State?" Hearings before Subcommittees of the *Select Committee on Small Business,* U.S. Senate, Ninetieth Congress (Washington, D.C.: GPO, June 29, 1967).

E. T. Grether and Robert J. Holloway, "Impact of Government upon the Market System," *Journal of Marketing,* Vol. 31 (April 1967), pp. 1–7.

Marshall C. Howard, *Legal Aspects of Marketing* (New York: McGraw-Hill, 1964).

Earl W. Kintner, "How Much Control Can Business Endure?" *Journal of Marketing,* Vol. 25 (July 1961), pp. 1–6.

Small Business Administration, "Trade Regulation and Small Business," from *Small Marketers Aids* (Washington, D.C.: Small Business Administration, June 1961).

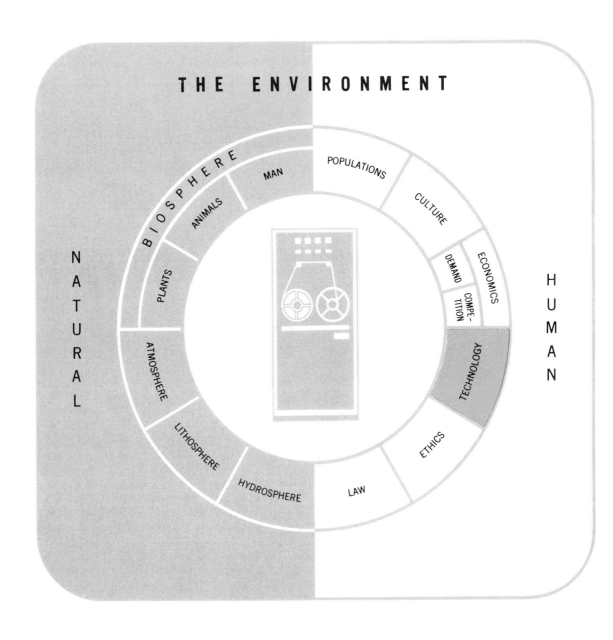

THE ENVIRONMENT

NATURAL

HUMAN

BIOSPHERE

MAN

ANIMALS

PLANTS

ATMOSPHERE

LITHOSPHERE

HYDROSPHERE

POPULATIONS

CULTURE

DEMAND

ECONOMICS

COMPE-
TITION

TECHNOLOGY

ETHICS

LAW

# CHAPTER 8
# THE FORCE OF TECHNOLOGY

*The consumer benefits from technology as marketing overcomes his resistance to change and delivers the fruits of invention to him. Technology also improves the marketing operation directly as it applies to transportation, information retrieval, and media. Marketing research and technical research are twin components of a corporation's thrust.*

In 1790 three patents were granted in the United States; in the 1860s President Lincoln suggested closing the Patent Office; in the 1960s over 600,000 patents were granted; and in the 1970s there seems to be no end in sight to the innovations pouring forth from modern technology. Following on the wake of the rapid development of modern science, the technological age has come fast. If the earth's history were compressed into one calendar year, practically all of modern science would occupy only the last one-half second of the year.

Technology means little to most of us, however, until its achievements have been made available. It is the role of marketing to "facilitate the translation of scientific and technological knowledge into profitable, want-satisfying products, processes, services, and distributive arrangements" (Clewett, 1966).

Technology is clearly an important environmental influence on marketing, one that interrelates closely with the other facets of the environment in a fantastically complex web in which nothing can be done without causing effects somewhere else. This concept of interdependence is not yet fully realized by most businessmen, who tend to lack the perspective of the poet, Francis Thompson, who wrote that "one cannot pluck a flower without troubling a star."

## TECHNOLOGY AND SOCIETY

The interrelationship mentioned above varies from society to society and especially between the primitive and advanced societies. Marketing without technology is simple. There is little specialization of labor, little private property, and little separation of producer and consumer.

The Igorots in the northern Philippines illustrate such a society. Living in one of the most beautiful but also most isolated spots in the world, the people of this region carry on their lives much as their ancestors did several thousand years ago. The terraces are communal, there is no industry, and the raising of sufficient quantities of rice and sweet potatoes to eat is the main productive effort. The people make their own clothing, repair their ancient huts, and raise a few chickens and pigs. The area is a paradise for the anthropologist but not for the student of marketing. Bare subsistence living is the rule, association with the outside world is minimal, and little if any money changes hands. There is little marketing in the villages, no marketing development work, no salesmen, no advertising, no supermarkets. Any signs of modern industrial technology would seem wholly out of place. As a matter of fact, a corrugated metal building erected a few years ago stands out as a sore intrusion. There is total lack of invention and innovation in the society, and indeed, these could cause serious upheavals in the way of life. The introduction of fertilizer, farm implements, and waterpower could transform the Igorots' whole culture. Not many miles away from this isolated area, in fact, are the modern cities of the Philippines, which show the marks of technological progress, the visible signs of a marketing economy, and a totally different society and culture.

In technologically more advanced societies businessmen have learned that innovation pays handsome profits and that failure to keep pace can cause the downfall of a firm or even an industry. The industrial producer and household consumer alike are fully aware of the impact of technology on almost everything they do or see. Some technological developments force radical reorientations on the part of the consumer. Among producers, well-trained personnel can find themselves outmoded, capital investment can become obsolete, and executives may have to sprint to keep up with the times. More often the changes are evolutionary, but their impact is recognizable. The simple box camera, for example, has gone through hundreds of changes so that a very elaborate mechanism is now available to the consumer. New products typically make the old products obsolete, and marketing personnel are required to develop new markets, persuade people to buy the improved item, and feed market information back to the producer. In the example of the camera it is interesting to note that the simple camera has found a recent market at the very time that the complex camera seemingly rendered it "obsolete."

## Invention and Innovation

Invention is the creation of something new. Innovation is the introduction of the new. In our frame of reference, innovation brings about the acceptance of invention as facilitated by the marketing system. The two terms, invention and innovation, encompass the processes by which new ideas are conceived, nurtured, developed, and finally introduced into the market as new products and techniques.

Products such as the digital computer, television, and the jet engine were not on the market at the end of World War II, but today they contribute approximately $15 billion to our GNP, provide work for almost a million people, and considerably affect all our lives. Yet most of us cannot identify the inventors of these products (see 8-1). Firms that have emphasized innovation as a way of life have exhibited high growth rates—for example, Polaroid, 3M, IBM, and Texas Instruments. Invention and innovation are not foolproof, however. There have been notable failures such as the Convair 880, the Edsel, and Corfam.

## The Visibility of Technology

Few forces in the marketing environment have the visibility of present-day technology. It often bewitches those who come into contact with it; yet for all those who worship it, there are some to whom it

## 8-1

**Some Important Inventive Contributions of Independent Inventors
and Small Organizations in the Twentieth Century**

Xerography
  Chester Carlson
DDT
  J. R. Geigy & Co.
Insulin
  Frederick Banting
Vacuum tube
  Lee De Forest
Rockets
  Robert Goddard
Penicillin
  Alexander Fleming
Cyclotron
  Ernest O. Lawrence
Cotton picker
  John and Mack Rust
Catalytic cracking of
petroleum
  Eugene Houdry

Zipper
  Whitcomb Judson/
  Gideon Sundback
Automatic transmissions
  H. F. Hobbs
Gyrocompass
  A. Kaempfe/E. A. Sperry/
  S. G. Brown
Jet engine
  Frank Whittle/Hans Von
  Ohain
Frequency modulation
radio
  Edwin Armstrong
Self-winding wristwatch
  John Herwood
Continuous hot-strip
rolling of steel
  John B. Tytus

Helicopter
  Juan De La Cierva/
  Heinrich Focke/Igor
  Sikorsky
Mercury dry cell
  Samuel Ruben
Power steering
  Francis Davis
Kodachrome
  L. Mannes and
  L. Godowsky Jr.
Air-conditioning
  Willis Carrier
Polaroid camera
  Edwin Land
Heterodyne radio
  Reginald Fessenden
Ball-point pen
  Ladislao and Georg Biro

SOURCE: Adapted from U.S. Department of Commerce, *Technological Innovation: Its Environment
and Management,* report prepared by Daniel V. DeSimone (Washington, D.C.: GPO, 1967), p. 18.

is anathema. This is not a new phenomenon, but today it is obvious
that it is a more pronounced one. People are touched directly by
technology; we need not go back to the invention of the wheel to
imagine its impact. Consider the changes that have taken place in the
last decade in transportation, household appliances, foods, and indeed
in virtually everything else.

These technological changes exert a great and visible influence over
any socioeconomic system in which they occur. They can cause cities
to blossom forth almost overnight, and they can cause cities to die
slowly on the vine. They affect jobs, which influence purchasing power,
which determines standards of living. We have become accustomed,
in part because of technological advances, to think in terms of *more*—
more food, more clothing, more variety, more comfort, more convenience, more complexity, more education, more pleasure, and more of
our own "thing." New products, as in the case of man-made fibers, have
stimulated new methods of production, modes of styling, advertising
programs, and habits of consumption; and in return consumers have
indicated their likes and dislikes in apparel through their patterns of
purchasing. The "votes" of consumers can thus influence technological
innovation, and an awareness of this influence is part of the marketing
concept of corporations.

### Progress and Disruption

Technology upsets work habits, modifies life expectancies, creates new mobility patterns, provides greater leisure, and determines new social norms. Sometimes it provokes serious upheavals from which few escape, but man, resilient as he is, has generally adapted himself to these changes.

> Man is on the move, from the East to the West, from the South to the North, from town and country to the city, from the inner city to the suburbs, and from one suburb to another. . . . Man is also socially mobile in our technological world. . . . Families move across the country in search of new opportunities and new income. . . . Man is mechanized in a technological society. . . . The great god production is surrounded in the pantheon by the lesser deities of efficiency, competence, science, technical education, consumption, and advertising. (Pitcher, 1961.)

As reported several years ago by a Presidential Task Force on Technology, the vast majority of people recognize that technological change "has led to better working conditions by eliminating many of the dirty, menial and servile jobs; that it has made possible the shortening of working hours and the increase in leisure; that it has provided a growing abundance of goods and a continuous flow of improved and new products." Even so, ". . . people are assailed by fears and concerns [of technology]."

Scientists have become alerted to potential problems and they have called for society to give new direction to technology, to modify the old drive to master, control, and even destroy man's natural environment. The concern is of immediate importance, for technology will continue to change business and society during the coming decades as ever more inventions are placed on the market. Marketing and production will adapt to these inventions in ways we cannot forsee at the present time. What happens in marketing is crucial since it is the liaison between the people in the marketplace and the producers and inventors: it is the medium for innovation.

## TECHNOLOGY'S IMPACT ON MARKETING

The impact of technology on marketing is diverse. It determines in large part what products will be handled by those in the various marketing functional areas—advertising, selling, pricing, distribution, and so on. It also affects the actual marketing tasks, as will be pointed out in this section.

A new product, for example, may require the development of new and different markets, with the result that the company's entire marketing operation may be affected by the handling of the single new innovation. Some product innovations, such as the computer, affect the handling of accounts, and air-type pallets alter the handling of items in warehouses. Other products create market opportunities and as a result new marketing institutions develop (e.g., snowmobile dealers), and still others expand media capabilities. New products influence consumption patterns, as television did. The influence of technology on marketing extends down through the entire operation; frequently a simple innovation calls for another innovation so that the dynamics are compounded. The credit card is a case in point: several marketing changes have resulted from the availability of the credit card, including the development of new kinds of insurance and the introduction of a machine to positively identify a credit card holder (through a hand-profile mechanism).

*Consumption.* It is obvious that consumption patterns change with innovation. Households, industry, and government all change their practices because of the availability of something new and better (see 8-2). Not all consumers change at the same time; thus marketing studies of the diffusion process have proven useful to business. Personal values can also change, as suggested in the following examples.

Fertility Control: The worldwide use of oral contraceptives, which became known in the 1960s, ties in with the need for population control. Education and religion are both responding to the new product and individuals have changed some basic beliefs.

Personality Control Drugs: It does not require a great deal of imagination to go beyond the tranquilizers and the hallucinogenic drugs now available. Psychologist Kenneth Clark has made the startling suggestion that world leaders all be given "peace pills" to insure a low level of aggression. On a more likely level, perhaps a person will be able to obtain antigloom pills or pleasure intensifiers that will transform his outlook and personality. What effects would these have on individual values?

Household Robots: Additional labor-saving possibilities exist for the home: computers, remote controlled appliances and yard equipment, picture phones, massaging machines. These, too, change individual ideas and values. (Gordon, 1969.)

*Media.* Television dramatically illustrates how technology can change advertising and media capabilities. Color television made possible further innovations. Cable television and computers for the home may foster additional novelties in advertising. Less dramatic innovations in printing occur continuously. Thus the entire field of communications is constantly adjusting to new technology.

*Selling.* The jet age caused many changes in personal selling techniques. The traveling salesman of today is far different from his counterpart a decade ago.

*Pricing.* In 1943 penicillin was selling wholesale at $20.00 per 100,000 units. With additional technology that yielded competitive substitute

## 8-2

**Consumption and Change**

One corporation obviously cannot figure it all out.

But—if you have a wide span of attention, think about the problems, put restless-minded people against them, do some innovative things, get into some unexpected businesses, and keep an earthy eye on profit—it's surprising to see how much one corporation can do.

Five "Markets of Change" and our relationship to them.

SHELTER
By 1975, our country could be spending $60 billion per year to remodel and replace old housing and build new. These homes will be modular, factory-manufactured, and virtually maintenance-free.

ENERGY
By 1975, U.S. demand for electric power will almost double. Aluminum, the world's most versatile and plentiful metal, will be the conductor. It already carries more than three times as much electricity per dollar.

FOOD
Two problems: grow enough to go around. And, then, get it around. Store it. Ship it. And serve it.

TRANSPORTATION
Since 1956, vehicle mileage increased 60%. Since 1960, use of ship-truck-rail containers increased seven times. Worldwide, this is just the beginning.

COMMUNICATIONS
In this field, an almost omnipresent use of aluminum. Items: Intelsat satellites which will soon hook-up the whole world on television. Community antenna cables which deliver superior tv pictures. Millions of feet of telephone lines. Memory discs which let the latest computers draw information instantly from data banks.

*SOURCE:* Adapted from *Kaiser Aluminum News,* 1970.

---

drugs, the price of penicillin dropped to $0.05 by 1956. Not all technology results in lower prices, of course, and some innovations add considerably to costs. The pricing effect illustrated by penicillin is considered a derivative of technology. A more direct effect of technology on pricing is the impact of the computer on calculating and printing prices for thousands of food products.

*Physical Handling.* Refrigerated trucks and rail cars, jet transport planes, money-changing machines, vending machines, computerized inventory systems—all are a part of this technological age. Larger equipment, faster delivery, and more rapid turnaround are the order of the day. The entire physical handling operation has been deeply affected by new developments of various kinds.

*Marketing Institutions.* Historically, marketing institutions have adapted themselves to all kinds of change. This flexibility has been vital, for once an institution no longer serves a purpose, it perishes. An examination of the kinds of wholesalers and retailers reported in each of the census years (1929–67) provides a picture of marketing's adaptation to technology. Not only have existing institutions updated their operations, but completely new institutions have also been formed to fill the needs caused by innovations. Hundreds of satellite operations surround the computer industry today, for instance, and almost all of these are newly formed enterprises.

Almost every part of the marketing process is subject to change because of technology. The innovations of tomorrow will cause marketers to adapt in order to remain competitive, and they will adapt in ingenious ways. The impacts from technology do not always come one at a time and the convergence of innovative trends can cause sudden and deep changes. On the other hand, various innovations may cause differing impacts and the dispersion that results may or may not create a need to change. It seems certain that marketing in the future will continue to adapt to the technological environment.

## TECHNOLOGY FOR THE MARKETPLACE

Technology is more than basic research: it ultimately must relate to the marketplace. But technology and marketing are not always compatible and one or the other (or both) has to adjust and adapt. Consider, for instance, the possible shift in automobiles from the internal combustion engine to the gas turbine, or steam, or battery-powered engine. Even if technologically the new power plants could be put on the assembly line today, could the changeover be made before the service system (garages, service stations, mechanics, parts, etc.) is fully operable? As innovators know, "Before you introduce an innovation you must understand the system [production, distribution, service, etc.]— understand among other things that it is frequently big and complex and slow to move. . . . Until then you are a neophyte, you are innocent, you are naive, and you will get bloodied up and thrown out" (Frey, 1969). It takes time for the marketplace to ready itself for innovation. The acceptance of the laser is a good example. There were high hopes for the utilization of laser beams in 1960 when the product was introduced, but it took ten years for the marketing and technical personnel to develop the potential to any considerable extent. By the early 1970s there were forecasts for a $1 billion market in lasers by 1980!

### The Feedback System

A market system typically provides an enormous amount of information to the businessman. The retailer, wholesaler, salesman, and others in the marketing network receive and send back various kinds of information. Each is concerned about consumer acceptance and ultimate profit from sales, and each is sensitive to the attitudes and actions of those further down the channel of distribution. Profit comes from sales and sales come from consumer acceptance. All links between the manufacturer and the consumer provide valuable feedback, which contributes to technological decisions.

The market in a sense, then, governs technological change. Getting information from the consumer helps guide the producer in his choice of products and his choice of technology. As Jacob Schmookler has pointed out, the influence of the market on technology suggests a role for consumer demand in the "dynamic aspects of economic development" (Schmookler, 1966). Marketing research provides the management with information about demand and this information can be the starting point of many product decisions.

The market feedback tells the producer if a product is desirable for the market; technological research tells him if the product is feasible to produce (see 8-3). The real world does not always work this way, however, and sometimes the market goes begging for an innovation with no answer from scientists, and sometimes technology is thrust upon the consumer when he really does not want it. Consider the furor

---

## 8-3

**Revolution on the Razor's Edge**

Stone Age man used sharpened *flintstone* or a clam shell. Ancient Egyptians used *bronze straight razors*. 3000 years later (1890) the *hollow-ground blade* was developed! By 1917, Gillette was selling 120 million blades a year. Schick invented the electric shaver in 1923 and today 6 million electric shavers are sold annually. In 1938 the *one-piece double-edge razor* was invented and in 1941 the one-piece injector razor appeared. The *adjustable safety razor* was developed in 1958 and the *Super Blue Blade* made its appearance in 1960. The British Wilkinson Sword Co., Ltd., introduced the *coated stainless steel blade* and in the next year sold 7 million of the new product in the United States (one-fifth of one percent of the total U.S. market). [By 1970 blades were made in part from platinum, and in 1971 the tandem razor was introduced.] Note: the average male grows 27½ feet of bristle in a lifetime.

SOURCE: Adapted from *The New York Times Magazine,* October 6, 1963, p. 58. © 1963 by the New York Times Company. Reprinted by permission.

over the SST. In 1969, when President Nixon decided to subsidize the development of the SST, the market was not clamoring for the new plane and relatively few orders had been placed by the airlines. The feedback system from the market shouted many warnings, but political and other forces pressed for the SST go-ahead. In 1971 Congress eliminated the government program amidst a good deal of public clamor which included nonbusiness as well as business voices.

### The Marketing System

The feedback system works from the marketplace backward toward the producer. Most of the other parts of the system operate "downstream" or toward the customer in the distribution of innovative products. The marketing system provides innumerable services in introducing an innovation, securing the acceptance, and gaining widespread distribution of it. After all there is typically a great deal of resistance to the acceptance of new technology.

Advertising carries a good deal of the burden by announcing a new product through direct mail, television, or print media, and by carrying on the campaign until the product is retired from the market. Personal selling also plays an important role. "Missionary" salesman are frequently employed by companies to educate wholesalers, retailers, and industrial customers. Whether the assignment is to sell a new paint, an electric drill, or a new kind of air-conditioning unit, the task is to educate the potential customer and gain product acceptance. Personal selling makes a significant contribution to the rate of adoption of a new product. Consider Harry R. Tosdal's conclusions about the role of selling:

> . . . selling determines the extent and rate of adoption of new consumer products and the rapidity with which development of new workers takes place and new processes are applied. Thus it [selling] determines the speed at which the results of innovation, research, and technical advances are brought into use for the benefit of all. (Tosdal, 1957.)

The marketing task is to take the innovation to the market, sell the buyer, and gain market acceptance. This task entails public relations releases, a sampling program, advertising campaigns, personal selling, design of new packages, and the physical distribution of the product itself.

If the innovation is a market success or failure, should marketing or technology be given the credit or the blame?

## MANAGING TECHNOLOGY

"Adaptation to change is the major marketing challenge facing us," reports one corporation president as he looks ahead. Another declares, "The single most important determinant of change in most markets is expanding technology: probably the greatest challenge facing any company in the marketing area today, both internal and external, involves the adaptation of the company to an environment reflecting the unhalting and accelerating march of technological change" (Pegram and Bailey, 1967). In coping with change, knowing about one's own company and industry is not enough.

> To manage innovation or change it is vital to have a knowledge of the environment—political, social, technological, and economic. In large part, this wide environment is unknown, and in order to grow, to innovate, to manage change, a business must convert its unknown environment to a known one. (Bruce, 1965.)

The influence of innovation on competition has become clear as the American economy has stepped up the pace of technological change. There is competition among similar or like products, as between a propeller-driven plane and a jet plane. There is the competition among different kinds of products that perform the same functions in different ways, for example, copying machines and photography. There is competition among different kinds of industries, as between the chemical-fiber and natural-fiber textile industries. Keeping competitive is a primary concern of the manager and managing innovation is a part of his task.

## The Need for Research and Development

It is no longer a question of whether a firm should engage in R & D: the question now is how much should be spent and for what. Theodore Levitt called attention to the misplacement of a company's resources because the firm had "marketing myopia" (Levitt, 1960). Levitt pointed out how companies would overlook obvious markets by not defining them properly, and as a consequence the firm did not allocate R & D funds optimally. The railroad industry defined its market in terms of trains in particular as opposed to transportation in general; the film industry thought narrowly of movies instead of broadly of entertainment; and the petroleum industry failed to envision its role in the general field of power. The proper definition of one's market has much to do with the allocation of funds toward R & D.

Technology can make a company obsolete overnight if management has not prepared itself adequately. Thinking about their R & D in terms of the market can help the executives keep abreast of the times and avoid developing serious "marketing myopia." For example, a firm that prints bank checks is in a profitable business today. But if we were to move to a checkless society, what would that firm have to offer the market? Marketing can help a firm diversify in a number of ways.

Marketing cannot dictate all R & D expenditures, however, nor can the marketing concept answer all R & D questions for management. Many products can indeed be developed as a result of the consumer orientation of that concept, but others may result strictly from technology. Both sides can be shortsighted; the counterpart of "marketing myopia" is "technological myopia" (Reynolds, 1969).

The proper management of R & D includes recognizing that innovations can come from either the market or the laboratory, from outside as well as inside. There is need in most large firms for (1) a fundamental research program, (2) exploratory research programs, and (3) applied product-development programs (Reynolds, 1969). Despite the different orientations that have developed, innovation is not an either/or proposition: it involves both marketing and technology.

Unfortunately, a serious gap can develop between laboratory and marketing staffs. Technical researchers are apt to isolate themselves from outside pressures, become preoccupied with scientific achievement, adopt a superior attitude toward less technically oriented colleagues (especially salesman), and lose touch with the marketplace. Marketing people may place too much reliance on their marketing studies, fail to grasp the technical significance of a product, regard research scientists as impractical oddballs, and lack an understanding of the R & D process. Most large firms try to bridge the gap, but many product failures can be attributed to poor marketing liaison (Danilov, 1967).

## The Firm's Environment

"There is a social, economic, and industrial climate that often controls technological progress" (Bright, 1965). Each firm must appreciate

**8-4** **Managing Technological Innovation**

| Condition | Characteristics | Problems |
|---|---|---|
| Business planning | Venture analysis<br>Directional planning<br>Business objectives control | Time value of money<br>Inbreeding<br>Lack of specific market experience<br>↕ Understanding |
| Experimental appraisal | Complex enterprise<br>R/D organization<br>Lacking certain technical skills | Entrepreneurs missing<br>Know-it-alls<br>Risk vs. cost emphasized<br>Extension of present businesses |
| Embryo business | Outside inputs needed<br>Incentives available<br>Continuing R&D effort | Failure to meet return on investment criteria in early years<br>Antitrust action<br>Key management |
| Successful growth business | Growths<br>Jobs<br>Products | Assimilation<br>Antitrust action |

*SOURCE:* Adapted from U.S.D.C., *Technological Innovation: Its Environment and Management* (Washington, D.C.: GPO, 1967), p. 26.

the need for this climate, for otherwise costly mistakes can be made. There is a need to develop an inside climate so that research efforts are properly executed.

The climate for technological development in a small firm is quite different from that of a large company, of course. The management of the small firm is more likely to be characterized by limited business experience and a total commitment on the part of the owners, who are probably the managers. It is usually in need of capital, operates often in a high-risk situation, and may have a limited market. The successful handling of technology may permit a small firm to expand its operation or, as is common today, to merge with a larger one. A large firm typically takes a smaller risk with a single venture because it is more diversified. Its marketing people are usually trained specialists as compared to the generalists that handle marketing in the small firm. No matter what a firm's size, however, the technological environment must be carefully developed (see 8-4).

## Forecasting Technology

An exciting problem in business is forecasting, especially of technology. In 1959 Francis Bellow tabulated the technological gains of the 1950s and then went on to forecast for the 1960s. Some examples from his work are included in 8-5. Bellow concluded his 1960 forecast of technology as follows:

> If wisdom and forebearance prevail, the Sixties could be filled with wonders—not alone for consumers and businessmen, but for everyone who can perceive the beauty and excitement in the great voyages of discovery now going forward in every region of science. (Bellow, 1964.)

**8-5** Technology in the 1960s as Seen in 1959

| Early 1960s | Mid-1960s | Late 1960s | Long shots |
|---|---|---|---|
| Battery TV | Borehole to "Moho" | Total synthesis of insulin | Computers with brainlike attributes |
| Ultrasonic dishwasher | Gas-turbine trucks | Electronic safety device for cars | 2000 mph VTOL (vertical take off and landing) airplane |
| Applications of fuel cell | Irradiated foods | Mural television | Atomic explosions in practical use |
| Operational ICBMs | Man in satellite | Man in flyable space ship | Man on moon |

SOURCE: Francis Bellow, in H. C. Barksdale, *Marketing: Change and Exchange, Readings from Fortune* (New York: Holt, Rinehart and Winston, 1964), pp. 78–79. Reprinted by permission of Holt, Rinehart and Winston, Inc.

**8-6** Possible Innovations by 2000

| Very likely innovations | Less likely innovations | Far-out possibilities |
|---|---|---|
| Multiple applications of lasers and masers<br>New sources of power for ground transportation<br>Three-dimensional photography<br>New and useful plant and animal species | "True" artificial intelligence<br>Room temperature superconductors<br>Artificial growth of new limbs and organs<br>Major use of rockets for commercial use<br>Automated highways | Almost complete genetic control<br>Interstellar travel<br>Practical extrasensory phenomena<br>Lifetime immunization against practically all diseases |

SOURCE: Reprinted with permission of the Macmillan Company from *The Year 2000* by Herman Kahn and Anthony J. Wiener. © 1967 by the Hudson Institute, Inc., pp. 55–57.

Forecasters have been at work on the 1970s. Herman Kahn and Anthony J. Wiener have provided a list of 100 inventions that could become available by the year 2000 (see 8-6). What influence has the market had in developing such ideas? And what role will marketing play if they come to pass? For the marketer, it is important to examine them with an eye toward how they could be taken to the marketplace and how advertising, selling, channels of distribution, and the retail network could be adapted to handle the new products and services.

Making technological predictions is more than an academic exercise. Even though forecasting is still in its infancy, it does help management to evaluate the probability and significance of future developments. A variety of techniques are used, including the so-called Delphi method, which uses panels of carefully chosen experts whose replies are placed in a data bank. Various probes of these experts are made: before each new probe a composite feedback of responses from all panel members is supplied to each. Identities are kept anonymous. The experts may be asked, for example, to indicate if they think a certain technology will be in operation by 1975. A Rand Corporation panel gave the following results from one Delphi study (*Business Week*, 1970).

| Technology | When scientific breakthrough will be achieved |
|---|---|
| Ultralight synthetic construction materials | 1978 |
| Economical desalination of sea water | 1980 |
| Reliable weather forecasts | 1988 |
| Popular use of personality control drugs | 2000 |
| Commercial production of synthetic protein foods | 2003 |
| Long-duration coma for time travel | 3000+ |

There are many limitations to such forecasts—unpredictable interactions, unprecedented demands, major discoveries, inadequate data—and they relate to both marketing and technology. One way to improve predictions is to monitor technology, by searching the environment for signals from the marketplace, identifying the possible consequences of cultural and other changes, choosing the parameters that should be observed, and presenting the data to management. The signals that James R. Bright identifies are many: literature, convention speeches, time series, industrial budgets, government budgets, population trends, leisure time, education, political environment, consumer polls, occupation trends, and others. (Bright reports that in 1940 an IBM marketing man spotted a news article about xerography, and though he alerted his firm, he got no response. Xerox later became a successful corporation by using the technology (Bright, 1970).)

Despite the work of the futurologists (see 8-7), there is much to be

---

## 8-7

### Shape of the Future

POPULATION—Modern technology must raise living standards faster than humans multiply.

COMPUTERS—Schools, medicine, and business will benefit but the misuse of data on individuals is feared.

NUCLEAR FACILITIES—These will help the U.S. meet the surging power demand which should triple by the year 2000.

AIRLINES of the future will exceed 4000 mph which will call for new materials and result in lower fares.

Increased SPACE EXPLORATION is seen for the future with such possible feats as a manned Mars landing.

SATELLITES of the future—Demand rather than technological considerations will determine speed with which communications innovations will be utilized. Cost will have to be "right."

The AUTOMOBILE of the future will undergo drastic changes. By 1975, electric propulsion, automatic controls, and traffic control stations linked to cars will be in limited use.

URBANIZATION will continue into the future, but efficient transit facilities and city planning provide a feeling of optimism.

ELECTRONIC DEVICES will make the housewife's tasks much easier and leisure time will be spent in educational or entertainment ventures.

EDUCATION will become a lifelong process with an emphasis on electronic aids.

MEDICAL gains will reduce heart and cancer deaths, reduce birth defects, but will not substantially increase the life span.

The U.S. is building a capacity for both a nuclear WAR and local conflicts through the use of orbiting weapons, missile defenses, advanced troop carriers and laser weapons.

SOURCE: *The Wall Street Journal,* issues in December 1966 and January–February 1967. Reprinted with permission.

done in marketing, for as Levitt observed: "Modern soothsayers, by combining computers with crystal balls, can parlay old dogmas into major disasters . . . There can be a need, but no market, or a market, but no customer; or a customer, but no salesman . . . Market plans must be tempered with common sense" (Levitt, 1969).

Marketing can be of use at several points in forecasting technology. It is helpful in identifying the basic trends of a society because it relates directly to the people. Marketing can determine needs and wants and can, through research, help determine potentials for new products. Technological forecasting must include marketing input if management is to handle innovation profitably and marketing information can help guide management in its R & D endeavors. As we have stressed, innovation is a joint operation.

## MARKETING AND TECHNOLOGY TOGETHER

> If science is knowledge about man and his environment; if technology is the application of this knowledge to achieve desired results; and if marketing is concerned with matching the needs and wants of potential buyers with profitable want-satisfying products and services through market transactions, then clearly, it is in the general interest of mankind everywhere to seek integration of science, technology, and marketing. (Clewett, 1966.)

Marketing may be headed for a more important role in the next decade than any it has had in the past. The public is making itself heard about safety, quality, pollution—without foregoing a "piece of technology." We Americans have a positive regard for technology, we believe in its capabilities, but we are beginning to demand more from it. Some believe that technology has moved so fast that we now have an "applied technology gap." They predict a decade of technological assimilation instead of a decade of invention. Last decade's research and development may become this decade's "hardware" (*Business Week,* 1969). The problem area may be primarily a company's ability to market innovation successfully.

The real task may be found in shifting emphasis. The simple problems have been solved, leaving tougher ones: we can produce easy-to-wash curtains, but not housing; fast cars, but not urban transportation; surgical lasers, but not universal medical care. These matters present a fresh challenge to marketing innovation and probably a much more difficult one than that with which we are familiar.

In dealing with these new challenges those in marketing and technology will have to cooperate even more than they have previously. People from both fields are going to have to learn to work with one another, despite differences in thinking; after all, they are working in the same environment and they share many of the same goals. Coordinating marketing research and technical research will be one of the most important places to start (see 8-8, which suggests the relationship

**8-8** Coordinating Technical Research and Marketing Research

| Phase | Focus of technical research | Focus of marketing research |
|---|---|---|
| Ideas | Experimentation<br>Technical solution of existing<br>problems | Interpretation of sales,<br>advertising, and related<br>marketing data<br>Outside sources |
| Investigation and exploration | Technical possibilities<br>Scientific problems<br>Technical practicability | Thorough preliminary<br>commercial evaluation |
| Research and development | Product characteristic and<br>design<br>Performance<br>Costs | Market potential<br>Market requirements<br>Share market goals<br>Competition |
| Testing | Process development<br>Control methods<br>Ingredient specifications | Pilot marketing:<br>Panel tests<br>Consumer tests<br>Market tests<br>Appraisal of sales<br>potentials and market-<br>ing plans |
| Initial sales and manufacturing | Aid to production in<br>manufacturing<br>Product specifications<br>for procurement | Thorough review with<br>sales and advertising of:<br>Product potentials<br>Consumer reaction |

SOURCE: B. F. Bowman, "Coordinating Technical and Marketing Research," *Cost and Profit Outlook*, Vol. 7 (July 1954), pp. 2–3.

between them). This is not a new problem, but it is being felt more now than in the past and many firms find it difficult to handle.

After research results are in from both the engineer and the marketer, management is going to have to strive for further coordination as crucial decisions are made about product emphasis. Each attribute of a product—quality, price, style, appeal, size, and so on—will reflect management's understanding of both the technical aspects of the product and the needs and wants of the consumer.

These are some of the challenges facing marketing in relation to technology. The public is entitled to the fruits of technology, and marketing has a vital role to play in seeing that the public gets them.

## THE NEED FOR A LONG VIEW OF TECHNOLOGY

The fruits of technology can be both bitter and sweet at the same time. The social impacts of technological change are being pondered by many persons, including those who have developed some of the blessings of yesterday that have become the monsters of today. DDT, nuclear power, and the internal combustion engine are three such examples. Technology induces changes in the physical world, multiplying and diversifying material and technical possibilities. It also induces changes in man's "image of himself and his world and in his conception of what is good" (Mesthene, 1967).

The need for some kind of criterion for innovation and invention is clearly upon us. Innovation in the future is likely to be subjected to some kind of societal "test" before it can be marketed. The reasons are several; as Joseph Wood Krutch pointed out:

> Science and technology can be catastrophic as well as beneficial. We cannot afford to wait and see what the effects of any specific application of new powers will be.
> Science for science's sake is no longer a tenable aim.
> Knowledge and power are good only insofar as they contribute to human welfare. (Krutch, 1969.)

Calls for caution come today from scientists and nonscientists alike, in sharp contrast to a few years ago when innovations were introduced without very much concern for the public. Kahn and Wiener warn as follows:

> . . . technology raises issues of accelerated nuclear proliferation; of loss of privacy, of excessive governmental and/or private power over individuals; of dangerously vulnerable, deceptive and degrading overcentralization; of decisions becoming necessary that are too large, complex, important, uncertain, or comprehensive to be left to mere mortals—whether private or public; of new capabilities that are so inherently dangerous that they are likely to be disastrously abused; of too rapid or cataclysmic change for smooth adjustment, and so on. (Kahn and Wiener, 1967.)

## Specific Product Examples

Many products introduced in the past have become matters of serious social concern. The *automobile,* loved by millions, is now being questioned for a number of reasons. As far back as 1957, however, it was recognized that the automobile had made a tremendous impact on our society as the following list shows (Allen, 1957):

| | |
|---|---|
| On transportation | On sex customs and morals |
| On population distribution | On education |
| On mobility of population | On attitudes |
| On vacation patterns | On housing |
| On business and industry | On mail service |
| On government—e.g., highways, licenses, law enforcement | On religion |
| | On language—e.g., "hot-rod" |
| On individual health | On social status |
| On the family | On fire protection |
| On rural life | |

Indeed, the direct social effects of the automobile are almost incalculable, and they relate to virtually all social institutions and to nearly all life activities. The derivative effects such as the proliferation of regional shopping centers, motels, and drive-in institutions—theaters, banks, laundries, and even mortuaries—are also phenomenal. It was marketing's task, and a tremendous task it was, to deliver the automobile to the consumer. New retailers, enormous quantities of advertising, special handling equipment and transportation, and ingenious credit terms are some of the adaptations made in marketing for the distribution of the automobile. Today there is the additional social emphasis which is being examined, and that is a different kind of problem for marketing and the automobile firms to handle.

As for other examples: *plastics* are used increasingly throughout the world, but we have now become aware of the problems of disposing of nondegradable items. *Insecticides, drugs,* and *enzymes* have conflicting costs and benefits. *Snowmobiles* caught on rapidly during the 1960s—starting from a production of a few units per year in the early part of the decade, the output rose to hundreds of thousands by 1970; in those few years snowmobiling became a $400,000,000 industry. Yet the fun of whipping over the snow is offset by hedge-chopping, noise-making, accidents, atrocities to nature, fences, and even man. The *Jumbo 747 Jet* was put into operation in early 1970 amidst predictions that there would be no cost advantage, no fundamental consumer advantage, awesome accident consequences, problems with insurance, and coolness on the part of the airlines themselves. (In this case, we saw a turnabout as companies found many advantages to the 747.) *Nuclear power* was put forth as the solution to fossil-fuel pollution, but conflicting scientific reports about radioactive and thermal pollution soon raised all kinds of questions about the desirability of building nuclear power plants. There are many other, less spectacular products introduced each year whose cost-benefit ratios bear examination—in advance of technological assessment.

## Impediments to Market Development

We Americans appreciate that new products can be easily introduced into our economic system. We like the vast array of goods that appear on the market. We want to clear the marketing road of any impediments that might prevent a company from introducing an innovation. Yet there are many impediments and the public may suffer from them.

In 1947 Dr. Edwin H. Land introduced a new polarized headlight system for automobiles consisting of polarizing filters on 125-watt lamps and a filtered viewer that could be pulled down in front of the driver's eyes. The purpose of the polarized system was to reduce glare from headlights of oncoming vehicles by reducing them to small blue dots; at the same time the roadway ahead of the auto was illuminated more brightly than with the existing headlight system. The system was referred by the Automobile Manufacturers Association to the American Association of Motor Vehicle Administrators for consideration but was not acted upon favorably (Land, 1948). Assuming that the system was feasible and economical, why wasn't it introduced?

In attempting to answer that question, you can begin to appreciate the impediments to innovation. For instance, these were some objections to the polarized headlight system:

Doubtful consumer acceptance
Cost of the product
Effectiveness achieved only with universal use
Transition problem
Single source of supply
Legal problems of licensing patents
Vested interests
Need for a larger generator
Alternative methods
Unlikelihood of uniform adoption

Automobile manufacturers resist adding anything to an automobile that will add to the cost. Still, a number of innovations that raised prices considerably have been introduced since then. Some of the questions raised about the Land system have been raised about safety features on autos. For the marketing manager the main one is, will people pay for safety?

## CONCLUDING COMMENTS

One of marketing's greatest contributions is its part in bringing the fruits of technology to the marketplace. An invention means little until it becomes available, and it only becomes available when it is distributed through the existing marketing system or through the system as modified to handle the innovation.

We seem to clamor for more than innovation today, for we are interested in the quality of life as well as in an unending parade of new products, of which many may be of questionable value. As a special panel of the National Academy of Sciences observed: "The challenge is to discipline technological progress in order to make the most of a vast new opportunity."

## STATEMENTS TO CONSIDER

A growing host of analysts and fortune tellers are flooding top management with glowing technologically based forecasts. But computer extrapolations are not enough. Market plans must be tempered with common sense. (T. Levitt)

Indeed, the central danger facing humankind in the latter part of the twentieth century lies not in the autonomy of technology or in the triumph of technological values but in the subordination of technology to the values of earlier historical eras and its exploitation by those who do not understand its implications and consequences but seek only their own selfish personal or group purposes. (V. Ferkiss)

Technology is expanding the old marketplace boundaries far beyond mere buyer and seller, involving even more "outside" parties—people who want *right now* technological fruits that the classical market isn't ready to provide, and people who fear bad side effects of technology evolving from the narrow interaction of buyer and seller alone. (A. Large)

The future of technology holds great promise for mankind if greater thought and effort are devoted to its development. If society persists in its present course, the future holds great peril, whether from the uncontrolled effects of technology itself or from an unreasoned political reaction against all technological innovation. (National Academy of Sciences)

There is no known example in which technology has been stopped being pushed to the limit. Technology has its own inner dynamic. (C. P. Snow)

There can be no question that technology is changing the traditional "American way of life" in a manner even more fundamental than those proposed by political revolutionaries. (M. Sibley)

No research pays unless, sooner or later, it leads to production of improved products that can be sold to create income.

The engineer's Hell is paved with brilliant technical innovations that failed because the company never solved the marketing, distribution, and service problems. Somebody was hollering down a rain barrel and all they got back was an echo. (D. Frey)

There is, to my mind, some absurdity in the exhortations we hear to adjust to a Technological Society. Why should we? Is it not more reasonable to harness the processes of innovation to procure a life rich in amenities and conducive to the flowering of human personalities. (B. de Jouvenel)

# QUESTIONS FOR REVIEW

**1.** What are your attitudes about modern-day technology? Have they changed in recent years?

**2.** Do you think that the role of marketing is different for a highly technical society versus one that is not technical?

**3.** Will the world beat a path to the door of the inventor of a better mousetrap?

**4.** What kinds of safeguards can marketing utilize to ensure that society reaps the benefits of beneficial technology?

**5.** Identify specific instances of where technology has had impacts on the marketing processes.

**6.** What major technological developments do you anticipate in the next five years? What role will marketing play?

**7.** Do you agree that consumers typically resist new technology? Explain.

**8.** What slows down the adoption of a product such as microfilm? Can marketing do anything about it?

**9.** Why have technical research people often been at odds with marketing personnel?

**10.** Will any of the technical forecasts in 8-7 have much of an impact on marketing?

## Further Readings

Kurt Baier and Nicholas Rescher (eds.), *Values and the Future* (New York: Appleton-Century-Crofts, 1957).

Robert L. Clewett, "Integrating Science, Technology, and Marketing: An Overview," in Raymond M. Haas (ed.), *Science, Technology, and Marketing* (Chicago: American Marketing Association, Fall 1966), pp. 3–20.

C. Merle Crawford, *The Future Environment for Marketing* (Ann Arbor, Mich.: University of Michigan, 1962).

Theodore Levitt, *Innovation in Marketing* (New York: McGraw-Hill, 1962).

Alvin Toffler, *Future Shock* (New York: Random House, 1970).

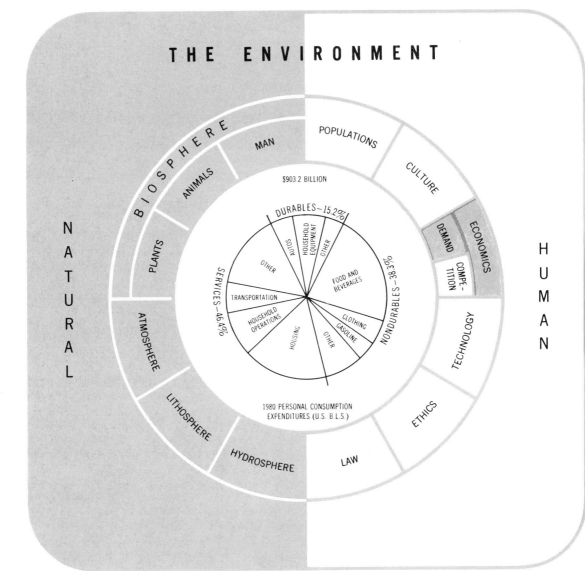

THE ENVIRONMENT

NATURAL

HUMAN

BIOSPHERE

MAN
ANIMALS
PLANTS
ATMOSPHERE
LITHOSPHERE
HYDROSPHERE

POPULATIONS
CULTURE
ECONOMICS
DEMAND
COMPE-
TITION
TECHNOLOGY
ETHICS
LAW

$903.2 BILLION

DURABLES—15.2%

AUTOS
HOUSEHOLD
EQUIPMENT
OTHER
OTHER

FOOD AND
BEVERAGES

NONDURABLES—38.3%

CLOTHING
GASOLINE
OTHER
HOUSING
HOUSEHOLD
OPERATIONS
TRANSPORTATION

SERVICES—46.4%

1980 PERSONAL CONSUMPTION
EXPENDITURES (U.S. B.L.S.)

# CHAPTER 9
# THE ECONOMICS
# OF DEMAND

**Determinants of Demand**

**The Ability To Buy:
Disposable and
Discretionary Income**

**Income**

**The Willingness To Buy**

*Tastes and Preferences of Consumers*
*Expectations of Consumers*
*    with Respect to Future Income*
*    and Future Prices*
*Price of Related and Substitute Goods*
*Number of Buyers in the Market*

**Elasticity of Demand**

*The ability and willingness to buy are determined by a buyer's level of income and his tastes and preferences. Income, a commonly used measure of market opportunity, is related to the sociopsychological factors of buyer behavior.*

Either formally or informally, any firm needs to assess its market opportunities. Since consumers are so central to these opportunities, an understanding of the intricacies of consumer demand is essential. Unfortunately, the term "demand" does not have a precise meaning used by everyone. To the layman demand usually means only the quantity sold, such as the demand for automobiles in a given year of 9,000,000. The layman thus assesses the resultant of demand rather than a market opportunity. To the economist, on the other hand, *demand is a schedule showing the various amounts of any product that consumers are willing and able to purchase at different prices during some stated period of time.* By definition a fundamental characteristic of demand is that as price declines the quantity of a specific good demanded rises. Conversely, as price increases the quantity demanded falls. Many actual marketing practices are based on this elementary but fundamental view of demand. Businessmen know that if their prices are set too high, consumers will shift their buying to substitute products or even withhold their spending. Similarly, bargain days, end-of-the-month sales, and the like are based on the theoretical constructs of demand.

## DETERMINANTS OF DEMAND

All too often consumer income is used as the sole determinant of demand. Although it is true that no demand can be registered without income, economists have long recognized that consumer behavior also determines demand. Note that the definition above implies that demand is influenced both by people's willingness and by their ability to buy. When a marketer estimates demand, it behooves him to consider those variables in addition to income that will more precisely determine the market demand. Many people may have the desire to own a Rolls Royce, which they regard as the ultimate in transportation; yet no willingness, if the ability to buy is lacking, will be forthcoming. Most consumers have whims, desires, and aspirations that may never materialize. Such mental processes do not constitute demand, but only mental exercises that most people can afford to enjoy.

On the other hand, in a capitalistic enomony consumer demand directs many noneconomic aspects of production. As consumers allocate their incomes among the numerous market offerings, they also register their demand for the esthetic and other noneconomic qualities found in goods and services. If consumers want home appliances in colors other than white, then an array of colored appliances will be manufactured. If they want processed foods that emulate French, Italian, Spanish, or Far Eastern dishes, these too become available. Consumer demand influences not only what is produced and at what prices, but also the numerous ramifications appended to market offerings.

Most economists recognize that the determinants of demand are quite compatible with the factors a marketing person must take into consideration in assessing market opportunities. These factors are (1) the money incomes of consumers, (2) the tastes and preferences of consumers, (3) the expectations of consumers with respect to their future income and future prices, (4) the prices of related and substitute goods, and (5) the number of consumers in the market. If one broadly interprets these demand determinants, they correspond either to the *ability to buy* (1) or to the *willingness to buy* (2 to 5) mentioned earlier in our definition of demand.

# THE ABILITY TO BUY: DISPOSABLE AND DISCRETIONARY INCOME

Businessmen and government officials are particularly sensitive to economic indicators that reveal tendencies toward increases and decreases in consumer demand. In the United States, as in other advanced economies, personal consumption expenditures made possible by the receipt of personal income are often watched closely. The relation of personal consumption expenditures, personal income, and other economic components to Gross National Product are shown in 9-1.

It is obvious that income is fundamental to consumer demand. It is perhaps not as obvious that income is also fundamental to the expression of social and psychological desires. Once a family or individual gains the position of being able to meet adequately the basic needs of life, remaining income may be used for the consumption of non-essential goods.

The potential purchasing power of consumers in the United States may be measured either by *disposable personal income* or by *discretionary income*. Disposable income is personal income less federal, state, and local taxes, as shown in 9-1. It is a measurement of the actual spending power in the hands of consumers. Normally, consumers do not spend all they earn, and hence personal outlays are the amounts received less the amounts saved. More important is the growth of disposable income. This may be seen in 9-2. With such marked increases in disposable income, the consumption of practically all goods, except the most mundane necessities, has also increased in recent years. Clearly much of our abundance of new goods and services can be attributed to the basic fact that consumers continue to enjoy increasingly higher levels of disposable income.

Perhaps even more meaningful to the individual consumer and some marketing people is the magnitude of discretionary income. Discre-

**9-1** The National Income and Product Accounts, 1970

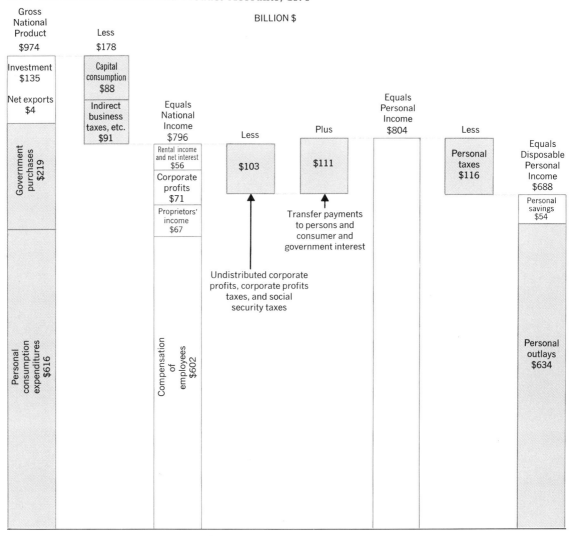

BILLION $

Gross National Product $974

Less $178

Investment $135

Net exports $4

Government purchases $219

Personal consumption expenditures $616

Capital consumption $88

Indirect business taxes, etc. $91

Equals National Income $796

Rental income and net interest $56

Corporate profits $71

Proprietors' income $67

Compensation of employees $602

Less $103

Undistributed corporate profits, corporate profits taxes, and social security taxes

Plus $111

Transfer payments to persons and consumer and government interest

Equals Personal Income $804

Less

Personal taxes $116

Equals Disposable Personal Income $688

Personal savings $54

Personal outlays $634

SOURCE: *Survey of Current Business* (July 1971), p. 12.

tionary income is found by subtracting from disposable income certain fixed, or nondiscretionary, expenditures. These are generally commitments to repay debts, obligations to pay real-estate taxes and rent, and amounts required for food, clothing, utilities, and other necessities. What is left is referred to as discretionary income because it may be spent or saved as the consumer desires. There have been marked increases in discretionary income enjoyed by American consumers. The consumer with such income has great latitude in how he spends it. He

## 9-2 Total and Per Capita Disposable Personal Income and Personal Consumption Expenditures, in Current and 1958 Dollars, 1929–71

| Year or quarter | Disposable personal income | | | | Personal consumption expenditures | | | | Population (thousands)[1] |
|---|---|---|---|---|---|---|---|---|---|
| | Total (billions of dollars) | | Per capita (dollars) | | Total (billions of dollars) | | Per capita (dollars) | | |
| | Current dollars | 1958 dollars | Current dollars | 1958 dollars | Current dollars | 1958 dollars | Current dollars | 1958 dollars | |
| 1929 | 83.3 | 150.6 | 683 | 1,236 | 77.2 | 139.6 | 634 | 1,145 | 121,875 |
| 1930 | 74.5 | 139.0 | 605 | 1,128 | 69.9 | 130.4 | 567 | 1,059 | 123,188 |
| 1931 | 64.0 | 133.7 | 516 | 1,077 | 60.5 | 126.1 | 487 | 1,016 | 124,149 |
| 1932 | 48.7 | 115.1 | 390 | 921 | 48.6 | 114.8 | 389 | 919 | 124,949 |
| 1933 | 45.5 | 112.2 | 362 | 893 | 45.8 | 112.8 | 364 | 897 | 125,690 |
| 1934 | 52.4 | 120.4 | 414 | 952 | 51.3 | 118.1 | 406 | 934 | 126,485 |
| 1935 | 58.5 | 131.8 | 459 | 1,035 | 55.7 | 125.5 | 437 | 985 | 127,362 |
| 1936 | 66.3 | 148.4 | 518 | 1,158 | 61.9 | 138.4 | 483 | 1,080 | 128,181 |
| 1937 | 71.2 | 153.1 | 552 | 1,187 | 66.5 | 143.1 | 516 | 1,110 | 128,961 |
| 1938 | 65.5 | 143.6 | 504 | 1,105 | 63.9 | 140.2 | 492 | 1,079 | 129,969 |
| 1939 | 70.3 | 155.9 | 537 | 1,190 | 66.8 | 148.2 | 510 | 1,131 | 131,028 |
| 1940 | 75.7 | 166.3 | 573 | 1,259 | 70.8 | 155.7 | 536 | 1,178 | 132,122 |
| 1941 | 92.7 | 190.3 | 695 | 1,427 | 80.6 | 165.4 | 604 | 1,240 | 133,402 |
| 1942 | 116.9 | 213.4 | 867 | 1,582 | 88.5 | 161.4 | 656 | 1,197 | 134,860 |
| 1943 | 133.5 | 222.8 | 976 | 1,629 | 99.3 | 165.8 | 726 | 1,213 | 136,739 |
| 1944 | 146.3 | 231.6 | 1,057 | 1,673 | 108.3 | 171.4 | 782 | 1,238 | 138,397 |
| 1945 | 150.2 | 229.7 | 1,074 | 1,642 | 119.7 | 183.0 | 855 | 1,308 | 139,928 |
| 1946 | 160.0 | 227.0 | 1,132 | 1,606 | 143.4 | 203.5 | 1,014 | 1,439 | 141,389 |
| 1947 | 169.8 | 218.0 | 1,178 | 1,513 | 160.7 | 206.3 | 1,115 | 1,431 | 144,126 |
| 1948 | 189.1 | 229.8 | 1,290 | 1,567 | 173.6 | 210.8 | 1,184 | 1,438 | 146,631 |
| 1949 | 188.6 | 230.8 | 1,264 | 1,547 | 176.8 | 216.5 | 1,185 | 1,451 | 149,188 |
| 1950 | 206.9 | 249.6 | 1,364 | 1,646 | 191.0 | 230.5 | 1,259 | 1,520 | 151,684 |
| 1951 | 226.6 | 255.7 | 1,469 | 1,657 | 206.3 | 232.8 | 1,337 | 1,509 | 154,287 |
| 1952 | 238.3 | 263.3 | 1,518 | 1,678 | 216.7 | 239.4 | 1,381 | 1,525 | 156,954 |
| 1953 | 252.6 | 275.4 | 1,583 | 1,726 | 230.0 | 250.8 | 1,441 | 1,572 | 159,565 |
| 1954 | 257.4 | 278.3 | 1,585 | 1,714 | 236.5 | 255.7 | 1,456 | 1,575 | 162,391 |
| 1955 | 275.3 | 296.7 | 1,666 | 1,795 | 254.4 | 274.2 | 1,539 | 1,659 | 165.275 |
| 1956 | 293.2 | 309.3 | 1,743 | 1,839 | 266.7 | 281.4 | 1,585 | 1,673 | 168,221 |
| 1957 | 308.5 | 315.8 | 1,801 | 1,844 | 281.4 | 288.2 | 1,643 | 1,683 | 171,274 |
| 1958 | 318.8 | 318.8 | 1,831 | 1,831 | 290.1 | 290.1 | 1,666 | 1,666 | 174,141 |
| 1959 | 337.3 | 333.0 | 1,905 | 1,881 | 311.2 | 307.3 | 1,758 | 1,735 | 177,073 |
| 1960 | 350.0 | 340.2 | 1,937 | 1,883 | 325.2 | 316.1 | 1,800 | 1,749 | 180,667 |
| 1961 | 364.4 | 350.7 | 1,984 | 1,910 | 335.2 | 322.5 | 1,825 | 1,756 | 183,672 |
| 1962 | 385.3 | 367.3 | 2,066 | 1,969 | 355.1 | 338.4 | 1,904 | 1,815 | 186,504 |
| 1963 | 404.6 | 381.3 | 2,139 | 2,016 | 375.0 | 353.3 | 1,982 | 1,867 | 189,197 |
| 1964 | 438.1 | 407.9 | 2,284 | 2,126 | 401.2 | 373.7 | 2,092 | 1,948 | 191,833 |
| 1965 | 473.2 | 435.0 | 2,436 | 2,239 | 432.8 | 397.7 | 2,228 | 2,048 | 194,237 |
| 1966 | 511.9 | 458.9 | 2,605 | 2,336 | 466.3 | 418.1 | 2,373 | 2,128 | 196,485 |
| 1967 | 546.3 | 477.5 | 2,751 | 2,404 | 492.1 | 430.1 | 2,477 | 2,165 | 198,629 |
| 1968 | 591.0 | 499.0 | 2,946 | 2,487 | 536.2 | 452.7 | 2,673 | 2,257 | 200,619 |
| 1969 | 634.2 | 513.5 | 3,130 | 2,535 | 579.6 | 469.3 | 2,861 | 2,316 | 202,599 |
| 1970 | 687.8 | 531.5 | 3,358 | 2,595 | 615.8 | 475.9 | 3,007 | 2,324 | 204,800 |
| 1971 | 741.2 | 550.6 | 3,581 | 2,660 | 662.2 | 491.9 | 3,199 | 2,376 | 207,006 |

[1]Population of the United States including Armed Forces overseas; includes Alaska and Hawaii beginning 1960. Annual data are for July 1.
NOTE: Superimposed graph line shows per capita disposable income in current dollars.
SOURCE: Department of Commerce, Bureau of Economic Analysis and Bureau of the Census.

may acquire a more expensive home, club memberships for more status, trips abroad, and a college education for his children. Since the holder of discretionary money incurs more long-term obligations, there is always the prospect of its diminishing unless his income (with other things remaining the same) periodically increases. Some middle- and higher-income consumers may have little discretionary money because of their greater obligations incurred by a more expensive way of living.

Durable-goods expenditures in particular are highly responsive to changes in discretionary income, because consumers can postpone or speed up their purchases of durables in direct relation to their freely available funds. Automobiles, appliances, new furniture, and vacations can normally be postponed if income is eroded by prior fixed obligations, or by an increase in taxes or a decrease in income. Likewise, consumers are quite willing to speed up such purchases when more discretionary income becomes available. If the free funds are insufficient, the consumer is likely to extend his purchasing power by using installment credit. Lenders are also quite willing to accelerate debt creation during periods of rising incomes. Less postponable items such as most nondurable goods and services are not likely to react as strongly to changes in income.

Of course, an economy does not reflect high purchasing power unless income is rather equally distributed among the people. The fortunate financial position of most United States families results from the continuing decrease in the proportion of people in the lower income levels.

The table in 9-2 also shows the advancement of per capita income and its relationship to the growth of personal consumption expenditures and population. These basic data reflect the economy's growth of marketing opportunities in a general way. Of course, if all segments of the population share equally in the growth of disposable income, the improvement of the economic position of American families will be felt in the marketplace.

## THE WILLINGNESS TO BUY

Perhaps all students have heard of "the economic man" who can carefully evaluate each purchase and hence order his consumption toward maximum satisfaction. No one can compare oneself with this mythical person, and few of us will ever know whether we actually have allocated our incomes to the best possible advantage. About all we can do is hope that we have made wise purchase decisions. The concept of the economic man, requires that each consumer have complete information (particularly on the prices of all related or competitive goods) and be able to forecast his future satisfactions in order to make perfectly rational purchase decisions. Many economists are aware of the limitations of this concept and presumably would prefer to interpret the determinants of demand broadly rather than be guided by an analysis dominated by perfect rationality.

With a broad interpretation of the tastes and preferences of consumers, the expectations of consumers with respect to future income and future prices, and the prices of related and substitute goods, the willingness to buy takes on reality. Some aspects of these determinants are economic, others are sociopsychological.

## Tastes and Preferences of Consumers

Tastes and preferences may include a complex array of influences that tend to shift and stimulate demand. For example, empirical evidence on the average annual expenditures for automobiles shows that higher-income families have substantially higher expenditures; the evidence also shows that these families are generally well educated, under fifty-five years of age and hence active, that they consist of three or more persons, and that they live in metropolitan areas. The origin of demand for most things is not evenly distributed among all persons in a given income bracket, however. Each individual and family spends money income in different ways.

The tastes and preferences of consumers form the dominant influence in determining the specifics of a purchase once the decision to buy has been reached. In some instances consumers' tastes and preferences actually determine *what* may be purchased. Most students will recall that an individual's demand curve slopes downward. A downward-sloping demand curve says that at a lower price one can buy more of a good at any given income, and that at the lower price the good becomes relatively more attractive compared to other things. Although it may be true that as individuals we conceive our demand for particular goods along a negatively inclined demand curve, this tendency does not explain consumer demand for a large number of things.

Brands, the characteristics of the point of sale, reputation, and other things combine with tastes and preferences to upset the postulated downward-sloping demand curve. Bayer aspirin is one of the leading sellers among aspirin products at 65 cents a hundred, yet many substitutes can be purchased for as little as 29 cents a hundred. Another exception is prestige goods. Mink coats, prestige automobiles, fine leather products, and very-high-quality watches may be bought because the price *is* high. Lowering the price of these products might jeopardize their "image" as status symbols. Even for such an everyday product as a cake mix, it is well known that a price increase of a few cents per package will expand sales volume, provided, of course, advertising of the product is intensified. This is one example of using a nonprice variable to advance sales even at a higher price. Nonprice variables often condition consumer tastes and preferences and hence may disrupt a strict theoretical model which is constructed on price, quantity, and given income. Much that is discussed in Chapters 10, 11, and 12 will be useful in considering consumer demand in light of a broadly interpreted concept of tastes and preferences.

## Expectations of Consumers
## with Respect to Future Income and Future Prices

Consumers' expectations have some bearing on present spending patterns. For a number of years the Survey Research Center of the University of Michigan has conducted studies of consumer buying intentions. More recently the Federal Reserve Board and the National Industrial Conference Board have also investigated consumer expectations and buying plans. In general, these studies attempt to identify planned expectations of spending behavior and saving. Apparently the central hypothesis of these studies is that consumer spending on homes, automobiles, appliances, furniture, and other durable goods is directly influenced by future expectations regarding income. If such expectations are favorable, optimism prevails and plans to purchase become realities in the near future. Pessimism prevails if expectations are negative.

George Katona, of the Survey Research Center, is regarded as the originator of studies of this nature, and he views economic psychology as having a marked influence on market demand. In recognizing demand as being determined by the interaction of economic and psychological variables, he states:

> Psychological factors, such as motives, attitudes, expectations, and group belonging, are intervening variables operating between the stimuli of market conditions and the responses to them in the form of economic decisions. The psychological factors do not alone determine the final decision, but under certain conditions they are powerful enough to alter individual as well as mass reactions and thereby influence the entire economy. (Katona, 1960.)

Most marketing professionals accept Katona's thesis, and it appears that the surveys have borne out the contention that willingness to buy cannot be analyzed in strictly economic terms.

## Price of Related and Substitute Goods

The price of related and substitute goods has long been regarded as a realistic determinant of demand by both economists and marketing students. In essence, according to common-sense, consumer demand is affected not only by changes in price of a given product but also by changes in prices of related and substitute goods. As the price increases for a good demanded by consumers, it results in a decline in the consumers' real income. This decline presumably tends to shift consumers to other lower-priced goods. To use the classic elementary textbook example, "the amount of oleomargarine purchased will depend on the price of butter." As the price of butter increases, consumers will redirect their consumption to the product substitute, oleomargarine. When the prices of two or more goods are directly related, they are referred to as substitute or competing goods. In setting the prices of their wares businessmen seldom ignore this basic principle.

One other aspect of this concept concerns *complementary* goods. Here again, as the price of a complementary good falls, it may set off expanded consumption. For example, when the price of long-playing records was lowered, the purchase of record players increased. Of course, one must be careful in attributing a shift of demand solely to price changes; the variables affecting purchasing behavior are so numerous and complex that they muddy cause-and-effect relationships. Empirical evidence during periods of strong price increases, however, lends support to the idea that consumer demand shifts to related or substitute goods.

## Number of Buyers in the Market

A remaining determinant of demand is *the number of buyers in the market*. As the number of buyers increases, the demand curve shifts to the right. More buyers may be a reflection of population increases, wider acceptance of a good once sold to the elite few, or even new or adjusted channels of distribution and marketing strategies. An example is the ever greater quantity of toys marketed each year in the United States. The increase is a result not only of an increased number of children but also of the increased number of parents and grandparents who actually buy the toys. Further expansion of the toy market was achieved by offering toys at an increased number of outlets and by marked changes in the distribution policies of toy manufacturers. All of these factors and more contribute to the increased willingness to buy toys at each possible price.

# ELASTICITY OF DEMAND

One of the more important and useful economic concepts for the businessman is the elasticity of demand. Unless businessmen, and marketing people in particular, can measure the responsiveness of consumers to changes in price, they are likely to make major price-policy blunders. The law of demand tells us that consumers will buy more of a given product as price declines. Even though this is not always true, one must be careful not to generalize from specific cases. Noneconomic factors often create special circumstances in which price changes generate little responsiveness or even tend to bolster demand if higher prices are equated with high quality and status. Consumers also tend to be affected by the quantities of a good held, and may have reached a point of diminishing marginal utility for further goods of like kind. Here, too, responsiveness to lower prices may be offset by this factor, which influences buying behavior. Despite the exceptions to the law of demand, the businessman should have some idea of the *degree* of responsiveness to price change. If this is known, a firm can estimate to what extent price changes will expand consumption, restrain it, or have little or no effect.

In 9-3 three hypothetical demand curves are depicted. Curve *a* is an

**9-3** Hypothetical Demand Curves

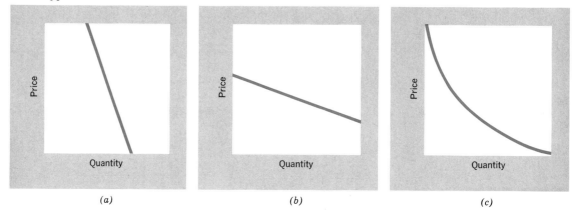

(a)                              (b)                              (c)

inelastic demand curve, curve *b* an elastic one, and curve *c* a unitary demand curve. To measure the degree of elasticity or inelasticity, economists use the following formula:

$$\text{Elasticity} = \frac{\% \text{ change in quantity demanded}}{\% \text{ change in price}}$$

Hence the elasticity of demand is the ratio between the relative change in quantity demanded and the relative change in price. Demand is said to be elastic (curve *b*) if the percentage of change in price brings about a larger percentage of change in quantity demanded. When demand is elastic the elasticity coefficient will be greater than 1. Demand is said to be inelastic (curve *a*) when the percentage of change in price results in a relatively smaller change in the quantity demanded. In this case the elasticity coefficient will be less than 1. Unit elasticity, or a unitary demand curve (*c*), occurs when the percentage of change in price is equal to the percentage of change in the quantity demanded.

From a marketer's standpoint, the real importance of the elasticity concept rests in the fact that a company's total revenue is affected by the prices it sets and the quantity sold at those prices. If the firm's demand curve is inelastic (*a* in 9-3), price changes will result in less than proportional changes in the quantity sold. In this case price increases may not seriously erode total revenue, and price decreases will not generate the same proportion of total revenue. Clearly the converse is true if the demand curve looks more like *b*. A unitary demand curve says that price changes will be exactly offset by changes in quantity; hence total revenue either expands or contracts by the same proportion. Examine the demand curves in 9-3 and adapt them to a number of real marketing situations.

# CONCLUDING COMMENTS

The basic factors influencing consumer demand include economic measures such as consumer income and consumer behavior. American consumers have experienced increased levels of income for many years. The greatest improvement in consumer income occurred in the postwar years from 1945 through the early 1970s. Disposable personal income is moving upward by many billions of dollars each year. As this trend continues we can expect more and more consumers to enjoy the abundance of products and services provided by the American economy. But this is a possibility only if all income levels share in the growth of personal income. Advancing levels of income also provide consumers the opportunity to express their sociopsychological motives in their purchase behavior. Marketing management is quick to recognize income improvement and also the stimulus it gives to the noneconomic character of consumer behavior.

# STATEMENTS TO CONSIDER

When demand is estimated under market conditions, an extended period of observation is required.

Generally advertising tends to speed up favorable trends of demand.

Pricing goods whose demand is perishable offers opportunities for profitable market segmentation.

We can assume that the typical consumer is rational and acts on the basis of rather well-defined preferences.

The theory of diminishing marginal utility says that the more an individual has of some object, the less will his satisfaction increase by obtaining an additional unit.

Expenditures for clothing do not remain a constant percentage of total expenditures as claimed in the so-called Engle's laws.

During the contraction and recovery phases of the four postwar business cycles, consumer incomes have followed strikingly similar patterns. Typically, purchases of nondurable goods have declined only slightly during recessions, and purchases of services have continued to advance, but less rapidly than during expansions.

The willingness to purchase durable goods may decline at a time of relatively high and stable incomes and may usher in a recession.

Stimulating, altering, and directing consumer demand is accomplished largely through advertising and personal salesmanship.

The starting point of any analysis of consumer demand must be the enabling conditions represented by income, assets, and debts, as well as by such demographic facts as population growth and the age distribution of the population.

**1.** When an economist uses the term "tastes and preferences of consumers," what is he referring to?

**2.** Should not marketing managers concern themselves with consumer income and its distribution more than any other consumer purchasing factor? Explain.

**3.** What factors in the economy, over which the consumer has no control, cause erosion of disposable income?

**4.** Explain the meaning of discretionary income. Does this kind of income relate to marketing some kinds of products and services?

**5.** A foreign person asks you to describe the needs and demands of a typical American consumer. What does a consumer demand during a year?

**6.** Do you consider demand to be a stable force in the economy? What forces affect demand for any given product?

**7.** Select a product and trace the demand for that product over a period of ten years.

**8.** In what ways is the concept of elasticity of demand useful to marketing managers?

**9.** What has been the trend of per capita disposable income during the past few decades?

**10.** Explain how consumers' expectations of future income and their expectations of future prices influence consumer buying behavior.

## Further Readings

Kenneth E. Boulding, *Economic Analysis: Microeconomics,* (New York: Harper & Row, 1966).

Robert Dorfman, *Prices and Markets* (Englewood Cliffs, N.J.: Prentice-Hall, 1967).

William Fellner, *Modern Economic Analysis* (New York: McGraw-Hill, 1960).

Hubert Henderson, *Supply and Demand* (Chicago: The University of Chicago Press, 1958).

H. S. Houthakker and Lester D. Taylor, *Consumer Demand in the United States: Analysis and Projections,* rev. ed. (Cambridge, Mass.: Harvard University Press, 1970).

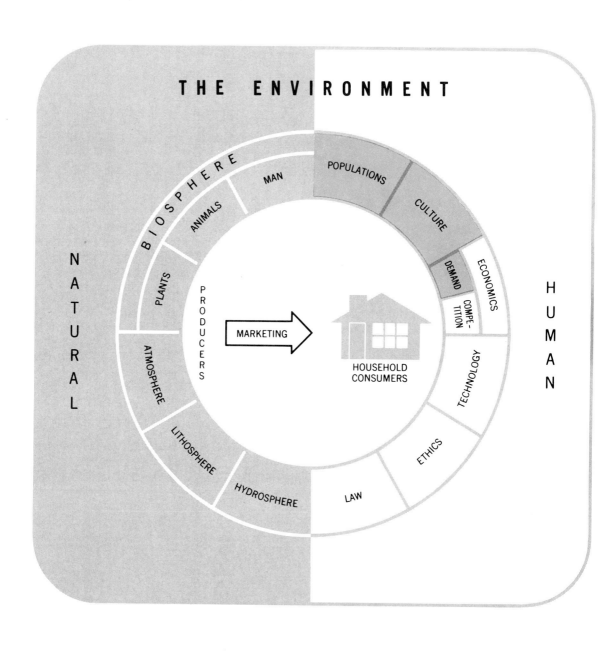

THE ENVIRONMENT

NATURAL

HUMAN

BIOSPHERE

MAN

ANIMALS

PLANTS

ATMOSPHERE

LITHOSPHERE

HYDROSPHERE

PRODUCERS

MARKETING

HOUSEHOLD
CONSUMERS

POPULATIONS

CULTURE

DEMAND

ECONOMICS

COMPE-
TITION

TECHNOLOGY

ETHICS

LAW

# CHAPTER 10
# HOUSEHOLD BUYER BEHAVIOR I
## AN OVERVIEW

*Consumers satisfy their wants and needs by purchasing a wide variety of goods and services. They have many reasons for buying and they are influenced by many forces in the marketplace, in the home, and in their everyday environments. Understanding buyer behavior is essential for any marketing manager.*

## IMPORTANCE OF THE CONSUMER

The consumer is the focus of marketing activity. Many years ago Adam Smith observed that "Consumption is the sole end and purpose of all production; and the interest of the producer ought to be attended to only so far as it may be necessary for promoting that of the consumer" (Smith, 1776). It is rather obvious that a successful matching of the firm's product to the consumer ought to be the goal of any business establishment. Yet failure to appreciate the central role of the consumer has led to a number of marketing disasters.

The automobile industry has learned a number of times about the role of the consumer. In its history in the United States the automobile industry has produced over 2000 brands of cars (and thousands of models), the vast majority of which eventually failed in some way to meet the market test though some had success for a period of years and some have thrived for more than a half-century. The Cord was too expensive for the Depression days; the Allstate lacked adequate distribution; the Packard failed to distinguish between its expensive and low-priced models; and the Edsel became the classic case of product failure for a number of reasons such as poor timing in the marketplace.

The threat of product failure haunts every business firm, but the possibility of success, of course, makes risks worth taking. Whatever the product—a ball of string, a bag of potatoes, or a lake cottage—the task of marketing is the same: to gain consumer acceptance for the offering and to deliver it to the consumer. The task lies not only with the introduction of the new product but also with established products. The ideal result is profit for the firm and satisfaction for the consumer.

The marketer facilitates the purchase process by bringing buyer and seller together. To do so he must know more than what people purchase. He also has to understand buyer behavior.* *Why* do people buy what they buy? Why do they *not* buy? *Where* do they buy? What *factors* influence their decisions? What is the actual *decision-making* process?

This chapter takes up those questions and provides background material for understanding the buying process. The next two chapters develop the factors important to decision making processes and exam-

---

*The terms consumer and buyer are frequently used interchangeably. In this text we have tried to distinguish between the terms since a buyer may or may not be the consumer. A housewife buys and consumes whereas a small child may consume but not buy.

ine the buying decision itself. These three chapters focus on the household consumer. A final chapter in this section deals with nonhousehold buyers such as industry, government, and institutions.

## SATISFYING NEEDS AND WANTS

Why do people buy? An obvious answer is that they buy in order to satisfy needs and wants. A task of the marketer, then, is to identify those needs and manufacture products accordingly. The following list by Theodore J. Kreps is one attempt to identify basic needs.

*Nine Basic Human Needs:*
1. Food and physical welfare (shelter, food, clothing)
2. Homemaking (recreation, opportunities for the family)
3. Desire for achievement
4. Desire for activity, variety, and novelty
5. Release for emotional tension
6. Security of status
7. Worthy group membership
8. Sense of personal worth
9. Sense of participation

Certainly many purchases can be classified according to these nine basic needs. And there are other ways to view human needs. Psychologist Abraham Maslow takes a different approach (though his list contains most of the above, at least in some form). He orders needs in a hierarchy of "prepotency"; as he explains it, "the appearance of one need usually rests on the prior satisfaction of another, more prepotent need" (see 10-1). The physiological needs are the most prepotent, for example, and until they are satisfied will compel an individual to push other needs into the background (Maslow, 1954).

**10-1** Maslow's Need Hierarchy

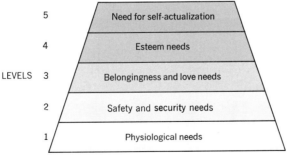

| LEVELS | |
|---|---|
| 5 | Need for self-actualization |
| 4 | Esteem needs |
| 3 | Belongingness and love needs |
| 2 | Safety and security needs |
| 1 | Physiological needs |

SOURCE: A. H. Maslow, *Motivation and Personality* (New York: Harper & Row, 1954), pp. 80–82.

Needs explain a lot of buying. We do, however, buy many items that are not needed, especially when we have the discretionary income to do so. Even the poor occasionally splurge, when they can, on apparent nonessentials in order to gain certain important satisfactions. Clearly, in our society people have learned to want many things, and we buy to satisfy those wants.

Marketers for many years have attempted to appeal to buyers and consumers on the basis of their buying motives. Fifty years ago Melvin Copeland (an early teacher of marketing) developed a list of buying motives divided into rational, emotional, and patronage categories, for advertisers to use in appealing to consumers (see 10-2).

His list still applies today, and many of these appeals can be found in current advertising. The ad for Mustang in 10-3 is extraordinarily open in its approach. But you can analyze any advertisement for the motives being appealed to.

The satisfaction of needs can be related to income in a variety of ways, as in the budget studies developed by the U.S. Department of Labor (10-4). The City Worker's Family Budget is based on a family of four persons. The "intermediate" budget reflects prevailing customs and a satisfactory standard of living. The "lower" budget represents a minimum level of acceptability, and the "higher" budget reflects a more comfortable level, or the "American standard of living."

## 10-2 Consumer Buying Motives

| Rational buying motives | Emotional buying motives |
|---|---|
| 1. Handiness | 1. Distinctiveness |
| 2. Efficiency in operation or use | 2. Emulation |
| 3. Dependability in use | 3. Economical emulation |
| 4. Dependability in quality | 4. Pride of personal appearance |
| 5. Reliability of auxiliary service | 5. Pride in appearance of property |
| 6. Durability | 6. Social achievement |
| 7. Enhancement | 7. Proficiency |
| 8. Enhancing productivity of property | 8. Expression of artistic taste |
| 9. Economy in use | 9. Happy selection of gifts |
| 10. Economy in purchase | 10. Ambition |
| | 11. Romantic instinct |
| **Patronage motives** | 12. Maintaining and preserving health |
| | 13. Cleanliness |
| 1. Reliability of seller | 14. Proper care of children |
| 2. Punctuality of delivery | 15. Satisfaction of the appetite |
| 3. Promptness in delivery | 16. Pleasing the sense of taste |
| 4. Securing exact fulfillment of specifications | 17. Securing personal comfort |
| 5. Variety for selection | 18. Alleviation of laborious tasks |
| 6. Engineering and designing service | 19. Security from danger |
| 7. Dependable repair service | 20. Pleasure of recreation |
| | 21. Entertainment |
| | 22. Obtaining opportunity for greater leisure |
| | 23. Securing home comfort |

SOURCE: Melvin T. Copeland, *Principles in Merchandising* (New York: A. W. Shaw Co., 1924), pp. 163–215. © 1924 by McGraw-Hill Book Company.

## 10-3

**Mustang Ad**

AMERICA'S FAVORITE FUN CAR
MUSTANG! MUSTANG! MUSTANG!

| *10 Solid Practical Reasons for Buying a Mustang* | *10 Wild Emotional Reasons for Buying a Mustang* |
|---|---|
| 1. Surprisingly low price | 1. A little excitement never hurt anyone |
| 2. Extras at no extra cost | 2. Be creative |
| 3. Safety features | 3. Be a disc jockey on wheels |
| 4. Thrifty but frisky Standard Six | 4. Take a plunge into ultra-luxury |
| 5. Strong, durable | 5. Become a stripe type |
| 6. Easy to handle | 6. If you're over 30, feel younger |
| 7. Comfortable | 7. If you're under 30, feel mature |
| 8. Easy maintenance | 8. Impress the neighbors |
| 9. Sensible fastback | 9. Buy for looks alone |
| 10. Proven winner | 10. All the world loves a Mustang |

SOURCE: Ford Motor Co. Advertisement. Reprinted with permission.

There may be no family that buys exactly according to the Bureau of Labor Statistics budgets, but the figures do show in a general way how needs and wants are translated into buying behavior. Further, the budgets reflect many of the factors that are important in buying: income, aspirations, values, and basic needs. Aside from basic needs, our buying behavior reflects our wants, which are influenced in part by the trends in our society.

Changing trends mean changing needs and wants and suggest that the need-satisfaction approach is essentially negative, since items are purchased to eliminate a problem, like aspirin for headaches. It has been suggested that we look elsewhere, to values, for a more fruitful explanation of consumer behavior, for "values, not needs, are at the basis of human behavior" (Lee, 1967). Needs arise out of basic values, and consumption is a response to the basic values of a person rather than simply a response to a felt need.

Buying patterns change, as do wants, needs, and values. At the present time, people think in terms of an affluent society (at least for the majority), with a great deal of time for leisure. But for many persons this idea gives rise to conflict because they have been taught the virtues of hard work and saving. The result is that we are not sure if we are reaping the fruits of decades of toil or if we are sick and decaying (Lazer, 1967). A changing mode of living has a profound effect on consumption patterns and consequently on the marketing of goods and

**10-4** City Workers' Family Budgets

| Urban United States Spring, 1970 | LOWER | | INTERMEDIATE | | HIGHER | |
|---|---|---|---|---|---|---|
| | $ | % of total budget | $ | % | $ | % |
| Total budget | $6,960 | 100 | $10,664 | 100 | $15,511 | 100 |
| Cost of family consumption | | | | | | |
|   Total | 5,553 | 79.8 | 8,205 | 77.0 | 11,346 | 73.2 |
|   Food | 1,905 | 27.4 | 2,452 | 23.0 | 3,092 | 19.9 |
|   Housing | 1,429 | 20.5 | 2,501 | 23.4 | 3,772 | 24.3 |
|   Transportation | 505 | 7.3 | 912 | 8.6 | 1,183 | 7.6 |
|   Clothing and personal care | 807 | 11.6 | 1,137 | 10.7 | 1,655 | 10.7 |
|   Medical care | 562 | 8.1 | 564 | 5.3 | 588 | 3.8 |
|   Other family consumption | 345 | 4.9 | 639 | 6.0 | 1,056 | 6.8 |
| Other costs* | 343 | 4.9 | 539 | 5.0 | 903 | 5.8 |
| Social security and disability insurance | 345 | 5.0 | 387 | 3.6 | 387 | 2.5 |
| Personal income taxes | 719 | 10.3 | 1,533 | 14.4 | 2,075 | 10.5 |

*Includes gifts, contributions, life insurance, and occupational expenses.

SOURCE: Adapted from U.S. Department of Labor, Bureau of Labor Statistics, *City Workers' Family Budget, December 1970* (Washington, D.C.: GPO, 1970).

services. The entire marketing process changes as it adapts to the dynamics of the environment.

Values, especially changing values, are being studied a great deal today by businessmen generally, not only by marketers, because of what they imply about buying needs and wants in the future. Today, when there are many suggestions (e.g., Galbraith) to the effect that the consumer is no longer "sovereign," there are also indications that business is paying increasing attention to him. Certainly those in business are trying to understand more about the consumer buying process.

## SOME OBSERVATIONS OF BUYER BEHAVIOR

Before examining buying behavior in detail we will make a number of observations at this point to provide an overall perspective. As you study the matter of buyer behavior you will develop an appreciation for those who must make important marketing decisions in the marketplace.

It is important to appreciate the *complexity* of the buying patterns of both the individual and buyers as a group.

> Man is a diversely motivated, complicated animal. Although he has much in common with other men, the pattern of one individual is different from the next. So there is no use expecting all of them to respond in the same way to the same stimulus. (Leavitt, 1958.)

It is also important to keep in mind that the buyer has *many alternative choices* in spending his money. There are vast quantities of goods and services available to him and countless appeals sent in his direction. We Americans have always prided ourselves on having these alternatives available, although recently our satisfaction with the possibilities of choice has turned to dissatisfaction with proliferation.

Buyer behavior is *dynamic* in nature: tomorrow's purchases are likely to be different from today's if only because of technology. There are other factors, too, such as changes in individual preferences, changes in income, a new environment resulting from relocation. Thus a changing person in a changing environment is supplied by an economic marketing system that is attempting to understand and reflect the trends of the times.

Studying buyer behavior requires a *multidisciplinary* approach. Economics, psychology, sociology, anthropology—all can contribute to our understanding. Any one discipline might provide the explanation for a single purchase or explain one aspect of another. For instance, anthropology can provide insight into cultural patterns, and psychology can explain specific motivations. Unfortunately, the real world is not divided nicely into academic compartments. In any purchase several interacting forces are operating simultaneously; certainly the buyer does not think in terms of anthropology or psychology when he ponders a buying decision. There is a kind of *totality* of buyer behavior, then, that has to be considered along with aspects studied by the various disciplines. In any case, marketers are interested in both the macro and micro aspects of buyer behavior—that is, both total consumption information and data on individual buying behavior.

The study of buyer behavior for the marketer is also *challenging* because of the linkage between potential profit and risk. Beyond being challenging, consumer or buying behavior is even *baffling* at times. A pharmaceutical firm, for instance, received "rave" reports from doctors and druggists about a new type of aspirin tablet that could be taken without the customary swallow of water, yet the product failed in the test market. Why? Because consumers prefer to take the swallow of water and they would not pay a premium to avoid it.

Buyers and their purchases can be *categorized* according to a number of psychological dimensions. One marketer established this breakdown about consumers:

1. A habit-determined group of brand loyal consumers, who tend to be satisfied with the last purchased product or brand.

2. A cognitive group of consumers, sensitive to rational claims and only conditionally brand loyal.

3. A price-cognitive group of consumers who principally decide on the basis of price or economy comparisons.

4. Impulse consumers who buy on the basis of physical appeal and relatively insensitive to brand name.

5. A group of emotional reactors who tend to be responsive to what products symbolize and who are heavily swayed by images.

6. A group of new consumers, not yet stabilized with respect to the psychological dimensions of consumer behavior. (Woods, 1960.)

And products which people buy and consume can also be categorized. Woods has divided products according to six psychological product classes.

1. Prestige products which become symbols (Cadillac).

2. Maturity products which are withheld from younger people (liquor).

3. Status products which impute class membership (big-name brands of many products).

4. Anxiety products which alleviate some presumed personal or social threat (deodorants).

5. Hedonic products which have an immediate and highly situational appeal (clothing, snacks).

6. Functional products which have little cultural or social meaning (staple food items). (Woods, 1960.)

Buying behavior is *difficult to influence.* Critics of marketing frequently state that business manipulates buyers at will, but few marketers have ever found them so easy to persuade. Any effort to arrest a downward sales trend is difficult—for example, the unsuccessful attempt by hat manufacturers to encourage men to wear hats again. The picture of cigarette consumption is still unfolding. Generally, however, basic consumer trends are quite powerful, either upward or downward as has been noted with purchases of small and large cars, for example.

Consumers are responsive to fashion. Public preferences in music, pets, eating habits, employment practices, and architecture all display the flux of fashion. So do formations used by football teams, popularity of colors, medical advice, and diets. Even services such as education have fashions that fluctuate from time to time. A "style" is a distinctive mode of expression and a style becomes fashionable when it is accepted by a large number of people. A style that develops fast and lasts a short time is known as a "fad." A fashion cycle in clothing is suggested in 10-5.

That fashion will change is certain. The challenge in any business is to predict the turning point in the acceptance of a style. Not every firm

## 10-5 The Clothing Cycle

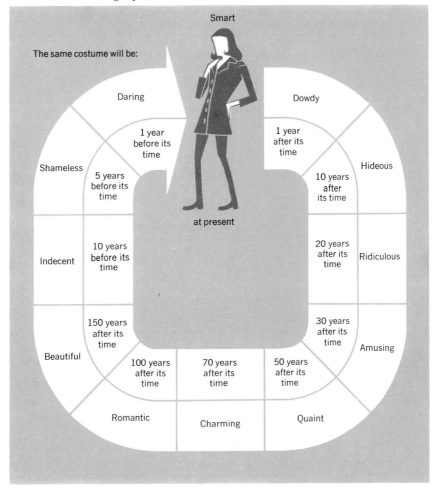

SOURCE: James Laver, *Taste and Fashion* (London: George G. Harrap, 1938), p. 202.

will enter a market at the beginning of a new fashion period; indeed, many firms prefer to enter when a style has become widely accepted and the risk factor has been lowered. When to enter is a crucial marketing decision, for it greatly influences a firm's clientele, and its pricing, promotion, and other marketing policies.

Finally, the consumer is said to be *sovereign*. Today there is considerable controversy on this point. Traditionally we learned that the buyer was sovereign and that he cast the votes that dictated which products the manufacturer produced and the retailer carried. The question is raised at this point and it will be further discussed in a later chapter, for it is an interesting and debatable matter.

# THE ENVIRONMENT OF BUYER BEHAVIOR

Consumers make their multitude of buying decisions in the context of the overall environment. Each good and service has in some way been "shaped" by the environment, as has the consumer himself. He buys in an *ethical* marketplace where most businessmen have integrity and where both buyers and sellers are generally satisfied with their transactions. Today there is a great deal of concern over "consumerism," yet millions upon millions of purchases are still transacted in an atmosphere of mutual trust between buyer and seller.

*Competition* provides the buyer with choices—of products, sizes, models, colors, manufacturers, and retailers. A competitive environment is vital to the consumer for he is protected from many evils of the marketplace by the very availability of choice. In contrast, in the ghetto frequently the low-income buyers are immobile and become prey to a few merchants in a relatively noncompetitive market.

*Technology* makes itself felt continuously. New products of all kinds are introduced in vast numbers. The consumer trades in one appliance for another and updates his car radio with a stereo tape player. The Post Office pleased millions of citizens when it replaced its old, scratchy pens with ball points. A university responds to enrollment pressures by utilizing closed-circuit television and self-learning programs. Not all the products of technology are accepted by consumers; indeed, it frequently takes an actual market test to determine what will be accepted.

The buyer responds to the *physical* aspects of his environment, as discussed in Chapter 5. Temperature, rainfall, geographic location, terrain, accessibility to water and other physical features all influence buyer behavior.

Much of our buying is regulated in some way by *law*. Potentially dangerous drugs may be removed from the market, cars must have safety features, liquor prices are regulated. The effect is not necessarily restrictive. Commercial airlines are regulated to a large extent—the government oversees aircraft safety, time schedules, prices, airport operations, and routes—still, the companies manage to develop and project separate and competitive images to the air traveler.

The *totality* of the environment, as well as individual forces, affects buying—that is, the interrelationship of factors produces second- and third-level effects. A change in interest rates, for instance, can affect housing starts, which in turn can affect not only furniture and appliance dealers, but also the employment, income, buying power, and purchases of many people only indirectly related to housing starts. The "multiplier effect" is detected quickly by marketing people.

# MARKETING AND BUYER BEHAVIOR

During the past two decades we have witnessed a rather considerable shift in emphasis on the part of companies from a production orientation to a marketing orientation. One corporation president traced his firm's development from its original production orientation, through a period of emphasis on selling, into the marketing era.

> We moved the mountain out to find out what Mahomet, and Mrs. Mahomet, wanted. The company's purpose was no longer to mill flour, nor to manufacture a wide variety of products, but to satisfy the needs and desires, both actual and potential, of our customers . . . our philosophy during the past decade was: "We make and sell products for consumers." (Keith, 1960.)

It seems logical that companies would place emphasis on the consumer. After all, production quotas are usually set on the basis of sales forecasts. And if the product matches the consumers well, success in the market may even call for expansion of production, but if buyers reject the product a reduction in output will follow. So it is surprising to find that a consumer-orientation is something new for a company, but this is still the case for many firms.

A company should obviously be geared to the marketplace, for it is in the marketplace where businesses *compete* for the buyers' dollars. And it is in the marketplace where business decisions are really tested. The marketing function is a liaison between the marketplace and the business firm, and so marketers do help guide the company in product, price, and other decisions. In this way, marketers give motion and dynamic thrust to the entire economic system as we know it.

Businesses see a buyer as someone who purchases particular products from certain outlets at a given price. Businesses also recognize that the buyer makes *decisions* that are influenced by many factors—some personal, some economic, some cultural, and some unknown. The consumer, or buyer, is a person who operates in a dynamic environment and who makes individual decisions, perhaps according to a number of private buying rules, after deliberation or sometimes on impulse. To identify potential buyers, the firm must deal in something more than sheer numbers of people: it also must ascertain something about the *why* of buying and the *why* of decision-making so that the marketing process can be made increasingly efficient.

A customer buys from a business *establishment*—the household customer from retailers and the nonhousehold customer from wholesalers and manufacturers. Firms have become more marketing- and consumer-oriented in recent years, though it should be pointed out that retailers, dealing in face-to-face contact, have always had to be conscious of the consumer. Even a mail-order house knows that fast service is necessary for sustained buying, and it gears its operations accordingly. The surroundings, the atmosphere of a store, influence the customer. Accordingly, stores tend to develop certain images and to attract particular clienteles. Failure to respond to the demands of the market can quickly and severely cost a store its patrons.

How a *product* or *service* is perceived affects buying behavior. Different consumers may see the product differently. What is a necessity to one may be a luxury to another. What is desirable to one may be undesirable to another. And with the traditional classification of consumer goods (convenience, shopping, and specialty), what is a shopping good to one buyer may be a specialty or convenience item to other buyers. The definitions of these consumer goods are as follows:

> *Convenience Goods*—Those consumers' goods which the customer usually purchases frequently, immediately, and with the minimum of effort in comparison and buying. (tobacco, soap, newspapers, chewing gum, many food products)
>
> *Shopping Goods*—Those consumers' goods which the customer in the process of selection and purchase characteristically compares on such bases as suitability, quality, price and style. (dress goods, furniture, shoes, appliances)
>
> *Specialty Goods*—Those consumers' goods with unique characteristics and/or brand identification for which a significant group of buyers are habitually willing to make a special purchasing effort. (fancy foods, hi-fi components, photographic equipment, men's suits) (American Marketing Association, 1960.)

The marketer interacts with the buyer on the field of *pricing* policy. Buying at the lowest price may be a decision rule for one buyer, but many other factors can be important for other buyers. "Odd" prices, which avoid round numbers, are used for psychological effect. A house may be priced at $29,999, a cosmetic item at 99¢, and two boxes of frozen broccoli at 39¢, because consumers are "trained" to think that an odd price is a better buy than an even one. On the other hand, some items are deliberately priced at "even" prices, which used to convey the notion of quality and high status. A woman, for instance, may prefer to wear a $50 gown than a $49.99 dress. Price conveys a great deal of information to the buyer, but some buyers equate price with quality, rightly or wrongly. In most instances buyers learn from experience approximately what something ought to cost, but unfamiliar products pose a problem. One of the authors presented to students a number of items unknown to them and asked for their estimates of prices. The range of estimates was considerable as was their inaccuracy. Steuben glass pieces costing $500 were priced from 39¢ to $5.00! When the students were told what each Steuben piece cost, however, their estimates of subsequent examples were greatly improved as they learned to look for cues such as size, etching, and intricacy of design. Try estimating what a Van Gogh painting might cost, or a signature of Abraham Lincoln.

The *package* for a product is important to consumers. Producers have attempted to offer convenience in packaging, as with reusable containers and nonreturnable bottles. The package is also important as a display, whether a velvet-lined box for a diamond ring, or a breakfast cereal package designed to attract the attention of a youngster who accompanies his mother on a shopping trip, or a portable typewriter in a case that can double as an overnight bag.

And, of course, the entire field of *persuasion* is clearly linked to the buyer. Many communications are sent to the potential buyer in order to persuade him to buy a given brand at a given store. The marketer through communicative techniques tries to persuade and to convince the buyer to try his particular brand. Sometimes the communication is designed to change attitudes, as illustrated by Renault's advertising several years ago. Renault admitted that their autos had not been made for rugged United States conditions. But, they said, they were now building their cars to withstand these conditions, so give them another chance.

Advertising attempts to develop a certain impression of a service or product. Each product may need a different kind of emphasis and appeal. Personal selling complements the advertising or in some cases completely substitutes for it, and vice versa. Product samples are often distributed to induce consumers to try a new toothpaste, a newly developed instant coffee, or a new soap product. There are many forms of persuasion and each is meant to relate directly to the consumer and to persuade him to buy the product. The relationship between marketing and the consumer is abundantly clear in the case of advertising (see 10-6).

## NEED FOR GREATER KNOWLEDGE

As our economy has developed, the marketing effort and the buyer-consumer have been given even greater attention. Considerably more effort has been placed on consumer research, with the result that much

---

## 10-6
### Demand Manipulation

Demand manipulation by its very name suggests that something is being done to consumers; that consumption programs are being fashioned, molded, twisted, or warped by some force outside of consumers themselves. Offering is pitted against offering, taste against taste, thrill against thrill, until the reader of advertisements may well be dizzy. This function of marketing is directed at the determination rather than the implementation of consumption. Consumption is the end and aim of sales promotion, right enough, but to manipulate demand does not necessarily further consumption. This is, however, one of the strongest forces influencing consumption. It plays upon the emotions, the prejudices, the whims, and the fancies of consumers; it creates mirages and will-o'-the-wisps; it leads to jealousy and covetousness and the drive to "keep up with the Joneses." But it also fires ambition, leads people out of the humdrum, and puts color into merchandise and thus into homes and into life itself. It leads people to aspire for a return from their income beyond the provision of food and shelter. If any point in industry merits the term "Business, the Civilizer," this is it.

SOURCE: Roland S. Vaile, "Consumption, the End of Marketing," *The Annals*, Vol. 209 (May 1940), pp. 17–18.

---

new knowledge of consumer behavior has been made available to students and marketers. But there is still much to be learned. It will become clear that you cannot understand buyer or consumer behavior by generalizing from your own experiences.

The exciting eclecticism of marketing scholars during the past ten or fifteen years has flooded the subject with new concepts and terminology. At the same time, the aspirations for a developed body of marketing theory have increased. Those aspirations suggest that the next decade will be characterized by a redefinition of marketing and of consumer theory. . . . (Tucker, 1967.)

Read the findings, hypotheses, and generalizations about consumer behavior in Statements to Consider at the end of this chapter. Whether you agree with them or not, thinking about them should open a number of doors to the important and intriguing subject of buyer behavior.

## STATEMENTS TO CONSIDER

There has been a change in marketing influence, as the retailer has become more passive and friends have become more influential.

The idea that marketers simply take advantage of impulses in passive and befuddled consumers is not as reliable as the idea that buyers make careful buying decisions to solve their problems and to gain satisfaction.

Consumers' attitudes toward products vary because of the lack of uniform information reaching them.

Cash customers are less quality-conscious than credit customers.

When a person wants advice about a product, he will seek out someone of the same social class, occupation, and life-cycle stage.

The higher a person's level of intelligence, the more likely it is that he will acquire information from communications.

All fashions end in excess.

Conspicuous consumption of valuable goods is a means of reputability to the gentleman of leisure. (Veblen)

"From each according to his abilities, to each according to his needs"— Karl Marx. Or was it Louis Blanc?—"Let each produce according to his aptitudes and his force; let each consume according to his need." Or was it the Bible, Acts 4:35?—". . . and distribution was made to each as any had need."

As the autonomy of consumers develops, the occupations of advertising, marketing, merchandising, and selling will become more professionalized. (Foote)

# QUESTIONS FOR REVIEW

**1.** Should the consumer be the focus of marketing?

**2.** Is the distinction between buyer and consumer a worthwhile one to make?

**3.** If a marketer understands needs and wants, does he not understand the buying process?

**4.** How relevant do you think Maslow's Need Hierarchy is to marketing?

**5.** What buying motives would you add to those listed in 10-2?

**6.** Consider the family budget shown in 10-4. Specifically, how do buying practices differ in different income categories (specific kinds of products)?

**7.** Do you concur with the statement in 10-6 that industry merits the term "Business, the Civilizer?" Substantiate your agreement or disagreement with this concept.

**8.** What broad generalizations of buying behavior would you list?

**9.** Does one buyer practice "price buying" and another "fashion buying," or do all buyers mix up their buying guides?

**10.** Why do fashion cycles occur?

## Further Readings

Steuart H. Britt, *Consumer Behavior in Theory and in Action* (New York: John Wiley, 1970).

James F. Engel, David T. Kollat, and Roger D. Blackwell, *Consumer Behavior* (New York: Holt, Rinehart and Winston, 1968).

John A. Howard and Jagdish N. Sheth, *The Theory of Buyer Behavior* (New York: John Wiley, 1969).

Harold H. Kassarjian and Thomas S. Robertson, *Perspectives in Consumer Behavior* (Glenview, Ill.: Scott, Foresman, 1968).

M. Venkatesan, Robert Mittelstaedt, and Robert J. Holloway, *Consumer Buying Processes: Contemporary Research in Action* (New York: Houghton Mifflin, 1970).

Various issues of the *Journal of Marketing*, *Journal of Marketing Research*, *Journal of Applied Psychology*, and the *Journal of Consumer Affairs* have articles dealing with consumer behavior.

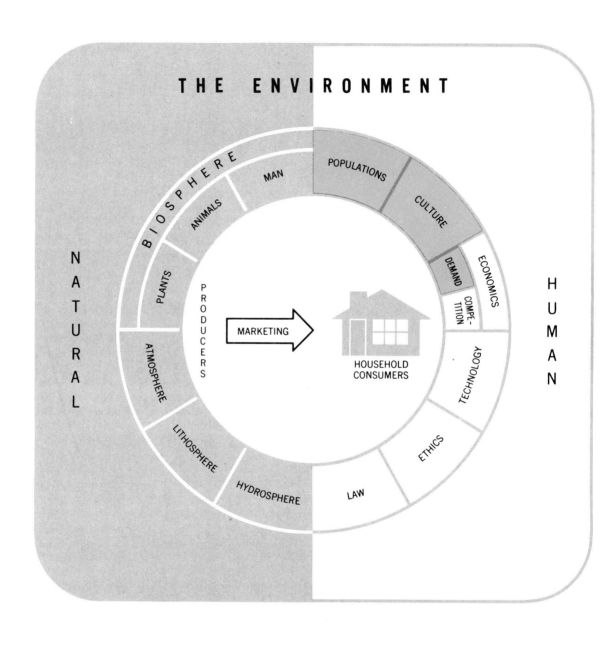

THE ENVIRONMENT

NATURAL

HUMAN

BIOSPHERE

MAN

ANIMALS

PLANTS

ATMOSPHERE

LITHOSPHERE

HYDROSPHERE

PRODUCERS

MARKETING

HOUSEHOLD
CONSUMERS

POPULATIONS

CULTURE

DEMAND

ECONOMICS

COMPE-
TITION

TECHNOLOGY

ETHICS

LAW

# CHAPTER 11
# HOUSEHOLD BUYER BEHAVIOR II
## THE FORCES OF INFLUENCE

**Internal Forces**

*Learning*

*Perception*

*Personality*

*Attitudes and Preferences*

*Motivation*

**External Forces**

*Cultural Forces*
*Mobility*
*Social Forces*
*Personal Influence*
*Interpersonal Interaction*

**Economic Forces**

**Marketing Forces**

*Buyers are influenced by many forces as they purchase goods. Some of these forces are internal—learning, perception, personality, attitudes, and motivation—and some are external—cultural forces, mobility, social forces, and personal influence.*

The household buyer is influenced in many ways by many forces in making buying decisions. It is the purpose of this chapter to identify the major forces of influence and to suggest how they operate. The list of forces is not exhaustive, nor does it delve into all the ramifications of any one force. Hopefully, however, you will acquire a fairly good picture of the forces at work in the buyers' environment. The next chapter will deal more specifically with the actual process of making decisions.

For any given buying situation, one force may be dominant or multiple forces may be at work. If you need to make a phone call you "buy" a service with which you are familiar; in effect this is a simple stimulus—response mechanism. But if you want to purchase a tent you readily become aware of a host of factors—price, material, size, design, weight, and durability, for example. There is probably no typical buying situation since each can be characterized by its own set of forces that influence the decision.

The forces of influence are of many kinds. Some are emotional, some rational. Some are felt frequently whereas others are occasional. One may be easily and separately identified and another may be interrelated with several others. Some are personal and internal, some external. Some forces are marketing factors, many are not. They may work slowly over long periods of time or work quickly and spontaneously. The diagram in 11-1 depicts some of the forces at work in an auto purchase decision. Whether a purchase is for an expensive item like an auto or a house, or for a parakeet, the influences can be identified so that consumer buying decisions can better be understood.

It is helpful to keep in mind that the subject of buying behavior is multidisciplinary in nature and often complicated. Various psychological, sociological, anthropological, and economic phenomena are related to individual buyers and their families as they make decisions on products, brands, and places of purchase (Burk, 1968). Some of these decisions may be quite effortless, but others may require days or even months of consideration.

In the process of receiving many influences a buyer accepts and discards bits of information, ultimately arriving at a decision. A simple model is:

Influencing Forces $\longrightarrow$ Buyer's Mental Process $\longrightarrow$ Buying Action

The approach to be used in this chapter is to divide the forces into two main categories, internal and external. Even though the forces will be emphasized, remember that the buying process should remain the

11-1 A Diagram of Consumer Decision-Making

IMPACT ON AUTOMOBILE MANUFACTURERS

EXPERIENCE

MARKETING          FORCES          INFLUENCING          DECISION

Technological innovations

Television commercial

Network of dealers

Stream of information from Detroit

Dealer service

Newspaper advertising

Announcements of new models

Prices

Company image

Brand image

Dealer image

Credit terms

Sales records, current year

Consumer Reports, Popular Science, etc.

Buys Cougar

Red
Convertible
Heater
Radio
St transmission
White sidewalls
Dealer financed
Other secondary decisions

Bank
Dealer
Agencies

Experience toward next car purchase

Experience: influence on acquaintances

Decides on Satellite Motor Co.

Alternatives:
Company 1
Company 2

Decides on Cougar

Decides on small car

Alternatives:
Maverick
Cougar
Mustang
Gremlin
Javelin
Charger
Barracuda
Pinto

Decides on new car

Decides to buy car

Desires car

Becomes aware of transportation need

Alternatives:
Bus
Walk
Taxi
Car

College student

Experience
Financial terms
Safety power
Company car
Appearance of car
Misc. information

Service on car
Size of car
Upkeep

Neighbors

Friends

Interaction
Climate
Income jumps
Conformity
Initial cost; trade-in prospects

Fellow employees

Buying triggers secure job upon graduation

Personal influence
Life cycle

Father

Girl friend

Hate to "bum" rides
Aspirations
Prestige

Lack of funds
Culture
Parents' cars
Friends own cars

Reference group

Dormitory mates

T  I  M  E    L  I  N  E

**11-2** The Forces of Influence

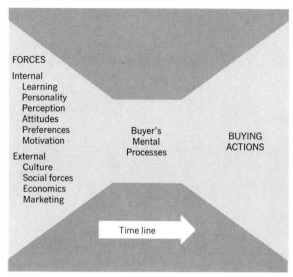

FORCES

Internal
   Learning
   Personality
   Perception
   Attitudes
   Preferences
   Motivation

External
   Culture
   Social forces
   Economics
   Marketing

Buyer's Mental Processes

BUYING ACTIONS

Time line

central focus. The diagram in 11-2 puts in schematic form the material to follow.* The forces are usually not mutually exclusive because they are related to the buying process in a total environment. However, we will treat them individually.

## INTERNAL FORCES

The principal internal forces to be discussed are learning, perception, personality, attitudes, and motivation. While these forces are obviously influenced by the external environment in many ways they are internal to the individual buyer.

### Learning

A buyer accumulates a reservoir of information about products, retailers, and manufacturers from experience, a powerful teacher. He does this by acquiring knowledge, by thinking, and by remembering. His buying process becomes modified time after time by his learning experiences. These learning experiences are in addition to his biological heritage and might be considered more of a social heritage. There is not complete agreement among psychologists on the way the learning process actually works, but we are aware of individual differences in

*This approach is used by M. Venkatesan, Robert Mittelstaedt, and Robert J. Holloway in *Consumer Behavior: Contemporary Research in Action* (Boston: Houghton Mifflin, 1970). The authors of this book acknowledge the organization developed by Venkatesan and Mittelstaedt.

taste which have been acquired through the learning process. Thus the French have a taste for snails, the Chinese for birds' nest soup, and the Americans for hamburgers. We learn a number of tastes such as classical music, and we learn to recognize certain cues to quality or style, for example, in the form of color, shape, weight, price, or smell. A darker color in vanilla ice cream may tell us that it is rich, and suds may tell us the soap or detergent will get our clothes clean. We learn to associate certain smells with cheap perfume or hair tonic and we may learn to associate price with quality, based on experience.

Aspects of learning are habit, thinking, association, repetition, observation, training, and reinforcement. As buyers we may purchase gasoline repeatedly from the same service station, and a habit of gasoline buying is thus developed. We may consider other purchases carefully as we observe other people, think through the situation, and consider the consequences of the purchase. We learn about companies and about brands, credit policies, and advertising. We learn which styles are acceptable, how to buy in a supermarket, and what to look for in a new portable radio.

When a person changes his residence he has to learn anew which doctor to use and which retailers, taxi companies, and service firms are reliable. He learns these things from a variety of sources—neighbors, advertising, and his own experiences. In one study of "new movers" (those with only three months' residence in a certain city), "older movers" (with 16 to 20 months' residence), and "residents" (those who had lived in the city for not less than three years), it was found that: (1) brand learning is done by new residents; (2) the overall pattern of brand learning is one of movement toward the norms of the community; and (3) brand learning involves the acquisition of knowledge about new brands and the forgetting of brands formerly purchased in the old community (Andreasen and Durkson, 1968).

The learning process is an important one for the buyer since he has to store enormous quantities of information in his head in order to derive the maximum satisfaction from his purchasing activities. It is an important process also for the marketer who should recognize that the marketing effort builds to an important extent on learning. An effective marketing effort should promote satisfaction on the part of the buyer-consumer so that repeat buying of the brand is realized.

## Perception

The process by which a buyer selects, organizes, and interprets his experiences in the marketplace is known as perception. His perception of a thing may not always be "accurate," but the subjective perception is usually more important in his decision-making than the objective actuality. Thus, if he has a strong liking for a Volkswagen, he may perceive it as being smaller than it actually is. A buyer's perception can also be influenced by packaging and advertising. A person may have a strong preference for a given brand of cola, cigarette, or beer, but in a blind test where he is dependent on taste alone, he may not be able to differentiate among various alternatives. Women have reported that bread in cellophane wrappers seems fresher than wax-paper-wrapped bread, even when the cellophane-wrapped product was two days old (Brown, 1958).

Associations incidental to a product can have an effect too. Tests have shown that the softness of the spring under the accelerator pedal of an automobile influences a driver's perception of the car's pickup capabilities. Price is another powerful influence. In one study 60 students who classified themselves as beer drinkers consumed beer under test conditions over an eight-week period. They were asked to evaluate unidentified bottles of beer that were identical except for price. The highest-priced beer received the highest ratings and the lowest-priced beer received the poorest ratings (McConnell, 1968). Toni Home Permanents had to raise price in order to convince consumers that the product was satisfactory in quality.

National stereotypes give rise to preconceptions that influence perception: we may believe that products made in Sweden are long-lived, that Italian products are stylish, that Dutch products are durable, that German items are unesthetic but sound in construction, that those from France are elegant but not durable, that English goods are utilitarian, and that products from the United States are practical but rapid-wearing (*Market Facts*, 1960). A marketing student from Japan—who perceived Japanese products as having quality, style, and appeal because he thought in terms of Sony, Toyota, Honda, Nikon, and Datsun—conducted a survey among U.S. businessmen and was dismayed to find that many of them saw Japanese products as imitative, cheap, and unattractive (Nagashima, 1970). Their perceptions were still reflecting stereotypes of pre-World-War-II Japanese imports. Hopefully today their perceptions would have caught up with the times.

It is popularly thought that retailers have the best insights into buyers' perceptions. One study of appliance retailers and buyers indicated, however, that this may not be so. It was found that retailers consistently underestimate the strengths with which buyers view the importance of service and warranty, ease of use, and style. Further, retailers tend to have either oversensitive or undersensitive images of specific attributes of competitive brands (McClure and Ryans, 1968).

Images are built by companies through their products and marketing efforts; even a trademark is thought to convey a company's personality to the public. The symbols in 11-3 suggest some different meanings that trademarks can have for consumers. These symbols, as with advertising, packages, displays, and store buildings are deliberately chosen in order to develop a desired image on the part of the buyer. In a study of the *Wall Street Journal* some years ago, it was found that the newspaper projected some fairly definite images to its readers. It was considered "authoritative," "clear," "intelligent," and "informative," but not "lively," "imaginative," "specialized," or "attractive-looking" (Bolger, 1960).

**11-3** Meanings Conveyed by Trademarks

| MODERN OR ABSTRACT | VS. | PICTORIAL OR REPRESENTATIONAL |
| TRADITIONAL OR HERALDIC | VS. | MODERN OR ABSTRACT |
| MASCULINE SYMBOLS | VS. | FEMININE SYMBOLS |
| BOLD LINES | VS. | DELICATE LINES |
| ANIMATE FIGURES | VS. | INANIMATE THINGS |

SOURCE: Adapted from "What Trademark Types Tell Consumers about a Company," *Business Week*, November 5, 1960, pp. 105–106.

## Personality

The third internal force is personality, perhaps the most distinctive feature of any individual. The personality is an overall pattern of many distinguishable characteristics of the individual. Making up the total personality are components, or traits—interests, attitudes, aptitudes, modes of behavior, capacities, and abilities, for example. Many attempts have been made to link personality traits to buying behavior, and even more attempts have been made to link personality traits to specific buying behavior such as the product and brand choice, risk-taking, and media choice. A contemporary novel highlighted this approach; it concerned a super-salesman who identified each person in his city with a lapel button that provided a color code to the person's personality. Clerks were then trained to use the selling technique that had been devised to sell the maximum amount to each personality type (Vercors, 1966). In the real world, some years ago Ford and Chevrolet owners were given personality tests in order to ascertain whether there was any substantial difference between them. Traits such as achievement, exhibitionism, affiliation, dominance, and aggression were used in the test. There was some tendency for Ford owners to see their brand as best for an athlete and for someone "up to date." Chevrolet owners rated their brand best for a woman, for a dignified gentleman, or for a person desiring job security. But on the whole the differences between the two groups were not significant enough to warrant predicting buying behavior on the basis of personality (Evans, 1959).

Another study indicated that the personality-consumer behavior relationship is equivocal. "Some studies indicate a strong relationship between personality and consumer behavior, a few indicate no relationship and the great majority indicate that if correlations do exist they are so weak as to be questionable or perhaps meaningless" (Kassarjian, 1970). One of the problems in such research concerns the validity of personality measuring instruments. Another is the selection of traits—18,000 terms referring to personality have been listed by psychologists! Thus, even though personality is thought to be important in buyer behavior, it is a difficult force to identify and to use in prediction. It remains an engrossing concept for marketers, however, because if one can identify personality-consumption relationships he has a key to the selling as well as the buying process.

## Attitudes and Preferences

An attitude is a learned predisposition to react in certain ways, and it may be negative or positive. A preference is the condition of liking A better than B. Attitudes and preferences are parts of a buyer's total person, and the marketer needs to identify and evaluate them in order to communicate properly. In some cases he attempts to strengthen attitudes, in others to change them. In all cases it is important to know just what buyers' attitudes are. In 1970, for instance, a public utility company misread the attitudes of the people in its market area and as a result made three poor decisions relating to power plant construction that caused serious problems in its long-range development program. The utility proceeded with new construction only to run into strong public opposition, which caused months of delay and considerable legal costs. They further assumed that customers would not pay more for electricity in order to reduce pollution, until a survey proved this assumption to be incorrect.

A study performed in Chicago revealed that, at least for scouring cleanser and coffee, brand preference was almost identical with purchase intention; about 96 percent of the subjects studied included their most preferred brands in their purchase intentions. Preference here was a good predictor of purchase (Banks, 1950).

It is, of course, one thing to ascertain an attitude or preference and quite another task to take advantage of this knowledge. In the competitive marketplace the consumer receives conflicting communications that may have a neutralizing effect. Nevertheless, attitudes and preferences are important forces that influence buying behavior.

## Motivation

This internal force is often used synonymously with wishes, drives, needs, desires, and the like. There is usually an incentive involved and the motivated behavior is internally activated. According to Maslow's hierarchy of wants and needs, introduced in the previous chapter, each level of need must be satisfied before there is much motivation to fulfill the needs at the next higher level. It is possible to assign goods and services to each level of Maslow's hierarchy and to ascertain a general order of priority for each of them. Fulfillment of basic physiological needs would come before any motivation to acquire nonessentials, for example.

An understanding of motivation would seemingly explain a good deal of buyer behavior, and would answer the "why" question involved in a purchase decision. Motivational research in marketing was developed to do exactly that, in order for marketing departments to design the proper products and advertise so as to meet the known motivation. Thousands of motivational research studies have been made about all kinds of marketing questions. How will doctors respond to a new type of suture? What are mothers' unsatisfied needs in breakfast cereals? What are the changing motivations and differentiated responses to color in the paper products field? What are the real forces of consumer resistance to a Wildroot shampoo for women? Motivational research is not a panacea for marketers, however, and indeed, the results are rather spotty. Before using motivational research, consider the following advice:

Be sure you really understand motivational research.
Don't expect it to solve all problems.
Ask for evidence on the methods proposed.
Make certain you use valid techniques. (Britt, 1965.)

A person's level of aspiration is related to motivation since he strives to reach a particular level of accomplishment. A consumer may aspire to owning two cars, a lake cottage, and a sailboat. Actually buyers'

**11-4** Food and Drink as Seen by Low-Income Families

Best World

10

| 9.05 | 5 years from now |

| 7.98 | Present |

| 5.43 | 5 years ago |

0

Worst World

Food and Drink
(Physiological)

SOURCE: Robert J. Holloway and Richard N. Cardozo, *Consumer Problems and Marketing Patterns in Low-Income Neighborhoods* (Minneapolis: University of Minnesota, 1969), p. 12.

aspirations tend to be realistic and they tend to adjust according to their situation. Just as a golfer's expectations about his score are tied to his experience on the course, so a buyer's expectations in terms of his standard of living are tied to his abilities. In one study, the Cantrill Self-Anchoring Striving Scale was used among low-income families in order to determine a number of their aspirations. The scale is simply a ten-rung ladder, the top of which represents the best possible world, the bottom the worst possible. Respondents are asked to place themselves on the ladder for each question being investigated. Illustrated in 11-4 are the results of the question: "With regards to food and drink, where on the ladder would you say you stand today? 5 years ago? 5 years from now?" The results provide some idea of their levels of aspiration and the changes that were taking place in these levels.

Marketing plays an important role in developing consumers' levels of aspiration. Mass communication, especially television, has been influential. Undoubtedly there are frustrations today because of the gap between achievement and aspiration, caused partly by our advertising.

Internal forces that act on buyer behavior provide part of the buying picture. They relate to the person himself, his personality, attitudes, preferences, motivations, aspirations, perceptions, and learning. But the buyer is exposed to the total environment, and he is therefore exposed to a multitude of external forces that must also be considered.

## EXTERNAL FORCES

External forces will be discussed under four main headings: cultural, social, economic, and marketing. These are forces that are external to the individual, but they are nevertheless influential in purchase decisions.

## Cultural Forces

Culture is an extremely broad and encompassing term. It includes what we have learned, our history, values, morals, customs, art, and habits. Cultural forces are not static; they change and adapt just as marketing adapts to its environment. Man passes culture along, so it is inculcated. Marketing takes place within a given culture, and, as you will recall from Chapter 4, many of the differences in marketing around the world are essentially cultural differences.

There are cultures, such as our own and that of the ancient Romans, and there are *subcultures,* such as those of southerners, blacks, teenagers, the poor, city-dwellers, and religious groups. The identification of a subculture may provide a firm with a segment of a market that it can develop. For instance, products have been developed in great quantity for the teenage subculture, and advertising has been directed to these consumers. Each subculture, like the larger cultures, has distinctive values, beliefs, and attitudes that the marketer must understand if he is effectively to exploit them. It is not always easy to identify differences among subcultures, however, and marketers disagree, for example, about whether there exists a black market that is distinct from a white market. Several studies provide some guidance about whether blacks spend their incomes in the same way as do whites. A summary of these studies in 11-5 reveals that blacks spend their incomes somewhat differently from what whites do in several expenditure categories.

It is easy to develop mistaken stereotyped notions about subcultures. For example, it may be surprising to learn that French women are more interested in durability than fashion in clothes and that blacks consume more Scotch whiskey per capita than whites. Studies show that Jews consume more instant coffee than Italians, but one must not generalize beyond the area of study for Jews in New York may have quite different buying habits from those of Jews in Sweden, for example. The marketer is interested in identifying any subculture as a potential market for his products. The advertising of many products in *Ebony* magazine is an

### 11-5 Summary of Findings: Do Negroes Spend More or Less than Comparable Whites?

| Food | Housing | Clothing | Recreation and leisure | Home furnishings & equipment | Medical care | Auto transportation | Nonauto transportation |
|------|---------|----------|------------------------|------------------------------|--------------|---------------------|------------------------|
| less | less | more | * | less | less | less | more |

*Four studies indicated less and three indicated more was spent by Negroes.
SOURCE: Adapted from Marcus Alexis, "Some Negro-White Differences in Consumption," *American Journal of Economics and Sociology,* Vol. 21 (January 1962), pp. 11–28.

illustration of selling to a subculture.

The aggregation of people by *demographic* variables has long been done by marketing research staffs. This is, of course, a way to study and measure the buying potential of a subculture, and it is usually based on rather well accepted demographic variables such as age (preschool, teenage, college, senior citizen), occupation (blue-collar, skilled, managerial, professional), income (low, medium, high), race (white, nonwhite), and religion (Protestant, Catholic, Jewish). These classifications are illustrative of demographic variables: others can be utilized and greater detail can be developed for any one of them.

All the demographic groups listed above may buy some of the same products, but each also has some unique needs and can, therefore, be classified as a separate market. The aged purchase some drugs made and marketed expressly for them, and preschool children influence the buying of cereals. This relationship between demographic variables and purchasing behavior has long been studied by those in marketing.

Closely related to demographic variables and subcultures is the concept of *social class,* a segment of society with similar income, values, occupations, and ambitions. Although social class distinctions may be crumbling, they have not disappeared from the scene, and a demographic characteristic such as occupation is still important in determining a person's social class. As with subcultures, marketers are interested in relationships between social classes and their buying behavior. In the Ford-Chevrolet study previously cited, there happened to be little relationship between social class and brand preference. In another study, it was found that professors tend to exhibit less conspicuous consumption than businessmen and that professors act more informally than businessmen (Porter, 1967). A study of credit card usage has indicated that the lower social classes tend to use their cards for installment payments, the upper classes for convenience (Mathews and Slocum, 1968). Lower-class persons shop the least and they generally perceive a narrow range of alternatives available for the improvement of their position (Bruce and Dommermuth, 1968).

Social classes can be related to *life cycles* and both factors can be related to a number of behavioral variables. In 11-6 it can be seen that there is more similarity among the middle classes than among the lower classes. For the marketer, it is important to recognize differences in buying behavior among social classes and also changes in buying behavior as a family proceeds through different life-cycle stages.

## Mobility

Another concept closely related to social class and demographics is that of *mobility.* Mobility refers to more than changes in residence; the concept includes changes in occupations, income, education, travel, associations with people, politics, and living styles. It has been suggested that people who are highly mobile tend to be the tastemakers of our society, and as such they lead in new product buying with obvious implications for marketing. An example of the relationship between mobility and consumption is shown in 11-7.

**11-6** Relationships of Social Class, Behavioral Variables, and Life Cycle

| SOCIAL CLASSES | BEHAVIORAL VARIABLES | FAMILY LIFE-CYCLE STAGES | |
| --- | --- | --- | --- |
| | | Young married | Older married |
| Middle class | Social mobility, aspiration | High | High |
| | Family income | High | Higher |
| | Role of the wife | Companion | Companion |
| | Occupation of the husband | Managerial | Managerial |
| | Marital relations | Good | Good |
| | Education | University | University, high school |
| Lower class | Social mobility, aspiration | Low | Low, downward |
| | Family income | Low | Low, decreasing |
| | Role of the wife | Companion, mother | Housewife, mother |
| | Occupation of the husband | Semi-skilled | Semi-skilled |
| | Marital relations | Poor | Poor, decreasing |
| | Education | High school | High school, elementary school |

SOURCE: Adapted from Richard H. Evans, "A Behavioral Model for Marketing Segmentation," *University of Washington Business Review*, Vol. 28 (Autumn 1968), p. 62.

## 11-7 High Mobiles and a Tastemaker Theory

The underlying concept of the tastemaker theory of change is *mobility*. Mobile people are those who are on the move with reference to:

| | | | |
| --- | --- | --- | --- |
| Occupation | Education | Travel | Politics |
| Residence | Ideas | Economics | New ventures |

High Mobiles lead in new product buying:

As adoption fans out, the High Mobiles account for a dwindling share of the total market.

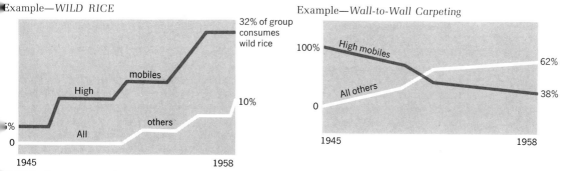

Example—*WILD RICE*        Example—*Wall-to-Wall Carpeting*

SOURCE: Opinion Research Corporation, *America's Tastemakers* (Princeton, N.J.: Opinion Research Corporation, 1959), p. 6. Reproduced by permission of the copyright owners.

**11-8** "Hippie" Life Style versus "Business" Life Style

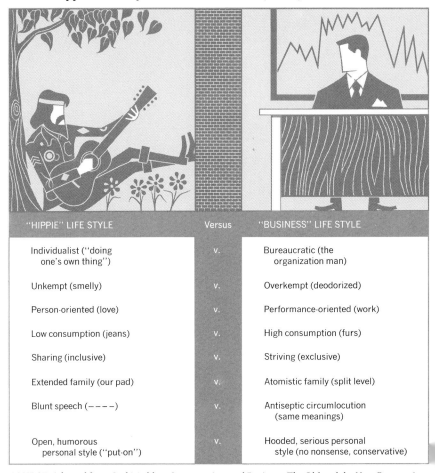

| "HIPPIE" LIFE STYLE | Versus | "BUSINESS" LIFE STYLE |
|---|---|---|
| Individualist ("doing one's own thing") | v. | Bureaucratic (the organization man) |
| Unkempt (smelly) | v. | Overkempt (deodorized) |
| Person-oriented (love) | v. | Performance-oriented (work) |
| Low consumption (jeans) | v. | High consumption (furs) |
| Sharing (inclusive) | v. | Striving (exclusive) |
| Extended family (our pad) | v. | Atomistic family (split level) |
| Blunt speech (– – – –) | v. | Antiseptic circumlocution (same meanings) |
| Open, humorous personal style ("put-on") | v. | Hooded, serious personal style (no nonsense, conservative) |

*SOURCE:* Adapted from Carl Madden, *Consumerism and Business: The Old and the New Perspective,* speech given at the American Marketing Association Meetings, Kansas City, April 1, 1970, p. 11.

The matter of *life style* is of utmost importance to the marketer who is handling consumer items. Consumers today are more expressive in terms of their life styles than they were formerly. Hippies and businessmen, for example, might be differentiated as shown in 11-8. Companies are now recognizing that they must relate to different and to changing life styles, as did the Pillsbury Company which announced its intentions to "change its approach to product development to meet the needs of this generation, modify existing products, and communicate differently" (Adler, 1970). It is virtually impossible to think in terms of any one life style today, and so the marketer is again faced with different and distinct segments of the market about which he must make certain decisions about products, prices, and other marketing matters.

"The times they are a'changin'," and marketers along with everyone else are trying to determine the impact of different life styles or marketing, and further what life styles will be in five and ten years from now. Although this kind of prediction seems difficult to make with any degree of accuracy, the awareness of changing life styles and the recognition of their relationship to buying behavior are easily understood.

## Social Forces

The second external force to be considered involves the influence of other persons on the buyer. There are three kinds of social forces: group influence, personal influence, and interpersonal interaction.

Groups importantly influence buyer behavior. Almost everyone belongs to groups of some kind, large or small, informal or formal, temporary or permanent. Groups to which a person belongs formally are membership groups, such as the Marketing Club or a fraternity; these tend to be rather small groups with face-to-face contact. Another kind is a reference group, with which a person identifies and by which he is influenced in his behavior. A person may belong to his reference group, or he may aspire to belong. People can have several reference groups at one time, of course, reflecting a variety of interests.

The relevance of the reference group to buyer behavior is that the group impact can determine to some degree a person's norms of buying behavior, as the group's norms are translated into personal buying practices. If your reference group is your immediate neighbor, your levels of aspiration and buying behavior will be influenced by their lawns, cars, and carpeting. This reference group is not equally determinative for all products. It can, however, operate in a variety of ways and can be effective on brands, services, and products. The matrix in 11-9 shows that reference group influence is strong for both brands and products in the case of cigarettes, but weak for both in the case of laundry soap.

It is probably not possible for you to ascertain the precise influence

**11-9** Reference Group Influence on Products and Brands

| BRAND | PRODUCT | |
| --- | --- | --- |
| | Weak − | Strong + |
| Strong + | Clothing<br>Furniture<br>Magazines<br>Refrigerator (type)<br>Toilet soap | Cars<br>Cigarettes<br>Beer (prem. vs. reg.)<br>Drugs |
| Weak − | Soap<br>Canned peaches<br>Laundry soap<br>Refrigerator (brand)<br>Radios | Air conditioners<br>Instant coffee<br>TV (black and white) |

SOURCE: Francis S. Bourne, *Group Influence in Marketing and Public Relations* (Ann Arbor, Mich.: Foundation for Research on Human Behavior, 1956), p. 8.

of your groups. But you can gain some idea of their importance by noticing how many items you have that are also possessed by the members of groups you belong to, desire to belong to, and refer to. There may be conflicts among these reference groups, forcing you to make a personal decision about which one will be determinative.

## Personal Influence

A remark by a friend, a conversation with a neighbor, and a phrase by a speaker are examples of potential personal influence. We are all clearly influenced by others, and this influence can affect our buying patterns. A clear example is the selection of a physician when a family is new to a community. Medical doctors do not advertise, and they do not provide a great deal of personal advice about one another. As a result, many persons select their physicians under the personal influence of a neighbor, friend, or colleague. In the entire field of personal services, indeed, the force of personal influence is considerable (Feldman and Spencer, 1965).

Personal influence is evident in the way new products and services are adopted. One theory is that opinion leaders influence the adoption of a new item. When it becomes known that an opinion leader has purchased a touch-tone phone, for example, others will conform by doing the same thing. In India an ongoing study is attempting to locate opinion leaders in the agricultural villages in order to promote better use of fertilizer. If opinion leaders can be located, perhaps they can be convinced of the virtues of fertilizers and encourage their "followers" to use them. In the medical profession doctors frequently discuss new drugs with opinion leaders in their field. For all of us a reliable personal contact may be the best and quickest way to receive an answer.

An obvious marketing strategy would be to identify opinion leaders and then convince them to use one's product. Aside from the difficulty of identifying leaders, there may be problems in getting a person to deliberately influence his friends. The testimonial advertisement is a way of putting the word of opinion leaders before the public.

## Interpersonal Interaction

Interaction is more than a process of passing along information—it includes discussion, argument, and nonverbal communication. Through a technique known as Interaction Process Analysis, it is possible to examine this interaction, and to develop an understanding of how it unfolds. During interaction an observer categorizes each comment and even each nod of the head into twelve categories, such as: agrees, asks for orientation, asks for opinion, shows tension, or disagrees. The total picture of the interaction can be quantified along a time sequence. To illustrate, the interaction between a car buyer and a salesman can be processed into the series of the twelve categories. As the picture of their interaction is finally examined in terms of the Interaction Process Analysis, we can learn what actually takes place in a buy-sell situation.

The amount of information requested and received, the kind of information, the way a salesman leads the buyer to decision, and the amount of tension and tension release can all be identified. As a result of studying interactions between successful salesmen and their customers as contrasted to unsuccessful salesmen, one should be able to teach car salesmen how to handle a sale. It is surprising that relatively little research has been done with the actual selling process.

Persons, reference groups, and interaction are three kinds of social forces that play roles in buyer behavior. Whether it is the child-family relationship or the housewife-neighbor relationship, there are likely to be influences which will affect buying decisions.

# ECONOMIC FORCES

Assets, their quantity and liquidity, and current income exert a major influence over a consumer's ability and even desire to buy. Ample assets and income encourage consumption. Lack of assets and income restrain and restrict; we postpone, cancel, and ignore purchases when our ability to buy is low. Assets are restrictive in another sense, too. If a housewife already has a complete set of glassware, she is unlikely to be interested in another set.

*Credit* has the same effect: lack of adequate credit restricts consumption, availability can encourage it. A consumer's willingness to spend may vary by several thousands of dollars on a house or several hundred dollars on an automobile depending on the credit arrangements.

Many theories relate income and consumption. Usually the explanation of consumer buying behavior in terms of income is oversimplified, leaving the notion that expenditures always follow income in a linear relationship. Aggregate data show this tendency over time, but income *per se* does not provide the complete answer to buying behavior.

Engel's laws (1848) propose a stable relationship between income and expenditures. According to these laws, expenditures for most categories increase as income rises. The *percentage* spent decreases for food, remains constant for housing, and increases for clothing, transportation, recreation, health, and education. Engel's laws probably held true well enough during the period of relative social stability from 1887 to 1914, but in recent years social and economic changes have often more than counterbalanced the effect of changed incomes on expenditures. Benjamin Loeb, who suggested this notion, "tested" the applicability of Engel's laws on a year-to-year basis from 1929 to 1953. The laws conformed only 45 percent of the time (Loeb, 1955). Thus, income provides no sure way to predict consumer expenditures.

The *absolute-income* hypothesis was furthered by economist John Maynard Keynes, who held that "Men are disposed, as a rule and on the average, to increase their consumption as their income increases, but not by as much as the increase in their income" (Keynes, 1936).

According to this view, aggregate consumption expenditures over time correlate highly with aggregate disposable income. This hypothesis has been questioned, however, because budget data have been difficult to reconcile in regard to savings. The *relative-income* hypothesis assumes that the savings rate depends not only on the level of income but also on the relative position of the individual on the income scale. This hypothesis recognizes the drive of people to attain a higher standard of living. Consumers want to close any unfavorable gap between themselves and their neighbor. Furthermore, once someone reaches a given level of consumption he tends to maintain it if at all possible even though his income decreases.

Another income hypothesis is the *permanent-income* theory put forth by Milton Friedman. Income is divided into two parts, permanent and transitory. A consumer determines his standard of living according to his expectations of returns from resources over a long period of time. These returns would be rather constant from year to year. The transitory income factors account for deviations in consumption from year to year. They amount to nuisance factors as far as the basic relationship between permanent income and consumption is concerned.

George Katona has stressed a "willingness to buy" factor. By asking consumers about their intentions to buy and their income expectations for future periods, he combines psychology and economics. It is quite possible that for many consumers, willingness to buy and actual purchases may move in the same direction.

Obviously a low-income consumer is more aware of economics as a restrictive force than someone with a large discretionary income. Various studies of the poor have been made, sometimes with conflicting results. One study summarized the buying of the poor as follows:

1. Although they spend most of their income on basic needs, those who buy durable goods make serious inroads on their incomes.

2. . . . many depend on merchants or relatives for judgments of what to buy.

3. Few have savings; most do not have life insurance; and only about half are covered by medical insurance.

4. It is doubtful whether many carry out home production activities to supplement cash purchases.

5. Many probably do not make full use of the programs established to provide services and goods free or at reduced rates. (Richards, 1966.)

Marketers frequently are in conflict with economics because economists assume the rational when the market may be nonrational. The mythical consumer is described in 11-10. Even so, economics must be drawn into the total picture of buyer behavior so that income is one factor that is weighted appropriately.

## 11-10

**The Economist's Mythical Consumer**

Economists hate to observe behavior, especially that of the individual consumer. By and large, they would rather be telling someone *how* to behave, preferably the President of the United States (or the chairman of the Federal Reserve Board). Few economists do not envy those who assist in the determination of national policy.

These understandable motives have left economics unwilling or unable to deal with marketing. Divided as it usually is, into the normative and the descriptive, and into macroeconomics and microeconomics, we find the normative-macro quadrant containing most economists and consequently most economic research. The other normative and macro quadrants take most of the remainder, leaving descriptive microeconomics shrunken and neglected. It is no surprise that from this depressed area of the economic economy has come a theory which is itself a victim of empirical malnutrition. Picture, if you will, the following consumer.

His preference patterns are constant. When he prefers *A* over *B* and *B* over *C*, he always prefers *A* over *C*. He knows all the products from which he may choose, and all their relevant attributes. This is easier than it sounds, because for him the products never change. He can discriminate every product from every other—no two ever seem alike. He can buy any part of a product he likes, e.g., half a Cadillac. He is totally uninfluenced by other consumers. He has a fixed income. As he buys additional units of some product, he enjoys each additional unit less and less. This is for two reasons. First, he tends to become satiated; second, he is forced to sacrifice more of alternative products as he uses up his income in the purchase of the first product. He is happiest when he has allocated his income among products and quantities of products such that the additional enjoyment of the next unit bought of each product is proportional to the product's price.

SOURCE: Charles K. Raymond, "Marketing Science: Stepchild of Economics," in Robert M. Kaplan (ed.), *The Marketing Concept in Action*, Proceedings of the American Marketing Association, June 1964, pp. 662–675.

## MARKETING FORCES

The final group of external forces is found in marketing efforts. The consumer is, after all, the focus of the marketer. The marketing forces are easily distinguishable from others because they are fully intended to influence the buyer. Neil Borden, who articulated the concept of the "marketing mix," describes the marketer as one "who is constantly engaged in fashioning creatively a mix of marketing procedures and policies in his efforts to produce a profitable enterprise" (Borden, 1964).

The mix is composed of the following ingredients:

| | |
|---|---|
| Product | Price |
| Brand | Channels of distribution |
| Advertising | Personal selling |
| Promotion | Packaging |
| Display | Service |
| Physical handling | Fact finding and analysis |

The *product* may be developed for a particular segment of the market or for a subculture, such as high-protein food items for the poor. The product is the principal objective for the buyer. The point is that through the right kind of product, the marketer can efficiently and effectively attain consumer acceptance.

The *price* is an important and difficult part of the marketing effort. The price may be the most important determinant of purchase in one instance and not even be considered in another. Most of the time a company must be mindful of the role of price and its effect on the consumer, for much of the time the consumer is certainly influenced by the price. Price may convey quality, and the ratio of price to quality conveys some notion of value to the buyer.

Another marketing force is the *brand*. The importance of brand names such as Nikon, Ford, Polaroid, and Gant is considerable. Consumers have brand images, which are sum totals of their impressions. They have brand preferences and brand loyalty, or at least they rebuy the same brand if they are satisfied. Clearly the brand is an important part of the marketing-buyer relationship.

Through the *institutions* of marketing the marketer makes goods available. The buyer patronizes certain retailers only for some products. For example, one buyer purchases camera film in a supermarket, another may prefer to visit a specialty store where a particular brand is available.

The marketer has the job of persuading the consumer to buy his product or service. Through *advertising*, *promotion*, and *personal selling*, the task is accomplished. This marketing effort, persuasion, is probably the most visible and one of the most important to the consumer, for the total buying process can become a difficult decision-making process since the persuasive forces "confront" one another. Personal selling, advertising, and promotion complement one another. Sometimes only one is effective and other times all are used. Together they represent the marketer's effort to communicate directly and persuasively to the buyer.

The marketer has many devices to persuade the buyer to select his product—the entire "marketing mix" is at his disposal. Thus, the tasks of marketing can be directed toward persuading the consumer to buy a given product at a given price with a certain package from a particular retailer. All of the marketing forces become a part of the total decision-making process that takes place millions of times each day by the world's buyers and sellers. The marketer wants to ascertain all the information possible from the consumer, and then direct his marketing efforts toward satisfying the buyer so that brand loyalty in the form of repetitive buying is the result.

## CONCLUDING COMMENTS

This chapter has presented many of the forces that influence persons to buy. The internal forces identified were personality, learning, perception, motivation, and attitudes. The external forces were cultural, social, economic, and marketing.

The forces act in different ways at different times on different persons, and even on the same person. Income, for example, may act as a *restraining* force at one time and an encouraging one on another occasion—as can degree of availability, variety of brand choice, and price. Some forces are *motivating* in that they move the consumer toward purchase. Some are *persuasive*, especially the marketing forces of advertising and selling. Some serve as *discriminating* forces, since they help the buyer to make selective decisions. Race, life styles, and experience would be examples. Some of the marketing forces, such as retailing are *enabling*, in that they make a product available. We can isolate the forces for identification, but they do not operate in isolation, rather they work together to form a totality.

It is the task of the next chapter, now that the inputs have been discussed, to describe and explain the consumer's decision-making process.

## STATEMENTS TO CONSIDER

Consumers desire and expect only slightly more than they presently have.

The style of a leader is determined more by the expectations of the membership than by the personal traits of the individual himself. (Berelson and Steiner)

The effect of college upon students is to homogenize them in the direction of the prevailing environment.

What our friends own, we own also, or shall own soon.

Women tend to be different; men tend to be similar. Or is it that men tend to be different; women tend to be similar?

People enjoy spending money. To learn how to be better spenders would remove much of life's satisfaction.

Conformity is more important in advanced societies than in less developed societies.

Buying becomes more and more irrational as one proceeds from the subsistence scale of living to that of ample discretionary income.

For each of the leisure items there is a hierarchy of goods typically purchased at each income level. (Fisk)

Marketing management has significance only if the concept of customer orientation is invoked. (Markin)

# QUESTIONS FOR REVIEW

**1.** Select any product and trace through every influence on the buying process that you can identify. A recent purchase of some significance would probably be the best kind of an item to choose.

**2.** How would you change the diagram of consumer decision-making (11-1) from your own personal experience?

**3.** List the cues you use in making purchases. (See section on Learning.)

**4.** Do you know of any instances in your own buying experiences when your perceptions of a product were quite different from the actual product?

**5.** Why do you think the building of images has become so important?

**6.** How much confidence can one place in personality characteristics insofar as predicting buying behavior is concerned? Explain.

**7.** Explain why culture is so important as a force in determining buyer behavior.

**8.** How much influence has the "hippie" life style had on consumption?

**9.** What accounts for the differences in the importance of reference groups on the buying of different household appliances?

**10.** As a general statement, what would you say about the relative importance of personal income as a buying force?

## Further Readings

*Note:* See the suggestions at the end of Chapter 10.

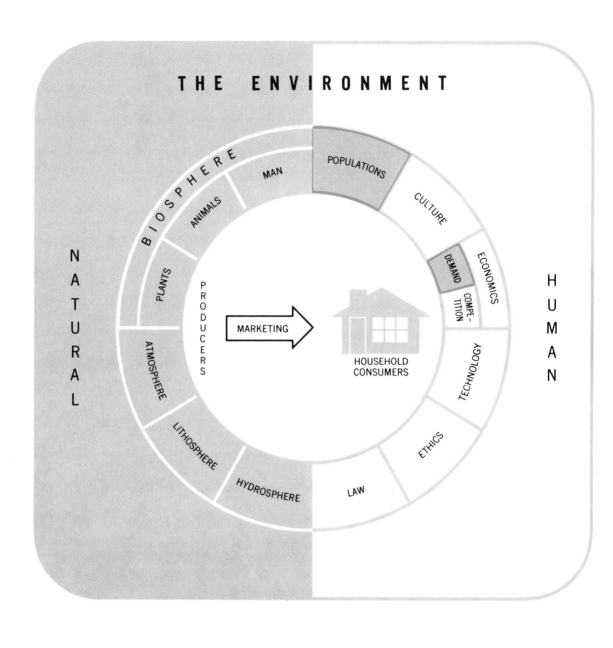

THE ENVIRONMENT

NATURAL

HUMAN

BIOSPHERE

MAN

ANIMALS

PLANTS

ATMOSPHERE

LITHOSPHERE

HYDROSPHERE

POPULATIONS

CULTURE

ECONOMICS

DEMAND

COMPE-
TITION

TECHNOLOGY

ETHICS

LAW

PRODUCERS

MARKETING

HOUSEHOLD
CONSUMERS

# CHAPTER 12
# HOUSEHOLD BUYER BEHAVIOR III
## THE BUYING PROCESS

**The Prepurchase Phase**

*Impulse Buying*
*Deliberation*

**The Actual Purchase**

*Risk*
*The Decision-Maker*
*Purchase Behavior and Strategies*

**The Postpurchase Phase**

*Satisfaction*
*Loyalty*
*Dissonance*

**Models of Buyer Behavior**

*The Katona Model*
*The Engel Model*
*The Andreasen Model*
*The Nicosia Model*
*The Howard-Sheth Model*

*The buying process can be examined in great detail although the buyer operates as a whole person. Throughout the buying process there is some amount of planning, handling risk, reacting to habit and confidence in sellers, and registering satisfaction upon purchase. Models of buying are useful in developing an understanding of the buying process.*

At a luncheon three marketing professors described their buying processes. One indicated that he searched diligently for the best buy each time he purchased a new car; the second explained that she decided on the make and style and then called for quotations over the phone, accepting the lowest price; the third admitted that he purchased his last car largely on impulse. Because a buyer, even a marketing professor, is influenced in many ways by many forces, the decision process varies a great deal. Some decisions are made with very little thought, whereas others require considerable deliberation; some involve large sums of money, many do not; some are made alone, and others require group consultation. The basic model

$$\text{Forces} \longrightarrow \text{Buyer} \longrightarrow \text{Purchase}$$

accurately describes all these decisions, but it does not offer any guides for distinguishing among them. The model certainly does not imply that there is some standard of buying behavior or of decision-making.

The examination of the actual buying process brings to a focus all the forces impinging on the purchase. We have discussed the *why* of buying; now we want to turn to *how, when,* and *where.* The prepurchase phase will be discussed first, then the actual buying decision, and finally the postpurchase phase. After that, we will introduce a number of buying behavior models in an attempt to integrate the work of these three chapters dealing with the household buyer.

## THE PREPURCHASE PHASE

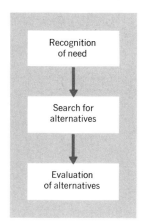

The prepurchase phase of buying may last a long time or it may be compressed into a very short period. We will consider this period of time as one unit of activity, but it can be broken down into several different parts as shown in the illustration at left (Engel, Kollat, and Blackwell, 1968).

The many forces examined in the previous chapter help a consumer to recognize the existence of a need. For a simple example, a person feels thirsty and so recognizes a need that might lead to a purchase. He might search out a vending machine with a choice of alternatives. He might then ponder the alternatives, weighing them carefully before making the decision. There are a number of possible determinants to recognizing a problem or need (Engel, *et al,* 1968).

Depletion of a previous solution
Dissatisfaction with a present solution
Changing family characteristics
Changing financial status
Recognition of other problems
Changing reference groups
Marketing efforts

Becoming aware of the existence of a buying need may in itself serve as a trigger to the purchase. Recognition of the need cocks the buying mechanism that may be actuated soon or it may be delayed until something else triggers the purchase.

## Impulse Buying

Marketers find it useful to distinguish between *impulse* and *deliberative* buying. The former applies to unplanned purchases made on the spur of the moment, as when a friend of one of the authors reported that he drove into a garage one rainy morning to get his windshield wiper replaced. A salesman happened to come by and asked, "Why don't you trade the car in instead of buying a new blade?" He bought!

In 12-1 are shown the results of one survey of purchases where the

### 12-1 Do Consumers Buy on Impulse?*

| Product group | IMPULSE PURCHASES (as a percentage of all purchases) | | | | |
| --- | --- | --- | --- | --- | --- |
| | Food stores | Drug stores | Variety stores | Dept. stores | Avg. all stores |
| Candy and nuts | 69.6 | 34.1 | 82.8 | 77.1 | 65.8 |
| Baked goods (sweet) | 67.1 | — | 68.7 | 76.7 | 70.1 |
| Cosmetics | — | 24.3 | 61.5 | 49.7 | 41.8 |
| Drugs and sundries | — | 32.2 | — | 44.0 | 38.0 |
| Stationery | — | 19.8 | 48.8 | 57.3 | 41.9 |
| Toilet articles | — | 27.5 | 37.8 | 47.6 | 37.6 |
| Notions | — | — | 37.2 | 54.7 | 46.0 |
| Dress accessories | — | — | 28.5 | 22.8 | 25.5 |
| Jewelry | — | — | 50.0 | 49.1 | 49.5 |
| Hardware and electrical supplies | — | — | 28.5 | 34.6 | 41.5 |
| Cutlery, kitchenware, glassware | — | — | 47.8 | 31.2 | 39.5 |
| Toys | — | — | 57.9 | 53.0 | 55.5 |
| Hosiery | — | — | 25.2 | 50.2 | 37.6 |
| Wearing apparel | — | — | 27.5 | 20.7 | 24.1 |
| †General averages—all items | 43.5 | 26.6 | 41.5 | 33.6 | 36.7 |

*Findings based on survey of 5300 Canadians in six cities.
†These averages are for all products surveyed in each of these outlets. They are not averages of only the product classifications shown above. Last figure shows that 36.7 percent of all purchases in the four types of outlets in all *six cities* are made on impulse.

SOURCE: C. John West, "Results of Two Years of Study Into Impulse Buying," *Journal of Marketing*, Vol. 15 (January 1951), p. 363.

degree of impulse buying varies with the product and store. Another study found that less than half of family food purchases included planned purchases, and further, that unplanned purchases of food did not alter the average expenditures for food or the allocation of expenditures among nine major food groups. Some items like eggs, head lettuce, and frozen orange juice were anticipated purchases by a fairly high percentage of buyers, whereas cookies, pickles, and canned pineapple purchases were characteristically not anticipated (Shaffer, 1960).

A later study, shown in 12-2, gives data on buying decisions in supermarkets according to degree of planning.

**12-2** Buying Decisions in Supermarkets, 1949–1965

| Year | CATEGORIES (Figures in percentages) | | | |
|------|------------------------|-------------------|----------------------|-----------|
| | Specifically planned | Generally planned | Brand substitution | Unplanned |
| 1949 | 33.4 | 26.7 | 1.5 | 38.4 |
| 1954 | 29.2 | 21.0 | 1.8 | 48.0 |
| 1959 | 30.5 | 15.9 | 2.7 | 50.9 |
| 1965 | 31.1 | 17.2 | 1.8 | 49.9 |

SOURCE: *Consumer Buying Habits Studies* (Film Department, E. I. duPont de Nemours and Company, Inc., Wilmington, Delaware, 1949, 1954, 1959, 1965).

Impulse is affected by a number of factors such as brands, shelf space, display location, product location, economics, time, and the buyer's personality and shopping habits. Impulse buying is typically, though not exclusively, associated with food items. Actually, there may be little to differentiate an impulse or unplanned purchase from a planned one. One study indicated that 87 percent of impulse purchases involved products that the customer had bought before (Kollat, 1968). Income and education do not seem to be associated with customer differences in unplanned purchasing; amount of the bill, frequency of purchase, use of shopping lists, and number of years of marriage seem to be variables that affect the proportion of unplanned purchases. The physical layout of a store and its promotional campaign certainly may cause a housewife to buy some items that she had not planned to buy. But many women deliberately shop with only a few basics in mind, fully expecting to be reminded of other purchases as they push the shopping cart down the half-mile or so of aisles.

### Deliberation

The extent of deliberation in buying decisions varies a great deal. Deliberation is typically measured by the time spent searching out information and evaluating the alternatives. A family planning next summer's vacation may deliberate over several months; they may extend the process for a new house over an even longer period of time. The process varies according to the item purchased, the cost involved, and

## 12-3 Length of Planning Period for Durable Goods Purchases

The question was: "Could you tell me how long you people were thinking or talking about buying a _____* before you actually bought it?"

| Length of planning period | Percentage of buyers |
|---|---|
| Several years | 8 |
| One or two years | 13 |
| Several months | 30 |
| One or two months | 9 |
| A few weeks | 19 |
| A few days | 13 |
| One day or less | 4 |
| Not ascertained | 4 |
| All cases | 100 |

*Durable goods such as TV, refrigerator, stove, washing machine.

SOURCE: Lincoln H. Clark (ed.), Era Mueller, and George Katona, "A Study of Purchase Decisions," in *Consumer Behavior* (New York: New York University Press, 1955), p. 44.

the people who are doing the buying. Typically most people do not prefer a long planning period, for when a need is identified they like to satisfy it as quickly as possible. Note in 12-3 the length of planning periods for purchases of durable goods. One-half of the buyers reported planning periods of more than two months. Another study, by General Electric, showed that among selected appliances radios required the shortest planning period and clothes dryers the longest (Pratt, 1967).

How much information a buyer looks for depends partly on the amount and quality of the information he already possesses, on the degree of risk he perceives in the contemplated purchase, and on the time and cost of searching for information. He may ask friends and relatives; he may read advertisements closely; he may examine *Consumer Reports;* he may rely on sales personnel; he may rely on his own judgments of quality and price. However he gathers it, he uses the information selectively, accepting and rejecting it, bearing in mind the authority of the source of any piece of information.

The search for information differs from one buyer to another and for the same buyer from one situation to another. The purchase of a home, one of the largest single expenditures most people make in their lifetimes, illustrates the search for information. The individual decisions made in purchasing a home, the duration of the active search period, and other search-related data are given in 12-4.

The effort involved in the search process in part determines the length of the prepurchase period. Many factors influence the search time. The time involved in the buying process is also influenced by the number of alternatives. Choosing between two similar items is quite different from making a choice among a number of dissimilar choices. Sometimes a consumer will spend considerable time on decisions requiring complex choices, but once the choice becomes too complicated, he is likely to become impulsive.

## 12-4 A Study of the Search Process of 129 Home Buyers

| Difficulty of decision in descending order |
|---|
| Price range to consider |
| When to purchase |
| Neighborhood to live in |
| Where to apply for mortgage |
| Whom to contact for assistance in finding houses |
| Whom to rely upon for financing |
| Style of home |
| Where to purchase household and property insurance |

| Duration of the active search period | Percentage of respondents | Number of houses entered for inspection | Percentage of respondents |
|---|---|---|---|
| <1 week | 12 | 1 | 14 |
| 1–4 weeks | 24 | 2–4 | 15 |
| 5–8 weeks | 15 | 5–9 | 30 |
| 9–12 weeks | 15 | 10–14 | 16 |
| 13–52 weeks | 23 | 15–20 | 16 |
| More than 1 year | 11 | 25+ | 9 |

| Factors extending search | Percentage of respondents |
|---|---|
| Could not find style, location, etc., combination | 45 |
| In no hurry | 11 |
| Time to find mortgage financing | 11 |
| Changing family situation | 10 |
| Unable to look around frequently | 5 |
| Need to find buyer for previous home | 5 |
| Husband/wife hesitant to buy home | 5 |
| Unfamiliar with town or area | 3 |
| Other | 15 |

| Factors reducing search | |
|---|---|
| Found good value; did not want to lose it | 48 |
| Buyer/owner wanted to occupy our former residence; lease expired | 22 |
| Husband/wife busy; wanted to minimize search time | 12 |
| Wife expecting baby, wanted to settle | 6 |
| Wanted to get settled before school started | 5 |
| Wanted to stop paying rent, avoid double payments | 4 |
| Living arrangements/funds provided by company running out | 4 |
| Other | 11 |

| Distribution of information sources | |
|---|---|
| Newspaper advertisements | 40 |
| Real estate agent | 8 |
| Walking or riding around | 21 |
| Friends | 7 |
| Coworkers, business associates | 6 |
| Builders and contractors | 2 |
| Newspaper articles | 2 |
| Magazine articles, pamphlets | 3 |
| Books | 4 |
| Yellow pages | – |
| Housing advisors/counselors | 3 |
| Lending institution personnel | – |
| Radio or television | – |

SOURCE: Donald J. Hempel, *The Role of the Real Estate Broker in the Home Buying Process*, Real Estate Report No. 7 (Storrs, Conn.: Center for Real Estate and Urban Economic Studies. The University of Connecticut, 1969).

**12-5** Range of Consumers' Predispositions To Buy

| | BUYING CONTINUUM | ATTITUDE SCALE |
|---|---|---|
| I | Firm and immediate intent to buy a specific brand. | "I am going to buy some right away." "I am going to buy some soon." |
| II | Positive intention without definite buying plans. | "I am certain I will buy some sometime." "I will probably buy some sometime." |
| III | Neutrality: might buy, might not buy. | "I may buy some sometime." "I might buy some sometime, but I doubt it." |
| IV | Inclined not to buy the brand, but not definite about it. | "I don't think I'm interested in buying any." "I probably will never buy any." |
| V | Firm intention not to buy the brand. | "I know I'm not interested in buying any." "If somebody gave me some, I would give it away just to get rid of it." |
| VI | Never considered buying. | "I have never heard of the brand." |

SOURCE: Adapted from William D. Wells, "Measuring Readiness To Buy," *Harvard Business Review*, Vol. 39, No. 4 (July–August 1961), p. 82.

The actual position of a potential buyer along the time line of buying may be of importance to the marketer who is attempting to estimate his sales for the coming period. It is possible to ask people where they stand in relation to the purchase of a given commodity. Their attitudes toward buying can be related to a buying continuum, as in 12-5, so that the marketer has some idea of their buying intentions.

## THE ACTUAL PURCHASE

The actual purchase, when the exchange of goods takes place, is the focus of marketing activity. In a sense, the buy/sell decision is the goal of marketing. The actual buying decision can be simple or complex. It may be one primary decision, as in the case of deciding to buy a new house, or it may be a number of smaller decisions (location, size, price, and style). It can be made by a group or by an individual. It can be a recurrent experience or a once-in-a-lifetime event. An illustration of a buying decision is shown in 12-6 where the buyer first recognizes a need, secures information, considers alternatives, and makes a decision to buy a particular brand of fertilizer at a given store. His level of satisfaction with the brand becomes input for the next fertilizer purchase. There are several elements to the actual purchase decision, such as risk-reduction, decision-making, and buying strategies, all of which will be discussed in this section.

### Risk

Most buying decisions are made with some degree of risk. Knowing this, a buyer takes steps to reduce the risk by relying on a familiar brand or retailer, reading advertisements carefully, asking friends, and keep-

**12-6** Stages of a Buying Decision

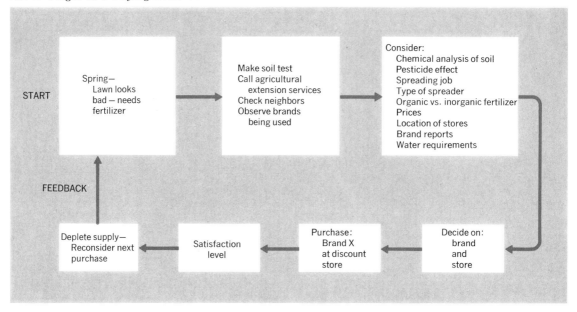

ing a mental note as to the satisfaction level of a previous brand's performance. Frequently the risk can be eliminated in the prepurchase buying phase, but there are times when the buyer is mindful of the risk at the very point of purchase. A study of telephone shopping illustrates the influence of risk. Telephone shopping can produce good sales and profits for a store and is of course convenient for consumers. Yet a study in New York and Cleveland showed that less than half of the housewives shopped by phone. Why? Because the housewives perceived elements of risk, the amount and kind of which varied from one product to another. In other words, the risk element was often too great to assure them that they would get what they wanted. Risk could of course be reduced by reading the information supplied in newspaper ads. But when a product involved a number of decisions, as contrasted with a single decision, the perceived risk was too high. For example, a woman's handbag requires more decision processes than the limited number of decisions involved in the purchase of bed linens. It is interesting to note those products considered to be "high risk" relative to "low risk" (Cox and Rich, 1964):

| High risk | | Low risk | |
| --- | --- | --- | --- |
| Blouses | 24 | Bed linen | 82 |
| Girdles | 30 | Stockings | 59 |
| Handbags | 13 | Men's underwear | 55 |

Figures represent percentage of women who would not worry about ordering the item by phone.

**12-7** Husbands' and Wives' Reports Regarding Decision-Making Patterns

| Answers | WHO IN THE FAMILY DECIDES . . . | | | |
|---|---|---|---|---|
| | When it's time to buy a car? | | When it's time to buy household goods and furniture? | |
| | Husbands say | Wives say | Husbands say | Wives say |
| Wife only | 3% | 3% | 24% | 25% |
| Wife predominates | 1 | 1 | 12 | 10 |
| Both equally | 31 | 23 | 53 | 51 |
| Husband predominates | 5 | 9 | 4 | 5 |
| Husband only | 51 | 54 | 4 | 6 |
| Other answers | 9 | 10 | 3 | 3 |
| | 100% | 100% | 100% | 100% |

SOURCE: Elizabeth H. Wolgast, "Do Husbands or Wives Make Purchasing Decisions?" *Journal of Marketing*, Vol. 23, No. 2 (October 1958), p. 153.

## The Decision-Maker

Who in a family makes the purchase decision? As 12-7 indicates, responsibility for the decision may be perceived differently by husbands and wives and may depend on the item being considered. Certainly we would expect purchase decisions to reflect the respective roles of the family members. In addition to husband and wife, the child today is important in the marketplace. Many items in stores and a great deal of advertising are aimed directly at the child market. In this connection it has been noted that a mother's purchase of her child's preferred packaged cereals is related to the child's assertiveness and her own child-centeredness (Berey and Pollay, 1968). Of course, many items are not available to a child except through an intermediary, but the child can still be quite influential.

## Purchase Behavior and Strategies

Research has indicated that women spend more time than men shopping in supermarkets, and that blacks spend more time than whites, morning shoppers more than late-afternoon shoppers, and the young more than the old (see 12-8). Buyers have preferences for days of the week, and Thursday, Friday, and Saturday tend to be the more popular shopping days. Further, more than half the shoppers patronize more than one supermarket (*Progressive Grocer*, 1965).

Buyers consciously or unconsciously develop guidelines or buying rules for themselves. These rules, or strategies, can be of many kinds. Some buyers are deal-prone, watching for specials much of the time. Describing a deal-prone buyer is difficult, but it is thought that the strategy can be related to the age of the buyer, to the number of brands and units purchased, and to his brand loyalty. Some buyers are

**12-8** Number of Minutes Spent Shopping

| Variables | TYPE OF NEIGHBORHOOD | | | | |
|---|---|---|---|---|---|
| | Small town | Blue-collar | Black | Young married | High-income |
| **Sex** | | | | | |
| Male | 17.8 | 19.5 | 22.4 | 17.3 | 16.0 |
| Female | 22.9 | 22.2 | 23.7 | 21.7 | 20.0 |
| **Age** | | | | | |
| Under 25 years old | 22.5 | 24.4 | 21.6 | 23.2 | 22.0 |
| 25–34 years old | 25.1 | 22.9 | 20.3 | 20.0 | 19.0 |
| 35–44 years old | 23.2 | 19.2 | 23.0 | 21.6 | 20.0 |
| 45–54 years old | 19.0 | 25.3 | 25.9 | — | 17.0 |
| 55 years old & over | 20.9 | 18.0 | 25.3 | — | 18.0 |
| **Time of Day** | | | | | |
| 9:00 a.m. to 12:00 noon | 24.1 | 21.9 | 26.4 | 21.2 | 20.5 |
| 12:00 noon to 3:00 p.m. | 20.8 | 20.3 | 23.5 | 22.7 | 19.3 |
| 3:00 p.m. to 6:00 p.m. | 21.6 | 22.2 | 19.2 | 19.5 | 16.7 |
| **Amount of Sale** | | | | | |
| Under $5 | 12.4 | 11.4 | 16.2 | 7.9 | 9.1 |
| $5–$9.99 | 15.4 | 18.8 | 23.6 | 16.4 | 17.3 |
| $10–$14.99 | 25.0 | 22.6 | 25.7 | 16.5 | 22.7 |
| $15–$19.99 | 27.6 | 27.3 | 27.3 | 24.4 | 25.7 |
| $20–$24.99 | 28.2 | 30.1 | 29.2 | 26.9 | 28.9 |
| $25– & over | 32.0 | 30.9 | 36.3 | 33.8 | 36.4 |

SOURCE: "Consumer Dynamics in the Supermarket," *Progressive Grocer*, 1965, p. K34.

brand-prone, a characteristic that seems to be related to family size, employment status of wife, education, and rate of consumption. Some buyers prefer private brands (those brands owned or sponsored by retailers or wholesalers) to manufacturer brands, and others have the opposite preference. Research suggests that private-brand buyers are likely to pay less than manufacturer-brand buyers, but this is not always so (Carman, 1969).

Buyers do not necessarily operate across the board with any one strategy. They may be brand-prone with some items and price- or store-prone with other items. In an emergency they may have to buy what is available at that time, whereas in other instances they may buy only when a special deal becomes available. Young married couples may buy differently as they gain experience with brands, products, and stores. Despite the differences in strategies among buyers and for the same buyer over time or in different situations, a retailer is more mindful of his total flow of business than he is the individual differences. And, of course, there are many similarities among buyers, even among American and British buyers (Ehrenberg and Goodhardt, 1968).

A housewife knows her family's preferences better for some products than for others. Products with highly visible brands (cereals) have strong buyer preferences. The housewife likes to maintain some stability in her brand selection because it simplifies her buying, but the degree of brand stability varies by person and by product. Beer and cigarette purchases, for example, show more brand stability than do cereals (Newman, 1966).

For many items a buyer relies on the salesman. The selling process here can be examined in terms of the interaction between the salesman and buyer. In one study of appliances the statements and questions were categorized by Interaction-Process Analysis, described in Chapter 11. The number of times each of several items was mentioned during the average sales presentation is shown as follows (Pennington, 1968):

| | |
|---|---|
| Price | 11.2 times per selling transaction |
| Product features | 6.5 |
| Timing of purchase | 3.0 |
| Brand | 1.9 |
| Terms | 1.7 |
| Delivery | 1.7 |
| Service | 1.2 |
| Guarantee | .9 |
| Product quality | .6 |
| Styling | .5 |

Pennington also reported that shoppers often attempted to change concession limits when they had shopped in several stores and had deliberated. Further, more than half the shoppers made purchases within two or three days of beginning their search and 63 percent did so within two weeks. When a purchase was actually made, delivery and terms were more important topics of discussion than when no purchase was made, as would be expected.

The actual purchase is the outcome of the entire purchase deliberation. It is the point at which all the marketing efforts toward influencing buyer behavior are ultimately tested.

## THE POSTPURCHASE PHASE

Since most buying is repetitive, the postpurchase aspects of buyer behavior are important to the marketer interested in repeat business. Most purchases involve learning, which can be quite influential in future purchases. We daily make decisions regarding products, services, brands, and retailers, and the outcomes of these decisions are filed away in our minds for future use. Most firms depend on repeat business, and as a matter of fact they cultivate it through credit cards, charge accounts, direct mail solicitations, and sale notices, as well as through value and service.

Each purchase decision initiates a feedback process that in turn becomes input into the buyer's next purchase decision. The purchase, ownership, and use of a product bring about negative and positive feelings toward the product, store, and manufacturer. These feelings feed into the complex network of the buyer's learning experiences and become important input to his buying processes. A study of auto buying suggests the role of brand experience in terms of both prepurchase and actual purchase—the "search for additional alternatives is higher when the first brand considered is not the brand owned. . . . [and] there is a direct relationship between repurchase of the currently owned make and previous ownership of that make" (May, 1969).

## Satisfaction

These findings lead directly into the matter of satisfaction, which in the marketing context is "a mental state of being adequately or inadequately rewarded in a buying situation for the sacrifice the buyer has undergone" (Howard and Sheth, 1969). The buyer is looking for value as manifested in the ratio of quality to price. He has expectations about the product, and the price he pays relates to those expectations and so establishes a satisfaction level.

The role of satisfaction in buying behavior is shown in diagrammatic form in 12-9. If a person is not satisfied with a brand, he may change brands. His level of satisfaction is determined by his level of aspiration,

**12-9** Role of Satisfaction in Buying Behavior

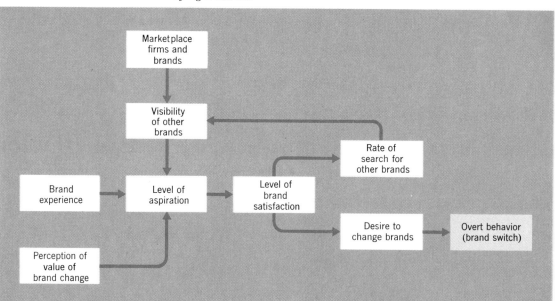

SOURCE: Adapted from Francesco M. Nicosia, *Consumer Decision Processes: Marketing and Advertising Implications* (Englewood Cliffs, N.J.: Prentice-Hall, 1966), pp. 110–111.

**12-10** Why Customers in Five Different Types of Neighborhoods Switched Stores

| Reason for switching | TYPE OF NEIGHBORHOOD (Answers in percentages) | | | | |
|---|---|---|---|---|---|
| | Young married | Small town | Blue-collar | Upper-middle-income | Black |
| Poor meats | 22 | 5 | 12 | 12 | 33 |
| High prices | 16 | 27 | 20 | 14 | — |
| Rude personnel | 4 | 16 | 12 | 9 | 10 |
| Unclean | 7 | 8 | 20 | 8 | 10 |
| Poor selection | 7 | 5 | — | 4 | 20 |
| Poor produce | 15 | — | — | 11 | 10 |
| Out-of-stock | 4 | 3 | 12 | 3 | — |
| Inconvenient | 2 | 10 | 12 | 10 | — |
| Poor services | 9 | 5 | — | 8 | — |
| Too crowded | 4 | — | — | 6 | — |
| General poor quality | — | 3 | 12 | 2 | — |

SOURCE: "Consumer Dynamics in the Supermarket," *Progressive Grocer*, 1965, p. K32.

which in turn is determined by his experience, his perception of the advantage of a brand change, and the visibility of other brands.

The concept of satisfaction is not simply academic, and it applies to retail stores as well as to brands. When housewives were asked in one survey why they switched stores, they gave the reasons shown in 12-10.

A laboratory experiment by Richard N. Cardozo indicated that customer satisfaction with a product is influenced by the effort expended to acquire it and expectations concerning it. If consumers spend considerable effort to obtain a product, they may have greater satisfaction than if it is easily obtained. Cardozo had subjects evaluate a gift item by indicating the price for which they thought it should sell: their effort was manipulated by varying the task in several ways. Relating efforts and expectations, Cardozo found that high effort combined with low expectations produced the highest product evaluation. High expectations combined with low effort provided the lowest product evaluation (Cardozo, 1965).

RATINGS OF GIFT ITEM

| Effort | Expectations | |
|---|---|---|
| | Low | High |
| Low | 51 | 35 |
| High | 54 | 44 |

Cardozo suggests that satisfaction may "depend not only upon the product itself, but also upon the experience surrounding acquisition of the product." Customer satisfaction, then, is undoubtedly more than simple product evaluation, for it includes selling, advertising, location of store, price, and other ingredients of the marketing mix.

In another study of satisfaction 300 urban families were interviewed about their buying practices and their satisfactions with purchases. The study identified "consumership components" that included the extent, length, and specificity of planning; the judgment process (information-seeking, consideration of alternatives, and guidelines for buying); and the usefulness of planning and judgment in terms of buying actions. The best predictor of satisfaction turned out to be judgment, a kind of economist's concept of the rational man. Thus the study "confirmed the assumption of the economist that rationality acts to increase satisfaction by joining more effectively ends and means, as compared with the situation in which irrationality and impulsive action characterize the decision-process" (Hill, 1963).

It is possible to construct an index that would indicate the degree of consumer satisfaction for brands, retailers, and manufacturers. The index, which could guide both consumers and business firms, would have to include many of the forces already described as well as environmental considerations previously ignored, such as pollution caused by disposable packaging.

Satisfaction influences future buying decisions through feedback by reinforcement, a fact that companies would bear in mind to their advantage.

## Loyalty

Loyalty is usually taken to refer to repeat purchase patterns, yet it implies, beyond mere repetition, a commitment to a brand, store, or manufacturer, a commitment that can persist for years. It is an elusive concept, as shown in 12-11.

Despite all the changes that take place in one's life, there is evidence to suggest that brand preferences linger on. In a study that examined preferences and usage of brands in 1941 and 1961 for the same people, it was found that the average amount of agreement between their stated 1941 preferences and their 1961 preferences was 26 percent. There was little indication that sex, intelligence, or marital status was related to persistence of preference. Age did have some effect, for older subjects seemed to stick with the same brands more than younger people. On this point, Lester Guest concluded:

> There still is no indication that there is a general loyalty factor in people. Rather it appears that it is related to specific products and brands, as well as to special pressures impinging on people . . . even early childhood experiences exert considerable influence upon later brand purchasing behavior. (Guest, 1964.)

Other studies of loyalty reveal some interesting findings. A study of beer drinking over a two-month period indicated that price can be taken

## 12-11

**Who Is Loyal to Brands?**

There are no socioeconomic characteristics associated with different degrees of brand loyalty for low-price, frequently purchased items (tentative). "In the absence of positive evidence to the contrary, manufacturers had better check carefully before they make the assumption that . . . they can distinguish between high-loyalty and low-loyalty families in their particular market by certain socioeconomic characteristics."

There is *not* a significant proportion of loyalty-prone families, that is, housewives who tend to have the same degree of brand loyalty in various product classes.

No truly significant correlation exists between brand loyalty behavior and store loyalty behavior.

There is no relationship between size of purchase and brand loyalty.

SOURCE: Ross M. Cunningham, "Brand Loyalty—What, Where, How Much?" *Harvard Business Review*, Vol. 34 (January–February 1956). pp. 116–128.

as an important cue to product quality and that perceived quality may be an important determinant of brand loyalty (McConnell, 1968). In another study, using data from a panel of housewives, James M. Carman hypothesized that the single most important predictor of brand loyalty is store loyalty. He also found that consumers who are not shopping-prone will shop in a very small number of stores and, within those stores, will remain loyal to a very small number of brands. Contrary to some findings, Carman also concluded that personal characteristics of consumers explain differences in store loyalty. Consumers most interested in status were the most loyal, and housewives who socialize with neighbors seemed to exhibit a higher degree of brand loyalty than those who did not (Carman, 1970).

A conclusion from another loyalty study suggests that "consumers tend to be less loyal toward products with many brands available, where number of purchases and dollar expenditures per buyer are high, where prices are relatively active, and where consumers might be expected to use simultaneously a number of brands of the product. Consumers are brand loyal in markets where brands tend to be widely distributed and where market share is concentrated in the leading brand" (Farley, 1964). And another study indicates that a buyer's loyalty to a store increased loyalty to private brands (distributor brands) carried by that store (Rao, 1969).

Most loyalty studies simply measure repeat sales, but they do not delve into the *attachment* felt by the consumer for a brand or store. It is clear that a great deal of repeat buying does exist, but it is also clear that considerable brand and store switching take place. Since any ingredient of the marketing mix can influence a buyer, brand loyalty has to contend with price competition, new products, advertising, product availability, and external forces such as personal influence. The evidence isn't very precise, yet intuitively it would seem that people do feel some attachment toward brands and stores. There is certainly an element of familiarity and experience that lessens the risk for the buyer. Clearly, there are many factors to take into account in attempting to generalize about the extent of and reasons for brand loyalty. And it is worth reminding ourselves that single elements in buying are seldom overpowering. Buyers will drop into and out of any brand pattern for all kinds of reasons.

### Dissonance

The theory of cognitive dissonance, first proposed by Leon Festinger, suggests that an individual consumer possesses many pieces of information, or cognitions, that he wishes to have consistent with one another. If the cognitions are inconsistent, he will find himself in a state of tension; in order to reduce the tension he will try to reduce the inconsistency, that is, to reduce the dissonance between his cognitions. Thus, whenever a consumer makes a purchase there is apt to be some dissonance. A housewife, for instance, may have chosen Brand A even though she was aware of favorable attributes of Brand B. Or she may have spent a considerable sum on a new dress and have to reconcile the satisfaction from the purchase with the sorrow of writing the check for it. Reducing dissonance is accomplished in many ways: most commonly, a person will actually change his cognitions or selectively admit information. The housewife may upgrade Brand A and downgrade Brand B or she might read advertisements about Brand A but not about Brand B. If dissonance cannot be reduced satisfactorily, she might switch to still another brand in a subsequent purchase decision. A number of factors causing dissonance are listed in 12-12.

A great deal of experimentation has been performed on dissonance-inducing situations, but because results are not consistent, some scholars question the theory as well as the applicability of the results to marketing. In the earliest marketing-dissonance study, new-car buyers were questioned about their reading of advertisements. It was found that buyers of Brand A tended to read advertisements about Brand A, Brand B buyers about Brand B, and so on, thus confirming the theory. A number of subsequent similar studies yielded results that are not wholly consistent with the theory, however.

Regardless of how reliable the theory turns out to be, we do know that it is important to please the buyer in order to gain repeat sales. Anything that can be done to make the buyer happy about his purchase would seem to be consistent with good merchandising practices. A follow-up letter to an appliance buyer telling him that he "now joins the ranks of thousands of satisfied customers" may help him reduce dissonance, if he feels any. But whether they feel dissonance or not, buyers are likely to switch brands and stores. The implication of dissonance theory for marketing, then, is that it may be a factor affect-

## 12-12 Dissonance and Buying Situations

| | Factors affecting dissonance | Buying situation | Conditions with high dissonance expectation | Conditions with low dissonance expectation |
|---|---|---|---|---|
| 1 | Attractiveness of rejected alternative | A high-school graduate decides which of several pictures to order. | Three of the proofs have both attractive and desirable features. | One of the proofs clearly is superior to the rest. |
| 2 | Negative factors in chosen alternative | A man chooses between two suits of clothing. | The chosen suit has the color the man wanted but not the style. | The chosen suit has both the color and style the man wanted. |
| 3 | Number of alternatives | A teacher shops for a tape-recorder. | There are eight recorders from which to choose. | There are only two recorders from which to choose. |
| 4 | Cognitive overlap | A housewife shops for a vacuum sweeper. | A salesman offers two similarly priced tank types. | A salesman offers a tank type and an upright cleaner. |
| 5 | Importance of cognitions involved | A child buys a present for her sister. | The sister has definite preferences for certain kinds of music. | The sister has no strong tastes for certain records. |
| 6 | Positive inducement | Parents decide to buy a photo-enlarger for their son. | The son already has hobby equipment and does not need the enlarger. | The son never has had a true hobby and needs something to keep him occupied. |
| 7 | Discrepant or negative action | A man purchases an expensive watch. | The man had never before paid more than $35 for a watch. | Fairly expensive watches had been important gift items in the man's family. |
| 8 | Information available | Housewife buys a detergent. | The housewife has no experience with the brand purchased—it is a new variety. | The housewife has read and heard a good deal about the product and has confidence in the manufacturer. |
| 9 | Anticipated dissonance | A small boy buys a model airplane. | The boy anticipates trouble at home because of the cost of the model. | The boy expects no trouble at home relative to the purchase. |
| 10 | Familiarity and knowledge | A family buys a floor polisher. | The item was purchased without much thought. | The item was purchased after a careful selection process. |

SOURCE: Robert J. Holloway, "An Experiment on Consumer Dissonance," *Journal of Marketing*, Vol. 30 (January 1967), p. 40.

ing the buyer's satisfaction and as such it can have a bearing on the next purchase decision and so should be taken into account.

The discussion to this point has focused on the decision process—the prepurchase phase, the actual purchase, and the postpurchase phase. We have looked at the total buying process, the forces that influence it, the deliberation preceding it, the way in which people buy, and the importance of feedback resulting from the decision. In the next section we will present a number of different models of buying behavior that will integrate all of the preceding information.

## MODELS OF BUYING BEHAVIOR

Because the buying process is so important in marketing, it would be ideal to have a complete model of buying behavior. A model is an attempt to diagram the elements and relationships among the elements, in this case buyer behavior forces and variables. A model is based on suppositions or assumptions that may or may not correspond exactly with the real marketing world but is, nevertheless, useful in helping us to understand what goes on in a buying process.

Scholars have attempted to further the understanding of buyer behavior by building models that show the relationships among a number of variables, such as the internal and external forces and the buying decisions. Such models show the system of buying, with its attendant relationships, as a logical flow process with the consumer proceeding down a time line toward a decision. Models help to explain the buying process, they can help to predict behavior, and they can be useful to marketing managers in serving the consumer, but they cannot be taken as precise descriptions of real-world situations.

Knowledge of buyer behavior is still in its infancy—human behavior is, after all, extremely complex—so a model can only be a beginning for understanding the process. But researchers continue in their efforts to shed additional light on the entire process of buying. It should be recognized, then, that the following models are not provided as the final word. They do not cover every known variable, but each proposal makes its own contribution. Indeed, precisely because each tends to emphasize something unique, we will present a number of models.

We have already given a simple model that deals very generally with forces, relationships, and decisions, but it does not provide other additional information.

$$\text{Inputs} \longrightarrow \text{Buyer} \longrightarrow \text{Outputs}$$

### The Katona Model

The *Katona* model, 12-13, is a morphological approach that explains the way in which a purchase decision is made. This model shows the environmental stimuli coming into contact with the internal forces that influence buyer behavior. The enabling conditions such as income

**12-13** The Katona Decision Process: A Flow Chart

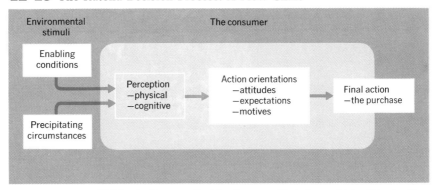

SOURCE: Francesco M. Nicosia, *Consumer Decision Processes: Marketing and Advertising Implications* (Englewood Cliffs, N.J.: Prentice-Hall, 1966), p. 95.

make it possible for a buyer to make a purchase. Precipitating conditions are "triggers," such as running out of milk or having a car accident. The intervening variables in this model are the forces, such as attitudes, that, of course, influence the decision.

## The Engel Model

The *Engel* model, 12-14, includes five principal stages: (I) problem recognition; (II) external search; (III) alternative evaluation; (IV) purchase processes; and (V) postpurchase evaluation. "This formulation attempts to describe the behavioral processes that occur from the stage where consumers recognize that some decision is necessary to the stage where postpurchase evaluation of the brand and its attributes affects those attitudes, values, and personality characteristics stored in the central control unit" (Engel, Kollat, Blackwell, 1968). The model shows how the various internal and external forces described in the previous chapter operate as influences on the buying process. It also shows that there are several paths for the buyer to take at each of the five major phases. A buyer does not have to be aware that he is passing through each of the phases and, as pointed out earlier, he may even skip the external search and/or the evaluation of alternatives. For a purchase that is made frequently, a person forms a habit so there would be little need to go through either of these two steps. Remember that the entire process shown in the model may take minutes or years.

## The Andreasen Model

The *Andreasen* model, 12-15, emphasizes attitudes and attitude changes. An attitude change is caused by exposure to all kinds of information that comes to the buyer over the time period: some he may seek and some may come to him involuntarily. The model shows a kind of information-processing cycle with stages of stimuli, perception, and filtration, disposition changes, and several outcome possibilities. The

**12-14** The Engel Model, Showing Outcomes of the Purchasing Decision

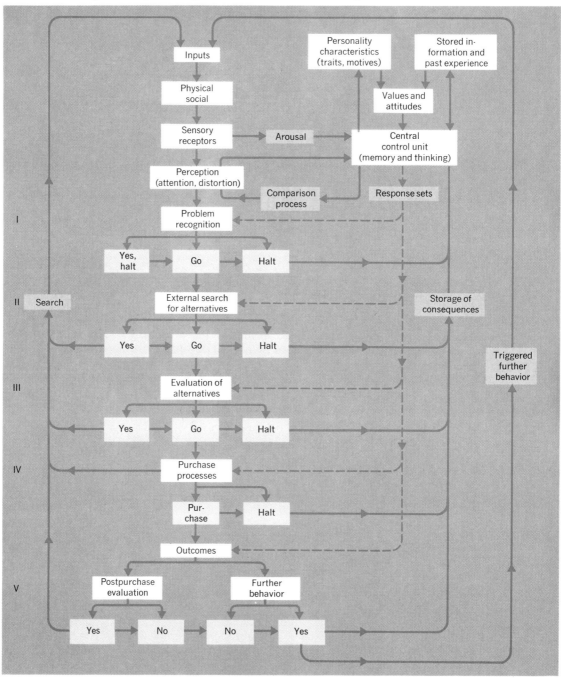

SOURCE: James F. Engel, David T. Kollat, and Roger D. Blackwell, *Consumer Behavior* (New York: Holt, Rinehart and Winston, 1968), p. 50.

**12-15** The Andreasen Model of Complex Consumer Decisions

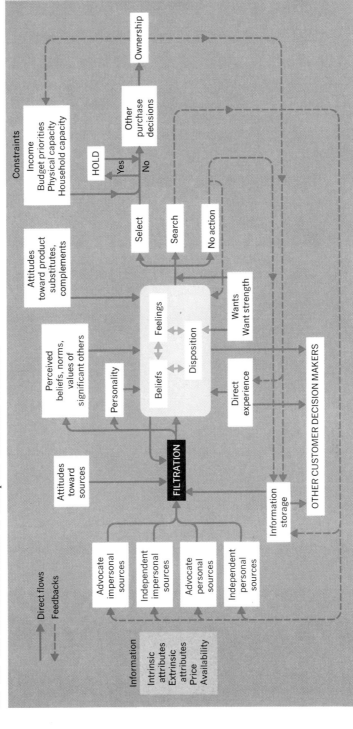

SOURCE: Alan R. Andreasen, "Attitudes and Customer Behavior: A Decision Model," from Lee E. Preston (ed.), *New Research in Marketing* (Berkeley: Institute of Business and Economic Research, University of California, 1965), p. 16.

model is based on cognitive theory and Gestalt psychology, which emphasizes the person as a whole rather than isolated behaviors. Andreasen suggests a number of questions raised by the model.

(1) What is the relationship between individual characteristics (such as age, education, family status, and personality needs for cognitive clarity) and number and kinds of information sources sought during some specified searching period? (2) What kinds of information tend to be sought from particular information sources? (3) How is information about sources combined with information about products and services, brands, and outlets? What is the interaction between them? (4) How are messages (advertisements) selected and/or distorted in the filtration process? (5) How does one measure attitude disposition valences?" (Andreasen, 1965).

### The Nicosia Model

The *Nicosia* model presented in 12-16 is a simulation of the consumer decision-making process. Nicosia uses the technique of computer

**12-16** A Structure of Consumer Behavior: A Summary Flow Chart (Nicosia Model)

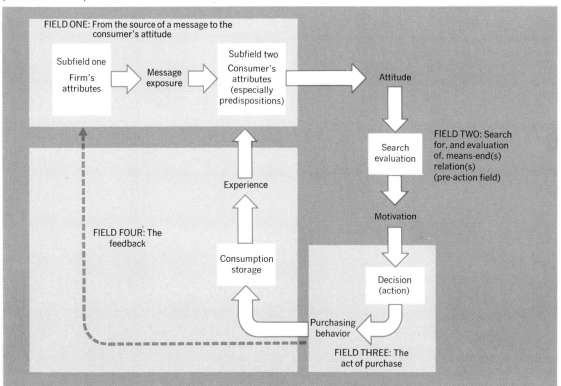

SOURCE: Francesco M. Nicosia, "Consumer Behavior and Computer Simulation," *Journal of Advertising Research,* Vol. 8 (March 1968), p. 32.

flow-charting to show the various forces involved and the relationships of those forces.

> By stating specific variables and their general interdependencies, it [the model] offers the necessary guidelines for data collection, and the technical bases for experimental simulations of the psychological, social, and economic processes it describes and of the possible reactions of these processes to different advertising policies. It also offers the necessary background for qualified interpretations of the results of experimental simulations. (Nicosia, 1968.)

The model is set up into four basic fields. Subfield One shows the flow of an advertising message to the consumer. (A new product is assumed in this model.) Subfield Two shows the merging of the advertising message with the person's psychological attributes. Coming from Subfield Two is an attitude toward the product that flows into Field Two where a search and an evaluation may be made. If the consumer is motivated to buy the product, the actual act of purchase occurs in Field Three. The results of the purchase become feedback into Field Four (Storage) that will be fed into the buying process the next time.

## The Howard-Sheth Model

The *Howard-Sheth* Model, 12-17, focuses on the element of repeat buying and presents the dynamics of purchase behavior over a period of time. The model shows that a person has motives and perceptions and that he may make a purchase decision which leads to learning. The model consists of input and output variables connected by the intervening variables—perceptual and learning constructs. The consumer has a set of motives and several courses of action: motives are matched with alternatives. With repeated purchases the decision process is simplified by the storing of information that has been fed back into the system.

This brief look at a number of buyer behavior models indicates some of the efforts made to understand the complicated process of buying. The models show interrelationships of the many variables, they stress different facets of the buying process, and they all attempt to provide an integrated and comprehensive picture of the total process as opposed to segments of the process. By understanding the buying process a marketer should be more effective in his efforts to satisfy buyers.

**12-17** A Simplified Description of the Theory of Buyer Behavior:
Howard-Sheth Model

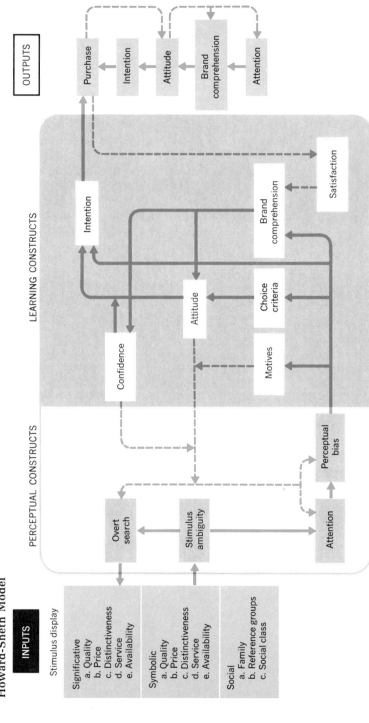

SOURCE: John A. Howard and Jagdish N. Sheth, *The Theory of Buyer Behavior*, (New York: John Wiley, 1969), p. 30.

# CONCLUDING COMMENTS

In this series of three chapters, we have attempted to locate the consumer in the total marketing environment. The many forces, internal and external, that influence the consumer have been briefly described in the earlier two chapters. The entire process has been examined in this final chapter, with models of the integrated process of buying serving as capstones.

Much has been learned through research about consumers. Much still remains to be learned. Each year some knowledge is added, some new theories are advanced, models are further developed, relevant variables are identified, and marketers determine more about how to serve consumers in a more efficient way so that satisfaction is increased.

Oh, you never plan. Planned consumption is almost as stifling as buying with cash. What I do is get out early in the morning with nothing very clear in mind and wander through the stores buying as impulse strikes. (Baker)

As we increase our ability to differentiate quality, our brand loyalty decreases.

Purchasing a known brand or a brand recommended by friends may be as intelligent a method of buying as carefully investigating the alternatives yourself.

As the size of the purchase increases, the planning period of buying lengthens.

The choice between two positive goals becomes more difficult and takes longer when they are seen as of equal value.

That spouse will dominate family decisions who is most closely tied to the prestige of kinship or to the material support of the family.

People tend to see and hear marketing communications that are favorable to their predispositions.

Buying decisions are not primarily the province of the husband. He may control the car decision but the wife makes the decisions for the home.

Buyers maximize returns received from devoting a given budget of time, effort, or money to shopping.

Advertising of durable, infrequently purchased products definitely and measurably stimulates purchases which otherwise would not be made.

Personal contacts seem to be most effective in changing opinion and behavior.

# QUESTIONS FOR REVIEW

**1.** Make a diagram (model) of one of your recent purchases.

**2.** What is impulse buying? For what kinds of goods does it become a factor?

**3.** What determines who in a family will become the dominant decision-maker?

**4.** List as many buying strategies as possible: e.g., always buy the private brand.

**5.** What is significant to the marketer about the postpurchase phase of buying?

**6.** Explain the relationship among the following terms: level of aspiration, satisfaction, rate of search, and value perception.

**7.** What is your understanding of the term "buyer loyalty"?

**8.** In what kinds of situations is cognitive dissonance likely to be a factor?

**9.** What does the Andreasen model (12-15) emphasize about consumer decisions?

**10.** How much of your buying is influenced by the desire to conform?

## Further Readings

*Note:* See the suggestions at the end of Chapter 10.

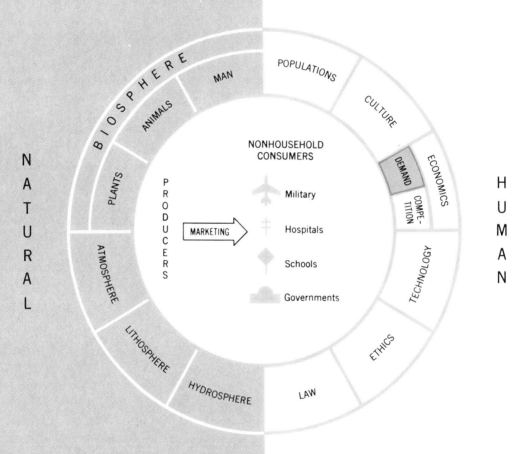

THE ENVIRONMENT

NATURAL

HUMAN

BIOSPHERE

MAN

ANIMALS

PLANTS

ATMOSPHERE

LITHOSPHERE

HYDROSPHERE

POPULATIONS

CULTURE

ECONOMICS

DEMAND

COMPE-TITION

TECHNOLOGY

ETHICS

LAW

PRODUCERS

MARKETING

NONHOUSEHOLD
CONSUMERS

Military

Hospitals

Schools

Governments

# CHAPTER 13
# NONHOUSEHOLD BUYER BEHAVIOR

*There are many important nonhousehold buyers—institutions, governments, and industries. Generally they buy in large volume and exhibit a rather high degree of professionalism. Emotional buying factors can be important, although rational factors predominate.*

This chapter focuses on the behavior of nonhousehold buyers, an extremely important economic activity that is frequently neglected in basic marketing courses. We are including material on three basic groups:

1. Institutional buyers that purchase for consumption and use, such as a college.

2. Government buyers that purchase primarily for consumption and use.

3. Industrial buyers that purchase for production as well as use, such as a manufacturer.

Nonhousehold buying takes place in environments quite different from those of the household buyers. The legal component of the nonhousehold environment is more important than that of the household because of the number, nature, and size of contracts. Technology is directly related to the nonhousehold market, especially for industrial and military markets. Demand, supply, and competition play vital roles in the economics of the nonhousehold marketplaces. The nonhousehold markets have a less personal orientation than household markets and the nonhousehold buyer is pictured as a more rational and professional buyer.

The individual purchase in nonhousehold buying is usually much larger than the typical household purchase. The department store buyer, for instance, who purchases household articles for resale will purchase appliances by the carload, dresses by the dozen or gross, and cosmetics by the case. The department store buyer has the consumer in mind at all times, but each part of his buying process reflects a more studied and professional approach than is usually the case with the household buyer. Lists of vendors are examined, alternatives are checked, competition is considered, and active negotiations with sellers (manufacturers) are maintained in order to get the best possible buys for the store. The store buyer is influenced by outside forces, such as customers and competition, and by inside forces, such as the goals of the management.

Nonhousehold buyers work in a variety of environments. The industrial buyer is deeply interested in profits and sees his buying activity as being closely related to the profit goal of his firm. Some institutional buyers too may be in profit-oriented environments, but many are not, as is the case with government buyers. Some are trustees of tax dollars and gear their activities to a service-oriented operation. We will first examine buying within the institution.

# INSTITUTIONAL BUYING

There are thousands of institutions—hospitals, libraries, schools, colleges, prisons, and associations—in the nonhousehold market. Some are government and others are private, but proper buying is critical for both types. Some items are secured for production but most are purchased for the use and consumption of the clientele of the particular institution. For example, the American Marketing Association publishes (or produces) two journals for its marketing members, the *Journal of Marketing* and the *Journal of Marketing Research*. A college library, on the other hand, purchases journals and books for the use of its readers.

*Hospital buyers* have a large variety of items to procure, from simple, inexpensive supplies such as paper tissue; through such articles as tape, sponges, catheters, stomach tubes, brushes, film, labels, powder, record forms, blood bank requests, scanning equipment, pencils, latex gloves, needles, sutures, drugs, microscopes, and food; to complex, expensive machinery such as X-ray equipment. A computer print-out of all the purchases would be hundreds of pages long. A good buyer can save a hospital a considerable amount of money. As an illustration the Fort Worth St. Joseph Hospital buyer substituted polyethylene-backed disposable diapers for rented linen reusable diapers. Though the monthly charge of the disposable diapers ran higher than the $500 rental charge for the linen variety, the plastic diapers were more effective in protecting bedding, with the result that laundry was reduced by 200 pounds per day, a savings of $1500 per year (Tanner, 1964).

The *purchasing department of a college* is another institutional buyer that is responsible for a bewildering array of goods and services. At one large university the buyers deal with 10,000 suppliers a year, handling everything from toothpicks for the cafeteria to monkeys for the laboratory. Their job is further complicated by administrative decentralization, which means that virtually every department and administrative unit submits its own purchasing requisitions. Policy manuals explain the process of centralized purchasing to staff members, but it is also necessary to have emergency and irregular purchasing routines. State universities typically require that every purchase in excess of some stated amount be offered on an open-bid basis. Vendors bid for the business and the bids are opened at a specified time and place where the winner is announced. The buying task of the university purchasing department can be made more vivid by the following list of actual responsibilities of each for several buyers.

Buyer A—Office equipment and contracts for vehicles, optical equipment, heating fuels, and elevator services

Buyer B—Animals, dry ice, gases, athletic uniforms

Buyer C—Air, boat, bus, and rail transportation

Buyer D—Hospital and laboratory equipment, nuclear instruments, office machines

Buyer E—Agricultural equipment and supplies, landscaping, laundry, musical supplies and instruments

Some items such as mimeographed paper may be purchased in carload lots for an entire university. Some items may be procured from other university units, as with photographic services or milk. Certain articles may be purchased on specifications set primarily by the using department—the Marketing department, for instance, may requisition a new typewriter with specified changeable typefaces, a requirement that would limit the competition to perhaps one supplier. If the requisition called for "one standard electric typewriter," however, bids could be requested from a number of firms handling different brands.

The university buyer operates within a number of restrictions in serving institutional needs. In a state university he may have to give preference to state or even local firms. He is subject to careful auditing, and therefore considerable paper work is necessary to verify the honesty of all purchasing. Not that safeguards are absent in the private sector, but typically governmental bodies build many safeguards to ascertain that the taxpayers' dollars are protected. The purchasing manager of a state university is both a governmental and college buyer, but he would belong to an association of college buyers and relate to them more closely than to government buyers outside the institution.

## GOVERNMENT BUYING

Thousands of government buyers annually place orders for vast quantities of goods and services. In describing some of the kinds of government buying, we will stress the federal government, but keep in mind that the same general environment exists for state and local governments.

Government buying in many ways is similar to other nonhousehold buying. A buyer recognizes a need and proceeds to locate a vendor who can supply the particular item involved. Frequently he buys according to routine requisitions. There are differences, notably the emphasis placed on the system of open bidding and honesty. The taxpayer must be protected, even at the risk of adding "protection" costs to the purchasing function. Thus government buyers have many restrictions and policies to follow in their procurement practices.

We will examine three broad categories of government buying: (1) The General Services Administration (GSA), (2) civil agencies, and (3) military departments.

### The Federal Government

*The General Services Administration* procures, stores, and issues items that are in general use by all government agencies. GSA offices, located throughout the nation, have responsibility for five major categories of goods and services.

Defense Materials Service—national stockpiles of strategic materials

Transportation and Communications Service—contract for services

Federal Supply Service—common services such as office supplies, refrigerators, vehicles, and stationery

Public Building Service—real estate and building construction

Utilization and Disposable Service—maintenance and disposal

The second main group is the buying done by each *civil agency*: the Atomic Energy Commission, National Aeronautics and Space Administration (NASA), Postal Service, Veterans Administration, and each of the administrative departments not mentioned above. NASA, which generally follows the regulations set forth in the Armed Services manual, employs a decentralized system of buying items ranging from routine office supplies to complex spacecraft systems. The buying for each of these agencies is dependent on congressional appropriations, and the funds vary according to congressional sentiment, war, and domestic priorities. If Congress decided to give additional priority to, say, pollution control, it might reduce expenditures for NASA or some other program.

The third category, *military buying*, has attracted a good deal of attention in recent years, especially as the conflict over war policies has focused the spotlight on military costs. Over a trillion dollars have been spent on military items since World War II. The amount of expenditures is part of the question but so also are waste and inefficiency. The environment of military procurement can be pictured as in 13-1.

The military buyer operates in a highly unusual market where technical capabilities often determine decisions, where few suppliers for certain products exist, where production frequently occurs after a sale is negotiated, and where many of the sellers are oriented more to government than to the private sector (Weidenbaum, 1968). There is considerable concentration in military business and there is some controversy over the amount of competition that actually exists. The military buyer operates in a fast-changing environment where technical advancements, sweeping procedural changes, and intelligence reports about foreign powers may force him to modify contracts already signed. One supplier has said that the military buyer is "more suspicious, more discriminating, more capable, more numerous, more cost-conscious, and more hedged about by restrictions and regulations imposed by his own superiors," than any other buyer (Durham, 1964). Critics of military procurement would deny this statement, pointing to overbuying, product failures, and known waste.

The Department of Defense is divided into four major buying organizations, each with its own buyers (both in Washington and at regional offices) who procure the multitude of items necessary to equip far-flung

**13-1** The Defense Marketing Function and Its Environment

Political eyeball

Oligopolistic supply

Competition

Market intelligence

Customer relations — Objective — Market planning

Change and obsolescence

Proposal formulation

Quasi-legalistic framework

Research orientation

SOURCE: Adapted from John J. Kennedy, "A Theory on Principles and Practices in Defense Marketing," in L. George Smith (ed.), *Reflections on Progress in Marketing*, American Marketing Association (December 1964), p. 449.

defense operations. For each organization an example of a specific subunit is given:

1. Department of the Army—e.g., Redstone Arsenal, Alabama, where the U.S. Army Missile Command is responsible for designing, procuring, producing, cataloging, and training personnel for rockets, guided missiles, air defense missile fire coordination equipment, and missile launching.

2. Department of the Navy—e.g., Submarine Base, New London, Connecticut, is responsible for compressed gases, dairy provisions, repair parts, submarine equipment, alarm and signal systems, sandblasting supplies, and disposal of radioactive waste material.

3. Department of the Air Force—e.g., San Antonio, Texas Air Material Area procures nuclear bombs, nuclear projectiles, nuclear war-

heads, batteries, time-measuring instruments, and hundreds of other items.

4. Defense Supply Agency, which supplies items common to the various military departments—e.g., Defense Construction Supply Center, Ohio, handles diesel engines, gardening implements, mining equipment, and many other items.

In most government buying all known responsible suppliers are, insofar as possible, given an equal chance to compete for contracts. The government publicizes its intentions by advertising in various media and by inviting bids from business firms on appropriate mailing lists.

In some instances, however, the government buys through direct negotiation with potential vendors. Negotiation is especially important in military and NASA procurement because there may be no existing technology to draw on and therefore research and development contracts may have to be let (see Rudelius, 1970). If the military wants a new device to seek out enemy forces, it may invite several companies to submit proposals. Firms that enter into such a contract face a high degree of uncertainty. It has been estimated, for instance, that $75 million were spent in developing proposals for the F-111 fighter. Buyers obviously must be highly skilled to appraise R & D contracts, and most generally, in fact, a group of experts will make the actual decision. (See 13-2, which illustrates an early military contract.)

**13-2** R & D Cycle for the Wright Brothers

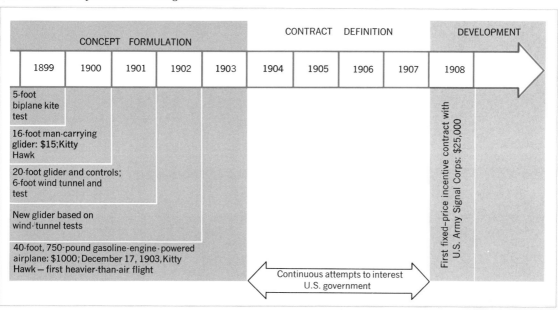

SOURCE: Martin Meyerson, "Price of Admission into the Defense Business," *Harvard Business Review*, Vol. 45 (July–August 1967), p. 122.

**13-3** The 71 Steps New York City Takes To Purchase Items like a Desk or a Truck (see text, p. 268)

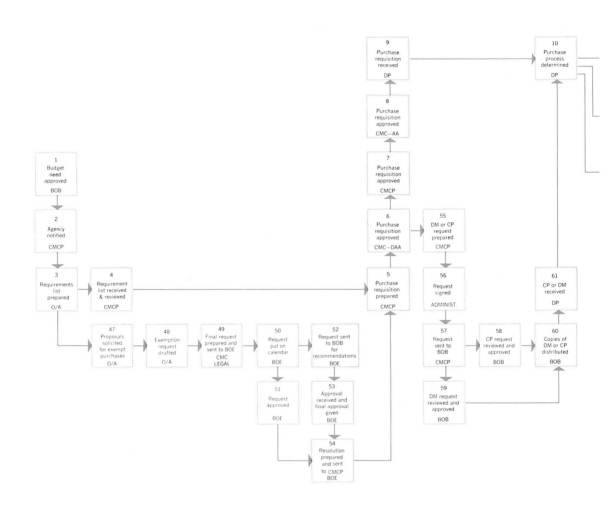

SOURCE: *The New York Times,* January 11, 1971, p. 36.

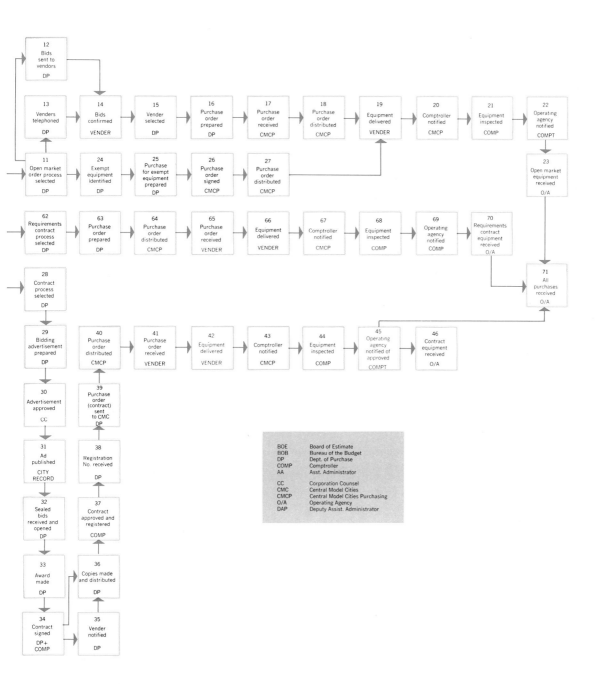

| | | |
|---|---|---|
| BOE | Board of Estimate | |
| BOB | Bureau of the Budget | |
| DP | Dept. of Purchase | |
| COMP | Comptroller | |
| AA | Asst. Administrator | |
| CC | Corporation Counsel | |
| CMC | Central Model Cities | |
| CMCP | Central Model Cities Purchasing | |
| O/A | Operating Agency | |
| DAP | Deputy Assist. Administrator | |

There are several kinds of government contracts. In the common "firm-fixed-price" contract the contractor delivers the item at the price he bids, regardless of the production costs. The "cost-reimbursement" contract bases profit on the original estimate of total costs. "Incentive" contracts provide a fee to the seller that is related to various combinations of cost, delivery, and performance. Clearly, buyers must be mindful of the nature of the contract.

There are also household buyers located within the framework of government. In the military, for example, there are commissaries instead of supermarkets and exchanges instead of department stores, ice cream parlors, and candy stores. In 1970 the military-consumer market amounted to $450 million on meats, poultry, and seafood; $220 million on drugs; and $209 million on soft drinks (*Army Times*, 1971). Household buyers in this case are military personnel and their dependents who spend hundreds of millions of dollars in the commissaries and exchanges. The purchasing agent for these government stores would be the counterpart to the department store buyer.

### Local Governments

In addition to the federal government, all the hundreds of other government units—states, counties, cities, and so on—also buy in enormous quantities; many of the same products are bought by means of the same processes. In smaller units of government a manager or even a town council member may do the buying, but in larger units the function will be located in a department of specialists. In a very large unit, such as New York City, the process can be very complicated indeed, as 13-3 shows.

# INDUSTRIAL BUYING

### Characteristics of Industrial Buying

Nonhousehold industrial buyers will be discussed in more detail than were institutional and government buyers because they function in a profit-oriented environment, which is the central setting for this text. Further, more is known about the actual industrial buying process than about the other nonhousehold operations.

Industrial buyers are concerned with items that are used in producing other goods. An item can serve both consumers and industries, of course, as does a typewriter. One classification of industrial goods is the following (Alexander, Cross, and Cunningham, 1961):

Major equipment
Minor or accessory equipment
Operating supplies
Fabricating parts
Processed materials
Raw materials

The market for industrial goods is enormous, both in the aggregate and for the individual firm. In the metal can industry, for example, materials account for approximately 66 percent of the sales dollar. For the diversified 3M Company in a recent year, when sales were $1,405 million, the cost of goods sold was $757 million, or 54 percent. The relation of purchasing costs to sales varies, of course, according to the mix of labor, materials, and other factors, but in most manufacturing firms purchasing accounts for over half the money spent.

The principal characteristics of industrial goods are numerous and varied, as shown in 13-4. An industrial buyer, who usually deals in large dollar amounts, buys in a market with a derived demand since his own company's purchases depend on someone else's purchases. In other words, a derived demand is a demand that stems from another market. The demand for steel, for example, depends on the demand for autos

---

## 13-4

### Selected Principal Characteristics of Industrial Marketing

1. Characteristics of the market or buyers
   a. Derived demand
   b. Rational buying motives
   c. Small number of buyers
   d. Geographic concentration
   e. Volume purchasing
   f. Multiple-buying responsibility

2. Product characteristics
   a. Technical
   b. Small fluctuations in price
   c. Specifications for details
   d. Bidding system
   e. Standardization

3. Characteristics of the operational setup
   a. Short channels
   b. Trade publications for advertising
   c. Reciprocity
   d. Seller makes contact
   e. Production for inventory

4. Other characteristics
   a. Speed and dependability of delivery
   b. Extensive sales training
   c. Low sales promotion expense
   d. Small number of women buyers
   e. Predominance of raw and semifinished products

SOURCE: Adapted from Industrial Marketing Committee Review Board, "Fundamental Differences Between Industrial and Consumer Marketing," *Journal of Marketing,* Vol. 19, No. 2 (October 1954), pp. 142–158.

---

and refrigerators. Price trends are important, though in the short run the buyer may purchase large quantities when the price moves upward and he may not buy when the price goes down because he is anticipating further movements in the price level.

Management has come to recognize that profits can be increased by saving money as well as by expanding sales. Indeed, to match the profit gain from a given amount of savings on expenditures, it takes a greater increase in sales. This purchasing-profit relationship is clearly shown in 13-5. In recognition of the gains to be made in savings, a few companies have placed their buyers on a carefully audited incentive basis, similar to salesmen's commissions. (A household buyer may also recognize that a dollar saved in buying is better than a dollar increase in salary.)

## Organizing for Buying

As with most business functions the organization for industrial buying differs from firm to firm. Traditionally, the buying function has been located in a department headed by someone called a Director of

**13-5** Purchasing-Profit Ratio

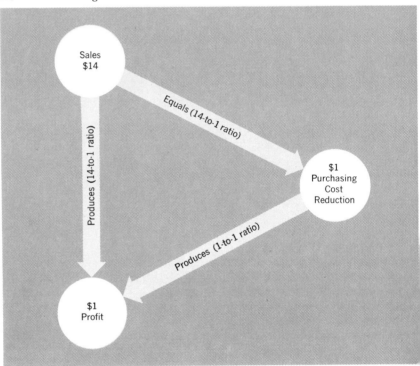

SOURCE: Victor H. Poole, "The Purchasing Man and His Job," in Paul T. McElhiney and Rober I. Cook, The Logistics of Materials Management (Boston: Houghton Mifflin, 1969), p. 14.

**13-6** Coordination of Activities of Industrial Buyers

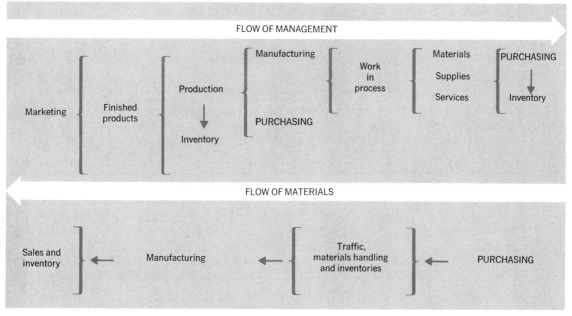

SOURCE: *Purchasing*, Vol. 38 (January 1955), p. 69.

Purchases (or some such title) and populated by buyers and assistant buyers who concentrate their buying efforts on selected products.

Since firms vary in their division of responsibilities, it is difficult to generalize on related purchasing activities such as stores, quality control, and transportation. Clearly, however, the activities of industrial buyers must be coordinated with those of all the departments they serve, as suggested in 13-6. During the past decade there has been a tendency to unite purchasing with related functions, and thus in some companies a Materials Manager has emerged with responsibility for all those activities associated with the handling of materials. Aside from degree of responsibility there are two other particularly vital factors in organizing for industrial buying. One is the matter of centralization versus decentralization in the firm. The second is the degree of importance management attaches to purchasing as indicated by its position in the hierarchy. Many directors of purchasing are vice presidents but a large number simply report to a vice president.

A very large corporation may employ hundreds or even more than a thousand buyers who, during the course of a year, may purchase from tens of thousands of vendors several hundred thousand items costing millions of dollars. With such financial responsibility at stake, it might be assumed that an industrial buyer has special status within a firm. Historically, however, this has not been the case. Many years ago the president of a company typically controlled the buying decisions and the orders were placed by a purchasing agent. The term "agent," which set the buyer somewhat apart from the regular management, carried down through the years, and it was not until 1967 that the National Association of Purchasing Agents changed its name to the National Association of Purchasing Management. This change reflects the current tendency to consider purchasing men part of management. It must be noted, though, that buyers in many enterprises still operate as clerks, in that they do not make the buying decision but do place the order. The upgrading of purchasing has occurred primarily since World War II. Profit squeezes, cyclical swings of surpluses and shortages, wars, recognition of the importance of cost factors, and the growing complexity of products have been contributing factors toward the improvement in status of the purchasing function (Poole, 1969).

## The Buying Process for Industry

Despite the economic importance of industrial buying, it has not generally been emphasized in marketing classes for a number of reasons, including lack of "glamour" and lack of adequate information. Indeed, much remains unknown about the process, but a considerable amount of knowledge has risen through the apathy of scholars in the field. The following generalizations summarize the kind of knowledge currently available (Webster, 1969).

1. The decision is made within an organization and by a number of individuals including users, deciders, and buyers.

2. The industrial buyer is often not the most important factor in the decision process, although he may serve as a kind of "gatekeeper" for the flow of information.

3. Decisions can be classed from the simple and routine to complex, expensive, and nonroutine.

4. There are stages in the buying process from initial awareness through to final buying action.

5. Buyers' uses and preferences for information vary according to the stage in the process and in relationship to other factors.

6. Buyers are motivated by a combination of individual needs and organizational needs.

7. There is a tendency to rely upon the familiar.

The industrial buyer's job is often described as purchasing the right materials, of the right quality, at the right time, in the right quantity, at the right price, from the right source, delivered to the right place. This may seem like an oversimplification, yet actually it is a fair general description of his task; only the degree of difficulty in accomplishing these goals varies from item to item. More specifically, buyers perform a number of well-defined tasks, as follows (Fine, 1964):

1. Determine the sources of supply.
2. Select the most economical method of delivery and routing.

3. Issue the purchase order.
4. Follow-up and expedite.
5. Receive and inspect the merchandise.
6. Check invoices and payment.
7. Control the inventory.
8. Conduct value analysis for materials.
9. Determine make-or-buy decisions.
10. Handle salvage and scrap disposal.

Selecting *suppliers* is certainly a key decision. The buyer must keep in mind such obvious considerations as price and service, but the task entails less obvious elements. He may, for instance, have to make a trip to a prospective vendor in order to examine his capabilities, to get to know the key people in order to judge their strengths and weaknesses. He will want to understand the labor situation and the firm's financial soundness. He must be wary of relying on a single supplier, for a strike or fire could put his source out of production, yet he wants to develop a strong relationship in order to improve service and secure the best possible terms.

The buyer may be responsible for the *transportation* decision and, as will be seen in Chapter 19, delivery costs are critical in terms of the total price of the purchased materials. The preparation of a *purchase order* is a routine function, but it can be a costly matter when a firm places thousands or even hundreds of thousands of orders each year. Fortunately this process for the most part can be automated. The real task is to determine a system for handling the necessary routine paper work; and from that point on it can be standard operating procedure. Failure to receive a shipment on time may shut down an entire plant and therefore the buyer must have a *follow-up* and *expediting* procedure. *Receiving* may or may not be the responsibility of the buyer, but some have the task of receiving, checking, and perhaps running *quality control* checks on incoming goods. Sometimes the buyer builds into the purchase order the responsibility of the seller for quality control. *Payment* is made by the accounting department after the buyer acknowledges that the shipment is in order. *Inventory control* has been greatly improved in recent years as buyers have learned how to handle the problem of determining the "economical order quantity" and how to signal order points. The various factors that enter into the inventory control decision are shown in 19-6 (see Ch. 19, p. 417).

The buyer is expected to make price and cost analyses rigorously since a small savings per unit can amount to large savings on a year's production. A buyer for a tractor company, for example, suggested using identical oil and water plugs, thereby saving the company hundreds of dollars. A buyer for an automobile manufacturer replaced the glass in a dome light with plastic and made considerable savings. In one year buyers at General Electric saved $500,000 in costs in one refrigerator plant (Stouffer, 1969). The technique of making these cost studies is known as value analysis or *value engineering*. Basically, the buyer asks three simple questions: What does an item, part, or process do? What does it cost? What else would do the job and at what cost? Other examples of value engineering include the following (Stouffer, 1969):

1. An electronic mechanism is required to open and close the 50-ton maintenance housing over a silo that holds a Minuteman missile. These mechanisms, as originally designed, cost $550,000 for each formation of Minutemen. Investigation turned up a commercial "off the shelf" hydraulic mule, used for routine hauling jobs, which would do this job effectively—at a cost of $80,000 per Minuteman formation.

2. The military version of the Electra prop-jet transport plane doesn't need external fuel gauges (although ground crews still find them important for quick-turn-around commercial flights). Each gauge costs $50, and there are eight tanks on each plane. One wooden dipstick that costs $12 now does the job of $400 worth of gauges.

Industrial buyers frequently face the question of making an item or buying it; actually, of course, both are ways of procuring the item for the company. The decision to produce an item within the company is likely if it is less expensive to do so, if there is idle plant capacity, if the part is difficult to transport, or if it is necessary to keep the item confidential. Conversely the *make-or-buy* analysis may show that it is less expensive to procure a part from an outside vendor, that the firm lacks the necessary skills, or that there are restrictive patents (Hubler, 1969). A buyer may develop a routine procedure for handling make-or-buy decisions, usually relying on accountants to aid in the cost accounting involved.

The buyer also must be a negotiator in his capacity as purchaser. It takes a great deal of skill to negotiate the many elements in a purchase: price, delivery, conditions of the contract, adjustments, changes in delivery points, changes in specifications, variations in quantity, price revisions under escalation, overhead rates for cost-plus contracts, termination settlements, acceptability of individual items, and provisions for handling other kinds of problems that might arise during the course of a contract.

Several other important aspects of industrial buying should be noted. One concerns *legal* implications. A buyer has to know when he has agreed legally to a contract and when he has a legal commitment from a vendor. This is a matter of legal interpretation subject to the laws regulating contracts and negotiations. A second aspect is *ethics*. The buyer is particularly vulnerable to attempts at influencing his decision through favors, gifts, even bribes. Industrial buyers can do their best job only when they are obligated to no one. In recognition of this problem some firms now provide buyers with expense accounts so that they do not become indebted to a supplier, even for a dinner. Other ethical problems in a buyer's behavior include placing duplicate orders and leading salesmen on. A company can be better assured of the best purchasing results if its buyers adhere to an ethical code such as that established by the National Association of Purchasing Management.

As an industrial buyer performs his tasks, he engages in actions similar to those of a household consumer, but he is far more thorough about them. For example, at several stages of the buying process he searches for *information* from both external and internal sources (see 13-7). It is clear that his search process is far superior to that of the household buyer. He accumulates more information; he has a good feedback system; he extends his search to the point where it no longer pays him to seek information; he undertakes in-plant testing; he has quality control standards; he learns from numerous salesmen; and he communicates directly with the manufacturer in many instances (Holton, 1970).

## Industrial Buyer Behavior

The material thus far has stressed the professionalism of the industrial buyer and the rational way in which he proceeds. The industrial

**13-7** Internal and External Information Flows to Purchasing

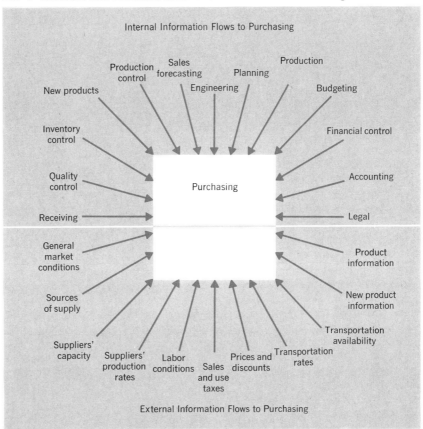

SOURCE: Wilbur B. England, *The Purchasing System* (Homewood, Ill.: Richard D. Irwin, 1967), pp. 121–129.

buyer is human, however, and is subject to the same kinds of internal and external forces as described for household consumers. Elbert Hubbard's description of the industrial buyer follows: (Boone and Stevens, 1970).

> The typical buyer is a man past middle-life, spare, wrinkled, intelligent, cold, passive, noncommittal with eyes like a codfish, polite in contact, but, at the same time, unresponsive, cool, calm, and damnably composed as a concrete post or a plaster of Paris cat; a human petrification with a heart of feldspar and without charm; or the friendly germ, minus bowels, passions, or a sense of humor. Happily they never reproduce, and all of them finally go to Hell.

Rational buying motives undoubtedly dominate the buyer's behavior even though in some buying situations he is motivated by emotion. For example, the purchase of office furniture for a corporate officer would probably reflect emotional motives whereas the purchase of cleaning rags for maintenance would not. The relevance of a motive depends in large part on the buyer, his environment, and the decision at hand. (For a list of buying motives, see 13-8.)

Further evidence of the industrial buyer's human qualities is suggested in the following quotation which brings to bear a number of relevant though frequently ignored considerations to a job in business.

> . . . fear is one of the major influences in industrial buying. Fear of displeasing the boss. Fear of making a wrong decision. Fear of committing the company to a substantial outlay. Fear of a mistake. Fear of losing face with the boss or with one's associates. Fear of losing status. Fear, indeed, in extreme cases, of losing one's job. . . . The buying influence is very much personally involved in this. He needs personal reassurance. He needs confidence. He needs to be able to have faith in people . . . let's not overlook the basic truth that purchasing executives are purchasing people, and that as long as people are people, they are going to continue to behave like people, to be influenced like people, and to buy like people. (Lazo, 1960.)

The industrial buyer's behavior is a complex phenomenon as is the behavior of other nonhousehold buyers. There are environmental factors, organizational constraints, psychological forces, and the flow of information. The framework shown in 13-9 is one pervasive proposal to summarize the determinants of behavior of the industrial buyer.

The multiplicity of the ways buying decisions are made in the radio, television, and communications equipment industry is shown in 13-10. It is interesting to note that buying decisions involve several corporate units and their relative importance in purchase decisions differ with the motive, kind of equipment, and even the choice of supplier. Also of interest is the minor role of the purchasing unit in initiating purchase, and in determining the kind of equipment, but its major role is determining the source of supply.

## 13-8

**Buying Motives Based on a Sample of the National Association of Purchasing Agents**

I. Heavy machinery
   A. "Product" motives
      1. Economy
      2. Productivity
      3. Dependability
      4. Time or labor saving
      5. Durability
   B. "Patronage" motives
      1. Reliability of seller
      2. Cooperation
      3. Low prices
      4. Quick repair service
      5. Past services rendered: satisfactory relationships

II. Raw materials
   A. "Product" motives
      1. Right quality
      2. Uniformity
      3. Dependability
      4. Purity
      5. Ability to increase salability of user's product
   B. "Patronage" motives
      1. Reliability of seller
      2. Continuous supply under all conditions
      3. Accessibility of seller
      4. Low prices
      5. Quick and reliable delivery of product

III. Supplies
   A. "Product" motives
      1. Right quality
      2. Dependability
      3. Uniformity
      4. Economy
      5. Durability
   B. "Patronage" motives
      1. Reliability of seller
      2. Continuous supply under all conditions
      3. Accessibility of seller
      4. Low prices
      5. Quick and reliable delivery of product

SOURCE: Delbert F. Duncan, "What Motivates Business Buyers," *Harvard Business Review*, Vol. 18 (Summer 1940), p. 453.

**13-9** A Proposed Framework for the Analysis of the Various Determinants of the Buyer's Behavior

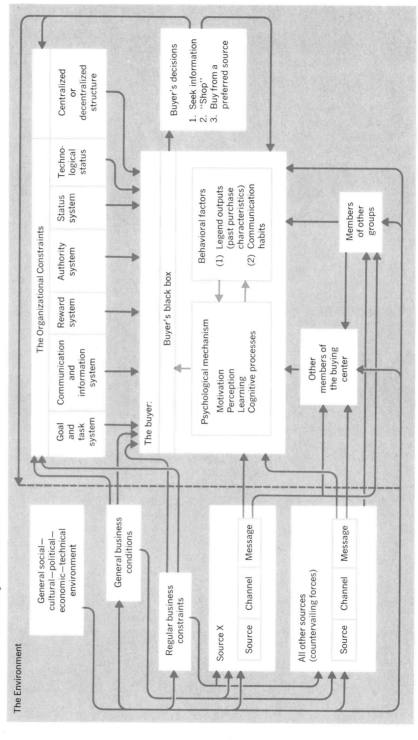

SOURCE: Patrick J. Robinson, Charles W. Faris, with Yoram Wind, *Industrial Buying and Creative Marketing* (Boston: Allyn & Bacon, 1967), p. 154.

## 13-10 How the Radio, Television, and Communication-Equipment Industry Buys Equipment

| | Who is most likely to initiate a project leading toward the purchase of new equipment to: | Overall corporate policy and planning | Operations and administration | Design and development engineering | Production engineering | Research | Finance | Sales | Purchasing | Others in company | Others outside of company |
|---|---|---|---|---|---|---|---|---|---|---|---|
| **MOTIVE** | Replace existing equipment? | 14.2 | 39.6 | 37.7 | 53.8 | 12.3 | .9 | .9 | 7.5 | 14.2 | 1.9 |
| | Expand capacity? | 44.2 | 43.3 | 24.0 | 42.3 | 3.8 | | 2.9 | 1.0 | 4.8 | 2.9 |
| | Change production processes? | 12.7 | 18.6 | 30.4 | 84.3 | 5.9 | | | 1.0 | 3.9 | 1.0 |
| | Take advantage of new materials? | 5.0 | 9.9 | 63.4 | 53.5 | 23.8 | | | 3.0 | 3.0 | 1.0 |
| | Manufacture new products? | 38.2 | 32.4 | 48.0 | 32.4 | 14.7 | 1.0 | 3.9 | 2.0 | 2.9 | 3.9 |
| **KIND OF EQUIPMENT** | Who surveys alternatives and determines kind (not make) of equipment? | 5.7 | 16.2 | 56.2 | 50.5 | 17.1 | 1.0 | | 12.4 | 8.6 | 1.0 |
| | Who determines specifications and characteristics to be met by the equipment? | 1.9 | 11.3 | 62.3 | 52.8 | 18.9 | .9 | | 5.7 | 12.3 | 1.9 |
| **MAKE OR SUPPLIER** | Who surveys available makes of the specified equipment and chooses suppliers from whom to invite bids? | 1.9 | 10.5 | 42.9 | 36.2 | 8.6 | | | 62.9 | 11.4 | 1.9 |
| | Who evaluates offered equipment for accord with specifications? | 1.0 | 8.7 | 57.3 | 52.4 | 16.5 | | | 9.7 | 19.4 | 1.0 |
| | Who decides which supplier gets the order? | 11.3 | 21.7 | 42.5 | 33.0 | 10.4 | 1.9 | | 58.5 | 10.4 | .9 |

Percentages indicate the frequency with which the various management functions were reported to participate in the successive steps of the purchasing process. Color highlights the three most-mentioned functions for each purchasing step.

| | | Percent of cases |
|---|---|---|
| When the radio, television, and communication-equipment industry buys equipment, the choice of make or supplier is limited by company preference or policy in setting up the required specifications and characteristics as shown at right: | Limited to one make | 27 |
| | Limited to two makes | 19 |

SOURCE: "How Industry Buys/1970," *Scientific American* (New York: Scientific American, 1969), p. 54.

## CONCLUDING COMMENTS

The nonhousehold buying sector includes institutions and government agencies as well as industry. Nonhousehold buyers are large in number and great in economic importance because they buy such enormous quantities and varieties of goods and services.

Industrial, government, and institutional buying practices are improving every day. They are taking advantage of computers, for instance, in many ways: improving inventory control, issuing purchase orders, calculating economical order quantities and price breaks, rating vendors by quality and delivery, preparing requests for quotation, preparing lists of slow or nonmoving items, preparing expediting notices, completing reports of dollars spent broken down by vendor, plant, and commodity (Gregg, 1965).

Further, industrial buying, at least, is increasingly subject to evaluation, whether informal or formal. A regular audit of a buyer's activities may include (1) company policy and organization, (2) purchasing department operations, (3) collateral operations, (4) records and reports, and (5) details on buying. Questions about choices of vendors, transportation, rush orders, allowances, lack of bids, delivery points and cross-shipping, and contract negotiations are usually raised in such audits (Arthur Anderson & Co., 1969).

In Chapters 10 through 13 we have attempted to provide a picture of both household and nonhousehold buying. To know buying is to know selling, and to know about those activities is to know a great deal about marketing.

## STATEMENTS TO CONSIDER

In summary, price means many things to different buyers and many things to the same buyer in different buying problems. Nevertheless, in all cases it is the real key to the buying decision, and the marketing manager who fully understands its real function will be able to develop the pricing strategy most likely to produce the maximum of business volume and profit. (Foster)

In summary, while there are undoubtedly some important functions performed by word-of-mouth communication in industrial markets, it appears reasonable to hypothesize that it is of less importance than in consumer markets for two reasons. First, the need is less, primarily because of the greater perceived adequacy of marketer-provided information. Second, channels of communication for interacting with other buyers are not as well established in industrial markets as in consumer markets. Both the need and the opportunity for word-of-mouth communication are therefore reduced. (Webster)

The studies usually demonstrate that functional responsibilities and job titles are not perfectly matched; buying responsibility is diffused throughout the firm. (Weigand)

The marketer, or for that matter the salesman, cannot directly influence an individual buyer. The sole means of influence lies in the changes which can be effected upon the individual's environment within the constraints of his ability to take account of such changes. (Robinson)

Once the Federal funds are dispersed, the identification of the market becomes difficult, the number of contact points become very numerous, and the cost of sales increases correspondingly. (Rothschild)

Many companies that attempt to sell aerospace technology to Government research agencies today find the selling operation to be more an extension of research and development than actual salesmanship. (Murphy)

Idea Number One: That purchasing is not a service function but a profit-making activity. (Hill)

The National Association of Purchasing Management has changed its name, but only individuals can change their game. (Bytwork)

Industrial buyers "do not stop being people when they enter the office." (Gross)

It is almost certain that a marketing and distribution system set up successfully to serve a defense customer will be dismally unsuited to marketing a consumer product. (Dunham)

**1.** How does marketing differ between household and nonhousehold buying?

**2.** Is the industrial buyer a completely rational buyer?

**3.** Could an individual household buyer conduct his buying in the same manner as an industrial buyer?

**4.** In what ways does a buyer for a university differ in his buying practices from a manufacturing buyer?

**5.** What purposes do the many kinds of military contracts serve? Do you think there is more poor buying among the military than among nonmilitary buyers? Why or why not?

**6.** Does the marketer perform the same function in selling new technology in military goods as in consumer goods?

**7.** What channels of distribution and media are used in industrial marketing?

**8.** Who makes the product decision in industrial buying?

**9.** Explain how value engineering contributes to the efficiency of buying.

**10.** Are the motives listed in 13-8 appropriate also for household buying?

## Further Readings

Marshall G. Edwards and Herbert A. Hamilton, Jr., *Guide to Purchasing* (New York: The National Association of Purchasing Management, Inc., 1969).

Paul T. McElhiney and Robert I. Cook, *The Logistics of Materials Management: Readings in Modern Purchasing* (Boston: Houghton Mifflin, 1969).

Patrick J. Robinson and Charles W. Faris, with Yoram Wind, *Industrial Buying and Creative Marketing* (Boston: Allyn & Bacon, 1967).

U.S. General Services Administration, *Doing Business with the Federal Government* (Washington, D.C.: GPO, 1966).

J. H. Westing, I. V. Fine, and Gary J. Zenz, *Purchasing Management: Materials in Motion* (New York: John Wiley, 1969).

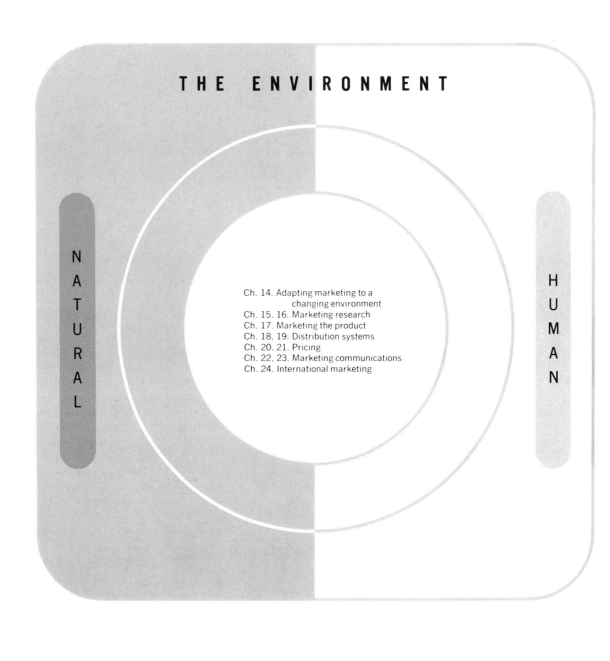

THE ENVIRONMENT

NATURAL

HUMAN

Ch. 14. Adapting marketing to a
changing environment
Ch. 15. 16. Marketing research
Ch. 17. Marketing the product
Ch. 18. 19. Distribution systems
Ch. 20. 21. Pricing
Ch. 22. 23. Marketing communications
Ch. 24. International marketing

# PART III

# MARKETING MANAGEMENT IN A CHANGING ENVIRONMENT

*Marketing is performed in a dynamic environment and it is largely through marketing research that the marketer receives pertinent data from the environment. Product, channel, logistics, price, and communications decisions are made for the marketplace, be it domestic or foreign.*

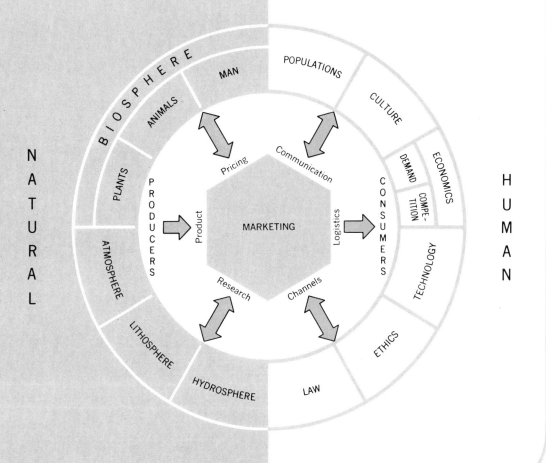

# CHAPTER 14
# ADAPTING MARKETING TO A CHANGING ENVIRONMENT

**Managing the Marketing Operation**

*Organizing the Marketing Department*
*Coordinating and Communicating*
*Gathering Information*
*Forecasting*

*Planning*
*Directing and Executing the Marketing Operation*
*Controlling the Marketing Operation*

**Integrating the Marketing Tasks**

*The environment of marketing interacts with all aspects of the mar-*
*keting mix. A marketing manager is well advised to blend his planning*
*of marketing efforts with environmental influences.*

The approach used in this text has been to lay the groundwork for an understanding of the environment in which marketing takes place. We began the text by examining society's expectations of the marketing function and immediately moved to a description of the environment in which marketing and all of business thrive. We examined in some detail the influential environmental forces—competition, laws, technology, geography, and demand. We noted that the environment in a total sense is a very complex system and that it has many subsystems such as the economic, legal, and communications systems as well as the natural ecosystems of air, land, and water. In addition, there are domestic environments and international ones for marketing, each influencing the kinds of roles marketing plays in each particular society.

We now shift from the marketing environment to the marketing process itself, that is, from the environment of marketing to marketing in the environment. As we examine the marketing process bear in mind that the goal is to satisfy the needs and desires of consumers who are attempting to adapt to the environment in which they live. The environment is where marketing takes place, where sales are made and lost, where competition, laws, changes in income, disappointments in the weather, and buying decisions occur. Marketing becomes functional when it reaches out to the consumer. This is the time when all the environmental factors and all the marketing operations interact in the kaleidoscope of the marketplace. This is marketing, this is business, this is the ever-recurring scene when buyers and sellers meet together. The fusion or the unity of the marketing process with the environment makes the environmental approach to marketing significant. As Philip L. Wagner has observed,

> An environment is only an environment in relation to something it environs, and is significant insofar as it interacts in some way with that thing. It is no easy matter to discover just where and why, much less how, some property of an environment does have significance for a process in which one may be interested. (Wagner, 1960).

In this chapter we move into the marketing operation by first examining each of the primary responsibilities of the marketing manager and then consolidating these responsibilities into a unified scheme. The chapter will provide an overview of marketing as it adapts to a changing environment. The success of the operation depends in large part on how well marketers understand the environment and its dynamics and then apply that understanding as they plan and direct the marketing operation.

# MANAGING THE MARKETING OPERATION

The marketing operation, though stressed in this text, is only one of the functions of business. Marketing must fit into the general scheme of the firm. Ideally a marketing manager will have a role in helping a firm determine its goals and objectives. This is not always the case, but a firm that is oriented to the customer and to society would do well to have a clearly defined marketing posture that top management takes into account in setting the firm's goals. (See 14-1 for one company's statement of objectives.) In any event, the marketing manager will be expected to develop various marketing objectives and strategies consistent with the broader corporate goals.

The broad managerial aspects of marketing can be classified in a number of ways, one of which is the following (after Urwick, 1956):

The Broad Managerial Responsibilities of Marketing

1. Organizing the marketing operation.
2. Coordinating and communicating within the marketing department and with other parts of the firm.
3. Gathering marketing information.
4. Making sales forecasts.
5. Planning marketing operations.
6. Directing the marketing effort.
7. Controlling the marketing effort.

Each of these seven responsibilities will be developed in the following pages.

## Organizing the Marketing Department

In a small firm one person might be responsible for all of marketing, but in a large firm the marketing department consists of a number of individuals each of whom specializes in one activity. These activities are shown in 14-2. Neil Borden, a long-time marketing scholar, suggested the term "marketing mix" as a way of describing the blending together of the marketing activities or ingredients (Borden, 1964).

In addition to the tasks shown in 14-2 there is the matter of gathering information, and this staff function must also be included in the marketing organization. In organizing these activities the firm selects some combination of marketing people who can perform the many tasks and collectively they constitute the marketing department. There is no perfect organizational solution applicable to all firms because so much depends on the size of the firm, capabilities and personalities of the personnel, product lines, geographic dispersion of the markets, and the company philosophy. A general type of organization is shown in 14-3.

## 14-1
**Corporate Objectives**

Swissair's Guiding Principles

1. Since our planes carry the Swiss flag into all parts of the world, Swissair Management and personnel have a moral obligation to uphold the good reputation of Switzerland and to strengthen and increase it through our activities and conduct.

2. As a landlocked country, Switzerland has a special interest in air transportation. Switzerland's industry, commerce, tourism and financial institutions have developed world-wide connections upon which its national prosperity is founded. Swissair recognizes that it has a duty, wherever it can, to serve the interests of the Swiss economy. Our activities, therefore, must be world-wide.

3. In the spirit of our country's humanitarian tradition, we also recognize our duty to serve as a link between and to promote understanding among all countries served by our network.

4. Our Company is determined to pursue a policy of financial independence. This means that we must cover our operating costs from our own revenues, provide for depreciation on our investment, pay interest on our stock, and build up necessary reserves. At the same time and in close co-operation with the federal and cantonal government authorities, we must uphold the general interests of our country.

5. We subscribe to the principle of fair and free competition, and we are convinced that Swissair will be able to meet competition by
—assuring maximum possible flight safety;
—operating all aircraft with maximum punctuality;
—offering all customers first class service according to
 the best traditions of Swiss hospitality.

6. We believe that the high demands we must make upon our personnel oblige us to provide good, up-to-date employment conditions. In this connection, we must take into account both local conditions and international standards.

7. We make especially high demands upon our flight captains, who bear full responsibility for the passengers, crew and property entrusted to them. Thus, we acknowledge our special obligations toward the flying personnel, and expect in return that the flight crews will be mindful of the high responsibilities to them.

8. We consider it our obligation towards the Company, its customers and its personnel to make such long-range plans as will enable Swissair to operate a reliable, economical and competitive fleet of aircraft.

## Coordinating and Communicating

In order for the marketing department to run efficiently and smoothly it should have adequate coordination and communication within the department and between the marketing personnel and other depart-

9. It is our opinion that we can attain the greatest success for our Company by giving our personnel on all levels the opportunity to develop initiative. Everyone should take an active interest in our Company's planning for both short- and long-range objectives. Company channels are not intended as a one-way street from top to bottom, but should also carry all ideas, suggestions and objective criticism of potential value to our common cause from the bottom to the top.

10. We consider strict discipline the necessary counterpart of this co-operation among personnel in the planning of the Company's work. There is no place in Swissair for anyone who refuses to follow instructions and directives. Democratic freedom does not mean absence of discipline, and discipline has nothing to do with servility.

11. In the development of our organization we follow the principle that authority should be delegated to the lowest level where the facts are available.

12. The duties and responsibilities of all supervisory and management levels must be precisely defined. At the same time, standards of performance must be set up which define the conditions prevailing when a given job can be considered well done.

13. We believe that co-operation among persons concerned with defining duties and responsibilities and setting up standards of performance represents an important medium for creating a good working climate. The results of periodic performance appraisals must not be kept from those concerned. Wherever deficiencies appear, it is considered the primary duty of the superior concerned to improve the performance through individual development and training.

14. Swissair is no exception to the rule that satisfied customers are the best form of advertising. Both our direct customer relations and the spirit within our organization contribute to making satisfied customers. In this sense, every employee plays a part in our most effective form of advertising.

15. Our activities in the service of a world-wide transport company must never allow us to become presumptuous. On the contrary, they impose upon us the duty of being modest toward our fellow men.

SOURCE: Swissair.

mental personnel in the firm. Many company decisions are, after all, company-wide in their nature: product decisions join marketing with finance, production, and research and development; pricing decisions are based on corporate philosophy, marketing information about competition, and cost data from several departments; marketing research solicits data from salesmen and provides them with various information; production gears its operations to the need of sales and also to labor, inventory, and the seasonal variations in availability of materials; accounting handles the billing and also provides cost data essential to controlling the marketing effort. Thus the tasks of coordinating and communicating are important marketing functions. Unfortunately some

**14-2** Marketing Activities: The Marketing Mix

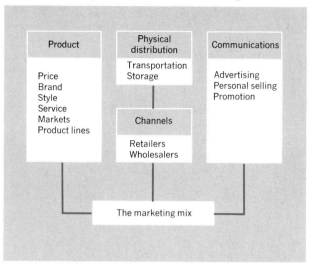

SOURCE: Adapted from William Lazer, *Marketing Management* (New York: John Wiley, 1971), p. 17.

firms make no provision for them and rely only on haphazard interaction.

## Gathering Information

Marketing research provides input to all marketing decision-making and in this way serves as a foundation for the marketing operations. Every firm sells a product or service in some market, and it is basic that information about those consumers in their environments be gathered, analyzed, and made available to the appropriate marketing personnel. Marketers consider themselves to be consumer-oriented and the only way they can achieve this goal is to know as much as possible about their consumers.

**14-3** A Functional Type of Marketing Organization

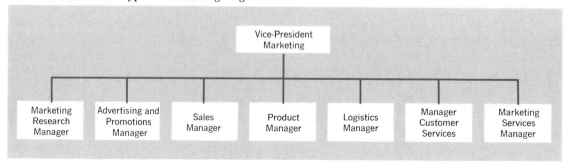

Various kinds of information are gathered. The simplest and perhaps most basic is an estimate of the number of potential customers. Beyond this a company needs information about competition, buyers' income, dispersion of population, availability of wholesale and retail outlets, climatic conditions, and current economic conditions. These and other data provide information for decisions about advertising, personal selling, credit, style, package size, and a host of other matters.

## Forecasting

The sales forecast is a basic instrument for an entire firm since marketing, production, finance, purchasing, and other departments base their plans on the number of units to be sold. The diagram in 14-4 shows how the sales forecast is the focus for integrative planning. The figure further shows how environmental factors are essential parts of the forecasting activity. It is to be noted that the internal (company) factors are controllable but the environmental factors tend to be uncontrollable. Nevertheless, the forecaster strives to include all pertinent information in his forecast so that it might be as accurate as possible.

## Planning

The planning of the marketing operation is one of the more important responsibilities of the marketer. Based on market information, forecasts, corporate objectives, and needs of other departments, the planning operation sets the stage for the effort to be made in the marketplace. Marketing plans are of several varieties. Some are long-term and others are short-run plans; some are general and others specific; some marketing plans are formal and written but others are oral; and plans may be formed from the top management group downward or from the lower echelons upward. The diversity in kinds of plans simply reflects differences in planning needs between companies and within the same company for different purposes. The reasons for planning, the procedure, the time period covered, and the totality of a plan may all vary from firm to firm, but the important point is that many firms now recognize the value of planning their marketing procedures.

Lyndall F. Urwick has carefully set forth some relevant ideas about planning.

The basic principle underlying planning is Order. That is why we plan, so that action may follow in a systematic, orderly way and not be checked or confused because this essential item has not been supplied or because that preliminary process has not been completed in time. Planning is essentially the analysis and measurement of materials and processes in advance of the event and the perfection of the records so that we may know exactly where we are at any given moment. . . . The principle underlying all planning is policy: planning must be the expression of policy or it is meaningless. . . . [With planning] it is possible to think logically and comprehen-

# THE ENVIRONMENT

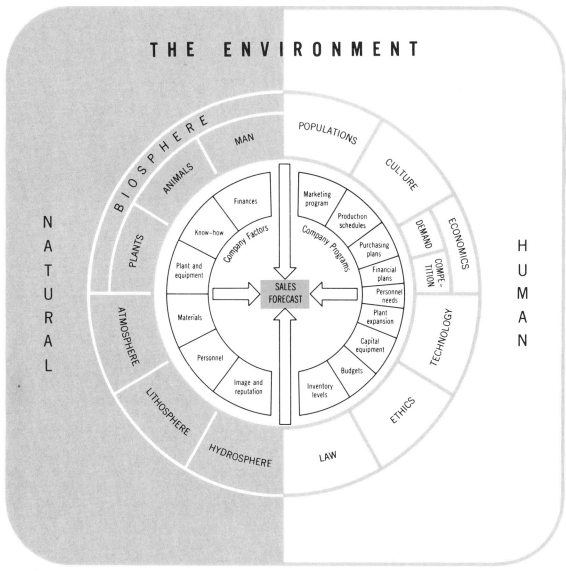

SOURCE: Adapted from William Lazer, "Sales Forecasting: Key to Integrated Management," *Business Horizons,* Vol. 2 (Fall 1959). p. 65.

sively about the process of management as a whole, to arrange our knowledge about grouping and correlating tasks and about directing and motivating groups, in some kind of pattern which includes almost everything that anyone in a position of authority has said about it. . . . (Urwick, 1956.)

Obviously marketing plans will differ from one another; nevertheless, we can enumerate some of the common elements. The list in 14-5 illustrates the ramifications of a marketing plan and program. A plan can be all inclusive and the effort in devising and later in executing it may be a formidable task. Planning is not meant to complicate the management of marketing but instead should simplify and give order to it.

The ideal marketing plan permits a firm to market its products in an orderly, efficient, and profitable manner. The characteristics listed below are essential to a successful marketing effort. You can see that violation of one of these can render a plan unworkable. For example,

## 14-5
**Elements of a Marketing Plan**

Sales Goals
  Measuring Opportunity
    Sales forecasts
    Market potentials
    Consumer behavior and motivation
    Market testing
    Industrial markets

Marketing programs
  Allocating Effort
    Product line
    Marketing channels
    Prices and discounts
    Sales budgets
    Marketing mix
    Advertising media
    Advertising appeals
    Sales compensation
    Production scheduling

Organization
  Mobilizing Capacity
    Organization structure
    Internal communication
    Standards and supervision
    Training and executive development
    Inventory policy
    Production and procurement base
    Investment planning
    Financing market expansion

SOURCE: "The Challenge of Marketing Management," *Cost and Profit Outlook*, Vol. 10 (January 1957), p. 1.

a plan that is not communicated to all pertinent personnel hardly has an opportunity to be put into effect. Or a plan that is not objective may be so unrealistic and so biased that it is far wide of the mark.

Characteristics of an Ideal Marketing Plan

| | |
|---|---|
| Objective | Balanced |
| Well-timed | Efficient in allocating resources |
| Simple | Developed through participation of |
| Based on clearly defined goals | several layers of management |
| Acceptable to both top and | Comprehensive |
| lower management | Integrated with all operations |
| Based on marketing intelligence | Accompanied by a schedule |
| Flexible | Controlled by periodic audit |
| Communicated to all concerned | Realistic |

Although it is unlikely that any marketing plan would fulfill all these prerequisites, they are desirable goals to aim for. In the business world, of course, compromises are necessary because of lack of agreement among managements, lack of data, inadequate resources, and the uncontrollable elements of the external environment.

## Directing and Executing the Marketing Operation

Marketers cannot play an intellectual game of planning and stop at that point. The marketing plan must be implemented: salesmen must be directed; advertising copy created and placed in appropriate media; wholesalers and retailers informed; and the entire marketing effort launched as effectively as possible. The direction and execution of the marketing effort takes place in the marketplace, in the environment of the consumer. Here the marketing effort is tested amidst competition and the seemingly whimsical forces of nature.

The viability of the plan becomes apparent when the actual marketing effort is set into motion. Those who perform the marketing services soon learn if they have taken the environmental factors into account and whether the strategy as planned is a proper one. Even the lesser segments of the marketing program are important. Packaging, for example, should reflect the desires of buyers who have been influenced in a variety of ways by environmental forces (see 14-6).

The marketers who operate shopping centers are aware of a number of environmental influences, as shown in 14-7. Both internal (company) and external environmental factors are shown as they play a role in shopping center activity.

The marketer who directs a foreign marketing operation must also be intensely aware of the environmental factors. Income distribution, cultural attitudes and traits, the state of technology, means of transportation, and the local political system are some of the environmental factors that shape the direction to his marketing effort (see 14-8).

## 14-6 The Package and the Buyer

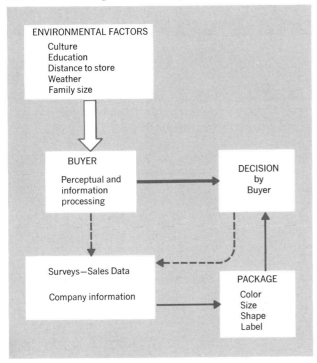

ENVIRONMENTAL FACTORS
Culture
Education
Distance to store
Weather
Family size

BUYER
Perceptual and information processing

DECISION by Buyer

Surveys—Sales Data
Company information

PACKAGE
Color
Size
Shape
Label

SOURCE: Adapted from David M. Gardner. "The Package, Legislation, and the Shopper," *Business Horizons*, Vol. 2 (October 1968), p. 57.

Thus environmental factors are not only important in planning but are also crucial in the actual marketing effort in the field. If each environmental factor were stable or controllable, implementation of the marketing plan would be simple, at least by comparison to the ever-changing environment that marketers are accustomed to.

## Controlling the Marketing Operation

Measurement and control of the firm's marketing effort is clearly desirable. Managers must know how effective their marketing is, and how their marketing program might be improved. A number of devices are available to management. A simple measure is to look at the absolute and percentage increase in sales from one month or year to the next, and in each of the territories, and by product. Share of the total market potential is another measure frequently used. Advertising is tested in a variety of ways for its effectiveness, although this task is not an easy one to perform.

The marketing control function may also be subject to periodic *audit;*

**14-7** The Shopping Center Environment

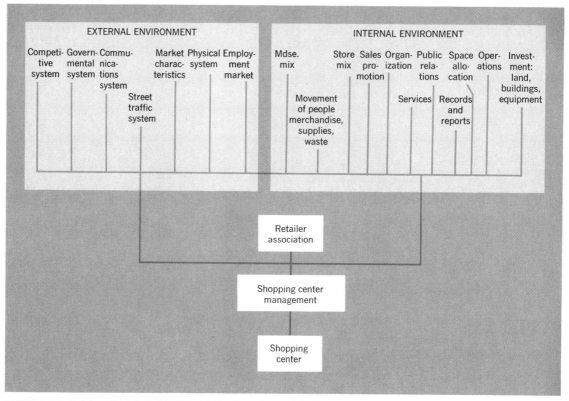

SOURCE: Adapted from Paul E. Smith, "Prescription for a Successful Shopping Center," *Business Topics*, Vol. 14 (Autumn 1966), p. 26.

. . . a systematic, critical, and unbiased review and appraisal of the basic objectives and policies of the marketing functions and of the organization, methods, procedures, and personnel employed to implement the policies and achieve the objectives. (Oxenfeldt, 1959.)

This audit is similar to an accounting audit. Some companies, stressing the need for an independent judgment, have the job performed by someone outside the firm whereas other companies rely on an internal audit. Regardless, an audit must be objective and thorough, and it should be done with the future in mind even though it is diagnostic in nature. The marketing audit is useful for *all* firms and should not be thought of only as a device to help an ailing company. (Kotler, 1967.)

## INTEGRATING THE MARKETING TASKS

The separate tasks of the marketer as described above need to be integrated, for each is only a part of the total marketing effort. An idea of an integrated effort is illustrated in 14-9. The consumer is shown at the beginning of the operation, where he influences the company's planning, and again at the end, where he is the target of the firm.

The diagram in 14-9 depicts the marketing concept that stresses (1) a consumer orientation, and (2) an integration of the total marketing effort so that marketers have charge of all those tasks associated with their responsibilities. The marketing concept also has (3) a profit orientation in lieu of a sales-volume orientation. When marketers unveiled the marketing concept in the 1950s, they added a good deal of credibility to marketing. The concept was attractive to everyone: ask the consumer about his needs; develop a product to fit those needs; plan and organize a marketing program that matches the market situation; and bring the product to the consumer.

Despite the attractiveness of the marketing concept, it has never reached its full potential. In a study of firms listed in the *Fortune 500*

**14-8** International Marketing: A Conceptual Framework

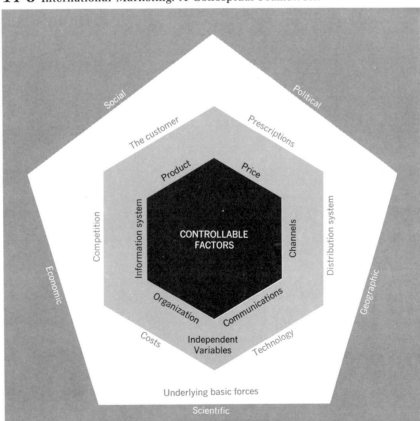

SOURCE: Warran J. Keegan, "Multinational Marketing Strategy and Organization—An Overview," in Reed Moyer (ed.), *Changing Marketing Systems* (Chicago: American Marketing Association, 1967), p. 204.

## 14-9 An Integrated Marketing Program

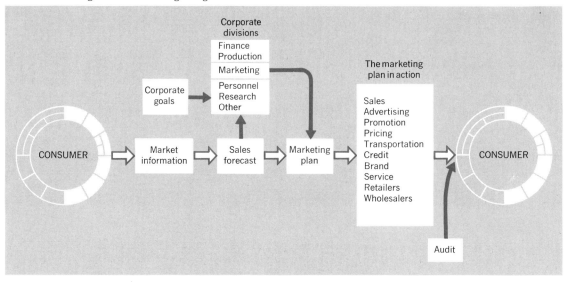

List almost three-fourths of the respondents were either uncertain or did not think the concept had been adopted by most business firms (Barksdale and Darden, 1971, and McNamara, 1972). The marketer used a narrow interpretation and looked at the customer only as someone to sell to. A genuine consumer orientation was not attempted by most companies. (See Bell and Emory, 1971.) Peter Drucker referred to the "shame of the total marketing concept" because marketers failed to adopt the consumer's point of view (Drucker, 1969). Leslie Dawson has also criticized marketers and has observed that their interpretation of the marketing concept was "limited in scope and one-dimensional in nature" (Dawson, 1969). Dawson suggested that marketers move into what he called the "human era," a concept more like the original rhetoric about the marketing concept.

One problem with the concept was that the trappings of implementation got in the way. Top management was proud to proclaim that a firm had become a marketing firm, and they demonstrated the new era by pointing to an increased staff in marketing, a newly created position of Vice President of Marketing, and increased marketing costs. But what was lacking was a "fundamental shift in thinking and attitude throughout the company so that everyone in every functional area places paramount importance on being responsive to market needs" (Ames, 1970).

The marketing concept need not be abandoned or given up as a lost cause, however, for it can be implemented any time management is ready to look at the market from the eyes of the consumer. Further, it can be strengthened by adopting the environmental approach so that the consumer is viewed in the broadest and fullest manner possible. This kind of approach seems so sensible that one wonders why it is not readily adopted by all firms. Management is certainly aware of the marketing concept, and indeed marketers enjoy telling how Henry Ford represented the antithesis of the marketing concept in practice when he commented, "Customers can have any color of car as long as it is black." As a result Ford almost failed during the 1920s for at that same time Chevrolet was offering its cars in several colors desired by consumers. There is more to the story, however, for Ford did have the marketing concept in 1913 when he provided customers with dependable and low-cost vehicles that were easy to repair. He sold Model T's by the millions then, but the changing environment for automobiles was not matched by a changing marketing policy. It was then that the marketing concept eluded Henry Ford.

## CONCLUDING COMMENTS

This chapter has attempted to serve as a transition from the chapters primarily concerned with the environment to the chapters in Part III that will discuss the primary marketing tasks. Hopefully, you will combine all these materials as you read so that you maintain an awareness of environmental forces in studying the managerial functions.

## STATEMENTS TO CONSIDER

The relation of man to his natural environment is always mediated by artificial agencies.

Natural, societal, and technical factors all exercise some control over every single element in an artificial environment and so over the whole artificial complex.

The broader framework of ecology holds greater promise for the development of marketing science than economics.

The ecological perspective offers criteria for marketing performance which transcend the limited measures of economic efficiency. (Alderson)

Marketing is concerned with the external relations of individual units or relations of organized behavior systems. (Alderson)

Our environmental problems are a result of our technological and economic successes and of our philosophical view of nature. Now we must learn to use our technology and our economic output better to bring us in harmonious relatonship to that environment. (U.S. National Goals Research Staff)

Wealth is our organized capability to cope effectively with the environment in sustaining our healthy regeneration and decreasing both the physical and metaphysical restrictions on the forward days of our lives. (R. Buchminister Fuller)

Planning does not superimpose any new authority.

When every activity of the corporation from finance to sales to production is aimed at satisfying the needs and desires of the consumer, the marketing revolution will be complete. (Keith)

Maximum effort should be made to assure the executives that the audit is primarily an attempt to find ways of improving marketing effectiveness and not to evaluate individual competences. (Kotler)

## QUESTIONS FOR REVIEW

**1.** Are the broad managerial responsibilities listed in the chapter applicable to all managerial functions or are they unique to marketing?

**2.** What is the rationale behind the term "marketing mix?"

**3.** Sketch out marketing organizations based on territories, products, and functions. What will be the differences in their operations?

**4.** Explain how sales forecasting is the focus of integrative planning within a firm.

**5.** Can you find any fault with Urwick's statement of planning?

**6.** What is it that makes a good marketing plan?

**7.** What are the most important ingredients of a marketing plan?

**8.** Make a diagram showing the environmental influences of a department store operation. Over which ones does the marketing manager have some element of control?

**9.** What is your understanding of a marketing audit? How can it be used?

**10.** What has happened to the implementation of the marketing concept?

## Further Readings

A. G. Abramson (ed.), *Operations Forecasting,* American Marketing Association (Chicago, 1967).

Leslie M. Dawson, "The Human Concept: New Philosophy for Business," *Business Horizons,* Vol. 12 (December 1969), pp. 29–38.

Robert J. Keith, "The Marketing Revolution," *Journal of Marketing,* Vol. 24 (January 1960), pp. 35–38. This article also appears in Holloway and Hancock, *The Environment of Marketing Behavior* (New York: John Wiley, 1969), pp. 254–259.

Eugene J. Kelley and William Lazer, *Managerial Marketing* (Homewood, Ill.: Richard D. Irwin, 1967).

Philip Kotler, *Marketing Management* (Englewood Cliffs, N.J.: Prentice-Hall, 1967).

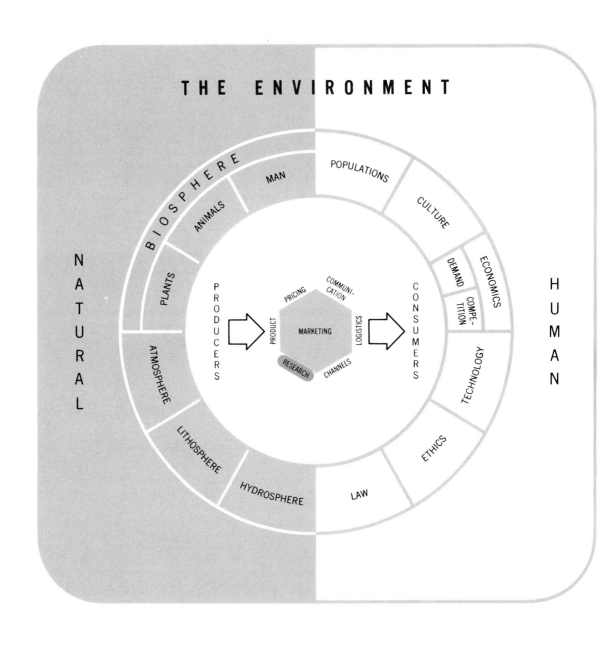

THE ENVIRONMENT

NATURAL

HUMAN

BIOSPHERE

MAN
ANIMALS
PLANTS
ATMOSPHERE
LITHOSPHERE
HYDROSPHERE

POPULATIONS
CULTURE
DEMAND
ECONOMICS
COMPE-TITION
TECHNOLOGY
ETHICS
LAW

PRODUCERS

CONSUMERS

PRICING
COMMUNI-CATION
PRODUCT
MARKETING
LOGISTICS
RESEARCH
CHANNELS

# CHAPTER 15
# MARKETING RESEARCH I

**Nature of Marketing Research**

**Marketing Information**

*The Value of Information*
*Environmental Information*

**Marketing Decisions**

*Basic Marketing Decisions*
*Decisions Relating to Competition*
*Other Research Applications*

**Organizing for Marketing Research**
**Marketing Information Systems**

*Environmental information about people, economics, and natural forces is especially useful to management. Marketing research is responsible for supplying management with all kinds of marketing information that can be used as an aid in making the basic decisions of the firm as well as many marketing decisions.*

One of the basic tasks of the marketing manager, as listed in the previous chapter, is to gather information that can be used to aid in his decision-making processes. In this chapter we examine briefly the nature of marketing research and its role in the firm, the information it provides, the decisions to which it applies, and the organization utilized to carry out the research function. In the following chapter research techniques will be examined.

## NATURE OF MARKETING RESEARCH

Marketing research is:

The systematic gathering, recording, and analyzing of data about problems relating to the marketing of goods and services. Such research may be undertaken by impartial agencies or by business firms or their agents for the solution of their marketing problems. . . . Marketing research is the inclusive term which embraces all research activities carried on in connection with the marketing work. (American Marketing Association, 1960.)

The process of "gathering, recording, and analyzing" data about marketing problems has steadily become expanded and formalized over the past several decades. Fortunately, many of the early people in the field were outstanding scholars and practitioners so that marketing research received a good start. Researchers for many years have assumed a professional posture. Though the early textbooks (circa 1920) were elementary by comparison to the advanced books of today, they did strive for quality, objectivity, and usefulness, all attributes that have stood the test of time. As a consequence of continuing high-quality work by researchers, company executives today have high expectations concerning the accuracy and relevancy of the data that marketing researchers provide them.

Today most large- and many medium- and small-size firms gather and analyze data about the market as they conduct their day-to-day affairs and plan for the future. Each of the using departments within marketing needs to know characteristics of potential buyers, sales performance of competition, and a myriad of other kinds of marketing information. The marketing research department today is capable of furnishing a wide variety of information to the various marketing managers in advertising, sales, product planning, and all other areas.

Some of the ways marketing research contributes to the success of the firm are as follows:

1. They delineate the significant marketing problems.
2. They keep a business in touch with its markets.
3. They reduce waste in marketing methods.
4. They develop new sources of profit through the discovery of new markets, new products, and new uses for established products.
5. They are insurance against unanticipated changes in the market which have the power to make a product or an industry obsolete.
6. They are used for sales promotion.
7. They reduce costs of production and other administrative expense.
8. They indicate the direction which technical research should take.
9. They infuse enthusiasm into the business organization.
10. They foster goodwill, both in the consumer market and in the industrial market. (Brown, 1955.)

## MARKETING INFORMATION

The gathering of information is so constant and necessary a part of life that we sometimes are unaware of it. Scouts look for good prospects for a college football team. Professional golfers carefully note distances and terrain features as they gather information during practice rounds. Generals and admirals make military decisions using available reports from their staffs. Senators make trips to diverse trouble spots in order to gain first-hand information. A United Nations agency sends observers for close and objective examinations of critical situations. We almost forget how much we depend on information, at least until we can't get it or when it is inaccurate.

Business executives, too, as they make hundreds of decisions in the face of competition and uncertainties, obviously rely on information, which has to be gathered, interpreted, and applied to each problem. Marketing information must be oriented to the specific problems of decision-makers in that area and, to a lesser but still important extent, to the nonmarketers who also base decisions on marketing data. In addition to its role in problem-solving, marketing information is also used in connection with planning, control, and public opinion, among other areas. Thus, both specific and general decisions are dependent on the information that can be made available. Of course, information does not replace executive judgment; it simply improves it.

Regardless of the type or size of industry, information is needed; regardless of the kind of business—manufacturer, foreign trader, retailer, or wholesaler—it serves as a basis for judgment; and regardless of location, executives require it. The awareness of this need is universal in marketing circles. In Europe the Organization for Economic Cooperation and Development strongly encourages the gathering of marketing data, and ESOMAR (European Society for Opinion Surveys and Market Research) was created especially for the improvement of marketing research, as was the International Marketing Federation (IMF). Information reaches those engaged in marketing in the Philippines through the periodical *Marketing Horizons,* in England through *Scientific Marketing,* and similar journals are available in other countries. The search for marketing information is not unique to the free-enterprise nations. Even the USSR employs vast amounts of marketing information in its economic planning. The curriculum in Soviet "Schools of Distribution" places some emphasis on information-gathering and on research methodology. In Eastern European countries such as Czechoslovakia, marketing research is used in a variety of ways by various marketing and economic offices, both in macro and micro situations.

## The Value of Information

The stakes in modern business are high, and information is valuable in many ways. To launch a new product may require a firm to invest millions of dollars, and for a product doomed to failure the consequence may be more than an embarrassing withdrawal from the market. Marketing research can save business from disaster in the same manner that military information serves the armed forces.

Marketing information can promote company growth as well as avert disaster. In 15-1, for example, growth is attributed to several factors, all of them based on information. Information also plays a vital role in increasing a firm's profits in a variety of ways. Supply schedules, for example, can be adjusted more accurately with knowledge about demand. Through the use of marketing intelligence, budgeting can be improved, pricing schedules can be better adjusted to the market situation, advertisements can be made more effective, and procurement of materials can be more efficiently handled. In short, a firm's marketing program will be more efficient when it is based on sound intelligence data. In one study of small business firms, specific benefits from marketing research cited by the owners included the following:

"We were able to prune down our product line."
"Product decisions are vastly improved."
"We revised our sales territories on the basis of the collected data."
"Research helped us to get product acceptance."
"We believe our marketing information stopped a downturn in sales." (Holloway, 1961.)

Information helps to eliminate waste and waste motion. Some of this reduction can be accomplished by time-studies, but other improvements require scrutiny of a variety of marketing figures on costs. As early as 1915 Arch W. Shaw lamented:

They [businessmen] guess at the most effective sales ideas which analysis of their product discloses, guess at the most forceful forms

## 15-1

**Why Companies Grow**

The study indicates that companies with high rates of sales growth usually have:

1. An affinity for growth products or fields,
2. Organized programs to seek and promote new business opportunities,
3. Proven competitive abilities in their present lines of business, and
4. Courageous and energetic management, willing to take carefully studied risks.

*SOURCE:* N. R. Maines, *Why Companies Grow* (Menlo Park, Cal.: Stanford Research Institute, 1955), p. 1.

of expressing these, and guess at the most efficient agencies and mediums for transmitting them to prospective purchasers. . . . The need of a search study of all the activities of distribution . . . is emphasized by the appalling waste of money, effort and merchandise due to this general lack of standardization in the materials of demand creation as well as all the other factors bearing on the efficiency of our marketing system. (Shaw, 1915.)

It is not easy to learn about the products, retailers, advertising, salesmen, packages, and other facets of marketing that fail each year since the evidence is usually removed from the market scene, unlike the vacant service station on the corner that testifies to mistakes made in allocating marketing resources. We do know that money is spent by some of our largest firms on products that have no market potential. It may surprise you to learn that approximately 2500 brands of automobiles have been withdrawn from the United States automobile market since the turn of the century.

Manifestly the economy benefits from the use of marketing information, for information also permits governments to anticipate needs in various areas, thereby improving the allocation of resources. Look at almost any government program and you will immediately note the important role played by information, whether routinely collected data such as population or the result of a formal research project such as a study on the effects of a postage-rate increase.

### Environmental Information

Vast amounts of information come to the marketer from the environment, most of it with little effort on his part. Much of the accessible information is, unfortunately, irrelevant, superfluous, and even unreliable. The marketer's task is to sort the data and use what fit his needs. When information is inadequate the research manager is forced to undertake a more formal program for collecting data. His goal, of course, is to use the information in preparing a product, complete with price, promotion, and package, and in developing plans for all other marketing activities. Thus in many ways *marketing operations and the environment are tied together through the information-gathering process.* The environment yields information and the firm responds with its products and services.

There are many sources of information in the environment. Economic information, of course, is everyday news which a businessman can avail himself of. Another important source of economic information is a firm's sales force, because the information it supplies is in the form of dollars of business lost or gained. Suppliers' salesmen also gather a certain amount of economic information that they pass on to management.

Technological information is announced through the press, trade publications, and governmental sources. Marketing people serve as the ears of the firm for learning about technological innovations or plans in the developmental stage. A marketer cannot wait to learn of technological development from his customer; if he does so, he will be too late. A company producing equipment for the care of golf-course greens, for instance, certainly should be aware of the development of artificial turf that requires no care.

Information about competition comes from printed sources, advertisements, customers, suppliers, and other sources. Corporate spies may provide some information, but this channel is in general disfavor. Rumors are common but difficult to evaluate. Some firms leave easy trails to follow, but others deliberately mislead their competitors. A few years ago a chemical company, for instance, placed a new brand of antifreeze (actually an old brand in a new package) on the market to conceal the development of a genuine new product. (The effort succeeded and the decoy product was carried for a number of years since it was purchased by a sizable number of car owners.)

The environment, then, is the principal source of marketing information for a firm. Information about customers and their attitudes, preferences, life styles, and socioeconomic characteristics; speed of innovation; competition; changing channels of distribution and retail trends; the economic outlook and government activity—all are relevant to the marketer. If he is at all receptive to the environmental forces, he cannot help but learn much that will improve his marketing efforts. With the great supply of information available, his task of collecting, sorting, evaluating, and using data to make decisions is not easy, but it is nevertheless essential.

## MARKETING DECISIONS

Marketing research provides information for decision-making but it is not the only source of marketing information any more than marketing managers are the sole decision-makers within the firm. The diagram in 15-2 shows other sources of information and influence in the decision-making process.

**15-2** Decision-Making Tree

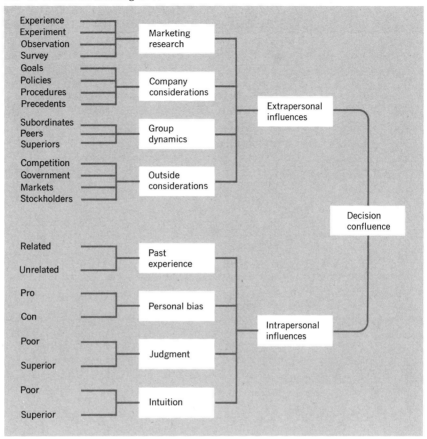

SOURCE: John G. Keane, "Some Observations on Marketing Research in Top Management Decision-Making," *Journal of Marketing*, Vol. 33 (October 1969), p. 12.

Marketing decisions range from the most vital to the most trivial matters. They include basic management problems, market development activities, and the details of packing a product for shipment. Most of these decisions have to be made over and over again. Each year advertising programs have to be devised, each quarter sales quotas may be adjusted, and each day inventories may be examined.

These decisions are not made in a vacuum, but in a fast-moving, competitive, complex business atmosphere that is exciting but potentially frustrating. The decisions involve risk and uncertainty, and this danger makes information indispensable. The situation may not be so critical as, for instance, the Cuban missile crisis of October 1962, when the late President Kennedy had to make critical decisions based on essential information provided by aerial photographs. Yet the same need for information to reduce risk in decision-making occurs in business time after time. A few years ago the management of a midwestern firm hired 1200 employees for a new plant set up to make TV tuning devices. After one year of operation it was suddenly discovered that the one plant alone had produced enough tuning devices to supply the entire TV industry for seven years. Needless to say, the plant was closed. The most elementary bit of marketing intelligence (at an extremely low cost) could have precluded this disaster (Shawver, 1971).

Decisions in marketing, as in other endeavors, involve alternatives. A quarterback may have an extensive repertoire of plays, each one representing an alternative. Information concerning the down, position of the ball, defense strategy, players' capabilities on both teams, time left, score, and other particulars of the game permit him to narrow the choice rapidly and to make a logical decision. Information serves the same useful function in marketing.

In our competitive society reliable information concerning competitive action can be among the most valuable pieces of intelligence a marketer can obtain. Ralph Cassady has observed: "The key to intelligent competitive activity is market research which seeks information about consumer wants and behavior patterns to serve as a basis for effective marketing activity" (Cassady, 1960). Knowledge of competitive plans relative to these wants and behavior patterns can have considerable influence on a firm's plans.

One of the most difficult tasks is to forecast market developments (see 15-3 for the predictive aspects of automobile production). Since the marketer is constantly thinking in terms of tomorrow, the informa-

---

## 15-3

### Prediction in the Auto Business

When It Comes to Predicting, Auto Men Look to These Factors:

*In General Business*

Gross National Product
Industrial Production
Personal Income
Wholesale Prices
Consumer Prices
Manufacturing Inventory-Sales Ratio

*In Their Own Business*

Prices: Autos versus Industrial
Prices: Used Cars versus New Cars
Car Sales Share of Disposable Income
New Car Registration as a Percentage of Cars on the Road
Car-buying Population
Installment Debt Repayments as a Percentage of Disposable Income
Percentage of Spending Units with Installment Debt

SOURCE: "Another Big Year Ahead," *Business Week,* September 14, 1963, p. 24. Copyright held by McGraw-Hill, Inc.

---

tion he wants and needs is whatever will help him improve his predictions. Marketing researchers have to be future-oriented for a management that works in tomorrow's terms.

## Basic Marketing Decisions

The most basic decisions for a marketer are actually the same as those of the firm as a whole; they transcend organizational lines. Not only are they the most basic, they are also among the most difficult. One, which is not so simple as it seems, is: *What* product(s) should the company sell?

In this day of rapid technological change, mergers, and diversification programs, the product decision can be overwhelming. What automobiles, appliances, frozen foods, or cosmetics will sell? What do the customers want? Can we produce what we can sell and can we sell what we are capable of producing? If we are established in consumer goods, should we enter the industrial market? Management examines many kinds of information during the product-decision process.

There are many check lists to follow in deciding on new products, and basic to all of them is the extremely difficult question of *quantity*: how many gallons of gasoline, cases of breakfast cereals, gross of ball-point pens, or freight cars of plywood can be sold? What follows from the answer to that question is the answer to questions on product features, plant, promotion, and other matters. Information does not magically produce precise forecasts, but it does narrow the range of error.

Another fundamental question is: *when* will customers buy? When will families vacation, buy new cars, or new houses, for example? When will companies install new hydraulic presses, or when will they replace their truck fleets? For staple or seasonal items, the answer may not be difficult, but for many other products demand may fluctuate so much that the answer will be hard to come by.

An additional basic decision concerns the *price* to charge. The impact of marketing information on price is seen most vividly in a futures pit of a grain exchange, where extremely small bits of information can provoke a change in price. In our competitive economy, price decisions are less rapid and less volatile; they are made primarily by business executives who study data on competition, demand, supply, and other factors. During times of emergency, government takes on the enormous task; in a planned economy, of course, government assumes the task continuously. Both the businessman and the government functionary, then, seek information relevant to pricing.

Still another basic decision for the marketer involves location: *where* should the company sell? The decision rests on information about shipping rates, competition, market potentials, and other factors. Expansion decisions may at times simply confirm a natural tendency to spread beyond a firm's original territory, but at other times they may reflect substantial changes in company policy. For example, a firm may decide after examining the appropriate information to invade another domestic market or even a foreign market. When Standard Oil of California after many years decided to invade the eastern market, both legal and market data were of paramount importance in the company's decision.

*How* to sell is obviously another basic marketing question. The entire plan for developing the market constitutes the answer. Since this topic will receive emphasis in the remainder of Part III, at this point we need only suggest that information plays a significant role in decisions on distribution, promotion, and other facets of market development.

These basic questions, applicable to all firms, involve analyses of the market, anticipations of demand, and an appreciation of immediate situations. Before settling basic market questions, information is collected and used as an aid to managerial judgment. As Percival White pointed out long ago:

> A market may be compared to a sponge, which absorbs the output of business. It is necessary to determine how much this sponge will absorb, how fast it will absorb it, and many other facts, before it is possible to understand and reckon intelligently with the possibilities and limitations of that market. (White, 1925.)

## Decisions Relating to Competition

At some point the basic decisions must be implemented in the marketplace. Market development plans are of necessity competitive. In these matters sometimes a marketer works by intuition, but where possible he prefers to base his decisions on a careful analysis of market information.

Following the broad decisions of pricing, producing, selecting a territory, and determining methods of selling, detailed and subsidiary operational programs must be worked out and these detailed programs should also rely on research. A firm deciding to enter the razor-blade market must spell out decisions on quality, price, packaging, and promotion to the letter. The name, the color of the wrapper, and the series of television ads must be carefully chosen. The exact appeal must be ascertained and commercials worked out precisely to take advantage of the market data. Commercials are scheduled for optimum hours of viewing as revealed by research information. Gillette, for example, has spent large sums of money in reaching the viewers of the World Series.

The package for a laundry soap is developed after preferences of housewives are ascertained; the name for a new shampoo is announced following a study of a thousand alternatives. Which is best remembered? Which is most pleasing? Which is easiest to pronounce? What meanings do various designs and names convey? A company examines competitors' lines of goods and then fills in gaps in the array it offers the consumer. Rival automobiles are taken apart, piece by piece, in order to determine manufacturing processes, materials, and features. An appliance manufacturer gathers information on returned merchandise and, on the basis of the resulting analysis, inaugurates a new repair service for small motors on washing machines, driers, and dishwashers.

A manufacturer of high-fidelity equipment learns from its dealers that warranty services must be decentralized if the firm is to remain competitive.

Information of this kind from the market tells the marketer a good deal about his competitive situation. He learns that his product has some special appeal to a particular occupational class, to a certain income, or to one life-cycle group of consumers. The information may help him to define the market segment he can exploit, in lieu of broadcasting his appeal to everyone in general and thus to no one in particular. Trade circles often provide advance information on a technological breakthrough. This intelligence could permit a firm to speed its own research and development in order to prevent a competitor from securing a market lead of months or even years. Marketing information frequently reveals facts about the market that were not recognized by the seller. For instance, a breakfast-food manufacturer became cognizant of a large institutional market (hotels, schools, and hospitals) when his market analyst discovered discrepancies between sales figures and research information.

These are only samples of the types of marketing decisions relating to competition that are made over and over again in any firm. Each decision is based on some amount of information and probably each could be improved with more. Ideally, such decisions would be made only after all the facts were in, but since the marketplace does not wait for anyone, they must frequently be made on the basis of insufficient information. And they are often made when rumors, confusion, and various pressures force action prior to a careful analysis of the circumstances. Nevertheless, whenever possible, the decision-maker prefers to have the facts before him.

## Other Research Applications

Many marketing decisions require much less effort than the foregoing. It is not that the decisions are unimportant but that they are easier to make. Furthermore, routinely collected data can simplify many managerial problems. For example, data on the method of shipment, important to buyer and seller, are fairly easy to gather (rates, insurance, shipping time, and packaging requirements), thus enabling the seller to make routine decisions that become standard procedure. Linear programming has supplied the seller with a technique to develop useful data that contribute to better efficiency for the entire physical distribution program.

Customer billings, too, are handled routinely. Underlying them are the terms of sale that have been agreed on. Once the basic policies have been determined, the more routine tasks of billing the customer are almost forgotten. Compensation of the sales force can be salary, commission, or a combination of both. Regardless, the marketing manager requires certain information in order to determine a compensation schedule that blends incentive with security and missionary work with selling effort.

The problem of identifying customers is aided in some instances by the simple expedient of having buyers return warranty cards. Usually a warranty card includes certain statistics about customer and distributor that enable a marketer who sells indirectly to ascertain who is buying his product. This routine method of handling information aids a firm in making a number of marketing decisions relative to market development.

The minimum size of a profitable order, another routine decision, is relatively easy to handle from cost data. Similarly, cost-of-distribution studies can yield significant data for the manufacturer or distributor without an expenditure of large sums of money. On the basis of these studies the marketer can distinguish between the profitable and unprofitable accounts.

The feedback of information from salesmen is often handled habitually during periodic sales meetings or in salesmen's reports. A tip from a salesman concerning a new use of one of the firm's products can be parlayed into many new orders simply by notifying the other salesmen. Although feedback is important, few firms systematize the information flow, perhaps because of the reluctance of salesmen to file reports.

Information collected routinely can often serve several roles. Gasoline gallonage, for example, is reported by oil companies for tax purposes, and it provides market information that aids in developmental decisions relating to location, demand analysis, and pricing. Changes in gallonage may be checked against new advertising campaigns, new pumps, gasoline additives, and competition, and marketing decisions are influenced from that one figure collected simply by reading the dials on the pumps.

## ORGANIZING FOR MARKETING RESEARCH

The development of a formal information system may not be the goal of every firm, but the development of a satisfactory system or organization for gathering crucial marketing data and information should be. Before examining the organizational questions, we will first look at the research activities as performed by companies.

Periodic surveys of marketing research activities are undertaken by the American Marketing Association. The 1968 survey of marketing research activities of firms is summarized in 15-4, where the research activities are grouped into four major categories with 34 subheadings. For all respondent companies as a group, the most common activities were: (1) determination of market characteristics, (2) development of market potentials, (3) market share analysis, and (4) sales analyses. Note that all of these depend on securing adequate information from the environment. Note also that there are some differences in research activities between consumer and industrial companies, especially in the category of "advertising research."

The activities of a marketing research department as enumerated in 15-4 suggest that a company must make an allocation of resources adequate to handle a sizable job. For an idea of what that means in

**15-4** Percentage of Companies with Research Departments
Performing Specified Research Activities

| Activity | Consumer Firms | Industrial Firms |
|---|---|---|
| Advertising research | | |
|   Motivation research | 60 | 22 |
|   Copy research | 71 | 38 |
|   Media research | 70 | 51 |
|   Studies of ad effectiveness | 81 | 58 |
|   Other | 17 | 14 |
| Business economics and corporate research | | |
|   Short-range forecasting (up to 1 yr.) | 95 | 95 |
|   Long-range forecasting (over 1 yr.) | 90 | 94 |
|   Studies of business trends | 87 | 93 |
|   Profit and/or value analysis | 90 | 87 |
|   Plant and warehouse, location studies | 83 | 81 |
|   Diversification studies | 85 | 86 |
|   Purchase of companies, sales of divisions | 79 | 86 |
|   Export and international studies | 75 | 78 |
|   Linear programming | 68 | 51 |
|   Operations research | 62 | 55 |
|   PERT studies | 55 | 52 |
|   Employees morale studies | 64 | 62 |
|   Other | 8 | 9 |
| Product research | | |
|   New product acceptance and potential | 98 | 95 |
|   Competitive product studies | 95 | 95 |
|   Product testing | 95 | 81 |
|   Packaging research design or physical characteristics | 86 | 62 |
|   Other | 9 | 8 |
| Sales and market research | | |
|   Development of market potentials | 98 | 97 |
|   Market share analysis | 98 | 97 |
|   Determination of market characteristics | 98 | 97 |
|   Sales analyses | 99 | 96 |
|   Establishment of sales quotas, territories | 95 | 94 |
|   Distribution channels and cost studies | 91 | 83 |
|   Test markets, store audits | 87 | 35 |
|   Consumer panel operations | 80 | 20 |
|   Sales compensation studies | 85 | 78 |
|   Studies of premiums, coupons, sampling, deals | 77 | 11 |
|   Other | 7 | 6 |

SOURCE: Dik Warren Twedt (ed.), *1968 Survey of Marketing Research* (Chicago: American Marketing Association, 1969), pp. 41, 44.

the real business world see the specific position descriptions in 15-5.

Studies of organizations show that the size of the marketing research department increases as the size of a firm increases, as might be expected. The median number of full-time employees for small firms is one or two and for large firms approximately 10. Advertising agencies have more research personnel than do manufacturing concerns, and the median number of employees for large agencies is 33. The median

## 15-5

**Marketing Research Position Descriptions**

GREEN GIANT COMPANY: DIRECTOR—MARKET RESEARCH, JOB DESCRIPTION[a]

Responsible to the Vice President—Marketing for administering the Company's market research activity.

*Responsibility and Authority*
  A. Operational
      1. Formulate and recommend investigations of marketing policies, programs, and procedures of the Company and other companies.
      2. Direct and supervise approved investigations of marketing activities.
      3. Direct the performance of tests:
          (a) To determine the relative market standing of Company products and competitive products, both overall and by individual marketing area.
          (b) To measure consumer reaction to proposed new products and new product ideas or actual new products.
          (c) To measure the impact of Company and competitive advertising.
          (d) To study consumer attitudes and feelings toward Company and competitive brands and products.
      4. Compile and maintain files concerning the marketing of Company products.
      5. Analyze and interpret such data so as to bring to management's attention various factors which may have immediate or long-term influence on the marketing of Company products.
      6. Initiate with aid of Brand Marketing Directors and Corporate Planning short and long-term Company sales forecasts.
      7. Recommend to the Director of Sales the purchase of canned goods when necessary.
  B. Organizational
      1. Train and maintain a market research organization adequate for the needs of the Company.
      2. Direct and supervise the activities of: Two Market Research Analysts and Sales Research Analyst.

*Relationships*
  A. Within the Company
      1. Coordinate his activities in obtaining shipping information from Controller's Department.
      2. Cooperate with Product Development Department by coordinating his activities in investigating consumer reaction to new products or new product ideas.
      3. Cooperate with other departments of the Company in developing and executing market research plans.
      4. Coordinate Market Research activities of Green Giant of Canada and the International Division.
  B. Outside the Company
      1. Conduct such relationships with outside research service agencies, government agencies, industrial and professional organizations as are necessary to accomplish his function.
      2. Maintain liaison with the Market Research Department of the advertising agency.

FORD MOTOR COMPANY: MARKETING RESEARCH
MANAGER, ADVERTISING & RESEARCH OFFICE,
STATEMENT OF FUNCTIONS[b]

1. Responsible for coordinating a comprehensive program of marketing research in all areas of the Company so as to provide data
   that is compatible to a total Marketing Research Information system.
2. Responsible for establishing marketing research standards for use
   throughout the Company and maintaining liaison with marketing research components to assure that uniform marketing research
   techniques are being used.
3. Responsible for organizing and interpreting marketing research
   data as it applies to broad Company problems.
4. Provide staff guidance and assistance to Company components
   in the development of research programs, recommend potential
   research opportunities and advise and assist in the development
   of such programs.
5. Coordinate and execute such marketing research studies as necessary to support his other responsibilities.
6. Responsible for representing the Company in various professional
   associations and with educational institutions as appropriate so
   as to assure that the Company is up to date on the latest research
   techniques and developments.
7. Maintain a central library and publish summary reports for management use on significant marketing research results.

SOURCES: [a]Courtesy of the Green Giant Company. [b]Ford Motor Co.

for small industrial firms is slightly higher than for consumer firms, but medium and large consumer firms have more marketing research employees than the industrials.

The number of new departments of marketing research continues to grow. Before 1918 there were five known departments and today there are approximately 500 new ones added every five years. One-third of the marketing research departments in consumer-product companies have originated since 1963, and 43 percent of the industrial depart-ments have been set up in this same period. In manufacturing approxi-mately two-thirds of the marketing research departments report to a vice president of sales or marketing. In advertising agencies about half report to the president or an executive vice president. Between 1963 and 1968 marketing research allocations increased 93 percent. Con-sumer companies have larger marketing research budgets than indus-trial companies: in terms of percentage of sales spent for marketing research, the median is .30 for consumer and .12 for industrial com-panies (Twedt, 1969). In addition to company research departments, there are independent research agencies, advertising agencies, and other commercial services that provide important services.

A businessman can make some approximations concerning the dol-lars-and-cents value of gathering information. He can estimate the costs of research, the costs of mistakes, and the probable gains from new data. A model for determining the value of information is shown in 15-6. After the maximum net value (AB) is reached, diminishing returns set in, that is, costs increase faster than value. Methods of evaluating the worth of marketing data may include sophisticated statistical studies or they may rely on executive judgment (intuition).

The role of the research department is to provide management with meaningful information that will improve decision-making. In this process a number of conflicts are inevitable as the marketing researcher is attempting to coordinate his work with departments both within and without marketing. Viewpoints of the technologist, production manager, or controller will naturally be different from those of marketing personnel. Further, the researcher has a keen desire to be free from any kind of pressure and strong motivation to perform well. He likes to be involved in decision-making, but much of his work is staff-oriented. Top management may see the marketing researcher as lacking in a sense of accountability, poor as a communicator, expensive, ritualized, given to qualifying statements, and too scholarly. The researcher, on the other hand, may see management as anti-intellectual, stingy with the budget, unsympathetic to the problems of the researcher, demanding, and, perhaps the worst, likely to ignore his research reports (see 15-7).

One study of research-management relations examined a number of the critical areas—lack of objectivity, lack of clarity, poor timing of research reports, and inclination to ivory-towerism—and found them to be diminishing in importance. One conflict area seemed to be gaining in importance—the desire of marketing research directors to take a more active part in management decisions is being met by the resistance of line and staff managers who are served by marketing research (Krum, 1969). There are going to be other understandable conflicts, including those between the bright young college student who enters marketing

## 15-6 Value of Information

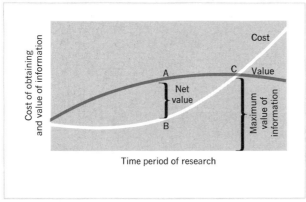

SOURCE: James H. Myers and A. Coskun Samli, "Management Control of Marketing Research," *Journal of Marketing Research,* Vol. 6 (August 1969), p. 268.

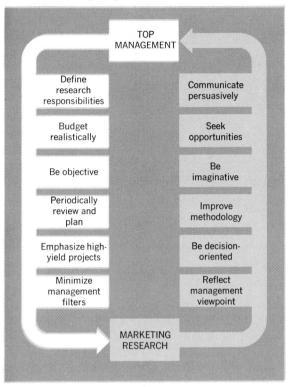

SOURCE: John G. Keane, "Some Observations on Marketing Research in Top Management Decision-Making," *Journal of Marketing*, Vol. 33 (October 1969), p. 13.

research and the sales manager who may have come up through the ranks as a former salesman on the "firing line."

## MARKETING INFORMATION SYSTEMS

A marketing information system has been defined as:

A structured, interacting complex of persons, machines, and procedures designed to generate an orderly flow of pertinent information collected from both intra- and extra-firm sources, for use as the bases for decision-making in specified responsibility areas of marketing management." (Brien and Stafford, 1968.)

Where MIS has been adopted it has become the all-embracing term, and marketing research is one part of the system. Marketing research may solve a number of problems, but it is not typically a continuous information-gathering process as is MIS. The role of marketing research depends on whether or not a MIS concept is in existence within the firm, for marketing research would probably have a narrower responsibility with an MIS program than without it, but at the same time it would not have to be responsible for routine information, thus permitting the research staff to undertake new ventures (Berenson, 1969).

The increasing complexity of marketing, the shortening product life cycles, the enormous investments, and the fast-changing marketing environment has called for more and better data and information. These factors, along with the computer, have encouraged many firms to develop an MIS program because it can offer a number of benefits.

1. It may provide more information within the time constraints required by the firm. Concomitantly, better performance could be achieved by the entire enterprise.

2. It may permit large and decentralized firms to use the information which is scattered in many places, and integrate it into a meaningful perspective.

3. It may permit fuller exploitation of the marketing concept.

4. It may provide selective retrieval of information—users can be given only what they want and need.

5. It may provide quicker recognition of development trends.

6. It may permit far better use of material which is ordinarily collected by many firms in the course of their business activities; for example, sales by product, by customer, and by region.

7. It may permit better control over the firm's marketing plan; for example, it may raise warning signals when something is amiss in the plan.

8. It may prevent important information from being readily suppressed; for example, indications that a product should be withdrawn. (Berenson, 1969.)

The anatomy of an information system is shown in 15-8. Although this is essentially a management system, it does depict the flow of data and information. Necessary marketing data can come from invoices, annual reports, professional and trade publications, and from marketing research efforts.

This kind of sophisticated information system requires a good deal of coordination since so many individuals are involved: top managers, salesmen, new product groups, systems analysts, statisticians, computer equipment experts, marketing managers, brand managers, marketing researchers, control and finance personnel, operations research people, model-builders, and programmers (Cox and Good, 1967).

The concept of an information system is still developing. A few firms have some rather advanced systems and many others have plans to start new ones. Most companies, however, are still operating with a marketing research department as the primary source of marketing information. This is not a criticism of either management or marketing

**15-8** The Marketing-Management Process and Information

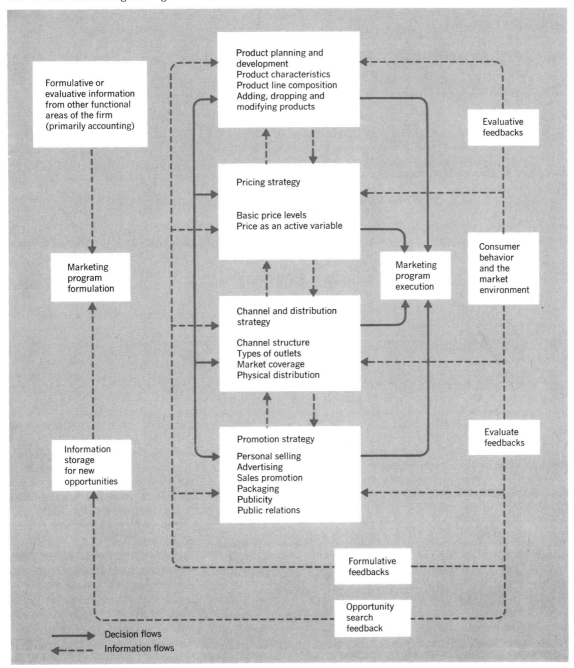

Product planning and development
Product characteristics
Product line composition
Adding, dropping and modifying products

Formulative or evaluative information from other functional areas of the firm (primarily accounting)

Evaluative feedbacks

Pricing strategy

Basic price levels
Price as an active variable

Marketing program formulation

Marketing program execution

Consumer behavior and the market environment

Channel and distribution strategy

Channel structure
Types of outlets
Market coverage
Physical distribution

Information storage for new opportunities

Evaluate feedbacks

Promotion strategy
Personal selling
Advertising
Sales promotion
Packaging
Publicity
Public relations

Formulative feedbacks

Opportunity search feedback

→ Decision flows
⤍--- Information flows

SOURCE: Adapted from Richard H. Brien and James E. Stafford, "Marketing Information Systems: A New Dimension for Marketing Research," *Journal of Marketing*, Vol. 32 (July 1968), p. 20.

research, for the MIS concept is new and it is not easy to implement. Further, it is probably unnecessary for many firms, especially small companies, to develop their marketing research function beyond its present level of activity.

Examples of MIS developments include IBM's Data Processing Division, which provides a manager with an immediate print-out of various types of information sales by product and customer, sales in relation to goals, and so on. Schenley has installed the Schenley Instant Market Reports system, which allows key executives to retrieve (via video display desk consoles and printers) current and past sales and inventory figures for any brand and package size for each of 400 distributors. Pillsbury's system enables marketing managers to obtain sales forecasts for each of 39 sales branches (Cox and Good, 1967).

The marketing information system is a logical and worthwhile concept. Any new concept, however, has to be implanted with care. Personnel changes, for example, must be made with caution. Despite its capabilities, an MIS cannot perform miracles and it does not serve all levels of management equally. Marketing people, like all managers, have much more to learn about what constitutes vital information: this need becomes especially important when computers are involved, for enormous quantities of data may be printed, with little worthwhile information available. With experience, however, the MIS concept holds promise of improving the role of marketing information within the firm.

## CONCLUDING COMMENTS

Marketing information is crucial to management decision-making and is used in the most vital and the most routine situations. Data must be gathered, analyzed, and interpreted for management. The reports of the marketing research department should be trustworthy and the entire research operation should be continuous and ". . . designed to help management set its objectives, plan for their accomplishment, implement the plans successfully, and evaluate the outcome so that better programs may be undertaken in the future" (Newman, 1962). The marketing research program today, just as Duncan pointed out in a series of propositions over 50 years ago, has an important place in serving the company.

1. The immediate and primary need of business today is intelligent direction and control . . .

2. Intelligent direction and control can be had only by a better knowledge of business principles.

3. A better knowledge of business principles can be derived only from a careful and comprehensive survey of business facts.

4. To secure a careful and comprehensive survey of business facts is a problem for business research.

5. Therefore, the immediate and primary need of business today can be met only by business research. (Duncan, 1921.)

In this chapter we have shown the role of marketing research and the value of information. We have also discussed the matter of organizing for research. The next chapter will concentrate on the methodology used by a researcher as he attempts to solve the many kinds of marketing problems posed by various managers within his firm.

## STATEMENTS TO CONSIDER

Marketing research is more responsive than creative.

As the emphasis in marketing shifts from the internal (company) to the external environment, management faces a relative shortage of information.

One of the major problems with marketing research is that both the researchers and the users think far too narrowly about research.

The important questions to which marketing research must be applied are really never answered permanently.

Research is probably more effective in unearthing new possibilities for action than in predicting the response to existing possibilities.

The more concerned top management is with an original research request, the more likely it is to be influenced by the results.

The strength of the research department is largely a function of the size of both the firm and the marketing research department.

One of the uncertainties about the role of research is how the researchers can become involved in day-to-day activities without sacrificing their objectivity. (Krum)

Perhaps the most important potential contribution of research in marketing comes from the relatively objective viewpoint that research encourages even those who do not directly execute it.

Important costs of marketing research include the misusing of information and the failure to obtain information that is available.

# QUESTIONS FOR REVIEW

**1.** Why is marketing research stressed today? For what kinds of problems is it best suited?

**2.** Does marketing research help solve the really difficult problems or is it applicable to only the superficial and factual kinds of problems?

**3.** In what ways would you expect marketing research to differ between socialistic and capitalistic economies?

**4.** What is the relationship between marketing research and the external environment of the firm?

**5.** What sources of information are available to the marketing manager?

**6.** In a product decision of a consumer-goods manufacturer, what kinds of information (specific) would be required to make an intelligent decision about introducing a new product?

**7.** How accurate do you think research data must be in order to be useful?

**8.** Do you consider competitive espionage ethical? Why or why not?

**9.** What possible conflicts do you see between a market researcher and a salesman in the field?

**10.** What kinds of differences would you anticipate in marketing research activities for industrial and consumer goods?

## Further Readings

Gerald Albaum and M. Venkatesan (eds.), *Scientific Marketing Research* (New York: Free Press, 1971).

Marcus Alexis, Robert J. Holloway, and Robert S. Hancock (eds.), *Empirical Foundations of Marketing: Research Findings* (Chicago: Markham Publishing Co., 1969).

Leo Bogart (ed.), *Current Controversies in Marketing Research* (Chicago: Markham Publishing Co., 1969).

Lyndon O. Brown (revised by Leland L. Beik), *Marketing and Distribution Research* (New York: Ronald Press, 1970).

Lewis W. Forman and Earl L. Bailey, *The Role and Organization of Marketing Research* (New York: National Industrial Conference Board, 1969).

David B. Montgomery and Glen L. Urban, *Management Science in Marketing* (Englewood Cliffs, N.J.: Prentice-Hall, 1969).

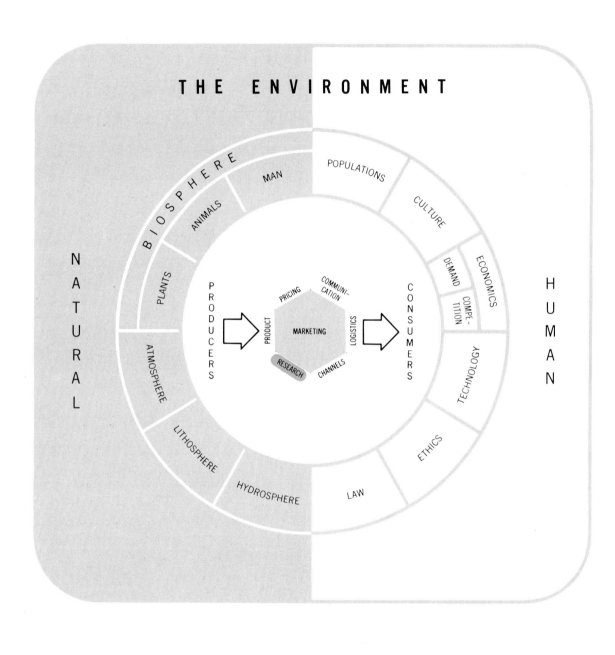

# CHAPTER 16
# MARKETING
# RESEARCH II

**Marketing Research in Operation**

*The Researchers*
*The Research Process*
*Collection of Data*


**Techniques in Marketing Research**

*Surveys*
*Panels*
*Observation*

*Cost Analysis*
*Sociometric Analysis*
*Content Analysis*
*Input/Output Analysis*
*Motivational Research*
*Media*
*Experimental Design*
*The Delphi Method*
*Statistical and Mathematical Techniques*

**Quality Marketing Research**

*The marketing research department in a firm is a highly professional group of individuals who have available many research techniques. These techniques—from mathematics, psychology, sociology, anthropology, economics, and other fields—are matched to a variety of marketing problems.*

In the last chapter we spelled out the role of marketing research and the organization for information-gathering in a firm. In addition, we pointed out the kinds of decisions to which such information ought to be applied. In this chapter we will emphasize research operations, beginning with the researchers themselves, continuing on with techniques, and concluding with some comments about the need for ethics in the field of research.

## MARKETING RESEARCH IN OPERATION

### The Researchers

We pointed out earlier that marketing research benefited from the high quality of people who have been attracted to the field. The professionalism that characterized the early researchers has, fortunately, continued until today. Sometimes a researcher has been criticized for being more "loyal" to his profession than to his firm, but his devotion simply reflects his intense interest in staying abreast of developments. In bygone days it was possible for a researcher to know almost everything published about methodology, but today he may be a specialist—in, say, stochastic processes or simulation techniques.

Persons from many fields engage in marketing research—marketers, advertisers, statisticians, psychologists, sociologists, anthropologists, and others. In common, they all examine data that they hope can improve the decision-making process, but with different emphasis. Still, there is need for the generalist as well as the specialist (Green, 1968). For both, the educational process typically continues on long after graduation from college. A properly programmed master's degree is desirable, and an increasing number of researchers, usually specialists in methodology, have Ph.D.'s.

Diversity characterizes research departments, which can range in size from one man to perhaps 50 people. A small company obviously needs a generalist to handle its many problems, whereas a large firm can afford the luxury of its own specialists. By hiring consultants for short periods of time, of course, a small marketing research department can avail itself of specialists. Independent marketing research firms offer service to companies that lack their own staffs or that want to supplement their staff's work. Again, consultant firms vary from small local companies to far-flung international agencies such as the A. C. Nielsen Co.

There are other types of research staffs. Many advertising agencies perform research for their clients and for their own edification; several of them are noted for fine work but a number lack distinction. Trade associations collect information for their members and sometimes suggest or even perform certain problem-centered research activities. Marketing research is also performed by various governmental agencies, which have published thousands of research reports. Universities, too, frequently have research bureaus. With or without these bureaus, faculty members engage in a substantial number of marketing research activities of their own choosing.

The diversity of market researchers and their backgrounds, interests, organizations, tasks, budgets, and other resources is healthy for the profession. The highly skilled psychologist, for example, learns from the statistician who, in turn, learns from the marketing management staff, and so on. Diversity probably helps to create and maintain an atmosphere in which researchers continually strive to gain new information, try new techniques, and expand their knowledge through journals, meetings, and books as well as discussions inside and outside the firm. The contributions of related disciplines to marketing research techniques is suggested in 16-1.

## The Research Process

Basically, marketing research is a process of gathering, analyzing, and interpreting information for marketing executives. The diagram in 16-2 illustrates the flow of marketing research from the formulation of the problem to its solution and the implementation of the decision.

The interaction of the research operation, the problem being studied, and the subsequent action taken by management is important to understand, for otherwise a researcher may gather unnecessary data and may also fail in gathering proper data for the solution to a marketing problem. This interaction can be shown diagrammatically as follows (Stewart and Haviland, 1951):

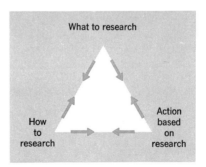

Whatever detailed research procedure is used, a researcher must use care with each and every step to avoid any weak links. Indeed, he ought to approach each marketing problem with the same care and attitude of a physical scientist. How *not* to conduct marketing research is told in 16-3.

## Collection of Data

Because data must be ferreted out of many places from many people, market researchers have to be resourceful individuals. For instance, since the principal source concerning pharmaceutical products is busy doctors, how does a researcher get them to provide valuable information about drugs and treatments? If the desired information concerns income, how does a researcher extract it from people who are reluctant to give it?

### 16-1 Measurement in Marketing

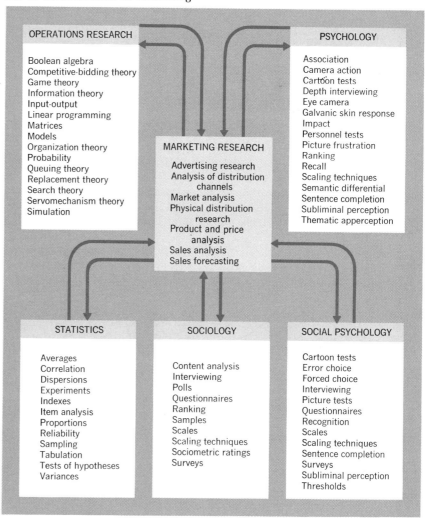

**OPERATIONS RESEARCH**

Boolean algebra
Competitive-bidding theory
Game theory
Information theory
Input-output
Linear programming
Matrices
Models
Organization theory
Probability
Queuing theory
Replacement theory
Search theory
Servomechanism theory
Simulation

**PSYCHOLOGY**

Association
Camera action
Cartoon tests
Depth interviewing
Eye camera
Galvanic skin response
Impact
Personnel tests
Picture frustration
Ranking
Recall
Scaling techniques
Semantic differential
Sentence completion
Subliminal perception
Thematic apperception

**MARKETING RESEARCH**

Advertising research
Analysis of distribution channels
Market analysis
Physical distribution research
Product and price analysis
Sales analysis
Sales forecasting

**STATISTICS**

Averages
Correlation
Dispersions
Experiments
Indexes
Item analysis
Proportions
Reliability
Sampling
Tabulation
Tests of hypotheses
Variances

**SOCIOLOGY**

Content analysis
Interviewing
Polls
Questionnaires
Ranking
Samples
Scales
Scaling techniques
Sociometric ratings
Surveys

**SOCIAL PSYCHOLOGY**

Cartoon tests
Error choice
Forced choice
Interviewing
Picture tests
Questionnaires
Recognition
Scales
Scaling techniques
Sentence completion
Surveys
Subliminal perception
Thresholds

SOURCE: William Lazer and Eugene J. Kelley, "Interdisciplinary Contributions to Marketing Management," *Marketing and Transportation Paper No. 5* (East Lansing: Bureau of Business and Economic Research, Michigan State University, 1959), p. 18.

**16-2** The Phases and Flow of Marketing Research

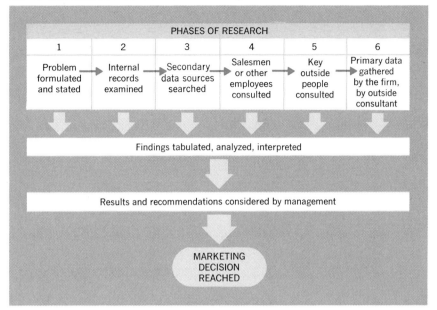

A good rule in collecting data is first to exhaust what is readily available. The data generated by a researcher's own firm are seldom fully used by management. Government data too are greatly underutilized, yet these are inexpensive and reliable. If a department store manager wishes to learn why customers return items, he does not have to commit himself to an expensive personal-interview survey. It is far easier, less expensive, faster, and more reliable to record systematically the actual returns of the firm's customers. Furthermore, unless up-to-the-minute information on population is needed, census data offer the researcher a true bonanza.

Data collection should be closely related to the solution of a specific problem, for often it is possible to settle a matter with data from company records. The point is to collect only essential data. When it appears that a problem can be solved with the data at hand, that is the time to solve it. The reason for belaboring this point is that data collectors become so involved in their task that they seemingly dislike to stop the collection process. Overcollection is a real temptation for a researcher who wants to do his job thoroughly. One lead may turn up another, and so on, until he has opened up vistas of information he did not know existed. Unfortunately he may devote so much time to that process that other phases of the research (for example, analysis and interpretation) will suffer.

The researcher leans heavily on secondary sources of information such as government and industrial statistics, journal articles, and internal company records. If the secondary sources do not suffice, he then gathers his own data through surveys and other research techniques.

## 16-3

**"How Not To Do Research"**

*Note:* Since the following ten rules have not been put into equation form (the style of countless dissertations), they should be easy to follow. Still, it may take time to master these rules, but with practice the average researcher should quickly become adept.

1. Begin the study before formulating a clear purpose or objective.

2. Do not prepare an operational plan or a budget so you can remain flexible, handle problems as they arise, and pester people for advice and money continuously.

3. Start the empirical work or data collection before specifying a hypothesis or theoretical basis.

4. If you are conducting a survey, carefully phrase the questions so they will give the expected answers.

5. On mail surveys, don't bother to follow up the nonrespondents.

6. In analyzing the data, don't bother to make significance tests.

7. To test whether a particular characteristic, say, education of family head, influences a variable such as consumer purchases, use bivariate comparisons.

7a. However, if you should do a multivariate analysis, mention the results only as an afterthought and base the conclusions on the bivariate comparisons.

8. If the data are to be analyzed by computer, let the programmer decide what kinds of analyses are easiest for him, then twist your study design so the objectives fit that kind of output.

9. In writing the report, be brief and vague when discussing the study's details and methods.

10. After you have bought your boss enough drinks so that he enthusiastically approves your report, send it to a journal editor indicating that you are magnanimously allowing him to choose which parts he wishes to publish.

*SOURCE:* Abbreviated from Robert Ferber, "How Not to Do Research—Editorial," *Journal of Marketing Research,* Vol. 5 (February 1968), p. 104.

---

This procedure is referred to as the collection of primary data. The relationship between secondary and primary data is shown in 16-4.

Secondary data are found in a rather small number of journals that provide a great deal of information about almost any marketing problem.

**16-4** The Relationship between Printed Data and Primary Sources

Selection of data and sources

| Data already available | | | | |
|---|---|---|---|---|
| Official statistics | Other published material | Unpublished reports | Internal records | Private information |

Not yet available data

| Surveys | Experiments |
|---|---|

Possible relationships between the data and the unknowns

| Economic | Psychological | Other relations |
|---|---|---|

Unknowns

Possible analytical tools

| Cross tabulation | Regression analysis | $\chi^2$ test | Other tools |
|---|---|---|---|

Type of solution

SOURCE: Robert Ferber and P. J. Verdoorn, *Research Methods in Economics and Business* (New York: Macmillan, 1962), p. 41.

## Marketing

Journal of Marketing
Journal of Advertising Research
Marketing Communications
Survey of Current Business
Business Horizons
Journal of Business
Management Science

Journal of Marketing Research
Industrial Marketing
Sales Management
Harvard Business Review
California Management Review
Business Topics

## Economics

American Economic Review

Quarterly Journal of Economics

## Statistics

Journal of American Statistical Association

Review of Economics and Statistics
Operations Research

Psychology

| | |
|---|---|
| *Journal of Applied Psychology* | *Journal of Personality and Social* |
| *Public Opinion Quarterly* | *Psychology* |
| | *Behavioral Science* |

Sociology

*American Sociological Review*

Trade publications such as the following are valuable sources:

| | |
|---|---|
| *Progressive Grocer* | *Iron Age* |
| *Motor Age* | *Women's Wear Daily* |
| *Electrical Wholesaling* | *Purchasing* |

The following organizations publish a great deal of pertinent material for the marketing researcher.

| | |
|---|---|
| American Marketing Association | Survey Research Centers |
| Opinion Research Center | (e.g., Universities of California |
| National Industrial Conference | and Michigan) |
| Board | American Management Association |

The United States Department of Commerce disseminates vast quantities of marketing information, including censuses of population, housing, retailing, wholesaling, manufacturing, services, and distribution. The Departments of Labor and Agriculture and the Federal Reserve Board also assist the marketer.

The foregoing citations of sources barely suggest the storehouses of information accessible to the researcher. But even with all the printed data available, many marketing problems would remain unsolved unless the marketer could collect information from primary sources, and thus consumers are the object of extensive research. A sensible researcher exhausts the company and printed sources first, or course, and then turns to more formal techniques.

## TECHNIQUES IN MARKETING RESEARCH

Before you leave your residence in the morning, you have a number of alternatives for securing information about weather conditions. You may look out the window, walk outside for a moment, listen to a late weather report, ask someone nearby, check a barometer for change in pressure, read a newspaper report, or call the weather station. Similarly a researcher has a number of alternative techniques for obtaining marketing data. A number of these techniques will be discussed on the following pages. Since this is an overall view of research techniques we have not provided full explanations of each technique. If you have already taken work in quantitative methods, you will find the techniques familiar; if not, you can at least become aware of the variety of tools with which the marketing researcher can solve problems.

## Surveys

Surveys take many forms. Widely used and widely misused, they are deceptively simple and their quality depends on each and every link involved—design, sample, questionnaire, interviewing, analysis, and interpretation. Surveys may solicit facts or opinions or, frequently, both. Many laymen consider the survey technique to be synonymous with marketing research since the term survey has been applied to almost any data-gathering by pollsters, marketing researchers, sociologists, and others. But surveys are only one particular research method.

A survey is simply a device to collect information of various kinds from a given population. A researcher may want to gather facts ("In what store does your family purchase most of its nonprescription drugs?"); or he may want to learn about the buyer's motivations ("Why does your family buy its nonprescription drugs in a _____ store?"). (See 16-5.) A number of other methods, such as projective techniques (to be discussed later), can be combined with survey methods. Surveys are flexible: the information may be gathered by mail, telephone, or personal interviewing.

The most expensive type of survey, personal interviews of a randomly selected audience, is considered the most reliable. Because of the expense involved, however, researchers have developed refinements of the random-sampling plan and improved interviewing techniques. You should bear in mind that the research technique chosen will be influenced by the problem, subsequent management action, and also by the financial resources available to the research staff.

Unless the population to be studied is extremely small and concentrated, the survey method will rely on some type of sampling design. To survey an entire population is most often impossible or at least impracticable, so it is advantageous to select a sample of the population that is hopefully representative of the whole. Even the Bureau of Census with its vast resources and the importance of its assignments utilizes sampling methods for its surveys and even for almost all of its collection of basic population data. The sample is one of the important links in the research chain.

One of the first tasks is to define the sampling unit, that is, the people who are to be surveyed. You may want to sample families in Nashville, adult males in the entire nation, housewives who shop in a supermarket in Manila, recent buyers of Buicks, or presidents of firms employing less than 500 persons. Once the sampling unit is decided upon, you need to determine the type of sample and the number of respondents to include in the sample. A number of sampling methods are used by marketing researchers; the two broad classifications are those that are based on probability and those that are not. A probability sample is one in which each person in the population has an equal chance of being selected in the sample—this is known also as a random sample. The researcher can calculate the degree of accuracy of a random sample and can say that the chances are 95 in 100 that the range "four to six" includes the correct number of radio sets that a typical household

**16-5** A Nationwide Sample of Households Surveyed via WATS (Wide Area Telephone Service)

Selected Questions

Question 1. "In what store does your family purchase most of its nonprescription drugs?"

Question 2. "Why does your family purchase most of its nonprescription drugs in a _____ store?"

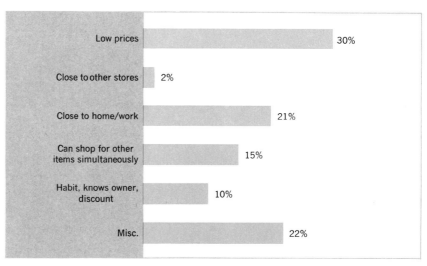

SOURCE: Adapted from Arthur C. Nielsen, Jr., "Convenience and Price—Keys to Drug Store Sales Progress," *The Nielsen Researcher*, Vol. 28, No. 1, (1970,) pp. 9 and 11.

owns. There are many varieties of probability samples. In the simple random sample a telephone directory may supply the listing of the population as defined in the study and the names could be drawn at random in such a way that each has an equal chance of being selected. A stratified sample would classify the population prior to the drawing of names: for instance, the names in the directory could be stratified according to location prior to selection. There are other varieties of probability samples such as cluster, area, quota, nonrepresentative stratified, and multistage sampling plans. There are also various kinds of nonprobability samples that rely on judgment, convenience, or perhaps known characteristics of the population. The big difference between the two major kinds of samples is that probability samples provide measures of confidence that are based on the mathematics of probability and the nonprobability samples cannot provide this information since they are based on judgment; thus it is not possible to say that each person has an equal chance of being selected.

The size of the sample can be determined from a formula that basically reflects the accuracy needed and the confidence desired—not the size of the population. A number of factors should be considered before a sampling formula is used, since the homogeneity and dispersion of the population, type of respondent, and information needed can either increase or decrease the size of the sample. A sample from a population of men aged 35–40 in the same occupation would be smaller than a sample from among men of all ages in all occupations. Thus a sampling plan includes both statistics and judgment. A researcher who knows sampling can reduce substantially the cost of a survey by employing the proper kind of sampling plan.

Once the sampling plan is designed there are decisions to be made about the questionnaire and the type of data to be collected. Each question needs to be worked out carefully and the researcher needs to know in advance that the kinds of answers he receives actually will be relevant to the problem he has formulated. Once the data are collected they must be tabulated, analyzed, and interpreted for management.

## Panels

A panel resembles a survey in that samples and questionnaires are used, but the respondents on a panel are interviewed over and over again. Participants in a panel may be included for several weeks or even indefinitely (see 16-6). The panel has the advantage of providing data over time so that a number of marketing operations can be examined, for example, changes in prices, impacts of new products, effects of commercials, and trends in buying. Analysts must be wary of any tendency of a female respondent, for instance, to lose her effectiveness as a "typical" housewife.

There are several varieties of panels. The Market Research Corporation of America, for instance, maintains a panel of 15,000 consumers

## 16-6

**A Description of the National Family Opinion Panel**

90,000 consumers who can answer any questions on ownership, use, brand preference, purchase expectations; or test any product requested.

Serves business firms and advertising agencies.

All data is treated as confidential.

40 separate on-going panels of 1000 families each, drawn from pool of 90,000.

Quota sample used—each panel consists of 189 strata, balanced against the latest projected census statistics.

The maintenance of a perfectly balanced panel is maintained. The costs must be amortized over many assignments.

SOURCE: *Marketing Knowledge from Consumer Facts* (Toledo, Ohio: National Family Opinion, Inc.).

that has value for many firms. (A consumer panel acquires buying information directly from the consumer, but it is possible to get the same kind of information from retail stores.) The A.C. Nielsen Company makes periodic checks of a group of food and drug stores in order to secure information on purchases, inventories, sales and store promotion, as shown in 16-7.

## 16-7

**Selected Information Secured Every 60 Days in Food Stores**

1. Sales to consumers
2. Special factory packs
3. Dealer support (displays, etc.)
4. Retail inventories
5. Prices (wholesale and retail)
6. Average order size
7. Retail distribution
8. Out-of-stock
9. Total food store sales

Broken down by brands, territories, county sizes, store types, package sizes, product types

SOURCE: Arthur C. Nielsen, "The Responsibilities of Marketing Research," speech given at Lucerne, Switzerland, September 20, 1966, p. 40.

## Observation

Trained observers can collect a good deal of information. Standing at a food store check-out counter, an observer can record a number of characteristics about customers, what was purchased, quantities of purchases, and even comments made to the checker (see 16-8).

The term "unobtrusive measure" has been given to techniques that

**16-8** Composition of a Shopper Population as Determined by Observers

| Shopper | PRODUCT (Figures in percentages) | | | |
|---|---|---|---|---|
| | Cereal | Candy | Detergent | Total |
| Housewife alone | 36 | 44 | '46 | 39 |
| With child or children | 16 | 11 | ' 7 | 13 |
| With husband | 16 | 9 | 12 | 14 |
| With other adult | 6 | 5 | 4 | 5 |
| Adult male alone, with other adult male, or with children | 22 | 23 | 27 | 24 |
| Child or children alone | 4 | 8 | 4 | 5 |
| *Base* (Number of episodes) | 1000 | 250 | 250 | 1500 |

SOURCE: William D. Wells and Leonard A. Lo Sciuto, "Direct Observation of Purchasing Behavior," *Journal of Marketing Research*, Vol. 3 (August 1966), p. 229.

do not require the cooperation of a respondent and that do not in themselves contaminate the response. For example:

1. The floor tiles around the hatching-chick exhibit at Chicago's Museum of Science and Industry must be replaced every six weeks. Tiles in other parts of the museum need not be replaced for years. The selective erosion of tiles, indexed by the replacement rate, is a measure of the relative popularity of exhibits. . . .
2. One investigator wanted to learn the level of whiskey consumption in a town which was officially "dry." He did so by counting empty bottles in ashcans. . . .
3. The degree of fear induced by a ghost-story-telling session can be measured by noting the shrinking diameter of a circle of seated children. . . .
4. Library withdrawals were used to demonstrate the effect of the introduction of television into a community. Fiction titles dropped, nonfiction titles were unaffected. (Webb, Campbell, Schwartz, and Sechrest, 1966.)

## Cost Analysis

Cost studies, which are performed both inside and outside marketing research departments, are intended to reduce various operating costs; thus the purpose of cost analysis is different from that of most marketing research, which is aimed at expanding sales. Nevertheless, the common goal is to improve marketing and profits. Calculations that prove helpful to management reveal profit as related to size of order, selling cost per customer, costs related to product lines, and shipping costs for orders. Internal company data are usually relied on, although outside statistics frequently enable a researcher to compare his company's costs with an industry "standard."

## Sociometric Analysis

Interaction among consumers is often studied for marketing purposes. The sociometric method permits a researcher to identify the most influential people in a particular setting. Consumers might be asked, "To whom in the neighborhood would you go to for advice about a dishwasher?" From this kind of neighborhood study a sociogram showing interrelationships could be developed. Further, relationships among others in the marketing chain (such as doctors, who prescribe drugs) are also subjected to analysis.

## Content Analysis

Content analysis is a technique for studying marketing communications. An advertisement, for example, can be examined word by word or thought by thought. By categorizing and quantifying the words and thoughts, a researcher can develop a picture of the communication that can be compared to competition and can be related to buying activity.

## Input-Output Analysis

The technique of input-output analysis was first developed to study the nation's economic structure on an interindustry basis. Each industry is listed twice: once in a row as an output; and once in a column as an input. By making a number of calculations a researcher can use the technique in forecasting, planning, budgeting, and in identifying markets. For instance, a firm selling materials to industries engaged in military activities might use the input-output technique to determine the impact of drastic cutbacks in military expenditures. The technique

**16-9** An Input-Output Matrix (Figures in Thousands of Dollars)

|  | Crude oil | Chemicals | Cellulosics | Synthetics | Plastics | Paints | Refined products | Gross* output |
|---|---|---|---|---|---|---|---|---|
| Crude oil | $ — | $ 18,463 | $ 3,640 | $ 592 | $ — | $ — | $ 66,769 | $ 103,514 |
| Chemicals | 2,869 | 21,488 | 40,882 | 55,462 | 56,166 | 15,761 | 1,711 | 355,350 |
| Cellulosics | — | 15,480 | — | 142 | 2,391 | — | — | 206,831 |
| Synthetics | — | — | 755 | — | 3,157 | — | — | 190.955 |
| Plastics | 305 | 2,662 | 5,557 | 616 | 25,059 | 930 | 24 | 130,078 |
| Paints | 1,188 | 286 | 271 | 4 | 586 | 7,677 | 193 | 109,404 |
| Refined products | — | 999 | 700 | — | 891 | 555 | 15,373 | 122,653 |
| Value added | 91,770 | 260,975 | 91,685 | 107,957 | 34,143 | 48,878 | 30,316 | — |
| Gross output* | 103,514 | 355,350 | 206,831 | 190,955 | 130,078 | 109,404 | 122,653 | 1,218,785 |

*Rows and columns do not total because columns for "other industrial sectors" and for "final demand" are omitted.

SOURCE: "Planners Put Big Picture on a Grid," *Business Week*, September 23, 1967, p. 62. Copyright held by McGraw-Hill, Inc.

has become useful to individual firms, but it is still not widely used because of its complexity and the relative scarcity of appropriate data (see 16-9).

## Motivational Research

The greatest strides toward finding out why purchasers behave as they do have been made through motivational research. Through an array of techniques researchers endeavor to ascertain the motivations behind a purchase, the reading of an advertisement, or the reaction to a brand name. Examples of some of these techniques are shown in 16-10.

## 16-10

### Determining Motivation—A Study of Automobiles

(Six Motivation Research Techniques)

(1) *Depth Interviewing:* "I'd like you to think of the most satisfying things about owning and driving a car. What would you say they are?"

(2) *Thematic Apperception Test:*

"The boy has asked Dad for advice about getting a car. Imagine that you are the parent; what would you tell him?"

(3) *Incomplete Sentences:* "People who drive convertibles . . . ."

(4) *Role Playing:* "Pick out a car from this list (on card) that goes with each person the best."

"He's a young guy, just starting out, bright and hopeful."

(5) *Attitude Study:* "What is the best thing and the worst thing about each of the following cars?"

(6) *Descriptions:* "Below are some descriptions of automobiles. Which car-make do you think fits closest to each description?"

"A quality car. Expensive, impressive but not flashy. It's built to last."

SOURCE: *Automobiles—What They Mean to Americans* (Chicago-Social Research, Inc.), pp. 6–14.

## Media

Many hours and much money are invested in evaluating techniques for all kinds of persuasive devices, yet the effectiveness of selling and advertising continues to be elusive. Most people are familiar with radio and television ratings that are based on telephone surveys, mechanical devices placed on sets, diaries, personal interviewing, or other techniques. The ratings are useful to advertisers and to those in charge of programs who want to know how many people watch any given program. Magazines and newspapers also have their methods to help advertisers evaluate the effectiveness of many kinds of printed media. The results of a readership study are shown in 16-11. The task of establishing the number of readers, listeners, or viewers is difficult enough, even for the purpose of defining a reader or a viewer. Even more difficult is the task of ascertaining the effectiveness of an advertisement on the reader. Evidence such as the following is frequently presented as proof of the effectiveness of television on buying practices. Forty percent of the television viewers are buyers in this example but only five percent of the nonviewers are buyers.

|  | 1000 Viewers | 1000 Nonviewers |
|---|---|---|
| Number of Buyers | 400 | 50 |
| Number of Nonbuyers | 600 | 950 |

## Experimental Design

The technique of experimental design is relatively new and little used by marketing researchers since the variables in a marketing situation are difficult to control in an experiment. However, social scientists—social psychologists in particular—have shown how to use experimental design in the study of human behavior, and as a consequence marketing researchers have taken up this technique. Successful studies related to the marketer's interests have been done of changes in attitude, recency-primacy, effort as related to satisfaction, and conformity. Experimentation has a substantial potential and will doubtless be used to a greater extent in the future. It is, indeed, the best way in which cause-and-effect relationships can be ascertained.

Some experiments can be conducted in a *laboratory,* such as a pilot test for an experiment that later may be taken to the field. The laboratory experiment is likely to receive increasing emphasis from marketing scholars as they seek answers to such questions as those involving brand loyalty, use of information, advertising stimuli, and personal influence. For an illustration of the design of a laboratory experiment, see 16-12.

With improvements in techniques *field* experiments will prove more useful to marketing practitioners than they have been in the past. Even now a number of them have been completed with adequate results—see

**16-11** Selected Results from a Starch Study* (of Men Readers) on *Life* (February 13, 1970)

| ADVERTISEMENT | COST Pennies per reader | RANK IN ISSUE Number of readers | RANK IN ISSUE Cost per reader | READERS PER DOLLAR Noted† | READERS PER DOLLAR Associated† | READERS PER DOLLAR Read Most† |
|---|---|---|---|---|---|---|
| Volkswagen passenger cars | 2.8 | 12th | 14th | 53 | 36 | 25 |
| Schlitz beer | 2.0 | 4th | 2nd | 57 | 51 | 13 |
| Maytag dishwasher | 2.2 | 16th | 7th | 57 | 46 | 4 |

*Daniel Starch & Staff, Inc., prepare the *Starch Message Report* for advertisements in a number of magazines and newspapers. In a typical year over 100,000 people are interviewed, and 75,000 advertisements and 1000 issues of 140 publications are studied.

†*"Noted" reader*: A person who remembered having previously seen the advertisement in the issue being studied. *"Associated" reader*: A person who not only "noted" the advertisement but also saw or read some part of it which clearly indicates the brand or advertiser. *"Read-most" reader*: A person who read half or more of the written material in the ad.

*SOURCE*: Daniel Starch & Staff, Inc., "Starch Scope, Method, and Use" (New York).

## 16-12 Effort, Expectation, and Satisfaction

*Hypotheses:* When customers expend little effort to obtain a product, those who receive a product less valuable than they expected will rate that product lower than will those who expected to receive, and do receive, the same product.

As effort expended increases, this effect decreases.

*Design:*

| Effort | Expectation Low | Expectation High |
|---|---|---|
| Low | A | B |
| High | C | D |

*The Experiment:* Consumers were placed in conditions of high and low effort combined with high and low expectations (A,B,C,D cells). They carried on an assigned task according to their cell and then made an evaluation of a product, shown below.

*Selected Results:* Index of mean product evaluation scores (Maximum = 100)

| Effort | Expectation Low | Expectation High |
|---|---|---|
| Low | 51 | 35 |
| High | 54 | 44 |

*Conclusions:* Hypotheses 1 and 2 were supported by the data.

*SOURCE*: Richard N. Cardozo, "An Experimental Study of Customer Effort, Expectation, and Satisfaction," *Journal of Marketing Research*, Vol. 2, No. 3 (August 1965), pp. 244-249.

16-13 for an example. Conditions are difficult to control in the field, of course, but the technique offers a wide variety of opportunities for studying the merchandising of consumer goods.

## The Delphi Method

Another recent development is the forecasting of technology. Among a number of techniques for forecasting the Delphi method is extensively used. In this method, opinions are gathered from experts in a field. The opinions received by the researchers are sent back to the panel of experts for a second opinion, but this time they have the benefit of the first-round responses. The process may be repeated several times. The idea is that the final result will provide the best possible forecast of the date when a given technology will become common or the kind of technology expected to be in use by, say 1990. The technique need not be confined to forecasting technology, of course, and marketing researchers can explore the application of the Delphi method to a variety of marketing problems.

## Statistical and Mathematical Techniques

There was a time when the only statistical and mathematical techniques employed by marketing researchers were random sampling

---

## 16-13

**Location Effects on Sales and Pilferage of Cigarettes**

*Problem:* To determine the effect of display location on the sales and pilferage of cigarettes in supermarkets.

*Design:* Three treatments were selected for the experiment:

1. An island shelving unit located in front of one of the store checkouts.
2. Rack shelving at the checkout end of one of the grocery aisles.
3. Regular grocery shelving.

*Selected Results:*

| Treatments | Sales (cartons) | Display space (sq. ft.) | Pilferage (cartons) | Pilferage (% of sales) |
|---|---|---|---|---|
| Checkout island | 8,195 | 133.6 | 479 | 5.84 |
| Grocery shelving | 8,807 | 158.5 | 613 | 6.96 |
| End aisle racks | 9,288 | 164.5 | 295 | 3.17 |
| Total | 26,290 | | 1,387 | 5.27 |

SOURCE: John R. Kennedy, "The Effect of Display Location on the Sales and Pilferage of Cigarettes," *Journal of Marketing Research*, Vol. 3 (May 1970), p. 211.

---

**16-14** The Growth Rate of Innovation in Advertising-Marketing Research

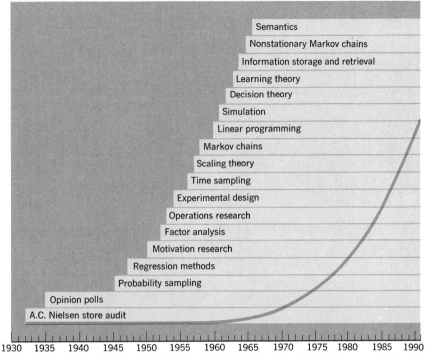

SOURCE: B. Lipstein, "Prospects for the Managerial Sciences in Advertising," *Management Science*, Vol. 13 (October 1966), pp. B-1 to B-9.

methods, correlation, and chi square analysis. But today the number of techniques available is most impressive, as suggested by the growth rate in 16-14. Various techniques and their applications are listed in 16-15, and two of the newer methods are illustrated in 16-16 and 16-17. The potentialities of marketing research have increased greatly because of these techniques, since they permit a widening array of problems to be examined and improved research on some of the older problems. Unquestionably, still more techniques will be developed in the near future, but even now the kit of the researcher is well stocked.

## QUALITY MARKETING RESEARCH

Business both performs marketing research and utilizes the results. It is important that the researcher and the manager understand each other and each other's tasks. In conducting research, a researcher should not combine personal selling with interviewing, for example. The researcher has the tools to make contributions of a high order and so both the doer and the user need to coordinate and cooperate (Hardin, 1969).

**16-15** Marketing Techniques and Applications

| | | Advertising research | Acquisition screening | Brand strategy | Customer segmentation | Customer service | Distribution planning |
|---|---|---|---|---|---|---|---|
| **MATURE TECHNIQUES** | Regression & correlation analysis | X | | X | | | |
| | Discounted cash flow (DCF) | | | | | | X |
| | Incremental analysis | X | | | | | X |
| | Multiple regression/ multiple correlation | X | | X | | | |
| | Random sampling | | | | | | |
| | Sampling theory | X | | X | | | |
| **MODERN TECHNIQUES** | Bayesian approach | X | | | | | |
| | Cost-benefit analysis | X | | | | | |
| | Critical path method (CPM) | | | | | | |
| | Decision trees | X | X | | | | |
| | Dynamic programming | X | | | | | |
| | Exponential smoothing | | | | | | |
| | Industrial dynamics | | | | | | X |
| | Input-output analysis | | | | | | |
| | Linear programming | X | | | | | X |
| | Markov processes | | | X | X | | |
| | Monte Carlo simulation | | X | X | | | X |
| | Nonlinear programming | X | | | | | X |
| | Numerical taxonomy | X | | X | X | | |
| | PERT | | | | | | |
| | Queueing models | | | | | X | X |
| | Risk analysis | X | X | | | | |
| | Sensitivity analysis | X | X | | | | |
| | Technological forecasting | | | | | | |

SOURCE: Joseph Dash and Conrad Berenson, "Techniques in Marketing Research," *Harvard Business Review*, Vol. 69 (September–October, 1969), p. 26.

| Market segmentation | Pricing strategy | Product life-cycle analysis | Product-line analysis | Product planning | R & D planning | Return on investment analysis | Sales forecasting | Test marketing | Venture planning |
|---|---|---|---|---|---|---|---|---|---|
| X | X | | | | | | X | | |
| | | | X | | X | X | | | |
| | X | | | | X | | | | |
| | | | | | | | X | | |
| | | | | | | | | | |
| | | | | | | | X | X | |
| | X | X | | X | | X | | | |
| | | | | | | X | | | |
| | | | X | X | X | | | X | X |
| | X | | X | | | | | | |
| | | | | | X | X | | | X |
| | | | | | | | X | | |
| | X | | | | | | | | |
| | | | X | X | X | | X | | X |
| | | | | | | | | | |
| | | | X | | | | | | X |
| | | | | | | | | | |
| X | | | | | | | | | |
| | | | X | X | X | | | X | X |
| | | | | | | | | | |
| | X | | X | | | | | | |
| | X | | X | | | | | | |
| X | | X | X | X | X | | X | | X |

## 16-16 Simulation Model

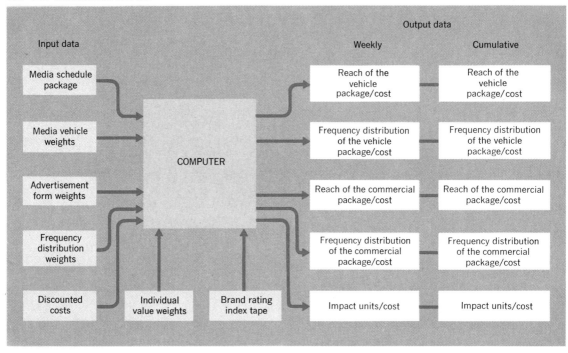

SOURCE: Dennis H. Gensch, "A Computer Simulation Model for Selecting Advertising Schedules,"
*Journal of Marketing Research*, Vol. 6 (May 1969), p. 205.

## 16-17 Bayesian Analysis

| Unit sales | Estimated probability | Profit or loss | OPPORTUNITY LOSS | | EXPECTED OPPORTUNITY LOSS | |
|---|---|---|---|---|---|---|
| | | | Introduce | Not introduce | Introduce | Not introduce |
| 1,800,000 | .10 | $450,000 | 0 | $450,000 | 0 | $45,000 |
| 1,600,000 | .25 | 200,000 | 0 | 200,000 | 0 | 50,000 |
| 1,400,000 | .35 | 0 | 0 | 0 | 0 | 0 |
| 1,200,000 | .15 | −150,000 | $150,000 | 0 | $22,500 | 0 |
| 1,000,000 | .10 | −250,000 | 250,000 | 0 | 25,000 | 0 |
| 800,000 | .05 | −400,000 | 400,000 | 0 | 20,000 | 0 |
| Total | 1.00 | | | | $67,500 | $95,000 |

Note: Bayesian analysis permits the assignment of numerical probabilities to unique rather than repetitive events. These probabilities can be subjectively determined. The probability of success can be predicted by the calculation of the opportunity loss for each action. For example, in the Bayesian analysis of a new-product introduction shown in this table, the overall expected opportunity loss for introducing the product is $67,500 and the opportunity loss for not introducing is $95,000.

SOURCE: James H. Myers and A. Coskun Samli, "Management Control of Marketing Research," *Journal of Marketing Research,* Vol. 6 (August 1969), p. 270.

Certain characteristics are essential to marketing research if it is to be worth a good deal to management. It must be:

Geared to the marketing problem; designed to answer the query; tailor-made to the situation.

Objective; free of bias from any source, from problem formulation to interpretation of results.

Deliberate; hurried research involves too many short-cuts and opens possibilities for errors.

Capable of making predictions; the marketer is concerned more about next month than last year.

Accurate to a sensible degree; well within the user's margin-of-error restrictions.

Presented in a report which is understandable, uncluttered, and free from difficult research terminology.

Common sense in its approach and direction; not divorced from the realities of the company and the marketplace.

Applied to the important problems; limited resources prohibit lavish expenditures for research.

The best possible information within the financial and personnel limitations of the firm.

Good marketing research provides an executive with evidence to help him decide on a plant acquisition, a coming television production, the number of price lines to feature, the size of his sales force, and a corporate symbol. Because the researcher occupies a staff job, he must integrate his results with his company's operations. His raison d'etre is to provide useful information to the manager.

Ethics is an important consideration; 16-18 contains a Code for marketing researchers. It is not a terribly confining Code. Few sanctions can at present be applied to violators. It does, however, offer some protection to both the researcher and the user of research. One study of research ethics found that top management and researchers have similar ethical standards and that both groups want "proper" research conduct. Some of the practices questioned by both groups included the use of ultraviolet ink, hidden tape recorders, and one-way mirrors (Crawford, 1970). Unless marketing research is kept on a high ethical plane, the results will be largely worthless because no one will trust the researchers.

In addition to ethical questions having to do with methodology, there are the questions relating to objectivity and kinds of research undertaken. For instance, some years ago an independent research organization was taken to task for conducting marketing research for a gambling casino. In another situation, a research company used the "research" results as information for personal selling efforts. In still another case, a company president asked a researcher to prove that the sales manager was ineffective in order to have cause to fire him.

## 16-18

**A Code for Marketing Researchers**

The American Marketing Association, in furtherance of its central objective of the advancement of science in marketing and in recognition of its obligation to the public, has established these principles of ethical practice of marketing research for the guidance of its members. In an increasingly complex society, marketing management is more and more dependent upon marketing information intelligently and systematically obtained. The consumer is the source of much of this information. Seeking the cooperation of the consumer in the development of information, marketing management must acknowledge its obligation to protect the public from misrepresentation and exploitation under the guise of research.

Similarly the research practitioner has an obligation to the discipline he practices and to those who provide support for his practice—an obligation to adhere to basic and commonly accepted standards of scientific investigation as they apply to the domain of marketing research.

It is the intent of this code to define ethical standards required of marketing research in satisfying these obligations.

Adherence to this code will assure the users of marketing research that the research was done in accordance with acceptable ethical practices. Those engaged in research will find in this code an affirmation of sound and honest basic principles which have developed over the years as the profession has grown. The field interviewers who are the point of contact between the profession and the consumer will also find guidance in fulfilling their vitally important role.

*For Research Users, Practitioners and Interviewers*

1. No individual or organization will undertake any activity which is directly or indirectly represented to be marketing research, but which has as its real purpose the attempted sale of merchandise or services to some or all of the respondents interviewed in the course of the research.

2. If a respondent has been led to believe, directly or indirectly, that he is participating in a marketing research survey and that his anonymity will be protected, his name shall not be made known to anyone outside the research organization or research department, or used for other than research purposes.

*For Research Practitioners*

1. There will be no intentional or deliberate misrepresentation of research methods or results. An adequate description of methods

---

The ethical problems are important, but fortunately they are relatively minor at the same time, for the issues involved seldom arise. The development of marketing research continues in part at least because of executives' confidence in it. A 1969 study indicates that companies are intensifying their marketing research efforts and moving away from very simple research concepts to "action-oriented, decision-oriented, problem-solving research." The same source points out that "many employed will be made available upon request to the sponsor of the research. Evidence that field work has been completed according to specifications will, upon request, be made available to buyers of research.

2. The identity of the survey sponsor and/or the ultimate client for whom a survey is being done will be held in confidence at all times, unless this identity is to be revealed as part of the research design. Research information shall be held in confidence by the research organization or department and not used for personal gain or made available to any outside party unless the client specifically authorizes such release.

3. A research organization shall not undertake marketing studies for competitive clients when such studies would jeopardize the confidential nature of client-agency relationships.

*For Users of Marketing Research*

1. A user of research shall not knowingly disseminate conclusions from a given research project or service that are inconsistent with or not warranted by the data.

2. To the extent that there is involved in a research project a unique design involving techniques, approaches or concepts not commonly available to research practitioners, the prospective user of research shall not solicit such a design from one practitioner and deliver it to another for execution without the approval of the design originator.

*For Field Interviewers*

1. Research assignments and materials received, as well as information obtained from respondents, shall be held in confidence by the interviewer and revealed to no one except the research organization conducting the marketing study.

2. No information gained through a marketing research activity shall be used directly or indirectly, for the personal gain or advantage of the interviewer.

3. Interviews shall be conducted in strict accordance with specifications and instructions received.

4. An interviewer shall not carry out two or more interviewing assignments simultaneously unless authorized by all contractors or employers concerned.

Members of the American Marketing Association will be expected to conduct themselves in accordance with the provisions of this Code in all of their marketing research activities.

SOURCE: American Marketing Association, Chicago.

---

sectors of management now embrace marketing research information as an aid . . . whereas they might previously have been inclined to view it as a threat to management prerogatives (Forman and Bailey, 1969). Other trends include the increased education of researchers, at both the university and post-university levels. And, of course, another trend is the development of more sophisticated techniques and information systems.

# CONCLUDING COMMENTS

Marketing information underlies the decisions made each day by marketing executives. The sources of this information are many, for each corner of the marketing environment yields some clues for operational and planning decisions. It is the marketer's job to look at the information and make decisions that will determine the success of the product or service involved. Essential to the soundness of advertising, selling, pricing, distributive, and other marketing plans is a well-organized program of marketing research. In summary,

> Market research is not magic. It takes time. It costs money. It performs no miracles. How much it can increase your profits and reduce your risks depends on you. Nobody else affects the results you get. You hire your research director. You appropriate his budget. You set the terms and conditions under which he works. You establish the general lines of inquiry he pursues. You get the results. You file and forget them or you use them . . . If you do not give him the tools he needs, that is your fault. If you do not put him to work on major problems, you will not get major results. (Fox, 1950.)

The task of the marketing researcher is not an easy one. He must know research methodology and the role research information plays for his company. He operates under budgetary constraints, yet his job is continuous, since the need for information never ceases. He wants to provide accurate answers at all times but recognizes that accuracy carried to an extreme can be prohibitive in cost. As the valuable intelligence arm of a company, he fills a vital staff job.

Under the best of circumstances, a researcher is going to make mistakes that may mislead management. These instances will be few in number if the researcher and his superiors understand the role of research. The research must not get "lost" in techniques and terminology. Management, on the other hand, must not demand the impossible in terms of quick results, nor should it suggest or compel the researcher to bias his results in any manner.

With the value of marketing information well accepted, the task becomes a matter of improving the information obtainable and the decisions based on it. As Fox (1950) has summarized:

Marketing research is an orderly way of determining:

Where
When
How
Why
By whom

competitive
alternative
our own

products
services

are

sold
bought
used

and

WHAT CAN WE DO ABOUT THESE FACTS TO INCREASE PROFITS?

# STATEMENTS TO CONSIDER

Marketing research does not relieve management from the responsibility for making decisions.

Motivation research practitioners are not capable of discovering people's hidden fears and desires.

The primary value of marketing research lies in its ability to make predictions for the marketing managers.

The recent emphasis on information has been largely responsible for the increased amounts of marketing research performed.

Unfortunately, marketing research does not apply to really important problems of the firm.

The businessman of today can reasonably expect that all his problems can be solved by one or more of the many techniques available to the researcher.

Management has more faith in research results than do the researchers themselves.

The current trends in research suggest that each researcher will be a rather narrowly trained person, skilled in one or two specific techniques.

Companies are probably ahead of academic institutions in their abilities to conduct research.

Unlike Gresham's Law, good research drives out bad research. (Hardin)

# QUESTIONS FOR REVIEW

**1.** What characteristics would you want your marketing researcher to possess?

**2.** How would you describe the measurement techniques available to marketing researchers?

**3.** Identify a marketing problem and trace through the research that would be necessary to solve the problem. Specify the problem carefully.

**4.** Elaborate on the relationship among what to research, how to research, and action based on research.

**5.** In what order should a researcher gather data from the various major sources of information?

**6.** What is meant by "secondary" sources? What kinds of information would you expect to find in them?

**7.** What guidelines would you prescribe for someone performing a consumer survey?

**8.** What "unobtrusive measures" can be used in conducting marketing research?

**9.** Why is motivational research so valuable to the researcher?

**10.** What characteristics does the experimental method have that most research techniques lack?

## Further Readings

*Note:* See the suggestions at the end of Chapter 15.

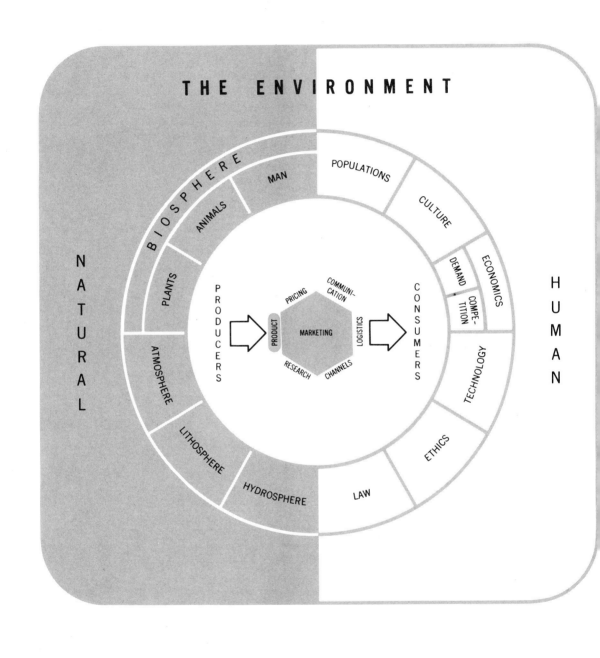

# CHAPTER 17
# MARKETING THE PRODUCT

**The Product and the Environment**

**Concepts and Product Strategy**
*Product Line and Product Mix*
*Product Life Cycle*

*Specific Strategies*
*Profit Analysis*

**Buyer Acceptance**

*The product offering is of utmost importance to the firm as a whole and to marketing in particular, for the entire range of marketing activities is directly and indirectly focused on the success of the product in the marketplace.*

A good product well fitted to a market means profit for the firm and satisfaction for the customer. No wonder that so much marketing effort is focused on the product and on the relationships between product and market and between product and company.

The ebb and flow of products continue year after year. Some succeed, and some fail. Old products are pruned from company lines and new products are added for reasons of diversification, competition, and expansion, and the like. The marketer, who straddles the gap between producer and buyer, has the task of matching the product with the buyer in the best possible way. In the early stages of product formulation, he feeds market information into the firm and later on he has to develop the market for the product finally decided upon.

What do we mean by "product"? Loosely, a product is any item that is for sale. But it is more. A product is "the sum of the physical and psychological satisfactions the buyer receives when he makes a purchase" (Hansen, 1967). It is the "total offering" of the product itself plus all the other ingredients of the marketing mix—the package, advertising, selling, price, brand, retail outlet, and so on. The total offering is the way the buyer perceives a product, though in a given situation the buyer may emphasize the price of coffee, or the brand of lipstick and cigarettes, or the location of a retailer of ice cream. The point is that a product is more than the "thing" purchased. Hormel's Cure 81 Ham (17-1) is a good illustration of the total product offering. Cure 81 was developed as a new product in the 1960s in order to combat the competition from foreign products. The ham was literally rebuilt in order to overcome the objections of the housewives to traditional hams. Bones and fat were removed and the ham was pressed back into conventional shape. Market testing of the new product provided information that proved useful. For instance, it was found that a code label listing production data caught the housewife's eye; as a result a cure-master label became a primary selling feature. The name originally was meant to convey the notion of a product of the future—1981—but housewives thought it referred to the number of attempts in developing the product. Either way the impact was favorable. The housewife perceives a total product in Cure 81—the brand name, company, cure-master's label, shape of product, lack of fat and bone, and price.

A product need not be *tangible* as with hams, cars, toasters, trousers, or ski boots, for it can be *intangible* as in the case of insurance, a theatre performance, hospital treatment, or education. Products can be categorized in various ways and these classifications are useful to the marketer, for he associates product characteristics with marketing strategies. *Manufactured* products are likely to have different supply

No other ham is numbered, registered and guaranteed. Cure|81. The world's most nearly perfect ham.

and demand characteristics from those of raw materials and thus will be promoted differently; *consumer* goods are sold through other channels than are *industrial* goods; expenditure patterns will vary for *durable, nondurable,* and *service* products; and *luxuries* will be promoted with different advertising appeals from those that are used for the *necessities* of life.

Further subdivisions are possible—for instance, consumer products can be categorized into *convenience, shopping,* and *specialty* goods. (See Chapter 10.) This traditional classification reflects the shopping effort by the buyer, and based on this classification the marketer knows whether his product should be "broadcast" through every available retail outlet (e.g., cigarettes), through a few outlets where housewives are comparing competing goods (e.g., dresses), or through specialty shops (e.g., expensive jewelry). This classification, while helpful, is not always clearcut and marketers have tried to improve upon it.

One extension of the traditional classification is the Aspinwall method that is based on five characteristics. (Aspinwall, 1962):

Replacement or turnover—the rate at which a product is purchased and consumed

Gross margin—selling price less laid-down costs

Adjustment—activity of an institution necessary to do its selling job

Time of consumption—time it takes to consume a product

Searching time—availability of goods; time and distance to the retailer

By means of these five characteristics, products can be classified as "red," "yellow," or "orange," arbitrary terms.

| Characteristics | Red | Orange | Yellow |
|---|---|---|---|
| Turnover | high | medium | low |
| Gross margin | low | medium | high |
| Adjustment | low | medium | high |
| Consumption time | low | medium | high |
| Searching time | low | medium | high |

The idea is that it requires a number of characteristics to determine the best marketing strategy. Based on the five characteristics above a marketer is able to classify products according to color or even a numerical scale. If an item is classified as red, the distribution system would be an indirect and long one—many wholesalers and retailers used—as with food, cigarettes, and similar items. If an item is yellow it should be distributed on a more direct, or short-channel basis as in the case of heavy machinery or a set of encyclopedias. Further, once the system of distribution has been decided on, the promotional scheme can be devised so as to parallel the distribution. This is known as the "parallel systems theory."

Another classification scheme takes into account nine characteristics (Miracle, 1965):

1. Unit value
2. Rate of technological change
3. Frequency of purchase
4. Significance of purchase to consumer
5. Technical complexity
6. Rapidity of consumption
7. Time and effort consumers spend buying
8. Need for service
9. Extent of usage

By classifying products into groups according to these nine characteristics, it is possible to develop strategy on price, promotion, distribution, and so on.

Each of these classifications has been developed to aid a marketer in understanding the kind of product he has and the kind of marketing best suited to it. Though the classifications will not be useful in every instance the process of thinking about the product in one of these ways should convey a good deal to the marketer.

# THE PRODUCT AND THE ENVIRONMENT

Every part of the marketing environment that we have discussed bears on the development and marketing of products. Laws, demand, consumer characteristics, technology, ethics, competition, and so on, all are important considerations in the marketing of products, though all do not bear equally on all products. Let us briefly consider some of the effects of environmental influences.

The *legal* influence is clearly discernible in the case of many products. Special laws, for instance, regulate the product and sale of alcoholic beverages, drugs, gasoline, and cigarettes. Labels and packages, too, are subject to legal requirements. Many consumer-protection laws that relate to toys, paint, and inflammable clothing, to name a few products, have been enacted, though these laws often provoke controversy (see 17-2). The patent system presents particular problems, for a company may want to proceed with its manufacturing and selling. Before the Reynolds Company could introduce the ball-point pen, its lawyers had to deal with patents going back to 1888 and with foreign patents as well. Once the firm cleared the legal hurdles, it sold $25 million of its new products in the first year.

Acceptance by the *buyer*, household and nonhousehold, is an essential consideration in the development of any product. The Boeing 747, a new product in 1970, was hardly an impulse item at $23 million. The manufacturer had to sell the plane to airlines, which in turn had to

## 17-2

### "Of Men and Mice"

*This is a story about three mice. Now these aren't the three blind mice, but they are three very sick little mice. The time of our story is in the year 1984. The place is a government testing laboratory. The kind of government testing laboratory that issues a proclamation every few months that scares the pants off you and me.*

*It is evening and two of the mice, Mickey and Freddie, are discussing the third mouse Walter who has been absent from their cage for the past six months.*

*Freddie:* I tell you (cough, cough) that Walter has lucked out. They're testing something really big on him. Mark my words, Walter (cough, cough) will go down in mouse history as the rodent who ruined some billion dollar industry.

*Mickey:* And here we are a couple of has-beens. You, still being forced to smoke 25 packs of cigarettes a day and me (burp) the mouse who caused the big cyclamate scare (burp) in semi-retirement.

*Freddie:* Cyclamates, boy that was a great day for you.

*Mickey:* I remember it now. They force-fed me Fresca. The equivalent of a human drinking 300 (burp) cans of Fresca a day for seven years. Then they tested me one day and found out I was a sick little mouse. They ordered champagne and celebrated. They issued a proclamation that cyclamates had to be taken off the market, but they forgot to mention that I was drinking 300 cans a day for seven years (burp). An obvious oversight.

*Freddie:* In 1970 they took tomato juice off the market. In 1971 it was apples. In 1972, candy. In 1973, ice cream. In 1974, spaghetti. In 1975, herring.

*Mickey:* I wonder what Walter's contribution to mankind will be? Hey, look, here he comes. Boy, does he look sick. Walter, Walter, what did they test on you?

*Walter:* One of the great experiments in history. I, Walter Mouse, shall go down in history as the mouse who ruined the cheese industry.

*Mickey:* Cheese?

*Freddie:* Cheese?

*Walter:* Cheese. We've proven beyond a shadow of a doubt that cheese, in massive doses, will destroy a mouse's health. And tomorrow everyone in the world will know that if you eat 600 pounds of cheese a day for 140 years, your health will be in serious danger.

*Mickey:* Gee, I used to love cheese.

*Freddie:* I must confess a fondness for cheese, too.

*Walter:* Boys, I feel the same way but we mustn't let our personal feelings get in the way of progress. Science (burp) marches on.

SOURCE: Jerry Della Femina, "Of Men and Mice," *Marketing Communications,* Vol. 298 (April 1970), p. 21.

convince their customers to ride in one. Each stage in the development of the 747 was expensive, and customer acceptance was a crucial question, for airline officials feared the public would form an image combining notions of a cattle car, crowds, noise, delays, bigness, less-frequent flights, and general uncertainty about any new plane. Then, too, the airlines were uncertain themselves. Because the new plane could accommodate so many passengers, the number of seats available would increase sharply. Could the marketing staffs stimulate those who have never flown to begin to travel by air? Could they get regular customers to take more air trips? In view of the tremendous investment required for a 747, one airline official thought that Calvin Coolidge may have had a good idea when he asked: "Why not buy one plane and let them take turns flying it?" Actually, the 747 has been well received. And only a few months after its introduction, Boeing announced a larger version that would seat 1000 passengers! Further, new hotels were planned because of the impact of the 747 on existing facilities.

The effect of *technology* on products is closely related to consumer acceptance. In the 1870s René Prudent-Dagron invented a way to photograph 1000 telegrams on a filmstrip small enough to be banded to the leg of a pigeon. Microfilm was thus born, but it took almost a century to develop a market of any size for the process. Now, after a number of fairly recent technological improvements, microfilm is being used by banks, airlines, libraries, and by many other businesses and institutions. Microfilm sales are now increasing at the annual rate of 18 percent. Technology and marketing moved along slowly together in this field; neither alone was sufficient to develop the product.

Microfilm may be an extreme case, but frequently it requires a long gestation period for consumer acceptance of a new product. Consider the elapsed time between the birth of the idea and large-scale marketing for certain familiar products (Adler, 1966):

| | |
|---|---|
| Birdseye Frozen Foods | 15 years |
| Crest Toothpaste | 10 years |
| Gerber Baby Foods | 1 year |
| Hills Instant Coffee | 22 years |
| Marlboro Filter Cigarettes | 2 years |
| Polaroid Color-pack Camera | 15 years |
| Talon Zippers | 30 years |

SOURCE: Lee Adler, "Time Lag in New Product Development," *Journal of Marketing*, Vol. 30 (January 1966), p. 19.

The *social* and *ethical* aspects of the environment are of increasing importance. Consumers have become disgruntled by obsolescence and products with a detrimental influence on society. Consider the social questions associated with the snowmobile. This product, which looks like a cross between a motorized toboggan and a bobsled, began appearing in significant numbers during the 1963–64 winter. The vehicles have been used by foresters, utility servicemen, farmers, and park workers. They have been invaluable in emergencies when no other vehicle could penetrate an area of heavy snow. But the recreational uses, for racing, hunting, fishing, and simply carefree driving, are of a different order and have frequently resulted in loss of lives, injury, and property damage. And the far-carrying, piercing noise of a snowmobile cannot be dismissed lightly. As one observer put it,

> Snowmobiles are great fun and they get you outdoors to winter's wonderland. Snowmobiles also are ear-shattering, dangerous and damaging to the delicate balance of our ecology. There are good and there are bad snowmobilers—but in both cases it is time for some control. (Olsen, 1970.)

The *natural environment,* as pointed out in Chapter 5, has become increasingly important to the marketer. A product may use nonrenewable resources and it may cause deterioration of the environment when it is used by the consumer. Thus products are related closely to the natural environment, from the raw material stage to the product's final resting place.

Another environmental consideration is product *competition,* an important part indeed of the marketing world. To be successful a firm must identify its competition and know the characteristics of the other firms as well as the advantages and disadvantages of their products. A firm's marketing strategy will to some extent be determined by the competitive situation: an auto firm introduces a new small car because the competition has one; Dynachrome sells hard against the competition of Eastman; a utility firm promotes its public image more than it does its product because it has little competition and is concerned mostly about rate increases.

## CONCEPTS AND PRODUCT STRATEGY

Product managers have to relate to corporate objectives, various departments within the firm, sales forces, researchers, distributors, advertising agencies, and ultimate consumers. The task is challenging as can be seen in the description of responsibilities in 17-3. Product management deals with all the elements of the marketing mix. *Packaging* of a product, for example, may provide product protection and it also may be a selling device. Packaging that serves as a selling instrument is of major importance for items subject to self-service, for those that are impulse and convenience items, and when the package can foster the strengthening of product differentiation. *Pricing* is another mix ingredient that is an important part of the product. Decisions regarding pricing may involve a number of persons because so much depends on it. *Channel* selection is sometimes rather automatic. When a firm adds a new product to the rest of its line, it may well follow established lines of distribution. On the other hand, a new channel may open up new markets. A large part of the product strategy rests with *persuasion* efforts—advertising, personal selling, and other kinds of

## 17-3

**The Product Manager's Position**

The critical importance of new-product development in the company's business cannot be overemphasized. It is the mainstream for product improvements and new applications so vital to the company's continuing growth and profitability.

The product development department is responsible basically for developing and testing new products and applications and for improving existing products and processes. The relationships of product managers with this department will be centered on the product development manager who is responsible for his assigned product line. The basic responsibility for recommending applications and product development goals and programs rests with the product development manager. However, in order to ensure a marketing-oriented point of view, the product development manager should rely heavily on the counsel of the product manager in determining the general nature of projects for his product line and the priorities that should be assigned to them.

An important responsibility of the product manager is to guide the efforts of the product development groups into the most profitable channels from a sales standpoint. He does this by keeping these groups closely informed of field needs, important market trends, and his own marketing plans. In effect, the product manager supplies the major part of the commercial intelligence needed by the product development department.

Ultimately, the director of product development and the vice president of marketing must collaborate in establishing the total applications and product development goals of the company, the over-all budget for this activity, and the priorities of major products.

Once project priorities and timetables are established, the product manager is expected to incorporate product development plans for his product line into his over-all product plans. And he is charged with the responsibility for keeping informed on the general status of projects for his product line and seeing that appropriate corrective action is taken when schedules bog down or planned goals are not achieved. To this end, he directs the discussions related to his product line in regularly scheduled development meetings and takes the initiative to secure the involvement of other departments when that is necessary.

SOURCE: B. Charles Ames, "Payoff from Product Management," *Harvard Business Review*, Vol. 41 (November–December 1963), p. 150.

promotion. Brands and trade marks are also to be decided on and need to be studied for their impacts and meanings. One approach to promotion is first to identify all possible product attributes, second to assign ratings to each of these, and then on the basis of their relative marketing potency to decide which attributes to promote (see 17-4).

As a marketer plans his product strategy he is guided most impor-

## 17-4 Rating Product Attributes

| STEP 1. Listing of typewriter attributes | STEP 2. Assignment of differentiation ratings — Compared with most competitive brands, our brand is . . . | | |
|---|---|---|---|
| | "Superior" + | "Equal" = | "Inferior" − |
| 1. Price | | = | |
| 2. Portability | + | | |
| 3. Esthetic design (geometric) | + | | |
| 4. Esthetic design (color) | + | | |
| 5. Versatility of use | | = | |
| 6. Availability | | = | |
| 7. Service guaranty | + | | |
| 8. Convenience of cleaning | | = | |
| 9. Convenience of replacing ink element | | = | |
| 10. Adjustability to different touches | | | − |
| 11. Convertability to different fonts | | = | |
| 12. Ruggedness and so forth | | | − |

SOURCE: Dik Warren Twedt, "How to Plan New Products, Improve Old Ones, and Create Better Advertising," *Journal of Marketing,* Vol. 38 (January 1969), p. 54.

tantly by the firm's goals for profit, growth, and stability. An example of an informal product planning statement is shown in 17-5. Notice that the product planning statement relates closely to the planning procedure as set forth in Chapter 14.

Product strategy can be aided by the organization within the firm and with identification of the tasks and assignments of responsibilities to those tasks. S. C. Johnson & Son, Inc. has defined a "product" as the matching of a technology and a market with two dimensions that can provide for newness. A classification can then be developed as shown in 17-6. The Research and Development Department is primarily responsible for the two cells labeled Reformulation and Replacement. Marketing has Remerchandising and New Use. Together, the two departments share the remaining four tasks. When new product information is sought, R & D is foremost in the Replacement and Product Line Extension cells, whereas marketing is primary in the New Use and Market Extension cells. Together, the departments handle Diversification. As a result of using this scheme the Company has noted many improvements in new and established product efforts (Johnson, 1957)

## Product Line and Product Mix

The concept of a product as a total offering has already been given but since almost all firms have more than one product for sale another concept, the product line, becomes relevant.

*Definition:* A product line is a group of products that are closely related either because they satisfy a class of need, are used together, are sold to the same customer groups, are marketed through the same type of outlets or fall within given price ranges. (American Marketing Association, 1960.)

A "product mix" is "the composite of products offered for sale by a firm or a business unit" (AMA). Thus toothpaste is a *product;* toothpastes, mouth washes, and allied products compose an oral hygiene

---

## 17-5

### A Product Planning Statement

PRODUCT PLANNING—— is the continuous process of fully integrating the planning,

*Here are those dynamic customer-oriented considerations!*

the timing, the pricing, and the servicing required to add the

*They control the product line!*

new, discontinue the undesired, and maintain, modify, and improve the existing products, so as most profitably to meet marketing

*Here's the Planning part!*

needs and to justify the manufacture of these products by the Company. This process is carried out by analyzing, organizing, and combining relevant facts as to the product and related company-wide interests (including every functional component)

*And here is the Programing!*

to obtain operating agreements and management decision for required

*Teamwork is essential!*

product programs and each product's total composition. This process embraces the business and requires understanding and cooperation of all functional components.

*Piloting the process is the Product Planning Manager's responsibility!*

Accountability for it rests with the general manager while integrating responsibility is vested in the marketing component.

SOURCE: *Product Planning Course, Marketing Services* (New York: General Electric Company, 1956).

**17-6** Classification of New Products by Product Objective

Increasing technological newness →

| PRODUCT OBJECTIVES | NO TECH-NOLOGICAL CHANGE | IMPROVED TECHNOLOGY<br>To utilize more fully the company's present scientific knowledge and production skills. | NEW TECHNOLOGY<br>To acquire scientific knowledge and production skills new to the company. |
|---|---|---|---|
| **NO MARKET CHANGE** | | *Reformulation*<br>To maintain an optimum balance of cost quality, and availability in the formulas of present company products. | *Replacement*<br>To seek new and better ingredients or formulation for present company products in technology not now employed by the company. |
| **STRENGTHENED MARKET**<br>To exploit more fully the existing markets for the present company products. | *Remerchandising*<br>To increase sales to consumers of types now served by the company. | *Improved product*<br>To improve present products for greater utility and merchandisability to consumers. | *Product line extension*<br>To broaden the line of products offered to present consumers through new technology. |
| **NEW MARKET**<br>To increase the number types of consumers served by the company. | *New use*<br>To find new classes of consumers that can utilize present company products. | *Market extension*<br>To reach new classes of consumers by modifying present products. | *Diversification*<br>To add to the classes of consumers served by development new technical knowledge. |

↓ Increasing market newness

    Area of the existing business

SOURCE: Adapted from Samuel C. Johnson and Conrad Jones, "How to Organize for New Products," *Harvard Business Review*, Vol. 35 (May–June 1957), p. 52.

*product line;* and soaps, cosmetics, dentifrices, drug items, cake mixes, and other items may constitute a *product mix* if marketed by the same company (AMA). The Nikon Photomic FTn 35mm single-lens reflex camera is a product of the Nikon Company. The Nikon FTn, Nikon F, and the Nikomat FTn comprise part of the Nikon camera product line. The cameras, along with the lenses, cases, filters, binoculars, and microscopes make up the company's product mix.

The Wrigley Company makes one product, chewing gum, but it does have a number of flavors and brands. As Wrigley observes, "It's a pretty simple business no matter how we try to complicate it" (*Wall Street Journal*, 1967). The chewing gum market is worth $325 million a year and Wrigley has approximately 45 percent of it. Three brands account for 90 percent of Wrigley's business. The company's marketing strategy has been to keep the product line simple and well known, and to handle all its own marketing activities.

By contrast the 3M Company has no single product line; it caters to no single industry. In 1969 it had 45 major product lines and 35,000 separate products. The firm's principle is that "No market, no end product is too small to be scorned; that with the proper organization, a myriad of small products can be as profitable, if not more so, than a few big ones" (3M, 1970).

Successful product lines come in all shapes and sizes from a single-product firm to one handling tens of thousands of separate products and many product lines. The number of separate product lines consti-tutes the *width* of the product mix and the number of products within a given product line constitutes the *depth* of the line. Though all kinds of patterns can be found in business today, the marketer should make certain that the products, lines, and mixes are the result of planning and not the lack of it. This means that a firm must constantly assess the value of each product in its line and each line within its total mix. It further means that the product line should be pruned because it is almost inevitable that some products will become unprofitable, for "Products, like men, are mortal" (Alexander, 1964). Each product should be examined periodically—for sales, market share, gross margin, mar-keting costs—in order to spot sick items and maintain the vitality of the firm's product line. The auto industry provides a good example for since World War II the Frazer, Crosley, Allstate, Henry J, Willys-Overland, Kaiser, Nash, Hudson, Packard, Edsel, DeSoto, Avanti, Stude-baker, Corvair, Marlin, Comet, and LeSabre have been withdrawn from the auto market.

A successful product line depends on the addition of new products as well as subtraction. The concept of newness in a product was suggested in 17-6 and is further elaborated in 17-7. Pressures to add products come from various sources: salesmen sense needs and report them back to the firm, technological developments open up new possi-bilities, and competition forces adjustments. A company can add prod-ucts through acquisition of other companies or through its own system of product evolution. In either case a systematic analysis of the sales potential for the product is in order because the rate of new product failure is very high. (Estimates of failures vary from 30 to 90 percent.) As products proceed through their evolutionary course they are sub-jected to "go/no go" decisions and at each of the decision points a number of the products are dropped from consideration. One study

## 17-7
**Ways a Product Can Be New**

A. Six novel attributes are positive, in the sense that they ease the job of introduction:

1. New cost—or, better yet, price—if lower.
2. New convenience in use—if greater.
3. New performance—if better, more dependable and in the range of experience of the prospect—if believable.
4. New availability, in place, or time, or both (including anti-seasonality).
5. Conspicuous-consumption (status symbol) possibilities.
6. Easy credibility of benefits.

B. At least four characteristics make the job more difficult, slow up market development, and usually make it costlier:

7. New methods of use (unless obviously simpler).
8. Unfamiliar patterns of use (any necessity for learning new habits in connection with performance of a task associated with the new product).
9. Unfamiliar benefit (in terms of the prospect's understanding).
10. Costliness, fancied or real, of a possible error in use.

C. Three others are ambivalent in their effect—that is, the effect on market development probably depends not only on their exact nature, but also on the cultural climate at the moment. However, extreme unfamiliarity would probably be negative in effect:

11. New appearance, or other sensed difference (style or texture, for example).
12. Different accompanying or implied services.
13. New market (including different channels of sale).

SOURCE: Chester R. Wasson, "What is 'New' About a New Product?" *Journal of Marketing*, Vol. 25, No. 1 (July 1960), p. 54.

indicated that out of 58 new product ideas presented for consideration, only one became a successful new product (17-8).

Management recognizes the need to introduce new products in order to sustain company goals of growth and profits, but at the same time they know that new products have a high death rate. In order to reduce the failure rate companies frequently design a checklist of factors to consider in order to remove some of the subjectivity and judgment that is inherent in new-product decisions. Some companies set up rating systems for new products in which the pertinent factors are considered as in the following list (adapted from O'Meara (1961):

I. Marketability
  A. Relation to present distribution channels
  B. Relation to present product lines
  C. Quality/price relationship

D. Number of sizes and grades
E. Merchandisability
F. Effects on sales of present products

II. Durability
A. Stability
B. Breadth of market
C. Resistance to cyclical fluctuations
D. Resistance to seasonal fluctuations
E. Exclusiveness of design

III. Growth Potential
A. Place in market
B. Expected competitive situation
C. Expected availability of end users

A new product would be rated *high,* for example, if major markets are reachable through present distribution channels, *average* if sales will rise and fall with the economy, or *very poor* if the product is similar to those presently on the market.

By rating the product according to each of the above factors, a marketer should be in a good position to pass judgment on it.

The maintenance of the product line, then, is a basic part of product strategy. The line must be evaluated on a continual basis and the necessary adding and subtracting of items carefully executed.

**17-8** **Mortality of New Product Ideas**
**(by Stage Evolution in 51 Companies)**

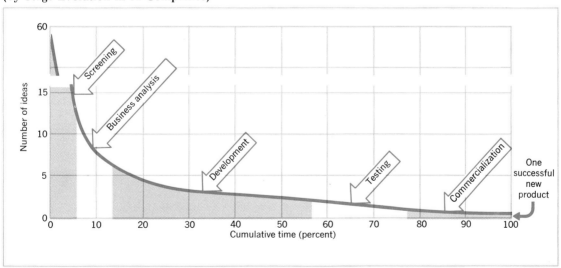

SOURCE: Booz, Allen, and Hamilton, *Management of New Products* (New York, 1968), p. 9.

## Product Life Cycle

The concept of product life cycle is one of the most widely accepted ideas in marketing. One definition of a product life cycle is: "a general pattern of growth in sales, use, or ownership which seems to fit the long-term histories of most products" (Buzzell, 1971). The concept is depicted in 17-9, where it is shown in five stages, from the introduction of a product to its decline in sales. The life cycle, which essentially reports product sales, therefore relates closely to the entire marketing operation. Two actual product life cycles are shown in 17-10. Note that in the cycle for cigarettes the general product class does not follow the basic life-cycle pattern, although one brand of nonfilter cigarettes appears to do so. Frozen orange juice concentrate exhibited the life cycle shown during the period 1946 to 1964. Actual products develop different patterns: some reach a saturation point when sales start to decrease; some stabilize at a given level; some reach a peak and then continue to increase at a rate lower than the initial sales period but still faster than population growth; and some overcome decline by a process known as extension, which will be discussed later (Scheuing, 1969). It is often a difficult matter to know where in a life cycle a particular product happens to be, as illustrated by the following quotation from an article written in 1926 by an able economist:

The automobile industry has proceeded through its introductory stage, in which sales to new users were difficult . . . The sale of cars

**17-9** The Basic Life Cycle of New Products

SOURCE: Booz, Allen, and Hamilton, *Management of New Products* (New York, 1968), p. 6.

**17-10** Examples of Product Life Cycles

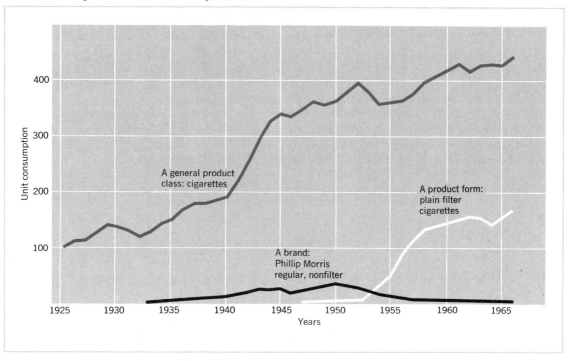

A general product
class: cigarettes

A product form:
plain filter
cigarettes

A brand:
Phillip Morris
regular, nonfilter

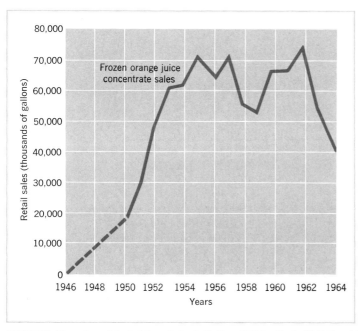

Frozen orange juice
concentrate sales

SOURCES: Cigarettes—Adapted from Rolando Polli and Victor Cook, "Validity of the Product Life Cycle," *The Journal of Business*, Vol. 42 (October 1969), p. 389. Orange Juice—Adapted from Eberhard E. Scheuing, "The Product Life Cycle as an Aid in Strategy Decisions," *International Management Review*, Vol. 9 (April–May 1969), p. 120.

at the present rate for a few years more will bring the number of cars in use to such a level that the replacement of those cars from year to year will demand a production about equal to the present output of the industry . . . In other words, the industry will have come to maturity and will take its place beside the iron and steel industry, the agricultural implement industry, shoe manufacturing, and other established, stable industries of the country. (Griffin, 1926.)

The strategy for marketing, clearly, is to adjust to the successive stages in the product life cycle. Consider the changing role of advertising as a product passes through its life cycle (Buzzell, 1971).

Introductory stage
    Consumer awareness, knowledge of product not yet developed
    Advertising designed to "educate" consumers
    Expenditures very high relative to sales
Rapid growth stage
    Declining advertising/sales ratio
    Beginning of shift to brand competition
    Usually, declining prices
Maturity
    Advertising/sales ratio stabilizes
    Brand competition and/or product improvement
Decline
    Advertising cut back or eliminated

Competition changes from stage to stage in the life cycle. In the beginning a company may face no competition: it is a pioneer facing the task of developing a market for a new product. As the company succeeds competitors enter the field, and as sales grow the number of companies competing for the business increases to a point where it becomes more and more difficult to retain a satisfactory share of the market. Prices also change throughout the cycle; frequently higher prices are charged at the beginning only to be lowered as competition enters the marketplace. The channels of distribution are also expanded over time; a product may enter a specialty house market but later become available in general stores and in discount stores.

The firm that pioneers a product may introduce it at high prices (and high profits) but then withdraw after the saturation point seems to be reached; alternatively it may attempt to extend the life of the product by introducing new models. Radio sales, for example, have not gone through the general life-cycle model. Instead, new models and uses have been added: auto radios, portables, stereos, and FM. This process of life-cycle extension, or "market stretching," is shown in 17-11. A firm can also stretch or extend the market by promoting more frequent usage, more varied usage, new users, and new uses (Levitt, 1965).

Another application of the product life-cycle concept relates to foreign trade following this sequence for a given product: the United States is first an exporter, then loses its export markets, and finally becomes an importer (Wells, 1968).

**17-11** Hypothetical Life Cycle—Nylon

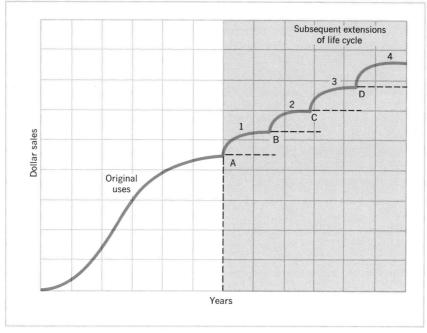

SOURCE: Theodore Levitt, *The Marketing Mode* (New York: McGraw-Hill, 1969), p. 42.

Earlier we mentioned that the product life-cycle concept is one of the most durable in marketing. It is interesting that, although it is a widely accepted concept and aids in the development of marketing strategy, little research has been done on the idea and many marketers do not utilize it at all. Levitt comments on this anomaly:

> . . . recent survey of executives found none who used the concept in any strategic way whatever, and pitifully few who used it in any kind of tactical way. It has remained—like so many fascinating theories in economics, physics, and sex—a remarkably durable but almost totally unemployed, and seemingly unemployable piece of professional baggage . . . The concept of the product life cycle is today at about the stage that the Copernican view of the universe was 300 years ago: a lot of people knew about it, but hardly anybody seemed to use it in any effective or productive way. (Levitt, 1969.)

## Specific Strategies

The management of the marketing mix is, of course, the manner in which marketing strategy is applied to the marketplace, and each ingredient of the mix can constitute a separate strategy—price, package, style, promotional strategies, and distribution. These strategies are all related to the overall product strategy in some way. In addition there are specific product strategies that deserve mention. *Segmentation* strategy, for one, is the dividing of a market into segments and offering a product for each selected segment. A watch market, for instance, might be divided into three segments: (1) people who want a reasonably good watch at a low price; (2) people who want good workmanship and a long-lasting instrument; and (3) those who want a good watch and also some glamorous qualities (such as a gold case). A different watch could then be developed for each of these segments (Yankelovich, 1964). Similarly, there can be different market segments for nearly any product and the segmentation can be based on geography, socioeconomic characteristics of the population, or product features. A company can spread into several segments or it may concentrate on one. Designer Victor Papanek thinks in terms of developing products for a "constituency base." He further points out that the development of products for given constituents typically excludes the poor, underprivileged, blacks, and those who do not match the "norms" of today's society (Papanek, 1972).

*Product differentiation,* another strategy, is the development of a product that is perceived by buyers to be different from the competitors'. The differentiation can be achieved by basic product differences or by minor variations in the product itself or in the brand name, package, color, or style. A firm might make only one watch, one that is distinct from the rest of the products on the market, or it might promote minor differences in order to develop some kind of differentiation. The two strategies of segmentation and product differentiation can merge, for a company can make a distinctive product designed for a particular segment of the market. And with either strategy the firm is concerned with the way its products are *positioned*—that is, the niche it carves out for itself, the place it holds among all similar products. For instance, a tobacco firm might place all cigarette products into groups of chosen product features such as length, filter, and type of package. The firm then might decide to position its new cigarette product where there are few if any existing products. The concept of positioning holds for almost any product, be it consumer, industrial, or institutional.

There are other product strategies, such as pioneering with new products as opposed to simply introducing "me too" products when it appears certain that there is buyer acceptance. Or a firm may have a policy of adding products by way of acquisition rather than through internal development. Whatever the strategy, it should be planned and not haphazard. Moreover, a firm should understand its market and what business it is actually in. If there are changes in the market, the firm may have to change its product line. For example, as the birth rate declined in 1971, Gerber Products Co. moved into life insurance, can-making, and infant accessories.

## Profit Analysis

Product strategy needs to be carried out with the benefit of various kinds of marketing analyses, such as subjecting the product to consumer-acceptance tests and collecting relevant secondary data in order to determine the approximate size of the market. Realistic analyses of profit opportunities are essential early in a product-development program. Break-even analysis is especially useful, for it shows how many units must be sold at various prices in order to recover fixed and variable costs. Boeing's break-even point with the 747 was calculated at 200 units, which means that the firm had to achieve sales of $4,600,000,000 before it began to show a profit. In 17-12, a variation of a break-even chart, you can see the planned profit at the planned price at the planned volume.

**17-12** A Break-even Chart for a Product

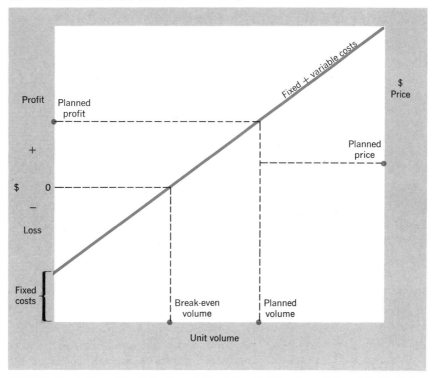

SOURCE: Adapted from John E. Smallwood, "Exploiting the Price-Demand Curve," in *The Professionals Look at New Products*, edited by Brand, Gruber, and Co. (Ann Arbor, Mich.: University of Michigan, Michigan Business Papers No. 50, 1959), p. 152.

## BUYER ACCEPTANCE

A major goal of the marketer is to gain buyer acceptance of the product, new or old. Buyer acceptance translates into sales volume, product life cycles, and profitability. Marketers want to know who will buy, how many will buy, how frequently and in what quantity they will buy, and whether buyers will become repeat purchasers. When a buyer decides to buy a product he becomes an "adopter," an early adopter if he buys early in the product life cycle or a late adopter if he is slow to catch on. Also of central interest is the "diffusion" process, which refers to the spread of the new product throughout the population. A good deal of research has gone into the adoption and diffusion processes, but much remains to be learned about how and why people adopt new products. Logically a new product that is closely related to an existing product (electric toothbrush) should meet with little buyer resistance, whereas a new concept (computer) would meet with considerable resistance (Robertson, 1969). Part of the marketing effort is to determine sources of buyer resistance and then to develop a promotional program to overcome this resistance.

A good product strategy, as stated at the beginning of the chapter, is one that provides profits for the firm and satisfaction for the buyer.

## STATEMENTS TO CONSIDER

The difference between the new product offered and the established product must be discernible, identifiable, and reproducible.

Products are initially purchased and tried on the basis of conceptual appeal; they are repurchased or discarded on the basis of tangible satisfaction. (Woods)

One of the problems in introducing new products is that companies make the assumption that the consumer is a competent individual, competent to judge intrinsic goodness in a product and to compare the desirability of competing products. (Brand)

Nothing sells itself, not even the most venerable and tantalizing of all commodities—sex. It has to be embellished, elaborated, amplified, enriched, perfumed, styled, corseted, colored and cosmeticized. (Levitt)

Airlines must think of their product as not travel alone, but including places to go and things to do—a total product concept.

The story of the Edsel is one of a firm proceeding carefully and methodically, working within the context of an elaborate marketing plan, doing most things right—and ending up with a total disaster. (Reynolds)

The major reason for new-product failure is a lack of a real consumer point of difference. (Angelus)

Inadequate product planning is a major factor inhibiting growth and profitability in international business operations today. (Keegan)

Product-line planning, whether it involves only product improvement, the development of new products, or the planning of mergers, must be a first consideration of top management. (Borden)

The fact is that as products and product lines increase numerically, the range of management problems seems to grow geometrically. (Kotler)

# QUESTIONS FOR REVIEW

**1.** Why is the product given so much attention in marketing? What is meant by a "total offering?"

**2.** How is the parallel systems theory of use to the marketer?

**3.** To which environmental forces would you say the product most closely relates?

**4.** How would you describe the job of a product manager?

**5.** What are the most essential ingredients of a product plan?

**6.** Discuss the relationship between marketing and technical research.

**7.** Are there any rules for developing a line of products for a given firm?

**8.** Are all new products really new? What is it that characterizes a new product?

**9.** What are some of the marketing reasons that products fail? Cite examples of market failures.

**10.** What is meant by "market stretching?"

## Further Readings

Thomas L. Berg and Abe Schuchman, *Product Strategy and Management* (New York: Holt, Rinehart and Winston, 1963).

Brand, Gruber and Co. (eds.), *The Professionals Look at New Products*, Michigan Business Papers, No. 50 (Ann Arbor, Mich.: University of Michigan, 1969).

J. O. Eastlack, Jr. (ed.), *New Product Development* (Chicago: American Marketing Association, 1968).

Theodore Levitt, *The Marketing Mode* (New York: McGraw-Hill, 1969).

Edgar A. Pessemier, *New Product Decisions* (New York: McGraw-Hill, 1966).

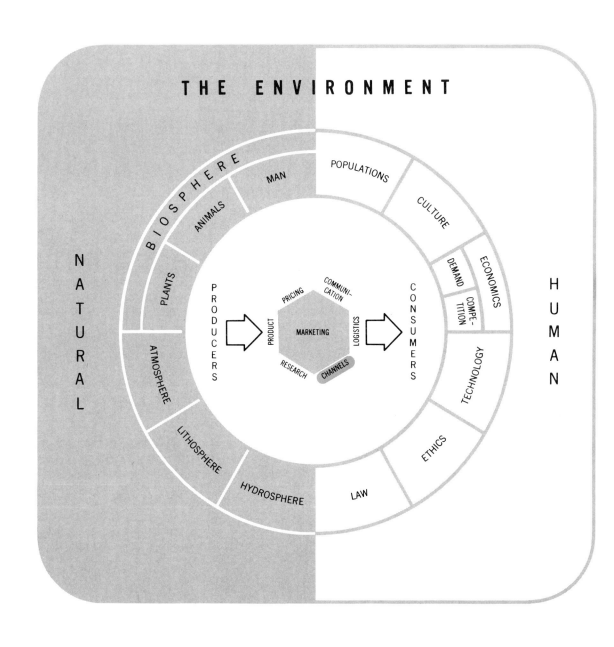

THE ENVIRONMENT

NATURAL

HUMAN

BIOSPHERE

MAN

ANIMALS

PLANTS

ATMOSPHERE

LITHOSPHERE

HYDROSPHERE

POPULATIONS

CULTURE

DEMAND

ECONOMICS

COMPE-
TITION

TECHNOLOGY

ETHICS

LAW

PRODUCERS

CONSUMERS

PRICING

COMMUNI-
CATION

PRODUCT

MARKETING

LOGISTICS

RESEARCH

CHANNELS

# CHAPTER 18
# DISTRIBUTION SYSTEMS I
## CHANNELS

**Elements of a Marketing Channel**

**Elements of an Exchange Channel**

**Channel Alignment**
*Justification*
*Channel Structure*
*Shifting of Functions*
*Interchannel Competition*

**Channel Selection**

**Channel Policies**

**Channel Administration**

**Channels of Distribution and the Environment**

This chapter was written by Frederick J. Beier, Associate Professor of Transportation and Business Logistics, School of Business Administration, University of Minnesota.

*Distribution channels offer marketers numerous opportunities to bring their product offerings into the marketplaces. The selection of a particular channel of distribution is determined by the firm's marketing goals.*

In this chapter we will discuss channels of distribution as a marketing system. We will identify the different elements of marketing channels and the different forms those channels take. We will also examine the various managerial decisions a firm makes in selecting and operating within a channel. We will discuss the distribution policies that a firm may choose as well as the problems and benefits of administering the channel as a single, multifirm "superorganization."

## ELEMENTS OF A MARKETING CHANNEL

In Chapter 3 we introduced the marketing channel as a sequence of marketing institutions between producer and consumer, in which each institution performs marketing functions and therefore helps to bring the product closer to the consumer (see 18-1). As we briefly indicated, marketing channels are not limited to the traditional marketing middlemen such as manufacturer, wholesaler, and retailer. There are many other firms that perform marketing functions and thereby facilitate the marketing process. For example, transportation carriers may provide physical movement of products outside the manufacturer $\longrightarrow$ wholesaler $\longrightarrow$ retailer chain, since many wholesalers take title to the goods but not physical possession. And further, manufacturers ship direct to retailers and on occasion to the household consumer. There are also facilitating agencies such as banks, advertising agencies, and marketing research firms that never assume ownership or physical possession of the goods. Finally, there are the consumers, who often perform marketing functions themselves, as they provide their own transportation between home and store.

The two ways in which channels are defined focus either on the flow of title from producer to consumer or the flow of physical product. The flow of title is called the *exchange channel*. This includes merchant and agent middlemen (see Chapter 3) who directly assist in the transfer of title. The second type of channel focuses on those firms that take *physical possession* of the product. This is referred to as the *logistics channel* and includes many of the same firms that also participate in the exchange channel. In addition, a logistics channel includes transportation carriers and warehouse companies. Logistics channels are discussed in the following chapter. The balance of this chapter will deal principally with the *exchange* channel.

**18-1** Flow of Food from Sources to Destinations, 1963

Agriculture
26.5 (net)

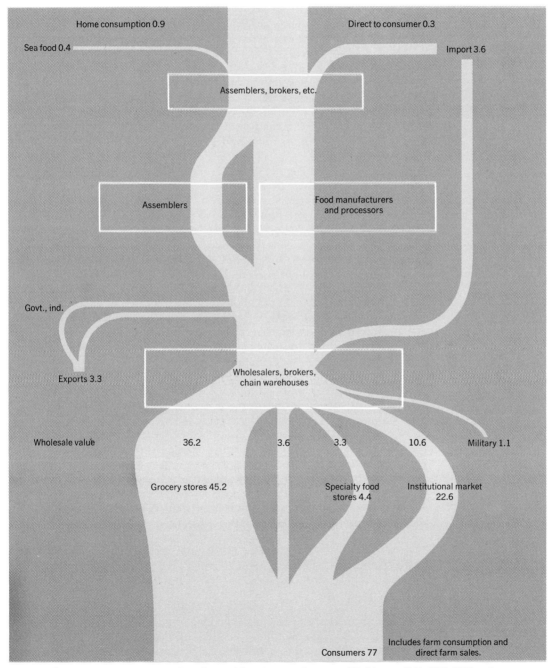

Home consumption 0.9

Direct to consumer 0.3

Sea food 0.4

Import 3.6

Assemblers, brokers, etc.

Assemblers

Food manufacturers
and processors

Govt., ind.

Exports 3.3

Wholesalers, brokers,
chain warehouses

Wholesale value          36.2          3.6          3.3          10.6          Military 1.1

Grocery stores 45.2                          Specialty food          Institutional market
                                            stores 4.4              22.6

Consumers 77

Includes farm consumption and
direct farm sales.

*SOURCE:* National Commission on Food Study, *Food from Farm to Consumer* (Washington, D.C.: GPO, 1966), p. 6.

# ELEMENTS OF AN EXCHANGE CHANNEL

Channels are characterized by more than a listing of marketing functions. Another way of looking at exchange channel alignments is to evaluate them in terms of four necessary elements: *market acceptance* of the product, *market access* of the product, *marketing expertise,* and *financial resources.* High product acceptance by customers indicates an unwillingness on their part to accept substitutes for a specific product. Market access refers to the manner in which contact is made with potential customers; for household goods market access refers to the number, type, and location of retail outlets, that is, how the product is exposed to the consumer. Marketing expertise refers to a channel participant's relative competence in performing marketing functions. Financial strength is a function of a channel member's ability to make funds available to finance business activities incident to producing and distributing goods.

Product acceptance and market access appear to be the primary requirements for the success of a channel. Furthermore, there is a complementary relationship between these two factors, that is, these resources may be partially substituted for each other in any particular channel. For example, a manufacturer that enjoys a strong brand image may not need a great deal of market access. Consumer pressure to buy the product may be strong enough so that most configurations of retail outlets will be satisfactory. Similarly, large resellers who control market access, such as J. C. Penney and Sears, have been able to limit or even avoid manufacturer brands by developing private labels that carry the prestige of the retail outlet. Because some minimum combination of these factors is required for channel success, and because they are typically controlled by different middlemen, most channels require a joint effort between manufacturer and reseller.

Product acceptance and market access are, of course, linked to marketing expertise and financial strength. Given time, financial strength can be converted into expertise, acceptance, and/or access. For example, many manufacturers, such as Procter & Gamble, Alberto-Culver, Avon, and Gillette, combine financial strength with great competence in mass-media advertising to create strong acceptance for a variety of branded products. Similarly, Federated Department Stores, S. S. Kresge, J. C. Penney, and Sears are distribution organizations that have, through financial strength and marketing expertise, created unusually strong market access in the form of national networks of retail outlets with strong appeals to consumers.

# CHANNEL ALIGNMENT

## Justification

Firms align themselves in a vertical channel structure in order to present products to consumers as efficiently as possible. Manufacturers rely on wholesalers and retailers to distribute their products because these middlemen are "in touch" with the consuming public and they carry many lines of products that can share the cost of the middlemen's operation. Without such middlemen a manufacturing firm would have to maintain its own sales force, warehouses, and retail outlets. For producers with limited resources and marketing expertise this policy is clearly out of the question. Even if it were financially possible it may simply be inefficient for a manufacturer to deal directly with consumers. Consider the problems of a manufacturer of auto parts who attempts to deal directly with retailers. For this type of product there are literally thousands of retail outlets including gas stations, discount stores, and parts stores. The manufacturer would have to contact each of them directly, thus requiring a substantial sales force and marketing expense. Further, the individual retail outlet may need supplies from many other manufacturers in order to present a full range of products to the ultimate consumer. Hence the retailer would have to maintain contact with other manufacturers of auto parts. If a wholesaler is used, however, the manufacturer can make one contact that in turn will contact a large segment of the retail trade. The retailer likewise can make one contact with the wholesaler and be confident that the wholesaler carries items from a number of manufacturers—thus eliminating the need to contact them individually. This situation is depicted graphically in 18-2. Notice also that the total number of contacts is reduced when a middleman is used, thus contributing to the overall efficiency of the marketing system. Hence a middleman must justify his existence by contributing efficiencies to the overall effort of the channel. If he cannot do so he will eventually be eliminated from the channel.

## Channel Structure

There is a great variety of exchange channel alignments (see 18-3). Manufacturers can deal directly with consumers, directly with retailers, through wholesalers then to retailers, or any combination of these. However, describing various channel structures in terms of different sequences of firms does not highlight the channel as a single, multifirm, cooperative system. Channel structure may therefore be more appropriately discussed by looking at the various states of cooperation, or interfirm organization, within certain channel systems. For example, to what extent does one firm dictate service or operating policies for the entire channel? Further, do the channel members see themselves as a part of a larger system or simply as individual entrepreneurs?

The various degrees of channel cooperation can be envisioned as a continuum. At one extreme is the *random channel* in which the channel alignment may last only until the current transaction is completed. In this channel, middlemen, including manufacturers, carry on a continuous search for short-run opportunities to buy and sell products. Such firms have been described as "transient" and in some cases have been charged with "disrupting the status quo by engaging in deviate, competitive activities, such as loss leader selling . . . and bait advertising" (McCammon and Little, 1965). Over time such unstable relationships may

## 18-2 Simplification of Contacts by Use of Wholesaler Institutions

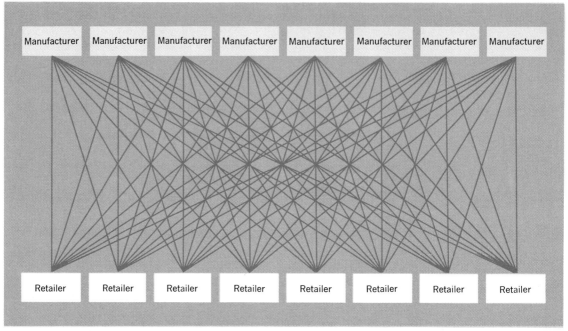

(a) Direct marketing

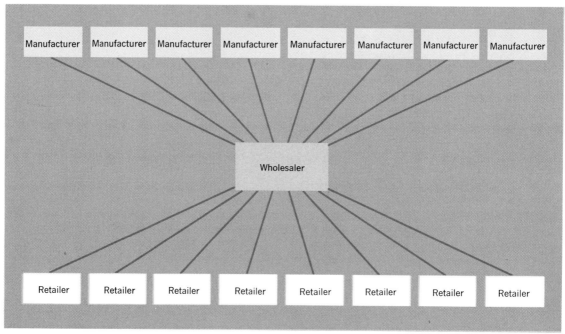

(b) Distribution through wholesalers

**18-3** Selected Channels of Distribution, 1967

| PRODUCT | SHIPMENTS (Percentages of total shipments) BY MANUFACTURERS TO: | | | | | | |
|---|---|---|---|---|---|---|---|
| | Wholesalers and manufacturers' own offices | Other manufacturers | Commercial, construction, governments | Households and farmers | Retailers | Federal Government | Export |
| Typewriters | 95 | — | — | — | 1 | — | 2 |
| Cigarettes | 82 | — | — | — | 10 | 5 | 3 |
| Photographic equipment | 66 | 7 | 2 | — | 6 | 7 | 10 |
| Tires and tubes | 45 | 26 | — | — | 24 | 2 | 1 |
| Fertilizers | 44 | 12 | — | 14 | 23 | 6 | — |
| Glass containers | 40 | 59 | 1 | — | 1 | — | — |
| Soft drinks | 23 | 6 | 3 | — | 66 | — | — |
| Ship building and repairs | 1 | 2 | 31 | — | — | 59 | 1 |

SOURCE: U.S. Department of Commerce, Bureau of the Census, *Census of Manufacturers, Special Report, 1967* (Washington, D.C.: GPO, 1967).

evolve into a *continuous routinized transaction channel.* In this case, manufacturers and resellers maintain an ongoing relationship and become familiar with one another's operations and procedures. The transactions between channel participants become more regular and routine, and searching for alternative alignments is substantially reduced. However, as is typical in the distribution of building materials, there is occasional testing of the market for better alternatives. Thus in neither the random nor the routinized transaction channel does any firm perceive itself to be part of an integrated channel system.

Another type of channel alignment, one that may also evolve from the routinized transaction relationship, is a *merchandise line channel.* In this system a manufacturer attempts to take an active part in controlling the method of presenting its products to the final user. All aspects of a product offering are programmed by the producer in order to control inventory levels, packaging, display arrangements, and so on. A manufacturer's line may represent only a portion of the reseller's total assortment of product offerings. Hence the reseller may have to deal with many such producers. For example, many discount department stores are made up of leased departments in which almost all decisions are controlled by the producer. Manufacturers attempt thereby to take advantage of the access to the enormous consumer market provided by discount stores and also to retain control over assortments and inventory levels, which may involve preticketing or pricing the item at the point of production. In the distribution of shoes through discount stores, it is the wholesaler and not the manufacturer who leases the department and assumes all other responsibilities for its operation, including the preparation and presentation of promotional materials.

When the merchandise line offered by the retailer is relatively narrow, the channel system may resemble a totally integrated organization.

For example, in the distribution of automobiles a retailer deals with only one manufacturer in offering a full assortment of items to the consumer. Both manufacturer and retailer see themselves as interdependent members of the same system even though they are controlled by separate ownerships.

Many merchandise line channels may be initiated and controlled by the retailer. For example, big resellers like Wards, Sears, and Penneys contract for all or a large portion of a manufacturer's output of a particular product. Manufacturers without a well-known product (limited market acceptance) often welcome this arrangement because of the large volume represented by a department store chain. This arrangement also permits manufacturers with limited marketing expertise and financial resources to conduct a promotional program to transfer these activities to the large retail organizations. Often, as with Penneys and Sears, the brand of the retailer will replace that of the manufacturer because the retailer has a stronger marketing image than an unknown manufacturer. It is interesting to note, however, that even well-known manufacturers supply goods for a retailer's "private label" program. For example, Whirlpool makes Kenmore (Sears) appliances while General Electric and Hotpoint produce Penncrest (Penneys) major appliances. Why do these manufacturers participate in private label programs? For one thing the private labels provide an outlet for excess production capability. For another, the retailers represent a significant volume of sales, and producers see this as a means of expanding profits.

At the other end of the continuum representing channel integration is a *total-support,* or *corporate, system.* Here, the manufacturing unit supplies the total product assortment to the retail unit, and all aspects of the system are under common ownership, including retail units. Examples of such total-support systems are Robert Hall apparel, Melville Shoes–Thom McAn stores, Sherwin-Williams paint, and Goodyear tires. In the case of Thom McAn the producer's line is a sufficient assortment for the retail outlet. In the case of Goodyear, merchandise lines have been added to the basic line of tires so as to improve the appeal of corporate stores. Thus Goodyear has supplemented its line by offering major appliances and television sets through its company stores.

Corporate systems can also be initiated and controlled by retailers and wholesalers. Sears, for example, integrated backward and assumed partial ownership of Whirlpool, Inc., and some of its other suppliers. Wholesalers, at the same time, have integrated forward by organizing retail chains; Super-Value, Western Auto, Our Own Hardware, and Ben Franklin Stores are typical of wholesaler total-support systems. While wholesalers may occasionally integrate backwards to assume the manufacturing function, their principal thrust has been forward to the retail institution.

During the past decade there has been an impressive increase in the amount of franchising—particularly in the fast-serve, convenience-food industry. Franchising is also a total-support system that demonstrates the degree to which marketing can be programmed. All basic decisions are made by a central franchiser organization, and little operating discretion is left to the retail units. The system decisions are made with the objective of minimizing the costs of transactions and distribution while maintaining product quality. The franchise headquarters establishes automatic reorder points and quantities, standard accounting systems, promotional displays, mark-ups, and so on. The advantage of the system is that decisions serve the single goal of the channel rather than the multiple and diverse goals of independent middlemen. Thus the opportunity for economy is enhanced when systemization is imposed on the channel. This advantage applies not only to franchising but also to other forms of total-support systems.

## Shifting of Functions

It should be apparent from our discussion of channel structures that no marketing function is the sole domain of any particular type of middleman. All functions can be shifted forward or backward in the channel to whoever is willing and capable to perform them. This shifting of functions has permitted self-service stores to emerge as the dominant form of merchandising in certain industries. Similarly, the willingness of consumers to select, transport, store, and finance their purchases has led to cash-and-carry stores in groceries, clothing, drugs, and lumber. The shifting of functions may result in cost savings that can be passed on to the consumer. Shifts may also take place between middlemen. For example, storage is being shifted backward in the channel for many lines of trade. Retailers thus can limit their stocks to display models only. When sales are consummated, direct shipments are made to the customer's home from a wholesale distributor's warehouse or even from the point of manufacturer.

This is not to suggest that middlemen can be eliminated from the distribution channel indiscriminately. For example, retailers will occasionally advertise that "we deal direct—eliminating the middleman." The implication is that the cost of a wholesaler's operation and his profit margin have been avoided. What is left unsaid is that the retailer must now assume the functions that a wholesaler would have otherwise performed—maintaining contact with manufacturers, arranging transportation and storage, financing, and so on. If distribution economies are to accrue the retailer must perform the assumed functions more efficiently than anyone else. For example, chain supermarkets have established their own warehouses that essentially perform all wholesaling functions for the individual supermarkets in the system. Such large-volume organizations as A & P, Kroger, and Safeway Stores are able to deal directly and efficiently with many manufacturers of food items. But where there is no large volume of homogeneous products and no expertise in wholesaling, an attempt to "deal direct" can only serve to increase the costs of distribution. Thus trying to eliminate entire classes of middlemen from the channel, such as wholesalers, should be approached with caution.

### Interchannel Competition

The degree of competition a firm faces depends obviously on the number of similar firms and the number of substitutable products but more subtly on suppliers or customers who are capable of integrating either forward or backward in a marketing channel. A wholesaler competes not only with other wholesalers but also with large retail organizations that may eventually assume their own wholesaling—as has happened in the grocery field. There is still another factor that affects competition: channels that offer similar or substitutable products. The marketing channel for Frigidaire appliances is actually a team that is competing against a team for General Electric appliances. If one channel is made more economical through some form of vertical cooperation or integration, it puts pressure on the other team to achieve similar economies. Thus a vertical perspective as well as a horizontal one is required in assessing a firm's competition. If one channel system is clearly inferior to another, the participants will have limited success regardless of the number of substitutable products or firms that exist. It is very important, then, to examine and evaluate competing channels when analyzing a distributive system.

Channel-versus-channel competition makes clear the interdependency of firms within the same channel. The manufacturer and wholesaler(s) are dependent on the retailer to make a suitable presentation of the product to consumers. Each retailer also depends on the suppliers to provide suitable merchandise in appropriate quantities at a specific point in time. Interdependency provides the motivation to eliminate superfluous activities and middlemen that do not contribute to the overall channel effort. The cost of not eliminating wasteful steps in a channel is the loss of ground to competitive distribution systems in the marketplace. Hence all participants of an inefficient channel will be penalized regardless of whether they themselves are contributing to the lack of efficiency. In an attempt to remove such uncertainty, large, financially able firms have assumed control, through integration of the functions of both suppliers and subsequent middlemen. Thus through a desire for control and for the elimination of interfirm dependency, a channel can come to be dominated by a single, powerful participant.

## CHANNEL SELECTION

One of the most important decision areas facing a manufacturer is the choice of distribution channel(s). Too often the choice is made in a haphazard fashion so that the manufacturer is not able to achieve the total potential impact in the marketplace. The choice is indeed extremely complex; since the decision is a function of the needs and capabilities of the producer, a firm must evaluate its own ability to perform marketing functions and then align itself with middlemen who can perform complementary marketing activities. There are numerous possible alignments, but they are basically variations on these four basic patterns:

1. Producer direct to consumer
2. Producer $\longrightarrow$ retailer $\longrightarrow$ consumer
3. Producer $\longrightarrow$ wholesaler $\longrightarrow$ retailer $\longrightarrow$ consumer
4. Producer $\longrightarrow$ agent middleman $\longrightarrow$ wholesaler $\longrightarrow$ retailer $\longrightarrow$ consumer

In dealing directly a manufacturing firm must be in a position to perform all of the marketing functions itself and *do so in an economical manner*. In general terms, it must not only enjoy market acceptance for its products but also control market access and have sufficient marketing expertise and financial resources. Even when it controls all of these factors, however, it still may not be economically feasible to deal direct with the consumer. Such a channel is feasible only when the following conditions exist:

1. Producer's product line is a sufficient assortment for a retail outlet.
2. The service requirements of the product do not require continuous and widespread representation in the marketplace.
3. The markets are relatively concentrated geographically and a large number of manufacturer-controlled retail outlets are not required. (The number of required outlets may also be a function of the typical gross margin and unit value of the product(s). Thus, the higher the value the greater the ability to deal direct.)

In the examples already cited—Robert Hall, Melville Shoes–Thom McAn stores, and Goodyear—company stores are located in major markets that are geographically concentrated and therefore the producers can handle their own warehousing and storage facilities. When postsale service is important, as for appliances, these activities may be shifted to either the original manufacturer or to independent service repairmen.

The use of independent retailers in a channel is advisable when a producer is not capable of establishing sufficient retail outlets itself, that is, the number of potential customers is sufficiently large and geographically dispersed so that a producer cannot establish enough retail outlets itself. Dealing through retailers is also advisable when a manufacturer's line does not provide a total assortment and should be mingled with other products at the point of retail sale. However, a direct manufacturer $\longrightarrow$ retailer channel is normally viable only when order quantities are large enough to justify transportation, transaction, and other distribution economies. Hence producer $\longrightarrow$ retailer channels involve large retailers that in turn control many individual outlets in a market territory. For example, Dayton-Hudson, Macy's, and discount department store organizations deal directly with many manufacturers.

This is also true for large supermarket chains such as Kroger and Safeway Stores and in the distribution of clothes such as Bond and Hart Schaffner & Marx.

Retailer-controlled private label programs, as previously discussed, represent another form of manufacturer-retailer channel. In general, producers may welcome such direct channel alignments because of the advertising, sales promotion, and selling support large retailers are able to give the product. These associations are also beneficial from the standpoint that a favorable retailer's image and reputation can also be transferred to the products they carry.

As typical order size and breadth of assortment declines and the need for market coverage increases, a wholesaler becomes valuable as an intermediary between manufacturer and retailer. This channel pattern is common in the distribution of low-margin, convenience-type goods that require the broadest exposure to the potential buyer. Wholesalers are members of the channels for patented drugs and sundries, hardware, and houseware products. Since many of the retail outlets that carry these items are small, the wholesaler performs many critical functions such as storing, breaking bulk, financing, developing promotional aids, and establishing accounting control systems. Because wholesalers buy in large quantities on behalf of many small retailers and represent many manufacturers, this type of channel alignment can achieve significant economies. For example, many independent grocery stores rely on strong wholesale organizations, such as the Independent Grocers Alliance, to keep them competitive with the larger supermarket chains.

The final type of channel, the addition of an agent middleman, is used by producers that have a small number of convenience items in their line or by those that are faced with seasonal constraints. For example, a small manufacturer who wishes to introduce a single convenience item may not be able to support his own sales force. Hence he will use an agent middleman as a substitute means of contacting wholesalers and/or retailers. This channel is also used in the distribution of fruits and vegetables between many small producers and the larger wholesale grocery establishments and chain store warehouses.

The foregoing discussion pertains primarily to the distribution of consumer goods. The distribution of industrial goods is generally more direct. Again, where the volume and order size are large, as with raw materials for large manufacturers (see 18-4), a direct channel will be adequate. But for tools, equipment, and other supplies an industrial distributor or agent middleman may be used to achieve adequate market contact. Another reason why industrial goods channels are direct is that products are often made to the specifications of the user.*
Unfortunately a manufacturer cannot always choose the most appropriate channel of distribution. For example, available middlemen may

*For a description of channel alternatives for industrial goods see R. S. Alexander, James S. Cross, and Ross W. Cunningham, *Industrial Marketing* (Homewood, Ill.: Richard C. Irwin, © 1961), Chapters 7 and 8.

**18-4** Flow of Ferrous Metals through the U.S. Economy in 1960

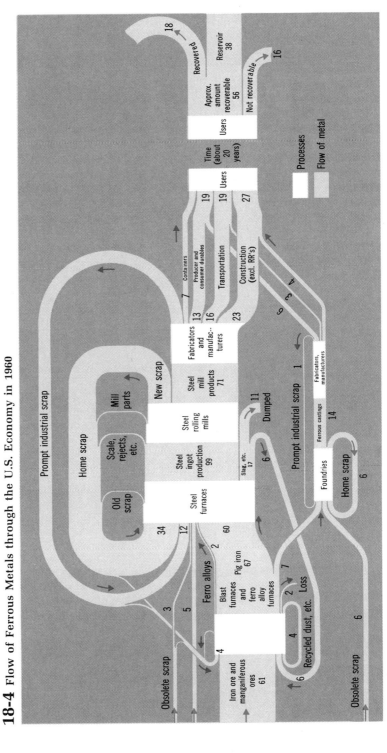

SOURCE: Hans H. Landsberg, *Natural Resources for U.S. Growth* (Baltimore; The Johns Hopkins University Press, 1964).

be unwilling to handle a product because profit potential is small or because they already have competitive lines of merchandise. Under these circumstances the producer will have to use whatever means are available. Should the market respond favorably to a new product, and its market acceptance becomes established, then more suitable channel alignments may become available. The distribution of baby foods produced by drug manufacturers has followed such a pattern. Initially these foods were distributed only through drug wholesalers and drug stores, this being the traditional channel used by the manufacturers. Eventually the consumer began demanding baby foods as a convenience item, that is, as a part of the regular food purchases from supermarkets. As a result new channels were established whereby the producers dealt with grocery wholesalers or chain store warehouses that were interested in adding the product to their grocery lines.

In summary, a manufacturer faces many variables in selecting an appropriate channel of distribution. The firm's own capabilities must be evaluated in terms of expertise, financial resources, and the consumer's acceptance of its products. It must then analyze the type of representation it needs in the market. Among the factors to be considered are the number of potential customers, the number and location of appropriate retailers, economic order sizes, and the characteristics of the product such as its value and service required after sale. In selecting a *particular* middleman a manufacturer must also look at the reseller's capabilities and willingness to push the product. Thus such factors as service capability, willingness to carry inventory close to the market, the availability of display space, and financial responsibility are important considerations. Further, the producer should insure that retail outlets are compatible with the image of the product. For example, a maker of a prestige line of stereophonic equipment may be reluctant to have the product distributed through discount houses. Finally, if a manufacturer is able to provide a complete assortment, then direct distribution may be used. If a producer cannot provide a full assortment, then he will probably have to use a longer channel with more intermediaries.

## CHANNEL POLICIES

There are three basic policies that a manufacturer can follow in the distribution of his product. For one, he may seek intensive distribution to gain the maximum possible market exposure. This policy generally involves using as many different channels of distribution as are available. The second alternative is to be more selective in terms of number and type of middlemen. This policy may also involve using more than one channel of distribution in order to reach different market segments. Finally, there is the policy of exclusive distribution whereby only specific middlemen are permitted to carry the manufacturer's line. In some cases the reseller will not carry competitive lines in return for an exclusive distributorship. Each of these policies is discussed below.

*Intensive distribution* is generally used when a product is considered a convenience item by consumers and is therefore subject to competition from other products. The policy is normally followed by food, drug, houseware, and hardware products. Consumers prefer one-stop shopping for many of the items in these lines. If a particular brand is not available at the store another brand will be selected. Hence the objective of the producer is to have his product available in as many retail outlets as possible.

A manufacturer needing intensive distribution may use many different channels. For example, a food producer can deal direct not only with large supermarket chains but also with the many brokers and wholesalers who represent large and small independent grocery establishments. In other industries the use of different channels will be a reflection of the markets' geographic dispersion or variations in typical order size. For example, a producer may establish his own selling organization within an urbanized, concentrated market, but in order to reach the potential customers in rural areas he will deal with agents, wholesalers, and retailers who maintain contact with this group of consumers. Similarly, a manufacturer may wish to service his very large customers directly while leaving the smaller orders to marketing middlemen. This pattern is particularly common in the distribution of industrial products and supplies.

When a manufacturer desires to exercise control over how middlemen handle his product, he may engage in *selective distribution*. This arrangement is used when the brand image is sufficiently strong and buyers will actively seek it out at only a limited number of retail outlets. Although the policy could be applied to convenience items, it is normally used for the distribution of shopping and specialty goods. There are numerous benefits for both producer and reseller in a selective distribution system. The middleman is protected from excessive levels of horizontal competition, since the identical product line may be available in only a limited number of outlets in the same marketplace. For example, one reason why some products are not distributed through discount stores is to protect the market for other full-line department stores. In return for this type of protection a reseller may be willing to make a greater commitment toward selling the product. A retailer may dedicate a large amount of display space to the product, run special promotions or advertising messages centered around the item, and carry large inventories. The manufacturer is therefore able to generate a substantial amount of enthusiasm on the part of retailers and still achieve rather broad distribution of his product. Selective distribution imposes conditions on the channel members. For example, a manufacturer may require retailers to carry a full line of items, to maintain a minimum inventory, and to adhere to a stipulated price. The retailer in turn may require promotional allowances and an exclusive sales territory. This distribution policy requires the cooperation of all channel participants and injects some cohesiveness into an otherwise non-integrated vertical alignment of independent firms.

*Exclusive distribution* is the extreme case of selective distribution.

According to this policy, a manufacturer may impose rather stringent requirements on the activities of resellers. As an example, resellers may be discouraged from carrying a competing line of goods.* Exclusive distribution agreements may be defined by formal contract containing any or all of the following matters (Beckman and Davidson, 1967):

1. Products covered by agreement.
2. Class or type of customers to be served.
3. The territory involved for exclusive sales.
4. Necessary inventories to be carried.
5. Prices to be paid to manufacturer and resale prices.
6. A sales quota for the reseller.
7. Advertising and sales promotion responsibilities.
8. Prohibition against competitive lines.
9. The duration and termination procedure of the contract.

Perhaps the best current examples of exclusive dealerships are the franchise operations. The advantage to the franchiser is that he controls most aspects of the total marketing effort. Exclusive dealerships are also used for specialty goods that have high unit values. For example, most new automobiles, fine jewelry, and expensive glassware are sold through exclusive distributorships. With the exception of automobiles, the markets for these products are rather narrow and the limited number of retail outlets will not normally pose a barrier to the interested buyer.

There is another channel policy that a manufacturer can follow—participation in *private label* programs with large wholesalers and/or retailers. From the manufacturer's perspective the decision may present competition for its own brand using conventional channels. Kenmore competes with Whirlpool appliances in the consumers' eyes even though the same manufacturer is involved. Usually a producer will make a modified product for a private label program to minimize this type of conflict. Retailers and wholesalers that establish these programs are able to impose their own favorable marketing reputation on the product and control all aspects of its distribution. From the producer's view dual distribution presents the opportunity for increased volume and utilization of excess capacity. As noted previously, well-known names such as General Electric and Whirlpool are participating in private label programs despite the potential increase in brand competition. Private label programs have had a major competitive impact on the conventional distribution of household appliances, food products, wearing apparel, automotive products, and other big-volume items. A brand-competition problem will be encountered by any manufacturer who distributes the same or similar products through different chan-

*The legal status of such restrictions is not entirely clear. Section 3 of the Clayton Act governs and essentially holds such exclusive dealerships illegal when their effect is to substantially reduce competition. See Chapter 7.

nels. There is no simple solution to "interchannel competitive conflicts," and a producer needs to appraise carefully any dual distribution policy.

## CHANNEL ADMINISTRATION

Much of the previous discussion has centered on the decisions of the manufacturer. The manufacturer is not always the dominant force in the channel of distribution. As a matter of fact there is mounting evidence in many industries that the real leadership of many channels rests in the hands of either wholesalers or retailers. The emergence of a leading firm within the channel of distribution can be a critical dimension to a channel's effectiveness.

It has been suggested that a single member of the distribution channel will naturally and inevitably emerge as a channel leader, or "captain" (Stern, 1965). Still, the ability of any firm to assume a leadership position depends on its influence. A manufacturer can clearly assume this role when it enjoys market acceptance of its products, market access, and a reservoir of financial resources. However, a producer may be able to maintain a relative position of leadership even without controlling all of the necessary marketing resources. For example, a producer may be able to attract sufficient access to the market through many small independent retail outlets that are not in a position as individual firms to assume a leadership role.* Examples of this type of channel relationship exist in most franchised operations and in the distribution of automobiles.

Resellers can achieve a clear position of channel dominance in essentially the same way manufacturers do. For example, large retailers can establish private label programs when their own brand image enjoys sufficient market acceptance. Such private label products have easy access to the consumer through the retailer's existing outlets. Middlemen may also assume dominance by representing a significant share of a manufacturer's output. Thus large retail organizations, such as supermarket chains and department stores, may be able to dictate terms to the manufacturer of a nondifferentiated or unknown product. When a manufacturing firm first enters the consumer goods field, access to the consumer is extremely critical, and the manufacturer may have to make substantial concessions to retailers in return for adequate display space.

A wholesaler may assume a leadership role when manufacturers and retailers are so numerous that none commands a significant share of the market. The hardware industry, for example, is characterized by many individual manufacturers and retailers, none of whom command enough of the market to be recognized as a channel leader. The whole-

---

*There have been cases where automobile dealers have banded together to counteract the dominance of manufacturers. Some of these confrontations are described in J. C. Palamountain, *The Politics of Distribution* (Cambridge, Mass.: Harvard University Press, 1955), Chapter V.

saler, almost by default, is able to control significant market access through the many individual hardware stores he supplies. The wholesaler can use this market access as a means of attracting suppliers of branded merchandise. In effect, both ends of the channel look to the point of greatest concentration: the wholesaler.

Although a single firm is likely to emerge as channel leader, the picture may not be as clear cut as the above examples imply. With the exception of totally integrated organizations that control everything from raw material supplies through the retail level, a channel is a cooperative effort and no single firm can do the job as efficiently as the group. Thus even the smallest firms make some contribution to the channels in which they participate. Unless their functions can be assumed by other channel participants even the weakest firms need to be retained in the system. It follows that all channel participants have some measure of influence. The role of the channel captain is to bring systematic cooperation between the various channel participants. The leader provides the impetus for securing agreement on channel-wide operating policies with the objective of improving the effectiveness of the system in terms of serving the customer.

## CHANNELS OF DISTRIBUTION AND THE ENVIRONMENT

One of the greatest challenges facing the environment and the marketing system is the recycling of waste material (Zikmund and Stanton, 1971). Although the technology exists for recycling many commodities, the appropriate channels are not yet organized. For example, the traditional channel is viewed as connecting manufacturer with consumer. In order to recycle waste there must be a channel that facilitates movement in the reverse direction. Beverage companies have developed a return-channel for their reusable bottles. The large proliferation of nonreturnable bottles, cans, and packaging wastes indicate, however, that a widespread implementation of a return-channel is needed. In certain cases this type of channel is made up of voluntary groups interested in preserving the environment. These groups act as collection points for the waste material, which is then shipped to the recycling plant. The recycled material is then sold to manufacturers as raw material. In other cases manufacturers themselves attempt to perform the recycling function.

Future research and study must be devoted to establishing efficient return-channels to facilitate the recycling of materials. This may mean the evolution of a totally new level of middlemen not currently involved in the marketing process. It may require manufacturers to take a position of leadership in controlling the way in which their customers dispose of waste materials. Whatever form such channels take, their establishment deserves a high priority from industry.

In addition to ecological concerns, channels of distribution must interact with other environmental aspects. They must therefore be flexible and responsive to changes in environmental factors. New channels of distribution must emerge when there are shifts in population characteristics. Self-service supermarkets, for instance, emerged as a dominant retail institution when population became centered in urban areas and automobile ownership became common. The legal environment can also cause changes in the structure of distribution channels. For example, the Robinson-Patman Act led to the elimination of a number of discriminatory practices by giant chain stores, including the establishment of dummy food brokers to act as purchasing agents. Such brokers added to the cost but not the efficiency of these channels. Finally, channels must be adaptable to changes in technology. In a very general sense the growth of mail-order marketing is a tribute to improvements in packaging, transportation, and certainly catalog preparation. Dynamic technologies, too, create the need for new methods to distribute innovative products. Hence exchange channels may always be in a dynamic state, changing according to the demands of a dynamic environment.

## STATEMENTS TO CONSIDER

Cooperation is as prevalent in marketing channels as is competition.

The more complex the marketing task becomes, the more necessary it is for a channel to operate as an integrated whole in order to attain efficiency.

Marketing channels change slowly in response to pressures generated by business and economic growth.

Vertical integration, by which short channels are achieved, tends to promote undesirable results from the point of view of the economy as a whole.

Legislation affects marketing institutions, and these in turn influence the form of the channel itself.

Basic functions are readily shiftable among the various business entities in the distribution channel and to others, including the consumer and specialized facilitating agencies.

The survival and prosperity of every firm in the channel is dependent on the success of the others. If the baker is inefficient, the miller is penalized almost as directly as by his own inefficiency.

The narrower the line, the more the manufacturer can afford to do in an effort to assure the success of his retailers and wholesalers.

There is considerable evidence that mass distributors tend to buy from small manufacturers and large manufacturers to sell primarily to small firms in the distributive trades.

The people who manufacture the goods and the people who move the goods into the hands of the ultimate consumer do not share the same business philosophy and do not talk essentially the same language.

# QUESTIONS FOR REVIEW

**1.** What are the likely channels of distribution used in distributing the products listed below? Why?

a. baseball bats

b. machine tools

c. jewelry

d. motion pictures

e. wheat

f. frozen vegetables

**2.** Of what impact is the normal size of purchase by the consumer on the structure of the distribution channel? How might this be related to a desire by a firm to move from a randomized channel to one that is more routinized and stable?

**3.** Define what is meant by a "shifting of marketing functions" and what it has to do with channels of distribution.

**4.** One of the implications of the claim "We eliminate the middleman" is that the use of middlemen is wasteful and does not contribute to marketing efficiency. Comment on this with specific reference to the wholesaler's position in the marketing process.

**5.** This chapter has suggested that the channel of distribution is a single system—a kind of superorganization. What factors would you examine to determine if one series of firms (acting as a channel) is acting any more as a superorganization than any other channel?

**6.** What are the elements of an exchange channel?

**7.** What is meant by a total support or corporate system?

**8.** What are the reasons that franchising has become so popular? Is it applicable to only food lines?

**9.** What are the implications of interchannel competition?

**10.** Would you choose intensive distribution for a new and expensive pipe tobacco? Why or why not?

## Further Readings

Bruce E. Mallen (ed.), *The Marketing Channel* (New York: John Wiley, 1967).

Phillip McVey, "Are Channels of Distribution What the Textbooks Say?" *Journal of Marketing*, Vol. 24 (January 1960), pp. 61–65.

Joseph C. Palamountain, *The Politics of Distribution* (Cambridge, Mass.: Harvard University Press, 1955).

Louis W. Stern, "The Concept of Channel Control," *Journal of Retailing*, Vol. 43 (Summer 1967), pp. 14–20.

Louis W. Stern (ed.), *Distribution Channels: Behavioral Dimensions* (New York: Houghton Mifflin, 1969).

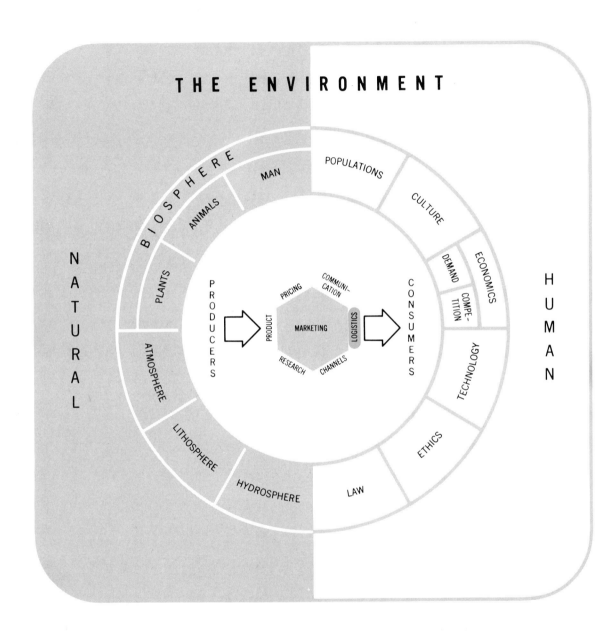

THE ENVIRONMENT

NATURAL

HUMAN

BIOSPHERE

MAN

ANIMALS

PLANTS

ATMOSPHERE

LITHOSPHERE

HYDROSPHERE

POPULATIONS

CULTURE

DEMAND

ECONOMICS

COMPE-
TITION

TECHNOLOGY

ETHICS

LAW

PRODUCERS

CONSUMERS

PRICING

COMMUNI-
CATION

PRODUCT

MARKETING

LOGISTICS

RESEARCH

CHANNELS

# CHAPTER 19
# DISTRIBUTION SYSTEMS II
## LOGISTICS

This chapter was written by Frederick J. Beier, Associate Professor of Transportation and Business Logistics, School of Business Administration, University of Minnesota.

*Logistics, an integral part of the distribution system, deals with the physical movement of goods from market suppliers to buyers. The management decisions should optimize the logistical support of the marketing program.*

Logistics has received major attention from industrial firms and marketing institutions since the end of World War II. There are two primary reasons for this interest. First, as a general trend, since 1945 markets have expanded rapidly and competition for the consumer's dollar has risen sharply. It was during this period that firms began adopting a marketing orientation, or the so-called marketing concept. Essentially this approach, as we have seen, dictates that the marketing effort be directed toward the satisfaction of the needs and wants of the consumer. Some of these needs may be measured in terms of providing the consumer with the desired product in the right place, at the right time, and at a reasonable cost. Logistics, therefore, represents an important part of a firm's service offering to its customers.

Second, logistics is a critical area for cost control. For many firms the costs of logistics far exceed the costs of manufacturing. More generally, two of the primary cost elements of logistics, that is, transportation and inventory carrying costs, account for approximately 15 percent of the GNP (Heskett, *et al.*, 1964). Hence logistics contributes significantly to costs that must be controlled if a firm is to remain competitive. Both the service and cost aspects of logistics make it an integral part of a firm's marketing program.

## LOGISTICS DEFINED

As with most business activities there are several definitions of logistics. It has commonly been defined as the coordination of physical supply and physical distribution to the end of creating time and place utility. That definition, however, does not highlight the close relationship between logistics and marketing. As an alternative we have adopted the following statement:

> Business logistics deals with the *coordination* of the physical movement aspects of a firm's operations so that a *flow* of raw materials, parts, and finished goods is achieved in such a way that *cost* is minimized for the levels of *service* desired. (Harper, 1964.)

A number of aspects of this definition warrant additional comment. Clearly it makes logistics an integrative concept. Before the physical movement of raw materials and finished products can be coordinated, a conceptual "pipeline" must be established throughout a channel of distribution so that all channel participants can mesh their activities.

Otherwise the different channel participants may be working at cross-purposes and thus fail to take advantage of operating economies. For example, the mismatching of pallet size and fork-lift equipment by a supplier and customer respectively may appear to be an obvious problem for which simple solutions are available. Yet the frequency of occurrence of this problem suggests that it is neither obvious nor simple to solve.

The definition also implies that logistics is not merely a synonym for transportation and traffic management. Indeed, logistics involves controlling an array of costs related to the physical movement of commodities. The challenge facing the logistics manager is to manage each individual cost element so that the net total cost to the firm is minimized. Further, these cost elements are interdependent, that is, changes in one may have impact on all others. Hence a rational decision by a firm may involve high transportation rates that are more than offset by savings generated by other cost elements. Logistics costs are discussed specifically in the next section of this chapter.

Finally, the above definition suggests that cost minimization is not the sole objective of the logistics manager. Rather, the goal is to accomplish the marketing mission while minimizing costs. Thus emphasis is placed on *minimizing costs for the level of service desired.* For example, a wholesaler of canned vegetables may have decided, because of the substitutable nature of the product and the large number of competing brands, that he does not want retailers who carry his private label line to be out of stock. The costs associated with maintaining such a service standard—in terms of larger inventories, fast premium transportation, and rapid order processing to keep retailers continuously supplied—may be far greater than if the wholesaler were willing to tolerate a certain number of stock-outs. Thus the absolute level of logistics costs does not provide evidence of an effective logistics system. Rather, the costs must be related to the marketing mission and its success that the logistics system is designed to support.

# LOGISTICS SYSTEMS

## Logistics Decision Areas

The categories of logistics activities are:

1. Transportation and traffic management
2. Warehousing and materials handling
3. Order processing
4. Inventory control
5. Production scheduling
6. Location of fixed facilities
7. Protective packaging

Essentially these are the activities that permit coordination of inbound raw materials, in-process storage, and the distribution of finished products. The relative importance of any specific activity varies with each individual firm. The important point is that a number of these activities must be coordinated simultaneously so that the overall cost to the firm is minimized.

The control of logistics activities is a form of "trade-off management." For example, in an attempt to reduce costs of movement, many firms ship in large quantities to qualify for a lower transportation rate. But increased quantities generate increases in inventory carrying costs, as well as possible complications in warehousing and production scheduling that also can lead to higher costs. Thus the net result of such "economy moves" may be to increase related costs over and above what is realized in transportation savings.

All such interrelationships between logistics activities demand attention. Changes in order processing—say, shortening the time between when the customer submits an order and when he can expect it—has an effect on inventory levels and the location of warehouses. Production scheduling—that is, determining when and how many of each item will be produced—has obvious relationships with inventory control, warehousing, and materials handling. Added investments in branch warehouses or multiple production facilities often result in decreased order-processing time and lower transportation rates. However, such changes also encourage the storage of more inventory in the system and thus increase inventory holding costs. Changes in protective packaging may be offset by higher transportation costs or the need to redesign the materials-handling system. The point of these examples is that a logistics manager must be willing to incur higher costs in one area if he can thereby achieve savings from another activity. A manager must be able to think through proposed changes, identify all the significant trade-offs, and evaluate their net impact on his firm. In 19-1 are some of the trade-offs that might be considered by a typical manufacturing firm.

### Complexity of a Logistics System

As noted earlier, logistics is an integrative activity. A total "logistics system" can be extremely complex. Consider that a manufacturing firm may have thousands of suppliers in widely scattered geographic locations, and it may rely on many retail outlets in order to reach consumers. The hourglass shape of the system for motor oil shown in 19-2 indicates that the oil is gathered from many sources (suppliers) and distributed to many retail outlets.

A system may be further complicated by the number of products involved. A manufacturer may produce a line of hundreds of items of different sizes, weights, colors, and so on. As the number of individual items increases so also does the average inventory within the system and the complexity associated with transportation, warehousing, order processing, and production scheduling. The impact of multiple product

**19-1 Typical Trade-offs between Logistics Activities for a Firm Producing and Warehousing Its Own Products***

| | Transportation and traffic | Warehousing and materials handling | Order processing | Inventory control | Production scheduling | Facility location | Protective packaging |
|---|---|---|---|---|---|---|---|
| Transportation and traffic | Increased† shipment size (−) | Increased size of warehouse to store inventory (+) | Decreased number of orders (−) | Increased average inventory (+) | Longer production runs encouraged (−) | | |
| Warehousing and materials handling | | Systemizing of warehouse and materials handling procedures (−) | | | | Inflexibility of facility location (+) | Inflexibility of packaging (+) |
| Order processing | Higher transportation rates for smaller shipments (+) | Larger warehouse facilities (+) | Increased time for order processing (−) | Higher average inventory (+) | | Warehousing moved close to markets (+) | |
| Inventory control | | Reduced size of warehouse (−) | Increased number of orders (+) | Reduction in average inventory (−) | Short lead time to replace stock-out items (+) | | |
| Production scheduling | | Larger warehouse facilities (+) | | Increased average inventory (−) | Minimized production changes (−) | | |
| Facility location | Increased shipping cost for longer distances (+) | Larger warehouse facility (+) | | Decreased average inventory in system (−) | | Minimizing of number of fixed facilities (−) | |
| Protective packaging | Increased transportation costs for handling of package (+) | Increased materials handling expense (+) | | | | | Package designed** to maximize sales (−) |

* Impact of cost saving measures (−) in diagonal element; on elements in same row, either (+) or (−).

† To be read as follows: Increased shipment size will reduce transportation costs but also have impact on costs of other logistics activities as noted in same row.

** Savings due to increased sales.

**19-2** The Channel of Distribution for Motor Oil

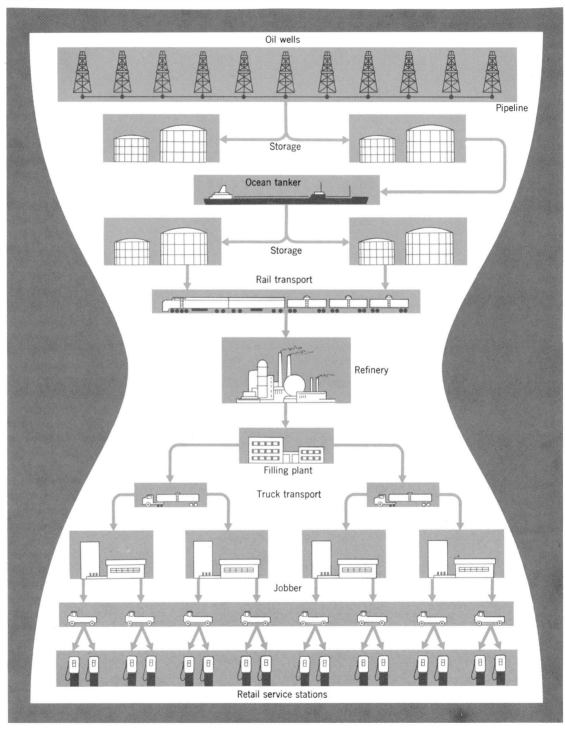

SOURCE: Adapted from Martin L. Bell, *Marketing, Concepts and Strategies* (Boston: Houghton Mifflin, 1966), p. 129.

lines is perhaps greatest on the wholesaling and retailing levels of the channel of distribution. For example, the retail supermarket must coordinate and account for 7800 items that pass through the average establishment (*Progressive Grocer,* 1971). Many of them have been forced to establish centralized warehouse facilities and purchasing procedures in order to facilitate the inbound movement of so many items.

## Objective of a Logistics System

We have already noted that the goal of a logistics system is to minimize cost while still maintaining a given level of customer service. A customer service standard can be expressed in many ways.

1. Maximize: $\dfrac{\text{Number of orders filled}}{\text{Number of orders requested}}$

2. Minimize time between order submission by customer and delivery of product

3. Minimize variance between estimated time of delivery and actual delivery

4. Minimize damage in transit to product

In actual practice firms will adopt all of these service standards but put emphasis on one or another according to circumstances. For a highly substitutable consumer product the manufacturer may wish to concentrate on maintaining a high ratio of orders filled to requests. The reason for this emphasis is twofold. First, by not satisfying a demand for a convenience item the producer loses the revenue from that potential sale. Often the retailer will not incur any loss since he may also carry the substitute product. Second, by not filling an order the producer may lose future potential sales. In other words, by being out of stock the producer has given his competitor a chance to service the buyer and the buyer in turn may decide that the competitor's product is better and stay with it.

An emphasis on other service standards may be more appropriate for other products or competitive situations. For example, one major consideration in purchasing a major appliance or other shopping good is how soon delivery can be made. Retailers normally cannot keep large inventories on high-cost items. This responsibility has been shifted back to wholesale distributors. These distributors are often located in primary markets so delivery time can be minimized. For industrial products that undergo processing at different stages of the distribution channel, precise scheduling may be most important. For example, high-value component parts, such as jet engines, are not kept in inventory but are scheduled to arrive at precise times for inclusion in the production line; a one-day delay in delivery may cause excessive costs incurred by a shutdown of the entire production line. Finally, minimizing in-transit damage is always important. The losses and expenses incurred from replacing and reclaiming damaged merchandise far exceed any added costs necessary to prevent damage in the first place. All of these aspects of customer service can be applied in varying degrees to any particular situation.

## Limits on Customer Service

Logistics as a marketing tool has its limits. Recall that the goal of logistics is to "minimize cost for the level of service *desired*." Management must select which level of customer service is most appropriate. The decision is a trade-off between the cost of supplying service and the incremental revenue derived from it (*Business Week*, 1961). An example may make this point clear.

Assume that an auto parts wholesaler wishes to maintain a 100 percent service level, which he measures in terms of the ratio of orders filled to orders requested. Thus the wholesaler wishes to service all the requests he receives from the many parts stores and gas stations with which he deals. In order to accomplish that objective the wholesaler would need a comprehensive inventory, storing special request items as well as more common, fast-moving items. The costs associated with this inventory can be calculated and plotted on a graph as in 19-3. Subsequent cost calculations for lower levels of customer service can also be plotted so that a continuous function is defined over all service levels. The shape of this curve indicates that logistics costs increase dramatically as the wholesaler approaches 100 per cent customer service. At the higher service levels the costs of carrying additional inventory far exceed added sales revenue. Below point S it is profitable

**19-3** Logistics Costs Associated with Various Levels of Customer Service versus Sales Revenue: Hypothetical Wholesaler

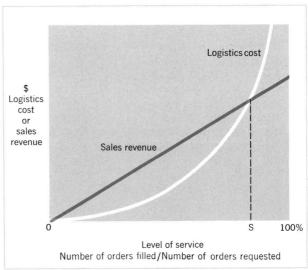

for the wholesaler to reduce lost sales by carrying more inventory. Beyond point S the costs of reducing lost sales makes these sales unprofitable. Thus the wholesaler's attempt to maximize revenue by increasing inventory will eventually cause higher costs and lower profits.

Although this example is expressed in terms of inventory costs, the same relationship prevails with other service standards. For example, if the goal is to minimize transit time, premium transportation must be used, thus substantially raising the level of movement costs. Providing 100 percent customer service, regardless of the standard, generally involves more costs than can be realized from increased sales revenue. This is the most basic form of trade-off that the logistics manager must be concerned with; it is also the most troublesome. The problems associated with establishing the customer service level will be discussed later in this chapter.

# MAJOR LOGISTICS DECISION AREAS

The three major logistics decision areas arc transportation and traffic management, inventory control, and the location of fixed facilities. They are the primary determinants of a system's effectiveness and account for the major cost areas in the overall logistics effort.

## Transportation and Traffic Management

The function of controlling transportation costs, that is, traffic management, is usually the first step toward establishing logistics responsibilities in most industrial firms. Hence some basic knowledge of the transportation industry is fundamental to understanding logistics. The transportation industry comprises five modes: rail, motor carrier, airline, water carrier, and pipeline. Each mode has varying degrees of government regulation. The Interstate Commerce Commission (ICC) regulates surface modes engaged in domestic transportation and regulation of interstate airlines is the responsibility of the Civil Aeronautics Board (CAB). Approximately 61 percent of motor carrier ton-miles are carried by nonregulated carriers, that is, industrial firms operating their own trucks or exempt carriers. The ton-mile and revenue statistics for the different modes of transportation are shown in 19-4. Although railroads account for the largest number of ton-miles, regulated motor carriers command a greater share of the total revenue.

Rail service is typically used for large-volume shipments over long distances. Indeed, many carriers do not accept shipments defined as "less than carload" (LCL), and in many cases this means that shipments less than 10,000 lbs. must either use alternative modes of transportation or consolidate their shipments through freight forwarders. Rail service has a great deal of flexibility in terms of the types of commodities it can carry. Further, the carriers have designed many special pieces of equipment for their clients. For example, there are now special cars

**19-4** Transportation Industry: Ton-Miles, Operating Revenue, and Revenue per Ton-Mile, 1968

| Mode | Ton-miles (in billions) | Percentage of total ton-miles | Revenue of regulated carriers (in thousands of dollars) | Revenue per ton-mile of regulated carriers (cents per ton-mile) |
|---|---|---|---|---|
| Rail (including express and mail) | 756.8 | 41.26 | 11,655,561 | 1.310 |
| Motor carriers (freight only) | 396.3 | 21.60 | 11,675,000 | 6.0 |
| Water (including Great Lakes) | 287.0 | 15.65 | 435,200 | .43 |
| Pipeline | 332.3 | 21.33 | 1,022,962 | .26 |
| Airlines | 2.9 | .158 | 333,562 | 19.98 |

SOURCES: *84th ICC Annual Report to Congress*, 1970, and *CAB Handbook of Airlines Statistics*, 1969 Edition.

for hauling automobiles and liquid products, and box cars that are designed to minimize in-transit damage to general freight.

In contrast to rails, motor carriers offer a more premium service. To offset their higher rates, highway carriers provide door-to-door service, with faster transit times over shorter distances. For example, the average freight train speed in 1969 was 20.1 m.p.h., not including the time a car spends in switching yards (Western Railroad Association, 1970). Thus a rail shipment of 400 miles can take five to seven days whereas highway carriers may be able to provide overnight delivery. The more rapid service and the lower shipment minimums established by highway carriers also permit a firm to reduce its average inventory and still maintain a high customer service level. A wide variety of available highway equipment permits bulk commodities as well as general cargo to use this mode.

Industrial firms also engage in private trucking. With such a fleet at its disposal a company can control the scheduling of shipments and provide more reliable service to customers. Private trucking is especially useful in making emergency shipments to prevent serious out-of-stock situations. Therefore, many firms consider it a valuable marketing tool, particularly in highly competitive industries. The successful economic operation of private trucking normally depends on a high volume of traffic and balanced hauls so that the number of empty truck-miles is minimized. Without these two conditions the costs of a private fleet are substantially above the rates offered by for-hire carriers. Nevertheless, many firms choose to pay the higher costs in return for significant improvements in service.

The growth of air freight is attributable to the recognition by industry that the costs of fast transportation may be more than offset by reductions in inventory and damage to the product. For example, in early 1960 Raytheon, a producer of vacuum tubes and related products, eliminated all its regional and field warehouses and concentrated inventory in a single location. Orders are sent directly to the main warehouse by the sales staff and shipments are dispatched by air freight—either directly to the customer or to a number of "break-bulk points" where they are again reshipped by surface carrier. This system, while incurring substantially higher freight rates and communication costs, has cut distribution costs by 17 percent. The source of savings is primarily from the lower average inventory and the reduced number of fixed facilities. In addition, service has improved in that transit times have been substantially reduced, thus reducing the inventory requirements of Raytheon's customers (Barrick, 1963).

In other cases air freight represents the key to reaching distant markets. The nationwide consumption of fresh Maine lobster is a good example. Further, with the introduction of new wide-bodied jet equipment, such as the Boeing 747, McDonald-Douglas DC-10, and Lockheed 1011, the airlines are greatly expanding their cargo-carrying capacity. These aircraft permit the airlines to attract additional traffic that has heretofore been out of reach because of physical size problems. If and when the Lockheed C5A becomes available, it has been suggested, automobiles could be imported from Europe by air at less expense than by present methods. These trends do not insure success for the future of air freight, however. The overall potential of this form of transportation is being jeopardized by the inefficiencies of ground-support systems—particularly airport congestion and the lack of standardized containers and materials-handling facilities for loading and unloading. Unfortunately, the new larger aircraft will complicate these problems by requiring specialized facilities at airports.

The remaining modes of transportation serve rather specialized users and need not be discussed in detail. For a summary of general service characteristics of the five modes of transportation see 19-5: speed measures door-to-door time; frequency refers to the number of times per day scheduled shipments may be made by any mode; dependability indicates the ability to conform to promised or scheduled delivery times; capability is the capacity of a mode to handle all manner of freight including odd-size shipments; and availability relates to the number of geographic points the mode is able to serve. In these very general rankings it can be seen that among the nonspecialized modes, highway carriers appear to rank above rail and air. However, these relative positions can change dramatically in specific cases. Note that costs have been excluded from this comparison.

## Inventory Control as a Part of the Logistics Effort

Inventory control occupies a central position in the task of the logistics manager, not surprisingly since inventory carrying costs can

**19-5** General Relationships of Service Characteristics of the
Five Modes of Transportation

| Characteristics | Ranking | | | | |
|---|---|---|---|---|---|
| | 1 | 2 | 3 | 4 | 5 |
| Speed | Air | Highway | Rail | Water | Pipeline |
| Frequency | Pipeline | Highway | Air | Rail | Water |
| Dependability | Pipeline | Highway | Rail | Water | Air |
| Capability | Water | Rail | Highway | Air | Pipeline |
| Availability | Highway | Rail | Air | Water | Pipeline |

SOURCE: Adapted from J. L. Heskett, Robert J. Ivie, and Nicholas A. Glaskowsky, Jr.,
*Business Logistics* (New York: Ronald Press, 1964), p. 71.

be as high as 30 percent of the value of a product per year. Inventory
costs include warehousing, taxes, damage, obsolescence, and capital
costs. The management of inventory demonstrates the process of trading off individual costs to achieve an overall minimum cost. In 19-6
you can see the type of trade-offs that must be considered when arriving
at an inventory policy. Thus as the quantity ordered becomes smaller,
certain costs increase, partially offsetting any savings. Similarly an
attempt to economize by increasing inventory size is accompanied by
increases in the level of other costs. The optimum inventory level for
a firm is a compromise between the various costs associated with
holding and ordering inventory.

Inventory control is also important for a logistics manager because
it is so highly interrelated with other activities. As indicated in 19-6
changes in inventory policy can have direct effects on transportation,
warehousing, order processing, and production scheduling. Although
activities such as order processing also appear to interact with many
aspects of the logistics effort, inventory involves a much larger expense
item. Because of this high interrelationship all the ramifications of a
change in inventory policy can be extremely complex. The logistics
manager must evaluate the total impact of such changes and attempt
to minimize total costs.

## Fixed-Facility Location

The location of plants and warehouses can have a profound impact
on the logistics costs of the firm. For example, the Pillsbury Company
has specialized production plants throughout the United States. Since
a typical order from a retailer consists of many different items in
varying quantities, it would not be practical to ship each item directly
from its point of production, for transportation costs would be excessive. Instead, the company has established a network of warehouses

**19-6** The Problem of Balance and Compromise in Control of Inventory Size

| *A* | *B* |
|---|---|
| Factors Associated with Costs of Maintaining a Small Materials Inventory | Factors Associated with Costs of Maintaining a Large Materials Inventory |

*A*

Factors Associated with Costs of Maintaining a Small Materials Inventory

1. Order costs
2. Excess of handling costs
3. Loss of quantity discounts
4. Service charges
5. Costly shortages
6. Added follow-up and expediting costs
7. Added transportation
8. Possible losses from price rises
9. Etc.

*B*

Factors Associated with Costs of Maintaining a Large Materials Inventory

1. Obsolescence
2. Insurance
3. Damage
4. Deterioration
5. Storage costs
6. Investment
7. Interest
8. Possible losses from price declines
9. Etc.

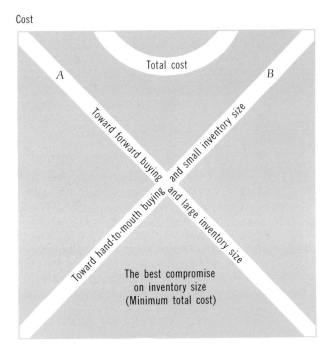

Cost

Inventory Size Axis

SOURCE: Stanley E. Bryan, "The Fundamental Elements of Effective Materials Control," *Purchasing*, Vol. 30 (May 1951), p. 97.

located close to their major markets. The distribution centers provide the opportunity for volume shipments to be made from each plant to each center, thus assuring low inbound transportation costs. Orders are made up at the distribution center and sent out for local delivery. The distribution centers are located so that they are within 24 hours by truck and 48 hours by rail of most potential customers.

A somewhat different approach may be taken by firms that elect to minimize the number of inventory locations in the field in order to reduce inventory costs. Rather dramatic savings can be generated with no reduction in customer service. For example, one company reduced the number of company warehouses from 50 to 25, thereby increasing transportation costs by 7 percent by cutting inventories by 20 percent and total logistics costs by 8 percent. Further, "this was accomplished at the cost of serving a few small markets (about 5 percent of the total) with second-day instead of first-day delivery" (Magee, 1960).

## LOGISTICS AND THE DISTRIBUTION CHANNEL

The study of logistics is an important aspect of distribution channels. Logistics requires some manner of agreement between suppliers and customers if it is to be totally effective since there are overlapping responsibilities for logistics activities. For example, consider the channel of distribution for ski boots: manufacturer direct to retailer. If the manufacturer wants to control his costs, he may wish to control the manner in which the boots are shipped to the retailer. The retailer, however, may also desire to control his inbound suppliers. The manufacturer's concern may be cost, the retailer's may be dependability and rapid transportation service to minimize inventory. Both characteristics may not be found in the same carrier. Hence either manufacturer or retailer will each attempt to get his own way, thus encouraging a conflicting, unstable relationship, or they may agree on a compromise. The latter is the probable outcome. The point is that logistics issues often require agreement between channel participants.

The overall objective for a logistics system is to serve the buyer at the end of the channel of distribution. Channel members must, therefore, recognize the interdependent relationship of participants in the same distribution channel. This is critical when analyzing the impact of trade-offs, for in order to be effective, cost trade-offs must result in some benefit to a firm's vendors or suppliers. "Intrafirm trade-offs which have no effect on external organizations either in the short run or long run are either ineffective or illustory" (Heskett, et. al., 1964). Hence failing to examine the impact of one firm's logistics decisions on the rest of the channel can seriously impair the firm's ability to compete. For example, assume that the ski boot manufacturer mentioned above intends to cut inventory and transportation costs by selling on the basis of F.O.B. origin. Title to the ski boots would thus change at the origin of the shipment with the retailer assuming all responsibilities in regard to liability for loss, damage, and transportation costs. The retailer must also finance the cost of inventory over a longer period of time, that is, the normal sales period plus transit time. Although the manufacturer may have reduced some of his costs it is not obvious that the product will be presented to the buyer with any more impact than in the past. In fact, unless the retailer is better able to carry inventory and coordinate inbound transportation than the manufacturer, the total costs of the channel will probably increase. Considering the small size of retail ski shops and their seasonal cash flow requirements, such a change would impose a hardship on the retailer. As a result the manufacturer's product would not be presented as effectively to the consumer, and some retailers might well shift to other boot manufacturers. Thus the consequences of not examining the impact of logistics decisions on other middlemen can be quite severe.

# PROBLEMS IN IMPLEMENTING
# A LOGISTICS SYSTEM

We have been rather optimistic about implementing a logistics system, but experience suggests that implementation is easier said than done. One of the major problems facing industrial and marketing organizations is providing an organizational structure for realizing potential logistics economies.

There are two primary problems that a firm must consider when developing an organizational pattern for logistics. First, there are obvious interdependencies between the various logistical subactivities. In 19-1 we pointed out some of the more obvious trade-offs between the various activities. The problem, however, is that these activities are normally delegated to autonomous departments within a firm. Consequently, there may be no interest in examining trade-off opportunities that involve other departments. For example, the interests of the marketing department may be to maximize sales. Therefore it may have little interest in attempts by some other department to reduce available inventory when the impact may be to lose sales.

This situation is reinforced by traditional accounting practices in which departments are held accountable for specific cost categories. For example, a traffic manager may be held accountable for transportation costs. Hence it may be difficult to convince him to reduce the average size of shipments and incur higher transportation rates so that some other department can reduce inventory costs. In theory top management should be able to evaluate the traffic manager on the basis of his contribution to the entire firm rather than his ability to minimize transportation costs. Most firms, however, do not have the internal management-information system to attain this goal. Until such a system is developed and incorporated into a firm's organizational structure people will make decisions based on self-interest without regard for the overall well-being of the firm.

There is a myriad of organizational alternatives available. At one extreme is:

the *centralized organization,* in which all logistics activities are located under a vice president or general manager of logistics. This type of organizational structure maximizes the amount of coordination among logistics activities, and thus helps to solve the dilemma of the traffic manager described above.

At the other extreme is:

the *dispersed organization,* in which the logistics activities are distributed throughout the firm. For example, transportation may be a part of the marketing department, production scheduling attached to production, and so on. There is no logistics department *per se* and emphasis is placed on promoting the interests of each of the traditional organizational functions, marketing, production, and finance, etc.

The most appropriate organization depends on the nature of the company, product, industry, and other factors. Producers of wide product lines for competitive markets may tend toward a centralized logistics department because of the need for coordination and customer service. Firms that produce a narrow line of products for industrial use may be able to use a dispersed organization.

## LOGISTICS AND THE ENVIRONMENT

Logistics is primarily a managerial subject, that is, it deals with making decisions in a certain area of the firm's operations. Even so, anyone dealing with logistics must face certain environmental questions. At the most basic level logistics is an activity that operates within the constraints imposed on it by the economic system. In a sense, this entire chapter has attempted to describe how logistics interacts with the total economic environment. For example, customer service demands may be the primary considerations when a firm makes logistics decisions. When new markets develop there are often significant changes required in the logistics system.

There are, however, other environmental issues that have an impact on logistics. At the current time there is great emphasis on protecting the natural environment. Such emphasis is often directed at the transportation system. Questions are being raised concerning the environmental impact of highways, airport location, and the development of navigable inland waterways. Attempts are being made to measure the social cost of the various transport alternatives. To the extent that social costs can be defined and measured, then, taxes may be levied against the users of that mode. Such a taxing scheme would apply to the transportation of passengers as well as freight. The inclusion of such costs, through a taxing mechanism, may have significant impact on competitive rate structures and cause a firm to reorder its thinking in its choice of transportation modes.

Logistics decision-makers will have to take the natural environment into consideration in other matters. For example, plant and warehouse locations must be made so that they are not damaging to the surrounding environment. Industrial firms must also continually evaluate new methods of protective packaging so as to reduce the amount of potential waste while still eliminating damage to the product. Thus, while logistics is essentially a managerial area, it faces a number of environmental challenges.

# STATEMENTS TO CONSIDER

Product changes are forcing new pressures on the distribution system—more items to carry, faster obsolescence, lower unit sales, and inventory turnover.

The nature of logistics does and will require that all firms interrelated in a channel of distribution be regarded as a superorganization greatly in need of decision coordination and control.

Managers should keep in mind that excessive commitments to high levels of customer service can be extremely expensive. System attributes of fast and consistent customer service have related costs. The higher each of these qualities of performance, the greater will be the required cost.

Unfortunately many firms still have not devoted special attention to the feasibility of a physical distribution organization. Internal pressures favored not upsetting the apple cart. So the functions of physical distribution in these firms remains neatly housed throughout the marketing, manufacturing, and financial departments.

Physical distribution is simply another way of saying, "the whole process of business." You can look at a business, particularly a manufacturing business, as a physical flow—the flow of materials.

The greatest savings in marketing in the future will come from physical distribution economies.

Physical distribution is marketing's dark continent. (Drucker)

Goods tend to move toward the point of final consumption at a rate established by the ultimate consumer. (Aspinwall)

Speed is the single most important element in obtaining market information through the flow of orders from customers. (Ivie)

The salesman is ultimately responsible for external coordination with customers: the logistician is likely to play the role of technical or expert adviser to the salesman. (Ivie)

# QUESTIONS FOR REVIEW

**1.** Considering the various characteristics of the individual modes of transportation what are the reasons that some forms of coordinated service, e.g., piggyback, are more practical than others, e.g., air-ship?

**2.** Contrast the emphasis placed on the different logistics activities by a firm manufacturing a narrow line of industrial products and one producing a wide line of consumer food items.

**3.** What are some of the conflicts which are likely to develop between a logistics manager of a wide-line consumer goods manufacturer and the sales or marketing manager?

**4.** What are the differences in the likely approach to logistics taken by a manufacturer, wholesaler, and retailer of consumer items?

**5.** Comment on the logistics implications of a customer service level implied in "The Customer is King."

**6.** Is logistics merely a synonym for transportation and traffic management?

**7.** Explain the meaning of trade-off management. How does it apply to the matter of logistics?

**8.** What is the implication of the hourglass shape of the figure in 19-2?

**9.** What impact does vertical integration have on logistics?

**10.** Explain how the factors associated with the costs of maintaining an inventory vary from firm to firm.

## Further Readings

D. J. Bowersox, E. W. Smykay, and B. J. LaLonde, *Physical Distribution Management* (New York: Macmillan, 1968).

Paul D. Converse, "The Other Half of Marketing," *Boston Conference on Distribution,* 1954, pp. 22–25.

J. L. Heskett, Robert M. Ivie, Nicholas A. Glaskowsky, *Business Logistics* (New York: Ronald Press, 1964).

John F. Magee, *Industrial Logistics* (New York: McGraw-Hill, 1968).

N. Marks and R. Taylor, *Marketing Logistics,* (New York: John Wiley, 1967).

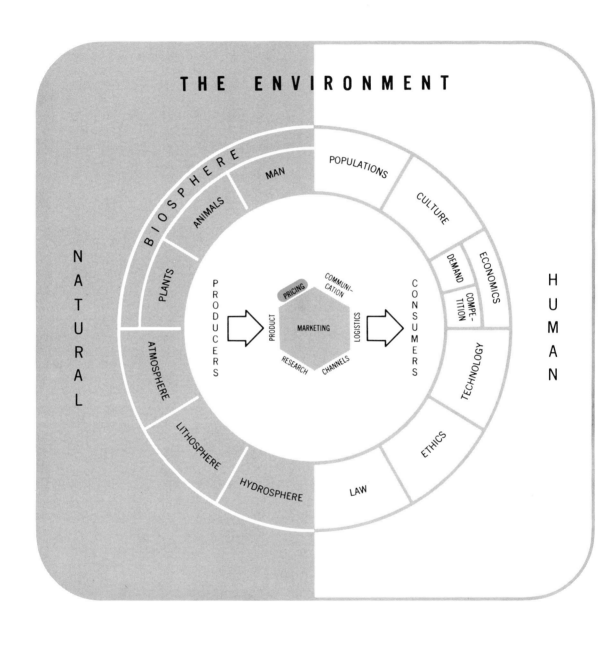

# CHAPTER 20
# PRICE INFLUENCES AND PRICE POLICIES

*The establishment of prices and the operation of the pricing system constitute one of the most important decision-making areas for marketing, since prices direct the use of resources in a capitalistic society and also help strike a balance between production and consumption.*

Pricing is the object of extensive study and research not only by marketers but also by students of other disciplines. Indeed, no other aspect of marketing is subject to the scrutiny and research given to pricing by economists, international trade experts, accountants, and other scholars. These experts have contributed a great deal of knowledge from their particular points of view. From a marketing standpoint, however, our principal concerns are how pricing affects customer acceptance of a product in the marketplace, how pricing influences the image of product and firm, how it affects the character of competition in the marketplace, and how it directly influences the revenue (and profits) flowing to a firm from the marketplace. Price in this context is an *element* of the marketing mix that *contributes* to a firm's success or failure.

## UNDERSTANDING THE ROLE OF PRICE

Both practitioners and students of marketing often misunderstand pricing, regarding the subject as highly complex and esoteric. Perhaps much of the misunderstanding results because segmented knowledge has been acquired from other disciplines. There is, for example, a common tendency to equate *price theory* with *price practice*. The economic theorist in describing the purely competitive market model tells us that at successively lower prices increased quantities of a good are demanded. As prices are increased the reverse reaction occurs. Similarly, the analysis and determination of costs for cost control and financial reporting as developed by the accounting scholar may not be appropriate for pricing purposes, and someone with knowledge about these accounting matters may easily overrate the importance of costs in determining prices. Jules Backman in a study for the National Industrial Conference Board comments that

> ... the cost theory of pricing is a nice, comfortable, easy-to-understand explanation—until a few key questions are asked: How are "costs" determined? What is included in "costs"? Are past, present, or future costs included? How is the break-even point determined? What time period is covered? What is done if your competitor has a higher or lower price? (Backman, 1961.)

Another factor complicating the understanding of price policies and practices is that no discernible pricing pattern exists among American companies. Some firms may follow a fixed policy in setting prices, but relatively few do have well-formulated policies. Moreover, manufacturers often adopt programs quite different from those of the distributive institutions. Unless the pricing objectives of a manufacturer are compatible with those of its distributors, there is little likelihood that a single workable policy can be applied. Finally, the pricing of industrial goods differs greatly from the pricing of consumer products.

For general guidance remember that the interrelationship of pricing and the other factors in the marketing mix is multidimensional. There are no easy answers to these basic questions: What is the best price for this product? How will our competitors react to a given price or price change? What price builds and fosters the product image? Can we optimize other marketing factors with price? For pricing is influenced by a host of economic and noneconomic factors. Despite the distressing lack of precision in available information, hopefully some useful guides may result from the following discussion.

## The Varying Importance of Pricing

In general, price decisions are an integral part of a firm's total marketing strategy. Sometimes, however, price decisions are of little importance to management. How can this be so? It is often assumed that consumers are motivated to buy because of a particular price. But it is more accurate to say that consumers respond to value or a "bundle of values" rather than to a single marketing element. If consumers tend to respond to noneconomic stimuli, then the pricing problem may be relegated to secondary importance. In that case marketing activities other than price play a more dominant role in the purchase-decision process.

Economic theory on pricing must be carefully applied to practical market situations because prices of products and services are rarely determined by the impersonal forces of the market. In Chapter 6 we pointed out that monopolistic competition and oligopoly more often characterize our economic structure than pure competition. Each of these conditions relates to differentiation. As we showed in that chapter, those industries (or markets) dominated by few sellers must boost their sales volume by nonprice variables. The few sellers recognize that price reductions can and will be met by the other few market participants and conversely that price increases if not followed by all will result in a marked decline in sales as customers shift their purchases to the close substitutes of other sellers. This state of affairs doesn't mean that pricing isn't important, only that price adjustments are restrained by the realities of the competitive situation.

Monopolistically competitive markets also give rise to differentiation. A marketer may emphasize price, but he will more likely base his market appeal on brands, symbolic meanings, styles, tastes, and other noneconomic factors. For most sellers in the American scene marketing policies do exercise an influence over consumers' market purchases.

These policies, of course, are designed to increase revenue. The importance of pricing in marketing policy depends on the specifics of a given industry or market situation.

Industrial purchasers buy under very different circumstances from those that pertain to individuals. An industrial buyer tends to be more objective and rational than a typical consumer. He is usually more knowledgeable about products, is governed by bid specifications, evaluates productivity versus cost, and seeks competitive bids. Of course, there are many knowledgeable consumers who might purchase a home lathe as objectively as a purchasing agent. But the "illusion of differentiation" that prevails among consumer goods is more difficult to achieve with industrial goods (Dean, 1951). Yet there is a growing tendency for industrial goods to be differentiated by psychological factors as well. Many industrial products, in their packaging and advertising, are no longer esthetically spartan. Lathes, bulldozers, computers, and trucks have been given stylish designs. Objectivity may not always prevail in the purchase of such goods, particularly if images and decor become matters of concern to management.

### The Interrelationship of Prices

Price is related (1) to many other prices, and (2) to the objectives of a firm. Rarely if ever can management set its own prices independently of other prices—those of its competitors, those of its suppliers, even those of other industries. Our economy functions through the delicate balance of prices. Any breakdown in the mechanism of adjustment is likely to affect a whole series of economic events. Jules Backman likens the interrelationship of prices between industries to the ripples in a lake:

> This interrelationship can be symbolized by the series of ripples that spread out when a stone is thrown into a lake. The ripples flow in every direction. A similar tendency is found in our economy. The prices of one industry are the costs of another, and the prices of the latter industry are the costs of a third industry, and so on until the ultimate consumer is reached. Thus, actions which cause prices to rise will be felt in many directions and may set in motion forces having results entirely different from those anticipated or desired. (Backman, 1953.)

The whole system is responsive to many factors. For example, if the general level of prices is rising, wage earners are likely to demand higher incomes to offset the diminishing value of their dollars.

Obviously the prices of goods on the shelves of wholesalers and retailers are closely related to the prices of goods in the hands of manufacturers, and these, in turn, are related to the prices of raw materials, capital goods, parts, and supplies. All of these prices are related to the prices in other trades, the prices of securities, and even the prices of services. The parallelism of various prices is illustrated in 20-1 and 20-2. These figures show the moderate upward movement of wholesale and consumer prices prior to 1966. After that period of stability in the early 1960s, inflationary pressures drove prices of most goods upward. From 1966 through 1971 no manufacturer, wholesaler, or retailer could avoid the effects of inflationary pressures, which increased the costs of doing business. Businessmen, as a result, rapidly moved up their prices, as reflected in the figures.

## The Setting of Price by a Firm

Just as prices in the economy are closely related to other prices and other economic factors, the prices set by a firm are related to its other prices. And they must correspond with the objectives and policies of the firm. Most firms would be unwilling to delegate the formation of price formulas to members of the sales force, for instance. The matter is too sensitive to delegate below the policy-making level. In a large firm overall price policy is usually determined by executives of several major departments, such as marketing, manufacturing, engineering, and finance or accounting. It is at this level that other major policies take shape, and because pricing influences the accomplishment of other corporate objectives it must be decided here. For example, take a company aiming for growth that has determined its dividend policy as some percentage of net earnings and desires to acquire its major financing from retained earnings. If the growth rate is set at X percent of sales each year and growth requires continuous investment, management knows that a profit margin of Y will be required. Prices will clearly have to be set to accord with the stated policies of the firm. In large corporations where there are many thousands of items to price, the overall price guidelines are developed at conferences of the major responsible executives. Once pricing policies that are compatible with the corporate objectives have been determined, the price structure for specific items, discounts, and geographic pricing problems can be worked out by employees at lower echelons.

Management also recognizes that price performs a rationing function. A firm's price tends to determine what will be produced, how much will be produced, and the way in which the good might be distributed. If price is too low, the competitors for the revenue received may be too great to warrant production and distribution. Price obviously influences the income of producers and hence serves to allocate the firm's resources. Likewise, prices that are too low relative to demand fail to induce the required capacity expansion needed to supply the demand. Thus resources that might flow to an industry are pulled elsewhere by more attractive prices. Conversely, when prices are too high they tend to cut off some of the demand, and a firm may not dispose of its output. This condition invites new entrants, usually at a lower price, thus increasing the quantities in the market. If an abundant supply appears unsalable, one or more firms in the industry may lower price to avoid

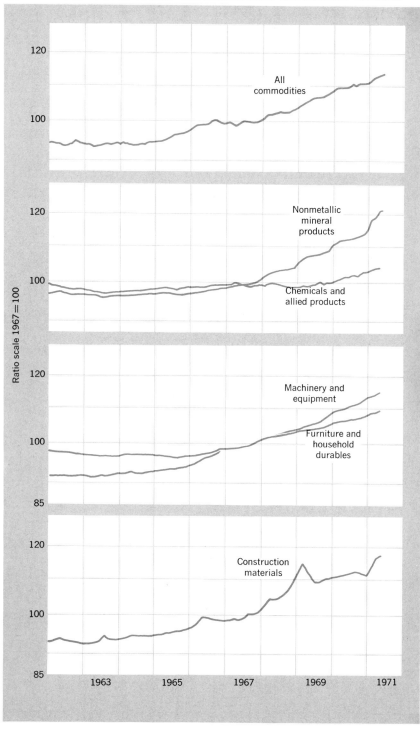

**20-1** Wholesale Price Trends—All Commodities and Selected Products

Ratio scale 1967 = 100

All commodities

Nonmetallic mineral products

Chemicals and allied products

Machinery and equipment

Furniture and household durables

Construction materials

SOURCE: Federal Reserve Chart Book, Board of Governors of the Federal Reserve System (June 1971), pp. 74–76.

**20-2** Consumer Price Trends—All Consumer Items and Selected Products

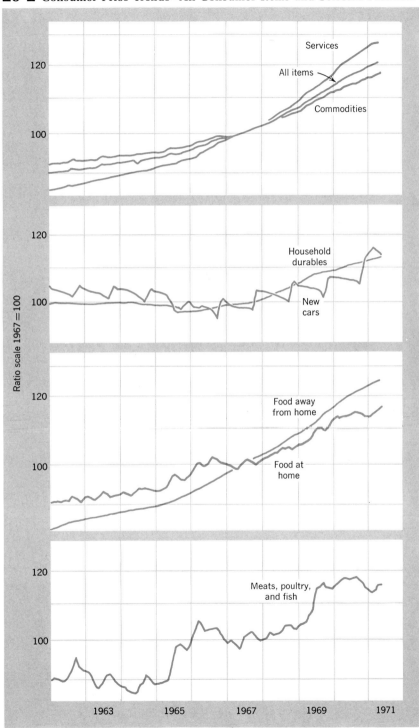

SOURCE: Federal Reserve Chart Book, Board of Governors of the Federal Reserve System (June 1971), pp. 72–73.

an inventory accumulation. This glut, of course, discourages entry into the industry. Although prices are not entirely a reliable regulator and rationer, they do operate within these broad limits.

# MAJOR INFLUENCES ON PRICING POLICIES

It is easy to say that it is desirable to develop well-formulated *price policies* and *price objectives,* but we must recognize the numerous influential conditioning factors. To develop policies that cannot be disrupted would be exceptional. Some idea of the number and complexity of influences may be obtained from 20-3. These influences are not of equal importance to all companies and industries because of differences in management, legacies of the past, character of the particular firm and its products, and other matters. Rather than discuss each factor in 20-3, we shall dwell only on some major influences and others that have general applicability.

## Character of the Product

For most firms the starting place in developing a price policy is the character of the product. The boundaries of price policy are set by the item's physical and market attributes, its production aspects, its degree of differentiation, and its newness.

With perishable products little opportunity exists for a seller to adopt a price policy that is insensitive to market demand. The unpredictability of the supply and the limitation of storage mean that selling prices, both wholesale and retail, are dominated by approximations of supply and demand. Unless these prices are administered by a pricing authority or some established formula (for example, milk prices), the seller can expect prices to be imposed by the perishable character of the product. Durable goods that lend themselves to storage, postponement of purchase, and some control by the manufacturer over raw material are much more amenable to company-controlled pricing.

Industrial goods are purchased because the buyer forecasts a market opportunity for goods or services he can produce with the industrial goods. This is a derived demand. In fact, the purchase of most industrial goods hinges on the opportunities in another market. For example, the automobile manufacturer's demand for automobile tires and parts is conditioned by the forecasts of the quantity of automobiles demanded. If automobile demand is sluggish, so will be the demand for tires and all other components. Price generally cannot play an incentive role in industrial goods when the ultimate demand for the goods to be produced is sluggish. Hence, when derived demand is present, price *per se* is not likely to be the dominant factor that determines whether a sale is made.

The concept of "joint" demand is also useful in determining prices of industrial goods. When numerous goods make up the overall cost of a product, individual prices are less likely to be responsive to de-

## 20-3 Factors Affecting Price Behavior*

I. Characteristics of the product or industry
   A. In terms of factors affecting demand
      1. Durability. 2. Producers' or consumers' goods. 3. Degree of processing—finished or semifinished goods or raw materials. 4. Joint demand. 5. Availability of substitutes. 6. Luxury or style goods or necessaries. 7. Standardized, unique, or differentiated. 8. Number of buyers. 9. Seasonality.
   B. In terms of factors affecting costs
      1. Rigidity of wage rates. 2. Price rigidity of materials. 3. Nonpostponable overhead.
   C. In terms of factors affecting physical supplies
      1. Ease of entry for new producers. 2. Number of sellers. 3. Time required to expand capacity and output. 4. Perishability of product. 5. Seasonality.

II. Law or administrative decree
   A. Governmental agencies—telephone, gas, railroad, electric, and water rates
   B. Minimum wage and maximum hour legislation
   C. Tariff
   D. Direct price control
   E. Indirect price control
      1. Production control. 2. Loan programs. 3. Marketing agreements.
   F. Making it possible for private interests to control prices
      1. Patents and copyrights. 2. Resale price fixing—Fair Trade Acts. 3. Limitations on sales below cost—Unfair Practices Acts.

III. Concentration of control
   A. Monopoly or oligopoly
      1. Producers. 2. Labor unions.
   B. Collusion—to restrict output, allocate production, share markets, etc.
   C. Price Leadership
   D. Central sales agencies
   E. Trade association activities

IV. Marketing techniques
   A. Suggested prices on packages
   B. Advertising of standard prices
   C. One-price policy
   D. Product differentiation
   E. "In between" prices

V. Structure of the market
   A. Organized or "unorganized" markets
   B. Scope of market area
   C. Marketing channels used

VI. Habits and customs
   A. Price of professional services
   B. Price lining
   C. Coinage system

VII. Contractual arrangements—long-term

* This listing was originally intended to explain price behavior and price inflexibility. With few exceptions the listing is also useful in categorizing the major influences on price policies.

SOURCE: Jules Backman, *Price Practices and Price Policies,* (New York: Ronald Press, 1953), pp. 59–60.

mand. The construction industry is often cited as an example of joint demand. The cost and demand for construction cannot be altered by a marked increase or decrease in the price of one of the component materials. The lowering of the price of insulation, for example, will not seriously affect the total cost of construction, because it accounts for a very small proportion of the total materials cost. The seller well knows that a reduction in his price of insulation would only result in a loss of revenue and not in an increase in sales. If however, the cost of all construction materials were either increased or lowered, the total cost of construction would be affected. Yet it should be recognized that some construction costs are seriously influenced by the price of a single product. Steel prices, for example, contribute heavily to the cost of construction when the proportion of steel used is high relative to other materials. Clearly this is not a joint-demand situation, but one wherein the importance of a single industrial material to the end product predominates.

Consumer goods are sometimes broken down into *convenience goods, shopping goods,* and *specialty goods.* This classification, which was also noted in earlier chapters, is based on the shopping effort and buying patterns of consumers. Convenience goods are low in unit price and are purchased frequently and in small quantities. Shopping goods are higher in unit price and are compared with the close substitutes offered; a buyer will expend some effort in seeking out the "best buy" among them. Specialty goods are often high in unit price and a buyer will go to considerable length before making the purchase; they are purchased only infrequently. The buyer of a specialty good is not as likely as a shopping goods' buyer to make comparisons with other goods. Despite definite limitations, the classification has an application to the development of price guidelines and the selection of channels of distribution.

From a price standpoint producers of convenience goods have little leeway in setting price. Their items command weak brand loyalty and are so slightly differentiated that their prices must fall within a narrow range of possibilities. If the price of a convenience good such as cigarettes, gasoline, or bread is out of line, the possibility of substitution is likely to occur.

Shopping goods open the door to price differentials because consumers can develop strong brand preferences and are susceptible to uniqueness of features, styling, and the like. The price of a shopping good often results in a major money outlay, but the time span between expenditures is often long. If a firm creates strong product differentiation it can usually command a somewhat higher price; consumers are quite adept at associating price with quality. Consumers are also believed to be less sensitive to the price of shopping goods because a substantial portion is purchased through installment credit. The amount of the installment payment, then, may be the critical factor.

Specialty goods give the seller a large amount of discretion in setting price. Since consumers will exert much effort to acquire them and since they fulfill particular needs, these goods are not purchased because of their price. High prices are in fact desirable for most specialty goods, particularly if the goods meet a prestige or status need. Fur coats, antiques, custom-tailored items, and rare jewelry are best priced high rather than low. Low prices would diminish their exclusive appeal. Another aspect of specialty goods is that they are usually sold in few outlets. The dealer who is significant to the buyer must convey the same kind of exclusive character as the product. For all of this the consumer *expects* to pay a price.

## Product Differentiation

Product differentiation can be a significant aspect of price policy for both industrial-goods and consumer-goods sellers. The fullest advantage of differentiation can be exploited when a company's product line has a distinct advantage over more standard competing products. If products do not offer this possibility, companies can develop differentiation in other aspects, such as delivery terms, service, and credit conditions.

Market strategists recognize that for a clearly differentiated product, price is subordinated in the purchase decision. Therefore they feature actual and psychological differences in their marketing effort. Advertising claims, package designs, distribution methods, and pricing build the concept of differentiation and hence strong brand or company preferences.

When a product itself is difficult to differentiate even in these ways, attempts can be made to distinguish the firm. Wholesale and retail firms particularly may exploit an advantage in their location, their array of services or lack of them, and the breadth and depth of lines of merchandise carried. Retail firms appear to have distinct possibilities to develop strong differentiation by virtue of their location, decor, price lines, and other assets. As noted in Chapter 6 differentiation leads to the steepening of the demand curve, which is why differentiation and price are so closely related. Businessmen seem to practice differentiation even though they may not recognize its influence on the demand for their products.

## Costs and Prices*

Perhaps the most widespread idea concerning pricing is that costs determine prices. This notion is a gross oversimplification of the issue and in most instances is erroneous. Certainly prices must cover all costs, but it is wrong to assume that every product's price must cover its own individual costs. There are too many variables influencing price for cost to be the sole determinant (see 20-3).

According to economic theory, in the long run price tends to equal the cost of production. This theoretical construction is a source of much

---

*For a somewhat detailed discussion of the relationship of costs to prices, see Jules Backman, *Price Practices and Price Policies,* pp. 119–148, or a brief but excellent discussion by Donald V. Harper, *Price Policy and Procedure,* pp. 49–59.

misunderstanding by those who ignore the fact that the economist does include a profit in his concept of cost of production. Perhaps the greatest drawback to the position that costs determine prices is that it completely ignores demand considerations.

Cost is more important in the long run than the short run. Economic doctrine is correct in telling us that when costs of production are above the market price, a firm will be forced, in the long run, to cease operations. Furthermore, if price is so high above the cost of production that it brings in large profits, new entrants will be drawn into the industry with ensuing pressure on existing prices. Thus, in the long run, effective competition tends to make prices equal the cost of production.

There are many instances in our economy where *costs are determined by prices*. Numerous products have their prices (or at least a range of possible prices) set by market forces. A firm then has to determine the price it can reasonably expect and work from that figure to see if it can profitably produce the item. When prices are determined by the market, manufacturers must seek cost-reduction measures through substituting raw materials, finding a lower-cost technology, and attempting to reduce distribution costs. In short, when market prices move downward, pressures are transferred to costs and firms attempt to reduce those items of cost that are controllable. When business is enjoying the reverse situation, rising costs exert pressures on prices. Prices will rise, but only to the limits permitted by market forces. The five-cent or ten-cent candy bar, for example, is what is known as a customary market price—and the manufacturer meets rising costs by reducing the quantity of the product. Other and more complex measures are faced by most other manufacturers.

Backman summarizes the complexity of the interrelationship of business conditions, costs, and prices in the following passage:

> In periods of rapidly changing business conditions, the importance of the psychology of a market situation should not be minimized, since the point of view of businessmen obviously exerts a very important influence upon market trends. In such situations it cannot be too strongly emphasized that the relation between costs and prices is not direct, mechanical, or exact. The cost structure of a concern and the condition of its market establish certain limits within which decisions must be made, but within these boundaries there may be a broad field for the exercise of individual judgment. . . . (Backman, 1953.)

Thus costs should be regarded as setting the lower limits on price, whereas the upper limit is the value of the product to the buyer. The decision to be made by the price-maker is to select a price somewhere between these extremes (Harper, 1966).

## New Products versus Mature Products

A firm's approach to pricing a new product varies depending on whether the product is completely original or similar to existing products. If a new product has existing substitutes, they provide the frame of reference for pricing. Unless influenced heavily by other factors, price will fall somewhere in the known price range of the other products.

If the product is completely new, then the problem is complicated by the lack of any experience or any established reasonable price range. Several attempts have been made to develop pricing approaches for new products. Perhaps the best known are Joel Dean's *skimming price* and *penetration price*. A skimming price, in Dean's view, is a high price accompanied by heavy promotional expenditures during the early phases of market development, followed by lower prices during later phases. This approach is widely practiced and has been successful in numerous instances. The reasons for its success are cited by Dean as follows:

1. Demand is likely to be more elastic with respect to price in the early stages than it is when the product is full grown. . . . Consumers are still ignorant about its value as compared with the value of conventional alternatives. . . . At least in the early stages, the product has so few close rivals that cross-elasticity of demand is low.

2. [An initial] high price is an efficient device for breaking the market up into segments that differ in price elasticity of demand. The initial high price serves to skim the cream of the market that is relatively insensitive to price. Subsequent price reductions tap successively more elastic sectors of the market. . . .

3. . . . facing an unknown elasticity of demand, a high initial price serves as a "refusal" price during the stage of exploration. How much costs can be reduced as the market expands and as design of the product is improved by increasing production efficiency with new techniques is difficult to predict.

4. Many companies are not in a position to finance the product flotation out of distant future revenues. High cash outlays in the early stages result from heavy costs of production and distributor organizing. . . . High prices are a reasonable financing technique for shouldering these burdens in the light of the many uncertainties about the future. (Dean, 1950.)

You can undoubtedly think of instances where the foregoing approach has been useful to specific firms or for specified goods. Firms find a high initial price, with subsequent price reductions, much easier to live with because it is obviously easier to justify lowering price than raising it.

A penetration price, in contrast, is a low price designed to capture mass markets early in the new-product stages. This policy has the advantage of encouraging sales to a wider segment of the market. Whereas a skimming policy may preclude the purchase by those with low incomes, the penetration policy has broad appeal to the lower-income groups. Dean believes that a penetration-price policy is worthy of consideration at various stages in a product's life cycle because new markets may be developed by examining price from product inception to its maturity. An often-cited example is the pricing policies of airlines, which have reduced fares to special groups on their charter flights, the 12-21 half-fares, adult standby fares, and the like. Each policy sharply appealed to new market segments. Dean cites the following conditions which are compatible with a penetration price:

1. . . . a high-price elasticity of demand in the short run, i.e., a high degree of responsiveness of sales to reductions in price. . . .
2. A substantial savings in production costs as the result of greater volume. . . .
3. . . . product characteristics such that it will not seem bizarre when it is first fitted into the consumers' expenditure pattern. . . .
4. . . . a strong threat of potential competition. (Dean, 1950.)

A "mature product" has different market and competitive conditions. Price practices at this stage too are vastly different. The symptoms of maturity are:

1. A deterioration of brand preferences caused by the close similarity of substitutes. Premium prices which once could be commanded are now not possible without losing market position.
2. The physical differences among competing products disappear and the better designs become standardized.
3. Private-label competition emerges.
4. The market is saturated and replacement sales represent a major proportion of all sales.
5. Production methods are stabilized; that is, technological innovation which may reduce costs may upset the stability enjoyed by an oligopolistic market condition. (Dean, 1950.)

Although it is difficult to state categorically the price action to be taken when the preceding conditions are observable, some generalized remarks can be ventured. Most firms facing product maturity can exercise little discretion in their pricing because only minor product differentiation exists. If price is higher than comparable substitutes, market position is jeopardized. Price reductions can be easily met by competition, but this action may also precipitate a lower level of prices for the industry with nothing but a reduced total revenue for the firm (unless, of course, market position improves, which is unlikely). Perhaps the best course of action, as suggested by Dean, is to meet the situation by reducing *real* prices. Rather than engage in open price warfare, a manufacturer can strengthen his position by giving more at the same price. Such an approach can mean product improvement, product refinements, better service, and other ways of upgrading the market offering.

## Other Price Considerations

Many firms face numerous other price considerations. The pricing of a product line, for example, raises a number of questions. How should differences in size be priced? What is the industry custom in pricing product lines? In general, a pattern of prices for a line should ease the entry of new additions. From the established pattern variations of product can be fitted into the company's line without serious price disruptions.

The number of buyers may also influence pricing practices and policies. In some instances thousands of buyers are in the market, while in others there may be only a few or even one buyer. In general, where the number of buyers is large, the influence of any one buyer on price is nil or at least small. When the market is populated by only a few, however, they have a greater opportunity to exert influence on the firm's price and price structure.

Finally, whether firms are large or small and sellers are many or few, all are influenced by legal considerations. In particular, the antitrust laws provide the legal environment within which all parties must operate. (Refer to Chapter 7 for a complete discussion of this aspect of pricing.)

## PRICING POLICIES

There is a good deal of confusion between pricing policies and pricing practices. Certain literature on pricing identifies *practices* such as customary prices, odd pricing, psychological pricing, and the like as price policies. Clearly these are price practices adopted more or less by the widespread use and convention of an industry. Price practices of this nature are discussed in the next chapter. In a few instances, some price policies have become so commonly adopted that a well-understood methodology has been adopted by its users. Return on investment pricing, for example, is a price policy, but also it has a clearly stated method so as to accomplish some predetermined rate of return. The methodology is a *practice* of a pricing policy, and this aspect of the policy also is discussed in the next chapter. Even though there is some confusion between the terms "policy" and "practice," it is well to explain *how* a particular pricing policy, or goal, is met.

One of the few well-known and highly authentic statements of actual company price policies resulted from a research study that was conducted some years ago. One result of this study is the table in 20-4; much of the interview material may be found in *Pricing in Big Business*, by A. D. H. Kaplan, Joel B. Dirlam, and Robert F. Lanzillotti. In this volume the authors isolate and identify the five most frequently encountered pricing policies as follows:

1. Pricing to achieve target return on investment.
2. Stabilization of price and margin.
3. Pricing to maintain or improve market position.
4. Pricing to meet or follow competition.
5. Pricing subordinated to product differentiation. (Kaplan, Dirlam, and Lanzillotti, 1958.)

**20-4** Pricing Goals of Twenty Large Industrial Corporations

| Company | Principal pricing goal | Collateral pricing goals | Company | Principal Pricing Goal | Collateral Pricing Goals |
|---|---|---|---|---|---|
| Alcoa | 20% on investment (before taxes); higher on new products [about 10% effective rate after taxes] | (a) "Promotive" policy on new products (b) Price stabilization | International Harvester | 10% on investment (after taxes) | Market share: ceiling of "less than a dominant share of any market" |
| American Can | Maintenance of market share | (a) "Meeting" competition (using cost of substitute product to determine price) (b) Price stabilization | Johns-Manville | Return on investment greater than last 15-year average (about 15% after taxes); higher target for new products | (a) Market share not greater than 20% (b) Stabilization of prices |
| A & P | Increasing market share | "General promotive" (low-margin policy) | Kennecott | Stabilization of prices | |
| du Pont | Target return on investment—no specific figure given | (a) Charging what traffic will bear over long run (b) Maximum return for new products—"life cycle" pricing | Kroger | Maintaining market share | Target return of 20% on investment before taxes |
| Esso (Standard Oil of N.J.) | "Fair-return" target—no specific figure given | (a) Maintaining market (b) Price stabilization | National Steel | Matching the market—price follower | Increase market share |
| General Electric | 20% on investment (after taxes); 7% on sales (after taxes) | (a) Promotive policy on new products (b) Price stabilization on nationally advertised products | Sears Roebuck | Increasing market share (8-10% regarded as satisfactory share) | (a) Realization of traditional return on investment of 10-15% (after taxes) (b) General promotive (low margin) policy |
| General Foods | 33⅓% gross margin: ("⅓ to make, ⅓ to sell, and ⅓ for profit"); expectation of realizing target only on new products | (a) Full line of food products and novelties (b) Maintaining market | Standard Oil (Indiana) | Maintain market share | (a) Stabilize prices (b) Target-return on investment (none specified) |
| General Motors | 20% on investment (after taxes) | Maintaining market share | Swift | Maintenance of market share in livestock buying and meat packing | |
| Goodyear | "Meeting competitors" | (a) Maintain "position" (b) Price stabilization | Union Carbide | Target return on investment | Promotive policy on new products: "life cycle" pricing on chemicals generally |
| Gulf | Follow price of most important marketer in each area | (a) Maintain market share (b) Price stabilization | U.S. Steel | 8% on investment (after taxes) | (a) Target market share of 30% (b) Stable price (c) Stable margin |

*SOURCE:* Adapted from Robert F. Lanzillotti, "Pricing Objectives in Large Corporations," *American Economic Review,* Vol. 48, No. 5 (December 1958), pp. 921-940.

Among these policies, target return on investment, the most commonly cited, refers to a percentage return on the investment required for the product or product line. The policy is sometimes modified to establish a target return on sales. The du Pont company, which cites target return on investment as its policy (see 20-4), states:

Our price is based upon the obvious elements of conducting business. The probable factory cost of manufacture is calculated. Expected sales and distribution charges are added. We then consider what return on investment is desirable, appropriate and consistent with our own long-term risk and tax exposure, and finally, we make an appraisal of the use value of the product to the consumer, as well as of its worth in relation to competitive counterpart or alternate materials. The end result is usually a compromise of these various factors. On occasion, I have even relied upon my . . . intuition to establish a price for a new article. (Kaplan, Dirlam, and Lanzillotti, 1958.)

Stabilization of price and margin is a policy sometimes practiced by firms faced by wide fluctuations in demand. Instability of prices can, of course, seriously upset production, marketing, and financial planning, and if a firm is successful in implementing this policy it reduces the risk of disturbances in established goals. Frequently the attempts to level out the peaks and valleys of prices are a counterpart to other policies, such as target return.

In those industries faced with aggressive competition the likely policy revolves around attempts to maintain or improve market position—20-4 cites A & P, Sears Roebuck, Standard Oil (Indiana), and Swift as adherents to this policy. Note that the industries within which these companies operate are all keenly competitive. The retail institutions (A & P and Sears) adopted a low-price policy in conjunction with their merchandising policies and, of course, have been successful in building their market shares profitably.

Pricing to meet or follow competition is a well-known and widely practiced policy. The firm that adopts this policy believes that a price above competition would only curtail sales, that an industry's prices are determined by the market, and that little control over price can be exercised by the firm. Lower prices than competition would only serve to reduce total revenue and not increase sales significantly. In other words, meeting or following competition corresponds with the concepts of oligopolistic pricing.

In earlier sections and also in Chapter 6 much has been said about pricing and product differentiation. A price policy related to product differentiation is seldom practiced without its being contributory to other price policies. The firm that has such a policy as an important factor in its pricing places much emphasis on its position in the industry and on the value of its brand name and other merchandising features.

Product differentiation is a significant aspect of price policy when a company features products that can offer the purchaser special satisfactions for which he will pay a price that yields a better than average return on the capital invested. To exploit this policy successfully, a company must have a product line that lends itself to innovations with marketable advantages over comparable standard products. Beyond that, the emphasis on making a product "different" in the consumer's estimate may be an indication of the research-mindedness of the company's management or its strong inclination to develop opportunities for upgrading product rather than cutting price. (Kaplan, Dirlam, and Lanzillotti, 1958.)

Note that the principal policies or goals of the firms listed in 20-4 have collateral pricing goals as well. The available empirical evidence on pricing policies supports the view that many companies have difficulty in isolating a single policy as being more important than another. Observation by the authors of this text strengthens the position that most price policies are multipurpose and that a combination of the major policies cited is more typical in real price situations.

## CONCLUDING COMMENTS

The problem facing marketing management in pricing is complex and has many facets. The discussion thus far has emphasized some of the difficulties encountered in understanding price and its implications, the interrelationship that prevails among prices of goods and services, the major influences on price policies, and the more commonly used price policies. These facets of pricing are more or less universal influences that affect the marketing manager in dealing with the price variable. Under many circumstances they may provide the basis for guidance in determining price policies and in actually setting prices. Clearly, as we have seen in this chapter, pricing is an administrative function; but it is one that is influenced by uncontrollable forces.

In the next chapter we offer additional guidance in dealing with the pricing process. Our attention now turns from the generalized influences affecting price to the more specific problem of setting actual prices, the use of pricing to accomplish market objectives, and some of the more common pricing practices.

## STATEMENTS TO CONSIDER

The discrepancy between economic theory and actual pricing policies, as observed by marketing specialists, is more apparent than real. (Hawkins)

Prices are still set by rules of thumb rather than systematic study.

The market system provides information about demand and prices that is lacking in controlled societies.

The negotiated price is the prototype of all price. (Alderson)

Prices are generally beyond the control of individuals.

The price leader is usually the largest firm in the industry; if there are two or more dominant concerns, one may serve as leader as a matter of custom, or more than one may lead in separate territories, or in turn.

Different price levels prevail because the commodities are in different places, rather than because a period of time has elapsed during which prices for the commodity have changed in all markets.

The price structures of individual retail firms selling to consumers are usually much simpler than those at the manufacturing or wholesale levels for the same goods.

Inelasticity of demand, or even the belief that demand is inelastic, acts as a strong deterrent to price flexibility.

All aspects of pricing by dealers are related to the buying habits and attitudes of buyers.

# QUESTIONS FOR REVIEW

**1.** How would you proceed to price a new industrial product?

**2.** Develop a pricing structure for an agricultural product as it proceeds from the farmer through wholesale markets through processors through wholesalers through retailers to consumers.

**3.** To what extent do we in the United States have price competition?

**4.** Price competition is really cost competition. Explain. Are loss leaders a form of price competition?

**5.** Evaluate each of the pricing policies listed on page 439.

**6.** Do you expect greater or less price competition as you proceed forward in the channels of distribution from raw-material producer to retailer?

**7.** Consider the price equation, X *Money* = Y *Goods*. List a number of ways you can change price by modifying the right side of the equation.

**8.** Does the lack of price competition in controlled economies cause any difficulties for the planners?

**9.** What industry would you say shows the greatest amount of price competition? What is your evidence? Is this also the most competitive industry overall?

**10.** In which area has legislation been more effective—price or non-price competition?

## Further Readings

Jules Backman, *Price Practices and Price Policies* (New York: Ronald Press, 1953).

Joel Dean, "Pricing a New Product," *The Controller,* Vol. 23, No. 4 (April 1955), pp. 163–165.

Clare E. Griffin, "When Is Price Reduction Profitable?" *Harvard Business Review,* Vol. 38, No. 5 (September–October 1960), pp. 125–132.

Donald V. Harper, *Price Policy and Procedure* (New York; Harcourt Brace Jovanovich, 1966).

Alfred R. Oxenfeldt, *Pricing for Marketing Executives* (Belmont, Cal.: Wadsworth, 1961).

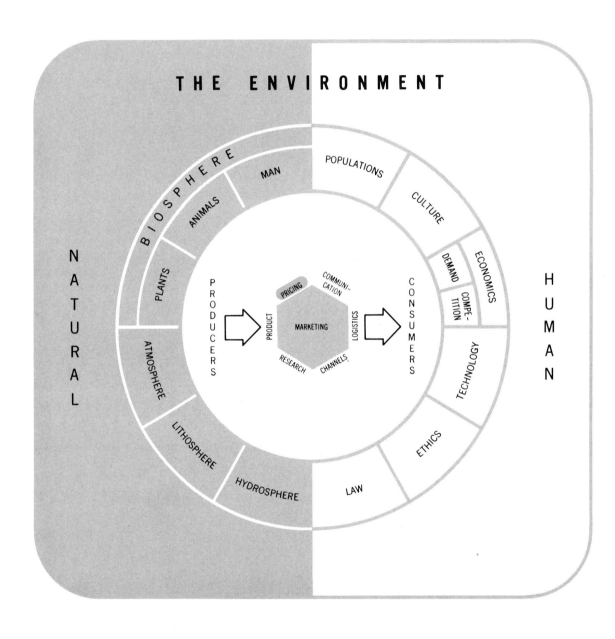

# CHAPTER 21
# PRICING PRACTICES AND PROCEDURES

*Pricing practices and procedures finally result in the setting of actual prices that all buyers pay for their goods and services. The price-maker tries to accomplish a predetermined goal for his firm, but prices are subject to customary differentials and some traditional practices. In setting an actual price the marketer needs to consider these common influences.*

Pricing policies, as we saw in Chapter 20, serve as overall guides of a firm in making pricing decisions. On the basis of these policies the firm gets into the mechanics of setting specific prices for goods or services through "pricing procedures and practices." Once the top management of a firm has established its basic pricing policies the mechanics can be delegated to lower managerial echelons.

## INFLUENCES ON PRICING PRACTICES

The price of a particular product or service is, of course, only one ingredient in the marketing mix and is naturally affected by the others. It is also affected by most of the environmental factors discussed in Part II of this book, including competition, technology, the influences of buyer behavior, and the economics of demand. The natural environment also plays an important role in pricing, for example, in the pricing of raw materials. Other influences and relationships were emphasized in Chapter 20.

In dealing with all these influences there are certain useful questions for pricing strategists to consider. For instance, how will price relate to members of the channel of distribution? Is a price high enough to permit distributors to earn their margins? Will there be geographic price differentials? What industry discount practices prevail? And, of course, marketing management must also pay heed to legal issues covered in Chapter 7—prohibitions against explicit agreements among sellers, discriminatory prices, and laws that foster and have as their intent the equality of buying advantage among competitors.

A general overview of some pricing relationships in consumer goods is shown in 21-1. This diagram makes clear the pervasiveness of government (the legal environment) in regulating pricing behavior and some of the principal influences affecting the price of a good or service as it moves through the channel of distribution. This schematic drawing also gives perspective to the effects of the marketing mix and competition. Note that manufacturers, wholesalers, and retailers face competition not only with firms like themselves but also with firms in other categories. (In 21-1 the two classes of competition are identified as "same category" and "different category.") For instance, food supermarkets compete with other food supermarkets and with discount stores that have a food department. Steel producers compete with other

**21-1** Pricing Relationships of Consumer Goods

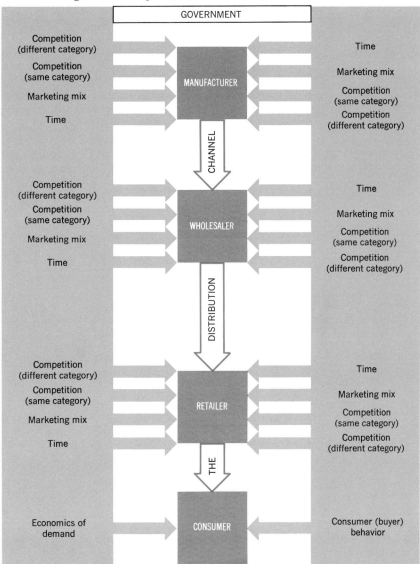

GOVERNMENT

MANUFACTURER
- Competition (different category)
- Competition (same category)
- Marketing mix
- Time
- Time
- Marketing mix
- Competition (same category)
- Competition (different category)

CHANNEL

WHOLESALER
- Competition (different category)
- Competition (same category)
- Marketing mix
- Time
- Time
- Marketing mix
- Competition (same category)
- Competition (different category)

DISTRIBUTION

RETAILER
- Competition (different category)
- Competition (same category)
- Marketing mix
- Time
- Time
- Marketing mix
- Competition (same category)
- Competition (different category)

THE

CONSUMER
- Economics of demand
- Consumer (buyer) behavior

SOURCE: Adapted from Benson P. Shapiro, *The Pricing of Consumer Goods: Theory and Practice* (Cambridge, Mass.: Marketing Science Institute, 1972), pp. 3–5.

steel producers and with manufacturers of aluminum, plastics, and other steel substitutes (Shapiro, 1972).

The question of whether to set a high or a low price provides a vivid example of the influences that affect pricing decisions. The criteria listed in 21-2, which relate to both products and marketing goals, indicate the array of factors to consider. For example, 21-2 shows a variety of conditions for a high-price strategy—if a product needs a great deal of promotion (advertising, merchandising, and personal selling), if it has a short life, if it has a slow inventory turnover, or if it is subject to rapid technological change. Conversely, price may be set low if market coverage is intensive (as with bread, cigarettes, and gasoline), if the stage of market development for the product is mature, if the channel of distribution is short, and if a product can be mass produced (Crissy and Boewadt, 1971). In general the criteria in 21-2 should be used with discretion. Not all factors have the same measure of influence on setting price and there are instances where price does not relate to these criteria because of offsetting influences, such as tradition, product line, and the impact of market behavior. This chart is, however, a useful device in explaining most of the elements affecting a firm's ability to command a high or a low price.

Let us now examine the methods and practices used in setting specific prices: we will discuss costs, discounts, geographical price differentials, price lining, odd-even pricing, psychological pricing, and prestige pricing. Some of these methods have a long tradition of use and others prevail because they ease problems in the channel of distribution or at point of sale.

**21-2** Should Price Be Set High or Low?

| Low price | Pricing Criteria | High price |
|-----------|------------------|------------|
| Little | Promotion | Much |
| Commodity | Product type | Proprietary |
| Mass-produced | Manufacture | Custom-made |
| Intensive | Market coverage | Selective |
| Long-lived | Product obsolescence | Short-lived |
| Slow | Technological changes | Rapid |
| Capital-intensive | Production | Labor-intensive |
| Large | Market share | Small |
| Short | Channels of distribution | Long |
| Mature | Stage of market | New or declining |
| Long-term | Profit perspective | Short-term |
| Single-use | Product versatility | Multiple-use |
| Much | Promotional contribution to line | Little |
| Few or none | Ancillary services | Many |
| Short | Product life in use | Long |
| Fast | Turn-over | Slow |

SOURCE: Adapted from William Crissy and Robert Boewadt, "Pricing in Perspective," *Sales Management*, June 15, 1971, p. 44.

## COST APPLICATIONS TO PRICING

In Chapter 20 we dealt with the common tendency to overemphasize the role of costs in determining price. But they cannot be ignored. Costs certainly do set the lower limits of price and all costs must be recovered in the long run. Pricing strategists have available to them several methods based on costs. Three rather well-known methods are: (1) full-cost pricing, (2) incremental-cost pricing, and (3) return-on-investment pricing.

## Full-Cost Pricing

Under the full-cost method selling prices cover all allocated costs plus a fixed or variable profit margin. Under this method a selling price is determined by adding total factory cost to an allowance for selling and administrative expenses and profit. On the surface this method appears logical enough. What is wrong with recovering total cost plus, say, a 7 percent profit? Full-cost recovery plus a desired profit margin is an obvious advantage, but it has three drawbacks.

First, full-cost pricing ignores the costs and market practices of competitors. If a competitor's costs are lower and he uses the same method for determining price, then his price would be lower. Unless the user of full-cost pricing has a distinct advantage such as strong product differentiation, a better sales force, better credit terms, or a more desirable location, it is doubtful that this method would be advisable.

Second, this method, being based on a stable price, ignores the dynamic character of market demand. Yet most prices are subject to demand elasticity and may rise or fall. Because the full-cost method does not divide fixed and variable costs, it is not possible to calculate the effect of a price change on profits.

Third, most firms have opportunities to accept additional business, and if full-cost pricing is used a company would be inclined to reject new business that does not cover total costs. The only flexibility available to the firm is to have a variable markup instead of a fixed percentage margin. A variable markup takes changing economic conditions into account. In periods of prosperity, sellers can adjust their margins upward and conversely adjust them downward during economic decline. If a seller must meet competitive price differences, a smaller margin can be added to the base cost to produce a lower price. This is not a common practice because it has a number of awkward aspects, notably the need for frequent estimates of demand, which involve much time and effort that many businesses are not equipped to invest.

## Incremental-Cost Pricing

The incremental-cost method has several advantages over full-cost pricing. Incremental cost is the increase in total costs resulting from an increase in a firm's volume of business, that is, "the costs that are of crucial importance in a pricing decision are the variable costs associated with producing or distributing additional amounts of a product or service or adding a new product or service" (Harper, 1966). Thus, whether an activity or new business should be undertaken is best determined by considering the incremental costs. For many price decisions, then, the incremental costs are the relevant costs. If, for example, a firm has unused capacity (and most firms do), it can accept new business or add new products so long as incremental revenue exceeds the incremental costs. Profits will expand as long as this condition prevails.

The airline industry has long recognized the advantage of incremental revenue. This industry has high fixed costs and often has unused capacity on its scheduled flights. Airline companies can and do improve their revenue position by retaining flight schedules that do little more than cover the incremental costs (variable costs) and some measure of profit. Additional business such as charter flights, extra flights abroad, and special travel plans for certain classes of customers can be attractively priced because incremental costs can easily be recovered along with a profit.

In most instances the incremental-cost user has the advantage over the full-cost user in attracting additional business, particularly when a firm has the opportunity to bid on business that would absorb unfilled capacity. The user of the full-cost method would usually be underbid, unless of course his full costs were lower than the variable costs of his competitor.

It is clearly desirable to employ incremental-cost pricing when unused capacity can be absorbed by additional business. In practice, however, it is advisable to have separate markets to which the additional products are sold.

> . . . variable-cost pricing for some portion of the total firm output and full-cost pricing for others can be employed only when markets can be separated from one another, that is, when demand prices for different products or services produced, for different outputs of the same product or service, or for the same product or service in different geographic markets are separate from one another. Businessmen often feel that variable-cost pricing is not a sound approach to pricing because they are afraid a low-variable-cost price for one segment of the firm's output will force them to lower prices on the rest of the firm's output as well, with the result that there is little or no contribution toward fixed expenses. However, as we have seen, this will not happen if markets are separated from one another. (Harper, 1966.)

### Return-on-Investment Pricing

In Chapter 20 we noted that return on investment was a pricing goal. Large corporations such as du Pont, General Motors, General Electric, Johns-Mansville cited this as their principal pricing goal (see 20-4). When a firm uses return-on-investment pricing, price will yield a predetermined average rate of return on the capital employed to produce and market its products. The concept is applied to product groups or lines and to new products and divisions. Return-on-investment pricing, if developed with flexibility, allows for cost considerations, demand fluctuations, and general market conditions.

The essential features of this pricing method are as follows:

1. Estimation of standard costs are based on standard volume. Margins are added to standard costs so as to yield a planned rate of return on investment over a long-run period. Margins are based on changing demand and market conditions and changes in volume.

2. It is assumed that the standard volume will be exceeded in some years, but not met in other years. The average rate of return on investment will fluctuate depending on the degree of variance from the "normal" volume. Over the long run, sales will average out to the standard volume.

3. Price flexibility can be practiced, particularly by applying this method to new products. A relatively high price, or a "skimming" price, may be used and markets "explored" before a lower price is adopted. A "penetration" price may be used to rapidly develop mass markets.

In the *long run* the planned rate of return will materialize if the anticipated market volume is realized and if the planned margins are sufficiently stable.

This method of pricing has been adopted by more and more companies because of the high success experienced by those major corporations who originally initiated this practice. It also has been successful in returning a "fair" or "reasonable" return as anticipated by managements (Spencer, 1968).

Break-even analysis and contribution analysis are other well-known approaches to pricing. Break-even analysis relates total costs to total revenue whereas contribution analysis establishes the difference between total revenue and variable costs at different levels of output so as to show the contribution of revenue to fixed costs and profits. Costs, as noted earlier, are just one of the many factors influencing price. They are best regarded as a guide to management in establishing minimum price. Full costs do not necessarily have to be recouped on all items and in all pricing situations, but in the long run and from the firm's overall pricing practices all costs must be recouped by prices.

# PRICE DIFFERENTIALS

Once a price for a product has been set, the market supplier is subject to price differentials. Although price differentials take on many forms the most common relate to geography, quantity, trade, and time. Each of the differentials is important to industrial, institutional, and governmental buyers. Geographical pricing practices oftentimes increase the delivered price to the buyer, whereas quantity, trade, and time differentials, or discounts, lower the price to the buyer.

## Geographical Pricing Practices

Every manufacturing and distributing institution is aware of the importance of transportation costs. Expenditures can run into many millions of dollars. In the United States, where the distances are great, the markets dispersed, and the transportation systems elaborate, the costs incidental thereto become significant. Consumers seldom come into direct contact with this aspect of pricing except when purchasing an automobile. Automobile prices are quoted f.o.b. (free on board) Detroit, some other assembly point, or port of entry. At purchase time the consumer learns that the delivered price is somewhat higher because of transportation charges.

In general, geographic pricing practices can be divided into two categories: f.o.b. pricing and delivered pricing. Under the former the seller quotes the same uniform price to all customers. The f.o.b. price includes the cost of preparing the goods for shipment and placing them on board the mode of transportation selected by the buyer. The buyer takes delivery and pays the transportation. The net return to the seller is the same regardless of the location of the buyer, but the cost to the buyer varies according to transportation cost.

A delivered-pricing system includes both the price of the goods and the transportation costs of getting the goods to the customer. Under this method the seller often receives varying net prices because transportation costs vary with distances. Delivered-pricing systems include zone prices, postage-stamp pricing, basing-point pricing, and freight equalization. These and other common terms used in delivered pricing are identified in 21-3. The particular method used is an important decision, since it may affect a firm's competitive position, the location of plant and suppliers, and the profitability of sales (Backman, 1953).

## Discounts

Discounts are a pervasive feature of pricing, used to accomplish various objectives. *Quantity discounts* are granted in recognition of the scale economies related to a large order or package size for a single order involving delivery to one location. Large orders can be processed by the seller at essentially the same cost as small orders, and thus reduce cost of selling, accounting, packing, delivery, and credit arrangements.

*Trade, or functional, discounts* are based on the trade classification of the buyer. For example, wholesalers, jobbers, and retailers occupy different trade positions in the channel of distribution. Furthermore they perform different marketing functions. Trade discounts are given in recognition of these differences and to encourage the performance of vital wholesaler or retailer services. Trade discounts must be sufficient to cover operating costs and profits for the market intermediaries. For example, a retailer might be quoted a 35 percent trade discount from the suggested retail price. Or if a product goes through both a wholesaler and retailer, the manufacturer might quote a chain discount to the wholesaler of 35 percent and 10 percent off the retail price. The wholesaler would get the 10 percent discount and the retailer 35 percent. Trade discounts vary from industry to industry, but they become so well known in most trades that they are recognized as customary practices. Because most trade discounts are well established the dis-

## 21-3

**Terms Frequently Used in Delivered Pricing Systems**

Basing-point mill: Any mill which quotes a "base price" from which a "delivered price" is arrived at by adding the actual freight to the customer's location.

Base price: What a basing-point mill combines with actual freight cost to determine what delivered price to quote provided its combination of base price and actual freight cost is lower than that of any other basing-point mill.

Freight equalization: The practice of charging a customer, not the seller's actual transportation costs, but the lower transportation cost at which the customer could get delivery from a competing seller.

Market interpenetration: The extension of seller's operations beyond the range of their respective transportation-cost advantages.

Mill net return: The difference between a producer's delivered price and his actual cost of making delivery.

Nonbasing-point mills: Producers who do not quote "base prices" and are left out of account in determining *the* basing-point mill and *the* delivered price to be quoted on any given piece of business.

Nonlocal seller: One who is making the sale in a territory in which his transporation costs impose a competitive disadvantage.

Phantom freight: The amount by which a nonbasing-point "mill net return" exceeds the base price of *the* basing-point mill for a given delivered-price quotation. (The same as the difference between its actual freight cost and that of *the* basing-point mill.)

Postage-stamp pricing: Quoting the same delivered price to all customers (usually to all customers in the United States), regardless of location.

Variable f.o.b. pricing: Quoting an f.o.b. price but not necessarily the same one to every customer. The "variable" means customer-to-customer differences, not time-to-time changes.

Zone pricing: Dividing the market into zones and quoting a single delivered price for each zone.

SOURCE: "Delivered Pricing and the Law" (Washington, D.C.: Chamber of Commerce of the United States, 1948), p. 9.

cretion of a manufacturer is limited. In setting his own prices a marketing manager must consider the discount structure of the trade. The alternative would be to market goods through other channels of distribution, but unless the market can be successfully developed by alternative means the *custom* of the trade will govern.

*Cash and seasonal discounts* relate to time. A cash discount encourages a buyer to pay his accounts receivable within a reasonable period of time. For example, a $1500 order might be invoiced 2/10, net 30, meaning that the buyer can take a 2 percent discount by paying the invoice within 10 days.

Seasonal discounts are typical in industries that are affected by seasonal demand variations that cause peaks and valleys in the production process. Wholesalers and retailers are offered seasonal discounts for taking preseason delivery on goods or for placing orders well in advance of peak season production. This practice results in better production scheduling for the manufacturer and may even shift the storage burden from him. For the wholesaler or retailer an attractive off-season price (seasonal discount) is the reward.

A price-maker must take into consideration the various discount practices that prevail in his trade. Discounts have been developed in most trades involving the production and sale of tangible goods. From time to time the legality of discounts has been questioned, as we discussed in Chapter 7, but they have a long and persistent history.

## PRICING BY WHOLESALERS AND RETAILERS

Wholesale and retail prices follow from the price-setting of the manufacturer or other market supplier. A manufacturer often may suggest wholesale or retail prices by establishing a trade discount structure. But in other instances the market intermediaries fix their prices by adding a margin to the cost of the item or product line purchased. In other words, both wholesalers and retailers might add a predetermined margin to their cost to cover their expenses and profits. A typical example of adding a wholesaler margin and a retail margin is shown in 21-4. In this case the imported Scotch whiskey incurs costs before it is taken into the wholesale distributor's inventory. The distributor's margin of $13.00 is added per case. The retailer adds his margin of $29.42, or 25.5 percent. The retailer in turn sells the product to a retail customer for $9.60 per quart. Many retail prices are determined in this way, though the margin varies from one line of merchandise to another.

## SUPPLEMENTARY PRICING PRACTICES

Over the years a number of supplementary pricing practices have evolved on the American business scene. These practices have little to do with actual price setting; rather they represent past pricing innovations that have achieved widespread acceptance. Their origin is not always discernible; some grew out of industry customs, some developed because of assumed shapes of demand curves, and others were formulated to develop customer goodwill, consistency of business dealings, and more simplified operational procedures. Whatever their origin, a price maker can do little about them because of their widespread use.

**21-4** Costs and Margins for Imported Scotch Whiskey, 1972
(One Case = 12 Quarts)

| Item | | Cost |
|---|---|---|
| F. O. B. Scotland (per case) | | $ 29.65 |
|     Import Tax & Duty | $33.33 | |
|     Ocean Freight to Los Angeles | 2.44 | |
|     Miscellaneous Costs—Shipping Broker/Insurance | .58 | 36.35 |
| F. O. B. Los Angeles | | 66.00 |
|     Freight from Los Angeles to Phoenix | .78 | |
|     State Tax | 6.00 | 6.78 |
| Cost to Wholesale Distributor, Phoenix | | 72.78 |
| Wholesale Distributor's Gross Margin—15.2%* | | 13.00 |
| Cost to Retailer | | 85.78 |
| Retail Dealer's Gross Margin—25.5%* <br> (i.e., package liquor store) | | 29.42 |
|     Total Costs & Margins | | $115.20 |

Note: Price to the retail customer is simply determined by dividing the per case cost by the number of items, i.e., $115.20 ÷ 12 = $9.60 per quart. The above price is in a resale price maintenance state.

* As a percentage of selling price.

## One Price to All Buyers

Retailers and industrial firms commonly offer the same price to all buyers for a purchase made under the same conditions. Indeed, for consumers this practice prevails for most goods (consider, in contrast, the bargaining carried on in the market of many foreign countries). Industrial firms use one price, which is often adjusted because of the quantities purchased, services performed by the buyer, or other cost-saving factors. The practice is attractive because it is easy to administer, simplifies the selling process, divorces price-making from sales-making, and nullifies the need for bargaining, which, of course, not all buyers can accomplish equally.

## Price Lining

When price lining is adopted, prices are set at specified levels for given classes or lines of merchandise. A retailer of men's suits, for example, may establish price lines of $89.00, $120,00, and $160.00. This procedure is duplicated in many retail firms and for much of their merchandise. Usually for a given kind of merchandise there are few price lines to avoid confusion. This practice not only facilitates the selling process but also simplifies the planning, accounting, and buying for the retail firm.

## Odd-Even Pricing

Many businessmen apparently believe that consumers react more favorably when prices end in certain odd numbers, as 59¢, 89¢, $1.09, rather than the next higher or lower even amount. The belief presupposes a demand curve like that in 21-5. This demand curve was originally developed by Edward R. Hawkins, who made one of the few attempts to integrate price theory with price practices. The odd-even demand curve tells us that each price ending in an odd figure will produce more sales volume than the next lower (and next higher) even price. Thus in 21-5 the $1.99 price commands more sales than $2.00, and $.99 more than $1.00. Is there any evidence to support the belief that odd prices generate more sales volume than even prices? No, there is not, but despite the lack of empirical evidence this practice is widely held to be effective. Historically, odd pricing came into popularity not as a result of demand analysis but as an administrative device: retailers believed that a sales clerk could easily pocket the proceeds of an even-price sale, whereas an odd price forced the clerk to ring up the sale and give change. Until solid evidence is produced to support the demand curve associated with odd-even prices, the validity and effectiveness of odd prices will remain unclear.

## Psychological Pricing

Similar to the matter of odd-even prices, but more provable, is psychological pricing, the demand curve for which is shown in 21-6. This curve is based on pricing experiments which have shown that

**21-5** Odd-Even Pricing

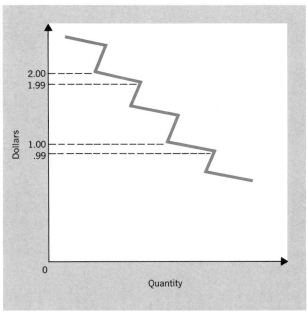

SOURCE: Adapted from Edward R. Hawkins, "Price Policies and Theory," *Journal of Marketing*, Vol. 18, No. 3 (January 1954), pp. 233–240.

## 21-6 Psychological Pricing

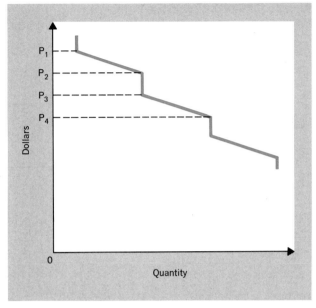

SOURCE: Adapted from Edward R. Hawkins, "Price Policies and Theory," *Journal of Marketing,* Vol. 18, No. 3 (January 1954), pp. 233–240.

certain price ranges have little effect on sales volume until some critical point is reached. Thus the price range from $P_2$ to $P_3$ is not as effective as the range from $P_3$ to $P_4$. The concept of psychological pricing does not rest (as is often assumed) on odd and even price points, but on those prices that are psychologically more attractive to consumers. The critical points are reached as price moves downward from $P_1$ to $P_2$, and from $P_3$ to $P_4$, and so on.

### Prestige Pricing

Because many consumers judge quality largely by price, some products carry prestige prices. The demand curve for this phenomenon is shown in 21-7, which indicates that price $P_1$ will generate more volume than the higher price $P_2$ and the lower price $P_3$. At point $P_2$ some buyers would be forced out of the market, but at point $P_3$ the quality-price relationship is not prestigious enough to attract the greater volume gained by pricing at $P_1$. This curve is appropriate to furs, high-priced autos, rare jewelry, and other luxury items. However, some potentially low-priced items such as health and beauty aids, though not prestigious, are more successful at a medium price; a lower price would only lead to suspicions of poor quality. In jewelry, for example, a $160 watch may tell no better time than a $12.95 utilitarian model, but most consumers would judge the timekeeping quality of the higher-priced watch to be superior.

**21-7** Prestige Pricing

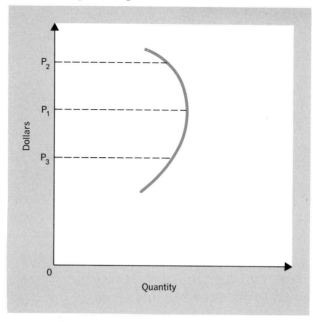

SOURCE: Adapted from Edward R. Hawkins, "Price Policies and Theory," *Journal of Marketing*, Vol. 18, No. 3 (January 1954), pp. 233–240.

## CONCLUDING COMMENTS

The pricing problem faced by marketing management is indeed complex. Many factors influence price-setting and management must evaluate them all and keep them in proper perspective. In pricing a product a manufacturer has several methods available to him. The most relevant costs to be considered are the incremental, or variable, costs. In the long run, however, *all* costs must be met by means of price. The members of the channel of distribution must also be considered, and sufficient margins for wholesalers and retailers must be provided for. Some pricing practices are of such a nature that the price-maker has little discretion but to accept the customary practices of the trade. Finally, buyers of all types respond to prices and their response is critical to the firm's marketing success.

## STATEMENTS TO CONSIDER

Price skimming is a safe method of pricing where product acceptability is uncertain and cost reductions difficult to predict.

A high price is indicative that demand is elastic.

A low price designed to achieve a large sales volume must be accompanied by low unit costs of production.

When a completely new product is introduced the company has no guides as to what price should be.

Costs play a minor role in marketing new products as contrasted with mature products.

Competition is a particularly powerful force in the pricing of gasoline and other petroleum products. The products of different companies are completely substitutable, and the motorist in the normal course of driving has a wide variety of alternatives in filling his needs for gasoline.

The reaction of the public to a company's pricing practices is of importance to many companies. Certainly, this factor must be considered in many large industries.

Although economists and businessmen emphasize the importance of the law of supply and demand, it is amazing how often public explanations of price change give major emphasis to costs.

Costs are so closely related to volume and to decisions concerning the allocation of research costs and starting-up expenses that almost any cost figure desired can be obtained.

When a product is differentiated markedly from competitive substitutes, a company has more freedom in its pricing than when it handles a standardized product.

(Statements to consider adapted from Jules Backman, *Pricing: Policies and Practices*, National Conference Board, 1961.)

**1.** Explain how price is influenced by: (a) the nature of the product; (b) competition; (c) the kind of promotion; and (d) technology.

**2.** Full-cost pricing is the logical approach to take in pricing a product line. Explain.

**3.** Explain how a reduced airline fare for special classes of customers might produce some profits? Does this help to explain special fares for the 12–21 age group?

**4.** Variable-cost pricing may force a firm to lower prices on its products to all customers. Explain.

**5.** Explain the principal features of return-on-investment pricing.

**6.** Wholesalers and retailers are regarded as having less freedom in setting price than do manufacturers. Is this a valid statement?

**7.** How do price differentials, such as discounts and geographical pricing practices, restrain the pricing latitude of a manufacturer?

**8.** Odd-even pricing is synonymous with psychological pricing. Is this a true or false statement? Explain.

**9.** Explain the nature of the demand curve as conceived by a business-man using odd-even pricing.

**10.** A prestige price can be lowered and more sales volume will result. Explain the validity of this statement.

## Further Readings

Mark I. Alpert, *Pricing Decisions* (Glenview, Ill.: Scott, Foresman, 1971).

Jules Backman, *Pricing: Policies and Practices* (New York: National Industrial Conference Board, Inc., 1961).

Edward R. Hawkins, "Price Policies and Theory," *Journal of Marketing,* Vol. 18, No. 3 (January 1954), pp. 233–240.

A.D.H. Kaplan, Joel B. Dirlam, and Robert F. Lanzillotti, *Pricing in Big Business* (Washington, D.C.: The Brookings Institution, 1958).

Robert A. Lynn, *Price Policies and Marketing Management* (Homewood, Ill.: Richard D. Irwin, 1967).

Elizabeth Marting (ed.), *Creative Pricing* (New York: American Management Association, 1968).

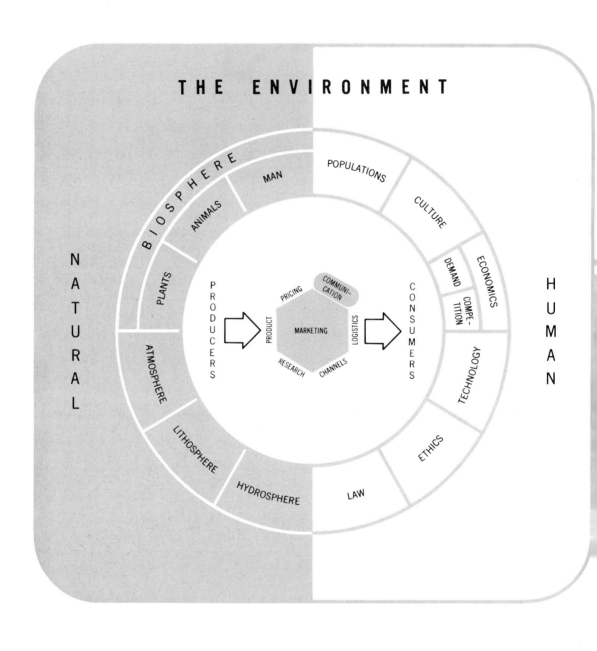

# CHAPTER 22
# MARKETING
# COMMUNICATIONS I

**The Use of Persuasion**

**Persuasion and the Environment**

*Environmental Influences*
*Magnitude of the Job*

**Broad Social Questions**

**Communications**

*Communications in the marketplace take a number of forms: adver-*
*tising, personal selling, and public relations. Marketing communi-*
*cations are geared to the promotion of the company's products and*
*the usual purpose of them is to sell more. The communications mix*
*is a part of the total marketing mix.*

One of the most important, most visible, and most controversial functions of marketing is that of communications—the persuasion elements of the marketing mix that includes advertising, personal selling, displays, publicity, catalogs, and other means of promoting and persuading (see 22-1). We will examine in this chapter the nature of communications and their roles in the marketing process. We will also relate communications to the environment and will delve into social aspects of the communications mix. In the next chapter we will concentrate on the management of the communications mix as we look into each of the ingredients and discuss the development of a communications program.

## THE USE OF PERSUASION

First, let us examine several definitions (AMA, 1960). The first is a general definition for "selling" in the broad sense of the term.

*Selling*—The personal or impersonal process of assisting and/or persuading a prospective customer to buy a commodity or a service or to act favorably upon an idea that has commercial significance to the seller.

We will use the terms "persuasion" and "communications" in lieu of "selling" because the latter term is often confused with the narrower term "personal selling." Personal selling and advertising are the two most important kinds of marketing communications. Their definitions follow:

*Personal Selling*—Oral presentation in a conversation with one or more prospective purchasers for the purpose of making sales.

*Advertising*—Any paid form of nonpersonal presentation and promotion of ideas, goods, or services by an identified sponsor. It involves the use of such media as the following:

| | |
|---|---|
| Magazine and newspaper space | Programs and menus |
| Outdoor (posters, signs, skywriting) | Motion pictures |
| | Novelties |
| Direct mail | Cards (car, bus) |
| Radio and television | Directories and references |
| Catalogs | Circulars |

**22-1** Persuasion Forces Combining To Make a Sale

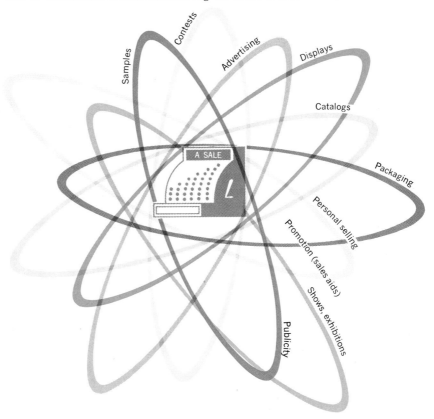

SOURCE: Adapted from Russell H. Colley, "Squeezing the Waste Out of Advertising," *Harvard Business Review*, Vol. 40, No. 5 (September–October 1962), p. 80.

A third kind of marketing communications is that of sales promotion:

*Sales Promotion*—In a specific sense, those marketing activities, other than personal selling, advertising, and publicity, that stimulate consumer purchasing and dealer effectiveness, such as display, shows and exhibitions, demonstrations, and various nonrecurrent selling efforts not in the ordinary routine.

All of us are thoroughly familiar with sellers' attempts to persuade us to buy, although we may not completely appreciate these efforts, even to the point of wishing to eliminate persuasion if we could. Would it not be better to shop without the many persuasive forces pressing against us? And beyond the marketplace would it not be better if we would study without "persuasion," if we would support the United Fund campaign without persuasion, if Congress would enact appropriate legislation without pressure, and if schools would be built without bond drives? In turn, what company would not like the world to beat a path to its door without having to spend large sums of money for persuasion?

Yet persuasion besieges us with thousands of messages each day. Persuasion is used in religious work, welfare programs, planned parenthood, international affairs, and political activities, but of course its greatest use is in business.

As Harry R. Tosdal, a marketing pioneer, has said of persuasion:

> Sometimes it is in bad taste, sometimes misleading, often inept; but it is so familiar that we take it for granted. At times we tolerate it, embrace it, and in particular condemn it; but by and large we are influenced by it to a degree which is little understood. We do not comprehend its social and economic implications. Because we do not understand it, we pass judgment upon the basis of its abuses. We sometimes endorse views which would tend to destroy or eliminate it and eventually wreck our own economy and its ability to maintain and raise standards of living for all the people. (Tosdal, 1957.)

Dexter Masters has a different viewpoint:

> In the jungle of the marketplace, indeed, the intelligent buyer must be alert to every commercial sound, to every snapping twig, to every rustle that may signal the uprising arm holding the knife pointed toward the jugular vein. (Masters, 1965.)

However it is evaluated, there is no question about the role of persuasion in the marketing process. It is used to influence, to convince, to coax, to move people to buy a company's product or service (see 22-2). Advertising and personal selling are twin manifestations of persuasion, and they function as integral parts of our competitive economic system. Would a totalitarian system in which we could abolish personal selling, advertising, and other forms of persuasion be a desirable alternative? Raymond A. Bauer and Mark G. Field have contrasted the Soviet and the United States drug industries—a particularly revealing choice since the industry has been criticized for its lack of social responsibility. In the Soviet Union where there were low promotion costs, no brand names, and no private responsibility, Bauer and Field did not find adequate information, well-informed physicians, adequate quality, sufficiently low prices, or ample supplies of pharmaceuticals. Bauer and Field concluded the United States fared better in these areas and further, that vigorous promotion is not necessarily socially undesirable, that brand naming is also not undesirable, that customer preference serves to stimulate full lines of drugs, and that our system has shorter research-to-market time periods than the Soviet system (Bauer and Field, 1962). Yet even the Soviet Union is beginning to see the value of advertising, as indicated in the following quotation by a manager of a textile store in Novosibirsk:

## 22-2

**"The Son Shows the Way"**

A man lived by the side of the road and sold hot dogs.
He was hard of hearing so he had no radio.
He had trouble with his eyes so he read no newspapers.
But he sold good hot dogs.
He put up a sign on the highway telling how good they were.
He stood by the side of the road and cried: "Buy a hot dog, Mister."
And people bought.
He increased his meat and roll orders.
He bought a bigger stove to take care of his trade.
He got his son home from college to help him.
But then something happened . . .
His son said, "Father, haven't you been listening to the radio?
If money stays 'tight,' we are bound to have bad business.
There may be a big depression coming on.
You had better prepare for poor trade."
Whereupon the father thought, "Well, my son has gone to college.
He reads the papers and he listens to the radio, and he ought to
  know."
So the father cut down on his meat and roll orders.
Took down his advertising signs.
And no longer bothered to stand on the highway to sell hot dogs.
And his hot dog sales fell almost overnight.
"You're right son," the father said to the boy.
"We are certainly headed for a depression."

SOURCE: *Sales Management*, Vol. 86, (March 17, 1961), p. 37.

> We should spare no effort in the organization of good advertising. Neither should we economize on advertising, because expenditures for it are repaid a hundredfold. (M. Argunov, 1966.)

Persuasion is not a twentieth-century anomaly. Neither is it a development of the affluent society, nor is it a monopoly of capitalism. Sellers have always tried to attract buyers. Stanley C. Hollander has described some early commerce-trading companies in Mesopotamia in 2500 B.C., trading codes in the time of the King of Ur Mannu (2100 B.C.), and Phoenician salesmen who sailed the Red Sea and the Persian Gulf in 1200–1500 B.C. (Hollander, 1953). Miriam Beard has written that the businessman was developing his skill at bargaining "enormously long" ago and that the traders were then "wise with the cunning of untold ages" (Beard, 1938). James P. Wood has located evidence of early singing commercials, product sampling, and other sales-promotion techniques that were used hundreds of years ago.

> For eyes that are shining, for cheeks like the dawn,
> For beauty that lasts after girlhood is gone,

For prices in reason, the woman who knows
Will buy her cosmetics of Aesclyptos. (Wood, 1958.)

Persuasion remains an effective way of urging people to buy—that is why it exists today. It is far from perfect, but it remains an integral part of our system, for persuasion facilitates the exchange of goods, aids in the marketing process, and expedites the profitable sales of the product. As one authority has pointed out, it is the "ultimate expression of the competitive effort" (Rathmell, 1964). In recent years persuasion has been used by those outside the business sector as programs of churches, theatres, symphonies, social agencies, the military, and educational institutions have been sold to the public. Though there is not a formal exchange of goods for money in all instances, there obviously is a marketing process at work.

In normal times it is the seller who employs the various forms of persuasion, but during unusual times such as wartime shortages, it is usually the buyer. In the Soviet Union buyer-expediters have been more influential than sales-oriented personnel. But in our society almost every business firm employs some kind of promotional strategy. Some attempt is made to persuade the buyer, to shift the demand curve to the right of where it would otherwise be. Critics call this effort "manipulation of demand," but one need not read anything sinister into it, as the following quotation suggests.

> The usual purposes of advertising, from the advertiser's viewpoint, are to effect sales, to create goodwill, and to improve understanding between a business and its public. The advertisement should, therefore, present a worthy picture of the firm and a true picture of the commodity . . . Advertising belongs to an economic order which has as its chief aim the making and selling of goods at a profit. The producer may be the backbone of the nation, but the country's economic prosperity depends upon its salesmen. They move goods into use by persuading people that they want the goods . . . [Persuasion] invites attention, makes a mental impression, rouses interest, offers benefits, and guides selection. It needs to go further than merely illustrating and describing the articles offered: it must add persuasiveness. (Royal Bank of Canada, 1968.)

## PERSUASION AND THE ENVIRONMENT

### Environmental Influences

Persuasion operates within the framework of the marketing environment. Technology, for example, both aids and limits the persuader. Selling techniques have changed dramatically as faster transportation for salesmen and improved printing processes for advertising have developed. The mail order catalog is now a colorful book of products, attractively presented, in contrast with the early black-and-white flyers of low-quality printing. Persuasion in turn promotes the adoption of new technologies and new products, such as computers, office-copying equipment, and improved dentifrices. Persuasion is essential in the development of markets for new products.

Persuasion takes place according to the legal and ethical rules of society. Because of abuses there has been an increase in the amount of legislation as well as in industry's efforts to improve the process of persuasion. The Truth in Advertising Act of 1971,* introduced by Senators McGovern and Moss, would require advertisers to give consumers the documentation used in support of advertised claims for products and services and also would require the media to inform the public that such documentation is available from advertisers. The Federal Trade Commission stepped up its control over advertising in the early 1970s. Regulations such as one known as the Green River ordinance restrict the activities of salesmen who are employed by companies located outside the city. Salesmen are also regulated by the Federal Trade Commission Act and the Wheeler-Lea Amendment that relate to such activities as bribes, tie-in selling, product claims, and misleading statements.

Persuasion adapts to culture. The various promotional techniques vary from one culture to another in terms of appeals, media, and quantity. A public speaker may be used in a market in South America, a traveling motion picture in the barrios of some islands in the Philippines, and direct mail in some isolated regions. Promotional techniques, like the rest of marketing, must adapt to the local culture.

Economics is obviously a determining influence. Companies sometimes base their advertising and selling appropriations on economic conditions and also on the competitive situation at the time. The effects of advertising on demand are not always easy to ascertain but some conclusions are the following:

> For many products advertising tends to speed up favorable trends of demand; that is, if underlying conditions are favorable to an increase in demand for the product.

> In the case of a declining trend in demand, advertising is powerless to halt or reverse the trend. It can do no more than temporarily delay it.

> Where possibilities of expanding a market do not exist, or where there is a declining trend of demand, cooperative industry advertising campaigns have not been able to succeed.

> By aiding in the expansion of markets through accelerating a rising trend of demand, advertising also helps to increase the elasticity of demand.

> The expansion of the market also makes it possible for new competitors to enter.

> There are situations in which it does not pay a company to adver-

*Senate hearings were held in 1972 but the bill was not reported out of committee.

tise, because of insufficient product differentiation, lack of strong consumer buying motives, insufficient size and frequency of sale, and so on, for instance, matches, wheat, and nails.

In the long run competitive forces tend to weaken the condition of a company which relies on advertising to bring about an inelasticity of its individual demand and thus enable it to ignore price competition, especially during periods of depression. (Borden, 1942.)

To be successful, persuasion must reflect an understanding of the consumer in his environment. What does he need, what does he want, how much can he pay, where does he live, and how much does he know about the product? What is ethical, what is legal, what technology is available? These are some of the questions that must be considered to improve the effectiveness of the persuasion process.

### Magnitude of the Job

Persuasion has a favorable impact on the environment in that it provides jobs for millions of people, though it must stand on its contributions to industries' selling programs. The data shown in 22-3 and 22-4 give some idea of the economic importance of advertising and selling. The people engaged in the persuasion process work all along the marketing system from the processors of raw materials, through the manufacturers, wholesalers, and retailers, and finally to the buyers in households, institutions, and governments. The communications effort is a costly one, estimated in 1970 at $32 billion for personal selling, $21 billion for advertising, and $3 billion for sales promotion (Buzzell, 1971). Thus persuasion in our environment is big business.

## BROAD SOCIAL QUESTIONS

Although most ethical questions will be raised in Chapter 25 we want to mention a number of issues in this chapter dealing with persuasion.

### 22-3 Magnitude of the Advertising Industry, 1967

| Type of service | Number of establishments | Receipts ($000) | Payroll entire year ($000) |
|---|---|---|---|
| Total advertising | 8,185 | 8,201,485 | 983,828 |
| Advertising agencies | 5,747 | 7,587,231 | 782,918 |
| Outdoor advertising services | 1,144 | 278,252 | 88,028 |
| Radio and television representatives | 290 | 64,667 | 29,116 |
| Publisher's representatives | 389 | 128,010 | 53,607 |
| Miscellaneous advertising | 615 | 102,825 | 30,159 |

SOURCE: U.S. Department of Commerce, Bureau of the Census, *Selected Services, United States* (Washington D.C.: GPO, 1967), pp. 1–8.

**22-4** Employment in Selling, United States, 1970

| Type of Selling | Number Employed | % Increase 1960–1970 |
|---|---|---|
| Advertising agents and salesmen | 62,676 | 84.9 |
| Auctioneers | 4,780 | 18.0 |
| Demonstrators | 37,854 | 56.3 |
| Hucksters and peddlers | 117,562 | 115.4 |
| Insurance agents, brokers, and underwriters | 455,624 | 25.0 |
| Newsboys | 61,622 | −68.0 |
| Real estate agents and brokers | 262,161 | 35.8 |
| Stock and bond salesmen | 97,279 | 240.0 |
| Salesmen and sales clerks (n.e.c.) | 4,019,531 | 7.3 |
|    Manufacturing | 411,757 | −11.4 |
|    Wholesale trade | 625,872 | 26.3 |
|    Retail trade | 2,731,966 | 4.8 |
|    Other industries (incl. not reported) | 249,936 | 40.5 |

SOURCE: U.S. Department of Commerce, *Census of Population: 1970*, Detailed Characteristics (Washington, D.C.: GPO, 1973). Figures for 1970 include Salesworkers allocated, 326,285.

Marketers must take cognizance of the criticisms of marketing communications, determine which are valid, and correct the problems.

One criticism has to do with advertising and consumer sovereignty:

> Practitioners of advertising have eaten the fruit of a new tree of knowledge. Many today openly proclaim their objective to be appeals to the irrational or the irrelevant. Even those who have paid out the highest fees to motivational researchers, though, have not actually intended thereby to destroy the theoretical basis of a free enterprise system. These very same advertisers who hold that sales appeals must be irrational point in the next breath to those sales as "votes for advertised goods"—as public acclaim of their efforts. They cannot have it both ways. If sales must be achieved through irrational means, then those sales are the empty votes of a disenfranchised electorate and merely represent consumer manipulation. . . . In the absence of rationality in purchase, consumer sovereignty becomes a meaningless concept. (Warne, 1962.)

That there is irresponsibility in advertising and selling cannot be denied. Whether the irresponsibility is greater or less than in other sectors of industry is not ascertainable. Informed advertising would certainly improve the buyer's knowledge, as would competent sales presentations, and the buyer would be in a good position to exercise his sovereign rights. However, the primary purpose of advertising and selling is to persuade a buyer to buy, and marketers have not believed that information *per se* is an effective selling device. (The advertisement in 22-5 is certainly informative—is it also persuasive?) This note of skepticism is not to deny that an informed buyer is a more competent buyer, but we suggest that a big change in the nature of communications from marketers as well as changes in buyer responses to information will have to take place before we see a move to informational advertising and selling. In the industrial area much more information is communicated to the buyer than is the case in the consumer area, so

What should a good turntable do? Easy to put into words...move the record at the exact specified speed, without variation, and without inducing distortion. Here's how the Empire Troubador turntable achieves that goal: • Empire 208 belt-driven 3-speed "silent" turntable • There are only two moving parts in the 208, the motor and the turntable platter—precise bearing tolerances in those parts • Each motor and each turntable are individually adjusted to perfect dynamic balance • Complete rumble isolation is provided by the motor suspension, flexible belt drive and the resilient nylon "seat" which supports and cushions the thrust of the main bearing • Total vibration limited to less than 1/1,000,000th of an inch • 3 speeds, 33⅓, 45, 78 rpm • Constant speed, heavy duty hysteresis-synchronous motor operates independent of variations in current fluctuation • Continuous flexible belt—perfectly ground to constant thickness ± .0001 inch, couples turntable directly to the motor pulley—no intermediate idlers • Acoustic isolation motor suspension • Fine speed control • Push button power control with on-off light • Optimum distribution of turntable mass; 6 pound heavy machined aluminum, individually balanced to precise concentricity • Machined heavy aluminum base plate • Safety suspension rubber mat • Retractable 45 rpm adapter • Rumble better than —65 db • Wow and flutter less than .05% • Satin-chrome or satin-gold finish turntable, $110. (slightly higher west of the Rockies) • Handsome walnut base for 208 turntable, $15. The "American Record Guide" (Larry Zide column) says of the Empire Troubador turntable: "I found speed variations—that is, flutter and wow—to be inaudible...vibration was extremely low... rumble figures have not been bettered by any turntable I have tested...the heavy turntable is driven via a belt by a synchronous motor, thus assuring the user of constant speed, regardless of minor line variations" • Don Hambly, station manager of KRE AM/FM, Berkeley, Calif. said: "We have long realized that belt driven tables would be the best to use, but had not been impressed with those on the market ...the Empire tables, however, have all the basic requirements of design and simplicity of operation and maintenance that we have sought" • "Audio" magazine's "Equipment Profile" of the 208 said: "A massive turntable with precise performance...individually balanced...we tried to induce acoustic feedback by placing the turntable on top of our large speaker system and turning up the gain: we were unsuccessful" • (Still with us?) • "High Fidelity" magazine said of the 208: "Bold appearance which suggests massive and reliable construction—an impression which is quite borne out by its performance tests...the various pieces of the turntable are carefully machined aluminum castings, thick enough to provide extreme rigidity...finely machined shaft...wow and flutter, with the Troubador', were completely undetectable by ear...rumble also was completely inaudible, even at high listening levels...the hum field above the platter was completely negligible...starting torque was good...speed accuracy very good" • What should a good arm do? It should hold the cartridge in place as the stylus follows the record in the groove...without detracting from the performance of the cartridge • Here's how the Empire 980 Arm achieves this objective: • Better dynamic balance achieved by locating the pivot points at the precise center of the arm's mass—equal mass on both sides of axis. Once in balance in one plane it is balanced in all planes. This permits the 980 arm to track at lowest levels, gives it its rock-like stability that will allow perfect tracking at any angle—even upside down • Lowest inertia achieved by critically calculated distribution of arm mass • Maximum compliance means it yields to the slightest impulse, responds and moves effortlessly, even with a tilted table, a badly warped record, or with the turntable turning upside down • Precision ball bearing suspensions—both the vertical and lateral pivot bearings of the 980 are suspended in precision steel-ball races, precision manufactured to instrument tolerances...vertical and lateral friction are both virtually unmeasurable, permitting high compliance and minimum hysteresis • Lowest fundamental resonance frequency: 6 cps (the lowest ever achieved in any arm), achieved by increasing the rigidity of the arm structure through weight distribution, and by making the cartridge shell an integral part of the arm • This permits the 980 5 wire circuit eliminates ground loops, hence eliminates the hum that gound loops induce • Easy plug-in installation...no wiring or soldering necessary • Self-latching arm rest...a slight push downward on the arm tube latches the arm in position. (Score yourself a fairly serious music lover) • Precise stylus force adjustment...calibrated knob dials any stylus force from 0 to 8 grams with an accuracy of 0.1 gram • Arm offset angle: 23.8° • Satin chrome or satin gold finish, $50. • Lowest tracking force possible, because of extreme compliance and low inertia • Counterweight zero balance adjustment for any cartridge from 2-25 grams • Maximum tracking error ± .650° • No acoustic feedback • Exact cartridge positioning, quick-release bracket-mount secures cartridge to arm shell. Stylus is aligned with front edge of cartridge mounting plate for exact overhang dimension • Dyna Lift (Patent Pending) lifts arm from record at play out • "High Fidelity" magazine's equipment report said: "The spring-loaded 12-inch 980 Arm moves exceptionally freely about its pivot points, indicating very well-made bearings" • "American Record Guide" (Larry Zide column) said: "One of the best available...substantial reduction in vertical mass...a cartridge of any dimensions can be aligned in the head for minimum tracking error...calibration is extremely accurate...Dyna Lift most useful...lateral and vertical friction is exceptionally low...exceptionally stable...steady even with shaky floors..." • "Audio" magazine's equipment profile said: "Much thicker walled tubing in the arm to reduce the fundamental resonant frequency, which is now below the lower limit of our test record" • (This settles it. Score yourself a dedicated music-loving audiophile for reading this far) • What should a good cartridge do? It should translate mechanical energy into electrical energy without introducing distortion. And for maximum life of the stylus and your records (not to mention reduced distortion) it should perform this function at as slight a stylus force as possible • Here's how the Empire 880p cartridge achieves these objectives: • Lowest dynamic mass, less than .5 x 10⁻³ grams • Highest compliance, 30 x 10⁻⁶ cm/dyne... Lower dynamic mass and higher compliance than any other cartridge made —eliminates distortion and makes possible many of the cartridge's other accomplishments • Performance range 6 to 30,000 cps, well beyond the range of human hearing • Channel separation more than 30 db—greater separation than any other cartridge means greater enjoyment of stereophonic sound • Tracking force as low as ¼ gram—lowest in the industry—at such low tracking force, the 880p not only eliminates record wear, but also eliminates distortion • Longest possible cartridge life insured by lightness of stylus and the low dynamic mass of the magnetic element. It's the last cartridge you're ever likely to buy • The amazing "Dyna-Life" Stylus (Patent Pending)—ultra-sophisticated hand-polished .6 mil diamond—world's lightest • Complete freedom from hum pickup: the Empire 880p incorporates a complete mu-metal shield to prevent stray hum in the cartridge • Fully compatible for stereo or mono • "Moving Magnet" principle • Balanced high output, 10 millivolts per channel ± ¼ db, etc. • Perfectly translates and responds to the intricate movements of the record groove • Stylus inertia approaches the irreducible minimum • Smooth, wide response • Inspected at each phase of its manufacture • Faithfully responds, instantly, effortlessly, favoring neither one wall nor the other • Empire 880p, $47.50 • Natural performance • The Empire 880p is so new, the country's hi fi magazines have not had an opportunity to test and publish their opinions... in the meantime, here's what a happy new owner of the 880p wrote us recently: "Most musical, noise non-existent, the sound is transparent, spacious, airy, exceptionally musical, violins sound like violins not cellos or steel wires, in a class by itself" • The Empire 880p is the cartridge that renders every other cartridge on the market today obsolete • If you've read this far you are by all means a music lover most seriously interested in highest quality record playback system. Above you have read a "few" of the reasons why we believe the Empire Troubador is for you. You've got the facts about the Empire 208 turntable, the Empire 980 Arm, and the Empire 880p Cartridge. But what about the integration of these three components? Every Empire component was designed and built for maximum integration with the Troubador system...no other manufacturer makes all three. • "High Fidelity" magazine said: "A precision-engineered product of the highest quality...in sum, the parts of the 'Troubador'—taken separately—stand up as first-rate audio components. Taken together, they form one of the handsomest record players available" • "Audio" magazine said: "Precise in appearance and performance...as a system, the 'Troubador' Model 398 is not inexpensive [$222.50 including base], but it just reaffirms something we all know: higher quality means higher costs. The Model 398 is an excellent buy for those who want the quality" • To you determined readers we can only say that we rest our case. (sigh...now you don't have to write for our brochure...you've just read it).

## Here are a few of the reasons why the EMPIRE TROUBADOR is called the "World's Most Perfect Record Playback System"

EMPIRE
SCIENTIFIC CORP • 845 STEWART AVE • GARDEN CITY, L.I. N.Y.

EXPORT: CANADA. Empire Scientific Corp., Ltd., Toronto, Canada • EXPORT EXCEPT CANADA. EMEC, Plainview, L. I., N. Y.

*Advertisement prepared by:*
Katz, Jacobs & Co., Inc.

SOURCE: *Printer's Ink*, July 26, 1963, p. 16. Reprinted by permission of Katz, Jacobs & Co., Inc.

it is not surprising to find less criticism of the marketing effort in the industrial sector. Though it is possible to provide information that would make the consumer more sovereign, it is an unfortunate truth that persuasion often concentrates on other matters.

Advertising is frequently lauded for its work on some nonprofit campaigns and in its public service efforts. Criticism has been voiced, however, about activities in the political arena to the point where presidential campaigns will have financial limitations placed on them in the future. The situation of the voter is probably analogous to the sovereignty of the buyer.

Another prime criticism of marketing communications has to do with quantity. Ben H. Bagdikian has stated:

> Communications are becoming increasingly efficient from a technological standpoint, but their content is becoming ever more meaningless. Advertising and propaganda are debasing our symbols so that there is a breakdown in real communications between different generations and different political groups. The solution may lie in the increase of noncommercial media that are not committed to playing the game of collecting mass audiences for sale. (Bagdikian, 1971.)

The thousands of advertising messages to which we are exposed, even on a daily basis, does suggest that advertisers do indeed bombard the public. On the other hand, we have internal mechanisms for shutting out of our minds many of the ads and for filtering many others. How should communications be limited in a society such as ours?

Critics fear that heavy advertisers can dominate the economy to the point that the small and the new firm cannot compete. Studies of the relationship between advertising and market share do not bear out this criticism, but the courts have on occasion ruled against the dominant sales-oriented firm because of its advertising. Merger regulations also include guidelines about the selling effort involved. Since the power of the advertiser is difficult to measure, the "watch dog" approach is probably the most viable policy at this time.

Businessmen themselves criticize advertising and they examine its merits on a continuing basis. If advertising does not produce results the effort is wasted and is ultimately reflected in higher prices to the buyer. In 1962 and 1971 studies of *Harvard Business Review* subscribers (93 percent businessmen among the respondents), a number of diverse findings were revealed.

> Businessmen today take a somewhat more critical stance toward advertising than they did nine years ago. This is true in areas of advertising's economic role, its social impact, and its perceived truthfulness.
>
> Executives still almost unanimously agree that advertising is essential to business and that the public places more confidence in advertised products than in unadvertised ones.

Respondents think that advertising speeds the development of markets for new products, helps raise our standard of living, and results in better products.

If advertising were eliminated, businessmen claim, selling expenses would have to go up. On the other hand, executives think too much money is spent on advertising. (Greyser and Reece, 1971.)

The respondents also criticized advertising for its conformity effects, but many also thought advertising led to diversity. They stated (57 percent) that advertising has an unhealthy influence on children, and 85 percent said that advertising often persuades people to buy things they don't need. Among the media used, trade publications received the best ratings since they seemed to be less annoying and offensive, and more informative and enjoyable. Direct mail advertising received the poorest ratings.

The Harvard respondents credited advertising agency people with various achievements but thought the agencies were also responsible for improvement of their field. Most respondents placed the ultimate responsibility, however, on the top management of the firm. Some companies have recently taken steps to get responsibility on behalf of the marketing departments and hopefully this development will improve the social impact of communications. Further, Secretary of Commerce Maurice H. Stans in 1971 requested 1200 corporate chief executive officers personally to review their company's policies and procedures on advertising and promotion.

Salesmen and sales managers also have their ethical problems. The sales manager has an important relationship to each salesman and also to his own superior. Matters of promotion, territorial assignments, compensation, and identification of house accounts are some of the areas that trouble managers. The salesman has allegiance to his company and he needs to be especially careful about information that he provides outsiders. The problem of a salesman resigning one company and taking his old customers to his new firm has been eliminated for the most part by laws that forbid him to sell for a competing firm in his old territory for a given period of time. The salesman also has responsibilities toward his customers, for they often give him information that should be kept confidential. Some of them are not above bribes of some kind—meals, gifts, or services. One of the authors once met a "salesman" whose sole job was entertainment. He purchased tickets for athletic events, operas, and plays; rented cabins at resorts, hired baby sitters, rented cars; and took customers out for the evening. He found the job fun for a few months and then found it became repugnant. There are selling jobs that permit the salesman to exert tremendous pressure on the customer. One salesman told one of the authors of a job he had selling cemetery lots. He found that he could have elderly couples in tears so that they became easy prey for his pitch. He, too, gave up his job. Fortunately many selling jobs are ethical, challenging, and personally satisfying, and the salesman can sense the mutual satisfaction that he and the buyer experience.

Persuasion at its best will still have its critics, but those critics should familiarize themselves with the total process, including alternatives to advertising and selling. There are benefits and there are costs and abuses. Advertising and selling do serve as a kind of "energizer" for the whole economic system and therefore deserve very careful examination.

# COMMUNICATIONS

To this point we have considered some of the broad issues of persuasion—the role of persuasion, its relationship to the environment, and social questions. We now focus on the communications process and on the elements of the communications mix.

Marketers communicate to their customers through the media of television, radio, direct mail, oral presentations, and so on. The communications process involves the imparting of information, opinions, and thoughts through the various media. The late Carl Hovland and his colleagues performed many experiments in an effort to enlarge our understanding of the processes of communication. Hovland pointed out that a communication contains three main classes of stimuli. The first relates to the observable *character* of the communication's personal source. A second class involves the *setting* in which the person is exposed to the communication. The third class comprises the *arguments* and *appeals* (Hovland, 1953). Hovland saw the persuasive communication as one involving a communicator, a communication content, audience predispositions, and responses. The marketer is a communicator; product information is the communication content; and buyers in the marketplace have various predispositions toward the product and the seller and also make certain responses to the communication. The marketer sends a communication in the form of a "recommended opinion" to the potential buyer, who may or may not think the communication is sufficiently persuasive to cause him to switch to the recommended brand. A variation of this pattern is shown in 22-6.

The overlap shown in 22-6 indicates that there has been communication. That is, the message sent means the same thing to the advertiser that it does to the prospective customer: only then is there real communication. "Noise" in the form of competitive communications can render the message useless.

The communication process seems simple enough when marketers are thought of as senders and buyers as receivers of messages. The attempt to persuade through communications is not simple, however, for there are many fine points to the process. Should a salesman or an advertisement present the competitive view as well as the one being promoted? Under what conditions should a salesman omit a relevant argument? What effect does a warning have on the receiving of information? That is, if a person is warned that he may receive information with which he has not agreed in the past, will he be more or less receptive to this negative information? Should the seller's views be

**22-6** Diagram of the Communications Process

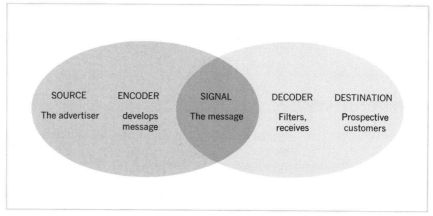

SOURCE: Adapted from Wilbur Schramm (ed.), *The Process and Effects of Mass Communication* (Urbana, Ill.: University of Illinois Press, 1954), p. 6.

presented first or last relative to those of a competitor? What is the role of persuasion after the purchase? This last point relates to the notion of cognitive dissonance, which was discussed in Chapter 12. Some advertising is directed toward the postpurchase period in order to help the buyer feel better about his dissonance.

To be effective, communications have to reach the right audience, and whatever the audience, persuasion attempts are launched in a "noisy" atmosphere where competitors are trying their best to recruit the same customers. For communications to reach the right audience, the advertising and selling techniques need to be carefully chosen. Any magazine will not do, nor will any salesman. The message itself must be tailored for the audience. The household buyer must be persuaded that a product tastes good, or looks good, or is owned by the neighbors, or is a sign of sophistication. The industrial buyer must be convinced of durability, safety features, or economy of operation. The goal of effective persuasion is to condition buyers to accept a message. Colin Golby illustrates how this conditioning might be done with a commercial (22-7). This example demonstrates an important principle in persuasion: no one part of the communication should ever be regarded as acceptable or believable in isolation from the rest of it.

There are many workable formulas for successful promotion. Sir William Crawford espoused: "concentration—domination—repetition" (Hobson, 1964). This formula simply means that the market is pinpointed or segmented, that all forms of persuasion are then gathered to create a dominant impact on the segment selected and, finally, that repetition is essential because readers of advertisements forget rapidly. Russell Colley visualizes four stages of commercial communications: awareness, comprehension, connection, and action (Colley, 1961). Herbert Krugman stipulates that successful advertising is based on three factors: information, reasoning, and emphasis (FTC Hearings,

1971). In the following communications, how much information and reasoning are used and what kinds of emphases are given?

... ABOUT THAT YELLOW STUFF ON THE CITY STREETS. IT'S A REVOLUTIONARY, NEW KIND OF SALT WITH A BUILT-IN "RUST INHIBITOR" TO PROTECT YOUR CAR. In tests it has reduced salt-induced auto rust an average of 85%. (Cargill Co.)

THE MAN IN THE PICTURE PAID $17,021 FOR HIS CAR. LET ME TELL YOU ABOUT THE VERY RICH. THEY ARE DIFFERENT FROM YOU AND ME. (Rolls-Royce.)

THE FORD RIDES QUIETER THAN A ROLLS-ROYCE. (Ford Motor Co.)

THINK SMALL. (Volkswagen.)

## 22-7

### An Example of a Conditioning Communication

| Statement | Response | Comment |
|---|---|---|
| 1. A nice complexion makes a woman more attractive. | "That's true." | Most women would likely agree. |
| 2. Toilet soap can help to keep the complexion nice. | "Yes, it can." | Follows first statement. |
| 3. Particularly a mild and gentle toilet soap. | "I suppose so." | Follows second statement. |
| 4. Lanolin helps to make a toilet soap mild and gentle. | "Yes." | Follows third statement. |
| 5. Brand Y contains lanolin. | "I see." | Notice the increase in particular-ness and decrease in generality. This prepares the way for the factual statement in statement 5. No. 5 completes the argument and prepares way for conclusion. |
| 6. Therefore Brand Y will keep her complexion nice and make her more attractive. | "I suppose that's true." | Conclusion now acceptable because of prior conditioning. |

SOURCE: Colin Golby, "Toward a Theory," *Scientific Business* (February 1965), p. 331.

MOST PEOPLE ARE SCARED WITLESS OF FLYING. Deep down inside, every time that big plane lifts off the runway, you wonder if this is it; right? You want to know something, fella? So does the pilot, deep down inside. (Pacific Air Lines.)

For the woman who has to meet the 6:22 there is a special kind of new program, of concise reporting and interesting features, scheduled with the busy housewife in mind. (WABC-TV, New York City.)

The communications process relates to almost every part of marketing. For example, it relates to the stages of buying as described in the chapters on buyer behavior. Different kinds of messages are appropriate for each of these stages, since enticing the nonuser may call for quite a different appeal from a campaign assuring someone who has already purchased a product. That is, the prospective buyer may be sent messages that increase his desire to buy, his awareness of the product, and information to facilitate his decision. After the purchase the messages should reassure the buyer and help him to sense satisfaction with his purchase.

The communications used by a marketer also relate to the product. The stage of the product life cycle, as explained in Chapter 17, necessitates different kinds of communications. The type of product typically influences the communications: industrial products are sold with rational appeals for the most part, whereas consumer items carry with them emotional appeals. Technical products need different communications from those for nontechnical items, and there are differences in the communications process as between impulse and planned purchases. The impulse items typically are promoted with heavy point-of-purchase communications whereas the planned items use advertising and personal selling.

Many products are sold to segmented markets, and these call for different kinds of messages as well as different media. Geographic markets, religious markets, and markets based on income, occupation, sex, age, and stage of life all influence the communications sent by the marketer.

Advertising man David Ogilvy has listed some of the things he has learned about communications:

Problem-solving communications are effective provided the sender does not cheat in some way.

Testimonials are effective if the celebrities are relevant and if their messages are credible.

Logorrhea (rhymes with diarrhea) drowns the receiver in a torrent of words.

Simple headlines telegraph what you want to say in simple language.

Use captions to sell since twice as many people read the captions under photographs as read the body copy.

Select your prospects and localize your message. (Ogilvy, 1971.)

In addition to discussing the role of persuasion and its relationship to the environment, we also have discussed communications in a general way, laying the groundwork for the management of communications that follows in the next chapter.

## STATEMENTS TO CONSIDER

Stimulation of selective demand cannot be easily accomplished for a product the identity of which is not obtrusive to the purchaser.

People tend to see and hear communications that are favorable or congenial to their predispositions.

The more trustworthy, credible, or prestigious the communicator is perceived to be, the less manipulative his intent is considered and the greater the immediate tendency to accept his conclusions.

People use their own changes of opinion, however recent or immediate, as blocks against further modification of opinion under the pressure of communications.

The communication of facts is typically ineffective in changing opinions in desired directions against the force of audience predispositions.

The higher a person's level of intelligence, the more likely it is that he will acquire information from communications.

Word-of-mouth or personal communication from an immediate and trusted source is typically more influential than media communication from a remote and trusted source, despite the prestige of the latter. (The seven statements above are from Berelson and Steiner, 1964.)

An individual's psychological characteristics play a role in his response to advertising.

Advertising will not reverse unfavorable trends based on changed socioeconomic conditions.

Stimuli that are pleasant, highly valued, and consistent with expectations are perceived more quickly and correctly. (The three statements above are from Halbert, 1965.)

## QUESTIONS FOR REVIEW

1. What do you consider the most important kind of marketing communication? Explain your answer.

2. Why is persuasion used at all in a controlled economy?

3. In what ways does advertising adapt to the social environment?

4. Argue the following point: About half the nation's advertising is wasted.

**5.** Is advertising powerful enough to create values and change attitudes?

**6.** Are there any indications that the proliferation of advertising is rendering it ineffective?

**7.** What happens to advertising expenditures during changes in the business cycle?

**8.** From the standpoint of society, can we ever be satisfied with the process of persuasion?

**9.** Break a marketing communication down into its various components.

**10.** What are the most effective advertisements you can remember seeing or hearing?

## Further Readings

James H. Bearden (ed.), *Personal Selling: Behavioral Science Readings and Cases* (New York: John Wiley, 1967).

Neil H. Borden, *The Economic Effects of Advertising* (Homewood, Ill.: Richard D. Irwin, 1942).

S. Watson Dunn, *Advertising: Its Role in Modern Marketing,* (New York: Holt, Rinehart and Winston, 2nd ed., 1969).

Claude Hopkins, *Scientific Advertising* (New York: Crown, 1966). (Original text 1923.)

Jerome B. Kernan, William P. Dommermuth, and Montrose S. Sommers, *Promotion: An Introductory Analysis* (New York: McGraw-Hill, 1970).

Taylor W. Meloan and John M. Rathmell, *Selling: Its Broader Dimensions* (New York: Macmillan, 1960).

William J. Stanton and Richard H. Buskirk, *Management of the Sales Force* (Homewood, Ill.: Richard D. Irwin, 1969).

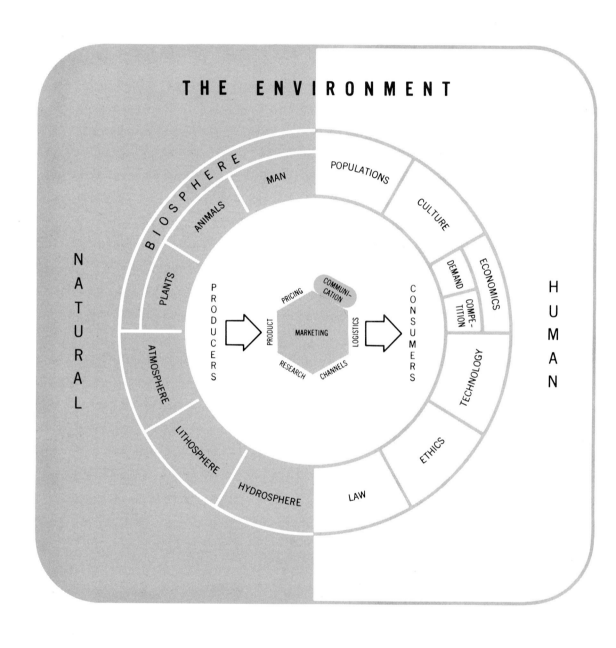

THE ENVIRONMENT

NATURAL

HUMAN

BIOSPHERE

MAN
ANIMALS
PLANTS
ATMOSPHERE
LITHOSPHERE
HYDROSPHERE

POPULATIONS
CULTURE
DEMAND
ECONOMICS
COMPE-TITION
TECHNOLOGY
ETHICS
LAW

PRODUCERS
CONSUMERS

PRICING
COMMUNI-CATION
PRODUCT
MARKETING
LOGISTICS
RESEARCH
CHANNELS

# CHAPTER 23
# MARKETING COMMUNICATIONS II

*The manager in charge of communications needs to make basic decisions about allocating his promotional resources. Media selection, the kind of advertising, the number of salesmen, and the selection of an advertising agency are some of the decisions facing the manager. Ideally he will develop an effective mix for the firm and an acceptable one for the public.*

The elaborate array of available persuasion techniques is impressive and offers alternatives to the one who must develop a promotions mix for a marketing program. The promotions or communications mix is only one part of the total marketing mix, and as such it has to dovetail with the rest of the marketing program. The one who develops the communications program must understand what is also being done about pricing, distribution, and the product and its package since each element of the total mix should complement the others.

Absolute precision cannot be achieved with a promotions program, of course, because there are many unknown factors. The marketer does not know exactly what the competition is going to do with its marketing program, nor does he know about the weather, economic conditions in the next year, or forthcoming technology. These are largely uncontrollable variables that will certainly affect sales. The marketer does have control over other variables—the amount of money to spend for promotion, the media to use, and the messages to communicate. In this section we will examine the communications mix, beginning with the task of personal selling.

## MARKETING AND PERSUASION

### Personal Selling

What is a salesman? When two groups of students were asked to write down the first five words that came into their minds in connection with the word "salesman" they responded as follows (Wilson, 1947). Note the difference between the two types of students.

| Order | Sales Students | Nonsales Students |
|-------|----------------|-------------------|
| 1 | Money | Fast talker |
| 2 | Appearance | High-pressure |
| 3 | Personality | Door-to-door |
| 4 | Work | Car |
| 5 | People | Pressure |
| 6 | Service | Buy |
| 7 | Knowledge | Speech |
| 8 | Professional | Hours |
| 9 | Help, helpful | Extrovert |
| 10 | Customer | Insurance |

## 23-1

**"The Salesman"**

A salesman is many things. He is a pin on a map to the sales manager, a quota to the factory, an overloaded expense account to the auditor, a book-keeping item called cost-of-selling to the treasurer, a smile and wise-crack to the receptionist, and a purveyor of the balm of flattery to buyers.

A salesman needs the endurance of Hercules, the brass of Barnum, the craft of Machiavelli, the tact of a diplomat, the tongue of an orator, the charm of a playboy, and a mind as fast as a Univac. He must be impervious to insult, indifference, anger, scorn, complaint, that tremendous burst of silence, and the effects of drinking all night with a customer.

He must be able to sell all day, entertain all evening, drive all night to the next town, and be on the job at 8 am, fresh as a water lily. He must be an expert as a golfer, card shark, story teller, business man, dinner companion, and listener to sad stories.

He wishes his merchandise were better, his prices lower, his commissions higher, his territory smaller, his competitors ethical, his goods shipped on time, his boss sympathetic, his advertising better, his customers human. He is a realist who knows none of this will ever be. He is an optimist, so he makes the sale anyway.

He rolls away his life in the tedium of planes, trains, and cars. Each morning he hoists on his back the dead weight of last year's sales record and this year's quota. He writes finis to the day with that special curse of the salesman—the daily report.

Despite all this there's nothing he'd rather do, and he'll be the first to tell you so . . . .

SOURCE: Herb Daniels, *Chicago Tribune*. Reprinted courtesy of the *Chicago Tribune*.

---

The college group is usually annoyed by salesmen who bother them when they are students. As a person expands his income, however, he becomes more appreciative of the salesman who can offer good advice on insurance, securities, housing, and other important purchases. Again, what *is* a salesman? Herb Daniels has given one answer in 23-1. It is no wonder that the salesman is many things to many different people, for there are millions of sales people in the nation who sell a multitude of products to different kinds of buyers. One salesman may instruct and inform garage mechanics about a new style of wrench—this is missionary selling. Another calls on industrial buyers at appointed hours. Others call on housewives on a house-to-house basis. Many are sales clerks in retailing establishments. Soft-drink bottlers hire salesmen who are combinations of public relations contacts, warehousemen, distributors, bill collectors, and who also handle the point-of-purchase advertising pieces.

The sales system in 23-2 shows the relationship of the environment to a generalized sales system. The management has control over its own

**23-2** A Simplified Model of the Selling Process

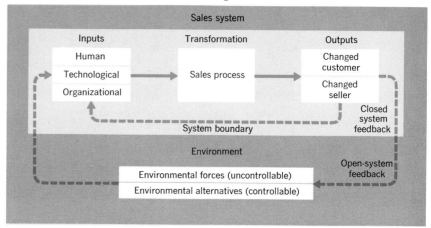

SOURCE: Thomas S. Robertson and Richard B. Chase, "The Sales Process: An Open Systems Approach," *Business Topics MSU*, Vol. 16 (Autumn 1968), p. 48.

selling decisions such as the number of salesmen, their territories, their incentive program, and so on, but it cannot control some of the environmental forces such as competition and new-product entries.

Over the years there has been a changing emphasis in sales management as shown in 23-3. This development parallels the overall evolution of the marketing concept as described earlier. There is more sophistication to the entire system today as salesmen are hired with the use of testing programs; they are trained by the firm's formalized training program; they are paid a combination of salary and commission in order to attain both security and incentive; and they are given various tools to help them sell. These tools include marketing research reports,

**23-3** Changing Emphasis in Sales Management in This Century

| | 1900  1910  1920  1930  1940 | | 1950  1960 | 1970 |
|---|---|---|---|---|
| Business response to perceived dominant environmental conditions | Production orientation | Sales orientation | Marketing orientation | Human orientation |
| Emphasis in management's conception of sales job | Personality art | "Scientific salesmanship" | Professionalism | Personal fulfillment |
| Emphasis in sales management | Tight supervision and control | Broadened responsibilities | Strategies and profits | Total human resource development |

SOURCE: Leslie M. Dawson, "Toward A New Concept of Sales Management," *Journal of Marketing*, Vol. 34 (April 1970), p. 37.

identification of prospects, and fast transportation. These aspects of a sales manager's job should not be taken lightly, for it is not easy to specify what makes a "good" salesman, what should be included in a training program, how the salesman should interact with his clients, what system of compensation is best, or how large a territory should be.

The changes listed above were verified by Edwin H. Lewis in a study of 30 manufacturing companies. Responding executives pointed out the major shift in personal selling has been from order-taking to presenting of merchandising programs, providing dealer support and counseling, training of distributor/dealer salesmen, and providing an increasingly broad range of technical services. The computer has largely taken over the reorder function for the salesmen. Another shift has been the emphasis from sales volume *per se* to promotional and merchandising programs, especially with lines sold through a distributor/dealer organization. Lewis points out that program selling creates in the minds of middlemen a strong brand image, which, in effect, consists of a combined service/product mix. In the same study executives reported the formation of a broader range of sales classifications—regular salesmen to national-account representatives, for example. And the hiring standards have been upgraded as sales managers today are looking for planning ability, creative ability, communication skills, a business sense, and maturity to deal with both small-business owners and top company managements. Increasingly, Lewis has reported, companies are finding that they need to sell services, systems, and merchandising programs rather than just products and product lines. This may be the most far-reaching implication for sales (Lewis, 1970).

Some of the principal concerns of the sales managers include turnover of salesmen, and Lewis found that in the 30 companies the turnover rate ranged from 5 to 50 percent. Another concern is motivation of the salesman, control of their activities, judgment of their performance, field communications, and the rise of personal selling costs.

Some companies operate with their own sales forces; others utilize agents of various kinds to handle the selling function; some use both. Mail order houses, however, rely on a catalog in lieu of a personal salesman, but all firms have a system for taking orders and for developing what they consider to be their market. In many cases the salesman is the principal or even the only contact with the buyer.

## Advertising

Another powerful instrument of persuasion is advertising. Advertising is a message to potential buyers, to actual buyers, and to almost everyone in some context, but it is not simple. (See 23-4.) It can be low-cost on a per-unit basis, it can be directed to a narrow audience through careful media selection, or it can be broadcast widely through television, radio, magazines, and newspapers. Still, few marketers are ever completely satisfied with their advertising programs, partly because they find it difficult to prove their effectiveness due to constantly

**23-4**

**The Sequence of an Advertisement's Synthesis**

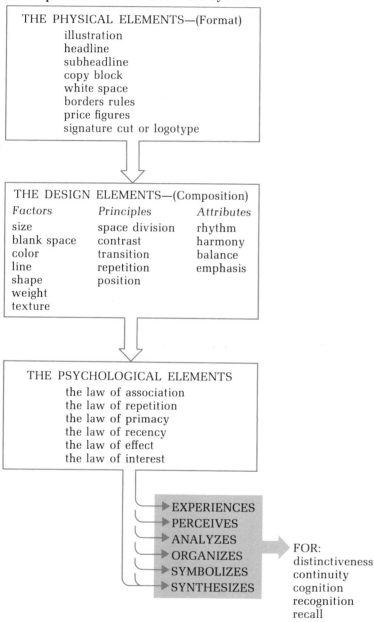

THE PHYSICAL ELEMENTS—(Format)
illustration
headline
subheadline
copy block
white space
borders rules
price figures
signature cut or logotype

THE DESIGN ELEMENTS—(Composition)

| *Factors* | *Principles* | *Attributes* |
|---|---|---|
| size | space division | rhythm |
| blank space | contrast | harmony |
| color | transition | balance |
| line | repetition | emphasis |
| shape | position | |
| weight | | |
| texture | | |

THE PSYCHOLOGICAL ELEMENTS
the law of association
the law of repetition
the law of primacy
the law of recency
the law of effect
the law of interest

EXPERIENCES
PERCEIVES
ANALYZES
ORGANIZES
SYMBOLIZES
SYNTHESIZES

FOR:
distinctiveness
continuity
cognition
recognition
recall

SOURCE: Reprinted by permission from John E. Mertes, "The Advertisement as Meta-communication," *Business Perspectives*, Vol. 6, No. 3 (Spring, 1970), p. 16. © 1970 by the Board of Trustees, Southern Illinois University.

changing conditions in the marketplace. This is a different situation from the year 1759 when Samuel Johnson stated, "The trade of advertising is now so near to perfection that it is not easy to propose any improvement." Today's advertisers are always seeking ways to improve their programs.

Lord Leverhume, John Wanamaker, and others have been quoted as saying, "I know about half my advertising is wasted, but I do not know which half." And as a society, we seem to feel that production is good, consumption is doubtful, and advertising is bad. We used to applaud the Hershey Chocolate Corporation because it sold its famous candy for 66 years without advertising. As a top company officer once explained: "All we do is make a good product, sell it at the lowest possible price, and do some promotional work with retailers and distributors" (Hughes, 1960). In fact, however, Hershey's policies were not opposed to advertising, and indeed the company sponsored cooperative advertising with retailers and advertised in trade publications. It used considerable point-of-sale advertising, and the millions of wrappers seen at more than one million retail outlets were excellent reminders to buy Hershey products. Even so, Hershey did not know how much better it could have done with media advertising, and in the 1960s the company launched a sizeable advertising campaign. Today there are few cases of well-known successful merchandising efforts that do not include advertising.

Let us look at some advertising data, both in the aggregate and for individual firms. The total U.S. advertising expenditures are shown in 23-5, selected company data in 23-6. The totals are impressive and so are the company figures that illustrate how different companies believe their advertising dollars should be spent. Even companies in the same industry show different allocations: General Motors spent 30 percent of its advertising budget on network television, Ford spent 40, and Chrysler 44. Variations in total advertising emphasis are shown in 23-7 for leading advertisers in the United States.

The task of allocating advertising dollars is difficult, as 23-8 suggests. How much should be spent? How should the money be distributed among the media? When does the firm reach the saturation point where buyers are very difficult to persuade? Advertising is used to increase sales to the point where profits are satisfactory, but this is difficult because of so many factors involved, some of which are uncontrollable. We need to know more about every facet of the persuasion process. We need to know the effect of an advertisement* on the market. We would also like to know how much the demand curve will shift to the

*One "perfect" measure has been suggested. Step-by-step, here it is:
—First, make a list of all the working functions of the business (research and development, maintenance, accounting, sales, etc., etc.). *But do not include advertising.*
—To each one of the listed functions, allocate the exact amount of sales or profit which can properly be credited to that activity.
—Add up the allocations.
—Deduct the sum of these allocations from the known total of sales or profit for the business.
—What remains is the contribution of advertising. (Wallace, 1966.)

**23-5** Estimated United States Advertising Expenditures in Millions of Dollars, 1970

| Year | Total | Newspapers | Magazines | Business publications | Farm publications | Television | Radio | Direct mail | Outdoor | Point of purchase displays | Agency income | Other expenditures |
|---|---|---|---|---|---|---|---|---|---|---|---|---|
| 1947 | 4,241 | 1,192 | 434 | 150 | 41 | 2 | 365 | 566 | 113 | 187 | 265 | 926 |
| 1948 | 4,907 | 1,410 | 482 | 163 | 42 | 9 | 408 | 671 | 115 | 194 | 309 | 1,104 |
| 1949 | 5,331 | 1,503 | 463 | 162 | 43 | 34 | 415 | 724 | 115 | 199 | 338 | 1,335 |
| 1950 | 5,864 | 1,641 | 481 | 164 | 42 | 106 | 444 | 739 | 132 | 202 | 373 | 1,530 |
| 1951 | 6,497 | 1,747 | 545 | 182 | 44 | 236 | 450 | 833 | 137 | 235 | 414 | 1,674 |
| 1952 | 7,161 | 1,879 | 592 | 210 | 46 | 324 | 470 | 907 | 145 | 262 | 459 | 1,867 |
| 1953 | 7,784 | 2,002 | 650 | 220 | 48 | 432 | 476 | 1,003 | 158 | 290 | 501 | 2,004 |
| 1954 | 8,080 | 2,059 | 646 | 228 | 48 | 593 | 449 | 1,040 | 172 | 288 | 520 | 2,037 |
| 1955 | 8,997 | 2,320 | 668 | 250 | 50 | 745 | 453 | 1,229 | 176 | 311 | 597 | 2,198 |
| 1956 | 9,674 | 2,476 | 680 | 275 | 53 | 897 | 480 | 1,308 | 189 | 345 | 675 | 2,296 |
| 1957 | 10,313 | 2,510 | 695 | 319 | 56 | 943 | 517 | 1,324 | 201 | 318 | 737 | 2,693 |
| 1958 | 10,414 | 2,459 | 652 | 302 | 55 | 1,030 | 523 | 1,419 | 219 | 344 | 757 | 2,654 |
| 1959 | 11,358 | 2,705 | 718 | 354 | 58 | 1,164 | 560 | 1,597 | 223 | 362 | 815 | 2,802 |
| 1960 | 11,900 | 2,821 | 769 | 383 | 55 | 1,269 | 598 | 1,658 | 242 | 387 | 859 | 2,859 |
| 1961 | 12,048 | 2,818 | 774 | 384 | 53 | 1,318 | 591 | 1,687 | 232 | 405 | 870 | 2,916 |
| 1962 | 12,919 | 2,930 | 797 | 378 | 50 | 1,486 | 636 | 1,758 | 230 | 416 | 955 | 3,283 |
| 1963 | 13,639 | 3,087 | 832 | 413 | 47 | 1,597 | 681 | 1,760 | 229 | 490 | 1,005 | 3,498 |
| 1964 | 14,824 | 3,411 | 873 | 451 | 47 | 1,793 | 732 | 1,890 | 241 | 554 | 1,085 | 3,747 |
| 1965 | 16,175 | 3,658 | 924 | 475 | 47 | 1,965 | 793 | 2,057 | 251 | 574 | 1,194 | 4,237 |
| 1966 | 17,511 | 4,130 | 997 | 528 | 47 | 2,203 | 872 | 2,277 | 270 | 597 | 1,293 | 4,297 |
| 1967 | 18,004 | 4,175 | 990 | 545 | 46 | 2,273 | 907 | 2,323 | 279 | 666 | 1,317 | 4,483 |
| 1968 | 19,054 | 4,446 | 1,020 | 560 | 46 | 2,521 | 1,023 | 2,434 | 310 | 706 | 1,441 | 4,547 |
| 1969 | 20,507 | 4,858 | 1,063 | 609 | 42 | 2,796 | 1,086 | 2,488 | 325 | 777 | 1,575 | 4,888 |
| 1970 | 20,838 | 4,936 | 1,019 | 579 | 42 | 2,853 | 1,128 | 2,548 | 362 | 839 | 1,597 | 4,935 |

SOURCE: Reprinted from Seymour Banks, Ronald Reisman, and Charles Y. Yang, "Ad Volume Rises 1.6% in 1970 to $20.8 Billion," *Advertising Age,* Vol. 42 (June 7, 1971). p. 27. Copyright 1971 by Crain Communications, Inc.

**23-6** The Top 20 National Advertisers of 1970 (Expenditures in Thousands of Dollars)

| Company | Total | Newspapers | Magazines | Farm publications | Business publications | Spot television | Network television | Spot radio | Network radio | Outdoor |
|---|---|---|---|---|---|---|---|---|---|---|
| Procter & Gamble Co. | $ 188,417 | $ 751 | $ 7,362 | $ 2 | $ 769 | $ 50,796 | $ 128,444 | $ 278 | $ 4 | $ — |
| General Foods Corp. | 121,509 | 9,140 | 11,858 | 135 | 270 | 49,259 | 44,642 | 5,263 | 502 | 438 |
| General Motors Corp. | 119,164 | 20,096 | 23,856 | 457 | 4,180 | 8,961 | 32,972 | 20,906 | 2,804 | 4,930 |
| Bristol-Myers Co. | 110,872 | 1,872 | 20,381 | — | 4,287 | 23,351 | 57,078 | 2,843 | 599 | 458 |
| Colgate-Palmolive Co. | 101,480 | 3,169 | 5,018 | — | 43 | 36,860 | 46,507 | 8,141 | 1,690 | 50 |
| American Home Products | 90,544 | 3,322 | 7,334 | 78 | 347 | 26,355 | 40,791 | 10,731 | 1,360 | 222 |
| R. J. Reynolds Industries | 83,986 | 1,661 | 9,731 | 254 | 176 | 14,401 | 52,405 | 4,304 | 804 | 246 |
| Ford Motor Co. | 79,745 | 11,220 | 14,544 | 1,214 | 1,797 | 7,544 | 31,345 | 7,430 | 1,676 | 2,970 |
| Sterling Drug Inc. | 73,212 | 1,169 | 10,003 | 162 | 442 | 12,940 | 41,324 | 4,195 | 2,975 | — |
| Warner-Lambert Pharmaceuticals | 73,123 | 223 | 3,108 | — | 4,334 | 17,853 | 46,200 | 1,087 | 315 | 1 |
| Lever Bros. | 67,019 | 2,009 | 3,734 | — | — | 20,893 | 38,554 | 1,331 | 496 | — |
| Philip Morris Inc. | 66,703 | 532 | 13,745 | — | 81 | 11,491 | 36,685 | 2,500 | 833 | 833 |
| American Brands | 58,572 | 7,397 | 15,438 | 5 | 661 | 2,092 | 31,365 | 899 | 15 | 706 |
| Coca-Cola Co. | 52,965 | 2,276 | 6,064 | — | 474 | 16,944 | 15,527 | 10,239 | — | 1,439 |
| Sears, Roebuck & Co. | 52,685 | 253 | 13,399 | — | — | 18,960 | 15,273 | 4,306 | 59 | 432 |
| Gillette Co. | 51,805 | 304 | 5,383 | — | 114 | 16,320 | 27,479 | 1,817 | 382 | 3 |
| General Mills | 51,777 | 1,752 | 7,004 | — | 395 | 17,940 | 24,152 | 117 | 386 | 13 |
| Kraftco | 50,073 | 6,307 | 8,897 | 16 | 1,844 | 13,181 | 18,359 | 1,025 | 108 | 308 |
| Chrysler Corp. | 48,714 | 7,034 | 9,366 | 40 | 491 | 3,926 | 21,341 | 4,869 | 930 | 646 |
| Distillers Corp.-Seagrams Ltd. | 46,986 | 11,883 | 25,825 | — | 751 | 254 | — | 202 | 150 | 7,920 |

SOURCE: Reprinted from *Advertising Age*, Vol. 43 (June 21, 1971), p. 41. Copyright 1971 by Crain Communications, Inc.

right if a given number of dollars is spent on advertising. A model may be used, and some are, to determine advertising appropriations, but no panacea has yet emerged. Well aware that the effects of his promotion program are buried among price changes, new products, competitors' actions, economic conditions, fashion changes, inventory levels,

**23-7** Advertising as a Percentage of Sales, 1970

| Rank in advertising expenditures among top 100 firms | Company (by type of business) | Expenditures as a percentage of sales |
|---|---|---|
| | Cars | |
| 9 | Ford Motor Co. | 0.6 |
| 70 | Volkswagen of America | 2.2 |
| | Food | |
| 65 | Borden Inc. | 1.5 |
| 48 | Nabisco | 14.1 |
| | Soaps, cleansers (and allied) | |
| 1 | Procter & Gamble | 8.3 |
| 6 | Colgate-Palmolive Co. | 22.4 |
| | Tobacco | |
| 19 | American brands | 2.4 |
| 28 | Brown & Williamson | 6.8 |
| | Drugs and cosmetics | |
| 76 | Merck & Co. | 3.1 |
| 65 | J.B. Williams Co. | 36.0 |
| | Gum and candy | |
| 100 | Mars Inc. | 7.8 |
| 80 | Wm. Wrigley Jr. Co. | 12.2 |
| | Liquor | |
| 82 | National Distillers | 2.1 |
| 16 | Distillers Corp. Seagrams Ltd. | 6.4 |
| | Beer | |
| 52 | Anheuser-Busch | 3.3 |
| 56 | Jos. Schlitz Brewing Co. | 5.2 |
| | Oil | |
| 99 | Standard Oil of California | 0.2 |
| 64 | Atlantic Richfield Co. | 1.0 |
| | Soft drinks | |
| 32 | Pepsi-Cola | 4.7 |
| 12 | Coca-Cola | 4.8 |
| | Airlines | |
| 94 | Trans World Airlines | 1.3 |
| 88 | Eastern Air Lines | 2.0 |
| | Toys | |
| 86 | Mattel Inc. | 5.6 |
| 97 | Topper Corp. | 21.9 |
| | Others | |
| 72 | Greyhound Corp. | 0.9 |
| 19 | Gillette Co. | 9.7 |

SOURCE: Reprinted from "100 Leading Advertisers as Percent of Sales," *Advertising Age*, Vol. 43 (August 30, 1971), p. 22. Copyright 1971 by Crain Communications, Inc.

**23-8** The Relation of Profits to Advertising Expenditure

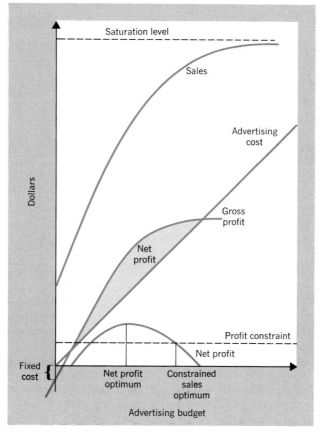

SOURCE: Wroe Alderson, "The Productivity of Advertising Dollars," *Cost and Profit Outlook*, Vol. 11 (February 1958), p. 1.

and other factors, the marketer nevertheless goes as far as he can toward making his advertising effort efficient and successful. Steuart Henderson Britt believes that the advertising program could be greatly improved if advertisers would ask and answer the following questions:

What facts do we have about the product or service to be advertised; and how can we integrate this information with other phases of our marketing mix?

What facts do we have about the people who might buy our product or service; and how can we use this information in developing our advertising messages?

What facts do we have about channels of communication; and how can we use this information in selecting our advertising media? (Britt, 1964.)

These are useful questions and they are helpful in aiding the marketer in meeting the challenge to make advertising an effective persuasive communication. Advertising is meant to propagandize, to persuade, to sell. It is meant to match a given product with a given market segment. Ultimately the sales figures tell the marketer how successful he has been.

The advertising function is carried out by a variety of organizations. The advertising agency performs a number of communication functions for the client company: planning, developing the copy, handling the art work, selecting media, conducting marketing research, producing, setting up radio and television programs, merchandising, public relations, and other tasks depending upon the needs of the clients (Dunn, 1969). Frequently an agency is organized around the above functions.

A company may use its own advertising manager for part or all of the advertising program. He may have a rather complete staff or he may be the marketing manager who "wears several hats." His most important task is to plan the campaign for the firm, and this job requires him to be a marketing man in the complete sense of the term as opposed to the narrower concept of an advertising man. Such a man would handle budgetary matters and would coordinate advertising with sales and other departments.

## The Sales : Advertising Ratio

For most companies the two most important ingredients of the communications mix are advertising and selling. Each of these complements the other. Some of the factors to consider in making choices between the two forms of persuasion are shown in 23-9.

It is impossible to generalize on what the sales:advertising ratio should be, and companies selling the same products use different ratios with adequate success. Avon products uses sales ladies to sell cosmetics on an in-house basis, paying approximately 40 percent commission for their efforts, and spends only about 1.5 percent on advertising. Revlon, by contrast, distributes its products through retail channels and pays between 35 and 40 percent markups on retail prices, but it spends approximately 7 percent of sales for advertising. Electrolux in 1970 paid its house-to-house salesmen about 33 percent commissions and spent nothing on national advertising. Hoover, by contrast, spent $1.5 million on advertising while retailers received about 20 to 25 percent markup (Buzzell, 1971). The results of a study in one metropolitan area showed similar variations in the sales:advertising ratios, as shown in 23-10. Edwin H. Lewis has commented as follows on the sales:advertising ratio:

> The development of a satisfactory sales:promotion mix by an individual company requires continuous study of the market and the competitive situation in it. The optimum mix probably is seldom attained, companies must continue to experiment with the several methods of sales promotion and to use them in various combinations in order to make their sales efforts more effective. (Lewis, 1954.)

**23-9** Personal Selling or Advertising?

| Personal Selling | Advertising |
|---|---|
| 1. Less opportunity for self-selection of messages by person being influenced. | 1. It must create or point out a need by identifying the circumstances under which it arises. |
| 2. Flexibility of timing and message to fit individual conditions. | 2. It must link the need to the possibility of fulfilling it with a general product, so that when the need arises the respondent will think of the product that will fulfill it. |
| 3. Immediate and personal award for compliance—through the approval and friendship of the influencer (salesman). | 3. It must differentiate the particular brand and its sponsor from other products which might satisfy the need approximately as well. |
| 4. Trust by the prospect in an intimate and respected source to select factors relevant to the prospect's specific case. | 4. It must connect the particular branded product with the place and the conditions under which it can be obtained. |
| 5. Decision on the basis of positive personal factors when there is no other element leading to a specific choice. (Rathmell, 1964.) | 5. It must show that the need is urgent and that the task of buying is easy. |
| SOURCES: John M. Rathmell, "The Salesman and Competition," in Taylor W. Meloan and Charles M. Whitlo (eds.), *Competition in Marketing* (Los Angeles: University of Southern California, 1964), p. 94, and Edmund D. McGarry, "The Propaganda Function in Marketing," *Journal of Marketing*, Vol. 23 (October 1958), pp. 131–139. | 6. It must give a rational basis for action, for people do not like to buy goods which they cannot justify to their own consciences. (McGarry, 1958.) |

The conclusions in 23-10 were based on the results of studies in 1954 and 1970. The two years showed surprising similarities: two of the companies (home furnishings and consumer durables) had increased the advertising component of the ratio and one (feed) increased the personal selling component.

## Other Communications

Though dominated by advertising and personal selling, persuasion takes many forms in the marketplace. The variations in products, customers, marketers, resources, channels, and competitive practices stimulate the development of different ways to promote products. A company likes to develop a niche in the market and sometimes this can be done through one variety of sales promotion. Brand names are used for products in order to provide identification and the brand becomes an important part of the promotional process. Names can be confusing (Glasstex batteries), difficult to remember and pronounce

**23-10** Personal Selling/Advertising Mix

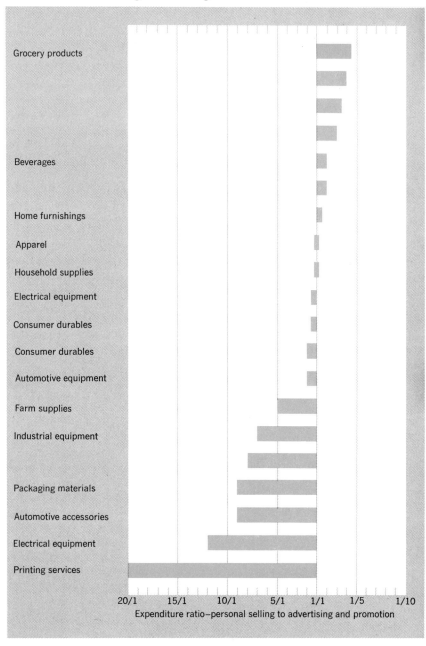

SOURCE: Edwin H. Lewis, "The Changing Dimensions of Field Selling," mimeographed report (Minneapolis: University of Minnesota, 1970), p. 13.

(Estrogenic hormone cream, Naugahyde Royalite plastics), and meaningless (Kordek binders, Tocco furnaces). Names can imply results (Wear-Ever utensils, Mum deodorant), and some meaningless names can even be given significance through advertising (Arm & Hammer baking soda, Zippo lighter, Arrow shirts, Dutch Boy paints) (McMurray, 1954).

Contests of all kinds are used among consumers, salesmen, and other employees. Gifts are used to a great extent by financial institutions. Trading stamps became a big business in the 1950s. A considerable variety of catalogs is used to promote business, and some of them are even sold to potential buyers. Premiums, bonuses, and other devices such as samples are also part of the array of sales-promotion techniques.

"Tie-ins" have also become important promotional devices. Millions of dollars are spent on auto racing as a sales tool. Goodyear, Firestone, and Goodrich tires; Gulf, Sunoco, STP, Wynn's, and Universal oil products; Champion and Autolite spark plugs—these are some of the products featured. Many car manufacturers subsidize racing teams. Even companies not directly related to autos sponsor the races: Topper Toys invests more than $250,000 in Al Unser's Johnny Lightning Specials. Soft drink, beer, cigarette, wax, luggage, toilet seat, bathtub, and food companies, along with motels, variety stores, and vacation resorts also put money into auto racing and hope that some of the charisma of racing becomes associated with their products (Radosta, 1971).

# DEVELOPMENT OF A COMMUNICATIONS PROGRAM

As mentioned in Chapter 14, much fun has been poked at Henry Ford for his remark, "Any customer can have a car painted any color that he wants so long as it is black." In 1909, when Ford made the statement, his marketing mix was simple and effective: build a mass-produced car, sell it at a low price, create strong dealerships, and advertise as needed. He stressed personal selling and wanted salesmen to know everyone in the territory.

As the environment changed, however, General Motors adapted faster than Ford. GM hired Richard Grant, one of the day's dynamic salesmen, who had learned to sell from John Henry Patterson of National Cash Register Company. Grant, too, stressed personal selling and he also used all kinds of advertising. The total marketing mix as he developed it pulled General Motors ahead of Ford (Chandler, 1964). The lesson here is that each element of a marketing mix should be strong, and if they are, the sales and profits should follow accordingly.

## Goals and Objectives

It is axiomatic that the communications program should be keyed to goals—corporate, overall marketing, and promotional goals. The goals are not automatically determined nor are they permanent. Typically, persuasion goals are multiple, and if achieved they perform a number of useful purposes. They may be to create an awareness for new products, to improve brand share in a competitive market, or to tell buyers where products can be obtained.

The setting of objectives for a company's communications program has a number of advantages, although the concept is not accepted by all companies. For one thing the communications, or persuasion, effort can be integrated so that advertising, selling, promotion, and all other communications are geared to the same end. Secondly, a statement of objectives provides the creative personnel with some guidelines for their work. Thirdly, the selection of media for advertising can be intelligently made because the markets have been specified and markets help to dictate the media to be used. Finally, stated objectives indicate what should be measured in postadvertising audits. Without objectives it may be quite difficult to determine whether advertising or sales departments fulfilled their "missions" (NICB, 1966). The diagram in 23-11 illustrates an overall promotional plan. A marketing objective in such a plan might be to gain a certain percentage of a market. The supporting advertising objective might be to describe a new product or to remind consumers to buy the product. Salesmen might be charged to do a certain amount of "missionary" sales work in order to familiarize customers with the product. The relationship between objectives is illustrated in 23-12.

If a marketing plan calls for the development of a *primary* market, the persuasion plan must be developed accordingly. A few years ago, when new concepts of office copying equipment were developed, office

**23-11** The Marketing Plan: Overall Marketing Objectives and Marketing Function Objectives

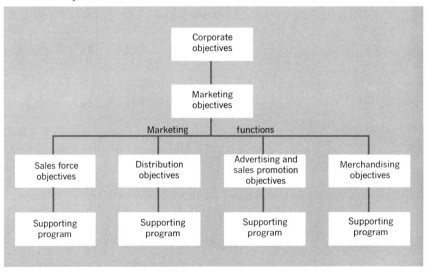

SOURCE: National Industrial Conference Board, "Setting Advertising Objectives," *Studies in Business Policy*, No. 118 (1966), p. 8.

## 23-12 Relationship between Objectives

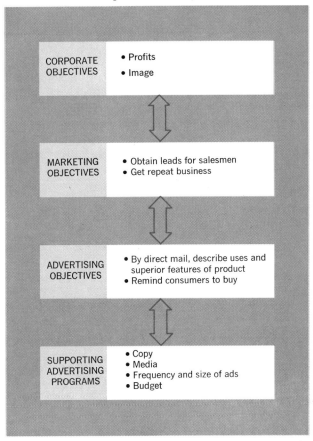

| CORPORATE OBJECTIVES | • Profits<br>• Image |
| SUPPORTING | |

SOURCE: National Industrial Conference Board, "Setting Advertising Objectives," *Studies in Business Policy,* No. 118 (1966), p. 9.

managers had to be persuaded that the concept was a good one—this activity was the development of a primary market. In the beginning competitors in effect worked toward a common goal because they knew that the job was not to sell Thermofax or Xerox but to sell dry-copying equipment. Similarly, steel companies joined together in association advertising promoting the use of stainless steel; only later did United States Steel become concerned about developing a *selective* demand for its particular stainless steel. The aluminum companies worked together in persuading people to use more aluminum for siding for homes; after the idea caught on Alcoa, Reynolds, and others changed their promotion goals to selective selling. Weyerhauser may work with other lumber companies through association or industry-wide advertising in promoting plywood; but it also does selective selling for Weyerhauser's Foursquare product.

The primary-demand campaign is aimed at information more than competition and the objective is to persuade a consumer to try the new product. Once the market has been developed, however, it becomes necessary to create and maintain brand shares. This is the phase of promotion where most of society's criticism is directed, because the advertising focuses on brand switching and loyalty, and small differences in products often are puffed up out of proportion. Failure to recognize the importance of the difference between primary and selective demand can lead to difficulties. Advertising for coffee, for example, has been largely aimed at maximizing brand shares. Yet young people are drinking soft drinks among other things, and it would appear that even a field as mature as the coffee market needs a greater effort directed to younger consumers—in short, advertising to develop a primary market (Leezenbaum, 1970).

*Derived* demand signals a particular kind of promotion program. A manufacturer of batteries, for instance, depends on new car sales, as does a manufacturer of tires. In both these cases there is, in addition to the new car market, a replacement market that has different demand characteristics. Steel also has a derived demand because steel sales depend on automotive, refrigerator, industrial construction, and other sales.

## Research and Evaluation

A marketer can draw on several sources of information to develop an effective persuasion program: his own company's records, secondary data such as government sources and association publications, and marketing research reports especially prepared for the marketing problem. An early example of the role of research in developing a promotion program was that of H. G. Weaver, who almost half a century ago found that 25 percent of General Motors' sales could be directly credited to dealer efforts. This research finding formed the basis of the firm's distribution program (Chandler, 1964).

Research serves many functions. Markets and people are surveyed before, during, and after marketing development efforts; copy themes and spot commercials are pretested; test markets are utilized; coincidental telephone surveys are made during television and radio programs; readership studies are performed; and consumer panels are used to test marketing programs as well as products. Indeed, it has become almost standard procedure for even the sales effort to be critically examined.

Research sharpens the persuasion tools. Identification of the market prior to the development program enables a company to pinpoint its efforts. When it is known, for instance, that a gelatin dessert is purchased because it is quick and easy to prepare, advertising copy stresses this feature. Offering complicated recipes would be wasteful and even dampen buyers' interests.

Inspired by research, bolstered by theories of persuasion, and aided by accumulated experience, the marketer develops his promotion plan synchronized with the rest of the firm's marketing effort. The General

Motors experience, rather oversimplified in the following statement, illustrates this point.

> Establish a complete line of motor cars from the lowest to the highest price that would justify production. Develop the best value in each price class which large volume, effective manufacturing methods, aggressive engineering and efficient means of distribution, all supported by large resources, make possible. (Chandler, 1964.)

# CONCLUDING COMMENTS

Clearly, promotion serves many needs. AT&T may advertise so as to maintain an image of a service company that is owned by many ordinary people. IBM may depend on informed salesmen to introduce a new type of computer. An automotive wholesaler may take along a missionary paint-spray salesman to demonstrate a new piece of equipment. A bottling company salesman may install a menu board in a restaurant. A petroleum company may sponsor a contest in order to bolster sales. A drug firm may sample doctors so as to familiarize them with the new product. The tasks of communications are many but so are the tools or ingredients of the communications mix.

Sellers have used persuasion tactics for centuries and will likely continue to do so. Hopefully the sellers will carry out the communications function efficiently for the firm and in a useful manner for consumers and buyers.

# STATEMENTS TO CONSIDER

If the ballyhoo and confetti of the competitive advertising man's carnival dies away, there will come a time of comparative quiet. It is at such times that the higher instincts and emotions are likely to emerge, and business may direct itself into channels dictated by a better social philosophy than now holds way. (Vaile)

A significant difference exists between the ratio of ad outlays to sales of consumer goods and industrial goods industries. (Halbert)

No single exposure of a single-print advertisement or commercial is likely to change consumer attitudes immediately toward buying a product or service. Instead, consumer attitudes usually change gradually. (Britt)

Industry is going to require salesmanship for as long as production exceeds spontaneous and necessary demand. (Hobson)

People interested in a topic tend to follow it in the medium that gives it the fullest and most faithful treatment.

The use, and perhaps the effectiveness, of different media varies with the educational level of the audience—the higher the education, the greater the reliance on print; the lower the education, the greater the reliance on aural and picture media.

People tend to misperceive and misinterpret persuasive communications in accordance with their own predispositions, by evading the message or by distorting it in a favorable direction.

In cases where the audience approves of the communicator but disapproves of his conclusions, it tends to dissociate the source from the content.

The nature of the source is especially effective in the case of ambiguous or unstructured topics.

The more communications are directed to the group's opinion leaders rather than to rank-and-file members, the more effective they are likely to be. (The six statements above are from Berelson and Steiner, 1964.)

## QUESTIONS FOR REVIEW

**1.** There are many variables associated with the communications process. What kinds of variables are uncontrollable by the marketer? Controllable?

**2.** What could the selling profession do to improve its image? Why should this be necessary when salesmen perform many useful functions?

**3.** What changes have been made in sales management during the past decade?

**4.** A corporation executive once remarked: "All we need to do is to continue to improve existing products, introduce one or two new products annually, protect them with patents, produce them on a quality basis, and sell, sell, sell." (Herbert Buetow, 3M Co., *The New York Times,* January 11, 1972.) Comment on this statement.

**5.** What psychological elements are involved in advertising?

**6.** Is there anything wrong with the philosophy: make a good product and it will sell itself?

**7.** What trends in media allocation are evident for the period, 1960–1970?

**8.** Advertising should normally run at about 5.0 percent of sales. Comment on this statement.

**9.** Explain how consumer surveys can improve the efficiency of advertising and selling.

**10.** Advertising and personal selling costs should be about equal. Comment.

## Further Readings

*Note:* See suggestions at the end of Chapter 22.

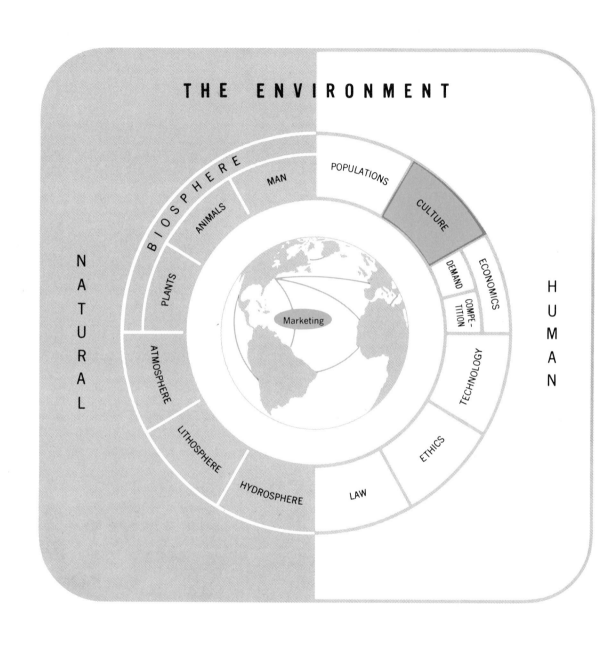

THE ENVIRONMENT

NATURAL

HUMAN

BIOSPHERE

MAN
ANIMALS
PLANTS
ATMOSPHERE
LITHOSPHERE
HYDROSPHERE

POPULATIONS
CULTURE
DEMAND
ECONOMICS
COMPE-
TITION
TECHNOLOGY
ETHICS
LAW

Marketing

# CHAPTER 24
# INTERNATIONAL MARKETING

*International markets offer the firm additional market opportunities to sell and profit. The organization for international marketing varies from the use of an agent to the world trading corporation. International marketing shows quite vividly the need to understand environmental conditions.*

In Chapter 4 on "Marketing in Different Environments" we emphasized the effect of environmental differences among countries on internal marketing. This chapter, although related to the earlier one, is concerned with the international marketing place.

International trade involves all the usual marketing functions, some in the country of origin and some in the importing nation. Arrangements are made for financing, shipping, advertising, insuring, selling, and packaging as a product makes its way from one marketing institution to another.

## REASONS FOR INTERNATIONAL TRADE

One nation has resources not possessed by others and this encourages trade among nations. The result of international trade should be the improvement of living standards around the world. For the individual firm, however, the principal reason for marketing in foreign countries is to expand sales and profits. As with domestic marketing, *money, specialization,* and the existence of *markets* are basic to the operation. Of course, all this oversimplifies the subject of international trade since governments may promote trade for imperialistic reasons, countries vary in their levels of development, and a certain amount of unrest complicates the marketing operation in the world today. Nevertheless, the international marketing transactions continue to be important to businesses, consumers, and governments. An example of one such transaction would be the user of a Caterpillar tractor in Liberia who needs a hydraulic press to remove the pin in a broken tread. The Rodgers Hydraulic Company of Minneapolis makes its profits by selling hydraulic presses to industrial customers around the world. Rodgers receives the order from an export agent in Chicago and ships the hydraulic press directly to the operator in Liberia. Thousands of such individual transactions make up the trade statistics in the complex international environment. Nations with state-controlled foreign trade have the same general incentives to trade as the capitalist nations, and they frequently handle their foreign trade through a state corporation.

## TYPES OF INTERNATIONAL MARKETING

Traditionally foreign trade has simply involved a *flow of goods and services* from one country to another. A company in the Philippines exports coconut-honey to a food distributor in this country. A Belgium firm sends umbrellas to Canada, a Japanese concern sells cars in various countries, and Italian film producers export their products internationally. In each case the product is processed by a local producer, exported to another nation, and handled there by the domestic marketing system.

Selected data for the United States are shown in 24-1. Some rather dramatic changes can be seen over the 35-year period, as in the increases in finished goods and decreases in industrial supplies (on a relative basis) for *both* exports and imports. Capital goods (excluding autos and military materials) accounted for most of the relative increase in the export of finished goods; and capital goods, autos, and consumer goods all showed relative increases in the finished-goods import category. In recent years Canada, Japan, the United Kingdom, and Western Germany have been our leading customers *and* our leading suppliers.

In a U.S. government study, a survey of 158 U.S. manufacturers indicated that sizeable future export increases were expected in machinery, transportation equipment, nonelectrical machinery, and chemicals. Somewhat slower growth rates were forecast for petroleum products; rubber and plastic products; stone, glass, clay, and concrete

**24-1** Value and Share of Principal End-Use Categories in U.S. Foreign Trade, Prewar and Postwar Periods

| | PREWAR PERIOD | | | | POSTWAR PERIOD | | | | | | | |
| | Average 1925–29 | | Average 1930–39 | | Average 1946–58 | | Average 1959–65 | | Average 1966–70 | | 1970 | |
| End-use category | Million $ | % of total | Million $ | % of total | Million $ | % of total | Million $ | % of total | Million $ | % of total | Million $ | % of total |
|---|---|---|---|---|---|---|---|---|---|---|---|---|
| **EXPORTS** | | | | | | | | | | | | |
| Total exports and reexports, including military grant-aid | 4,990 | 100.0 | 2,604 | 100.0 | 14,974 | 100.0 | 22,650 | 100.0 | 35,584 | 100.0 | 43,226 | 100.0 |
| Finished (final) products, including special category (military-type goods) | 1,238 | 24.8 | 764 | 29.3 | 6,520 | 43.5 | 10,319 | 45.6 | 18,203 | 51.2 | 22,132 | 51.2 |
| Industrial supplies and materials | 2,806 | 56.2 | 1,477 | 56.7 | 5,735 | 38.3 | 7,833 | 34.6 | 11,222 | 31.5 | 13,767 | 3.18 |
| Foods, feeds, and beverages | 825 | 16.5 | 304 | 11.7 | 2,334 | 15.6 | 3,907 | 17.2 | 5,163 | 14.5 | 5,826 | 13.5 |
| All other | 123 | 2.5 | 60 | 2.3 | 385 | 2.6 | 591 | 2.6 | 996 | 2.8 | 1,502 | 3.5 |
| **IMPORTS** | | | | | | | | | | | | |
| Total general imports | 4,267 | 100.0 | 2,142 | 100.0 | 9,864 | 100.0 | 17,064 | 100.0 | 32,348 | 100.0 | 39,963 | 100.0 |
| Finished (final) products | 474 | 11.1 | 222 | 10.4 | 1,060 | 10.7 | 3,812 | 22.3 | 12,420 | 38.4 | 17,288 | 43.3 |
| Industrial supplies and materials | 2,803 | 65.7 | 1,281 | 59.8 | 5,805 | 58.9 | 8,854 | 51.9 | 13,491 | 41.7 | 15,117 | 37.8 |
| Foods, feeds, and beverages | 945 | 22.1 | 590 | 27.5 | 2,740 | 27.8 | 3,607 | 21.1 | 5,150 | 15.9 | 6,158 | 15.4 |
| All other | 44 | 1.0 | 49 | 2.3 | 259 | 2.6 | 791 | 4.6 | 1,287 | 4.0 | 1,399 | 3.5 |

SOURCE: Adapted from Max Lechter, "OBE's End-Use Classification of Foreign Trade," *Survey of Current Business*, Vol. 51 (March 1971), p. 23.

products; and primary metals (U.S. Department of Commerce, 1969).

The major forces favoring U.S. exports are: (1) foreign market growth, (2) introduction of new products, (3) planned direct investment abroad, and (4) more vigorous promotion. Forces hindering U.S. exports are: (1) increased third-country competition, (2) limitations imposed on direct investments, (3) nationalism, (4) nontariff barriers, and (5) increasing costs. The early 1970s showed how fast the international scene can change, causing adjustments on the parts of firms in all sectors of the world. In 1971 the textile agreement worked out with Japan, the monetary crisis, import duties, Common Market negotiations, new trade agreements with the USSR, and the United Nations' admission of mainland China were important factors that registered their impacts on export opportunities.

The traditional kind of foreign trade has now become less important than the marketing by the *multinational* firm. A multinational private firm has investments in several foreign countries, actually holds and manages physical assets, does its own marketing, and arranges its own financing in various countries. In a common pattern of development such a firm starts out by exporting to foreign countries, later establishes sales organizations abroad, still later grants licenses for the use of its patents to foreign firms, and finally establishes its own manufacturing facilities, sets up a management structure from top to bottom, and owns corporate stock in each country involved. This kind of direct investment and management characterizes and defines the multinational firm (Jacoby, 1970).

As an illustration of how important this kind of operation can be, IBM reported sales of $7.2 billion in 1969, of which $2.5 billion were foreign sales. The latter are handled by IBM's World Trade Corporation, which operates in 108 nations, has 105,000 employees, 18 plants, 336 branch offices, 248 data centers, 7 development laboratories, and 8 regional and area headquarters. This is multinational marketing on a grand scale. Only a part of the $2.5 billion was accounted for by goods shipped from the U.S. firm to an importing company abroad. Most of it derived from goods produced and sold outside the United States.

For centuries international trade was controlled by what were essentially trading organizations. It was not until the early part of the twentieth century that the early multinational companies were formed—British Petroleum, Standard Oil, International Nickel, Anaconda Copper, Singer, Coca-Cola, and Woolworth. Multinational investments spread further after World War I and by 1940, 600 American firms had invested in Britain. The depression stifled further gains, but American companies led the world trend toward multinationalism after World War II, although there were other multinational firms based in foreign countries. Shell Oil, Nestlé, and Bayer are examples of foreign operations (Jacoby, 1970). Sales volume of the United States industry abroad now constitutes the third largest economy in the world out-ranked only by the domestic economies of the United States and the Soviet Union: in addition, foreign production of American firms has grown faster during the past decade than has domestic production.

There are a number of reasons for going the route of multinationalism. Starting in the early 1960s management began to undergo many changes so that today it plays a central role in developing a multinational corporation: ". . . management is not only a key resource, it is *the* key resource both in terms of people and systems" (Leighton, 1970). The task of handling a complex multinational firm in several countries is enormous and requires able people to do the job successfully. Another factor is the desire to overcome barriers such as tariffs and quotas: with a multinational firm a product becomes in essence a domestic product wherever it is produced. Further, with a multinational set up firms can adapt their products and their marketing programs to local needs. The rise of the Common Market encouraged a good deal of investment in European nations since companies anticipated larger markets as trade barriers were removed. Other reasons include political stability, desire to diversify geographically, competition, technology, and surplus funds.

A multinational firm has or can have fairly complete control over the production and distribution of its product, an achievement difficult under old-style international trade. The marketing advantages alone are attractive to the multinational firm: no tariffs or quotas, lower cost of transportation, lower inventory requirements and savings in warehousing, access to service markets, less sales resistance, and better efficiency of promotional efforts (Kolde, 1966).

The expansion of U.S. companies has encountered opposition, however. Many Europeans fear the power that direct investment gives the U.S. firms. Similar fears have been voiced in Latin America and in Canada. (In 1971 legislation was introduced in Canada that would provide a Tribunal with the power to veto or undo mergers in the case of foreign ownership.) Since certain multinational firms have sales that exceed the GNP of some small countries, we should not be surprised that fears are being expressed. If the trend toward the multinational firm continues, it is likely that international agreements will be reached concerning control. It is clear that many advantages can accrue to a foreign nation in which a multinational firm invests, but it is possible that exploitation can occur more easily under conditions of heavy foreign investment. For instance, a powerful firm might be able to gain tax benefits not available to a domestic firm, to wield too much influence on the economy, or to prevent nationals from creating their own industries.

As you read of developments in the international sector you should bear in mind that conventional import and export figures do not tell the entire story. The multinational firm has added a new dimension that complicates the simple foreign trade concept. Investments are made by the multinational firm and profits may be sent back to the parent company or they may be reinvested elsewhere. Regardless, the balance of trade statistics do not accurately mirror the world marketing situation as it exists today.

# THE ENVIRONMENT OF INTERNATIONAL MARKETING

An experienced foreign trader always warns a novice about the necessity for understanding the foreign environment. With our environmental approach, we second the warning. As the material on comparative marketing pointed out, differences in cultures, levels of living, philosophies, geography, and marketing institutions cause wide variations in the potential market for a product. Differences in personal manners, eating habits, sources of pride, ideas of status, negotiating tactics, and even color preferences are important to understand. One sign of a culturally aware person is his sensitivity to such differences.

When a company decides to examine trade possibilities or investment opportunities a number of variables have to be considered. When the decision involves foreign countries the importance of environmental considerations becomes especially clear. In 24-2 a list of investment variables is shown and an examination of this list reveals a variety of physical and social/political factors. In addition, a country's national interests have to be taken into account. It may have problems with its balance of payments, anxieties over its defense, or a need to develop several infant industries. It may want to favor its own manufacturers, may be wary of foreign nations, and may have strong international alliances.

The technological segment of the environment is important since international trade results in a transfer of technology. There are several methods by which this is accomplished: licensing agreements, know-how contracts, formal training of operators and users, patent exchanges, research and development contracts, and investments in foreign plants. The most common mode of transfer, however, is simply through the sale of products, the transfer being effected through observation and imitation. These methods may not appear to be marketing matters, but in fact they directly affect the marketing practices that evolve in each particular situation.

The legal and political environments also have profound effects on marketing practices, which must adjust to antitrust laws both here and abroad, patent legislation, tariffs, quotas, exchange restrictions, and nationalization laws. The political environment can be most favorable for the exporter or multinational firm if the host nation desires to attract the merchandise or company, but on the other hand the host nation can also impose all kinds of barriers if it so desires. The early years of this decade certainly provided evidence of the impact of political negotiations.

The amount and kind of competition in foreign markets varies with the situation. Competition can be intense since it can involve the host country's firms as well as firms from all over the world. Ford Motor not only competes with Volvo in Sweden but also with Volkswagen, Toyota, General Motors, and Fiat, for example. A list of computers in use in Germany (24-3) suggests the international flavor and competitive environment of that market.

## 24-2

**Variables To Consider in International Investments**

*Financial Considerations*

1. Capital acquisition plan
2. Length of payback period
3. Projected cash inflows (years one, two, and so forth)
4. Projected cash outflows (years one, two, and so forth)
5. Return on investment
6. Monetary exchange considerations

*Technical and Engineering Feasibility Considerations*

7. Raw materials availability (construction/support/supplies)
8. Raw materials availability (products)
9. Geography/climate
10. Site locations and access
11. Availability of local labor
12. Availability of local management
13. Economic infrastructure (roads, water, electricity, and so forth)
14. Facilities planning (preliminary or detailed)

*Marketing Considerations*

15. Market size
16. Market potential
17. Distribution costs
18. Competition
19. Time necessary to establish distribution/sales channels
20. Promotion costs
21. Social/cultural factors impacting upon products

*Economic and Legal Considerations*

22. Legal systems
23. Host government attitudes toward foreign investment
24. Host attitude toward this particular investment
25. Restrictions on ownership
26. Tax laws
27. Import/export restrictions
28. Capital flow restrictions
29. Land-title acquisitions
30. Inflation

*Political and Social Considerations*

31. Internal political stability
32. Relations with neighboring countries
33. Political social traditions
34. Communist influence
35. Religious/racial/language homogeneity
36. Labor organizations and attitudes
37. Skill/technical level of the labor force
38. Socioeconomic infrastructure to support American families

SOURCE: James R. Piper, Jr., "How U.S. Firms Evaluate Foreign Investment Opportunities," *MSU Business Topics*, Vol. 19 (Summer 1971), p. 14.

The U.S. Department of Commerce study referred to earlier forecast that, of 89 manufactured commodities, 55 percent will maintain or improve their competitive position by 1973, 35 percent which seem to be deteriorating can be restored, and 10 percent will likely worsen in their competitive position. Third-country competition, especially from Western European and Japanese firms, is a concern of a number of U.S. exporters; increased competition from domestic firms is apparently less feared. The international firm has to learn how to compete abroad and how to take advantage of any superiority it may have.

International marketing involves both the environments of the importing and exporting nations—both sovereign—*and* in addition the new environment that is created when two nations trade across national boundaries. The same is true with multinational corporations, although

**24-3** Computers in Use in Germany, July 1970

| Manufacturer | Number of installations | Manufacturer | Number of installations |
|---|---|---|---|
| AEG-Telefunken | 141 | Honeywell | 237 |
| BBC | 17 | IBM | 3,895 |
| Bull/GE | 616 | ICL | 20 |
| Burroughs | 21 | Litton | 14 |
| CDC | 61 | NCR | 97 |
| CII | 27 | Philips | 30 |
| Dietz | 24 | Raytheon (Dynatec) | 23 |
| Digital Equipment | 350 | RR-Univac | 589 |
| EAI | 10 | Saab | 1 |
| Elliott | 7 | SEL | 3 |
| Eurocomp | 92 | Siemens | 583 |
| Facit | 1 | Varian | 28 |
| Ferranti (GRA) | 13 | Zuse | 251 |
| General Automation | 23 | | |
| Hewlett-Packard | 79 | Total | 7,253 |

SOURCE: *German-American Trade News,* (February 1971), p. 5.

there is a real question about its allegiance that has not yet been answered. To whom does it owe its allegiance? The worldwide type of multinational firm "sees the planet as its province, and its ownership and control are widely diffused" (Boddewyn, 1970). So the environment for international marketing of any kind is even more complex than the domestic environment of one marketing organization. The following quotation sums up the environmental considerations.

As a company transcends a national setting, its environmental framework changes progressively in countless respects. New ground rules as defined by law, custom, and culture; new values, new contradictions, interactions, and balances among external forces; and new opportunities as well as uncertainties arise. The wider the company's international scope, the greater become the environmental diversities and multiversities surrounding it. To make rational choices among the alternatives available to it in different countries, the company must be able to identify, understand, and anticipate the negative and positive forces of the international diversity. (Kolde, 1966.)

## THE INTERNATIONAL MARKETING PROCESS

In international marketing the usual considerations of market size and potential, cost of distribution, channels of distribution, competition, and promotion must be integrated with the other usual considerations such as finance, engineering, and production, as well as with the social and cultural environment. Interviews with leading international executives by James R. Piper indicated that one of the important problems today is the inadequate treatment of economic, political, and social variables. The executives were not suggesting that all the variables could be programmed into a computer for easy manipulation, but they stressed the importance of getting a "kind of feel" about the variables. They also pointed out that official government analyses may reflect ideological bias, so that a marketer should do his own research work (Piper, 1971).

We have already noted that international trade takes place between two sovereign nations and that in this unique environment management has a complicated job. The job is characterized by the following considerations:

1. Transaction and transmission of resources across borders in exchange for other resources.
2. Innovative operation in different social systems. This requires knowledge and acceptance of foreign ways and means, as well as skills about introducing change abroad.
3. Synergism of the multinational corporation. Here the requirements are for "third-power" management, cutting across the three related organizational dimensions of product, function, and geography.
4. The international firm must reconcile its own interests with those of the host nation and of its home country. (Boddewyn, 1970.)

In its unique international environment the company must face up to questions of organization, marketing research, product, promotion, channels, and pricing, the topics to be discussed at this time.

## Organization

The international trading firm has a number of alternatives in organization. At one extreme it can set up nothing special and simply sell its merchandise through an export agent in this country, and at the other extreme management can set up an elaborate world company that is completely separate from the parent firm. In between these extremes are various combinations of agents in this country and in the importing nation, joint ventures with foreign companies, licensing arrangements, franchised distributors, branch-plant assembly operations, sales and service branches, and merchant wholesalers. These organizational arrangements are shown in 24-4, which depicts both middleman and foreign control. Two other organizations are shown in 24-5: a traditional export department and a world organization.

The organizational decision depends on the nature of the business, size of the firm, desires of management, and the probable importance of future export business. Since World War II there has been a tendency to decentralize foreign operations, to place more control in the host country, and to take more managerial personnel from the host country. Using management from the foreign country eliminates some criticism of the operation. The criticism is completely understandable, for some

## 24-4 International Business Arrangements

The vertical axis is labeled "Degree of foreign principal's control and participation" ranging from 0% to 100%. The horizontal axis is labeled "Degree of middleman control and participation" ranging from 0% to 100%. The business arrangements are positioned diagonally from top-left to bottom-right:

- Principal's wholly owned manufacturing subsidiary
- Branch-plant assembly operation
- Sales and service branch
- Franchised distributor
- Merchant wholesaler
- Joint venture
- Licensing arrangement
- Agent's wholly owned manufacturing operation

SOURCE: Adapted from Isaiah A. Litvak and Peter M. Banting, "A Conceptual Framework for International Business Arrangements," in American Marketing Association, *Marketing and the New Science of Planning* (1968), pp. 460–467.

U.S. firms used to hire all American management and hired host nation personnel for laboring jobs. The use of local management also enables the exporting firm to understand the needs of the local population.

The multinational firm, of course, operates as a complete unit in the foreign country, whether decentralized or highly centralized in structure. It is a separate organization complete with manufacturing and marketing facilities and thus is the most highly integrated kind of foreign marketing. With most multinational firms there exist various central controls, but in the ultimate world corporation the operation would be completely decentralized.

## Product

Executives must recognize several basic realities in selling products in international markets. Product design obviously demands adaptation

**24-5** A Traditional Export Department (top) and a World Organization (bottom)

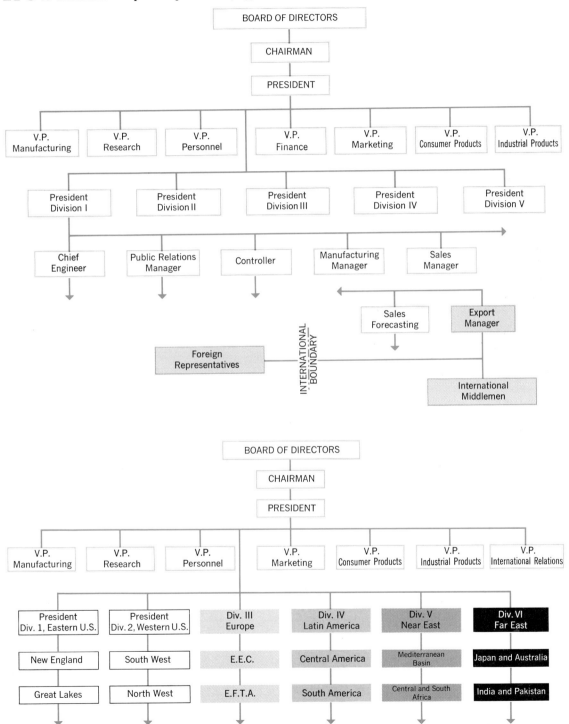

SOURCE: Endel J. Kolde, "Business Enterprise in a Global Context," *California Management Review*, Vol. 8 (Summer 1966), pp. 38, 40.

to foreign markets. Automobile speedometers have to be changed to kilometers, steering wheels moved to the right side, and headlights fitted with different bulbs. Dials on equipment have to be adjusted to the metric system. Power-driven units have to be replaced by hand-operated devices. The illustrations are many: the product must fit the needs of the foreign consumer. Richard D. Robinson has usefully summarized this sensitivity, as he identified the environmental factors to consider in designing an exportable product (24-6).

Second, management must recognize that the products may not yield the same kind of economic and social benefits that accrue to buyers in this country. A product may be successful here because of labor-saving attributes that are entirely irrelevant abroad. Third, both buyer and seller must reckon with the political implications of their products. A simple cola drink may be excluded from some countries because of the shortage of foreign exchange for a "luxury" item.

Of course, many items are successfully marketed abroad. The elec-

## 24-6

**Environmental Factors Considered in the Design of an Exportable Product**

| | |
|---|---|
| Level of technical skills | → Product simplification |
| Level of labor cost | → Automation or manualization of product |
| Level of literacy | → Re-marking and simplification of product |
| Level of income | → Quality and price change |
| Level of interest rates | → Quality and price change (Investment in high quality might not be financially desirable.) |
| Level of maintenance | → Change in tolerances |
| Climatic differences | → Product adaptation |
| Isolation (heavy repair difficult and expensive) | → Product simplification and reliability improvement |
| Differences in standards | → Recalibration of product and resizing |
| Availability of other products | → Greater or lesser product integration |
| Availability of materials | → Change in product structure and fuel |
| Power availability | → Resizing of product |
| Special conditions | → Product redesign or invention |

SOURCE: Richard D. Robinson, "The Challenge of the Underdeveloped National Market," *Journal of Marketing,* Vol. 25 (October 1961), p. 22.

tronic calculator provides an interesting example, since it has been imported from Japan and the product has been widely accepted. Marchant has even run advertisements (*Wall Street Journal*, November 23, 1971) explaining that of seven electronic calculator leaders, three import all their machines from Japan, three import several models, and only Marchant does all its calculator manufacturing entirely in the United States.

| Brand Name | Manufacturer |
|---|---|
| Burroughs | Sharp, Japan |
| Dictaphone | Sanyo, Japan |
| Friden | Hitachi, Japan |
| Monroe | Canon, Japan |
| NCR | Nippon, Japan |
| Remington | Casio, Japan |
| Marchant | Marchant, U.S.A. |

## Communications

Language presents a special problem in international marketing. In addition to the obvious spoken and written language problems, there are those of the "silent language" about which Edward Hall has written:

Language of Time—Decisions are made in accordance with very different time scales in foreign countries.

Language of Space—Different nationalities have different customs concerning the distance people maintain between themselves when carrying on a conversation.

Language of Things—There are different values: money versus friendship versus tasteful arrangements versus dependability.

Language of Friendship—It takes different amounts of time to develop friends in various countries.

Language of Agreements—Rules and customs vary a great deal. (Hall, 1960.)

Advertising is used in nearly all countries, though to different degrees and in different ways (see 24-7). Even in state-controlled nations such as the USSR there are means of advertising foreign products. Successful advertising campaigns in Yugoslavia, for instance, have changed consumer habits. In one case, consumers were successfully encouraged to purchase canned soup instead of preparing soup in the home as had been done for many years. In another instance, industrial firms were persuaded to substitute paperboard packing for wooden packing cases (Skobe, 1965).

An exporting firm may use its domestic advertising agency abroad if there is a branch or it may use a local agency operating within the importing nation. In 1970, of the world's ten largest agencies, only one—Dentsu of Japan—was located outside the United States; Hakuhodo (Japan) ranked 19th. The choice of agency is important, of course,

## 24-7 Distribution of Total National Advertising Expenditures by Medium*

| Medium | Belgium | Brazil | France | Israel | Japan | Lebanon | Peru | Turkey | United Kingdom | United States |
|---|---|---|---|---|---|---|---|---|---|---|
| Newspapers | 27.1 | 32.5 | 22.4 | 49 | 38.7 | 28 | 31.5 | 30.0 | 31.2 | 29.8 |
| Magazines | 14.5 | 11.6 | 28.1 | 6 | 6.0 | 22 | 3 | 7.4 | 17.4 | 12.9 |
| Outdoor and transportation | 10.6 | 8.1 | 8.1 | 8 | 8.6 | 10 | 5 | 21.1 | 6.8 | 1.4 |
| Cinema | 3.1 | Neg. | 7.1 | 5 | 1.8 | 9 | 4 | 2.7 | 1.1 | Neg. |
| Radio | 2.2 | 14.0 | } 9.1 | 4.7 | 7.3 | None | 18 | 4.8 | Neg. | 5.7 |
| Television | 0.3 | 9.3 | | None | 28.9 | 18 | 27.5 | None | 18.2 | 15.0 |
| Direct | 17.4 | 21.0 | } 12.5 | 10 | 4.7 | 4 | 2 | 23.1 | 9.1 | 15.6 |
| Exhibitions, etc. | 7.7 | NA | | 10 | } 2.1 | 3 | NA | NA | 3.8 | "Misc." |
| Display and point of sale | 7.7 | NA | 11.5 | NA | | 2 | 2 | 4.1 | 7.1 | "Misc." |
| Promotional schemes | "Misc." | 2.9 | NA | 3 | NA | NA | 5 | NA | 3.5 | "Misc." |
| Reference publications | NA | NA | NA | NA | NA | "Misc." | NA | NA | "Misc." | "Misc." |
| Miscellaneous | 9.4 | 0.6 | 1.2 | 4.3 | 1.9 | 4 | 2 | 6.8 | 1.8 | 19.6 |
| Total | 100 | 100 | 100 | 100 | 100 | 100 | 100 | 100 | 100 | 100 |

*Figures in percentages. NA = not available. Neg. = negligible. "Misc." = included in "Miscellaneous."

SOURCE: John Fayerweather, *International Marketing* (Englewood Cliffs, N.J.: Prentice-Hall, 1965), p. 108. © 1965.

because of the need to make advertising compatible with the culture of the country involved. Hakuhodo has advertised in the United States in an effort to convince U.S. companies to use its facilities: part of one advertisement stated the following:

> . . . Japanese consumers don't have the same pattern of responses as American consumers. The Japanese *do* want American products. But Japan very definitely remains Japan. A separate and a different culture.
>
> Fortunately there exists a bridge. The Japanese advertising agency.
>
> Japan has had advertising agencies almost as long as the U.S. One of the oldest—and one of the biggest—is Hakuhodo.
>
> Hakuhodo has watched Japan's market change. And helped it to grow.
>
> With its total marketing services, Hakuhodo can help you build a share of the amazing new mass market called Japan. ARE YOU SELLING? (Hakuhodo Incorporated, 1971.)

The entire promotional program in an international marketing context is similar to the domestic task. One has to select the media and the message, and to determine how much and where to spend the promotional budget. If advertising can be standardized—that is, transferred from the domestic to the foreign market—both money and time can be saved. See 24-8 for criteria that can be used in appraising the transferability of advertising. In one study at least 90 percent of the reporting firms attempted to make some use of standardized campaigns. (The "tiger in the tank" theme of one oil company in the 1960s was usable in most nations of the world.) But only 17 percent estimated that they used standardized advertising as much as one-half the time. Only 16 percent simply translate copy into the appropriate language and make no other changes. Most rewrite at least some of their copy (Ryans and Donnelly, 1969).

## Pricing

Pricing, never an easy task, is even more difficult in international markets than in domestic markets. It is complicated by special relationships, shipping risks, government regulations, and the seller's unfamiliarity with the foreign environment. The decision is dependent on the same factors in both settings, but local customs such as haggling may be the customary mode of exchange. How do you set a price to accommodate that custom? Or there may be state-controlled prices or regional price differences to contend with. Some exporters dump products at low prices into a foreign market, thus creating special problems. For instance, the Japanese people were outraged in 1970 to learn that Sony color TV sold for less in the U.S. than in Japan.

## Channels

The channels of international marketing differ only in particulars from those in domestic marketing. The principles are the same. The channels may be short, as when a large company in the United States

---

## 24-8

**Criteria Used in Appraising the Transferability of U.S. Advertisements**

Market Criteria
  Competition
  Distribution system

Cultural Criteria
  Psychological barriers to acceptance of the product
  Friendliness of people toward U.S.
  Extent to which people accept advertising
  Importance of religion
  Acceptance of authority
  Class consciousness
  Level of sophistication

Media Criterion
  Availability of the same media used in the U.S.

SOURCE: Modified from S. Watson Dunn, "The Case Study Approach in Cross-Cultural Research," *Journal of Marketing Research*, Vol. III (February 1966), p. 29.

supplies its branches abroad. They may be long and involved, as when a seller in this country ships through an intermediary to yet another intermediary in the importing nation. If it is a multinational operation, the proper domestic channels are used in the same way that a local manufacturer would distribute his products.

Insofar as possible, channels are closely tied to a company's organization. An exporter can sell directly to the buyer abroad or he may turn over his exporting to a middleman who specializes in foreign marketing. An importer may buy through import houses or may buy directly. Many American department stores, for instance, send their buyers abroad to place direct orders with foreign manufacturers. The channel alternatives vary from nation to nation and the decision will rest on the type of product, the size of the foreign business, and other factors not unlike domestic distribution decisions. As in domestic marketing, there have developed marketing institutions (wholesalers and retailers) to handle each kind of situation.

The intricacies of foreign trade permit some curious things to take place. For instance, the USSR is the world's second-largest watch manufacturer. But United States tariffs on Soviet watches are 70 percent higher than on watches from Switzerland and Japan since the USSR is not a "most-favored" nation. Even so, the USSR is selling its watches in the Virgin Islands and Guam where they are assembled into cases and thus become "American" watches. In Great Britain, through a similar transformation, Soviet watches become British watches (Carson and Wortzel, 1970).

Japan illustrates some of the differences in channels of distribution, since her channels have been characterized as being more diverse, complex, and longer than those in the United States. It has not been unusual in Japan for the use of three wholesale links. Wholesalers there include sales subsidiaries, service wholesalers, cash wholesalers, locals, along with special-product, primary, and secondary wholesalers. The Japanese have also used multiple wholesalers for the same product more than we do. The reasons for this pattern are that the population dwells in diverse kinds of places ranging from huge Tokyo to tiny rural villages. Also there existed no traditional wholesalers for the many new products that were introduced in the country after World War II.

The Japanese distribution system today is highly fragmented, with a large number of small establishments and a small number of large concerns at both the wholesale and retail levels. In recent years the large manufacturers have attained extensive control over their channels of distribution, and the power relationship between manufacturers and marketing institutions has changed accordingly. Whereas in the past the large wholesaler and trading firms dominated the marketing system, a more recent situation is for manufacturers to dominate a newly created vertically integrated distribution system (Elgass, 1961, and Yoshino, 1971).

## Marketing Research

The diversity of unfamiliar markets and a paucity of reliable statistical data complicate foreign marketing research. In some of the less-developed countries mail may be unreliable, respondents for surveys are quite inaccessible, telephones are uncommon, and there may be a number of dialects to contend with. In the more advanced countries, however, are marketing research agencies well staffed for gathering primary data. Some advanced research methods can be used in connection with selected marketing problems, but often the best that can be hoped for is informed estimates. See 24-9 for a study of movie preferences, which could be helpful to both an exporter and an importer. The data are old but they suggest the kind of research that can be accomplished. The range of the quality of marketing research is staggering, from almost nothing to the most sophisticated practices. Eastern European nations and the USSR have increased their marketing research efforts in the last decade; research in Far Eastern countries is spotty but improving, both in quality and in quantity; and research in Great Britain and Western European nations is quite good.

## Standardization of the Marketing Operation

Some companies have successfully standardized their marketing operations for all geographic areas, while other firms have failed in the international area because of not making some adjustment in their products or in their marketing programs to fit the local conditions.

**24-9** Audience Preference for Picture Types

|  | Country | 1st | 2nd | 3rd | 4th | 5th | 6th |
|---|---|---|---|---|---|---|---|
| LATIN AMERICA | Brazil | Musical | Drama | Action | Comedies | Slapstick | Mystery |
| | Chile | Musical | Action | Drama | Slapstick | Mystery | Comedies |
| | Colombia | Musical | Drama | Action | Mystery | Comedies | Slapstick |
| | Cuba | Musical | Drama | Action | Mystery | Comedies | Slapstick |
| | Mexico | Action | Drama | Musical | Mystery | Comedies | Slapstick |
| | Panama | Musical | Action | Drama | Comedies | Mystery | Slapstick |
| | Peru | Musical | Drama | Action | Mystery | Comedies | Slapstick |
| | Puerto Rico | Musical | Drama | Action | Mystery | Comedies | Slapstick |
| | Venezuela | Musical | Action | Drama | Mystery | Comedies | Slapstick |
| NEAR EAST | Egypt | Action | Musical | Mystery | Slapstick | Comedies | Drama |
| | Iraq | Action | Musical | Drama | Mystery | Slapstick | Comedies |
| | Lebanon | Action | Musical | Drama | Mystery | Slapstick | Comedies |
| FAR EAST | Hong Kong | Musical | Action | Slapstick | Drama | Mystery | Comedies |
| | India | Musical | Action | Slapstick | Drama | Mystery | Comedies |
| | Indonesia | Action | Musical | Slapstick | Drama | Mystery | Comedies |
| | Japan | Action | Musical | Drama | Slapstick | Mystery | Comedies |
| | Malaya | Musical | Action | Slapstick | Drama | Comedies | Mystery |
| | Philippines | Action | Musical | Drama | Mystery | Slapstick | Comedies |
| | Thailand | Musical | Action | Slapstick | Drama | Comedies | Mystery |

SOURCE: Ronald Carroll, "Selecting Motion Pictures for the Foreign Market," *Journal of Marketing*, Vol. 17 (October 1952), p. 167.

Soft-drink bottlers, notably Pepsi Cola and Coca-Cola, have been able to standardize their products, bottles, trucks, and even much of the advertising. There are many advantages in being able to conduct a company's operations abroad in the same manner as domestic operations are handled. Cost savings, particularly with the manufacture of the product, are obviously desirable. A standardized product becomes better known than nonstandard products. Standardized advertising may lead to some synergistic advantages in the same way.

Not every company can standardize, and actually most do not sell a completely uniform product or use a uniform marketing program. A number of the obstacles to standardization are summarized in 24-10. Some of the obstacles are rather superficial but others are deep-seated. Stage of industrial development, for one instance, can profoundly influence many aspects of a marketing program. The public goals of a developing nation, for another, must be balanced against a seller's desire for profits. The point is basically the same one we have been making throughout this text—a firm must first understand its customers *and* their environment and then create a marketing program that reflects the peculiarities of the local situation. Both a small manufacturer who operates indirectly through foreign-trade intermediaries and a large multinational firm with local production facilities in several nations face the decision of whether to standardize or modify in order to succeed in its foreign operations.

The same marketing functions, as we have said, are carried out in international as in domestic marketing, but often with different emphasis because of the environmental conditions. The specimen export transaction work sheet (24-11) illustrates some of the detail involved in an export to Brazil. Pricing, transportation (domestic and foreign), handling, insurance, and other needs have to be taken care of by the exporter and/or importer. There are financial worries that are greater than in the domestic shipment, but the proper kind of credit document (letter of credit) overcomes most of these obstacles.

## CONCLUDING COMMENTS

Marketing in any form to other nations is both a challenge and an opportunity to a firm. Profits can certainly be made in the additional markets. But management must realize that it is dealing with different environments from those in the domestic market and that it may have to adapt its marketing program in a number of ways. Some of the program may be standardized—that is, similar to the regular domestic program—but part of it may be modified to fit the particular environment into which it is being carried. The following list of rules and warnings suggests some of the concerns of the international marketer (Nielsen, 1959).

## 24-10 Obstacles to Standardization in International Marketing Strategies

| Factors limiting standardization | ELEMENTS OF MARKETING PROGRAM | | | | |
|---|---|---|---|---|---|
| | Product design | Pricing | Distribution | Sales force | Advertising and promotion, branding and packaging |
| **Market characteristics** Physical environment | Climate Product use conditions | | Customer mobility | Dispersion of customers | Access to media Climate |
| Stage of economic and industrial development | Income levels Labor costs in relation to capital costs | Income levels | Consumer shopping patterns | Wage levels, availability of manpower | Needs for convenience rather than economy Purchase quantities |
| Cultural factors | "Custom and tradition" Attitudes toward foreign goods | Attitudes toward bargaining | Consumer shopping patterns | Attitudes toward selling | Language, literacy Symbolism |
| **Industry conditions** Stage of product life cycle in each market | Extent of product differentiation | Elasticity of demand | Availability of outlets Desirability of private brands | Need for missionary sales effort | Awareness, experience with products |
| Competition | Quality levels | Local costs Prices of substitutes | Competitors' control of outlets | Competitors' sales forces | Competitive expenditures, messages |
| **Marketing institutions** Distributive system | Availability of outlets | Prevailing margins | Number and variety of outlets available Ability to "force" distribution | Number, size, dispersion of outlets | Extent of self-service |
| Advertising media and agencies | | | | Effectiveness of advertising, need for substitutes | Media availability, costs, overlaps |
| **Legal restrictions** | Product standards Patent laws Tariffs and taxes | Tariffs and taxes Antitrust laws Resale price maintenance | Restrictions on product lines Resale price maintenance | General employment restrictions Specific restrictions on selling | Specific restrictions on messages, costs Trademark laws |

*SOURCE:* Robert D. Buzzell, "Can You Standardize Multinational Marketing?" *Harvard Business Review,* Vol. 46 (November–December 1968), pp. 108–109.

## 24-11 A Specimen Export Transaction

DATE _September 16, 19—_

QUOTATION ☐        OFFER ☒        SALE ☐

BASIS (check) FAS VESSEL

         C&F _____

         CIF _X Santos_____

MATERIAL _Portland Cement_____

CONSIGNEE _Brazil Imports of São Paulo_____

PORT _____Santos_____

QUANTITY _10,000 bags_____

| | | |
|---|---|---|
| BASE PRICE _$.76_ | per _bag_ | $7,600.00 |

SHIPPING BASE      PACKED IN _6-ply paper_

(check)

     Ex Factory          MEAS. _____

     FOB Cars           GROSS _95#_____

     FAS Vessel _New York___    TARE _1#_____

                         NET _94#_____

                         _Profit Markup_

                         _(5¢ per bag)_      500.00

| | | | |
|---|---|---|---|
| INLAND FREIGHT _____ lbs. | @ _____ | | |
| CARTAGE _____ lbs. | @ _____ | | |
| HANDLING _____ | @ _____ | | |
| OCEAN FREIGHT _950,000#_ | @ _$18.00/2,240 #_ | 7,633.93 | |
| SURCHARGE _____ | @ _25%_ | 1,908.48 | |
| _____ | @ _+10¢/2,240#tax_ | | |
| PORT & HANDLING CHARGE ___ | _+$6.00 per B/L_ | 48.41 | |
| HEAVY LIFT CHARGE _____ | @ _____ | | |
| MARINE INSURANCE _$19,790_ | @ _$1.30%_ | 257.27 | |
| (Coverage _A/R—2% shortage_) | | | |
| CONSUL FEES _____ | | 42.00 | |
| MISCELLANEOUS _____ | | | |
| | TOTAL | $17,990.09 | |

TOTAL UNIT PRICE _$1.80_ PER _bag_

SOURCE: Philip McDonald, _Practical Exporting_ (New York: Ronald Press, 1949), p. 287.

1. Adapt the product to the market.
2. Gauge the impact of custom and tradition.
3. Exploit markets in proper sequence.
4. Remain politically tolerant.
5. Build a strong local management.
6. Beware of language barriers.
7. Study differences in advertising.
8. Identify the company with the local scene.
9. Know the trade channels.
10. Understand the consumer's views of price and quality.
11. Appraise the degree of acceptance of free enterprise.
12. Explore government regulations.
13. Insulate against restrictive legislation.
14. Invest for the long pull.
15. Interchange information between the home office and the foreign office.

The marketing effort will probably be inadequate without a thorough examination of the foreign market scene. Relying on myths and preconceptions can be misleading. American managers in Japan, for instance, are often misled by the mistaken notion that knowledge of management flows only one-way, from the United States to Japan (Tsurumi, 1971). During 1972, Japanese business interests sent a mission to the United States to teach American businessmen how to improve their marketing in Japan. The Japanese of course recognized that unless the U.S. trade balance with Japan improved, the U.S. might place import quotas on Japanese goods. Marketing executives have a great deal to learn from the foreign scene, and those who tailor their marketing programs to the local environments are likely to be the ones who succeed.

## STATEMENTS TO CONSIDER

The theory of comparative advantage is perhaps the most useful concept for a company to utilize.

Channels of distribution are quite different in advanced nations from those in less-developed countries.

Only one country appears today to have the potential to challenge U.S. exports seriously; that country is the U.S.S.R. It has the population, is achieving the income, and is developing the basic technology. All that has been missing is an understanding of and access to Western markets, and it is developing these. (Carson and Wortzel)

The more advanced a nation's domestic marketing system is, the more apt it is to engage in foreign trade.

Students today have a better picture of the world situation than do their professors.

A campaign for advertising which works in the U.S. will probably work in Europe.

Marketing policies employed in advanced nations cannot be expected to work in less-developed countries.

Exporters should be more aware of market segmentation than domestic producers and sellers.

U.S. antitrust laws were written for another era and consequently should be overhauled for this day of the multinational firm.

Knowledge flows from nation to nation are more important today than money flows. (Quinn)

## QUESTIONS FOR REVIEW

**1.** What are the characteristics of a multinational corporation?

**2.** Why do companies enter the field of foreign marketing?

**3.** How are multinational operations reflected in the balance-of-trade statistics?

**4.** What kinds of factors will determine the U.S. trade picture during the next ten years?

**5.** What kinds of responsibilities do exporting firms have insofar as the importing nation is concerned?

**6.** Which is more important for foreign trade—environment or management know-how? Comment.

**7.** Discuss the different kinds of competition the foreign trader encounters.

**8.** Which kind of export organization for a large corporation do you favor? Why?

**9.** In what ways might an exporter have to adapt a power lawn mower, for example, for the importing nations?

**10.** What do you think about transferring U.S. advertisements to other nations?

## Further Readings

David Carson, *International Marketing: A Comparative Systems Approach* (New York: John Wiley, 1967).

John Fayerweather, *International Marketing* (Englewood Cliffs, N.J.: Prentice-Hall, 1965).

John M. Hess and Philip R. Cateora, *International Marketing* (Homewood, Ill.: Richard D. Irwin, 1966).

John K. Ryans and James C. Baker (eds.), *World Marketing: A Multinational Approach* (New York: John Wiley, 1967).

U.S. Department of Commerce, *U.S. Foreign Trade: A Five-Year Outlook* (Washington, D.C.: GPO, 1969).

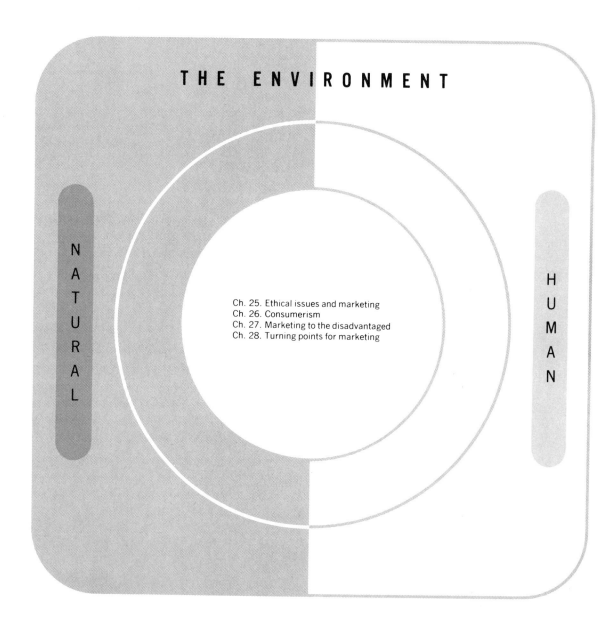

THE ENVIRONMENT

NATURAL

HUMAN

Ch. 25. Ethical issues and marketing
Ch. 26. Consumerism
Ch. 27. Marketing to the disadvantaged
Ch. 28. Turning points for marketing

# PART IV

# SOCIAL ISSUES IN A MARKETING ENVIRONMENT

*Since business, including marketing, has the privilege of operating within the social environment, it seems obvious that marketers should examine the social issues most closely related to their activities. All social concerns need to be identified and dealt with as best as possible.*

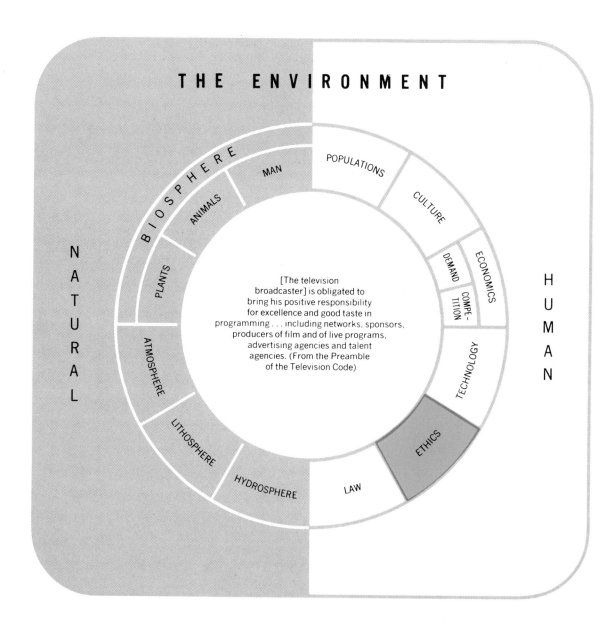

THE ENVIRONMENT

NATURAL

HUMAN

BIOSPHERE

MAN

ANIMALS

PLANTS

ATMOSPHERE

LITHOSPHERE

HYDROSPHERE

POPULATIONS

CULTURE

DEMAND

ECONOMICS

COMPE-
TITION

TECHNOLOGY

ETHICS

LAW

[The television broadcaster] is obligated to bring his positive responsibility for excellence and good taste in programming . . . including networks, sponsors, producers of film and of live programs, advertising agencies and talent agencies. (From the Preamble of the Television Code)

# CHAPTER 25
# ETHICAL ISSUES AND MARKETING

*Marketers are expected to be responsible executives—responsible to whom? They are expected to operate ethically—what does this mean? They should be aware of the areas where questionable practices are not uncommon and they should knowingly evolve their own conduct standards.*

Ethical behavior in marketing is an old problem, but since the early 1960s the ethical and moral responsibilities of businessmen have become a matter of serious social concern. Hardly a corporation, trade association, or professional society has avoided considering the subject or exploring it in some detail. Academicians from several disciplines—philosophers, sociologists, economists, and, not the least, marketers—have paid considerable attention to business ethics. The impetus for this attention comes, to a large extent, from two opposing efforts operating almost simultaneously. One is the search for a moral philosophy by those engaged in business endeavor, and the other is the age-old attacks on business as renewed by critics who have been examining the practices, policies, and judgments of the business community. But new criticism has come to the fore: "In days gone by the businessman was said to oppress people and profit by their poverty; now, with the dramatic rise in the standard of living, the businessman contributes to the sins of affluence" (Robinson, 1963).

The marketplace in many respects is a scene of honesty and integrity. Millions of transactions are consummated daily in an atmosphere of mutual trust. Credit is granted, checks are accepted, assurances accepted, and promises made. As Kenneth Boulding has observed, "An exchange system cannot flourish in the absence of a minimum of simple honesty because an exchange system is an exchange of promises, and honesty is the fulfillment of promises" (Boulding, 1969). On the other hand, the marketplace has its share of swindlers, crooks, and operators who dodge social responsibility.

The marketplace contains examples of marketing from the most ethical to the most unethical. Peter Drucker offers a positive picture of marketing: ". . . in an economy that is striving to break the age-old bondage of man to misery, want, and destitution, marketing is also the catalyst for the transmutation of latent resources into actual resources, of desires into accomplishments, and the development of responsible economic leaders and informed economic citizens" (Drucker, 1958). Richard Farmer, on the other hand, has pointed out that because marketing is both unethical and irrelevant, "If that nice young man who has dates with your daughter turns out to be a marketing major . . . I would chase him off the premises fast. Who wants his daughter to marry a huckster?" (Farmer, 1967).

The authors believe that marketing, like all of business and even nonbusiness institutions, must confront squarely the matter of ethical conduct. More explicit standards will be required in the years ahead. More rigorous enforcement of the standards will also be needed. The purpose of this chapter is to provide an airing of the issues in order that we all can better determine what ethical conduct means.

# ISSUES IN ETHICS

Ethics basically refers to a systematic study of moral choices. In our context, it refers to what is right and good in the moral choices marketing managers make. It is related to, and distinguished from, law and morals. Commonly morals refer to definite, specific rules of conduct, ethics to general principles. Law refers to a set of rules passed by a government, restraining and enabling legislation as interpreted by courts and regulatory agencies. What is legal may not be ethical, although some businessmen have indicated that they thought this to be the case:

> So long as a businessman complies with the laws of the land and avoids telling malicious lies, he's ethical. If the law as written gives a man a wide-open chance to make a killing, he'd be a fool not to take advantage of it. If he doesn't, somebody else will. . . . If the law says he can do it, that's all the justification he needs. There's nothing unethical about that. It's just plain business sense. (Quoted in Albert Z. Carr, 1968.)

In relation to business practices, there are many aspects of ethics to consider, for a person makes his choice of behavior from among many personal value systems. (See 25-1 for some philosophical statements.) Also, a person has several roles: a marketer, a businessman, a father or mother, a husband or wife, and a member of society. His values are influenced by his culture and he in turn influences his own culture. He sees conflicts between his behavior and values and he cannot apply pure logic and reasoning to all his actions. Further, his actions always reflect environmental influences for he is not "an island, entire of itself."

A business system is organized primarily through the institution of exchange and the buyer-seller relationship is a critical one for considerations of ethical behavior. For marketing the problem is matching what is "right" according to general cultural standards with what is good business. As Robert Bartels has stated, ". . . ethical decision under private capitalism is a moral decision impelled by social sanction but modified by economic exigency" (Bartels, 1967). Actually making such decisions is no easy job. Albert Levi has neatly summarized the confusion that prevails:

> 1. Ethics is ethics and business is business. Profits are one thing and moral squeamishness is another. You have to make your choice.
> 2. I'm a businessman and I try to be ethical, but when others in my field cut corners morally, I don't see how I can stay in business if I don't follow suit.

## 25-1

**Thumbnail Ethics**

With which philosopher do you agree?

| Agree | Not sure | Disagree | The Statement | The Philosopher |
|---|---|---|---|---|
| _____ | _____ | _____ | Wise action is that which is directed toward the ideal situation. | Plato |
| _____ | _____ | _____ | Right actions avoid undesirable extremes. | Aristotle |
| _____ | _____ | _____ | Wise action increases pleasure and avoids pain. | Epicurus |
| _____ | _____ | _____ | Right action conforms to the common sentiments of mankind. | Hume |
| _____ | _____ | _____ | Right action conforms to a rule that you would be willing to make the universal law. | Kant |
| _____ | _____ | _____ | Wise action leads to the greatest possible happiness of the greatest number. | Bentham |
| _____ | _____ | _____ | Right action fits into the historical trend of the evolving nation. | Hegel |
| _____ | _____ | _____ | Right action conforms to laws or principles revealed by God or by nature. | Thomas Aquinas |
| _____ | _____ | _____ | Moral actions are grateful responses to God's love—even if we know that we do wrong. | Tillich |
| _____ | _____ | _____ | Intelligent action reduces the conflicts which impede social advance. | Dewey |

SOURCE: Philip W. Van Vlack, *Management Ethics Guide* (Brookings, S.D.: South Dakota State University, 1965), p. 92. Reprinted by permission of South Dakota State University.

3. Morality is terribly vague, it seems to me. The churches say one thing, the bosses of my company another, and I guess the government even something different. Who is right?

4. Business as a whole is ethical. Of course you'll always find a few cheaters and crooks, but they're built that way. They'd cheat at whatever they worked. (Levi, 1967.)

What is the relationship of marketing to our value structure? There is confusion on this point that reflects very real differences of opinion on serious issues. Some argue that marketing influences and even creates social values. If so, businessmen must take into account the kinds of social values that are created and those that are violated by marketing practices. Others, however, maintain that business is not the guardian of social values and that marketing plays little part in shaping them. Some marketing scholars, along with some businessmen, contend that American marketing activity merely reflects society's norms. The environmental approach to marketing stresses the interactions of all forces in society and thus the authors believe that marketing does indeed influence social values just as it is also influenced by them.

Another ethical issue concerns the people engaged in marketing. As J. M. Clark wrote many years ago, "The individual is so molded in body, mind, and character by his economic activities and relations, stimuli and disabilities, freedoms and servitudes, that industry can truly be said to make the men and women who work in it, no less truly than the commodities it turns out for the market" (Clark, 1926). The products of our system are not only goods and services but also the character of the people working in it. Unfortunately the marketing system provides opportunities for marketers to profit by the sacrifice of moral principles. What is the effect on the marketer who is guilty of making false or misleading statements to his customers in order to sell them a product or service? What is the responsibility of the businessman who corrupts the integrity of an employee by asking him to perpetuate falsehoods?

Marketing occurs under the watchful eye of the public. Directed to masses of people, it is openly judged, sometimes harshly, by numerous persons. Everyone on occasion finds something objectionable about a product or a marketing tactic, and complains, "There ought to be a law . . ." As noted in Chapter 7, legislation has frequently been a response to unscrupulous behavior that ignored fair competition or consumer welfare. In fact, legal restraint is a primary alternative to voluntary ethical behavior. If businesses, and especially marketers, value freedom as they so often protest, it behooves them to consider the ethical aspects of their operation.

# ETHICS PAST AND PRESENT

Whether marketers today are more concerned about consequences of their actions than were their counterparts in earlier days is difficult to prove. A look into the past does reveal unethical practices. In a 1340 *Manual for Confessors*, for example, a list of the evils of trade included:

1. Selling as dear as one may or buying as cheaply as one may.
2. Lying or foreswearing to sell wares.
3. False weights and measures.
4. Selling on time.

5. Failure to comply with sample.
6. Hiding the truth about latent defects.
7. Making a thing look better than it is. (Stone, 1963.)

As early as 1750 in the United States, John Woolman expressed misgivings about trade:

> . . . my trade increased every year, and the road to large business appeared open, but I felt a stop in my mind. . . . The increase in business became my burden; for though my natural inclination was toward merchandise, yet I believed truth required me to live more free from outward cumbers. . . . I lessened my outward business . . . told my customers of my intention that they might consider what shop to turn to; and in a while I wholly laid down merchandise. . . . Though trading in things useful is an honest employ, yet through the great number of superfluities which are bought and sold, and through the corruption of the times, they who apply to merchandise for a living have great need to be well experienced in that precept which the prophet Jeremiah laid down for his scribe; "Seekest thou great things for thyself? seek them not." (Whitney, 1950.)

The nineteenth century had its unscrupulous businessmen, Robber Barons, "Public be damned" attitudes, and notorious exploitation of workers and public. In our time we have had unsafe products, misleading advertising, "What is good for General Motors is good for the country" statements (admittedly overcriticized and taken out of context), and rigged sales contests. Because of public concern ethics are being applied to much of marketing—price fixing, price cutting, deceptive labeling, and advertising; noteworthy is the observation that "responsibility for ethics in marketing is attributed increasingly to individuals on the higher management levels" (Bartels, 1967).

Whether today's marketer is more or less ethical than his earlier counterpart may not be proven. J. Howard Westing suggests that there is little difference between marketers of today and yesterday and that the real point is that the *environment* is different today. Westing believes that we are not struggling as much with our material needs and therefore can afford to turn to matters of ethics—". . . when one is destitute he is less likely to indulge his ethical impulses than when he is comfortable or satiated" (Westing, 1967). Today the issues of a century ago may appear clear to us, though at the time there was undoubtedly confusion and uncertainty, just as there is today on a variety of marketing issues. Regardless of the period of time we can find both ethical and unethical operations and our task today is to make the marketing effort as ethical as possible.

## MARKETING VERSUS NONMARKETING ETHICS

How do marketing ethics compare with those in other fields such as medicine, law, and education? No precise comparison is possible, of course, since ethics is a matter of values not quantities. According to Westing:

> . . . at a given time, the level of ethics in all major occupational groups of a society is very nearly the same. With no social barriers and few economic barriers to the entry into various occupational fields it is unlikely that they would attract people of widely varying ethical standards. It seems more likely . . . that any differences which exist result, not from intrinsic differences in the moral standards of individuals or groups, but from the fact that the moral temptations and pressures may be greater in some fields than others. (Westing, 1967.)

One thing is possible to measure: public attitudes. Unfortunately, surveys indicate that marketers have poorer public images than those in most other professions. In a study by John Hess, clergymen, medical doctors, college professors, teachers, bankers, and military officers, in order, were felt to have higher ethics than businessmen; lawyers, civil service employees, newspapermen, and the general public rated about the same; and advertising men, labor union officials, and politicians ranked lower. Hess also compared a variety of businessmen, with the results shown in 25-2.

**25-2** Opinion Leaders' Views of the General Ethical Level in Business

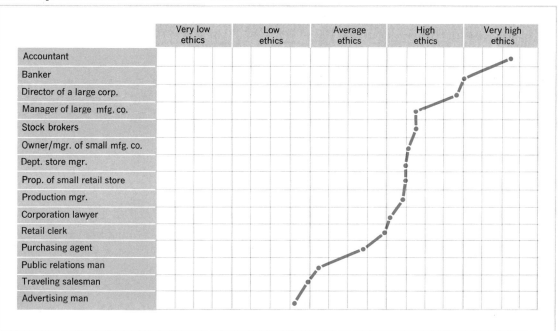

SOURCE: John Hess, "Public Policy as a Function of Perception of Business Ethics," *Economics and Business Bulletin*, Vol. 20 (Spring 1968), pp. 31-32.

The public image of professions changes over time. Recent studies also show that institutions generally have lost favor with the public. A Harris Survey in 1971 indicated changes in confidence for a variety of institutions, as shown in 25-3.

**25-3** Public Trust of Institutions*

| Institution | 1966 | 1971 |
|---|---|---|
| Major companies | 55 | 27 |
| Organized religion | 41 | 27 |
| Education | 61 | 37 |
| Executive branch, federal government | 41 | 23 |
| Organized labor | 22 | 14 |
| The press | 29 | 18 |
| Medicine | 72 | 61 |
| Television | 25 | 22 |
| Banks and financial institutions | 67 | 36 |
| Mental health and psychiatry | 51 | 35 |
| The U.S. Supreme Court | 51 | 23 |
| Scientific community | 56 | 32 |
| Congress | 42 | 19 |
| Advertising | 21 | 13 |
| Military | 62 | 27 |
| Local retail stores | 48 | 24 |

*Figures show percentage of Americans expressing a "great deal" of confidence in the institution.

SOURCE: "The Harris Survey," The Chicago Tribune, New York News Syndicate, Inc., October 25, 1971.

# CONTEMPORARY ATTACKS ON MARKETING

Any modern marketing system populated by thousands of manufacturers, wholesalers, and retailers and supplying millions of customers is certain to generate criticism. The attacks on marketing range from the kind of economic order it creates to specific charges against advertising, pricing, and product characteristics. The critics of the critics sometimes reply that the attacks lack logic, are highly emotional and hence unsound, or that the originator of the attack (that is, from a nonbusiness discipline), does not understand the complex ramifications of business life. Another common method of dealing with a critic is to contend that the ends justify the means. For example, many advertising men defend themselves on the grounds that they are promoting economic growth. Frequently the "delivering of the goods" theme is cited:

It's demonstrably evident that our system, vis-à-vis any other form of economy that mankind has ever known, has delivered the goods, and that the action today in our country, whether it is social or economic, is in business. . . . I believe very deeply and sincerely in the efficacy of the free enterprise system. (Rep. Jack Kemp, R–N.Y., 1971.)

Evidence that something is wrong and that some marketing is not conducted on a high ethical plane was gathered from business executives themselves in one study. The study, conducted at the Harvard Graduate School of Business Administration, included among other things a question concerning business practices that the respondents would like to see eliminated. In 25-4 which summarizes these practices, it is evident that items 1 through 7 involve marketing. The respondents felt that industry self-regulation would contribute to the elimination of such practices.

As already mentioned, marketing is exposed to the eyes of the public more than other business activities. The entire marketing system is in a sense under surveillance. Advertising is directed toward the consumer; packages are designed to catch the eye of buyers; personal selling is tête-à-tête; the price is frequently debated by buyer and seller at length; credit terms are spelled out; trucks and freight cars are highly visible; and the product and the institutions of marketing are clearly exposed. Several of these points will be discussed following a look at the economic system.

## Criticism of the Economic Order

Perhaps the best-known contemporary criticism of our economy's excesses is John Kenneth Galbraith's book, *The Affluent Society*. Galbraith sees a social imbalance in our system because the abundance of privately produced goods has caused a crisis in the supply of public services. In one of his more caustic passages he describes the consequences:

The family which takes its mauve and cerise, air-conditioned, power-steered, and power-braked automobile out for a tour passes

**25-4** The Business Practices Executives Would Like To See Eliminated

| Unethical practices executives want to eliminate | Percentage of total specifying the practice |
|---|---|
| 1. Gifts, gratuities, bribes, and "call girls" | 23 |
| 2. Price discrimination, unfair pricing | 18 |
| 3. Dishonest advertising | 14 |
| 4. Miscellaneous unfair competitive practices | 10 |
| 5. Cheating customers, unfair credit practices, overselling | 9 |
| 6. Price collusion by competitors | 8 |
| 7. Dishonesty in making or keeping a contract | 7 |
| 8. Unfairness to employees, prejudice in hiring | 6 |
| 9. Other | 5 |
| | 100   $n = 1531$ |

SOURCE: Raymond C. Baumhart, "How Ethical Are Businessmen?" *Harvard Business Review*, Vol. 39 (July–August 1961), p. 160.

through cities that are badly paved, made hideous by litter, blighted buildings, billboards, and posts for wires that should long since have been put underground. They pass into a countryside that has been rendered largely invisible by commercial art. (The goods which the latter advertise have an absolute priority in our value system. Such aesthetic considerations as a view of the countryside accordingly come second. On such matters we are consistent.) They picnic on exquisitely packaged food from a portable icebox by a polluted stream and go on to spend the night at a park which is a menace to public health and morals. Just before dozing off on an air mattress, beneath a nylon tent, amid the stench of decaying refuse, they may reflect vaguely on the curious unevenness of their blessings. Is this, indeed, the American genius? (Galbraith, 1958.)

Rather than concentrate our resources on private satisfactions, Galbraith argues, society would be better served by allocating more resources to schools, better parks, and other public services. This, he contends, would maximize our satisfactions more readily than the buying of bigger automobiles.

Critics of excessive materialism have generally argued that industrial civilization inverts social values, so that material gain rather than moral values becomes the sole motivating force in society. J. P. Marquand's *Point of No Return*, R. H. Towney's *The Acquisitive Society*, Aldous Huxley's *Brave New World*, and a host of other books were forerunners of Galbraith's critique, and they all attacked the excesses of materialism.

Another criticism of the economic order challenges the drive for profits. What is the proper role for profits today? Should profits be the end goal of business or only a measuring stick? *Fortune* has put the case for the former matter squarely enough: "The single-minded pursuit of profits is the discipline that reconciles conflicting interests; it is the wind of reality that blows away executive cobwebs; it achieves renewal when businesses falter and it keeps business alive as a vital force" (*Fortune*, 1969). On the other hand, Lyndall F. Urwick, an international business consultant, has written:

> But profit can no more be the objective of a business than betting is the objective of racing, making a score the objective of cricket, or eating is the objective of living. Profit is a stimulus to individuals who participate in business activities; sometimes it is an almost exclusive stimulus, just as one meets people who live to eat. But, and more important, it is also a measuring rod, a test, if a rough one, of the success with which the real objectives of the business are being obtained. One must live to eat. And similarly, one cannot usually continue to conduct a business for long unless one makes a profit. But that stimulus and test cannot be the real objective of a business. To say so is almost equivalent to suggesting that one conducts one's business in order to keep accounts . . . and the true objective of any business undertaking must be to make or to distribute some product or service which the community needs. (Urwick, 1943.)

Excessive drive toward profits or even sales can undoubtedly bring about a number of ethical problems. But it would also seem that it is possible for profits and ethics to be compatible with one another. Perhaps it is that excessive kind of drive toward profits which takes us over the line.

## Criticism of Advertising and Selling

We are told by critics that persuasion raises the costs of products unnecessarily, that persuasion influences people to buy the wrong things, to buy the right things for the wrong reasons, and to buy harmful goods; that the entire selling effort is untruthful and insincere, resulting in fraud, sharp practice, and deceit; and that selling causes people to be too materialistic. The charges are not groundless. We all have experienced offensive selling practices. We resent any attempt by anyone to wield power over us or any force that interferes with competition. We abhor any device that makes prices higher than they "should be." We dislike being cheated in any way. Our goal as consumers is to make wise decisions in order to be able to derive maximum satisfaction from our expenditures of limited funds. If persuasion obstructs attainment of this end, we consider it unethical.

In defense of the marketer's persuasion efforts, most businessmen claim that relatively few are guilty of abuse. They also point out that many safeguards exist in addition to laws. They are not in business to sell only once; to succeed, they need repeat sales. This in itself imposes restraints on persuasion. Moreover, they ask, does not the buyer know that someone is selling him, that someone is trying to persuade him? "To be forewarned is to be forearmed." Does not a buyer trim out the unacceptable persuasion? Does anyone actually believe there is a tiger in the tank? But puffery of claims through advertising and personal selling has little to be said for it. Nor do efforts to influence young children as they watch television on Saturday mornings. By age 14 a child may have seen 18,000 human beings killed on TV (Johnson, 1971). No wonder that the Federal Trade Commission has stepped up its activities in regulating the persuasion efforts of business. No wonder that businessmen are trying to improve on their own self-regulation.

The criticisms of advertising can be classified in various ways in order to help us examine the social issues involved. One such classification scheme is shown in 25-5. The effects on values are serious ones for this chapter on ethics. Most of the points were covered in Chapter 22 but it is useful to summarize them at this point because advertising is a principal means of affecting influence and change of values.

Many thoughtful people have raised ethical questions about advertising. Howard R. Bowen, former college president, is one such person. He has asked:

Should the businessman conduct selling in ways that intrude on the privacy of people?

Should he employ "high pressure" tactics in persuading people to buy?

**25-5** Advertising and Social Issues

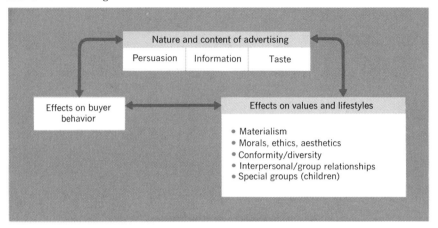

SOURCE: Stephen A. Greyser, "On the Social Impacts of Advertising," remarks prepared for the Federal Trade Commission's hearings (October 1971), p. 3.

Should he try to make people dissatisfied with what they have? Should he emphasize sex in his advertising appeals?

Should he attempt to set himself up as the arbiter of good taste and "proper" living standards through his advertising and selling activities? (Bowen, 1953.)

Vance Packard has been an angry critic:

They [admen] have . . . become major wielders of social control in America. . . . About 40 percent of the things we buy . . . are unnecessary. . . . We are persuaded that the old product has become hopelessly inadequate to meet our needs. . . . Advertising men call this "creating psychological obsolescence." (Packard, 1957.)

Some of advertising's supporters believe, however, that the attacks on advertising are based on a false assumption, namely, the assumed *power* of advertising. One of them contends: "This sense of power is overdrawn. A more realistic view suggests that advertising as akin to casting in a stream when the fish are biting. It does not lure fish into hitherto uninhabited waters" (Walton, 1962.)

Advertising gets into trouble in many ways. For instance, when cigarette ads were barred from television at the end of 1970, cigarette manufacturers doubled their advertising in magazines. Senator Frank E. Moss called the increase "shocking" and suggested that it would strengthen the case for a strong mandatory health warning in all cigarette advertisements (Morris, 1971). But if Congressmen believe that cigarette smoking is bad for one's health, why do they not ban the product?

Advertising is insulting, the critics say. Is it ethical to advertise in a way that insults the intelligence of the public?

Advertising is often false and misleading. There is much "double-talk" and claims that are made cannot be substantiated in many instances. As products are similar to one another, great effort is made to distinguish between minor differences.

Advertising promotes offensive products in an offensive way. "Why, you'd think from watching the tube that everyone's got bad breath and stinky underarms" (Colihan, 1969).

In the Harvard study referred to in Chapter 22, businessmen responded as follows to a number of ethical issues (Greyser and Reece, 1971):

Advertising:

| | |
|---|---|
| downgrades public taste | 41 percent |
| improves public taste | 37 |
| has healthy influence on children | 17 |
| has unhealthy influence on children | 57 |
| often persuades people to buy things they don't need | 85 |
| often persuades people to buy things they don't want | 51 |

Advertising has also been severely criticized for its ads on environmental matters. Companies felt the need to tell the public of their efforts toward combating pollution, but critics stated that the ads were attempts to capitalize on a vital issue. One study of pollution ads analyzed a special *Readers's Digest* supplement that was distributed to 50 million Americans. Three kinds of questionable ads were detected: (1) "environmentally irrelevant ads" that use the environmental issue as a gimmick to sell products; (2) "misleading ads" that create a corporate image through simple slogans and claims; and (3) "patently false" ads (*Economic Priorities Report,* 1971). Further in the same study, of 289 pages of environmental ads ($6 million worth) run in *Time, Business Week,* and *Newsweek,* over half were traced to the five industries classified by McGraw-Hill as having the "biggest clean-up job to do."

So there are many ethical issues with advertising. Potentially it can be a positive factor and in many ways it actually is, but there obviously remains much room for improvement.

## Product Criticisms

One of the most unethical practices as viewed by critics is planned obsolescence, that is, making frequent model changes that are superficial in nature in order to stimulate sales. To others, product obsolescence is necessary and even desirable, for it brings consumers improvements in product design and it helps provide full employment. Is it ethical to plan for product obsolescence and to encourage consumers to buy new models that they really do not need when their existing products still are serviceable? There are manufacturers such as Volkswagen that have built their marketing programs around the opposite strategy—consistent styling—with advertising that tells of hidden product improvement. Is the Volkswagen firm more ethical than the American firm that changes models frequently? There is some evidence that the American firms are examining their model-change philosophy, and in 1971 an executive of the Ford Motor Co. stated: "Excesses in size, flamboyance, in needless styling changes, which were gobbled up in the 1950s, are behind us" (Petersen, 1971). Ralph Nader, on the other hand, commented: "The automobile has the overwhelming lock on surface transportation, and I don't see it changing soon" (Nader, 1971).

The auto industry serves as an illustration of another practice that is questioned by the critics: is it ethical for a manufacturer to encourage standards, which in this case put the car near the top of a person's value structure? The critic points out that the car has been a consumer's alter ego, an escape into an imaginary life of sex, prestige, and power. Or take pet food, which is now a $1.4 billion market compared to cereals at $814 million and baby food at $390 million. Many cats and dogs eat far better than many humans (Tracy, 1971). Critics of marketing question the ethics of a system that permits such aberrations. They also question the ethics of firms that produce items that are unsafe, poisonous, or injurious to the user or to the environment. Is it ethical, they ask, for the marketing system to sell hand guns, master keys, and low-quality patent medicines? Drugs in particular are being studied by governmental agencies, but hundreds of other products are also being scrutinized. (Chapter 26 will discuss these issues in more detail.)

Closely related to the product is the *package*. Some manufacturers have misled the public with their packaging methods, and have deceived buyers about the quality, quantity, composition, and price of the product. One candy manufacturer redesigned his package to hold less candy in the same space for the same price. This unethical deception was soon emulated by his two closest competitors who found themselves at a competitive disadvantage in terms of profit. Congress spent more than six years debating the packaging issue, and finally in 1967 enacted a "truth-in-packaging" law. The unhappy experience with the new law suggests that some unethical marketers have been able to sidestep the law and continue with a variety of unethical packaging programs.*

## Pricing Practices

Because pricing practices are perhaps the most esoteric of the marketing functions, critics of pricing are less vocal and numerous than critics of other marketing activities. Business executives themselves have, however, named price discrimination, unfair pricing, and price collusion as practices they would most like to see eliminated. In the illegal and grossly unethical electrical conspiracy referred to in Chapter

---

*In 1972 an Advisory Committee to the Secretary of Commerce developed a set of Guiding Principles for Responsible Packaging & Labeling. National Business Council for Consumer Affairs (Washington, D.C.: GPO, 1972).

7, one of the defendants was reported to have rationalized the conspiracy as follows:

> "One of the problems of business is what is normal practice, not what is the law," he said. "If it's normal practice, it's ethical—not legal, but ethical."
>
> Bolstered by his own brand of ethics, this executive, even in the aftermath, felt no sense of guilt. His only reservation was that the conspiracy, once embarked upon, had gone too far; it was wrong to allocate business, he felt, but he still found nothing wrong about rigging prices because "the customer buys total value in which price is only one significant factor." (Cook, 1963.)

Though the Minnesota State Pharmacy Board prohibit druggists from posting prices of drugs, a retail drug chain has challenged the regulation by posting prices in its stores. In 1972 the State Consumer Council sided with the drug chain and took action to make it legal to post drug prices. Is it ethical to prevent buyers from knowing the prices of the drugs they buy?

Consumer criticism is generally leveled at rising prices during periods of apparent abundance. Housewives usually charge that food prices rise because "those middlemen are raising prices for their own profit." Few realize, however, that the pricing of food items is complex and often based on the scarcities or abundances that must be forecast by the price maker. The prices of canned food, for example, fluctuate with estimates of the quantity and quality of the next crop. Too much rain, too little rain, hail, wind, and numerous other variables influence the quality of crops. Housewives are also especially aware of prices during times of price controls, as in 1971–72, when even the Internal Revenue Service was hard put to enforce the approved prices.

The marketing system is geared to greater efficiency and higher profits. Men are not measured on the basis of their moral contributions to the business enterprise but in quantitative terms of "how much" the firm grows with their actions. Hence they become caught up in a system where there is always the temptation to push harder even though there are infractions of the "rules of the game."

The character of competition and the degree of its intensity are keenly felt by every businessman, and they are often placed in a position of electing either lower profits or lower ethics. The entire marketing mix, as already suggested, is subject to pressures toward unethical practices. In an effort to overcome aggressive rivals, a firm may tend to exaggerate claims and "puff" its market offerings. The temptations to promote false claims, cheat on the package, deceive about pricing, and lower quality to unsafe levels abound in competitive economic systems. Though most manufacturers are undoubtedly honest, we have to face the fact that there still exists in marketing much unethical activity. Much of the pressure comes from outside marketing to be sure, but it is implemented through the marketing program.

Sometimes the boundary between truth and deception is not easy to establish. Does ethical behavior require a marketer to tell about the bad as well as the good features of a product? This question is particularly pertinent to products that might cause injury or even death—for instance, power tools, electrical devices, automobiles, and power mowers. Is it ethical to claim that price denotes quality? In many instances this is a truism, but with aspirin, for instance, it is known to be a falsehood. Should a gasoline be touted as being superior to all other products when in fact it holds no such superiority? Such questions are not always easy to resolve, but they illustrate some of the ethical problems faced by marketers today.

The entire marketing program has to be examined from the standpoint of ethics. The marketing plan as described in Chapter 14 should do more than make a gesture toward developing a socially acceptable program. Bert Elwert believes that modern marketing management does look outside the firm and this should help the firm get a social view:

> . . . the modern managerial model . . . makes pricing decisions, plans new products and modifies old ones, plans promotions and campaigns, evaluates alternative channels of distribution, organizes sales units and dealer relationships, participates in trade associations, promotes a favorable corporate image, and generally regards *nothing in the firm's external environment* as beyond their interest. (Elwert, 1968.) [Emphasis supplied by authors.]

## ALLEGIANCE TO WHOM?

The practical day-to-day ethics of a marketer depends to a large extent on his loyalties, which may conflict. He is responsible to the management of the firm on whom he is economically dependent. He accepts the *primacy* of the corporation. He is responsible for profits and is aware of stockholder pressure. He wants to be fair to his employees, creditors, and various professional and business contacts. If the marketing concept holds sway, he owes allegiance to the customer.

Wilmar F. Bernthal has suggested a "value hierarchy" that illustrates how decisions at any level are influenced by values at a higher level. (See 25-6.) Seeking profits will be affected by the allocation of resources, for example, and the allocation of resources will be influenced by what is considered to be a "good life." The snowmobile, cited earlier, gave the individual an opportunity to have fun in the winter; society saw it as part of the "good life"; companies allocated resources to build and distribute them; and the company made profits as a result. As other individuals complain about personal injustice because of the snowmobile, the influence down through the hierarchy becomes felt, and if voluntary restraints are not effective, society will demand strict legislation for the use of the product.

Robert Bartels has developed a model for ethics in marketing that assumes that marketing is a part of the economic system which is a

**25-6** The Value Hierarchy—A Model for Management Decision

|  |  | THE DECISION CRITERION | GOALS OR OBJECTIVES |
|---|---|---|---|
| LEVELS OF VALUES | IV | The individual | Individual welfare<br>Freedom<br>Opportunity<br>Self-realization<br>Human dignity |
| | III | Society | Social welfare<br>"The good life"<br>Culture<br>Civilization<br>Order<br>Justice |
| | II | The economic system | Consumer welfare<br>Allocation of resources<br>Production and distribution<br>of goods and services |
| | I | The business firm | Ownership welfare<br>Profits<br>Survival<br>Growth |

SOURCE: Wilmar F. Bernthal, "Value Perspectives in Management Decisions," *Journal of the Academy of Management*, Vol. 5 (December 1962), p. 196.

part of a social process and that marketers have commitments within and without the marketing process (Bartels, 1967). Marketing is only one social institution and marketers relate to several others—family, church, school, economy, government, and leisure, for example. Ten role positions, inside and outside the company, are identified for the marketers:

| | |
|---|---|
| Managers | Intermediate customers |
| Employees | Resources |
| Owners | Competitors |
| Financiers | Government |
| Consumers | Community |

Bartels further assumes that the expectations of the participants in the marketing roles are known, subject to change over time, increasing, and becoming more clearly articulated. Ethics, as he sees it, is a matter of social sanction and evolves from the interaction of people in their various roles. To show this, Bartels devises four matrices. Matrix # 1 includes the influence of the culture on the institutions, including marketing: law, respect for individuals, and property rights, for example are related to the family, church, marketing, and so on. From this competitors determine what is fair play and consumers derive their expectations of honest merchants. In Matrix #2 the institutions are shown as influencing the ten roles, previously given. The church may influence consumption patterns and a socialist government may restrict competition. In Matrix #3 the people in their ten roles interact with others in their roles and thus sellers may guarantee their products and make refunds in order to assure satisfaction. Ethics of doing business evolves as a result of role interactions. Finally, in Matrix #4 the roles are shown in relation to managers' bases of decision, that is, self-interest, laws, social standards, and convictions. Thus marketing ethics evolve from many different kinds of relationships and influences—culture, different roles, institutions, and several bases of decision. The marketer is not loyal to only one entity and his ethics reflect a multiple kind of allegiance. There is no one set of ethics that is universal to all.

## IMPROVING MARKETING ETHICS

One of the best ways to raise the standards of marketing ethics is *education,* not merely through formal schooling but also through continuing professional activities. Members of marketing associations discuss the subject frequently and many articles are published in their trade journals. A number of associations have standing ethics committees to deal with problems brought before them by their members. It is difficult to gauge how effective these groups are, but at least they encourage marketers to behave in a professional manner. The authors believe that there is much to be gained by fostering a professional attitude. Henry O. Pruden has provided a model that incorporates three types of ethics: an individual, organizational, and professional (Pruden, 1971).

As shown in 25-7 the three ethics relate to one another. In the *individual-organization* interaction the individual produces and creates within the firm, and the firm rewards the individual. In the *individual-professional* linkage the individual behaves in accordance with the standards and otherwise supports the profession, which in turn supplies him with technical knowledge and behavioral standards. The *organizational-professional* interface calls for the support of the profession by the firm and also expects the firm to aid the professional in his determination to advance the state of the arts: the profession should provide data, techniques, and interpretations about the market as well as publicize standards of behavior.

The individual's own ethics are undoubtedly the most important, but professional ethics may help him to adhere to his own values when the organization is pressing him to deviate from them. Further, the individual can develop his professional ethics simultaneously with his professional competence through continuing education.

*Codes of ethics* represent another way to heighten the standard of conduct. Many individual businesses have formulated codes of good business practice, as have industry groups and professional associa-

**25-7** Frames of Reference for the Marketer

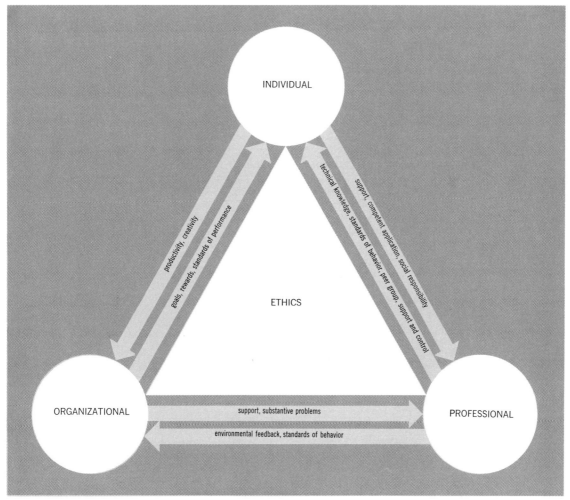

SOURCE: Henry O. Pruden, "Which Ethic for Marketers?" in John R. Wish and Stephen H. Gamble (eds.), *Marketing and Social Issues: An Action Reader* (New York: John Wiley, 1971), p. 100.

tions. The American Marketing Association, for instance, has a Marketing Research Code of Ethics. The American Management Association has a Business Ethics Advisory Service which has gathered a large number of existing codes for use by businessmen. A code in a somewhat controversial marketing area is shown in part in 25-8. To be effective in influencing behavior, a code must meet three tests: first, it must be specific and concrete rather than general; second, the standards should be revised as economic, social, and marketing conditions change; and third, some method of self-policing is needed. A summary of information on codes is shown in 25-9.

## 25-8

### "The Television Code" (March 1971)

#### General Advertising Standards

1. This Code establishes basic standards for all television broadcasting. The principles of acceptability and good taste within the Program Standards section govern the presentation of advertising where applicable. . . .

2. A commercial television broadcaster makes his facilities available for the advertising of products and services and accepts commercial presentations for such advertising. However, a television broadcaster should, in recognition of his responsibility to the public, refuse the facilities of his station to an advertiser where he has good reason to doubt the integrity of the advertiser, the truth of the advertising representations, or the compliance of the adveriser with the spirit and purpose of all applicable legal requirements.

3. Identification of sponsorship must be made in all sponsored programs in accordance with the requirements of the Communications Act of 1934, . . . and the Federal Communications Commission.

4. Representations which disregard normal safety precautions shall be avoided. Children shall not be represented, except under proper adult supervision, as being in contact with, or demonstrating a product recognized as potentially dangerous to them.

5. In consideration of the customs and attitudes of the communities served, each television broadcaster should refuse his facilities to the advertisement of products and services, or the use of advertising scripts, which the station has good reason to believe would be objectionable to a substantial and responsible segment of the community. . . .

6. The advertising of hard liquor (distilled spirits) is not acceptable.

7. The advertising of beer and wines is acceptable only when presented in the best of good taste and discretion, and is acceptable only subject to Federal and local laws.

8. Advertising by institutions or enterprises which in their offers of instruction imply promises of employment or make exaggerated claims for the opportunities awaiting those who enroll for courses is generally unacceptable.

9. The advertising of firearms/ammunition is acceptable provided it promotes the product only as sporting equipment and conforms to recognized standards of safety as well as all applicable laws and regulations. Advertisements of firearms/ammunition by mail order are unacceptable. . . .

10. The advertising of fortune-telling, occultism, astrology, phrenology, palm-reading, numerology, mind-reading, character reading or subjects of a like nature is not permitted.

11. Because all products of a personal nature create special problems, acceptability of such products should be determined with especial emphasis on ethics and the canons of good taste. Such advertising of personal products as is accepted must be presented in a restrained and obviously inoffensive manner.

12. The advertising of tip sheets, race track publications, or organizations seeking to advertise for the purpose of giving odds or promoting betting or lotteries is unacceptable.

13. An advertiser who markets more than one product should not be permitted to use advertising copy devoted to an acceptable product for purposes of publicizing the brand name or other identification of a product which is not acceptable.

14. "Bait-switch" advertising, whereby goods or services which the advertiser has no intention of selling are offered merely to lure the customer into purchasing higher-price substitutes, is not acceptable.

15. Personal endorsements (testimonials) shall be genuine and reflect personal experience. They shall contain no statement that cannot be supported if presented in the advertiser's own words.

SOURCE: National Association of Broadcasters, The Television Code (New York: 1971, 15th Ed.), pp. 13, 14.

## 25-9 A Summary of Information on Codes

### Types of Problems Dealt with by Codes of Ethics

Competition among members of the profession

Conflict among members

Relations between practitioners and clients, consumers, or users of the services

Relations of practitioners with superiors, or executives

Relations of practitioners with sources of supplies needed in the profession

Relations between the more general practitioners and the highly developed specialists—acute in several professions

### Kinds of Codes

Codes combining general principles or precepts and specific rules for practice. (Most codes could probably be so described)

Codes containing largely particular rules of ethical practice. (Some of the newer professions tend to adopt documents of this type)

Codes containing only the more general principles, leaving all matters of application to the individual's interpretation and conscience; or, in a few professions, permitting a committee or other group to advise with respect to applications based on a set of facts.

### Advantages of Codes of Ethics

1. Codes may formulate the mature experience of a profession and the traditions that are recognized.

2. Codes may provide a balancing of public interest and private interest; or the general good and protection of the profession.

3. Codes may offer guidance to young persons entering the profession.

4. Codes may furnish a focus of the interests of members which may become subjects of fruitful discussion; this may take the form of questioning the validity of the accepted code.

5. In certain instances, codes provide the bases of disciplinary action against offenders, or the ways and means of reconciling offending members with the standards of the profession.

### Limitations of Codes of Ethics

1. Some codes are written and adopted, only to be ignored or forgotten.

2. Some codes are formulations only of a vague idealism, with no practical application.

3. Some codes are adopted and then seldom discussed, thus indicating that they are not significant aspects of professional organization.

4. Some codes deal with old situations and not with the new, thus ignoring the effects of rapid change.

5. Thus some codes are used to resist changes that portions of the members may deem necessary.

6. Some codes are regarded as so authoritative that they prevent discussion by members who fear discipline for dissenters.

SOURCE: Philip W. Van Vlack, *Management Ethics Guide* (Brookings, S.D.: South Dakota Dakota State University, 1965), pp. 96–97.

Codes that meet these prerequisites can be helpful to a businessman, can promote the general good of the field of endeavor, and can be in the public interest. A well-built code provides guidance for new employees, especially young people entering the field. And, finally, through its enforcement measures, the code provides the basis for remedial or disciplinary action.

The Canadian Association of Broadcasters put a new advertising code for children into effect in 1972, and it has provision for enforcement, jurisdiction, inquiries, and complaints. Several of the code's provisions are quoted below in order to illustrate the sensitivity of it.

> Children, especially the very young, live in a world that is part imaginary, part real, and sometimes do not distinguish clearly between the two. Advertisements should respect and not abuse the power of the child's imagination. . . .
>
> To avoid undue pressure, advertising must not urge children to purchase, or urge them to ask their parents to make inquiries or purchases. . . .
>
> The personalities or characters on children's programs shall not be used to promote products, premiums, or services, on their own programs.
>
> Toy advertisements shall not make direct comparisons with the previous year's model, or with competitive makes—even when the statements or claims are valid—because such references may undermine the child's enjoyment of present possessions or those that may be received as gifts. . . . (Canadian Association of Broadcasters, 1971.)

## A NEW MARKETING ETHIC

The late ecologist Aldo Leopold proposed "The Land Ethic" as an attempt to change public attitudes toward the use of land and to develop an ethic of ecology (Leopold, 1970). Leopold saw an ethic, ecologically, as a "limitation on freedom of action in the struggle for existence"; in a general philosophical sense, an ethic is a "differentiation of social from anti-social conduct." Leopold recognized that land has been considered strictly as an economic object, "entailing privileges but not obligations." His land ethic changes "the role of Homo sapiens from conqueror of the land-community to plain member and citizen of it." Can this approach be applied to marketing? Can the marketer look at the marketplace as something more than a place to make money? Can he conceive of himself a citizen of the marketplace rather than a conqueror of it? Leopold saw land as "not merely soil but as a fountain of energy flowing through a circuit of soils, plants and animals." In the same vein can we visualize marketing as a way to sell goods to consumers and also as a way to allocate and distribute goods and services in the best interests of those consumers? Such a viewpoint would provide a fruitful starting point for a new marketing ethic.

The cultivation of such a marketing ethic would certainly change the marketplace and the activities of people in it. Marketers could be more professional in their stance. They would be a part of the marketplace, not an adversary, but more sensitive to the needs of others. Personal values would undoubtedly dominate organizational demands, and personal gains at the expense of others would not be as rewarding as they are today. Being a marketer would be a privilege with obligations to serve the consumers. He would be in harmony with consumers and would not feel the need to press so hard for sales. He would be aware of his impact on personal values. The firm's management might be forced to accept a lower rate of growth and perhaps lower profits as defined today. The firm would not rely on government, nor entirely on economic norms, but would have a broader kind of definition of marketing. The marketers would find that many of their problems would be resolved with this kind of ethic.

A Leopold-type of marketing ethic may seem to be a naive and unrealistic solution to the ethical problems of the marketer today. Many would say that our system simply cannot work with this kind of philosophy. But on the other hand we have absorbed many kinds of changes and the system itself has evolved as it has adapted to changing conditions. Is it necessary that businessmen continue to be the perpetual ogre? It has been suggested that the marketing situation is analogous to the person who owns a beautiful house on a cliff overlooking the sea. The view is wonderful but the waves slowly undermine the foundation. Marketers cannot be content merely to enjoy the view, for it carries with it a moral burden to stop the erosion (Feldman, 1971). We should be aware that marketing does influence social values; that the individual's character and integrity are influenced by the nature of his economic endeavor, and that the alternative to ethical marketing behavior is public policies. These are central issues in marketing ethics and reasons for marketers to adopt high standards.

Perhaps the marketing concept as originally postulated did not mean to put the buyer in a position of primacy over the corporation and its profits, but certainly it did mean to give new and added emphasis to the responsibility of the marketer. The extension of the marketing concept to a marketing ethic could help the entire economic system and the people who rely upon it and it would provide those who do the marketing with a great deal more satisfaction with their tasks. And satisfaction, after all, is what a lot of marketing is all about.

## STATEMENTS TO CONSIDER

Ethics, legality, and profitability all suffer from three fundamental weaknesses: incompetence, cowardice, and myopia. (Garret)

. . . to explain the marketing leader in ethical conduct we must make the assumption that he hungers and thirsts after righteousness. (Alderson)

We cannot arrive at a rule of choice which will always give us the best personal ethic by a process involving pure logic, without reference to the world of experience.

In every culture or subculture there is an ethical system which both creates it and is created by it.

The marketing type of executive tends to view himself as a commodity to be exchanged. He also sees others as commodities. (Fromm)

A marketing manager should stick to his marketing and leave the problems of the world to others.

The whole world, including the United States, appears to be moving in a direction in which marketing is decidedly *not* prepared to go. (Farmer)

Marketing wields enormous influence upon our goals and values—upon our beliefs and assumptions as to what and how much is good, important, worth doing, or worth working for. (Borton)

If he be tame and have been rydden upon then *caveat emptor*.

It is a hard skeptic indeed who, given prevailing market conditions, would not view the widening scope for personal responsibility with greater enthusiasm than the old iron law of supply and demand. (Walton)

## QUESTIONS FOR REVIEW

**1.** What are the differences between operating legally and operating ethically, or are there any differences?

**2.** Comment on the Levi statements, pages 536–37.

**3.** Do you think it is possible for marketers and other businessmen to operate ethically and without legislation?

**4.** Compare the ethics of those in marketing with those in other areas of business. With occupations outside of business. Why does the public have the views shown in 25-2?

**5.** Is it possible for marketing to satisfy society if it is criticized when there are few goods to distribute and also during properous times when many worthless items are purchased by the people?

**6.** Comment on Galbraith's statement on pages 541–42.

**7.** Is advertising to be blamed for the values we hold today?

**8.** From the point of view of a businessman, comment on Howard Bowen's questions on pages 543–44.

**9.** Evaluate the automobile from the standpoint of its impact upon our values and quality of life.

**10.** Assume that you are employed in some part of a marketing staff. What kinds of ethics will you be able to maintain? At what point do you decide that you do what is told in contrast to what you prefer to do?

## Further Readings

Robert Bartels (ed.), *Ethics in Business* (Columbus, Ohio: The Ohio State University, 1963).

Robert J. Lavidge and Robert J. Holloway (eds.), *Marketing and Society,* (Homewood, Ill.: Richard D. Irwin, 1969), AMA series.

Lee E. Preston (ed.), *Social Issues in Marketing* (Glenview, Ill.: Scott, Foresman, 1968).

Joseph W. Towle (ed.), *Ethics and Standards in American Business* (Boston: Houghton Mifflin, 1964).

John R. Wish and Stephen H. Gamble (eds.), *Marketing and Social Issues: An Action Reader* (New York: John Wiley, 1971).

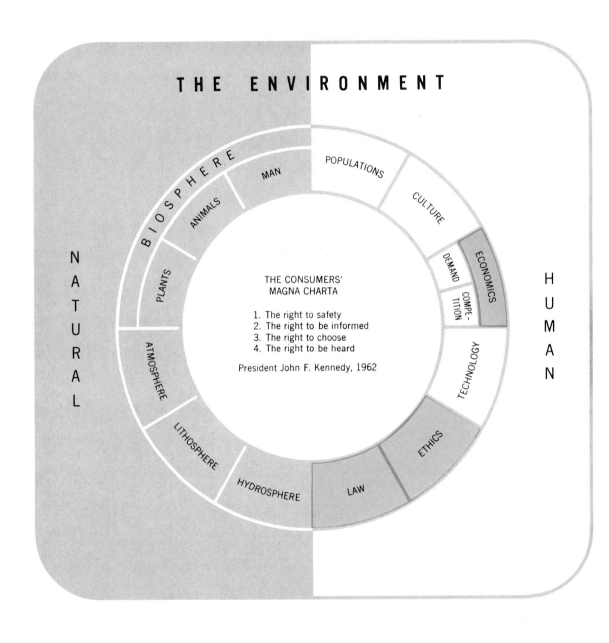

THE ENVIRONMENT

NATURAL

HUMAN

BIOSPHERE

MAN
ANIMALS
PLANTS
ATMOSPHERE
LITHOSPHERE
HYDROSPHERE

POPULATIONS
CULTURE
DEMAND
ECONOMICS
COMPE-TITION
TECHNOLOGY
ETHICS
LAW

THE CONSUMERS'
MAGNA CHARTA

1. The right to safety
2. The right to be informed
3. The right to choose
4. The right to be heard

President John F. Kennedy, 1962

# CHAPTER 26
# CONSUMERISM

*The consumerism movement is not to be treated lightly or ignored. It clearly calls for responses from business, government, and consumers themselves. The movement provides ample evidence that improvements need to be made by business firms and that many of these improvements will be implemented by marketers.*

Ethics, which we considered in the previous chapter, is of course important in any consideration of the marketer-consumer relationship. One could make a good case for including all the chapters in this section under the topic of ethics. But consumerism and low-income marketing (Chapter 27) are important and identifiable issues that need special attention. Further, consumerism relates to more than the ethical segment of the environment, since it is also concerned with legal, technological, economic, and physical segments. The implications of consumerism apply more broadly than to marketing. But since it is the marketer with whom the consumer comes into contact, marketers have assumed the problem to be theirs, at least to a large degree. Yet marketing alone cannot solve the consumerism issue, for it is a broad societal problem.

Movements on behalf of consumers have existed off and on throughout history. In the United States mail-fraud laws are almost 100 years old. The Food and Drug Administration was formed in 1906 and the Federal Trade Commission in 1915. Business set up Better Business Bureaus in 1914. Consumers formed Consumers' Research, Inc. in 1928 and Consumers Union in 1936. Franklin D. Roosevelt in his first inaugural address commented on the failure of the exchange system, and during the Great Depression of the thirties there was widespread interest in cooperatives as a way to improve upon the market system. The current movement is different from the previous ones in that it is more permanent in nature, more widespread, better led, and receiving much more attention. The movement has many implications for marketing, especially in the selling, advertising, credit, pricing, and product decision-making areas. Consumerism could well temper the force of the persuasion effort.

Consumerism is not a fad and it is not a phenomenon limited to the United States. In Britain, for example, in response to consumer pressure a number of substantial changes have been made in the advertising and pricing of detergents and a number of government studies have been undertaken. In Canada, certain marketing and consumer issues have also been studied and the consumer is represented by a minister at the cabinet level. In the Soviet Union there are consumer clubs that try to improve the quality of production. The Minister of Consumer Services, Aleksandr N. Gandurin, spends much time appeasing consumers. Consumerism is disquieting to many businessmen, and completely unwelcome by some, but it is a key subject that demands the attention of business, government, and consumers.

It is logical, though seemingly ironic, that consumerism should hav developed at a time when we think in terms of an "affluent society," a "high mass-consumption" economy, the "final stage of economic development," and the "age of opulence." Our educational levels are at an all-time high, our sophistication has been rising, and we pride ourselves on our standard of living. But prosperity, education, and sophistication have combined with general unrest and with specific concerns about war and pollution. Aaron Yohalem explains it nicely:

> Consumerism is a distinct sociopolitical development of our changing and troubled times—a collection of deep-rooted and volatile questions and challenges that go far beyond the ordinary concerns of the marketplace as we have traditionally known it. Consumerism is a concomitant phenomenon of the great unrest of our cities; of the unprecedented revolt of our youth; of the extraordinary rise of inspired, militant, and articulate minorities. It is a reflection of the thoughtful search for excellence by our great middle class. (Yohalem, 1970.)

More ironic is the observation that consumerism has followed on the heels of the "marketing concept." But as pointed out in earlier chapters, marketers failed for the most part in looking at marketing from the standpoint of consumers.

In the remainder of this chapter we will describe consumerism, causes for its growth, and responses to it by business, government, and consumers themselves. We want to identify the reasons for consumer dissatisfaction and we want to explore solutions to the problems involved. Recognizing the existence of consumerism and suggesting changes in the marketplace are not threats to our economic system: indeed, failure to face up to the consumerism phenomenon is the threat.

## MEANING OF CONSUMERISM

There is no one definition of consumerism, and the meaning seems to change from month to month as consumerism responds to new societal concerns. The changeability reflects the fact that it is an evolving concept, broadening in scope. Concerns about pollution, for example, are now tied to consumerism (see Chapter 28). Low-income marketing problems are a part of it (Chapter 27). Nevertheless, we offer several typical definitions that show the scope of the movement.

> Consumerism is the search for getting better values for the money. It is the challenging of that goal of our society that calls for an ever-increasing amount of material goods through time. (Ferber, 1970.)

> Consumerism means that the consumer looks upon the manufacturer as somebody who is interested, but who really doesn't know what the consumer's realities are. He regards the manufacturer as somebody who has not made the effort to find out, and who expects

the consumer to be able to make distinctions which the consumer is neither able nor willing to make. (Drucker, 1969.)

Consumerism is a social force within the environment designed to aid and protect the consumer by exerting legal, moral, and economic pressures on business. (Cravens and Hills, 1970.)

Consumerism—The contemptible acquisition of things. Revolting in itself as well as by virtue of the capitalist manipulation and materialist philosophy which underlie it. To be rebelled against by the massive purchase or theft of such austere objects as fast cars, elaborate motorcycles, love beads, Indian bands, parkas, ponchos, handcrafted sandals, ornate boots, mod suits, skirts and unisex pants, leather jackets, jade necklaces, stereo sets, Apple records, guns, skis, snorkels, fancy wigs, tonsorial equipment, bongo drums, original Picassos, binoculars, eight-track tape recorders, strobe lights, German cameras, aphrodisiacs, Tarot cards, gourmet meals and/or health foods, and cut but not cut-rate narcotics. (Rosenberg, 1970.)

Consumerism is anything consumers say it is. For marketers, it's the why behind who buys what from whom. (*Marketing Horizons*, 1969.)

So consumerism means a lot of things to a lot of people, mostly however, dissatisfaction with the marketplace and remedial efforts. Many groups are involved because of the multiplicity of issues and the inclusion of business, governments, and consumers. The interrelationships of the various groups are shown in 26-1.

## LEADERS OF THE MOVEMENT

Although it would be impossible to list all the leaders of the consumer movement, there are certain preeminent persons who should be identified. The Number One consumer advocate is Ralph Nader, a lawyer who has become identified with a variety of ventures that have had substantial impact. Nader challenged General Motors on the safety of the Corvair, and he has since challenged Congress, the Federal Trade Commission, the Federal Drug Administration, and the Transportation Department on their work in product safety. Senator Philip Hart (Michigan) has introduced a number of consumer bills, as has Senator Warren Magnuson (Washington), Senator Lee Metcalf (Montana), Senator Walter Mondale (Minnesota), and Senator Gaylord Nelson (Wisconsin). Hart and Magnuson have championed a number of consumer causes, Metcalf has worked primarily on electrical power issues, and Mondale on meat-packing bills. Representatives Emanuel Celler (New York), Wright Patman (Texas), Benjamin Rosenthal (New York), and Leonor Sullivan (New York) have all been leaders in the House. Bess Myerson became the protector of the consumer in New York City and launched a number of improvement campaigns such as unit pricing

**26-1** The Consumerism System—Group and Information Flows

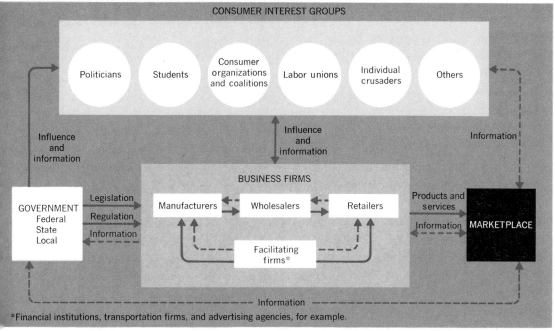

CONSUMER INTEREST GROUPS

Politicians  Students  Consumer organizations and coalitions  Labor unions  Individual crusaders  Others

Influence and information

Influence and information

Information

GOVERNMENT
Federal
State
Local

Legislation
Regulation
Information

BUSINESS FIRMS

Manufacturers  Wholesalers  Retailers

Facilitating firms*

Products and services

Information  MARKETPLACE

Information

*Financial institutions, transportation firms, and advertising agencies, for example.

SOURCE: Adapted from David W. Cravens and Gerald E. Hills, "Consumerism: A Perspective for Business," Business Horizons, Vol. 13 (August 1970), p. 25.

A number of women have been appointed by Presidents as special assistants for consumer affairs. Helen Canoyer, Cornell Dean of Home Economics, was appointed by President Kennedy, as was Esther Peterson from the Department of Labor; Betty Furness from television was appointed by President Johnson; and Virginia Knauer of Pennsylvania was appointed by President Nixon. Each of these women played important roles in the consumer movement of the past decade as have, of course, the Presidents themselves. Beyond these national figures have been hundreds of people working in independent agencies, in state and local governments, in professional business associations, and in business firms.

The consumer movement has been supported by both major political parties. Leaders in all walks of life have organized various segments so that it now has substantial support everywhere. Generally it is thought that the middle classes and the more educated people are the ones who have fostered the movement, but 26-2 includes information to the contrary. The books, articles, laws, and programs that have appeared suggest that articulate and educated people do support the movement. They may not consider consumerism as important as stopping war or saving the environment, but they nevertheless do take active roles in improving the marketplace.

## 26-2

**Excerpts from a Survey on Consumerism**

Based on 714 returns, 25 percent considered consumerism most important among seven issues. Personal finances, morality, ecology all rated higher.

In order of importance, the following elements were rated important in the consumerism cluster of questions.

Quality of medical care
Auto safety
Food shortages
Dishonest advertising
Consumer protection
Adequate nutrition
Truth in packaging

Who is concerned about consumerism?

(Figures show percentage considering the issue most important.)

| Income | | Education | | Age | |
|---|---|---|---|---|---|
| Over $15,000 | 9 | College Graduate | 9 | Under 35 | 8 |
| 10–15,000 | 12 | Some College | 10 | 35–44 | 13 |
| Six–10,000 | 17 | High School Graduate | 17 | 45–54 | 19 |
| Four–6,000 | 23 | Trade School | 22 | Over 54 | 27 |
| Under $4,000 | 28 | Grade School | 37 | | |

Conclusions:

1. Consumerism is an issue of middling importance.
2. Those who are concerned tend to be the older, poorer, less educated, and generally less able to cope with the world.
3. If there is a new, young, educated, activist consumer, he is drowned out by the young, educated consumer who is really not interested in the problem.

SOURCE: John. S. Coulson (Leo Burnett Co. Inc), "New Consumerists Breed Will Fade Away," *The Marketing News*, Vol. 4 (Mid-June 1971), pp. 5, 7, 8.

## CAUSES OF CONSUMERISM

We will first list some of the complaints of the consumer and then examine the underlying causes of consumerism.

| | |
|---|---|
| Deceptive advertising | Unsafe products |
| Unfair tactics in selling | Junk products |
| Proliferation in packaging | Cheating of the poor |
| Unfair pricing practices | Impersonal selling |
| Merchandising tricks | Poor service |

| | |
|---|---|
| Inflation economy | High credit costs |
| "Free" goods | Stress on quantity instead of quality |
| Debt-collection deception | Lack of communication between consumer and businessman |
| Refusal to make refunds | |
| Used for new products | Complexity of technology |
| Promotion of superficial values | Misleading warranties |
| Planned obsolescence | Bait and switch practices |
| Proliferation in products | Phony contests |
| Lack of competition | Deceptive packaging |
| Exploitation of children | Substitution of merchandise |
| | Lack of information about products |

President Kennedy, in his 1962 Special Message on Protecting the Consumer Interest, spelled out four basic rights. The first was the *right to safety*. Many products are dangerous in one way or another—drugs, appliances, insecticides, foods, automobiles, and even rugs have been causes of many accidents. It is not surprising, therefore, that product-related accidents were a major spur to consumerism. By January 1972 more than 200 toys had been banned by the Food and Drug Administration (FDA) during the two-year period the Toy Safety Act had been in effect. Dangerous darts, rattles that lose beads, and toys with sharp wires, poison paint, and small pieces of breakable plastic have been among those removed. The FDA announced in early 1972 that it would undertake the first overall review ever attempted of the safety and efficacy of the more than 100,000 nonprescription drugs on the market. Automobile safety, of course, has been in the news for several years. And consumers have been greatly distressed to learn that items they eat, appliances they use daily, their cosmetics, and even their soap and tobacco are unsafe. The right to safety is one of the principal demands of the consumer groups.

The second right—*to be informed*—is very closely related to marketing. Advertising, personal selling, labeling, packaging—nearly all company information has become suspect. Consumers should know what a product really is, how is it to be used, and all other pertinent information. Few of us know precisely the definitions related to wool, for instance—reprocessed versus reused wool, or virgin wool. Cheap furs have been given high-sounding names in order to sell them at inflated prices—Baltic Lion instead of rabbit skin or Hudson Seal for sheared muskrat. What are these generic names that apply to man-made textiles—modacrylic, azlon, spandex, vinyl, and anidex? What is the total cost of an item that is purchased on a credit plan? What is hamburger and what is in a weiner?

The *right to choose* is the third right of the consumer named by Kennedy. Many consumers feel that competition is not working adequately and that the range of choice has deteriorated. Others complain of the proliferation of products, brands, and packages that confront them in the retail store. Some say that sellers adopted a "take it or leave it" attitude so that a woman, for example, had to choose a new fashion because that was all that was offered to her. The bombardment of the buyer with advertising and merchandising gimmicks led one disenchanted consumer to write:

> I would like:—freedom from coupons . . . —freedom from stamps that can be collected for prizes . . . —freedom from liquor ads in my mailbox addressed to Occupant . . . —freedom from fancy, expensive packaging; and from buying six big refrigerator covers I don't want to get the three little ones I need . . . —freedom from contests and prizes . . . —freedom from opulent chrome and nauseous color combinations . . . —freedom from advertising pressures based on stimulated wants, not needs; and appeal to motives that are false. (*Christian Advocate,* 1955.)

The fourth right—the *right to be heard*—was suggested because so many consumers found that their grievances were poorly handled. Many executives seriously underestimated the level of discontent and did not even respond to complaints. Better Business Bureaus received thousands of complaints but they could not take care of all of them. Many consumers, of course, did not complain: they simply quit buying Brand X. But many did complain, by letters to the editor, by letters to company officials, and letters to the President's consumer advisor. Yet government agencies were poorly equipped to do anything, and in many states there were no consumer services at all.

Violations of these four consumer rights unquestionably were important causes for the rise of consumerism, but there were other stimuli as well. The growth of *population* with its attendant problems, not felt before, made people more aware and sensitive to all kinds of consumer concerns. The population focus related to environmental problems, and it seemed to convey an impersonal crush of humanity dependent on mass production with its image of quantity, sameness, and plastic ingredients. Large populations surely were targets of businesses and suddenly the people who make up the populations resented it. Pollution, the war in Vietnam, civil rights, law and order, and morality were all *social concerns* that provoked further resistance on the part of the consumer.

With advances in *technology,* products were becoming more complicated. As President Kennedy said, "The march of technology—affecting, for example, the foods we eat, the medicines we take, and the many appliances we use in our homes—has increased the difficulties of the consumer along with his opportunities." Products had simply become too complicated for ordinary maintenance and repair let alone operation of the equipment. Technology in the form of many products seemed to be a two-edged sword.

The *legal* sector, too, was changing as governments at all levels began to pay attention to the consumer. As consumers began to accept increasing government intervention, they accepted the view, "If business will not correct its faults, then government will have to step in."

The *economy,* with its inflationary trends, caused further disenchantment with things in general. Products and services cost too much and even increases in income did not offset higher prices. Mistakes by *business* spurred on the consumer movement. Consumers were questioning the role of advertising and marketing in general. Should buyer expectations be raised by Madison Avenue only to find high prices, shoddy workmanship, or lack of safety factors when an item was purchased? The proliferation of brands, products, and packages also antagonized consumers, by inducing confusion, irritation, and finally resentment. In general, business seemed to advocate a "throwaway" economy, to plan obsolescence, to apply pressure to buy more and more, and at the same time to produce what were perceived as low-quality items.

Many consumers found business to be impersonal. They reacted against corresponding with a computer and being a number. (Some companies have removed from their computer records the names of all customers who have filed complaints.) Critics felt that mergers were eliminating too many small firms and their intimate identity with products. Many consumers felt that the buyer-seller balance had tipped in the favor of big business and away from the individual buyer. With ever more products, increasing complexity of products, confusing prices, and uninformative advertising, many consumers felt that they had to devote more time to buying, which they could ill afford, or press for changes in the system. Marketing was geared simply to provide more and to persuade people to buy more in an expanding, mass-consumption society. But the marketing environment was changing in the ways mentioned; as a result efforts boomeranged and consumerism began to flourish.

The riots in our large cities further focused attention on marketing because it became clear that some of the rioters blamed local merchants for a number of things. Though this topic will be discussed in the next chapter we should point out that the emergence of problems of the *underprivileged* added more strength to the consumer movement.

So the causes for consumerism are many. When a buyer pays his hard-earned money for a product or service he expects to receive satisfaction, be told all important information, receive a safe product, have an adequate choice, and get redress from retailer and manufacturer when something goes wrong. Yet "the consumer is king" belief no longer holds, and if consumers are not masters of their own purses, if they do not control their own decisions, if they cannot have significant impact on the allocations of resources, then the concept of consumer sovereignty has to be examined. This issue goes to the heart of our system. Economist Paul Baran has explained the Marxian viewpoint:

> . . . The real problem . . . is whether an economic and social order should be tolerated in which the individual, from the very cradle on, is so shaped, molded, and "adjusted" as to become an easy prey of profit-greedy capitalist enterprise and a smoothly functioning

object of capitalist exploitation and degradation. The Marxian socialist is in no doubt about the answer. Holding that mankind has now reached a level of productivity and knowledge which make it possible to transcend this system and replace it by a better one, he believes that a society can be developed in which the individual would be formed, influenced, and educated not by a profit- and market-determined economy, not by the "values" of corporate presidents and the outpourings of their hired scribes, but by a system of rationally planned production for use, by a universe of human relations determined by and oriented toward solidarity, cooperation, and freedom. (Baran, 1962.)

American businessmen would have a different kind of answer and so would our government and most other governments. The answer would be that we have to improve and adjust within our total environment so as to eliminate the kinds of problems now plaguing consumers. In the next section we will examine some of these responses by government, business, and consumers to the consumerism phenomenon.

## RESPONSES TO CONSUMERISM

Responses to consumerism by the various segments of society have been different in each case—and for good reason, since each group sees the issue differently. One survey among business, consumer, and government spokesmen revealed some of the different attitudes on consumerism that prevail; selected findings are given in 26-3.

### Consumer Responses

In acts ranging from the quiet refusal to repurchase a particular item to the looting and destruction of retail establishments, consumers have responded unmistakably. They have organized in many kinds of groups, some temporary as in the case of price strikes in Denver, and others permanent as with state consumer organizations. Citizens are reading consumer publications and books on consumerism. They are supporting lobbying activities to influence their state and federal governments. They are writing to their congressmen and they are voting for candidates who support consumer protection. Through many associations and groups to which they belong consumers have encouraged favorite programs and positions. Thousands have written to the President's advisor on consumer affairs, and thousands have gone to Better Business Bureaus and have sent protests to individual companies.

Consumers are better organized today than they were a few years ago. Their interests are broader. They have tasted victory in the form of new laws and pronouncements from manufacturers. Their goals are not depression-bound or war-bound but are of a more permanent nature, not tied to emergencies. Of course, the consumer movement is diffused in a real sense, and it tends to move into a wide variety

**26-3** Consumer vs. Government vs. Business—Selected Findings

| | | Answers in percentages | | |
|---|---|---|---|---|
| | | Business | Consumer | Government |
| "Consumerism is an attempt to preserve the free enterprise economy by making the market work better." | Agree | 12 | 82 | 76 |
| | Disagree | 68 | 6 | 16 |
| | Uncertain | 20 | 12 | 8 |
| Opinions about the nature of consumerism: "Consumerism is primarily: . . . ." | Political in nature | 67 | 29 | 47 |
| | Economic in nature | 5 | 29 | 39 |
| | Social in nature | 14 | 21 | 0 |
| | Other | 14 | 21 | 14 |
| Possible underlying causes | A feeling that business should assume greater social responsibilities | 64 | 75 | 100 |
| | A bandwagon effect | 68 | 54 | 50 |
| | Political appeal of consumer-protection legislation | 88 | 67 | 77 |
| | Widening consumer-information gap | 25 | 74 | 85 |
| | A deterioration of business ethics | 9 | 61 | 0 |
| | Lack of public awareness of the legislation which already exists | 70 | 26 | 8 |

SOURCE: Ralph M. Gaedeke, "What Business, Government and Consumer Spokesmen Think About Consumerism," *Journal of Consumer Affairs*, Vol. 4 (Summer 1970), pp. 10–15.

of areas of concern. Some of the active groups in consumerism include: The National Organizations Advisory Committee on Consumer Interests, NAACP, cooperatives, libraries, National Urban League, United Church Women, Camp Fire Girls, PTA, YMCA, National Council of Jewish Women, credit unions, and National Farmers Union. Nader has organized many campuses with thousands of students now taking active parts in changing existing situations. Another Nader innovation has been the formation of "Mini-Nader" crews: private consumer crusaders who have learned the basic tenets of aggressive watchdogging from Nader and who concentrate on specific consumer complaints. There is a crew for auto safety, children, household products, foods, and promotion.

Despite this array of activity, all citizens do not completely support consumerism. There has even been a great deal of opposition to consumerism, although no analysis of this attitude has been made. Many consumers have other interests that they consider primary: for example, most marketers whether in sales, advertising, or transportation would put those interests ahead of consumer interests. Further, the effectiveness of the movement is complicated by misperceptions of both businessmen and consumers. Unfortunately, meaningful dialog is often impossible because of differences in perceptions. For example, a consumer may demand safety in his automobile and declare that it should be very easy to build safety into the auto. A manufacturer, on the other hand, may assert that it is speed and glamor that sell cars and that safety features cost a great deal more than they are worth to the consumer. Even so, attempts at having dialogs are still worth trying.

### Government Responses

In the 1960s politicians discovered the consumers and the consumers discovered the politicians. New agencies were created, old ones were spurred into action on behalf of consumers, laws were passed, speeches were made. A decade or so ago the consumer bills introduced annually in Congress numbered five or ten, but by the early 1970s there were several hundred bills being introduced on an annual basis. There were 42 agencies in the federal government dealing with over 400 consumer programs. And by 1972 there were 43 states with their own consumer-protection agencies, most of them closely related to the state attorney-general. In one state the attorney-general proposed to train each of the county attorneys in consumer law so that the effectiveness of the attorney-general's office could be expanded enormously. (He left office that year and his successor did not press for the change.) Four states by 1972 installed toll-free "consumer hot lines" so that consumers could call in their complaints to the state agency. These states were Georgia, Kentucky, Washington, and Delaware. A few cities have offices of consumer affairs, the most notable one being New York City with Bess Myerson.

President Kennedy, as we indicated, set the stage for consumer legislation with his consumer message in 1962. The following are excerpts from his speech.

> Consumers, by definition, include us all. . . . But they are the only important group in the economy who are not effectively organized, whose views are often not heard. . . . If consumers are offered inferior products, if prices are exorbitant, if drugs are unsafe or worthless, if the consumer is unable to choose on an informed basis, then his dollar is wasted, his health and safety may be threatened, and the national interest suffers. . . . The housewife is called on to be an amateur electrician, mechanic, chemist, toxicologist, dietitian, and mathematician—but she is rarely furnished the information she needs to perform these tasks proficiently. . . . Marketing is increasingly impersonal. Consumer choice is influenced by mass advertising utilizing highly developed arts of persuasion. The consumer typically cannot know whether drug preparations meet minimum standards of safety, quality, and efficacy. He usually does not know how much he pays for consumer credit; whether one prepared food has more

nutritional value than another; whether the performance of a product will in fact meet his needs; or whether the "large economy size" is really a bargain. . . . To promote fuller realization of these consumer rights, it is necessary that existing Government programs be strengthened, that Government organization be improved, and, in certain areas, that new legislation be enacted.

Kennedy asked for:

I. Strengthened programs
  1. Food and drug protection (Food and Drug Administration and Department of Agriculture)
  2. Safer transportation (Federal Aviation Agency, Commerce, Public Roads)
  3. Financial protection (Securities and Exchange Commission, Postmaster, Justice)
  4. More effective regulation (ICC, CAA, FTC, FPC, FCC, SEC)
  5. Housing costs and quality
  6. Consumer information and research—and representation (Housing, Agriculture, Food and Drug, Labor, Commerce, HEW, and a new Consumers' Advisory Council)

II. New legislative authority
  1. Strengthening of regulatory authority over food and drugs
  2. Requiring "truth-in-lending" information
  3. Manufacturing of all-channel television sets
  4. Truth-in-packaging laws

President Johnson continued the consumer movement with several voiced expressions of support, including the following:

1964—The consumer is moving forward. We cannot rest content until he is in the front row. . . . [I want to] assure that the best practice of the great American marketplace—where free men and women buy, sell, and produce—becomes common practice. To fight, side-by-side with enlightened business leadership and consumer organizations, against the selfish minority who defraud and deceive consumers, charge unfair prices, or engage in other sharp practices. To identify the gaps in our system of consumer protection, information, and choice that still need to be filled.

1966—Every domestic program of the Federal Government in a very real sense is directed toward the consumer. When we work to stem pollution, improve transportation, or rebuild our cities, we promote the welfare of the American consumer.

1968—It is the government's role to protect the consumer—and the honest businessman alike—against fraud and indifference. Our goal must be to assure every American consumer a fair and honest exchange for his hard-earned dollar.

Legislation that President Johnson called for included the following:

1. Inspection of foods, over-the-counter drugs, cosmetics, therapeutic, diagnostic and prosthetic devices
2. Warning labels for many products
3. Screening of pesticides
4. Meat and poultry inspection
5. Elimination of unfair trade practices
6. Truth-in-packaging
7. Truth-in-lending
8. Truth-in-securities
9. Better housing
10. Child safety act
11. Drug safety act
12. Aids for the poor
13. Interstate land-sales full-disclosure
14. Additional controls for mutual funds
15. Medical-device safety
16. Clinical-laboratories improvement
17. Protection against hazards in the home: product safety, flammable fabrics, fire safety
18. Electric power reliability
19. Natural gas pipeline safety
20. Crackdown on fraud and deception in sales
21. Major study of automobile insurance
22. Elimination of radiation hazards from television sets
23. Prevention of death and accidents on our waterways
24. New meaning to warranties
25. Government attorney to represent the consumer

In 1969 President Nixon stated in his consumer message:

> Consumerism in the America of the 70s means that we have adopted the concept of "buyer's rights" [intelligent choice, accurate information, health and safety, right to register dissatisfaction, personal freedom, better business]. . . .
>
> Our goal is to turn the buyer's bill of rights into a reality, to make life in a complex society more fair, more convenient and more productive. . . . Our action is intended to foster a just marketplace—a marketplace which is fair both to those who sell and those who buy.

Programs recommended by President Nixon included the following:

1. New Office of Consumer Affairs in the White House
2. Expanded powers for the FTC
3. New Division of Consumer Protection in Justice
4. New law with provisions for consumer class-action*

*Class-action provides consumers the right to sue as a group or class and not only as individuals; in this way they can divide the law suit costs among them.

5. New products-testing law
6. New commission on consumer finances
7. New laws on product safety
8. Stronger enforcement of food and drug laws
9. Expansion of consumer activities in the Office of Economic Opportunity
10. Strengthening of state and local consumer programs
11. New look at warranties and guarantees

Do all these laws help? How much help do consumers need from government? This is certainly a debatable issue. In 1969 Secretary of Commerce Maurice H. Stans stated that the nation had to consider "whether we are going to let the wave of consumerism move too far and destroy the freedom of consumers." Some consumer advocates among the congressmen have also voiced concern about "overkill" legislation. The programs of the past three administrations have been consumer-oriented and the trend seems to be continuing. Yet there is concern that government as a kind of "bargaining agent" may soon stand tall between the manufacturer and consumer. To get an idea of the scope of these programs, let us look at two consumer issues, truth-in-packaging and product safety.

President Kennedy asked for a truth-in-packaging law in 1962 and President Johnson asked for it each year thereafter until it was finally passed in 1966. Five years were spent in debate, with consumers fighting for it and business opposing it. The law, officially known as "Fair Packaging and Labeling Act" has this declaration of policy:

Informed consumers are essential to the fair and efficient functioning of a free market economy. Packages and their labels should enable consumers to obtain accurate information as to the quantity of the contents and should facilitate value comparisons.

Since the law was passed, the government reached voluntary agreements with certain industries, such as the following:

| Products | Reduction in number of package sizes | |
|---|---|---|
| | From | To |
| Dry cereals | 33 | 16 |
| Detergents | 24 | 6 |
| Green olives | 50 | 20 |
| Tooth paste | 57 | 5 |

Because of such achievements the law was considered a victory for the consumer. But the law has a number of imperfections and the results have not entirely been what consumers wanted or expected. For example, the enforcement of the law is divided among several federal agencies. In addition, the wording of the regulation is imprecise. One of the tasks of the Secretary of Commerce is to figure out what phrases such as the following mean: "undue proliferation," "reasonably comparable," "impairs the reasonable ability of consumers to make value comparisons." Consumers are also finding that the new law does not guarantee that a buyer will be able to make comparisons. An experiment was performed in California in 1962 with college-educated housewives who were given a shopping list of 14 items, ranging from pancake mix to shampoo, and were instructed to pick whichever package contained the largest amount of each product at the lowest price. In 1962, before the truth-in-packaging act, 34 of 70 choices were incorrect. In 1969, after truth-in-packaging, the experiment was repeated and this time the housewives made 38 incorrect choices. A few comments on this study and the law should be made. Clearly a number of businesses are operating within the letter but not within the spirit of the law. But in addition the number of choices for the housewives increased in the seven years between experiments as new brands have appeared on the shelf almost daily. It takes a long time to make effective changes in something as numerous and varied as packages and labels; even so, legislation is no cure-all.

Product safety is another important area for consumer interest. One way to achieve product safety is through specifications and standards. The United States has had product standards for many years and today there are over half a million of them. The problem is that they are industry standards that facilitate production and interchangeability but do not relate to consumer safety. Standards for rugs, for instance, might regulate sizes but not necessarily flammable materials, and the result would be that many people lose their lives because their rugs catch on fire. Most standards have resulted from voluntary and successful cooperation between business and government. With consumerism there has been a move to develop standards that would particularly promote product safety.

The need for product safety has been underscored with widely publicized reports on the dangers of cigarettes, cyclamates, automobiles, glass doors, pesticides, ladders, cancerous chickens, fish poisoned with mercury, appliances, carpets, plastic sheets, paints, glues, eyeglass frames, and children's products. In 1971, for instance, the FDA issued a warning against a toy shaving kit that contained infection-causing bacteria. In 1972 a test of 76 children's sleeping garments found that 75 did not meet flammability standards and could be burned easily with a candle.

The National Commission on Product Safety produced its report in 1970. It estimated that almost 15 million injuries are sustained annually from the consumer products studied. Appliances accounted for 500,000, ladders for 180,000, and power mowers for 140,000 accidents annually. The Commission found that hazards exist in many consumer products: fire in color television sets; 300–400 degree temperatures in floor furnaces; thin, breakable glass for bottles; poor stability in high-rise bicycles; hotwater vaporizers that upset easily; lack of guards on power tools; and carbon monoxide from unvented gas heaters. Hazardous, also, are electric blankets, eyeglasses, ski bindings, snowmobiles, minibikes, boats, and cosmetics. Insurance companies reported that their three biggest headaches come from glass bottles, beauty aids, and stairways. The Commission examined the topic from almost every viewpoint and then made a number of recommendations:

1. An omnibus Consumer Product Safety Act should be passed.
2. An independent Consumer Product Safety Commission should be established.
3. Information should be collected, standards be set, consumers be educated.
4. The FTC should promulgate rules for those who certify safety of products.

If you think through the ramifications of protecting the consumer through packaging and safety laws, you will come to a better understanding of the scope of the problem and of the nature of consumerism itself. Legislation in food, drugs, toys, appliances, credit, pricing, and selling have undoubtedly helped the consumer—but legislation is not a panacea.

Before leaving the subject of government responses we want to point out the increased activity of regulatory agencies on behalf of the consumer. Whether inspired by the administration, the Congress, or by Nader's raiders, the effect has been one in favor of consumers. Enforcement by the FTC has been stepped up in several areas such as advertising claims, unordered merchandise, deceptive pricing, and warranties. In July 1971 the FTC announced that it ordered seven automobile manufacturers to document 60 advertising campaigns such as "over 700 percent quieter" (Ford), "109 advantages" (General Motors), "lowest priced compact in America" (American Motors), and "30 miles a gallon from your new Dodge Colt" (Chrysler). The FDA has been busy with food and drug items along with toys. The Public Health Service has made a number of statements on cigarettes and on television violence.

## Business Responses

President Johnson observed in 1965:

> I believe the time has come to bury forever the myth that furthering the interest of the consumer must be at the expense of the producer. There is, I am convinced, a common interest between Americans in their capacity as producers and in their capacity as consumers. This mutuality must be emphasized.

American business has responded to the challenge of consumerism. A new industry of consumer-consulting firms has even sprung up to service the movement. Existing organizations have taken various steps. The Grocery Manufacturers of America now has a Council on Consumer Affairs and sponsors the Consumer Research Institute. The National Association of Food Chains, the National Consumer Finance Association, The National Gas Association, and the Shoe Retailers

Association have taken steps to help the consumer by establishing advisory councils and furnishing more consumer information. The National Association of Manufacturers offers a booklet, "TIPS" (Techniques in Product Selection), that is a catalog of self-helps for consumers. The American Pharmaceutical Association and the National Paint and Varnish Association have also taken some action toward helping the consumer. RCA-Whirlpool, Maytag, J. C. Penney, Sears-Roebuck, and Procter & Gamble have taken certain steps such as improved quality control, better warranty agreements, dependable repair service, point-of-sale information, and information for low-income buyers. "We listen" campaigns with toll-free telephone numbers were developed by appliance and automobile manufacturers. American Motors offered a "Buyer Protection Plan" for 1972 that included a straight-forward guarantee, a better factory-checked car, and a direct line to Detroit. Ford published a book, "Car Buying Made Easier," that provided a good deal of information about cars. Allstate Insurance continued to offer discounts for insurance on cars that had bumpers that met certain specifications, thus cars meeting the 1973 federal specifications would qualify for a 10 percent reduction in rates. Allstate also offered a 20 percent discount for any car the manufacturer certifies, through independent tests, can take a five mile an hour crash into a test barrier, front and rear, without any damage.

Some Better Business Bureaus were strengthened to take care of the demand of consumers and to increase their educational efforts. The advertisement in 26-4 suggests that not all business is willing to support consumers to the extent that may be necessary.

The U.S. Chamber of Commerce established the Consumer Issues Committee and made recommendations to its members on quality,

---

## 26-4

**"Open Letter to the Businessmen of This Area from the Better Business Bureau of Greater Minneapolis"**

Business today finds itself in "the awe of the consumer." There is a steadily increasing volume of public inquiries pertaining to the record of firms in this area and an even greater need for detailed and objective investigation of consumer complaints. Yet, in the face of this mounting demand for its services, your Better Business Bureau has had to reduce its staff and curtail operations since September 1 because of a budget deficit of $17,000.

Ethical and farsighted businessmen of Minneapolis founded the first bureau of the BBB movement in 1914. Unless their successors rally now to support the bureau by their firm memberships, in 1970, it may have to close its doors *at a time when bureau services are needed the most in its 56-year history!*

SOURCE: Advertisement in *The Minneapolis Tribune,* May 11, 1970. (Note: The BBB was formed by the Vigilance Committee of the Minneapolis Advertising Club in 1914.)

---

## 26-5

**United States Chamber of Commerce Code for Business-Consumer Relations**

**1.** Protect the health and safety of consumers in the design and manufacture of products and the provision of consumer services. This includes action against harmful side effects on the quality of life and the environment arising from the technological progress.

**2.** Utilize advancing technology to produce goods that meet high standards of quality at the lowest reasonable price.

**3.** Seek out the informed views of consumers and other groups to help assure customer satisfaction from the earliest stages of product planning.

**4.** Simplify, clarify, and honor product warranties and guarantees.

**5.** Maximize the quality of product servicing and repairs and encourage their fair pricing.

**6.** Eliminate frauds and deceptions from the marketplace, setting as our goal not strict legality but honesty in all transactions.

**7.** Ensure that sales personnel are familiar with product capabilities and limitations and that they fully respond to consumer needs for such information.

**8.** Provide consumers with objective information about products, services, and the workings of the marketplace by utilizing appropriate channels of communication, including programs of consumer education.

**9.** Facilitate sound value comparisons across the widest possible range and choice of products.

**10.** Provide effective channels for receiving and acting on consumer complaints and suggestions, utilizing the resources of associations, chambers of commerce, better business bureaus, recognized consumer groups, individual companies, and other appropriate bodies.

SOURCE: United States Chamber of Commerce.

warranties, complaint systems, sales training, pricing, product safety, ethics, and Better Business Bureaus. The Chamber also prepared program guides for local chambers of commerce in order to "revitalize business-consumer relations." The organization issued a 10-point code for consumer relations which is shown in 26-5. In these ways the Chamber indicates that it aims to stimulate the development of business-consumer programs among 2700 local chambers and 1100 associations, which they calculate would "motivate 37,000 business members to put these principles into effect. . ." This would, they hope, mobilize five million businessmen and women. Certainly the effort will have a significant effect even if only a small percentage of the businessmen participate in the programs.

Businesses have taken many constructive steps toward solving the problems posed by consumerism. These actions are far better than for business to deny the existence of any problem or to contend that government regulation is an evil. But for the statements of business to be effective there must be force behind them. Workers on the production line, advertisers, salesmen, and everyone concerned with the product must know that top management is truly behind the statements and that the whole thing is not simply a public relations program.

Consumerism looks like a threat to many businessmen. Many consumer demands create additional costs, impinge upon the freedom of business operation, and push business in the direction of uniform standards and sameness. But if American business ingenuity is a fraction as good as most of us believe there should be no difficulty with consumer programs.

## Other Responses

There are other responses to consumerism that are worthy of brief mention. Foundations such as the Arthritis Foundation published leaflets telling of arthritis quackery, a $403 million "racket." The Foundation stated that for every $1 spent each year in legitimate research on arthritis, more than $25 are spent on useless quack cures and remedies. Unions such as the AFL-CIO stepped up its efforts in lobbying for consumer education programs and many local unions conducted classes for consumers. Universities and schools added courses related to the consumer. Some high schools decided that consumer education is as important as driver training. Television stations and newspapers instituted consumer programs that handle consumer complaints. Hundreds of articles and dozens of books on consumerism have been published since the late 1950s. Consider the following list:

| Books | Authors |
|---|---|
| *Dollars and Sense* | Joseph Bensman |
| *The Intelligent Buyer's Guide to Sellers* | Dexter Masters |
| *The Real Voice* (drug industry) | Richard Harris |
| *The Dark Side of the Marketplace* | Senator Warren Magnuson |
| *The Medical Messiahs* | James Young |
| *Hot War on the Consumer* | David Sanford, Ralph Nader, James Ridgeway, and Robert Coles |
| *The Innocent Consumer vs. the Exploiters* | Sidney Margolius |
| *You are a Consumer of Clothing* | Pauline G. Garrett and Edward J. Metzen |
| *The Hidden Persuaders* | Vance Packard |
| *The Consumer and His Dollars* | David Schoenfeld & Arthur A. Natella |
| *Quota* | Vercors |
| *The Great Discount Delusion* | Walter Nelson |
| *The American Way of Death* | Jessica Mitford |

| **Books** (*continued*) | **Authors** (*continued*) |
|---|---|
| *The Poor Pay More* | David Caplovitz |
| *Silent Spring* | Rachel Carson |
| "The Nader Report" on the FTC | Edward F. Cox, Robert C. Fellmeth |
| | & John E. Shulz |
| *Unsafe at Any Speed* | Ralph Nader |
| *The Consumer* | Gerald Leinwand (Ed.) |

The causes of consumerism have been many and varied and so have the responses by business, government, and consumers themselves.

# CONCLUDING COMMENTS

It will take some time before the responses to consumerism, especially those of business, have crystallized and before they can be evaluated. However disturbing it may be, it is a challenge that business should accept, for the benefits that can be derived, not just for the consumer but for business itself, are enormous. As Robert Ferber has suggested, consumerism can serve "to provide ideas and hypotheses for testing the shortcomings of one's products as well as possibilities for remedying these shortcomings" (Ferber, 1970). Discussions with consumers can suggest to business, ways to close the gaps between them and the buyers. Another marketer put the case for paying attention to consumerism this way:

> The challenge we face, then, is to recognize and respond voluntarily to merited consumer demands, so we can assure that the thrust of consumerism manifests itself through the normal machinery to the maximum feasible extent—so the merits can be examined carefully and thoughtfully and the issues resolved in orderly and rational legislative or regulatory change. If this is not done, it is perfectly conceivable that consumerism ultimately could pose a serious challenge to the core of private enterprise: the profit system itself. (Yohalem, 1970.)

We generally feel that if people are provided with adequate information they will arrive at the correct decision. Marketing communications are a key to this information. Consumer education courses and point-of-purchase materials help considerably, of course. Several groups of consumers are especially in need of information—low-income households, senior citizens, young married couples, and high school students (Holton, 1966). Better labels, more informative advertising, improved and increased standards, and availability of testing information are other ways to inform the buying public. (See 26-6.)

## 26-6

**"To Advertising Men Who Are Also Businessmen:"**

### Why the Consumer Is
### Looking for More
### Informative Advertising.

Don't be fooled by the mini skirt. Today's woman wants, and is demanding more informative advertising.

She's a brand new breed in more ways than one. Better educated. More sophisticated. Often just off a campus where her classmates were questioning everything their mothers once took for granted.

She's eager, open, honest, inquiring, experimental—and often skeptical.

She's interested in your product—*really* interested—and she wants to know *all* about it. Not just the name and a jingle signature.

She wants to know what it does, how it works, what's in it, why it's better, how to maintain it, how long it will last—and what you'll do if it doesn't.

She knows more about chemistry, biology, health, nutrition and home economics than the class of '50 ever did. And you can put that knowledge to work for you—if you'll just give her the facts to work on.

SOURCE: Excerpted from a *Good Housekeeping* advertisement, *The New York Times*, May 14, 1970, p. 76.

---

The questions raised by consumerism obviously affect marketing profoundly. As E. T. Grether, a professor of marketing, points out: "The competitive market system is not a mechanical, closed system; it does and must react to law, regulation, and social value systems. It should not in itself inculcate and establish community standards and values" (Grether, 1966). The questions of consumerism affect other aspects of business as well. The point is that improved marketing alone cannot eliminate the problems of the consumer. Ultimately management at the highest level is responsible for what a firm produces and distributes. At *that* level the question to be faced is: What is the responsibility of the businessman—to give the consumer what he demands, what the businessman thinks is best for the consumer, or a combination?

Consumerism goes to the heart of our economic system, to matters of creditability, sovereignty, competition, representation, information, and concern for the consumer. It will not go away and it cannot be ignored. Marketers can play a lead in bringing consumers and management together in a positive thrust to solve the problems that have been uncovered. Many, indeed, can be solved on a voluntary basis, a course that is preferable to laws forcing compliance. But if voluntary compliance is not forthcoming, consumers will undoubtedly press for legislation. What will it be?

The evidence suggests that the consumer is nowhere near using the information now available to him. (Crichton, advertising)

If marketing fights consumerism as "socialism"—as the American Medical Association fought Medicare—the end result will be increased regulation that will put marketing into the straightjacket of a quasi-utility. (Weiss, advertising)

Roofs leak. Shirts shrink. Toys maim. Toasters don't toast. Mowers don't mow. Kites don't fly. Radios emit no sounds, and television sets and cameras yield no pictures. Isn't anything well made these days? (*Wall Street Journal*)

A prime secret of the success of the U.S. competitive enterprise system has been the great freedom of interaction between buyers and sellers. That freedom has generated the most dynamic and productive economic system in the world. (Stans, government)

The least appropriate, if not the most foolish, response is to deride consumerism as a threat to the free enterprise system. (Burson-Marsteller, public relations)

The supermarket, glossy symbol of our affluence, is today the scene of the greatest swindle since the serpent sold Eve on the forbidden fruit. (Mowbray)

What is new today about consumerism is the fact that consumers' concerns today are much more directly focused on the human values and environmental considerations involved in today's economic decisions than they are on the more strictly "economic" problems of obtaining the highest quality goods at the lowest possible price. (Mary Gardner Jones, FTC)

Let's give the American consumer the freedom, protection, and justice he deserves. Let's eliminate the fraud and the gimmick. Let's insist on quality control and safe products. Marketing is an exacting profession. The pace-setter that fails may be your own. Let's make our durables really durable. Let's write simple and effective guarantees, warranties that warrant, labels and instructions that give accurate and adequate information. Let's take the puff out of packaging, the proliferation out of sizes, and the confusion out of claims. (Virginia Knauer, President Nixon's consumer advisor).

Government is by no means convinced that business is doing as much as it should for the consumer. (Furness, government).

Reduced to its absolute essentials, consumerism challenges business to do better. (Yohalem)

# QUESTIONS FOR REVIEW

**1.** What evidence is there that the consumerism movement is not a fad?

**2.** What have been the reasons for the success of Ralph Nader?

**3.** What is your own appraisal of the causes of consumerism? Where do you place most of the fault?

**4.** Are the consumer rights as listed by John F. Kennedy adequate? Or are they excessive?

**5.** What is your answer to Paul Baran? (Pages 567–68)

**6.** What do Gaedeke's results (26-3) seem to tell you?

**7.** What do you conclude about the politics of consumerism?

**8.** Is there a better way than legislation to handle the problems of the consumer? What?

**9.** What business firm are you aware of that is doing a splendid job with consumers? In what way?

**10.** How far do you think consumer information can go in aiding the consumer?

## Further Readings

David A. Aaker and George S. Day (eds.), *Consumerism: Search for the Consumer Interest* (New York: Free Press, 1971).

*Freedom of Information in the Market Place,* A Collection of Opinions Expressed During the Ninth Annual Freedom of Information Conference. (Columbia, Mo.: School of Journalism, 1966).

Y. Hugh Furuhashi and E. Jerome McCarthy, *Social Issues of Marketing in the American Economy* (Columbus, Ohio: Grid, Inc., 1971).

Gerald Leinwand (ed.), *The Consumer* (New York: Washington Square Press, 1970).

See copies of the following periodicals: *Consumer Bulletin, Consumer Reports,* and *Journal of Consumer Affairs.* Also, see FTC reports.

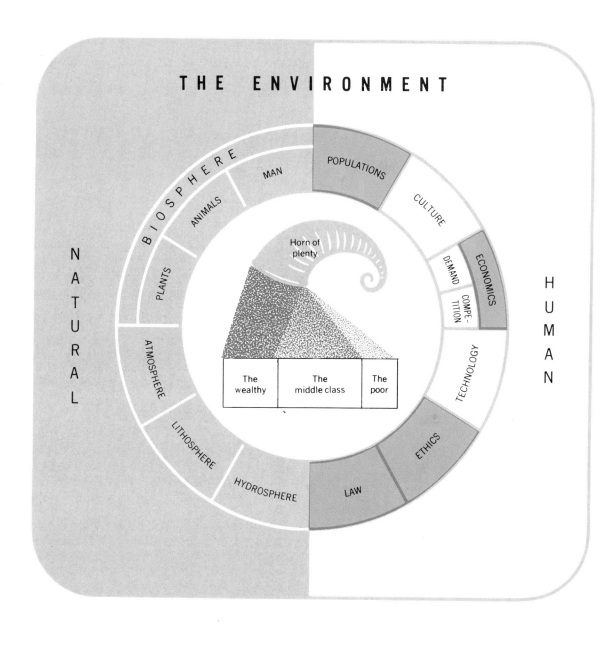

THE ENVIRONMENT

NATURAL

HUMAN

BIOSPHERE

MAN

ANIMALS

PLANTS

ATMOSPHERE

LITHOSPHERE

HYDROSPHERE

POPULATIONS

CULTURE

DEMAND

ECONOMICS

COMPE-TITION

TECHNOLOGY

ETHICS

LAW

Horn of plenty

| The wealthy | The middle class | The poor |

# CHAPTER 27
# MARKETING TO THE DISADVANTAGED

*The delivery of the standard of living has not meant affluence for millions of Americans, let alone those living in the Third World. How to provide adequate goods and services to the disadvantaged, through the present marketing and economic systems, is indeed a challenge.*

> *A definition:* Marketing is the deliverance of the standard of living."
> (Mazur, 1947.)

This chapter is concerned with the marketing of products and services to low-income consumers, primarily those who reside in our inner-cities. The disadvantaged sector includes all those people who are not reaping the economic benefits that characterize our affluent society, who are not being "delivered" the American standard of living. The chapter includes material on poverty, the buying habits of the poor, the problems of both buyer and seller, and finally solutions that have been tried in the inner-city areas. First, however, we want to consider the question of the responsibility of marketing.

## HAS THE MARKETING SYSTEM FAILED?

Responsibility must be considered in the total environmental framework since the problems of the disadvantaged are rooted in all segments of the environment. We are addressing ourselves to the marketing problems of the disadvantaged, but these are related closely to income, race, housing, the law, ethics, transportation, competition, and the physical surroundings of the areas in which the disadvantaged live.

If marketing is "the deliverance of the standard of living," has it failed in its task by neglecting to serve approximately 30 million who are poor citizens? Consider this description of the marketing system in a ghetto.

> The most concrete fact of the ghetto is its physical ugliness—the dirt, the filth, the neglect. In many stores walls are unpainted, windows are unwashed, service is poor, supplies are meager. . . . When tumult arose in ghetto streets in the summer of 1964, most of the stores broken into and looted belonged to white men. Many of these owners responded to the destruction with bewilderment and anger, for they felt that they had been serving a community that needed them. They did not realize that the residents were not grateful for this service but bitter, as natives often feel toward the functionaries of a colonial power who, in the very act of service, keep the hated structure of oppression intact. (Clark, 1965.)

The distribution of affluence has been uneven, most uneven, and those not a part of the affluent society have, in a sense, been forgotten. The marketing researchers, who have cast about the metropolitan areas for choice locations have understandably overlooked the inner-city ghetto areas. Instead they have recommended the building of new shopping centers in the fast-growing suburbs where the middle- and high-income people are locating. Advertising has been geared to a high consumption level and has given the impression that every American family has a station wagon, a boat, air-conditioning, and a patio grill. Blacks and other minorities have usually been pictured as maids or someone on the "outside." The one part of the marketing system that has served the poor consists primarily of "mom and pop" stores, which are characterized by low turnover, high costs, shabby interiors and exteriors, and poor service. No one has yet examined systematically the marketing system that "serves" Indians on reservations, but available evidence suggests that it provides the same low quality. Of course, marketing is not entirely to blame for these shortcomings. Society in general and many groups and institutions in particular have failed to serve the poor: people in education, religion, the law, the courts, real estate, transportation, urban redevelopment, and even welfare work all bear responsibility. And, of course, the poor themselves can shoulder some of the blame, although this is a debatable and only partially understood point.

The marketing system has responded best to those with adequate incomes. They are in the system! Business gravitates toward profit-making activities and away from low-income sectors. Low-income people do not have enough money: the problem is as simple and ridiculous as that.

One way to appreciate the failure of marketing is to contrast an inner-city neighborhood with a suburban area. Most of the readers of this book have probably never been inside a ghetto store, or even in a ghetto community, but a visit to such a neighborhood would be enlightening. The contrasts in dress, housing, schools, playgrounds, and retail stores would be most obvious. Where in the ghetto area are the big clean supermarkets and the expansive shopping centers?

The riots of the sixties forced those in power to look at the plight of the disadvantaged. This is not to suggest that marketing practices sparked the riots, only that consumer grievances were contributing factors. The Kerner Commission was authorized by the President to probe ghetto residents for grievances. Consumer grievances ranked thirteenth in the list, well behind grievances concerning police practices, employment, housing, and education, for example (Report of the National Advisory Committee on Civil Disorders, 1968). A study of the Detroit rioters indicated that 43 percent thought the possible riot causes included "anger with local business people"; police brutality was reported by 57 percent; reasons for the riots given by respondents were multiple (Detroit Urban League, 1967). How respondents rated various types of stores for fairness or unfairness is shown in 27-1.

Since the retailer is the businessman most well known to inner-city residents, retail stores become convenient targets during a riot, especially because looting offers some immediate reward. Not surprisingly, retailers bore the brunt of property damage during some of the major riots.

## 27-1 Rioters' Attitudes toward Merchants in Detroit

*Question:* In your own neighborhood, do you think that the merchants in the following kinds of businesses treat Negroes fairly or unfairly? After I read each type of business, tell me if you think the merchants are fair or unfair to Negroes. (Answers given in percentages.)

| Type of store | Fair | Unfair | Don't know, no answer |
|---|---|---|---|
| Shoe stores | 49.9 | 17.4 | 32.7 |
| Grocery stores | 38.9 | 53.8 | 7.3 |
| Clothing stores | 45.3 | 29.1 | 25.6 |
| Dry cleaning shops | 65.2 | 21.1 | 13.7 |
| Appliance stores | 39.4 | 27.0 | 33.6 |
| Variety stores | 49.0 | 20.4 | 30.6 |
| Car dealers | 19.7 | 36.2 | 44.1 |
| Furniture stores | 28.6 | 39.6 | 31.8 |
| Drug stores | 64.1 | 25.9 | 10.0 |
| Gas stations | 61.8 | 12.4 | 25.8 |
| Bakery shops | 52.9 | 8.7 | 38.4 |
| Jewelry stores | 27.9 | 22.2 | 49.9 |
| Automobile repair shops | 23.3 | 36.2 | 40.5 |
| Hardware stores | 49.9 | 18.3 | 31.8 |
| Real estate agencies | 15.6 | 46.9 | 37.5 |
| Insurance agencies | 34.6 | 38.7 | 26.7 |
| Record shops | 62.5 | 6.9 | 30.6 |
| Restaurants | 50.8 | 18.3 | 30.9 |
| Magazine and book stores | 47.6 | 8.5 | 43.9 |
| Bars | 32.0 | 14.9 | 53.1 |
| Home improvement companies | 14.4 | 46.9 | 38.7 |
| Department stores | 58.8 | 22.9 | 18.3 |
| Loan offices | 16.9 | 48.5 | 34.6 |
| Liquor stores | 46.7 | 11.4 | 41.9 |
| Pawn shops | 14.6 | 26.8 | 58.6 |

SOURCE: Detroit Urban League, *A Survey of Attitudes of Detroit Negroes after the Riot of 1967,* Coordinated by the *Detroit Free Press* (Detroit 1967), p. 11.

Another study attempted to identify the kinds of people who riot. As it turned out, they were not the poorest of the poor, the least educated, nor the hard-core unemployed. Neither did they express frustration because of the gap between their situations and their expectations. According to the "relative-deprivation" theory, as it applies to marketing, advertising builds up expectations so high that frustration finally erupts when the expectations are unfulfilled. Mostly, however, the rioters reported that the problem was one of "blocked opportunity" to move ahead economically (Caplan and Paige, 1968). Jobs for blacks did not exist, nor did adequate housing and education. Again, the issue is bigger than marketing, although the forces of marketing are related.

A decade ago, even before the riots, sociologist David Caplovitz's book *The Poor Pay More* alerted many people for the first time to the problems the poor face in pricing, selling, advertising, and credit policies in New York City (Caplovitz, 1963). Since then, hundreds of articles and books have focused on the failures of marketing in the inner-cities. As one senator observed,

... the recognition of domestic poverty has slowly begun to sink into our social awareness. ... The ghetto is one place Adam Smith's "invisible hand" hasn't reached. ... Ghettos are like inland lakes, cut off from the marketing mainstream. Walk around a ghetto. What do you see? Inefficient stores; low-quality goods; marginal merchants. ... You [in marketing] can no longer ignore the ghetto. You must become involved. The challenge is to change perceptions, to create, to innovate, to transform. (Mondale, 1968.)

The riots that shook the nation in the 1960s bewildered and embarrassed many who had assumed that the business system was functioning perfectly, or at least properly. Businesses, governments, and communities all responded to the newly discovered needs. Some retailers in ghetto areas rebuilt; some departed the scene. New jobs were created, capital was put into the areas, black capitalism was promoted, and public awareness to the problems of the ghettos mounted. Some action-oriented steps such as neighborhood cooperatives were taken by those who sensed the crisis. Most marketing people, however, did not have ready answers, for indeed they did not even understand the situation, the problems, and the people. An obvious approach to overcome this failure was to gain vital information by studying the poor, their buying habits, their attitudes, and their needs, along with the existing retailing structure and merchandising practices.

## THE LOW-INCOME CONSUMER

A definition of low-income was adopted by a Federal Interagency Committee in 1969.* The index is based on a sliding scale of income, adjusted for price changes, family size, sex and age of the family head, the number of children, and farm-nonfarm residence. At the core of the definition is a nutritionally adequate food plan. According to this definition, some 25 million people in the United States were living in poverty conditions in 1970. Of course, if comparisons were made between the poor in the United States with the poor in many other nations, our poor would be affluent by comparison, but within the United States those families falling in the low-income category are poor.

The new interest in the poor revealed a few basic facts about them. The incidence of poverty is higher for the young and old than for intermediate age groups (see 27-2 and 27-3). There are more poor white than nonwhite but the incidence of poverty is higher for nonwhites; more poor in family units but higher incidence with unrelated individuals; more poor in nonfarm residences but higher incidence on farms; more poor in metropolitan areas but higher incidence in nonmetropolitan nonfarm residences; and more poor whites in all family sizes but higher incidences in all Negro groups. More poor people live in urban than in rural areas but the incidence of rural poverty is higher. What do you think the incidence would be for a Negro family of seven

*For 1971 the poverty income figure for a family of 4 was $4137.

**27-2** Persons and Families below the Low-Income Level, 1970*

| Category | Number (000) | Percentage† | Percentage distribution below low-income level** |
|---|---|---|---|
| **ALL PERSONS AND FAMILIES** | | | |
| Total | 25,522 | 12.6 | — |
| In families | 20,499 | 11.0 | — |
| Head | 5,214 | 10.0 | — |
| Related children under 18 years | 10,493 | 15.0 | — |
| Other family members | 4,792 | 7.3 | — |
| Unrelated individuals 14 years and over | 5,023 | 32.7 | — |
| **RACE AND SPANISH ORIGIN** | | | |
| Total persons | 25,522 | 12.6 | 100.0 |
| Spanish origin | 2,177 | 24.3 | 8.5 |
| White | 17,484 | 9.9 | 68.5 |
| Negro | 7,644 | 33.6 | 30.0 |
| Other races | 394 | 16.3 | 1.5 |
| **AGE OF PERSONS** | | | |
| Total | 25,522 | 12.6 | 100.0 |
| Under 14 | 8,541 | 15.7 | 33.5 |
| 14 to 21 | 3,709 | 12.6 | 14.5 |
| 22 to 44 | 4,801 | 8.3 | 18.8 |
| 45 to 54 | 1,654 | 7.1 | 6.5 |
| 55 to 64 | 2,107 | 11.4 | 8.3 |
| 65 and over | 4,709 | 24.5 | 18.5 |
| **RESIDENCE OF FAMILIES** | | | |
| Total families | 5,214 | 10.0 | 100.0 |
| Farm | 435 | 18.5 | 8.3 |
| Nonfarm | 4,779 | 9.6 | 91.7 |
| Metropolitan areas | 2,654 | 7.9 | 50.9 |
|   Inside central cities | 1,583 | 10.9 | 30.4 |
|   Outside central cities | 1,071 | 5.7 | 20.5 |
| Nonmetropolitan areas | 2,561 | 13.8 | 49.1 |
| **SIZE OF FAMILY** | | | |
| *All Races:* All families | 5,214 | 10.0 | 100.0 |
| 2 persons | 1,951 | 10.7 | 37.4 |
|   Head 65 and over | 936 | 16.4 | 18.0 |
| 3 and 4 persons | 1,586 | 7.7 | 30.4 |
| 5 and 6 persons | 964 | 9.7 | 18.5 |
| 7 persons or more | 713 | 22.8 | 13.7 |
| Mean size of family | 3.93 | — | 3.93 |
| *White:* All families | 3,701 | 8.0 | 100.0 |
| 2 persons | 1,581 | 9.5 | 42.7 |
|   Head 65 and over | 793 | 14.9 | 21.4 |
| 3 and 4 persons | 1,115 | 6.0 | 30.1 |
| 5 and 6 persons | 605 | 6.9 | 16.3 |
| 7 persons or more | 399 | 16.6 | 10.8 |
| Mean size of family | 3.61 | — | 3.61 |
| *Negro:* All families | 1,445 | 29.3 | 100.0 |
| 2 persons | 359 | 24.4 | 24.8 |
|   Head 65 and over | 135 | 38.8 | 9.3 |
| 3 and 4 persons | 440 | 25.1 | 30.4 |
| 5 and 6 persons | 341 | 33.3 | 23.6 |
| 7 persons or more | 303 | 44.4 | 21.0 |
| Mean size of family | 4.71 | — | 4.71 |

*See Table 27-3. †All totals in the several categories are as a percentage of total U.S. population. Detail of each category is as a percentage of the total in that particular category (e.g., there are 8,541,000 persons under 14 years of age in low income, or 15.7 percent of everyone under 14). **Represents the proportion of the particular category in low income.

SOURCE: U.S. Bureau of the Census, "Characteristics of Low-Income Population, 1970," P-60 #81 (November 1971), pp. 3-7.

**27-3** Weighted Average Thresholds at the Low-Income Level in 1970 by Size of Family and by Farm-Nonfarm Residence

| Size of Family | Total | Nonfarm Total | Farm Total |
|---|---|---|---|
| All unrelated individuals | $1,947 | $1,954 | $1,651 |
| Under 65 years | 2,005 | 2,010 | 1,727 |
| 65 years and over | 1,852 | 1,861 | 1,586 |
| All families | 3,580 | 3,601 | 3,147 |
| 2 persons | 2,507 | 2,525 | 2,131 |
| Head under 65 years | 2,569 | 2,604 | 2,218 |
| Head 65 years and over | 2,328 | 2,348 | 1,994 |
| 3 persons | 3,080 | 3,099 | 2,628 |
| 4 persons | 3,944 | 3,968 | 3,385 |
| 5 persons | 4,654 | 4,680 | 4,000 |
| 6 persons | 5,212 | 5,260 | 4,490 |
| 7 or more persons | 6,407 | 6,468 | 5,518 |

SOURCE: Adapted from U.S. Bureau of the Census, "Characteristics of Low-Income Population, 1970," P-60, #81 (November 1971), p. 20.

living on a farm? Surprisingly, most of the poor are employed: their incomes simply are meager. Almost half of those living in urban areas will probably always be poor, because they are too old to work, or are physically or mentally handicapped, or are female heads of households with little or no opportunity to find employment, sometimes because of racial or sexual discrimination.

The poor live in what anthropologist Oscar Lewis has called a "culture of poverty." Lewis sees the culture of poverty as a "subculture of Western society with its own structure and rationale, a way of life handed on from generation to generation along family lines." Some of the characteristics of the culture are the following: nonintegration of the poor with respect to the major institutions of poverty; production of little wealth; chronic unemployment and underemployment; low wages; lack of property; lack of savings; absence of food reserves in the home; and chronic shortage of cash. Lewis observes, ". . . by the time slum children are six or seven they have usually absorbed the basic attitudes and values of their subculture. Thereafter they are psychologically unready to take full advantage of changing conditions or improving opportunities that may develop in their lifetime" (Lewis, 1966).

The poor are handicapped by a feeling of powerlessness, deprivation, and insecurity. When the poverty-urban-racial crisis erupted in the 1960s many of them made it clear that they saw "the economic and political systems as essentially malign rather than benign, antagonistic to humane values rather than supportive of them" (Fusfeld, 1972). The cry of "cop-out" when the nation turned to environmental matters underlines the attitudes held by many of the disadvantaged.

Poor blacks, whites, Mexican-Americans, and others have been counted and studied, ad nauseam. There are a great many of them, but they have not offered the marketer an attractive potential and as a result they have not been ably served by the nation's marketing and business systems. Marketers know too little about the poor, their attitudes and life styles. Business as a whole knows too little about serving people who lack the income necessary to pay for the items they need.

## Buying Habits of Low-Income Consumers

An understanding of their buying habits would help improve marketing for inner-city and other underprivileged persons. Unfortunately, despite a number of recent studies, few concrete generalizations can be made about the buying habits of the poor, for each study has been made under special conditions. One rather obvious point that *can* be made is that the poor buy less—food, housing, clothing, transportation, or whatever—than the more affluent. But beyond that one generalization, the conclusions are not clear-cut. For example, one hypothesis is that low-income consumers (especially blacks) are prevented from buying some items, such as homes in certain areas, and therefore spend their money on automobiles as "compensatory consumption." Others refute this notion and point out that whites spend more for automobiles, income being a constant. A sampling of the literature does provide certain information about the buying practices of the disadvantaged, as the following shows.

Most of the poor do not use more deliberation, consult more sources, or shop more widely, to get the best buys. Instead, many depend on known merchants or relatives for judgments of what to buy. . . . Although they spend most of their income on basic needs, those who buy durable goods make serious inroads on their incomes. (Richards, 1966.)

Half the food shoppers in the area [Model City, Columbus, Ohio] did their major shopping at supermarkets within the area. More than half traveled over one mile to make their major food purchases. Quality, convenience, and price were the most important reasons for selecting the stores. (Marion, Simonds, and Moore, 1969.)

The disadvantaged [in Minneapolis-St. Paul] have several shopping strategies. One is to buy the lowest-priced item; a second is to patronize higher-quality department and specialty stores in order to avoid poor value; a third is to shop at Penneys, Sears, Wards, etc. (a popular strategy); a fourth is to shop at Goodwill Industries; and the fifth reported strategy is to shop where items can be easily returned. (Holloway and Cardozo, 1969.)

Low-income buyers as compared to middle-income buyers are more aware of available brands, buy more private-branded food items; are less knowledgeable about price, and consider price as less important than other store characteristics (location, accessibility to transportation, hours, and credit). (King and DeManche, 1969.)

It can be argued that inner-city residents are in effect prisoners. Their physical mobility is restricted and commodities tend to come into use as currency. Mobility is as important in determining inner-city shopping behavior as in determining shopping behavior elsewhere. . . . Environment is the key to everything. (Alexis, Haines, and Simon, 1970.)

Purchases of many food store items are similar regardless of level of income. Some of the differences, however, are interesting to examine. In one study of Cleveland shoppers, industrial neighborhood shoppers had incomes averaging $138 per week as contrasted to higher-income neighborhoods of $238. The blue-collar store reported sales of frozen Italian products of 14 percent of the higher-income store, 12 percent for relishes, 18 percent for Maraschino cherries, and 19 percent for frozen juices. On the other hand, the high-income stores had sales of 10 percent of the blue-collar stores in dried beans, 14 percent in apple butter, 14 percent in beans and peas. (*Progressive Grocer*, 1965.)

Some of the low-income buying studies concentrate on the differences between blacks and whites. Here is a sample of these studies:

The Negro is acutely quality- and brand-conscious. Blacks purchase more meat, especially pork and poultry, more bread, and more canned vegetables. As they go up in income they switch from canned to fresh and frozen products. As contrasted to the high-income stores, black-patronized stores (in Cleveland) report sales of the high-income stores to be 0.8 percent of the black stores in corn and potato meal, 15 percent in canned milk, 20 percent in shortening and 26 percent in hot cereals. The Negro stores sales were 7 percent of the higher income stores in frozen juices, 9 percent in frozen Italian products, 11 percent in cranberry sauce, 14 percent in oriental foods, and 17 percent in frozen cookies and gourmet foods. (*Progressive Grocer*, 1965.)

Forget about race. Race does not affect consumption. (Alexis, Haines, and Simon, 1970.)

Whites [in Chicago] have higher ownership of automobiles. The Negro preferences for autos is a function of income rather than race. Almost 61 percent of Negroes own either a Chevrolet or a Ford as contrasted to 44 percent of whites. There is no evidence that Negro shoppers prefer "mom and pop" stores. Negroes tend to purchase more cooked cereal, cornmeal, rice and flour than do whites. Whites purchase a greater variety of liquors than do blacks but about the same percentage of families purchase Scotch whiskey, the leading liquor purchased by Negroes for home consumption. Whites seem to buy more hair spray, shampoo, regular coffee, soups, cosmetics, and dietary soft drinks. Negroes preferred Colgate toothpaste over Crest by a 10 to 1 margin: whites divided almost equally between Colgate and Crest. (Larson, 1968.)

Negro women [in a southwestern city] do more of their shopping in downtown stores than do white women. As income for the Negroes increases, the percentage of shopping downtown decreases substantially. The study showed that more whites had shopped in discount stores within the past six months than had blacks, but when this was controlled for income changes, there was no difference. For mail order shopping, whites use the service more than blacks—40 percent versus 26 percent. More whites have charge accounts with department stores, but when controlled for income there seems to be no difference. 58 percent of the whites had gasoline credit cards as contrasted to 17 percent of Negroes. (Cox, Stafford, Higginbotham, 1971.)

A lower percentage of blacks with incomes under $3000 own refrigerators, freezers, washing machines, and washer-dryers, though the differences are not great except in the case of washing machines. The same kinds of differences hold for higher incomes although the percentage figures are of course higher in all cases. For example, only one percent of Negroes with less than $3000 income reported washer-dryer ownership whereas 15 percent of Negroes making over $8000 reported ownership. On health care, low-income whites see physicians and dentists more frequently than blacks. (Oladipupo, 1970.)

Negroes seem to be more brand-conscious for products in those categories which they regard as important, and less brand-conscious in those categories which they regard as less important. This would refute the common impression that Negroes are brand-conscious to an extreme. (Bauer and Cunningham, 1970.)

A summary of Negro-White expenditures is shown in 27-4. Blacks seem to spend more proportionately on clothing and nonautomobile transportation, but many of the expenditures are quite similar between the two groups. Many marketers believe in the existence of a Negro market and they expect to find differences in consumption patterns, forgetting that blacks read the same newspapers as whites, watch the same television commercials, and buy from retailers who are served by the same wholesalers. As one study concluded, "The research which has been done on consumption is remarkable for its lack of policy implications. This, it may be speculated, arises from the use of race as a dummy variable to cover a host of differential cultural and environmental factors which affect consumption. Policy implications could arise from research on differential consumption patterns only if the effect of environmental factors which affect consumption were explicitly measured" (Alexis, Haines, and Simon, 1970). Another study confirmed this: "Negroes are like all consumers everywhere. They will purchase those products and brands which maximize their satisfaction—physical, psychological, and sociological" (Larson, 1968).

Certainly most of the environmental factors were not controlled or measured in most of the above studies. Take the use of the media, for instance, and examine the differences between white and black. The poor are as likely to have TV as the general population, but they are less likely to use the other media. The poor are not media-poor, since

**27-4** Negro vs. White Distribution of Family Expenditures for Current Consumption*

| | Average percentage of current consumption | |
|---|---|---|
| Expenditure category | White† | Negro |
| Total food expenditures | 25.7 | 24.4 |
|   Food prepared at home | 20.7 | 20.0 |
|   Food away from home | 5.1 | 4.4 |
| Tobacco | 1.8 | 2.0 |
| Alcoholic beverages | 1.7 | 2.3 |
| Shelter | 16.1 | 16.1 |
|   Rented dwelling | 8.5 | 11.3 |
|   Owned dwelling | 7.1 | 4.7 |
|   Other shelter | 0.5 | 0.1 |
| Fuel, light, refrigeration and water | 4.8 | 4.6 |
| Household operations | 5.8 | 6.3 |
| House furnishings and equipment | 4.6 | 5.3 |
| Clothing, material and services | 8.9 | 12.5 |
| Personal care | 2.8 | 3.8 |
| Medical care | 7.1 | 4.5 |
| Recreation | 3.5 | 3.7 |
| Reading | 1.0 | 0.9 |
| Education | 0.9 | 0.5 |
| Transportation | 13.1 | 11.9 |
|   Automobiles | 11.4 | 9.5 |
|   Other travel and transportation | 1.8 | 2.4 |
| Other expenditure | 2.2 | 1.4 |
| Expenditure for current consumption | 100.1 | 100.3 |

* Controlled for income: $1,000–$14,999 income inclusive. Income control was obtained by "averaging averages"—that is, the percent for each income group was weighted by 1, summed and divided by 8, the number of income categories. Income categories under $1,000 and over $15,000 were excluded from the analysis. Total sample size was *8000* families.

† For whites (controlled for income), 25.7 percent of the total expenditures for current consumption was spent on food.

SOURCE: Raymond A. Bauer and Scott M. Cunningham, "The Negro Market," *Journal of Advertising Research*, Vol. 10 (April 1970), p. 10.

97 percent report ownership of TV, 93 percent have at least one radio, 75 percent have a newspaper delivered, and 77 percent have phonographs and records (Greenberg and Dervin, 1970). Other environmental factors have to be considered before one can draw any kind of conclusions about black-white differences in consumption. Housing, transportation, geographic distribution of population, occupations, and other factors all influence consumption as we have already seen.

The above sampling of low-income and black-versus-white buying practices does not yield a nice clear-cut picture, nor is it very complete, for we have little or no data on other disadvantaged segments of society such as Indians, the rural poor, and the handicapped. The data do suggest that income is more important than race in determining consumption practices, and this finding emphasizes the importance of understanding low-income consumers in general. With continued efforts in this direction, there will doubtless be less discussion about a "Negro market" and more about meeting the needs of inner-city ghettos, rural areas, and the disadvantaged in less-developed nations.

## Marketing Problems Reported by Low-Income Consumers

One way to understand low-income consumers is to examine their grievances. The problems listed below have been reported, in a variety of studies, by those living in the inner-city areas. They may not all be accurate statements of conditions from an objective point of view, but they are accurate descriptions of the way the poor perceive the conditions. The problems can be categorized in four parts as related to: (1) the merchant; (2) marketing system; (3) legal system; and (4) consumers themselves. No attempt will be made to elaborate on the individual problems since they are self-explanatory, but behind each are many tales of woe, such as the following story of a 41-year-old Puerto Rican husband whose family was on welfare: "I was cheated on a TV set I bought. At first the price was supposed to be $220. After I signed the contract I found out that it was really $300. But then it was too late" (Caplovitz, 1963).

### Merchant-related problems

Substitution of merchandise

Over-selling, high pressure tactics

Poor service

High prices

Bait and switch advertising

False and misleading statements

Misleading guarantees

Low-ball tactics

Misleading installment contracts

Failure to reveal full purchase price

Deceptive pricing

Fake drawings, contests, telephone surveys, and scholarships

Selling used merchandise as new

Fictitious wholesale price lists

Intimidation of customers

Low quality of products

Discrimination in serving customers

### Problems related to the system

Lack of competition and choice of retailer

Poor transportation facilities

A market place of "mom and pop" stores but few if any modern shopping centers

Inadequate housing

Problems of credit which go beyond the merchant's activities

High insurance costs

High land costs

Lack of available personnel in areas

Cycle of poverty—(A person gets a job, buys appliance on credit with garnishee provision, fails to make payments, wages garnished, loses job, loses appliance)

Inadequate educational opportunities

Lack of employment opportunities

The "culture of poverty" problem

### Problems with the legal system

Police intimidation, brutality

Law protects the establishment

Merchants never punished for fraud

Garnishment

Repossession, and sheriff sales

Consumers have nowhere to complain

Lack of funds to prosecute swindlers

Merchants, financial agencies, banks, everyone protected by law except consumer

Violations of licenses, inspections, sanitation, etc. not dealt with by law

Bill collectors with marked cars intimidate

### Problems related to the consumers

Do not report fraud and other violations

Lack information about buying—consumer ignorance

Do not take advantage of bargains when possible

Do not take advantage of stores out of the inner-city when such stores do exist nearby or on the fringe of the area

Unfamiliarity with legal recourse

Lack of budget skills

Presence of some who intimidate retailers who are accepted in the area

Basically, many low-income consumers do feel that they are captive in their environment, that they are preyed upon by malicious merchants who cheat and defraud them, that they pay higher prices than necessary, that they lack adequate choice, and that they are victims of the cycle of poverty. Findings such as these have been reported from most every major city. Not all merchants are guilty, of course, but the point is that retailers need to improve on their marketing practices in low-income sectors. There actually is no reason for any of the above problems to exist in any marketplace.

One question in particular has intrigued marketers: *Do the poor pay more?* The Caplovitz study, previously referred to, certainly indicated that they do. Again, the evidence is inconclusive. Some studies have reported that they pay more because they buy from small stores that have high costs. But others indicate that there are no differences in prices. Still others claim that prices are raised on welfare day when the people have checks in their hands. The problem is a difficult one to research, for prices have to be compared for the same products, brands, sizes, and dates of purchase in both inner-city and outer-city stores. Once again the data are inconclusive, as in these price studies:

Without exception, low-income market retailers had high average markups and prices. On the average, goods purchased for $100 at wholesale sold for $255 in the low-income market stores, compared with $159 in general market stores. (Federal Trade Commission, 1968.)

Differences in prices charged for clothing by stores in the two income areas were negligible when the same quality, brand, and style were compared, but generally higher-quality, higher-priced items were carried by stores in higher-income areas. Reported prices for drugs showed widespread price variations among stores but no discernible differences between low- and high-income areas. Prices for service items generally were lower in the low-income areas. (U.S. Department of Labor, 1966.)

Because they shop at competitive stores, going outside their residence area to do so if necessary, the poor do not pay more for food in this area [Philadelphia]. (Goodman, 1968.)

Price differences for comparable products are explained by the type of store rather than by store location . . . it is necessary to know where low-income families make their purchases, and what they purchase. (Dixon and McLaughlin, 1968.)

Generally, prices in both areas [Watts and Culver City] were quite similar. On the basis of the data collected for food items in general, the poor do not pay more; in fact . . . the cost of food in the ghetto area is actually slightly lower than in the nonghetto area. (Marcus, 1969.)

. . . there are some low- and high-priced stores in each area; thus, no matter where you live, in terms of price, it pays to shop around. (Teach, 1969.)

For equivalent rents, poor families get poorer housing than families with higher incomes. Food prices are associated with the kind of store rather than with the geographic area. In buying food, the poor pay more if they shop in the small independent stores rather than in the large independents and the chain stores, whose prices are lower. For clothes, appliances, and other items, the survey results are inconclusive. What is confirmed is that the poor do not buy the same items as the better off. (Groom, 1966.)

In a comparison study of 15 other pricing surveys, Donald Sexton found that "five indicated that consumers in black or in low-income areas either paid or were charged more for food products. The ten remaining studies found that the black or the poor did not pay or were not charged higher prices." Sexton continues, however, to point out the need for additional research since the studies already undertaken are "too equivocal and too restricted" (Sexton, 1971). Future studies will need to go further, into service and quality differences as well as price differences.

## THE MARKETER

Who are the merchants that serve the poor? It is important to know because, as the Kerner Commission Report declared, "Retail merchants are one of the most important and continually functioning interfaces between Negro communities and the large white societies." The Report indicated that of several occupational groups serving the ghetto the merchants have the widest range of age, have the largest percentage of immigrants, and are the least well educated. More vote Democratic than Republican; 39 percent are Jewish, 35 percent Protestant, and 24 percent Catholic. They are not joiners: at least most have not been active in civil rights movements. Only 23 percent live in the neighborhood where they work.

The Kerner Commission found that merchants' attitudes toward Negroes are a source of difficulty. Retailers are most likely to see Negroes as violent, criminal, and unreasonable in their desires for equality. Further, the merchants are unsympathetic to the plight of the ghetto Negro. Some merchants engage in unethical practices, and some are apt to treat Negro customers considerably less well than white customers. The Report concluded: ". . . a sizeable percentage seems to do business in a way that leaves many improvements to be desired. As long as these improvements are not made, the retail merchant in our urban ghettos will continue to be one of the primary targets of Negro antagonism" (Supplementary Studies for the National Advisory Commission, 1968).

But the retailer has his problems, too! Doing business in the inner-city during the past decade or more has not been an easy task. Riots, physical destruction, tension, intimidation, high insurance costs, and other problems have raised havoc with the retailer. What are the merchants' versions of an extremely difficult situation? They talk of shoplifting and vandalism. They report that their customers are frequently intoxicated, rude, and disorderly. They have to be wary of personal checks, and they dare not keep large sums of money in order to cash "safe" checks, a service very much desired by local residents. They say that their customers do not accept buying advice, a reflection, of course, of the distrust the buyer has for the merchant. Retailers in turn do not understand their customers, and they find it difficult to adapt to the environment in which they operate their business.

Just running a business is difficult. Merchants complain of the antibusiness attitude which they say prevails. Few attempts have been made to help the merchant and most of the ghetto studies have been derogatory. The retailers also claim that the hand-to-mouth purchasing of their customers means small-volume business, which causes high costs of operation. Credit and collection costs are high as well. It is difficult for them to find employees, white or black, and those they have they criticize as being late, lazy, and dishonest, while the manager himself frequently puts in long hours six and seven days a week. Retailers in the ghettos complain of the service from wholesalers. The wholesalers are geared for large-volume operations and so the small ghetto store receives infrequent delivery service. Often the lack of storage space means that the wholesaler has to pile boxes in the aisles, thus bothering the customers in the store. Problems of credit also exist between the retailer and wholesaler.

Inner-city buildings are old, making it costly and risky to expand and improve. Parking and delivery space is usually minimal if it exists at all. Often new freeways and urban renewal programs cut through the inner-cities, so that a merchant may find himself cut off from half his former customers. Merchants also complain that as the residents get decent jobs and incomes, they move out of the area and consequently the businesses are serving an ever-lower-income group.

A number of merchants have tried to do something about improving the marketing services to their low-income areas. Certainly some of the malpractices have been eliminated, service has been improved, and some new facilities have been built and old ones rebuilt. In some areas, however, the residents have less adequate retailing facilities than before the riots. Stores that the rioters demolished have not always been rebuilt and new capital has not been forthcoming.

## ATTEMPTS TO REMEDY THE PROBLEMS

Since the problems of the poor have been thrust into the public consciousness, just about every conceivable sector of society has put forth some effort toward alleviating them. The following suggests what has been done.

### Business Sector

A number of new stores have been built in inner-city areas by retail chains, private citizens, and cooperatives. Wholesalers, too, have helped to set up new stores and a good wholesaler-retailer relationship is vital to these kinds of operations. In a few instances there have been new shopping centers built, as in Philadelphia. Exact figures on the number of new stores—and the number of closings—in inner-city areas are not available. One survey indicated that from 1965 to 1970 in the 40 largest U.S. cities, 53 new supermarkets and 5 shopping centers were added, but 26 stores closed down (Wright, 1970). Although the authors believe that the situation has improved somewhat, there is still little evidence to indicate the extent to which the ghetto retailer has improved his marketing practices, adapted to his customers' needs, and eliminated his unfair and fraudulent dealings. This is a difficult sector of marketing to do very much about: these are small, independent businessmen who do not have time, for instance, to attend classes in order to learn more about retailing to the poor. The ghetto residents would undoubtedly benefit a great deal if new supermarkets were built in their areas so that competition would force a better marketing climate. But how many new stores will be built is open to question for it is difficult to see what will entice private business to invest in many of the poverty regions around the nation. Private capital does not easily flow into unattractive areas.

Business has aided the black capitalism movement in a number of ways, through gifts, training, consulting, and legal and accounting aid. The attempt to get black capitalism started in the ghetto areas has been a debatable issue. Some argue that this is the way to help new entrepreneurs, to gain confidence of the residents, and to eliminate cheating. Others argue that blacks should be encouraged to enter business in all areas, not only the ghettos, and that whites should enter the ghettos. They point out, further, that black-operated supermarkets are "just as vulnerable to the problems of the ghetto environment as white-operated businesses" (Bloom, 1970).

Most approaches to the problems have been piecemeal and narrow in scope. Kelvin A. Wall has proposed taking a broad systems approach to the ghetto problem, that is, an approach which would weave sociological and economic considerations of the community with marketing functions and implications. Distribution, advertising, new products, package size, wholesaler functions, outlets, sales coverage, employment practices and training, joint ventures, and public relations would all be covered by this approach (Wall, 1969).

## Residents

One of the ways ghetto residents have attempted to improve their marketing facilities has been through the formation of cooperatives. The cooperative movement which flourished during the thirties has gained some prominence in recent years as disadvantaged neighborhoods have given cooperatives their support. This is a natural development since it involves local citizens, gives them control and ownership, eliminates the criticisms of outside management, and holds prices down. The Harlem River Consumer Cooperative, for example, was started in New York in 1968 with help from businesses. The Harlem community has provided most of the board members and 4300 cooperative members purchased $264,000 in shares. In 1969 the volume was $2 million, but later, because of a number of problems, revenue dropped to $4000 per week (Cox and Seidman, 1969). A second venture has been Jet Food Corporation, established in 1966 as a franchise program: a prototype store was opened in Baltimore and another cooperative was set up in Cleveland. The Hunter's Point Coop in San Francisco opened in 1965, but it had a variety of problems including a robbery and in 1969 was receiving help from a private chain operation. In Minneapolis the Peoples' Cooperative Union opened in 1969 with black militants as its managers. They received considerable help from local business and church groups, but the real effort was on the part of the militants and local residents, including many children who helped the store become a reality. Unfortunately the store burned nine months after opening and in 1972 the residents were waiting for a new inner-city shopping center to be built.

## Universities

Universities have established special courses for those serving low-income areas. The training of blacks by the universities has helped a number of persons who had not had business experience. Through marketing research, students and faculties have examined various facets of inner-city environments and they have prepared the basic studies for new ventures in the inner-cities. Attempts have been made to encourage more minority groups to enter the business schools in order that they can move directly into the mainstream of business rather than be restricted to their own inner-city environments. In some universities, students have had class assignments that included work with a minority enterprise.

## Government

Almost every governmental agency has had one program or more dealing with poverty. During President Johnson's administration, every federal office inventoried its efforts on behalf of the poor. The Department of Commerce has had a number of programs that have ranged from black entrepreneurship to marketing. The Secretary of Commerce established the National Marketing Advisory Committee to advise him on marketing matters, and for several years the focus of the committee was on low-income marketing. Some research was sponsored by the committee, cases for university students were prepared, a *Bibliography of Low-Income Marketing* was compiled, and Guideline Questions were made available to those serving the ghetto areas. (See 27-5.) The purpose of the Guideline Questions was to raise issues that marketers moving into the ghetto for the first time should definitely consider, since it was found that some efforts did more harm than good.

Some improvements in legislation and in the legal system have been made but little documentary evidence is available. Much of the general consumer legislation on marketing practices, product safety, truth-in-packaging, truth-in-lending, and drugs should alleviate some of the ghetto consumers' problems. Government can encourage a variety of practices, but in marketing the job of implementing programs eventually falls to private business.

## 27-5

**"Guideline Questions"**

(The following questions are a checklist of factors to be considered in evaluating potential marketing activities in low-income areas. They also can be adapted for use in judging current programs which might be continued or expanded.)

1. Will there be adequate demand for the goods or services which will be made available to low-income consumers?

2. Will low-income consumers have a better range of choice in facilities, goods, and services?

3. Will low-income consumers get more for their money?

4. Will low-income consumers get more satisfaction from their marketing experiences?

5. Will the people to be served be involved in the planning?

6. Will helpful marketing information be more available and be put to better use?

7. Will unethical business practices be reduced?

8. Will the physical facilities in low-income areas be improved?

9. Will the financial resources needed for marketing facilities in low-income areas be expanded?

10. Will the drain of resources out of the low-income areas be reduced?

11. Will improved use be made of existing facilities?

12. Will employment and job-training opportunities for residents of low-income areas be expanded?

13. Will needed managerial skills be provided?

14. Are the costs of operating in low-income areas being considered realistically?

SOURCE: U.S. Department of Commerce, *Guideline Questions for Projects to Improve Marketing Services to Low-Income Consumers* (Washington, D.C.: GPO, 1969).

## CONCLUDING COMMENTS

The problems of the disadvantaged consumer have now become apparent to businessmen as well as to government and the ordinary citizen. Many attempts have been made to improve the plight of the inner-city resident, but little has been done for those disadvantaged persons living outside the inner-city. Further, there is a long way to go before anyone can say that marketing is doing a good job in most of our areas. It is, as was suggested at the outset, more than a marketing job. True, the retailers are a key to the situation, but the present retailing structure is not one that will bring a good deal of improvement and change into the areas. The solutions proposed are varied, ranging from eliminating the ghettos, to helping the consumer become a more intelligent buyer. But surely marketing can do more than this. As Roy Alexander has commented:

> Who better [than the marketer?] The business-to-business marketer has a proved record of getting things done—on time. He's trained in persuasion and communications—two indispensable elements. He's people-oriented. He's seasoned in unsnarling complex problems. The marketer relates effectively to other fields—legal, construction, accounting, social—because he's a generalist . . . on balance, the marketer has the best chance to succeed. (Alexander, 1969.)

The low-income marketing problems offer an environmental picture for study and action. The culture of residents is important since it is different from that of the affluent society. Their life styles, politics, and attitudes are not understood by the outsider. The geography and physical environment of ghettos have distinctive characteristics. The transportation system is typically poor. Housing conditions are deplorable. And the marketing system has for many years consisted of "mom and pop" stores with little choice and relatively high prices. The result is a situation where, as the able marketing scholar Marcus Alexis pointed out, "The environment is everything."

## STATEMENTS TO CONSIDER

> The distinctive nature of the Negro revolution is that it is not a revolution to overthrow the established order so much as it is a revolution to achieve full membership in that order. . . . The basic dilemma of Negroes is whether to strive against odds to attain these middle-class values (and the goods which come with them), or to give in and live without most of them. (Bauer, Cunningham, Wortzel)

> Whether the poor consumer, and especially the black resident of a low-income area, will fare better in the years to come may well depend on whether we succeed in bringing the competitive market to him, or whether he will become the pawn of those who would use him as their protected preserve. (Goodman)

> . . . the products and services available, their prices, and the stores in which he buys are vital, everyday concerns. They affect his standard of living, the ways in which he spends his time, and his attitudes toward his community and U.S. society. (Lavidge)

> The dilemma of the low-income consumer lies in these facts. He is trained by society (and his position in it) to want the symbols and appurtenances of the "good life" at the same time that he lacks the means needed to fulfill these socially induced wants. (Caplovitz)

...consumer problems in the curfew area [of Watts] are not due to systematic racial discrimination but rather result from the traditional interplay of economic forces in the marketplace, aggravated by poverty conditions. (Governor's Commission on the Los Angeles Riots)

Our slum areas show very little evidence of realization of the promises and hopes that were held out for their residents in the early 1960s, when America rediscovered poverty. (Sturdivant)

The discipline of the marketplace as the primary regulating force of our economy has broken down in the ghetto. . . . What we learn from the choice we make and the actions we take will shape the next evolutionary steps in the development of our entire marketing system. Out of the solutions to our ghetto marketing crisis can come productive and profitable improvements of wider applicability. (Hamilton)

I think it is wrong for some people to line their pockets with tattered dollars of the poor. So the first thing we should pledge ourselves to do is to take the profit out of poverty. (Lyndon Johnson)

The Negro customer is difficult to characterize due to the rapid and significant changes that are occurring in social status of Negroes in every major metropolitan area. . . . By far, the majority remain in the substandard situations they have known all their lives, and themselves create classes within their own racially classed society. The food store operator cannot apply the same common denominators to all Negroes as consumers; but, rather, he must learn to recognize and understand the motivations that characterize the distinctly different groups that are emerging today. (*Progressive Grocer*)

I must again in candor say to you members of this Commission [Kerner]—it is a kind of Alice in Wonderland—with the same moving picture reshown over and over again, the same analysis, the same recommendations, and the same inaction. (K. Clark)

## QUESTIONS FOR REVIEW

**1.** Has the marketing system failed the disadvantaged?

**2.** How important do you think marketing is to the low-income consumer?

**3.** Is there such a thing as a "culture of poverty?"

**4.** What are the important problems of the low-income consumer?

**5.** Do differences in consumption patterns exist between black and white consumers? How about between the affluent and the disadvantaged?

**6.** Would a small amount of consumer education give the disadvantaged a great deal of help or are his or her problems unrelated to buying practices?

**7.** What do you conclude about comparative pricing of food items in low-income versus high-income areas?

**8.** Evaluate the efforts of the marketers to solve the marketing problems of the disadvantaged.

**9.** Can the ghetto marketing problems be solved in a profit-oriented economy?

**10.** Comment on the statement by Alexis: "[For the disadvantaged buyer] the environment is everything."

## Further Readings

Raymond A. Bauer and Scott M. Cunningham, *Studies in the Negro Market* (Cambridge, Mass.: Marketing Science Institute, 1970).

David Caplovitz, *The Poor Pay More* (New York: Free Press, 1963).

*Journal of Advertising Research*. See the entire issue of Vol. 10 (April 1970).

Frederick D. Sturdivant, *The Ghetto Marketplace* (New York: Free Press, 1969).

U.S. Department of Commerce, *Bibliography on Marketing to Low-Income Consumers*, Revised, Robert J. Holloway and Frederick D. Sturdivant (eds.), (Washington, D.C.: GPO, 1971).

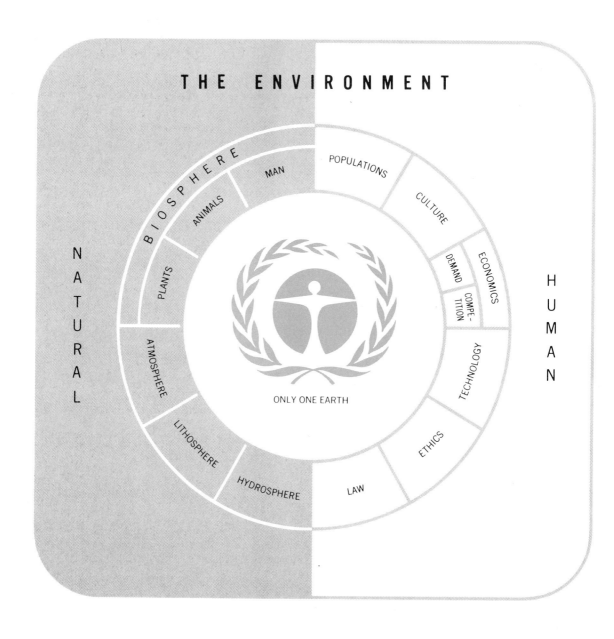

# CHAPTER 28
# TURNING POINTS
# FOR MARKETING

*The job of the marketer spans the total decision-making, executive, and evaluation process in matters of public policy affecting marketing. The posture of marketers may well change from year to year as they meet the turning points that become evident to those with social consciences.*

This book contains much of the traditional material of marketing, such as the institutional framework within which marketing functions and the various tasks of the marketing manager. In addition, we have tried to deal with the social responsibility of marketing managers, a complex issue well recognized by both businessmen and academicians. David Rockefeller has stated: ". . . it seems to me that businessmen have no choice but to respond by becoming reformers themselves, making a conscious effort to adapt the operation of the market system to our changing social, political and technological environment" (Rockefeller, 1971). And Wroe Alderson has commented: "Looking outward, the executive must be concerned with the habitability of the environment or habitat. . . . Thus, as he surveys the inside of the organization, the leader will be concerned with conditions that insure survival and externally he will be concerned with habitability" (Alderson, 1969).

We have attempted to identify the relationships between marketing and all other parts of the environment—government, technology, population, the legal system, and the natural environment. Marketing takes place in a kaleidoscope of subsystems, clusters, and constellations all of which interact simultaneously in an almost incomprehensible manner. Marketers are beginning to examine more than the primary consequences of their actions on profits, sales, and brand shares. They know that brand names can insult minority groups; advertising can degrade the poor; and packages can worsen the problem of solid-waste disposal. It is perhaps a great deal to expect a marketing manager to be equally aware of society and his firm, because he naturally will concentrate on his primary duties. To take a comparable example from government, the National Aeronautics and Space Administration is supposed to conduct its operations so as to benefit other national programs, but to no one's surprise NASA officials are primarily interested in the space program. The traditional and narrow focus of agencies and companies has served its purpose.

Ideally the marketing system has worked for everyone, as observed by Maurice H. Stans, former Secretary of Commerce: "The main characteristics of the American business system are the use of the market mechanism and the profit motive to allocate the productive resources of our society in accord with the wishes of society." Given the goals of the past, marketing has served well. It has helped business make profits and it has given consumers new models and fashions and an ever-increasing abundance of goods. But goals, assumptions, values, and our way of life are changing, and marketing is coming to a number of turning points in the road.

In response to the new values and demands of life, a new stage is developing in the evolution of marketing, a stage that has been called the "broadening of marketing" (Kotler and Levy, 1969). A part of the broadening process has included, as we mentioned earlier, the use of marketing techniques by museums, theatres, symphonies, the March of Dimes, politicians, churches (28-1), the military, and the government. Marketers are helping in bringing to public attention ideas having to do with pollution, care of natural resources, population control, and safety in the use of products. Not all of this extension of marketing is well received, however. When the Navy in 1971 signed a one-year advertising contract for $120,000, there was sharp criticism by those who feel that the military has already oversold itself to the people. And

**28-1** The Broadening of Marketing

THE GREEKS HAD A WORD FOR IT.

WE DO, TOO. THE SAME WORD.

AGORA.

IT MEANS MARKETPLACE.

Lately we've branched out. We still have church in church, but we also have it at the Oakbrook Shopping Center in suburban Chicago. We have a man in Las Vegas and on the ski slopes of Squaw Valley. And in a coffee shop in Lancaster, Pennsylvania.

We figure if you won't come where we are, we'll come where you are. We call it a listening ministry.

Our local ministers are good listeners, too.

United Church of Christ
a union of
The Congregational Christian Churches
and The Evangelical and Reformed Church

*Source:* The Office of Communication of the United Church of Christ.

in relation to the arts, some worry lest the selling of tickets becomes more important than the production itself. Nevertheless, marketing practices are steadily being adopted by many groups considered to be nonprofit or cultural in nature.

There is another side to the broadening process, the increased emphasis on social concerns—pollution, poverty, population, racism, and natural resources. In the three preceding chapters, we examined values, consumerism, and poverty in some detail. In this chapter we will discuss marketing as it relates to the quality of life, and we will identify some of the turning points with which marketers must struggle. These turning points are controversial and they are complicated.

## MARKETING AND THE QUALITY OF LIFE

We have over many years built institutional structures to handle the many marketing tasks dictated by our needs. These structures worked well to fulfill the needs of "a materialistic, acquisitive, thing-minded, abundant market economy. . . ." (Lazer, 1969). The system did what was expected of it, but with new societal concerns the system has been brought into question; it is obsolete in some respects and simply does not mesh well with contemporary values. Arthur Miller has made us think about values:

Tragedy is when you lose your boat.
Life is preparation for retirement.
To succeed as a woman you have to have a car.
Brotherhood is when two men have the same mother.
Sacrifice is a car sold at a ridiculous price.
Beauty is teeth, deep skin, and the willingness. (Miller, 1969.)

Values, life styles, interests, and norms all relate to the quality of life. But in order for governments and businesses to establish priorities, assessment and direction are needed. Over the past decade a number of groups have studied the question of goals, and their various focuses are shown in 28-2. Several studies are presented because they illustrate both diversity and changing conditions. The first one is the President's Commission on National Goals (1960), which produced a list of 11 goal categories that have been used by many persons who are trying to establish a sense of direction and who are attempting to evaluate our way of life. An attempt to measure the quality of life on a state-by-state basis, according to the 1960 goals, is shown in 28-3. The question is: how does marketing relate to these indicators of the quality of life? For some indicators the relationship is close, for others it is quite remote. We will not go through the lists seriatim but instead will identify a smaller list of turning points that we will discuss after each of the studies has been introduced.

In 1968 the Brookings Institution prepared a series of detailed memoranda on the substantive issues facing the incoming adminis-

**28-2** Five Studies of Goals, Issues, and Ingredients of the Quality of Life

| A<br><br>1960 President's Commission<br>on National Goals | B<br><br>1968 Brookings Institution<br>Substantive Issues | C<br><br>1970 President's National<br>Goals Research Staff |
|---|---|---|
| Status of the individual<br>Equality<br>Democratic process<br>Education<br>Arts and sciences<br>Democratic economy<br>Economic growth<br>Technological change<br>Agriculture<br>Living conditions<br>Health and welfare | Budget alternatives after Vietnam<br>Jobs, training, and welfare for the underclass<br>Raising the incomes of the poor<br>The Negro and the urban crisis<br>Realistic housing goals<br>Unemployment, inflation, stability<br>U.S. and Western Europe<br>U.S. and Soviet Union<br>Transpacific relations<br>The dollar and the world economy<br>U.S. and low-income countries<br>Military strategy, forces, and arms<br>Crime and law enforcement<br>Better schools<br>Challenges to the colleges<br>Managing the federal government<br>The Middle East<br>American foreign policy | Population<br>Basic natural science<br>Environment<br>Consumerism<br>Education<br>Technology assessment |

| D<br><br>1971 Blueprint for<br>Changing National Priorities | E<br><br>1971 World Dynamics<br>Cornerstones   &   | Quality of Life<br>Components |
|---|---|---|
| Full employment, growth, stability<br>Equal opportunities for all people<br>Guarantee of basic necessities<br>Balance revenues between federal, state, and local governments<br>National security against military threats<br>Assist development of world's less-developed nations | Population<br>Capital investment<br>Natural resources<br>Fraction of capital devoted to agriculture<br>Pollution | Material standard of living<br>Crowding<br>Food<br>Pollution |

SOURCES: (A) President's Commission on National Goals, *Goals for Americans* (Englewood Cliffs, N.J.: Prentice-Hall, 1960). (B) Kermit Gordon (ed.), *Agenda for the Nation* (Garden City, N.Y.: Doubleday, 1969). (Originally published by the Brookings Institution, 1968.) (C) National Goals Research Staff, *Toward Balanced Growth: Quantity with Quality* (Washington, D.C.: GPO, 1970). (D) Robert S. Benson and Harold Wolman, *Counterbudget: A Blueprint for Changing National Priorities* (New York: Praeger, 1971). (E) Jay W. Forrester, *World Dynamics* (Cambridge, Mass.: Wright-Allen Press, 1971).

# 28-3 The Comparative Ranking of Individual States in Terms of the Quality of Life

| State | Final ranking | Status of the individual | Equality | Democratic process | Education | Economic growth | Technology change | Agriculture | Living conditions | Health and welfare |
|---|---|---|---|---|---|---|---|---|---|---|
| California | 1 | 3 | 17 | 6 | 4 | 1 | 1 | 1 | 3 | 14 |
| Minnesota | 2 | 10 | 1 | 4 | 9 | 3 | 11.5 | 19 | 10 | 1 |
| Connecticut | 3 | 2 | 6 | 2 | 6 | 13 | 14 | 16 | 1 | 9 |
| Massachusetts | 4 | 1 | 3 | 1 | 10 | 19 | 4 | 25.5 | 9 | 12 |
| Washington | 5 | 6 | 5 | 19 | 2 | 7 | 13 | 10 | 12 | 20 |
| Colorado | 6 | 14 | 14 | 10 | 3 | 15 | 19 | 7.5 | 24 | 6 |
| New York | 7 | 4 | 20 | 15 | 15 | 16 | 2 | 32 | 2 | 2 |
| Oregon | 8 | 7 | 8 | 12 | 1 | 8.5 | 32 | 29 | 11 | 11 |
| Wisconsin | 9 | 8 | 26 | 7 | 18 | 6 | 11.5 | 25.5 | 22 | 7 |
| Iowa | 10 | 13 | 2 | 26.5 | 7 | 11 | 26 | 6 | 29 | 13 |
| Illinois | 11 | 9 | 27 | 14 | 19 | 8.5 | 10 | 17 | 14 | 21 |
| Delaware | 12 | 20 | 30 | 31 | 16 | 4 | 29 | 7.5 | 8 | 3 |
| New Jersey | 13 | 11 | 9 | 8 | 35.5 | 33 | 9 | 24 | 4 | 24 |
| Hawaii | 14 | 21 | 18 | 3 | 22 | 10 | 40 | 15 | 7 | 27 |
| Rhode Island | 15 | 5 | 4 | 13 | 24 | 34 | 37 | 39 | 6 | 4 |
| Michigan | 16 | 12 | 13 | 20 | 27 | 2 | 8 | 46 | 13 | 41 |
| Utah | 17.5 | 25 | 36 | 5 | 5 | 27 | 22 | 22 | 20 | 40 |
| Ohio | 17.5 | 16 | 19 | 23 | 32 | 20 | 6 | 42 | 17 | 30 |
| North Dakota | 19 | 22 | 11 | 34 | 25 | 21 | 41 | 12 | 33 | 8 |
| Nevada | 20 | 23 | 37 | 9 | 30 | 24 | 44 | 4 | 5 | 35 |
| Pennsylvania | 21 | 18 | 23 | 17 | 37.5 | 37.5 | 5 | 48 | 16 | 16 |
| Maryland | 22 | 31 | 39 | 33 | 40 | 5 | 15 | 36 | 21 | 5 |
| Arizona | 23 | 29.5 | 40 | 21 | 8 | 29 | 28 | 2 | 31 | 38 |
| Wyoming | 24 | 17 | 15 | 35 | 11 | 43 | 46 | 5 | 28 | 32 |
| Indiana | 25.5 | 27 | 25 | 28 | 17 | 12 | 17 | 30.5 | 34 | 47 |
| Kansas | 25.5 | 19 | 24 | 32 | 12 | 27 | 31 | 20 | 38.5 | 34 |
| Vermont | 27 | 32.5 | 28 | 16 | 23 | 30 | 45 | 30.5 | 25 | 10 |
| Idaho | 28 | 28 | 21 | 22 | 26 | 31.5 | 43 | 9 | 18 | 44.5 |
| New Hampshire | 29 | 15 | 7 | 30 | 34 | 35.5 | 42 | 49 | 19 | 22 |
| Florida | 30 | 39 | 44 | 26.5 | 37.5 | 18 | 7 | 3 | 37 | 42 |
| Montana | 31 | 24 | 31 | 24 | 28 | 47 | 47 | 13 | 23 | 19 |
| Nebraska | 32 | 29.5 | 22 | 38 | 29 | 31.5 | 39 | 14 | 40 | 29 |
| Oklahoma | 33 | 32.5 | 38 | 39 | 13 | 45 | 23 | 23 | 43 | 17 |
| Alaska | 34 | 26 | 29 | 18 | 21 | 41.5 | 49 | 40 | 26 | 25 |
| Virginia | 35 | 43 | 42 | 11 | 41 | 14 | 16 | 41 | 42 | 26 |
| Texas | 36 | 41 | 45 | 37 | 20 | 22 | 3 | 11 | 50 | 49 |
| South Dakota | 37 | 34 | 10 | 42 | 35.5 | 48 | 48 | 18 | 35 | 18 |
| New Mexico | 38 | 37 | 35 | 29 | 14 | 46 | 36 | 21 | 32 | 43 |
| Maine | 39 | 36 | 12 | 25 | 47 | 49 | 50 | 43 | 15 | 23 |
| North Carolina | 40 | 45 | 41 | 40 | 33 | 28 | 18 | 33 | 44 | 33 |
| Missouri | 41 | 38 | 32 | 41 | 39 | 37.5 | 20 | 44 | 36 | 28 |
| Tennessee | 42 | 44 | 34 | 36 | 42 | 23 | 22 | 47 | 38.5 | 37 |
| West Virginia | 43 | 35 | 16 | 48 | 50 | 50 | 34 | 50 | 30 | 15 |
| Georgia | 44 | 48 | 48 | 44 | 44 | 17 | 24 | 28 | 45 | 39 |
| Louisiana | 45 | 40 | 46 | 43 | 31 | 41.5 | 25 | 35 | 49 | 31 |
| Kentucky | 46 | 42 | 33 | 50 | 48 | 26 | 30 | 45 | 27 | 46 |
| Arkansas | 47 | 46 | 43 | 47 | 43 | 44 | 35 | 27 | 41 | 36 |
| Alabama | 48 | 47 | 50 | 46 | 46 | 39.5 | 21 | 38 | 47 | 44.5 |
| South Carolina | 49 | 49 | 47 | 45 | 49 | 39.5 | 33 | 34 | 48 | 50 |
| Mississippi | 50 | 50 | 49 | 49 | 45 | 35.5 | 38 | 37 | 46 | 48 |

Note: The final ranking reflects the average of nine goal areas.
SOURCE: Minnesota Department of Economic Development, The Quality of Life in Minnesota, prepared by John O. Wilson, Midwest Research Institute (Kansas City), (St. Paul: Minnesota Department of Economic Development, 1968).

tration. Only 18 of the initial list of 40 topics were finally presented, and a number of critical issues such as mass transportation, pollution, and medical care were among those omitted. Again, a number of the issues relate closely to marketing and others are quite remote. Surely marketing research is of value to the firms facing postwar conversion problems, desiring to sell to the poor, or hoping to increase trade with various nations in the world.

On July 4, 1970, the President's National Goals Research Staff made public its report, "Toward Balanced Growth: Quantity with Quality." The report was meant to serve as a basis for discussion and as an aid to decisions by businesses and governments. It defines the questions, analyzes the arguments pro and con, and examines the alternative sets of consequences. The questions raised by President Nixon in his State of the Union Message in 1970 can be raised with each of the six emerging debates listed in the report:

> In the next 10 years we shall increase our wealth by 50 percent. The profound question is—does this mean we will be 50 percent richer in a real sense, 50 percent better off, 50 percent happier? Or does it mean that in the year 1980 the President standing in this place will look back on a decade in which 70 percent of our people lived in metropolitan areas choked by traffic, suffocated by smog, poisoned by water, deafened by noise, and terrorized by crime?

A National Urban Coalition study (1971) set up six major goals relevant between 1971 and 1976, as shown in 28-2(D). These goals, like the others, were culled from a long list of possibilities. Marketing relates most closely, of course, to the goals of economic growth, basic necessities, and the development of some of the poorer nations.

In the last study, Jay Forrester has identified and related the problems of growth and the equilibrium solution. Forrester has identified five key variables (28-2), made some 40 assumptions, and has worked out mathematical equations to show what happens with the interaction of the variables. Moreover, he has been specific as regards the *quality of life,* defining this to include four variables: (1) material standard of living, (2) crowding, (3) availability of food, and (4) pollution.

The above five studies have identified many issues, goals, and ingredients of the quality of life. As mentioned, marketing is only remotely related to many of the basic issues facing us today, but it *is* closely related to others. It is those issues that are defined here as the turning points of marketing.

## SELECTED TURNING POINTS OF MARKETING

Two turning points have already been discussed: the refocus of the marketer toward the consumer was examined in Chapter 26 and the inclusion of the poor within the framework of marketing was the subject of Chapter 27. Six additional turning points are presented in this chapter. Each reader might well prepare a different list, but some of these points would undoubtedly appear in some way on every list made by those in marketing.

### Resources—Technology—Products

Earl Cook has asked: "Are we drunken miners? We act like miners drunk with the riches of energy, trying to find new ways to spend, petulant when we can't satisfy fully two conflicting desires (energy and environmental quality; energy and low cost)" (Cook, 1972). And Harrison Brown wrote: ". . . the first major penalty man will have to pay for his rapid consumption of the earth's nonrenewable resources will be that of having to live in a world where his thoughts and actions are ever more strongly limited, where social organization has become all-pervasive, complex, and inflexible, and where the state completely dominates the actions of the individual" (Brown, 1954). The turning point is easily defined: marketing has helped to persuade people to buy more and businesses have produced an ever-increasing variety and quantity of products. Household consumers, for example, buy and rebuy dryers, ironers, washing machines, dishwashers, disposals, freezers, ranges, refrigerators, water heaters, electric blankets, blenders, can openers, radios, television, knife sharpeners, toasters, electric shavers, dehumidifiers, humidifiers, air conditioners, corn-poppers, electric tooth brushes, and heating pads, just to name a few of the home appliances. Almost 600,000 recreational vehicles costing $1.5 billion are purchased in one year. Seven hundred manufacturers, 10,000 dealers, and more than 10,000 campground operators receive income from the use of the recreational vehicle.

These products raise our standard of living but they consume valuable resources, some of which are nonrenewable. Betsy Gelb and Richard Brien have pointed out that marketing is at the "cutting edge" of the environmental question and that it will be up to the marketing manager to carry out the overall corporate responsibility as regards resources and the environment (Gelb and Brien, 1971). There is a balance with nature that must be appreciated (Gillespie, 1971). Technology has brought us new products but the parade of these products is now of concern. The turn for marketing will come when marketing managers and their firms learn to make a *prior assessment* for the new product. The assessment will enable the firm to determine whether or not the new product *should* be marketed. The entire marketing mix is involved—products, selling, advertising, pricing, packaging, and transportation. As the Friends of the Earth stated in an advertisement: "We need every adman we can help keep alive . . . advertising people can, by eloquently protesting and by educating the unconcerned" do much to alleviate the problems involved with our natural resources.

The SST was a vivid example of how public pressure killed or at least badly wounded a national allocation of resources for a questionable product. Little assessment of its virtues had been made public prior to the debate. The systematic planning operation encompassing options and costs of potential technology, known as technology assessment, should be made for all products. Perhaps the day is passed when Americans worship technology and the day is present when we show a concern for our resources.

An illustration of the change that is taking place is a comparison of the 1946 Employment Act that spoke of using "all practical means . . . to promote maximum employment, production, and purchasing power," with the National Environmental Act of 1969 that spoke of "the policy of the Federal Government . . . to use all practical means and measures . . . in a manner calculated to foster and promote the general welfare, to create and maintain conditions under which man and nature can exist in productive harmony, and fulfill the social, economic, and other requirements of present and future generations of Americans." This concern for resources is an important turning point for marketing. Changes in consumption will take place. Women may not enjoy wearing furs from baby seals or leopards and men may scorn at those who wear alligator shoes and boots. And advertisements will change by not promoting the use of products that are in question.

## Growth versus Demarketing

The once sacrosanct goal of economic growth suggests another turning point for marketing. Related to the first point—resources, technology, and products—the growth debate reminds us that GNP is a measure of output, not of well-being. Marketers used to look at the population forecasts and drool over the expanding markets of almost every item. Every new baby requires 56 million tons of water, 21 thousand gallons of gasoline, 10,150 pounds of meat, and prodigious amounts of other goods in his lifetime since wants are ever-expanding (Rienow and Rienow, 1967). Emphasis has been on growth—for instance, airlines, between 1960 and 1970, increased their jet fleets from 388 to 3771 and each year more and bigger jets are being added. In 1971, not a good year for that industry, scheduled airlines alone flew the equivalent of 100 empty 707s across the Atlantic every day (Lindsey, 1972).

We accepted the arguments for economic growth and extolled its virtues without question for many years. Consider the following quotation from the U.S. Department of Commerce in 1966:

When we consider that as citizens of the United States, we occupy only 7 percent of the world's land area and represent only 6 percent of the world's population, we can well be proud of our country's economic accomplishments. We produce 33 percent of the world's electrical energy. We drive 56 percent of the world's passenger cars and 40 percent of its commercial vehicles. We use 49 percent of the world's telephones, 47 percent of its radios, and 41 percent of its television sets.

By 1980, if our current rate of expansion and our stability continue, we shall have achieved a constantly rising standard of living for growing numbers of Americans. By so doing we shall prove to the world that our free enterprise system is working better than ever in bringing more benefits to more people than any system under the sun.

These are goals worth striving for!

We recognized that growth made possible an increase in the standard of living (material level of consumption); employment to increasing numbers of people; modern technology for the military; space shots; funds with which we could fight wars, poverty, and pollution; higher productivity and earning power; more goods and services with fewer hours on the job; and capital investment for the less-developed nations. Economists taught that the real GNP per capita has advanced even after adjusting for increases in population, prices, and pollution, and that a rise in social welfare has accompanied the rise in output of goods and services (Heller, 1971).

Marketing has delivered the products of this growth, and indeed it has grown right along with GNP. The marketing task was relatively easy with an expanding population coupled with an increase in income: more goods were produced and more were sold to a ready buyer. But now the entire concept of growth is being questioned. Is growth a good thing? Is the problem economic growth itself or the *kind* of economic growth? How limiting are such factors as natural resources, pollution, overpopulation, and shortage of food? Could we stop economic growth if we wanted to? Consider that it is anchored in population growth and increased levels of training, experience, and education of the population; improvements in the state of our scientific and managerial technology; and increases in investment in equipment, plant, and machinery.

Actually we have had no comprehensive growth policy for the nation, it has been the composite result of many decisions. The National Goals Research Staff suggests that the growth issue is one for the people to decide, individually through their private institutions and through their governments. Further, the Staff advises that we should have a growth policy with a relatively long-term perspective, and that this approach might help us discontinue our practice of defining our successes in yesterday's terms.

If marketers were to change their stance toward growth, a great deal of marketing effort would undergo change. The term "demarketing" has been suggested to refer to "that aspect of marketing that deals with discouraging customers in general or a certain class of customers in particular on either a temporary or permanent basis" (Kotler and Levy, 1971). It would be a turning point indeed, if marketers undertook to persuade consumers not to buy! Yet this eventuality is certainly conceivable. For instance, some public utilities are now teaching their customers how to save on the consumption of electricity. The same kind of marketing could be applied to many products. The growth debate will continue, however, since the facts are not yet available for any final decision and our system is simply not yet ready, let alone convinced, that demarketing is the answer.

## Ecology and Economics

This next turning point, relating to ecology, involves the role of marketing in an economy that has elements of "doomsday" at one end and "paradise regained" at the other. The problem is not unique to our economic system: capitalism, socialism, and communism have been making equally generous contributions to despoiling the earth—the death of the Caspian Sea, for example. While man is involved with environmental deterioration as both producer and consumer, it is to his role as a consumer that we address ourselves. Since everybody is a consumer of the environment, its quality is everbody's business. Of course, one of the major problems is that consumers do not actually consume the many products they buy since they use them and discard them in some way. At some time everything the consumer uses becomes waste, and so marketing has a vital role in this matter of the quality of the environment.

Industrial wastes accumulate rapidly: the big offenders are paper, organic chemicals, petroleum, and steel, all items of utmost importance to the consumer. There are over 1000 oil spills every year that are reported. The waste from one large farm's feedlot equals a small city's sewage. Sulphur oxide, particulates, carbon monoxide, hydrocarbons, nitrogen oxides, and photochemical oxidants come from energy sources, factory chimneys, transportation, refineries, and engine exhausts. The resulting dirty air costs each family $309 per year. Noise from subways, riveting, freeway traffic, and snowmobiles are frustrating and annoying, to say the least; they can also be physiologically harmful. Poisons used by consumers are killing fish, mammals, and birds (National Wildlife Federation, 1971). Our containers are unusable; we waste products through inadequate crating; and we pollute food by storing it next to poisons. As a sign of the extremity of the problem, waste has been called the "end of the marketing cycle" and our society has been described as a "no deposit, no return" society.

We have thought of the earth as a "throughput" model, where natural resources are put into the economic system with outputs of finished goods and waste products that are set aside or dumped conveniently. Some economists such as Kenneth Boulding have pointed out that the earth is a spaceship, in which we must travel on a very long voyage, reprocessing and reusing everything in this finite space (Dolan, 1969). Marketing, as with the rest of the economic system, has been operating on a throughput philosophy, and as we adjust to the spaceship concept another turn in marketing will take place.

Consider each of the major kinds of pollution. Marketing has played a major role in persuading housewives to use detergents with phosphates, yet today we recognize that phosphates promote excessive growths of algae and affect our water systems. The air is polluted by the factories that turn out consumer products and by some consumer products themselves. The solid-waste disposal problem has become critical: President Nixon has described it as the "discarded left-overs of our advanced consumer society." What is to be done with one ton of solid waste per person that is generated each year? A survey in

Maryland in 1966 (exclusive of the eastern shore counties) located 51,000 abandoned vehicles. The package problem also is enormous. Walk through a supermarket and observe the packaging of shampoo, toothpaste, slices of cheese, packaged meat, soft drinks in nonreturnable bottles, wax milk containers, double grocery bags, and extra plastic wrappings. The package is a part of the marketing process, and vending and fast food firms in particular utilize enormous quantities of packages. The problem is not only the single package, for frequently an item is covered by several packages and then placed in a sack and then in a box. Packaging wastes are increasing at the rate of 6 percent a year, as compared to a one percent increase in population (Grinstead, 1969). Surely marketers can do something about this. Millions of cans, 8 million old TV sets, 8 million autos, 100 million old tires, 3.5 billion tons of garbage, and other items have to be disposed of somehow, and in a spaceship that is a closed system. The noise problem caused by power lawnmowers, vehicles, jet planes, amplified musical instruments, and saws, and snowmobiles constitute yet another unsolved, but not unsolvable, problem. And general use of land by marketing establishments must be examined. Shopping centers may or may not contribute to the environment. A store may or may not enhance the shopping area. Pipe lines may damage millions of acres of land. The empty service station, so prevalent in the United States, certainly is a kind of pollution.

Why does not the marketing system prevent the problem of pollution? Is it not possible to incorporate the necessary values in the marketplace? Is it necessary to distort other values in the process of selling merchandise? Does the competitive economic system necessarily lead us on toward more and more waste and pollution, or does the situation represent a possible turning point for the marketing process? Many persons see economics and ecology as contrasting viewpoints, as opposing extremities. The economic system has permitted consumers to vote through their purchases and as a result businessmen have not attempted to be concerned about environmental values. But at the same time the marketing system offers us an opportunity to solve many of the new serious problems, for it is through the price mechanism that consumers can be encouraged and discouraged from buying many items. By internalizing pollution costs, by charging the consumer for polluting society, changes in consumption patterns can be effected. Costs of cleaning the air, cleaning the streams, and handling solid wastes are an appropriate charge to the product involved. This policy would mean, of course, an adjustment in the marketing of products. Two European professors have suggested that what is developing is a "socioecological" product in which the traditional product concept as a bundle of need satisfactions gives way to a sum total of all positive and negative utilities which must be accepted by society as a whole (Cracco and Rostenne, 1971). The idea is that a user of a product will receive the product only if the society, including nonusers, approves the item as having a positive balance of utilities. Marketing's priorities would change as follows:

| Traditional Priorities | Socioecological Priorities |
|:---:|:---:|
| Individual | Environment |
| ↓ | ↓ |
| Corporation | Society |
| ↓ | ↓ |
| Society | Individual |
| ↓ | ↓ |
| Environment | Corporation |

The traditional market is user-oriented in that companies attempt to satisfy, for a profit, the user's needs even though these needs may be in conflict with society and the environment. The turning point would place the environment at the top of the priority and a company's success would be evaluated in terms of social contribution as well as profit.

There are many ways in which marketing can help alleviate the problem of environmental deterioration. Take the assessment of products. The Ford Motor Company has indicated that the Maverick was designed to meet shifts in consumer preferences that included small size, durability, fuel economy, and low maintenance and repair costs (Ford, 1970). The National Industrial Pollution Control Council has prepared reports that show industry how to examine their operations in terms of environmental concerns. Plans are being made to handle junked cars, including building the product in such a way as to be more salvageable; the marketing system too would be designed to handle the cars once they are no longer in service. This procedure in effect would put marketing in the business of handling wastes. Zikmund and Stanton have pointed out that the recycling problem is essentially a reverse-distribution process in which a "backward" channel returns the product to the manufacturer (Zikmund and Stanton, 1971). Marketing can also help to make consumers aware of the need to recycle and reuse and to buy those products that do not worsen the environmental quality. An enormous contribution would be made if some of the tips in "The User's Guide to the Protection of the Environment" were stressed (Swatek, 1970). Swatek tells how to conserve on water, how to manage waste in the home, how to avoid problems of chemicals, how to save on transportation, and how to conserve energy in the home. But to do all the necessary things to avoid further environmental deterioration obviously means that many groups are going to have to cooperate. As with problems of resources, poverty, and consumerism, the problem of pollution in our nation is going to require joint efforts by marketers, manufacturers, governments, and consumers. The issue is political, technological, economic, cultural, legal, and even psychological—and it definitely is a turning point for marketing.

### Relevancy to Today's Environment

Marketing, like the economic system in which it operates, has been relatively silent on today's social problems. Yet marketing, "because of its inherently social character, impinges upon virtually every major social problem confronting society today" (Dawson, 1971). Let us examine briefly some of the issues.

The Metric System—The United States is one of the few nations in the world not using the metric system—Barbados, Muscat, Nauru, Tonga, and Sierra Leone are some of the others. Actually we are partially on the metric system since pharmaceutical firms gave up the drams, grains, and minims bit a decade ago and much scientific equipment, many machine tools, swimming pools, skis, and photographic film are based on the metric system. This is an important issue for marketers and they are tardy in their analysis of the costs and benefits that would accrue from a transition to the new system. (The metric system was developed in the late 1700s in France because individual towns found it difficult to trade with one another.) At a time when foreign trade is important to our firms it would seem logical for marketers to urge our adoption of a metric system that would make our products compatible the world over without costly adjustments. (See DeSimone, 1972.)

*Trade Barriers.* For over 40 years the United States moved steadily in the direction of more liberal trade arrangements. Those in foreign marketing recognize the need for us to import in order for us to export. In 1970, however, pressure began to build for more stringent import controls. For instance, the American Footwear Manufacturers Association and Tanners' Council of America placed full-page ads in newspapers during the 1970 hearings on the "Save-American Jobs" bill. The advertisement in part is shown in 28-4.

Closely related to trade barriers is the matter of our trading with communist nations. A few marketing men have been working to free the trade apparatus between the United States and the communist countries. They know that they have large potential markets in each

---

## 28-4

### A Union-Sponsored Advertisement

A *no* vote on the "Save-American Jobs" (Mills) Bill is a vote to "export" your job. To countries where imports manufactured at minimum wages like 22¢ an hour are putting American businesses out of business. And American workers out of work. Like the shoe industry, where the tide of imports rushed from 26 million pairs in 1960 to over 210 million pairs in 1969! And more than 50 American shoe factories went under. Thousands upon thousands lost their jobs . . . Pick your pen up. And put your foot down. Tell your Senators and Congressmen you don't mind sharing but charity begins at home. . . .

PUT YOUR FOOT DOWN! SAVE JOBS—CURB IMPORTS

SOURCE: American Footwear Manufacturers Association and Tanners' Council of America advertisement, *The Washington Post*, June 24, 1970.

---

of those nations, whether for computers or clothing. The Cold War between communistic and capitalistic nations has been a stifling influence on worldwide marketing.

*Boycotts in Retail Markets.* During the latter part of the 1960s the California grape boycott became a national issue. Retailers over the nation were asked to curb their buying of table grapes. Consumers were asked not to buy them and to boycott stores that sold grapes. On the one hand was the argument that the grape pickers were disadvantaged workers who were paid too little and were furnished inadequate housing and other services, and that the only way for them to improve their situation was to promote boycotts since they had no legal bargaining privileges. On the other hand was the argument by some retailers that their duty was to provide choice for the buyer. If a buyer did not want to purchase grapes, all right, but the retailer would make them available in our free market for those who wanted them. No consistent pattern of response developed across the country. In one large chain-store operation, for instance, some managers refused to buy grapes and others bought them. The issue was not simple: it involved pickers, growers, retailers, consumers, labor legislation, agricultural policy, and social conditions, and it was being fought out in the marketplace. If marketing people decide they can become more policy-oriented, they may well assume more of a leadership role in solving issues such as the dispute between grape growers and pickers instead of acting as passive middlemen. The boycott may well be used more in the future with problems of pollution, war, and other social issues.

*The Women's Liberation Movement.* There are several ways in which marketing relates to women's liberation. First, in terms of employment, along with most of the rest of the business world marketing can make greater use of the talents and intelligence of women. Marketing managers can explore the contributions women can make to the field rather than hiring them primarily for the low-paying clerical jobs. Marketing research has more to offer women than simply interviewing. Approximately 30 million women are in the work force and three-fifths of them are married. Women are clearly becoming a force in the job market; narrow and belittling marketing approaches ought to become passé (Leezenbaum, 1970).

*Sales of Weapons.* There is a large market in international sales of military equipment—guns, ammunition, planes, trucks, and all kinds of weapons are sold by governments and private companies, not in military aid programs, but through exchanges of goods for money in an international military arms market. Since World War II some $66 billion of conventional arms have been placed on the world markets, $50 billion from the U.S. From 1962–68, $819 million of F-4s, $569 million of C-130s, $534 million of combat vehicles, and $320 million of Polaris missiles have been among the "best sellers." In addition to government sales, there are private sellers, such as International Armament Corporation, that sells close to $100 million a year (*Business Week*, May 23, 1970). Should marketers have no restrictions on the kinds of products they are willing to sell?

These kinds of issues drag marketing into the social arena. Marketers can deny that they have any responsibility, but an examination of past practices will certainly show that marketing has had a great deal to do with life styles and attitudes. The question is, how does marketing properly face up to these kinds of issues? And if marketers begin to display a new set of values regarding today's social problems, another turning point will have been passed.

## Humanism in Marketing

A humane marketplace requires more than affluence and economic growth. "It requires a social environment that brings a sense of community and fellowship into human relationships. It demands compatibility among man, his technology, and the natural environment" (Fusfeld, 1972). Humanism in marketing includes everyone connected with it—employees, suppliers, customers, users of products, and those who are affected in any way by the marketing effort.

In one area—minority groups and marketing—marketing for decades was a white man's province. There were no minority racial groups represented among retail clerks, advertisers, salesmen, or other jobs that might cause management any embarrassment. After all, marketers made the contact with the public and those contacts had to be white ones. But today retailers are hiring all colors of people, not just because it is the law, but because it is good business. Perhaps, too, it represents a change of attitude. There are blacks in advertising agencies. A few minority groups are now in selling, though the number is small. Approximately 15 auto agencies in the early 1970s were operated by blacks, a 400 percent increase in a decade. A black in a service station signals to the public that the company supports equal rights, and this proclamation helps tear down the walls of the past. A minority-group retail clerk conveys to customers the store's attitudes toward minorities. A truck-driver salesman for a soft-drink company "tells" retailers a story about the policies of the bottling firm. Much more than was ever realized, marketing can play an important role in helping the nation overcome one of its most difficult problems.

*Racism* in advertising is a problem that marketers once ignored. A recent ad by a shirt manufacturer showed neatly dressed whites with colored shirts and ties. In the background was an American Indian in native attire. Part of the advertisement read as follows:

> Swinging squaws go for braves in the untamed colors . . . Brave, brawny in-colors . . . Join the . . . tribe and make yours an Indian summer . . .

Offensive ethnic stereotypes have been used indiscriminately. A potato chip ad showed fat Mexicans toting guns. A corn chip ad used a

Mexican thief called the bandito. A cigarette ad suggested that Mexicans are lacking in perseverance and incapable of finishing what they begin. One TV ad showed a Mexican sleeping next to a television set. A deodorant ad suggests that if the product will work for an unwashed Mexican, it will work for everyone (Bernstein, 1970). Two senators in 1970 called on the advertising agencies and networks to eliminate stereotypes of Mexicans and to make that the "next industry-wide effort in your battle against intolerance and discrimination."

Because of national consciousness of the black revolution improvements have been made in the use of blacks in ads. Much research has been performed, and while the results are sometimes contradictory they do spell progress. For example, consider these results of research that were taken from articles appearing in the *Journal of Advertising Research* (Vol. 10, April 1970), a special issue devoted to research on Negroes:

> White respondents were found to be indifferent to well-conceived integrated [blacks and whites] advertisements. (Stafford, Birdwell, Van Tassel.)

> Portrayal of Negroes in realistic Negro roles [in TV ads] is yet to come. (Dominick and Greenberg.)

> Advertisers need not be fearful of using Negro models or integrated advertising. (Guest.)

> Attitudes toward integrated advertisements are shown to vary by degree of racial prejudice, and ads with all-Negro or all-white principals may be more effective than integrated ads. (Cagley and Cardozo.)

> Integrated advertising in five major magazines increased markedly during the past twenty years, and has shifted occupational roles of Negroes from cooks, maids, butlers, etc., to businessmen, students, and consumers. (Keith Cox.)

This notion of humanism that is popular today is applicable to international marketing as well as domestic marketing. It can be another turning point for marketing.

## The Questioning of the Sacred Cows

There are many concepts in marketing that have been sacred cows in the past but they are being questioned by many today. For instance, there is this view of the American economy: ". . . an engine powered by uncoerced, inner-motivated decisions of legions of ardently competing businessmen and hordes of their customers . . . success is ultimately related to individual merit and application— . . . economic power and income gravitate toward those who, like successful quarterbacks and attorneys, mingle grit and determination with superior mental or physical attributes" (Lekachman, 1972). But how do the oil, shipping, airlines, communications, farming, utilities, and broadcasting industries match that view? How important has competition and consumer demand been in relation to regulatory agencies, Congress, and the White House?

Consider the following concepts. Are they viable today? Are they desirable? How do they fit into the marketing system in a realistic way?

| | |
|---|---|
| Profit system | Consumer sovereignty |
| Competition | Full employment |
| Economic growth | Freedom of choice |
| Marketing concept | Economic man |
| Freedom of entry | Private enterprise |
| Informed population | Small business |
| Price-directed marketplace | Mergers |

The examination of concepts such as the above coupled with a more realistic marketing system can mean that marketing will have made an important turn in the road. There are many crises today and marketing cannot be blind to them: inflation, failures in less-developed nations, poverty, militarism, unemployment, and racism. It is essential that those in all fields, including marketing, become aware of these issues and begin to appreciate that their actions are a part of the whole system.

## 28-5 Public Willingness To Pay for a Cleaner Environment

| Are you willing to pay 10% more for—or do you think the problem is not that serious? | Figures in percentages | | |
|---|---|---|---|
| | Willing to pay | Problem not serious | Undecided |
| Detergents if it turns out to be the only way to eliminate their pollution of water supplies | 69 | 17 | 13 |
| Gasoline if it turns out to be the only way to eliminate the pollution caused by automobile exhausts | 68 | 16 | 15 |
| An automobile if it turns out to be the only way to eliminate the pollution caused by the exhausts | 67 | 17 | 17 |
| Electricity if it turns out to be the only way to eliminate the pollution caused by power plants | 64 | 22 | 14 |
| Magazines and newspapers if it turns out to be the only way to eliminate pollution caused by paper mills | 60 | 20 | 20 |
| Airplane tickets if it turns out to be the only way to eliminate pollution caused by their exhausts | 59 | 18 | 22 |

SOURCE: From *The Roper Report* (October 1971), published by the Roper Organization Inc., New York, N.Y.

# PROGRAMS FOR TURNING POINTS

Fortunately there are many reasons to be optimistic about the future. In a national cross section of the population, the Roper Organization found that the majority of people are willing to pay 10 percent more for a cleaner environment (see 28-5). This is only an indication, of course, but it surely suggests that the public is concerned and that it does want cleaner air, land, and water. Not all pollution-free products have received good receptions, an apparent contradiction of Roper findings. But on the other hand, the public is skeptical about many so-called ecological products because some have been misrepresented. Further, the government has confused the public in a number of cases such as phosphates and hexachlorophene.

A second survey was made by the American Marketing Association of 1400 of its members. Respondents were asked to indicate whether or not they agreed with a number of statements, selections of which are shown in 28-6.

**28-6** Responses from Marketers on Public Issues

| Issue | Figures in percentages | | |
|---|---|---|---|
| | Agree | Disagree | No opinion |
| The most critical problem facing the U.S. is environmental pollution. | 44 | 55 | 1 |
| Marketing abuses are more common than they were ten years ago. | 19 | 67 | 14 |
| Retailers should be required to provide unit price information. | 84 | 14 | 2 |
| When health or safety is involved, compulsory product and service standards should be established and adhered to . . . | 94 | 5 | 1 |
| Consumers are adequately protected against health hazards. | 26 | 72 | 2 |
| The "consumer movement" is likely to result in more harm than good for society. | 16 | 80 | 4 |
| Business has a responsibility to help improve the marketing of goods and services to the poor. | 84 | 15 | 1 |
| When developing marketing plans, greater consideration should be given to minimizing environmental pollution than to profitability. | 48 | 49 | 3 |
| A corporation's duty is primarily to its owners and secondarily to its employees, customers, and the public. | 42 | 56 | 2 |

SOURCE: From a survey of its members conducted by the American Marketing Association under the Chairmanship of Robert J. Lavidge of Elrick and Lavidge, Inc., 1972.

Both of these surveys indicate that there is a good deal of appreciation for improving the handling of social problems. Further, the marketing people responded in a way to indicate that many of them want marketing to play a more active role in the social arena.

A third bit of optimistic evidence comes from the establishment of a Public Policy and Issues Division within the American Marketing Association. The Division's first statement was released in early 1972, part of which is reproduced in 28-7. The full statement includes positions on professional standards and ethics and public policy as well as implementation procedures.

There are other bits of evidence to show that marketers are making significant turns in their endeavors. They are doing more to educate consumers. They are participating in conferences in an effort to develop a new set of social indicators for the nation and for individual firms. They are involved with impact studies that might eventually be part of companies' standard operating procedures. They have established departments that are given responsibility for helping companies do a better job for the environment. They are helping to develop products that will minimize pollution. At the same time we still have efforts by business to put their heads in the sand: the Trans-Alaska pipeline issue may be a case in point. The environmentalists do not think that the companies have satisfactorily answered many questions and that the firms simply want the oil to serve the expanding markets regardless of the environmental consequences. For instance, the questions of pipeline leaks, effects of earthquakes, permafrost, river crossings and runoff, glacial flooding, corrosion, avalanches, monitoring, impacts on wildlife, toxicity, air pollution, gravel needs, and pipeline mechanics are among the questions bothering environmentalists (Sierra Club, 1972).

There is evidence, then, that marketers are reaching some vital turning points and that some are moving toward a socially oriented position. It is too early to know how many are doing so and to what extent this is happening. It is too early to know if it is happening in time.

## CONCLUDING COMMENTS

In this chapter we have attempted to expand the horizons of marketing, especially in terms of social responsibility. We have included a variety of illustrations that take marketing into the nonprofit sectors. We have made it clear that marketers have a positive and strategic role to play in society because they are the connecting link between the consumer and the producer.

Marketers should feel no compulsion to carry out antisocial activities. They can make it their task to identify social issues and to help companies avoid activities that are damaging to society, not as a public

## 28-7

**"The Public Interest and the American Marketing Association:
A Policy Statement, January 1972"**

### Public Policy: The AMA Commitment

As an organization of professional people, the AMA is vitally interested in bringing the expertise of its members to bear on matters of public policy formulation and enforcement of relevance to marketing. Government and business relations affecting marketing have been the traditional focus here. More recently, the relations of government to consumers, and consumers to business, have moved to the forefront among matters of public interest in marketing—as have ecological aspects of marketing activity. In the future, the AMA will have to extend its attention to the marketing by public bodies of their own products, services, programs and policies, to intergovernmental relations affecting international marketing, and to policies of trade associations and other forms of organized business as they impinge on issues of public interest in marketing. These developments are in tune with the emerging pluralist view of democratic society.

The AMA commitment spans the total decision-making, execution, and evaluation process in these matters of public policy affecting marketing. Thus, the Association strives to:

*stimulate member interest* in questions of public policy and social responsibility affecting marketing at individual and chapter levels

*identify* issues of public interest before they become "political," to permit their professional research and evaluation

*inform* the membership about public policy developments

*promote research* on potential and actual public policies and their effects, thereby contributing to the factual basis needed for intelligent action by decision-making and enforcement bodies and for well-grounded opinion-formation among members of the Association and the public at large

*encourage debate* among interested parties in all walks of life on matters of public concern in marketing

*articulate professional opinion* and recommendations from the membership

*provide expert testimony and advice* to decision-makers and enforcement officials, and

*bring about independent evaluation* to current public policies here and abroad by marketing professionals.

SOURCE: "Set Public Interest Statement Policy," *The Marketing News*, March 1, 1972, p. 4.

relations "smoke screen" but as a watchdog activity, a preassessment of the impact of a company's action on the environment and the people living in it. This development would update what has been an outstanding system of marketing, for it would merge corporate interests with natural and human environments as depicted in 28-8.

**28-8** Interaction of Business and Environment

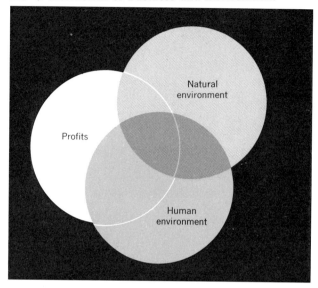

## STATEMENTS TO CONSIDER

One of the hallmarks of a profession is its adherence to an ideal of social service which transcends the immediate tasks with which its members are occupied. (Bogart)

In the ever-renewing society what matures is a system or framework within which continuous innovation, renewal and rebirth can occur. (Gardner)

It is only a slight exaggeration to state that American business, given the right incentives and conditions, can respond to almost any quantitative challenge. (Yankelovich)

Increasingly during this decade, marketing has been interpreted as a social process having for its principal goal the more satisfactory fulfillment of the needs and wants of buyers, consumers, and others. (Beckman and Davidson)

. . . besides merely providing the economic base necessary to support the physically productive capacities, marketing may also provide a stimulating force for the cultural development of society. (Kelly and Lazer)

In the abstract, marketing is always a system of total corporate action operating in accordance with the appropriate social parameters. . . . In the particular, marketing is often a system of fragmented corporate frolic operating at or near the peril point of the antitrust laws. It is designed to outmark and outmaneuver competitors and to transfer risk to someone else. (Castle)

Business can answer its critics, revitalize its ranks, and provide itself with an unlimited future through acceptance of the spirit of the human concept. (Dawson)

It is in marketing, as we now understand it, that we satisfy individual and social values, needs, and wants. . . . Marketing is thus the process through which economy is integrated into society to serve human needs. (Drucker)

A society in which consumption has to be artificially stimulated in order to keep production going is a society founded on trash and waste, and such a society is a house built upon sand. (Sayers)

Rather than a consumer-oriented, profit-motivated cooperative, we want to build an institution which is socially useful and which allows real participation and individual growth. . . . we here in Delano know (this) to be true—man must reverse the present order of things and bring about a system where human values and concerns are paramount and in which the economic system fosters this end. (Cesar Chavez)

# QUESTIONS FOR REVIEW

**1.** Are we kidding ourselves to think that marketers can reform many of the practices of business?

**2.** Make up your own list of priority issues for today's marketer. Identify only basic issues.

**3.** Will the "broadening of marketing" have a wholesome effect on society or is it simply a case of another group being concerned about selling more tickets?

**4.** Relate marketing to the quality of life. First, what is the quality of life?

**5.** Do you see any kinds of trends as you look over the five studies that are summarized in 28-2?

**6.** Evaluate the best you can the comparative rankings of states, as shown in 28-3.

**7.** Times change rapidly. What turning points would you now identify for marketing?

**8.** Do you think that it is possible that "demarketing" will become a common practice?

**9.** Relate and evaluate the matter of economic growth as it relates to marketing.

**10.** What steps should be taken by marketers to handle the problems of our natural environment?

## Further Readings

Raymond A. Bauer (ed.), *Social Indicators*, (Cambridge, Mass.: M.I.T. Press, 1966).

Kermit Gordon (ed.), *Agenda for the Nation* (Garden City, N.Y.: Doubleday, 1968).

Norman Kangun (ed.), *Society and Marketing* (New York: Harper & Row, 1972).

Donella H. Meadows, Dennis L. Meadows, Jorgen Randers, and William W. Behrens III, *The Limits to Growth* (New York: Universe Books, 1972).

National Goals Research Staff, *Toward Balanced Growth: Quantity with Quality* (Washington, D.C.: GPO, 1970).

*Journal of Marketing*, Vol. 35 (July 1970), entire issue.

John Silk, *et al.*, "Does Economics Ignore You?" *Saturday Review*, January 22, 1972.

THE ENVIRONMENT

NATURAL

HUMAN

# PART V

# MARKET PERFORMANCE AND THE FUTURE ENVIRONMENT

*Marketers must evaluate, improve, and plan insofar as possible for tomorrow. The evaluation and the plans for the future must include environmental considerations both internal and external to the firm, both profit-oriented and society-oriented.*

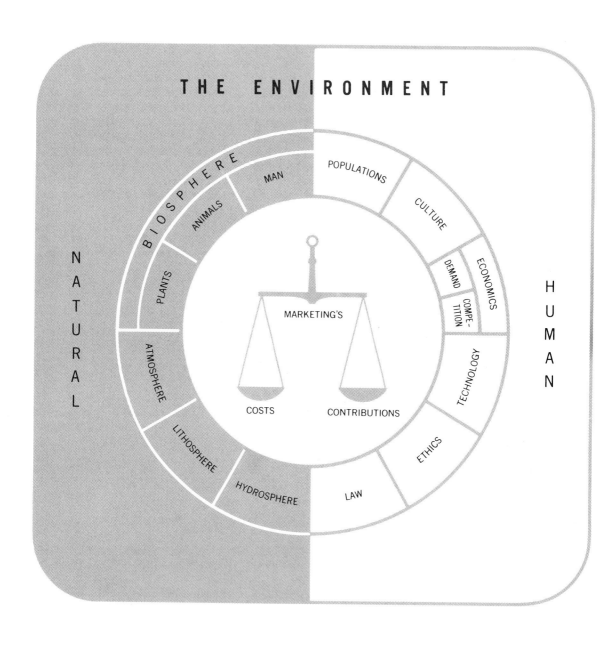

THE ENVIRONMENT

NATURAL

HUMAN

BIOSPHERE

MAN

ANIMALS

PLANTS

ATMOSPHERE

LITHOSPHERE

HYDROSPHERE

POPULATIONS

CULTURE

DEMAND

ECONOMICS

COMPE-TITION

TECHNOLOGY

ETHICS

LAW

MARKETING'S

COSTS

CONTRIBUTIONS

# CHAPTER 29
# AN EVALUATION
# OF MARKETING

**Different Kinds of Evaluations**

**A Social Evaluation**

**A Company Evaluation**

*Marketing, like other activities, should stand the test of evaluation. As students of marketing we are interested in marketing's performance, and the economy and society demands high performance in terms both of helping the firm make profit and of rendering a service to each segment of the total environment.*

Throughout the book we have stressed that marketing is influenced by technology, a legal system, codes of ethics, economic conditions, consumers' needs and desires, competition, and other internal and external segments of the global environment. We have attempted to show how marketing functions through research, persuasion, channels, and marketing strategies. Now in this chapter we want to focus on the question: *Is marketing doing a good job?* The question concerns not only the past, but the present and future as well.

As a consumer, you have the privilege of asking this crucial question and demanding a satisfactory answer. As a businessman or woman you also have the responsibility of making sure that the marketing effort is an efficient one or it will not be competitive. If marketing is not doing a good job, its faults should be identified and corrected. You will probably never be satisfied, but that is preferable to extolling the virtues of an unexamined system.

## DIFFERENT KINDS OF EVALUATIONS

Evaluations of marketing from the standpoints of the consumer, of government, of labor, of stockholders, or of society in general all differ. Business is essentially profit-oriented. The consumer by contrast is satisfaction-oriented. He or she wants choice, availability, credit and delivery, adequate packaging, and information. Government stresses legal aspects such as competition and compliance with consumer laws. Employees are interested in salaries and working conditions, and society in general may want to measure marketing's performance in a quality-of-life framework.

The definitions of marketing in Chapter 1 illustrated the diversity and complexity of the marketing process. One definition in particular, suggested the many different points of view of marketing:

> . . . a business activity; a group of related business activities; as a trade phenomenon; as a frame of mind; as a coordinative, integrative function in policy making; as a sense of business purpose; as an economic process; as a structure of institutions; as the process of exchanging or transferring ownership of products; as a process of concentration, equalization, and dispersion; as the creation of time, place, and possession utilities; as a process of demand and supply adjustment; and as many other things. (The Ohio State University Marketing Faculty, 1964.)

The Ohio State faculty also pointed out that "the ends served by the marketing process are, hopefully, the more complete satisfaction of human, business, and public wants, and at the same time provision for the highest attainable degrees of utilization of our technological and human resources." All this suggests a large task for marketing, and, moreover, as we broaden our concept of the marketing function we broaden the task of evaluation.

In this chapter we will be examining marketing from two points of view: (1) how well does marketing serve society? and (2) how well does marketing serve the firm?

# A SOCIAL EVALUATION

Social audits for marketing have been almost nonexistent. "The nation has no comprehensive set of statistics reflecting social progress or retrogression. There is no Government procedure for periodic stock-taking of the social health of the Nation. The Government makes no Social Report" (U.S. Department of Health, Education, and Welfare, 1969). We do not have for marketing any neat social report, yet such a social report would make the social problems of marketing more visible and would help marketers to evaluate the public value of their efforts.

One contribution to marketing knowledge has been the estimation of total marketing costs. The first such estimate was made by the Twentieth Century Fund, using 1929 data. That report noted:

> The idea that it costs too much to distribute goods and that modern methods of distribution are wasteful and inefficient has taken root in the public mind. Every day the consumer is exposed to sights and sounds which seem to confirm this impression—the spectacle of four gasoline stations, one on each corner of a crossroads, the constant bombardment of costly radio programs selling everything from cigarettes to pianos, and the frequent complaint of the farmer who gets only four or five cents of the fifteen cents we pay for a quart of milk.
>
> Quite naturally the automobile driver and the cigarette smoker and the housewife begin to wonder if all the costs of placing goods at their disposal are necessary and warranted. And since they themselves have to pay all these costs, they question so great a toll on their purchasing power. Added to this is the general belief that while invention and scientific management have increased the efficiency and lowered the costs of making goods, the cost of distributing them has remained high. (Stewart and Dewhurst, 1939.)

Unfortunately the Fund's estimate that marketing took 59 percent of the consumers' dollars became a widely accepted figure even though it was only an estimate and subsequent estimates provided a lower figure. The marketing cost data are not always separated neatly from other costs of doing business, and the figures gathered on national product, investment, inventories, consumption expenditures, prices, and value added by manufacturing do not provide any precise measure of marketing costs. A few added figures on the Census of Business forms would provide considerable insight into marketing costs and functions. Unfortunately the concept of "value added by marketing" seems to be difficult for many persons to comprehend. They can easily visualize how a manufacturer adds value to a product, but the contribution of marketing is blurred and little understood by comparison. People seem to recognize that marketing institutions do indeed exist, but they have not yet accepted the total contribution of marketing. Perhaps many still accept Karl Marx's attitude toward distribution: "The general law is that all expenses of circulation . . . do not add any value to the commodities" (Karl Marx).

The task of gathering marketing cost data without a Census Bureau operation is enormous. A single raw material goes into multiple manufacturing processes, wholesaling and retailing channels, and ultimately to many different kinds of consumers. Consider a coconut tree: there are products from the leaves, shell, husk, dust, root, trunk, meat, water, and pith. These products go into hats, candy, brooms, yarn, rope, buttons, charcoal, medicine, poultry feed, and soap, for example. Tracing the costs of distributing coconut products is in itself an enormous task. Or take the components of a house—hundreds of items that come from different sources are processed and handled by many people, and they finally come together in an acceptable sequence so that a builder can combine them into a house. One item studied by Cox and Goodman was a window unit that was processed from a variety of materials, shipped by truck and rail over 2000 miles, stored, priced, and eventually moved to the building site. The wood that went into the unit was traced back through the channels to the forest—a 331-day trip was involved from the forest to the building site (Cox and Goodman, 1956).

Despite the obvious difficulties, marketing scholars have made estimates of total marketing costs and these are shown in 29-1. The studies are not uniform but they provide some idea of what marketing costs the American consumer.

The total cost of distribution is a large figure on the basis of either dollars or percentages of the consumer's dollar. You cannot jump to the conclusion that marketing costs too much, however, because reduction of the costs would mean reduction of benefits, and for many years the American consumer has been willing to pay for variety, convenience, and availability. After looking at other aggregate cost data, we will probe further into the social questions of marketing costs. In addition to the total cost picture we can look at the costs *industry by industry,* and here we find considerable variation (29-2).

Marketing costs vary both by *function* and by *industry.* Analysis of costs show transportation costs ranged from 2.4 percent of final purchase for textile products to 10.2 percent for lumber and wood products. Warehousing and storage costs were fairly low and constant for most items. Advertising varied from 0.7 percent for lumber and wood products to 5.0 percent for chemicals and allied products (Cox, 1965). Cox

**29-1** Estimates of the Cost of Marketing

| Year | MARKETING COSTS (as a percentage of the consumer dollar) | | | |
|---|---|---|---|---|
| | Stewart and Dewhurst | Converse | Barger | Cox |
| 1869 | — | — | 32.7[b] | — |
| 1909 | — | — | 36.5 | — |
| 1929 | 59[a] | 49.0[a] | 37.0 | — |
| 1939 | — | 50.5[a] | 37.3 | — |
| 1947/48 | — | 48.1[a] | 37.4 | 41.7[c] |
| | | | | 45.3[d] |

[a] Value added percentage (1948 value added by manufacture was 51.9).

Converse's estimates of marketing costs in billions:
| | |
|---|---|
| 1929 | $39.4 |
| 1939 | 29.4 |
| 1948 | 89.8 |

[b] Cost of distributing goods through wholesalers and retailers.
[c] Value added excluding public utilities, services, and miscellaneous.
[d] Considers only goods distributed to households.

SOURCES: Paul W. Stewart and J. Frederick Dewhurst, *Does Distribution Cost Too Much?* (New York: Twentieth Century Func, 1939). Paul D. Converse, Harvey W. Huegy, and Robert V. Mitchell, *Elements of Marketing* (Englewood Cliffs, N.J.: Prentice Hall, 1958), pp. 742–745, © 1958 Prentice-Hall. Harold Barger, *Distribution's Place in the American Economy Since 1869,* published by National Bureau of Economic Research (Princeton, N.J.: Princeton University Press, 1955), p. 68. Reavis Cox, *Distribution in a High-Level Economy* (Englewood Cliffs, N.J.: Prentice-Hall, 1965), © 1965 Prentice-Hall.

points out that advertising is likely to be important for products which lend themselves particularly well to differentiation by aggressive promotion of brand names (drugs, medicines, tobacco, and alcohol). Transportation contributes more market value when long distances are involved, as in the shipping of sugar from Puerto Rico or the Philippines or the shipping of heavy items far distances as with lumber or steel.

Cox found that the *wholesale* contribution ranged from 3.6 percent for leather and leather products to 15.2 percent for paper and allied

**29-2** Marketing Costs by Selected Industries

| Function | COSTS (Cents per dollar of final purchases) | |
|---|---|---|
| | Printing and Publishing Products | Primary Metal Products |
| Advertising | 1.3 | 1.3 |
| Warehousing and storage | 0.1 | 0.1 |
| Transportation | 3.0 | 3.2 |
| Retailing | 13.9 | 25.1 |
| Wholesaling | 3.8 | 10.8 |
| Total | 22.1 | 40.5 |

SOURCE: Reavis Cox, *Distribution in a High-Level Economy* (Englewood Cliffs, N.J.: Prentice-Hall, 1965), p. 135, © 1965.

products. *Retail* market value added ranged from 13.1 percent for food and kindred products to 26.1 for fabricated metal products. Wholesaling is likely to be relatively important when items have low unit values and are dangerous to transport and store (for instance, alcohol). Large inventories, bulk, fragility, and government regulations can also increase the amount of wholesaling costs. Thus, high marketing costs are found with medical, optical, and photographic equipment. Retailers carrying a wide assortment of goods with low turnover (for example, jewelry and musical instruments) will likely have high costs.

Still another way to examine marketing costs is to look at *products;* see 29-3 and 29-4, which give costs for milk and beer. These examples show how marketing adds value and costs to products and how the products proceed through their circuitous routes from producer to consumer. For other food products there is also considerable variation in costs of marketing. From 1964 data furnished by the Department of Agriculture, the high and low extremes in 29-5 can be identified.

A product line that is undergoing special scrutiny today is drugs. Because of rising medical costs and the increased roles of government and large private organizations, pressure is being brought to bear on the pharmaceutical industry to reduce marketing costs. E. B. Weiss has suggested that $1 billion annually could be saved in drug marketing costs. The solution, he points out, is to computerize the operation, centralize all drug information, substitute generic for brand names, and call on the computer to do the jobs formerly performed by detail men, advertising, sampling, demonstrations, seminars, trade shows, house organs, and the tedious jobs performed by the pharmacist such as

### 29-3 Cost of Milk

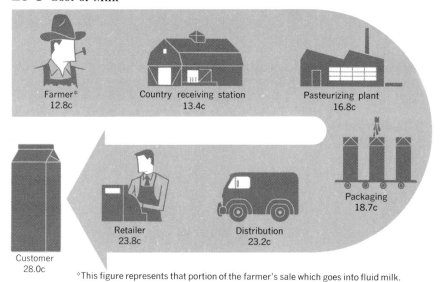

| | | |
|---|---|---|
| Farmer* 12.8c | Country receiving station 13.4c | Pasteurizing plant 16.8c |
| | | Packaging 18.7c |
| Customer 28.0c | Retailer 23.8c | Distribution 23.2c |

*This figure represents that portion of the farmer's sale which goes into fluid milk.

SOURCE: Robert E. Dallos, "Milk: Case History of a Rising Price," *The New York Times,* August 7, 1966.

**29-4** Barley Costs as Part of the Total Cost Structure of Beer

Cost of barley production at farm level   $25.00 per acre
Average yield of barley in bushels per acre:
20 bushels per acre; some yields as high as 50 bushels

| Item | Cost per bushel |
|---|---|
| Price of a bushel of barley on the farm | 0.90 |
| Country elevator margin | 0.05 |
| Freight to Minneapolis Market | 0.25 |
| Commission firm's charge | 0.02 |
| Terminal handling charge | 0.04 |
| Minneapolis price for barley | $ 1.26 |
| Freight to Milwaukee Market | 0.13 |
| Procurement and interest charges | 0.06 |
| Cost of converting barley to malt | 0.40 |
| Maltster margin | 0.05 |
| Milwaukee price for malt | $ 1.90 |
| Cost of converting malt to beer | 1.00 |
| Advertising costs for beer | 2.50 |
| Transportation costs for beer | 0.70 |
| Packaging costs for beer | 1.30 |
| Federal tax on beer | 9.00 |
| State tax on beer | 2.00 |
| Brewers margin | 1.00 |
| Beer cost to wholesaler | $19.40 |
| Wholesaler margin | 3.40 |
| Cost to retailer | $22.80* |
| | (or 95¢ per 6-pack) |
| Sales price to consumer | $27.60 |
| | (or $1.15 per 6-pack) |

*1 bushel = 24 6-packs

SOURCE: Harvard Business School, Pabst Brewing Company, Case, 1961.

**29-5** Marketing Costs as a Percentage of Retail Price

| Cost item | High | Low |
|---|---|---|
| Marketing margin | 89 Breakfast cereals | 30 Butter |
| Labor | 56 Pork | 15 Evaporated milk |
| Buildings and equipment | 19 Butter | 4 Canned tomatoes |
| Containers and supplies | 36 Evaporated milk | 5 Beef and pork |
| Advertising and promotion | 22 Breakfast cereals | 3 Apples (Washington Delicious) |
| Transportation | 21 Fresh fruits and vegetables | 4 Canned tomatoes, corn, bread |
| Administration and other | 28 Processed fruits and vegetables | 8 Pork |
| Profits before tax | 15 Breakfast cereals | 4 Fresh fruits and vegetables |

SOURCE: National Commission on Food Marketing, *Food From Farmer to Consumer* (Washington, D.C.: GPO, 1966), pp. 16–17.

counting out 50 pills and typing labels. Experimental work now being carried out suggests that the $1.50 cost of filling a prescription can be substantially reduced by new methods of marketing (Weiss, 1969).

Society asks many questions about the efficiency of marketing. How much advertising should be used? How many retailers should be operating? Is the high failure rate of retailers necessary? Does the market-place keep prices as low as they ought to be? Is there a limit to be placed on choice? Is each function of marketing being performed as efficiently as it might be? What kind of an assortment of marketing institutions is optimal? Certainly it is possible to reduce marketing costs substantially by restricting the individual entrepreneur, but our choice in the United States thus far has been to permit a relatively free marketplace to operate.

The social aspects of marketing costs are both important and complex. It is not a simple matter, for example, to control any segment of the business system, and so we consumers hope that the marketplace will adequately express our desires (see 29-6).

As social indicators are developed there may well be modifications of the present system. And as we do a better job of examining both costs and benefits we should also expect improvements in the system. Even a proposed law can be examined on a cost/benefit basis in order to determine if society will benefit from this addition to marketing legislation. Consider the truth-in-packaging law. The problem was to improve decision-making on the part of the consumer, especially in food-store buying. The goals of the proposed legislation were to eliminate deceptive packaging and proliferation of packaging, and to improve the consumers' ability to make value judgments on "best buys." There were several alternatives open to Congress since it could have specified voluntary or mandatory compliance, various kinds of labels and package sizes, and certain kinds of information that had to be included in advertising.

The benefits to be expected would be the goals suggested above. In addition there might be reductions in costs and therefore in prices. A better relationship between consumers and businesses should develop. There might be fewer law suits. But there would also be costs since the business sector might have to develop new packages, sustain losses on present inventory, increase advertising expenses, accept a lower return, and experience a lower volume of sales. Such a cost/benefit analysis can be used widely in the marketing field and it can serve both the consumer and businessman well.

In addition to evaluating marketing from the standpoint of cost, the social evaluation would today include other considerations. How is marketing relating to the problem of poverty? How well does it serve the disadvantaged, both here in the United States and abroad? How well does marketing inform the public? How well does marketing deliver a quality of life? Does marketing help to conserve scarce natural resources? Does marketing help to eliminate problems of pollution? Are marketers helping to eliminate racism? Is marketing serving the widest possible market, nonprofit as well as profit; government as well as

## 29-6

**The High Cost of Distribution**

Some services are not sheltered from market discipline, and the outstanding example is wholesale and retail trade, which in 1968 provided no fewer than 16,700,000 jobs, or 35 percent of all service employment. Here competition has forced employers to find ways of improving their productivity, and they have come up with advances such as computerized warehousing and inventory controls, new accounting methods, and self-service. Wholesaling accordingly has achieved some impressive productivity increases, and to a lesser extent so has retailing. A lot of the chain stores' success in reducing the cost of retailing, however, is the result not so much of real productivity increases as of making the manufacturer and the consumer perform services formerly performed by the storekeeper. The manufacturer prepackages, prelabels, and presells. The consumer does his own selection, delivery, and financing (i.e., he often pays a charge for credit).

There is little likelihood that large capital investments can pay off in improving the productivity of retail trade. It seems forever burdened with the rising cost of personal contacts. Unless some wholly new impersonal technique of distribution is invented, the cost of distributing goods is bound to keep on mounting faster than the cost of making them. Mail order is no alternative, for it uses enormous amounts of labor and so costs even more than store sales. Appropriately enough, therefore, employment in trade is rising considerably faster than employment in manufacturing. In 1948 trade employed 12 million people, 70 percent as many as manufacturing; by 1980 it will employ nearly 21 million, nearly as many as manufacturing. Distribution accordingly will become more expensive, and offset to some extent the high productivity growth and lower cost of making goods.

SOURCE: Gilbert Burck, "There'll Be Less Leisure Than You Think," *Fortune*, Vol. 81 (March 1970), p. 165.

---

private; services as well as products; industries, institutions, and corporations? Is marketing, as carried on, helping to make the economic system a stronger and more viable one?

## A COMPANY EVALUATION

Aggregate cost data for marketing are not of much help to a manager who is primarily interested in his own marketing costs and how they relate to his competitors'. The kind of cost analysis performed by the individual firm is referred to as *distribution cost analysis*. Although many firms have sophisticated cost systems, the information is usually of a proprietary nature and thus there is relatively little information readily available about corporate costs of marketing.

Techniques for making the cost analyses, however, have been developed over many years. One such method has been described by the marketing research director of Standard Oil Company of California.

*First,* natural elements of expense are subdivided into functions. These elements include such things as salaries, commissions, fees, depreciation, taxes, advertising, etc.

*Natural expenses* divided in *14 functions,* the most important of which are wholesale distributor commissions, plant depreciation, plant expense, solicitation expense, accounting, field administration, special customer expense, credit, advertising.

*Second,* all volume, income, and marketing expenses are separated by *7 sales areas* (Alaska and Washington, Hawaii, Oregon, California (several), Nevada and Arizona).

*Third,* expenses are then broken down by 6 means of distribution—wholesale, direct shipment, company transport fleet, truck, wholesale distributors, and the Pacific operations.

*Fourth,* the expenses are then divided into *16 trade classes* using SIC classifications (agriculture, railroads, state, heating fuel distributors, airlines, etc.)

*Finally,* expenses are categorized by *19 separate product* groups which are separate groupings of hundreds of separate products—gasoline, diesel fuel, furnace oil, industrial oils and greases, etc.

When you multiply the above categories—14 functions × 7 sales areas × 6 means of distribution × 16 trade classes × 19 product groups—it is realized that there are 178,752 "little boxes into which many millions of dollars of marketing expense must be divided." The company considers it one of the basic ways in which it can maintain marketing efficiency. Basic problems and opportunities are identified and marketing functions and marketing employees can be better controlled and assigned. Further, the results can help considerably in planning for the future. (Gardner, 1969.)

A distribution cost system can provide the marketer with a good deal of valuable information, for many decisions will be made on the basis of cost. Benefits to the firm as well as to its customers must be weighed in terms of costs. Attention to costs permits the manager to locate waste and accordingly to eliminate it, and this can provide the firm with competitive advantages in the marketplace. Cost analyses can be examined in the aggregate or in minute detail, but they do not necessarily provide an evaluation of marketing itself. For example, the identification of the high cost of serving a small customer does not dictate whether the firm continues to serve that customer, for there may be other reasons. Similarly, the cost of distributing old parts may be a losing proposition, but a firm may continue to do so in order to maintain a reputation for always serving its machinery. On the other hand, cost information can be useful for virtually every function of marketing. Some examples follow.

The promotion cost of securing 10, 20, 33, or 50 percent of a given market

Profit by size of account

Selling costs by salesman, by customer type, by geographic area

Alternative costs of selling to customers

The company's cost ratios versus industry averages

Costs of marketing research

Packaging costs

Transportation costs

Costs of filling orders

Costs of returned goods

The marketer can perform a kind of cost/benefit analysis as each decision is made on product, price, transportation, storage, advertising, packaging, and personal selling. Further, he can analyze each existing marketing procedure being used. Distribution cost analysis is a tool that can help marketers keep their operations efficient: it is a way to evaluate the company's marketing program.

# CONCLUDING COMMENTS

Evaluation of marketing relates to all the activities of the firm and to the firm's relationship to society as well. Evaluation cannot be a static exercise since perspectives change from day to day and so do expectations of good and bad performances. Marketing operates in a given environment, but it is a changing environment, and therefore marketers must respond adequately to environmental pressures and concerns. Clearly an evaluation of marketing should reflect a number of different viewpoints.

We have stressed cost anaylsis as the way of determining whether or not a company is doing a good job and whether or not marketing as a whole is doing a good job. But we have also pointed out that during the past decade marketers have become concerned with many new societal problems, and these must be considered in any evaluation today. In the past marketing has been mostly evaluated according to how well it has delivered a high standard of living. As the emphasis shifts to a broader meaning—quality of life—marketing may have severe adjustments to make in order to maintain a high performance level.

Whatever criteria are used, a satisfactory performance by marketers must satisfy interested parties—the firm's management, the owners, the consumers, and the government. Marketing cannot operate for any one group—marketing itself is a transaction of exchange. Both buyer and seller expect to gain from it and in our system, complex as it is, society as a whole has to be taken into account. A firm expects to profit as a result of its marketing effort, but not at the expense of society. Unfortunately some of the most important determinants in any evaluation are also the most intangible. That is, a firm may know precisely what it costs to distribute a hi-fi set and the customer may also know precisely what the set costs him. The nebulous part is the degree of satisfaction the customer receives from the purchase. Although attempts have been made to measure customer satisfaction, the results remain less precise than the cost data.

Americans believe in an economic system in which there is considerable freedom—freedom to buy and sell, to produce, and to consume. We want a system that operates without violence, according to law. Believing in the gains to be had from competition, we stress competitive effort in many ways. All this is a part of our total environment, and any evaluation of the marketing process has to recognize the kind of a system in which marketing exists. Further, we are aware that other economic systems that are characterized by a high degree of planning lack the vital information that the marketplace provides. Indeed, socialist countries are attempting today to work elements of the marketplace into their planned systems.

As consumers, we like to have brand choice and manufacturer choice. We want to think that the price system accurately reflects supply and demand. Of course we are aware of those parts of our system that do not employ the marketplace in this way—utilities, for example. We hope that manufacturers and distributors make intelligent decisions based on information. We want a marketing system that helps deliver a good standard of living without ruining the environment. But we also want efficiency in our marketing. Specialization and standardization provide the consumer some measure of efficiency. Labor-saving devices, new marketing institutions, adjustments to the dynamics of society, competition, research, and the training of people also reflect the efficiency of the distributive process (See Beckman, 1940).

As a citizen, a stockholder, an employee, a consumer, a student, or merely an observer of the passing scene, you will in the years ahead ask yourself many times about the quality of the marketing job. Perhaps you will find ways in which the marketing process can be improved; certainly you owe it to yourself to make this one of your goals. There are a number of questions you might ask. Does the system work for all? Is efficiency enough? What factors are really important in an appraisal? After exhaustive study, Reavis Cox concluded:

> Obviously, in a very important sense, the system works. The society dependent upon it not only has survived; it has grown and prospered enormously. Year after year stupendous quantities of goods and services are produced, processed, sorted, moved about, transferred from owner to owner, and eventually delivered to millions of terminal buyers. Billions of transactions supported by billions of units of transportation, storage, finance, and all the rest are arranged and carried into effect. The end result: A much vaunted level of living. . . . Specifically, [marketing] must be judged in our society by what it

does to serve rather than abuse the consumer interest, however that interest may be conceived. (Cox, 1965.)

Another authority suggests:

The legitimacy of the system is high, since all transactions within it are voluntary and the government exercises no formal authority. . . .

In this connection it may be well to survey the difficulty of the problem. Any industrial society must make decisions about goods— what to produce, with what factors, and so forth—for the whole society. This decision requires some sort of technique for aggregating many preference systems into a single preference system—at least in a society which pays attention to individual preferences. Viewed in this light, it is difficult to imagine any technique of social decision-making which could give more continuous and detailed attention to individual preferences. (Kuhn, 1963.)

Of course not all would agree:

In the market, the fetishistic power of commodities affects the capitalist differently from in the workshop. Whereas production is characterized by the discipline of an artificially constructed order, in the market the most perplexing anarchy prevails. There, commodities escape from the hands of their creator, engage in the maddest dance. They assume prices according to fancies of their own; make journeys; change owners; collect themselves into heaps, or scatter themselves to all the winds of heaven; store themselves away in warehouses, to rot there sometimes and thus fail to achieve their purpose; or speed from person to person, from town to town, to be consumed in the predestined way. Forming a fantastic world of their own, they lead therein an autocratic life, independent of the will of the producer. (Ruhle, 1929.)

The authors of this book believe that marketing has done a good, in some ways an amazing, job in incorporating "a delicately calibrated system of penalties and rewards which records the preferences of individuals and creates pressures to honor those preferences" (Oxenfeldt, 1957). The social trends have shown us that the job today, however, is bigger than ever and there remains much yet to accomplish.

Marketing, as one component of the total business and economic system, is analogous to one of the cells in the human body. The cells specialize and work together. Each in itself is unimportant; what matters is its contribution to the whole. Marketing definitely contributes to our society in a positive way. There are faults that remain to be corrected, efficiencies yet to be gained. The marketing task has been performed well in terms of the goals set for it, but as the goals change so must the marketing effort.

## STATEMENTS TO CONSIDER

In distribution, the economies of scale are sometimes much less than in manufacturing; they may even be nonexistent.

As production becomes larger in scale and more specialized, as products are manufactured to stock and not to order, and as consumers demand a greater and greater variety of goods, marketing becomes more and more important and more and more costly.

The key to distribution cost analysis is a thorough analysis of marketing expense which must be segmented into understandable and communicable elements.

Marketing costs are becoming an integral part of the protect-the-consumer movement.

Circulation (distribution) sweats money from every pore. (Marx)

The primary criterion of marketing performance is "whatever makes money"; "whatever I can get away with": anarchy plus the policeman.

Advertising can be evaluated easily. First, make a list of all the functions of business. Second, allocate the exact amount of sales or profit which can properly be credited to that activity. Third add up the allocations. Fourth, deduct the sum from sales or profit total. What remains is the contribution of advertising. (Wallace)

To be of worth, and to know how to show it, is to be worth double. (Gracian)

The fundamental economic criterion for appraising marketing activities is the efficiency with which they are performed. (Preston)

Estimates of costs and profits comprising the price spreads for individual foods cannot be made with complete precision and must be treated as approximations. (U.S. Department of Agriculture)

## QUESTIONS FOR REVIEW

**1.** Is marketing doing a good job? What criteria are you using?

**2.** Does marketing cost too much? If you answer in the affirmative, who in marketing receives too much for his services?

**3.** How would you go about reducing the wastes that come as a result of our system—e.g., failures of firms that had the freedom to enter?

**4.** Do you think that examination and licensing procedures for marketing personnel might improve the quality of people engaged in marketing?

**5.** Where is the resistance to improving the marketing system? What can we do about it?

**6.** In what areas of marketing would you expect distribution cost analysis to be the most useful?

**7.** Set up an evaluation of marketing for an industry and compare the performance of several firms operating within that industry.

**8.** Why do we have so much difficulty in making social evaluations of firms?

**9.** Do you think our system of marketing better or worse than that of the socialistic nations? Compare them the best you can.

**10.** How useful would "value added by marketing" information be to an evaluation of the marketing operation?


## Further Readings

Harold Barger, *Distribution's Place in the American Economy Since 1869* (Princeton, N.J.: Princeton University Press, 1955).

Chamber of Commerce of the United States, *Value Added by Distribution* (Washington, D.C.: 1956).

Reavis Cox, in association with Charles S. Goodman and Thomas C. Fichandler, *Distribution in a High-Level Economy* (Englewood Cliffs, N.J.: Prentice-Hall, 1965).

Stanley C. Hollander, "Measuring the Cost and Value of Marketing," *Business Topics,* Vol. 9, No. 3 (Summer 1961), pp. 17–27.

United States National Commission on Food Marketing, *Food From Farmer to Consumer* (Washington, D.C.: GPO, 1966).

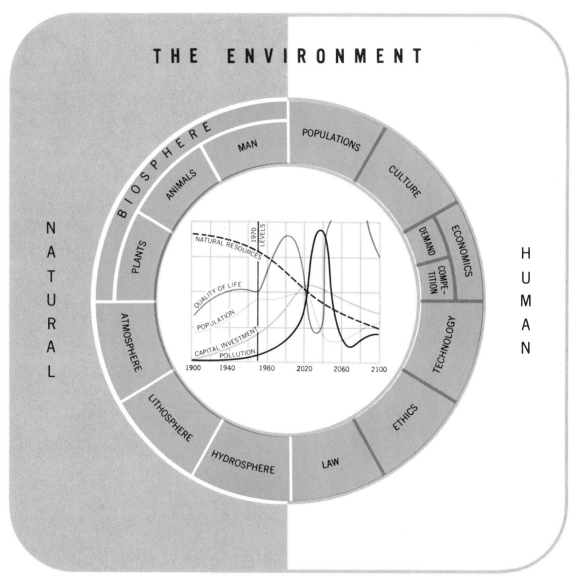

# THE ENVIRONMENT

NATURAL

HUMAN

BIOSPHERE

MAN
ANIMALS
PLANTS
ATMOSPHERE
LITHOSPHERE
HYDROSPHERE

POPULATIONS
CULTURE
DEMAND
ECONOMICS
COMPE-
TITION
TECHNOLOGY
ETHICS
LAW

NATURAL RESOURCES
1970 LEVELS
QUALITY OF LIFE
POPULATION
CAPITAL INVESTMENT
POLLUTION

1900   1940   1980   2020   2060   2100

SOURCE: Jay W. Forrester, *World Dynamics* (Cambridge, Mass.: Wright-Allen Press, 1971), p. 70.

# CHAPTER 30
# MARKETING AND THE FUTURE

Marketing in the 1960s

A Look into the Future

Selected Trends

*The future will present new problems and new opportunities to marketers. Those who are futuristic in their thinking are perhaps on the threshhold of helping marketing gain a new authenticity in tomorrow's society. In any case, trends point toward bigger-than-ever challenges in the years ahead.*

The managers of the year 2000 are now you students in the schools of business. You obviously need knowledge of the way things are now, but in addition you need some idea of probable trends for the future since your decisions are really future-oriented. It is important to prepare yourself mentally to cope with change, for change there will be.* Fortunately you can keep abreast of changes through the literature, meetings of professional associations, management development programs, and extension classes at universities and via television.

The purpose of this chapter is to help you develop a receptive mental state for coping with change and of thinking about what might happen in the next decade or so. To this end we have divided the chapter into three parts: (1) a look at changes that occurred during the 1960s; (2) selected forecasts that provide some bases for marketing decisions in the next decade; and (3) a look into the future.

## MARKETING IN THE 1960s

A brief look backward provides some realism to the notion of change. In every sector there were adaptations by marketers to the changing environments in which they worked. The decade of the 1960s began with people confident of a continuing high standard of living in our country and hopeful that we could help other nations emulate our economic success. The outlook was for a "sizzling sixties": smoke billowing from the factory chimney was reassuring and DDT was proof of our ability to control nature. But then we witnessed waves of social-political-religious movements erupting in Watts, Milwaukee, Selma, Chicago, Memphis, Newark, Kent State, Washington, D.C., and many other places. A host of new movements swept in, all well-marketed—Ecology, Black Power, Women's Lib, Chicano, and Anti-war, in the Age of Aquarius.

We experienced rapid change in our technology, political system, economic situation, and way of life. We began to question our values and especially our materialistic goal. Most of the chapters in this book have referred to changes that have taken place, as subsequent paragraphs review.

Marketers demonstrated that they could adapt. Low-calorie and organic food items, small cars, modular housing, men's cosmetics, instant TV replay, nuclear power, miniature calculators, "old" clothing,

*See Alvin Toffler, *Future Shock*, (New York: Random House, 1970).

and hundreds of other new items were produced for and distributed to the marketplace. This ability to adapt suggests that changing life styles of the future will offer no problem to the marketer in terms of his satisfying the customer.

Prices became important in the latter part of the decade because of inflation. Unit pricing was introduced in an effort to provide the buyer with adequate price information.

The conglomerate merger boom of the 1960s exceeds all previous merger periods in our history. Patterns of competition changed as well-known product lines fell under new ownership. The growing importance of foreign goods, especially from Japan, began to frighten some U.S. manufacturers. Other firms began to develop as multinational companies.

Marketing institutions relocated, especially in the suburbs, as they followed a traditional pattern of going with the population. Discount house operations became "legitimate," and Sunday shopping spread throughout the nation. Franchised operations appeared in almost every conceivable kind of operation.

Changes in physical distribution improved marketing efficiency. The use of the container and the increased use of air freight with the new large planes became commonplace. Trucking firms advertised, "If you have it, a truck brought it," a fair reflection of their role in hauling products of all kinds. Computers directed the distribution and storage of millions of products. Packaging became a solid-waste problem.

Advertising continued to expand and also to be under attack by its critics. Racial integration in ads became noticeable, and advertisers directed many of their messages toward the newly discovered nonwhite and youth markets. In the social sector, with problems of inflation, racism, poverty, and war, marketing wrestled with consumerism.

Changes in the environment elicited adaptations on the part of marketing during the 1960s. This is not to suggest that marketing performed perfectly: the point is that there is always change and marketers must be alert to that inevitable phenomenon.

## SELECTED TRENDS

Marketers make many of their decisions after examining and interpreting data that have relevance to the marketplace. The trends are especially useful in identifying market segments and in estimating the size of those segments. The best available indicators are gathered and estimates of the future are then made based on various assumptions about the future such as growth patterns, technological innovation, and war or peace. We are presenting a number of trends, not to suggest what tomorrow will be, but to suggest the kinds of information that interest marketers. The assumptions underlying the projections could change overnight—international climate, armed forces expenditures, the institutional framework of our economic system, technological breakthroughs, monetary policies, and the emphasis on combating pollution—and so the marketer has to modify the projections frequently.

One of the most basic trends for the marketer is that of population (30-1) for population represents market potentials.

The birth rate presents a problem in forecasting population since the attitudes of people toward large families, abortions, zero population growth, and marriage blend with economics, immigration, wars, and other factors. Different assumptions give different forecasts. (See 30-2.)

The total size of population, however, is not sufficient information for the marketer who needs better definitions of his market segments. One useful kind of information is the regional distribution of population (30-3).

Another population factor that can have an influence on marketing is the place of residence (30-4).

The age distribution of the population (30-5) is another important trend for marketers who know that some products reach only certain age groups and that advertising appeals must fit the age group constituting the market segment.

Household formation is obviously important to many in marketing, but especially to those who distribute housing materials, household furnishings, and appliances. Projected households to 1980 are shown in 30-6.

**30-1** U.S. Population and Growth Rate

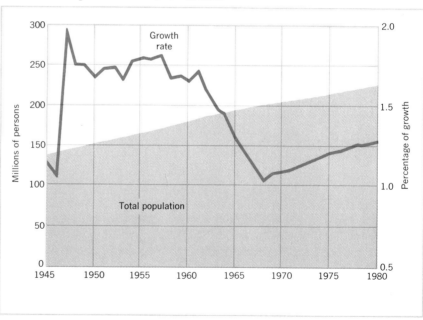

SOURCE: Fabian Linden, *The Consumer of the Seventies* (New York: National Industrial Conference Board, Inc., 1969), p. 11.

## 30-2 Births and Fertility Rates

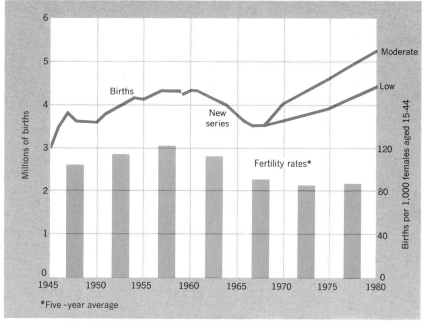

SOURCE: Fabian Linden, *The Consumer of the Seventies* (New York: National Industrial Conference Board, Inc., 1969), p. 13.

## 30-3 Regional Population

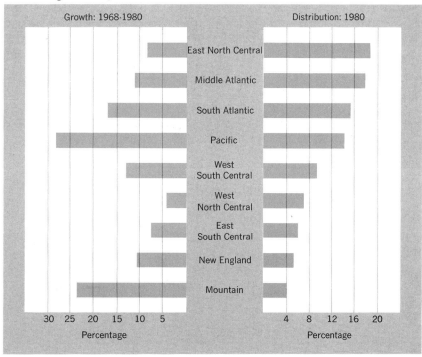

SOURCE: Fabian Linden, *The Consumer of the Seventies* (New York: National Industrial Conference Board, Inc., 1969), p. 49.

## 30-4 Population by Metropolitan and Nonmetropolitan Areas

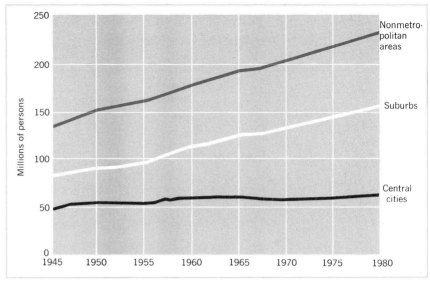

SOURCE: Fabian Linden, *The Consumer of the Seventies* (New York: National Industrial Conference Board, Inc., 1969), p. 41.

## 30-5 Population Growth by Age Groups

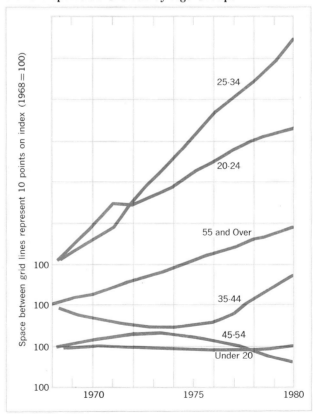

SOURCE: Fabian Linden, *The Consumer of the Seventies* (New York: National Industrial Conference Board, Inc., 1969), p. 21.

**30-6** Households and Net Household Growth

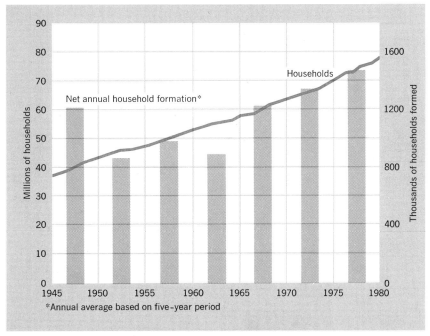

SOURCE: Fabian Linden, *The Consumer of the Seventies* (New York: National Industrial Conference Board, Inc., 1969), p. 27.

Other population characteristics influence the nature of marketing. Education, for example, signals the degree of sophistication of the consumer, tastes for products, and desires for services (see 30-7).

Effective market demand consists of people—with money—and money is earned through employment. Employment in major occupational groups is shown in 30-8.

In the area of employment the number of working wives has a real influence on buying decisions in the homes (see 30-9).

Gross National Product forecasts are basic to many marketing analyses. The forecast in 30-10 shows 1980 GNP at approximately $1.4 trillion. (A Chamber of Commerce estimate, with different assumptions, suggests planning for a 1980 GNP of $2.0 trillion.)

GNP concerns the economy as a whole. But what of individual consumers? The income available to individuals—disposable personal income—is shown in 30-11 along with per capita forecasts. Changes in the regional distribution of personal income (30-12) are obviously relevant to sales planning too.

The diagram in 30-13 illustrates successive steps in projecting demand for a few selected products. Basic indicators are at the top of the diagram; you read down to locate the estimated demands for goods and services as well as the resulting requirements for basic materials.

## 30-7 Educational Level

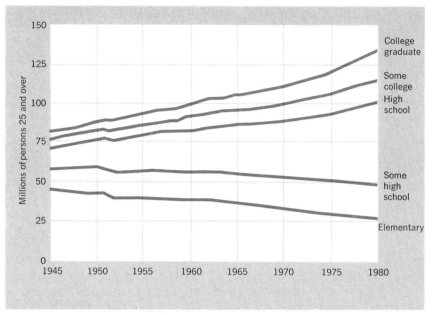

SOURCE: Fabian Linden, *The Consumer of the Seventies* (New York: National Industrial Conference Board, Inc., 1969), p. 23.

## 30-8 Employment Trends in Goods-Producing and Services-Producing Industries

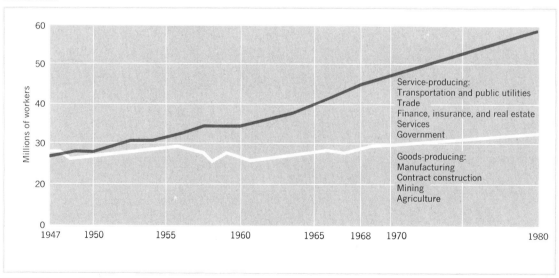

SOURCE: National Goals Research Staff, *Toward Balanced Growth: Quantity with Quality* (Washington, D.C.: GPO, 1970), p. 183.

**30-9** Working Wives

SOURCE: Fabian Linden, *The Consumer of the Seventies* (New York: National Industrial Conference Board, Inc., 1969), p. 57.

**30-10** Gross National Product

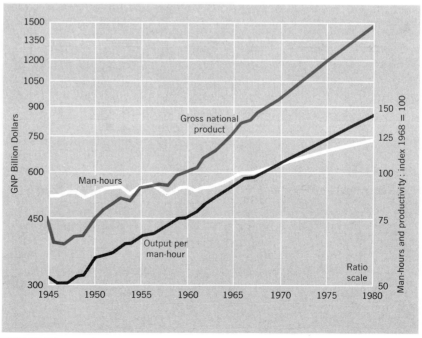

SOURCE: Fabian Linden, *The Consumer of the Seventies* (New York: National Industrial Conference Board, Inc., 1969), p. 9.

**30-11** Disposable Personal Income

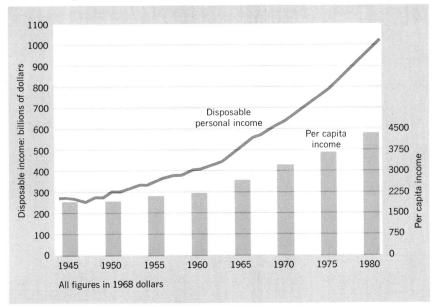

SOURCE: Fabian Linden, *The Consumer of the Seventies* (New York: National Industrial Conference Board, Inc., 1969), p. 51.

Differences in future demand structures depend on a number of factors, such as the demands for services and durable goods. The next diagram, 30-14, shows the differences in demand structure in a services economy and in a durables economy. The services economy is based on a continuation of the long-term shift toward the purchase of more consumer and public services whereas the durable-goods economy assumes a slower growth in the trend toward services with correspondingly greater emphasis on durable-goods production. The differences lie in the composition of final demand and its related components, a factor most important to marketers.

The distribution of the consumers' dollars is shown in 30-15. Relative increases in expenditures for shelter, medical care, and automobiles are matched by decreases in food, clothing, alcohol, and other expenditures.

There are other ways to examine future trends than mere extrapolation of trend lines. Simulation, for instance, permits one to build a model in which changes can be simulated in order to ascertain the effect. The "World Dynamics" model by Jay W. Forrester, referred to in Chapter 28 (28-2), is one such model of the way the world "works." The computer holds the basic information including the model's five basic variables: (1) population, (2) pollution, (3) natural resources, (4) capital investment, and (5) the fraction of capital devoted to agriculture

Assumptions include the following: crowding, pollution, and a high material standard of living decrease the birth rate and food increases it; the quality of life is increased by food and by material standard of living and decreased by pollution and crowding; capital investment increases pollution, which in turn reduces food production. An updated version of the world model by Dennis L. Meadows is shown in 30-16, a very complicated picture of interaction but one undoubtedly more realistic than projections that are concerned with only one variable

**30-12** Relative Differences among Regions in per Capita Personal Income as a Percentage of U.S. Averages

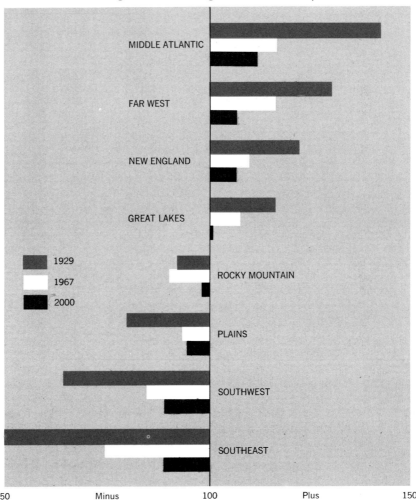

SOURCE: National Goals Research Staff, *Toward Balanced Growth: Quantity with Quality* (Washington, D.C.: GPO, 1970), p. 187.

## 30-13 Resources and Economic Growth: How the Demand Projections Were Built Up

The chart illustrates successive steps in projecting demand for a few selected products. Starting with projections of population, labor force, households, and gross national product at the top, the diagram traces, as one reads down (1) the estimated demands for goods and services, (2) the resulting requirements for key materials, and (3) the demand for basic resources and resource products of which there are many more than those shown on the bottom line. The chart also suggests the way in which different elements in the economy combine to create the level of demand for particular resources.

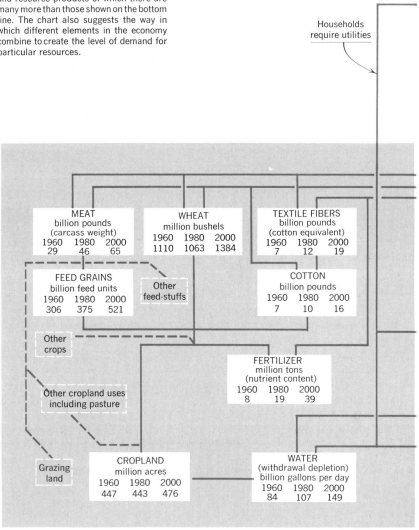

Households require utilities

| MEAT billion pounds (carcass weight) | | |
|---|---|---|
| 1960 | 1980 | 2000 |
| 29 | 46 | 65 |

| WHEAT million bushels | | |
|---|---|---|
| 1960 | 1980 | 2000 |
| 1110 | 1063 | 1384 |

| TEXTILE FIBERS billion pounds (cotton equivalent) | | |
|---|---|---|
| 1960 | 1980 | 2000 |
| 7 | 12 | 19 |

| FEED GRAINS billion feed units | | |
|---|---|---|
| 1960 | 1980 | 2000 |
| 306 | 375 | 521 |

Other feed-stuffs

| COTTON billion pounds | | |
|---|---|---|
| 1960 | 1980 | 2000 |
| 7 | 10 | 16 |

Other crops

| FERTILIZER million tons (nutrient content) | | |
|---|---|---|
| 1960 | 1980 | 2000 |
| 8 | 19 | 39 |

Other cropland uses including pasture

Grazing land

| CROPLAND million acres | | |
|---|---|---|
| 1960 | 1980 | 2000 |
| 447 | 443 | 476 |

| WATER (withdrawal depletion) billion gallons per day | | |
|---|---|---|
| 1960 | 1980 | 2000 |
| 84 | 107 | 149 |

SOURCE: Hans H. Landsberg, *Natural Resources for U.S. Growth* (Baltimore: The Johns Hopkins University Press, 1964), pp. 8–9.

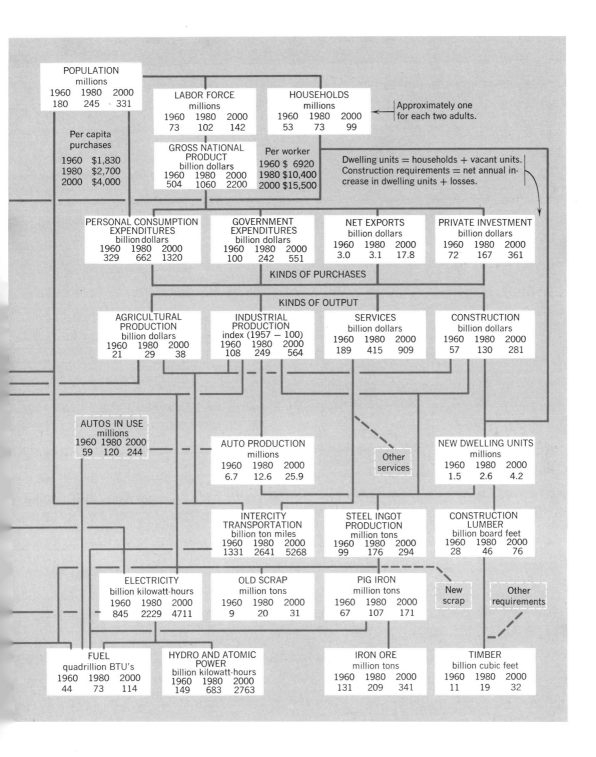

POPULATION
millions

| 1960 | 1980 | 2000 |
|---|---|---|
| 180 | 245 | 331 |

Per capita purchases

| 1960 | $1,830 |
|---|---|
| 1980 | $2,700 |
| 2000 | $4,000 |

LABOR FORCE
millions

| 1960 | 1980 | 2000 |
|---|---|---|
| 73 | 102 | 142 |

HOUSEHOLDS
millions

| 1960 | 1980 | 2000 |
|---|---|---|
| 53 | 73 | 99 |

Approximately one for each two adults.

GROSS NATIONAL PRODUCT
billion dollars

| 1960 | 1980 | 2000 |
|---|---|---|
| 504 | 1060 | 2200 |

Per worker

| 1960 | $ 6920 |
|---|---|
| 1980 | $10,400 |
| 2000 | $15,500 |

Dwelling units = households + vacant units.
Construction requirements = net annual increase in dwelling units + losses.

PERSONAL CONSUMPTION EXPENDITURES
billion dollars

| 1960 | 1980 | 2000 |
|---|---|---|
| 329 | 662 | 1320 |

GOVERNMENT EXPENDITURES
billion dollars

| 1960 | 1980 | 2000 |
|---|---|---|
| 100 | 242 | 551 |

NET EXPORTS
billion dollars

| 1960 | 1980 | 2000 |
|---|---|---|
| 3.0 | 3.1 | 17.8 |

PRIVATE INVESTMENT
billion dollars

| 1960 | 1980 | 2000 |
|---|---|---|
| 72 | 167 | 361 |

KINDS OF PURCHASES

KINDS OF OUTPUT

AGRICULTURAL PRODUCTION
billion dollars

| 1960 | 1980 | 2000 |
|---|---|---|
| 21 | 29 | 38 |

INDUSTRIAL PRODUCTION
index (1957 − 100)

| 1960 | 1980 | 2000 |
|---|---|---|
| 108 | 249 | 564 |

SERVICES
billion dollars

| 1960 | 1980 | 2000 |
|---|---|---|
| 189 | 415 | 909 |

CONSTRUCTION
billion dollars

| 1960 | 1980 | 2000 |
|---|---|---|
| 57 | 130 | 281 |

AUTOS IN USE
millions

| 1960 | 1980 | 2000 |
|---|---|---|
| 59 | 120 | 244 |

AUTO PRODUCTION
millions

| 1960 | 1980 | 2000 |
|---|---|---|
| 6.7 | 12.6 | 25.9 |

Other services

NEW DWELLING UNITS
millions

| 1960 | 1980 | 2000 |
|---|---|---|
| 1.5 | 2.6 | 4.2 |

INTERCITY TRANSPORTATION
billion ton miles

| 1960 | 1980 | 2000 |
|---|---|---|
| 1331 | 2641 | 5268 |

STEEL INGOT PRODUCTION
million tons

| 1960 | 1980 | 2000 |
|---|---|---|
| 99 | 176 | 294 |

CONSTRUCTION LUMBER
billion board feet

| 1960 | 1980 | 2000 |
|---|---|---|
| 28 | 46 | 76 |

ELECTRICITY
billion kilowatt-hours

| 1960 | 1980 | 2000 |
|---|---|---|
| 845 | 2229 | 4711 |

OLD SCRAP
million tons

| 1960 | 1980 | 2000 |
|---|---|---|
| 9 | 20 | 31 |

PIG IRON
million tons

| 1960 | 1980 | 2000 |
|---|---|---|
| 67 | 107 | 171 |

New scrap

Other requirements

FUEL
quadrillion BTU's

| 1960 | 1980 | 2000 |
|---|---|---|
| 44 | 73 | 114 |

HYDRO AND ATOMIC POWER
billion kilowatt-hours

| 1960 | 1980 | 2000 |
|---|---|---|
| 149 | 683 | 2763 |

IRON ORE
million tons

| 1960 | 1980 | 2000 |
|---|---|---|
| 131 | 209 | 341 |

TIMBER
billion cubic feet

| 1960 | 1980 | 2000 |
|---|---|---|
| 11 | 19 | 32 |

**30-14** Differences in Demand Structure in a Services Economy and in a Durables Economy, 1980

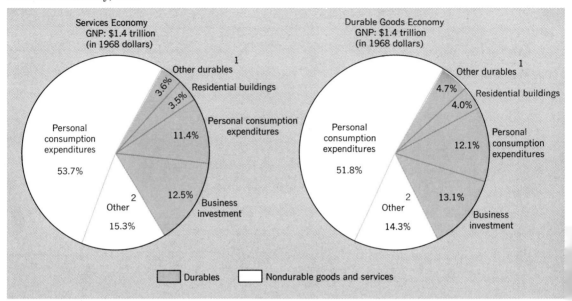

Services Economy
GNP: $1.4 trillion
(in 1968 dollars)

Other durables¹

Residential buildings

3.6%

3.5%

Personal consumption expenditures

11.4%

Personal consumption expenditures

53.7%

Other²

15.3%

12.5% Business investment

Durable Goods Economy
GNP: $1.4 trillion
(in 1968 dollars)

Other durables¹

4.7%

Residential buildings

4.0%

Personal consumption expenditures

12.1%

Personal consumption expenditures

51.8%

Other²

14.3%

13.1% Business investment

☐ Durables      ☐ Nondurable goods and services

¹ Includes net exports and government purchases.

² Includes government compensation and household services.

SOURCE: U.S. Department of Labor, Bureau of Labor Statistics, *The U.S. Economy in 1980*, Bulletin 1673 (Washington, D.C.: GPO, 1970), p. 9.

at a time. Meadows has listed some of the conclusions from the simula tions:

> There is no possibility of sufficient technological and cultura progress occurring in the next 100 years to sustain as many as 1 billion people on our globe.
>
> There is no possibility of bringing the vast majority of those livin in the developing countries up to the material standard of livin enjoyed by the developed nations.
>
> There is a strong probability that the Western nations will witnes a marked decline in their own material standard of living within th next three or four decades.
>
> There is no unique, optimal long-term population level. Rathe there is an entire set of trade-offs between personal freedom, materia and social standard of living, and the population level.
>
> There is, in theory, no fundamental human value which could no be better achieved through a substantial lowering of the glob population base.

There is a very strong probability that the transition to global equilibrium will involve a traumatic decline in population. (Meadows, 1971.)

An example of the way Forrester used his simulation model to predict events is shown in 30-17 where natural resources are shown to be one-third depleted by the year 2000 and two-thirds depleted by 2100. Population peaks around the year 2020 and then because of resource shortage turns downward. Quality of life, of considerable interest to the marketer, has already peaked and is on its way down. If the consumption of natural resources is reduced to one-fourth the normal rate,

**30-15** Distribution of the Consumer Dollar

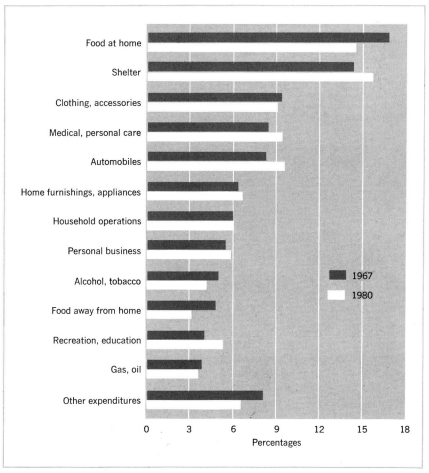

Total expenditures each year = 100%

SOURCE: Fabian Linden, *The Consumer of the Seventies* (New York: National Industrial Conference Board, Inc., 1969), p. 65.

**30-16** "World 3"

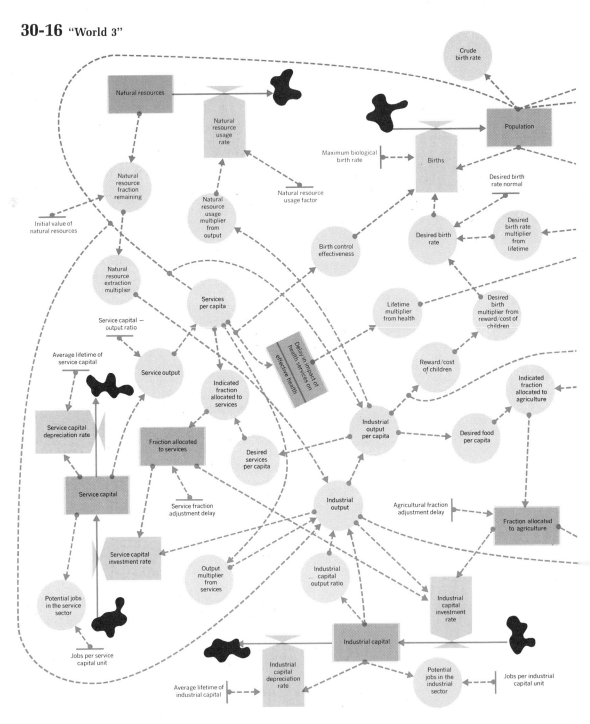

SOURCE: Dennis L. Meadows, "The Predicament of Mankind," *The Futurist*, Vol. 5 (August 1971), pp. 140–141. Chart drawn by Nancy Montague of *Futurist* staff.

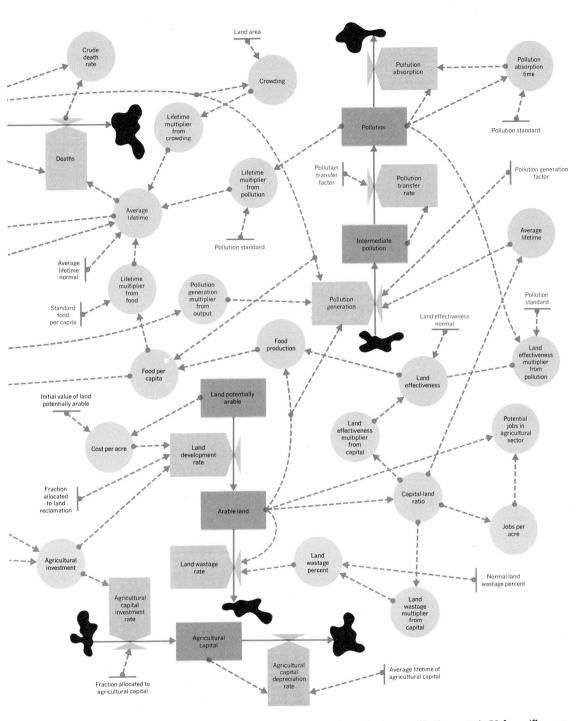

The rectangles represent "levels" (population, pollution, etc.). Valves (figures suggesting fire extinguishers) are "rates" (birth rate, death rate, etc.), which directly determine levels. Circles are "auxiliaries"—various factors that strongly affect rates. (Birth control effectiveness is one auxiliary.) Clouds (irregular figures) are levels that are considered to be unimportant in the simulation.

**30-17** Basic Behavior of the World Model, Showing How Industrialization and Population Are Suppressed by Falling Natural Resources

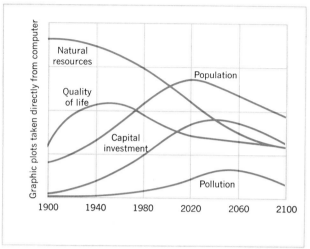

SOURCE: Jay W. Forrester, *World Dynamics* (Cambridge, Mass.: Wright-Allen Press, 1971), p. 70.

population peaks a little later as shown in 30-18; industrialization increases more; pollution multiplies five-fold by the year 2020 and then goes off the graph. Pollution then governs man's fate.

Is all this relevant to the marketer? We believe so, for the marketer

**30-18** How Reduced Usage Rate of Natural Resources Leads to a Pollution Crisis

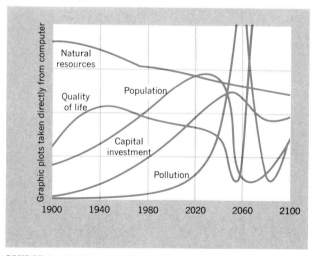

SOURCE: Jay W. Forrester, *World Dynamics* (Cambridge, Mass.: Wright-Allen Press, 1971), p. 75.

is jointly responsible for the allocation of his firm's resources and the products they produce. He should attempt to understand to the best of his ability the impact of his decisions on the environment and the effects of the environment on his firm.

# A LOOK INTO THE FUTURE

At the end of the 1960s *Business Week* predicted:

> Economic growth will continue at a brisk clip, carrying the U.S. to levels of output and income never seen before and not even imagined two decades ago. Rising population and rising incomes will open new markets, and advancing technology will provide new ways to serve these markets. But neither growth nor increasing affluence will relieve the tensions that are building up. Through most of the Seventies, the U.S. will seethe with conflicting emotions as it strives to find answers to problems that are social and even philosophical rather than simply economic. (*Business Week*, 1969.)

The emphasis above on emotional, philosophical, and social matters suggests that the mere extension of trend lines into the future is totally inadequate. We need to go deeper in order to have any real understanding of where we are going. Actually when most of us think of the future we think only of some fuzzy modified present, and we sit back and wait for it. Sometimes we wait in fear and sometimes we see it as an opportunity to plan so as to achieve our desires. Some marketers let technology dictate to them and others utilize it for future endeavors. Some marketers capitalize on social trends and others are relatively unaware of them. The awareness and anticipation of change permits the marketer to do more than collect forecasts. The broader view of marketing and the environment proposed in this book means that the marketer must consider many factors, some of which have not in the past concerned marketing—and herein lies one of the changes for the future.

Francesco Nicosia and Charles Glock have suggested an accounting scheme, 30-19, for affluence and social changes. A decade ago this kind of scheme would have seemed inappropriate for marketing, but today with the broadening of marketing, its increased integration into the main stream of society, and computer capabilities of handling information, such a scheme suggests a plausible approach to getting a focus on social change and its meaning for marketing. Each item in the scheme is deserving of consideration.

Changes in *life styles* affect sales of products. Consider the impact on marketing from trends toward personalization, cultural self-expression, mysticism, personal creativity, return to nature, pleasure for its own sake, blurring of the sexes, greater tolerance of chaos and disorder, and living in the present (Yankelovich, 1971). The new life styles will demand a new view on the part of the marketer, and he will have to

## 30-19

**Affluence and Social Changes: An Accounting Scheme**

I. STYLES OF LIFE
   1. Consumption expenditures
   2. Content of baskets of goods bought
   3. Time budgets
   4. Activities by types of behavior

II. TECHNOLOGY
   1. Technical
   2. Administrative

III. VALUES
   General, nonobject-specific norms, rewards sanctions, etc. concerning:
   1. God
   2. Sex
   3. Perceptions of time, life
   4. Achievement, equality
   5. Free will, individual's responsibility
   6. Justice
   7. Pluralism: From *one* hierarchy of values to many and relative hierarchies

IV. OTHER SOCIAL AND CULTURAL FACTORS
   1. Institutions
      Military, business, arts, economic system, schools, families, governments, labor unions, social classes, religious, place of residence
   2. Political structure and processes
   3. Religion
   4. Communication
      Mass media, others
   5. Welfare
      Facts, structural aspects
   6. Systemic conflict
      Pluralism, specialization
   7. Population
      Facts, characteristics, interactions
   8. Black and other populations
      Facts, integration, expenditures, social-cultural
   9. Age
   10. Education
      Students, teachers, the school
   11. Occupations
   12. Woman
      Within and outside the family
   13. Economics
      Spending, earning, saving, assets, international, production, research
   14. Arts-culture
   15. Legislation
   16. International

SOURCE: Adapted from Francesco M. Nicosia and Charles Y. Glock, "Marketing and Affluence; A Research Prospectus," in *Marketing and the New Science of Planning*, Robert L. King (ed.) (Chicago: American Marketing Association, 1968), pp. 525–527.

reconcile conflicts among them as he modifies his thinking about consumers in the marketplace.

Another item suggested in the Nicosia-Glock scheme is that of the relationship of business and social *institutions*. A Delphi study by the Institute for the Future suggests that marketing must expect continued turmoil, militant actions against business, various means of protest (litigation, sit-ins, and federal action), public relations work in the social arena, new types of business establishments, *and* continued profitable business operations (Institute for the Future, 1971).

The foregoing comments about the future are general in nature. More specific comments about marketing could be made, although they may turn out to be perishable or short-sighted whereas the general remarks may be long-lasting. One can certainly safely forecast that new products will be introduced. Some, such as automatically controlled automobiles, may require little if any modification of the role of the marketer. Home information centers with a computer, two-way video, and printer communications, on the other hand, could bring about drastic changes in food marketing. It has been predicted that food store volume will reach $239 million by 1980, a 62 percent increase over 1968. An increase in population during the next decade of 26 million people would match the total population in the combined states of Montana, Wyoming, Colorado, North Dakota, South Dakota, Nebraska, Kansas, Minnesota, Iowa, Missouri, Wisconsin, and Illinois (Graf, 1970). But if the home computer becomes a reality, it should not be necessary to add thousands of new stores to serve the expanded population. Another possibility for this decade is a new home power package that will change the work of the housewife and husband. Product innovations usually bring about new retailing and wholesaling facilities as well as manufacturing.*

The systems concept may well bring about changes in marketing management. More complete integration of the marketing functions and better integration between marketing and the other business activities should take place. Accounting and marketing, for instance, have a good deal in common and a total approach to problem-solving should help them integrate their efforts. There will be better coordination between research and development and marketing and between sales and marketing research. Better information systems should smooth many of the communications problems among different departments.

Techniques of all marketers will improve. Marketing researchers certainly are continually improving their research methodology; wholesalers, retailers, advertisers, and salesmen are also increasing their efficiency with new methods. The seventies will see continued attempts to measure the effectiveness of advertising, more sensitivity to the marketplace and to society in general, more ads in tune with environmental problems, more careful listing of product benefits, and some "demarketing" efforts. Wholesalers, always aware of the integration pressures from retailers and manufacturers, will do more to improve the physical handling of goods, computerizing accounts, and providing new services (Lopata, 1969).

The future of international trade is clouded, as always, by uncertainty because of international politics. It is expected that U.S. imports and exports will increase considerably during the next decade (imports $66 billion and exports $70 billion by 1980), but trade data tell only part of the story since multinational marketing will be growing during this

*A number of these observations are based on a special feature in the *Journal of Marketing*, Vol. 34 (January 1970), pp. 1–30. Contributors included Eugene J. Kelly, Robert D. Buzzell, William R. Davidson, Philip Kotler, Paul E. Green, John A. Howard, Elmer P. Lotshaw, Robert J. Lavidge, and Robert Ferber.

same period and sales of firms in that field are not reflected in the conventional trade statistics. Competitive pressures, momentum from present operations, world peace, and greater standardization of markets are all factors that are likely to increase world trade.

# CONCLUDING COMMENTS

Writing scenarios of the future is a fun thing to do: see 30-20. But even with current attempts to develop improved ways to study the future, predicting what will happen in marketing is an overwhelming task. Marketing is influenced by too many environmental factors—economics, psychology, sociology, and geography, the law, new ideas in advertising and selling, and the way people will behave years from now—for prediction to be easy or reliable. Although it is difficult to know which human and physical forces of the environment will have important meaning for marketers in the future, you can be rather sure of some things. For instance, much of marketing as it takes place today will be with us in the near future. Also, marketing will be able to adapt to new life styles and even to problems such as consumerism. The more difficult struggles will be with basic changes such as controlled growth, the internalizing of external costs of pollution, and changes in the mix of private and public influence.

The emphasis in this book has been on the fundamental and general as opposed to the specific. Hopefully you have learned the basics of the marketing system and have developed an attitude for making changes when they should be made. Hopefully, too, you see the associations between marketing and each identifiable part of the environment and can trace first, second, and even third-order effects of various marketing decisions. You have been reinforced in wanting to conduct your marketing program in keeping with societal goals for a higher quality of life, improving standards of living for many including those who have not previously enjoyed them, providing better information for buyers, and giving greater satisfaction to consumers—all with a satisfactory rate of profit for management and owners. It may seem like an impossible task, but it presents marketing—indeed, all of business—with an aim higher than any in the past; the attempt to reach that higher aim will hopefully produce improvement in many aspects of marketing. Marketing can become the instrument for the delivery of a high quality of life for all.

## 30-20

**Blueprints for the Businessman of 1980**

### Alternative A

Drawing on the technology that we already have or can reasonably expect to have in the near future, you could blueprint a world for the businessman of 1980 that would look something like this:

He will spend the afternoon running simulations of new marketing strategies for Indonesia through the company computer, working, of course, from a terminal at his own desk. With his plans perfected, he will instruct the computer to transmit them to Tokyo for branch office attention.

Leaving the office, he will pick up his all-purpose electronic identification card from his secretary, who had been using it to order his wife's birthday present. He also will pocket a couple of TV tape cassettes containing interoffice reports and his homework for the evening, an instruction tape on new applications of probability theory to market research.

A high-speed turbotrain will rush him to his suburban stop, and at the station parking lot he will unplug his electric runabout from the combination parking meter and battery recharger. There will be no need to feed in quarters because both the parking fee and the electricity will be billed by direct wire to his bank account when he put his ID card in the slot.

*After hours.* On the way home, he will stop by his doctor's office for a booster shot of anticancer vaccine. Coming out, he will note with approval that demolition of the electric transmission towers on the hill behind town is proceeding rapidly. All transmission lines will be underground by then.

At home, after a quick supper, he will look over some bills and his daily bank statement, all transmitted over the printer attached to his television set. Then he will settle down for a couple of hours with his tapes. Toward the end of the evening, he will call an old friend by Picturephone and play Scrabble with him for an hour. And so to bed.

### Alternative B

For an alternate picture of the businessman in 1980, try this:

He will spend the afternoon working on plans to protect company property from vandalism, and before he leaves there will be a meeting to consider the new government order shutting down three of the company's biggest plants because of an air-pollution emergency. The chief of Indonesian marketing will report that the new nationalistic regime is demanding 99% ownership of all foreign operations.

On the way to the station he will make a detour of several blocks to avoid a confrontation between the police and a militant new group agitating for "poverty power." His commuter train will be two hours late, and his car will be balky because the last mechanic to work on it had no idea what he was doing.

On the drive home, his nose will start dripping and he will suspect that he is catching another cold. On arrival, he will find his wife waiting with her coat on.

"We'll have to go out to dinner, dear," she will say. "The power has been off again since three o'clock and I can't cook anything. I tried to phone you but all the circuits were busy."

*SOURCE:* "The Seventies—Super But Seething," *Business Week*, December 6, 1969, pp. 77, 80. Copyright held by McGraw-Hill, Inc.

# STATEMENTS TO CONSIDER

Either we will choose the future or the future will choose—and destroy—us. (Harrington)

Never before in human history has a civilization been so intoxicated with change. At a fundamental cultural level, this intoxication with the future can be said to stem from the Christian element in Western civilization. (Ferkiss)

What we anticipate seldom occurs; what we least expect generally happens. (Disraeli)

My interest is in the future, because I am going to spend the rest of my life there. (Kettering)

Change is the essence of progress; but its magnitude—the sheer speed with which change is rushing toward us—can overwhelm us unless we are prepared for it intellectually and emotionally. (Cole)

If management and educators make the progress which can be anticipated we will add to the marketing knowledge base, expand the role and importance of corporate marketing in a consumeristic society, and add stature and importance to the role of marketing. (Kelly)

By changing what he knows about the world, man changes the world he knows; and by changing the world in which he lives, man changes himself. (Dobzhansky)

Change is the very essence of growth—less addition than it is substitution, less accumulation than transformation. Projects are born, grow, reach their peak, decline, and die in the fervor of creative destruction. (J. J. Servan-Schreiber)

The most successful companies in the future will be those that are creatively concerned not only with increasing the nation's wealth but also with enhancing the people's welfare. (D. Rockefeller)

Marketing historians in the year 2000 will most likely look back at the decade of the 1970s as an era of great transition in the marketing field, an era when a things-first, people-second culture reasserted itself as a people-first, things-second culture. (Berry)

# QUESTIONS FOR REVIEW

**1.** What will happen to marketing if our society moves to a people-oriented versus a material-oriented focus?

**2.** What do you expect to happen with our ideas of economic growth, concentration of industries, mergers, multinational firms, environmental concerns, and races?

**3.** Trace the impact on the economy of a zero growth rate in population for the next 20 years.

**4.** If you could buy five pieces of information and you were the marketing researcher for a large consumer goods firm (e.g., cosmetics), what information would you buy?

**5.** What would you list as the ten most outstanding marketing events of the 1960s?

**6.** What would you list as the ten areas in which we can anticipate major changes in marketing during the next ten years?

**7.** What is the significance of becoming more "service-oriented?"

**8.** Design a program for marketers where the basic assumption is that we must restrict our consumption or perish.

**9.** What changes do you sense taking place in society today—right now—that will have impact on marketing for tomorrow?

**10.** Identify the ten most important things you have learned about marketing.

## Further Readings

C. Merle Crawford, *The Future Environment for Marketing* (Ann Arbor: University of Michigan, 1969).

Editors of *Fortune, Markets of the Seventies: The Unwinding U.S. Economy* (New York: Viking Press, 1968).

Jay W. Forrester, *World Dynamics*, (Cambridge, Mass.: Wright-Allen Press, 1971).

Herman Kahn and Anthony J. Wiener, *The Year 2000: A Framework for Speculation on the Next Thirty-Three Years* (New York: Macmillan, 1967).

*The Futurist*, World Future Society, Washington, D.C. All issues.

# GLOSSARY OF
# MARKETING DEFINITIONS

Compiled by Ralph S. Alexander and the Committee on Definitions of the American Marketing Association, *Marketing Definitions: A Glossary of Marketing Terms* (Chicago: American Marketing Association, 1960), pp. 9–23.

## A

**ACCESSORIES—See Equipment.**

**ADVERTISING**—Any paid form of non-personal presentation and promotion of ideas, goods, or services by an identified sponsor. It involves the use of such media as the following:

> Magazine and newspaper space
> Motion pictures
> Outdoor (posters, signs, skywriting, etc.)
> Direct mail
> Novelties (calendars, blotters, etc.)
> Radio and television
> Cards (car, bus, etc.)
> Catalogues
> Directories and references
> Programs and menus
> Circulars

This list is intended to be illustrative, not inclusive.

*Comment.* Advertising is generally but not necessarily carried on through mass media. While the postal system is not technically considered a "paid" medium, material distributed by mail is definitely a form of presentation that is paid for by the sponsor. For kindred activities see "Publicity" and "Sales Promotion."

**ADVERTISING RESEARCH—See Marketing Research.**

**AGENT**—A business unit which negotiates purchases or sales or both but does not take title to the goods in which it deals.

*Comment.* The agent usually performs fewer marketing functions than does the merchant. He commonly receives his remuneration in the form of a commission or fee. He usually does not represent both buyer and seller in the same transaction. Examples are: broker, commission merchant, manufacturers agent, selling agent, and resident buyer. The Committee recommends that the term Functional Middleman no longer be applied to this type of agent. It is hardly logical or consistent in view of the fact that he performs fewer marketing functions than other middlemen.

**ASSEMBLING**—The activities involved in concentrating supplies or assortments of goods or services to facilitate sale or purchase.

*Comment.* The concentration involved here may affect a quantity of like goods or a variety of goods. It includes the gathering of adequate and representative stocks by wholesalers and retailers.

**AUTOMATIC SELLING**—The retail sale of goods or services through currency operated machines activated by the ultimate-consumer buyer.

*Comment.* Most, if not all, machines now used in automatic selling are coin operated. There are reports, however, of promising experiments with such devices that may be activated by paper currency; machines that provide change for a dollar bill are already on the market.

**AUXILIARY EQUIPMENT—See Equipment.**

## B

**BRANCH HOUSE (Manufacturer's)**—An establishment maintained by a manufacturer, detached from the headquarters establishment and used primarily for the purpose of stocking, selling, delivering, and servicing his product.

**BRANCH OFFICE (Manufacturer's)**—An establishment maintained by a manufacturer, detached from the headquarters establishment and used for the purpose of selling his products or providing service.

*Comment.* The characteristic of the branch house that distinguishes it from the branch office is the fact that it is used in the physical storage, handling, and delivery of merchandise. Otherwise the two are identical.

**BRANCH STORE**—A subsidiary retailing business owned and operated at a separate location by an established store.

**BRAND**—A name, term, sign, symbol, or design, or a combination of them which is intended to identify the goods or services of one seller or group of sellers and to differentiate them from those of competitors.

*Comment.* A brand may include a brand name, a trade mark, or both. The term brand is sufficiently comprehensive to include practically all means of identification except perhaps the package and the shape of the product. All brand names and all trade marks are brands or parts of brands but not all brands are either brand names or trade marks. Brand is the inclusive general term. The others are more particularized.

See also NATIONAL BRAND and PRIVATE BRAND.

**BRAND MANAGER—See Product Management.**

**BRAND NAME—**A brand or part of a brand consisting of a word, letter, group of words or letters comprising a name which is intended to identify the goods or services of a seller or a group of sellers and to differentiate them from those of competitors.

*Comment.* The brand name is that part of a brand which can be vocalized—the utterable.

**BROKER—**An agent who does not have direct physical control of the goods in which he deals but represents either buyer or seller in negotiating purchases or sales for his principal.

*Comment.* The broker's powers as to prices and terms of sale are usually limited by his principal.
The term is often loosely used in a generic sense to include such specific business units as free-lance brokers, manufacturer's agents, selling agents, and purchasing agents.

**BUYING POWER—See Purchasing Power.**

# C

**CANVASSER—See House-to-House Salesman.**

**CASH AND CARRY WHOLESALER—See Wholesaler**

**CHAIN STORE—CHAIN STORE SYSTEM—**A group of retail stores or essentially the same type, centrally owned and with some degree of centralized control of operation. The term Chain Store may also refer to a single store as a unit of such a group.

*Comment.* According to the dictionary, two may apparently be construed to constitute a "group."

**CHANNEL OF DISTRIBUTION—**The structure of intra-company organization units and extra-company agents and dealers, wholesale and retail, through which a commodity, product, or service is marketed.

*Comment.* This definition was designed to be broad enough to include (a.) both a firm's internal marketing organization units and the outside business units it uses in its marketing work and (b.) both the channel structure of the individual firm and the entire complex available to all firms.

**COMMERCIAL AUCTION—**An agent business unit which effects the sale of goods through an auctioneer, who, under specified rules, solicits bids or offers from buyers and has power to accept the highest bids of responsible bidders and, thereby, consummates the sale.

*Comment.* The auctioneer usually but not always is a paid employee of an auction company which is in the business of conducting auctions.

**COMMISSION HOUSE (sometimes called Commission Merchant)—**An agent who usually exercises physical control over and negotiates the sale of the goods he handles. The commission house usually enjoys broader powers as to prices, methods, and terms of sale than does the broker although it must obey instructions issued by the principal. It generally arranges delivery, extends necessary credit, collects, deducts its fees, and remits the balance to the principal.

*Comment.* Most of those who have defined the commission house state that it has possession of the goods it handles. In its strict meaning the word "possession" connotes to some extent the idea of ownership; in its legal meaning it involves a degree of control somewhat beyond that usually enjoyed by the commission merchant. Therefore, the phrase, "physical control," was used instead. The fact that many commission houses are not typical in their operations does not subtract from their status as commission houses.

**COMMISSARY STORE—See Industrial Store**

**COMMODITY EXCHANGE—**An organization usually owned by the member-traders, which provides facilities for bringing together buyers and sellers of specified commodities, or their agents, for promoting trades, either spot or futures or both, in these commodities.

*Comment.* Agricultural products or their intermediately processed derivatives are the commodities most often traded on such exchanges.
Some sort of organization for clearing future contracts usually operates as an adjunct to or an arm of a commodity exchange.

**COMPANY STORE—See Industrial Store.**

**CONSUMER RESEARCH—See Marketing Research.**

**CONSUMERS' COOPERATIVE—**A retail business owned and operated by ultimate consumers to purchase and distribute goods and services primarily to the membership—sometimes called purchasing cooperatives.

*Comment.* The Consumers' Cooperative is a type of cooperative marketing institution. Through federation, retail units frequently acquire wholesaling and manufacturing institutions. The definition confines the use of the term to the cooperative purchasing activities of ultimate consumers and does not embrace collective buying by business establishments or institutions.

**CONSUMERS' GOODS**—Goods destined for use by ultimate consumers or households and in such form that they can be used without commercial processing.

*Comment.* Certain articles, for example, typewriters, may be either consumers' goods or industrial goods depending upon whether they are destined for use by the ultimate consumer or household or by an industrial, business, or institutional user.

**CONVENIENCE GOODS**—Those consumers' goods which the customer usually purchases frequently, immediately, and with the minimum of effort in comparison and buying.

Examples of merchandise customarily bought as convenience goods are; tobacco products, soap, newspapers, magazines, chewing gum, small packaged confections, and many food products.

*Comment.* These articles are usually of small unit value and are bought in small quantities at any one time, although when a number of them are bought together as in a supermarket, the combined purchase may assume sizeable proportions in both bulk and value.

The convenience involved may be in terms of nearness to the buyer's home, easy accessibility to some means of transport, or close proximity to places where people go during the day or evening, for example, downtown to work.

**COOPERATIVE MARKETING**—The process by which independent producers, wholesalers, retailers, consumers, or combinations of them act collectively in buying or selling or both.

### D

**DEALER**—A firm that buys and resells merchandise at either retail or wholesale.

*Comment.* The term is naturally ambiguous. For clarity, it should be used with a qualifying adjective, such as "retail" or "wholesale."

**DEPARTMENT STORE**—A large retailing business unit which handles a wide variety of shopping and specialty goods, including women's ready-to-wear and accessories, men's and boy's wear, piece goods, small wares, and home furnishings, and which is organized into separate departments for purposes of promotion, service and control.

Examples of very large department stores are Macy's, New York, J. L. Hudson Co. of Detroit, Marshall Field & Co. of Chicago, and Famous, Barr of St. Louis. Two well-known smaller ones are Bresee's of Oneonta, New York, and A. B. Wycoff of Stroudsburg, Penn.

*Comment.* Many department stores have become units of chains, commonly called "ownership groups," since each store retains its local identity, even though centrally owned. The definition above stresses three elements: large size, wide variety of clothing and home furnishings, and departmentization. Size is not spelled out in terms of either sales volume or number of employees, since the concept keeps changing upwards. Most department stores in 1960 had sales in excess of one million dollars.

**DIRECT SELLING**—The process whereby the firm responsible for production sells to the user, ultimate consumer, or retailer without intervening middlemen.

The Committee recommends that when this term is used, it be so qualified as to indicate clearly the precise meaning intended (direct to retailer, direct to user, direct to ultimate consumer, etc.).

*Comment.* The phrase "firm responsible for production" is substituted for "producer" in the old definition so as to include the firm that contracts out some or all of the processes of making the goods it sells direct, for example the drug house that has its vitamin pills tableted by a contractor specializing in such work.

**DISCOUNT HOUSE**—A retailing business unit, featuring consumer durable items, competing on a basis of price appeal, and operating on a relatively low markup and with a minimum of customer service.

**DISCRETIONARY FUND**—Discretionary income enlarged by the amount of new credit extensions, which also may be deemed spendable as a result of consumer decision relatively free of prior commitment or pressure of need.

*Comment.* These are the definitions of the National Industrial Conference Board, which publishes a quarterly Discretionary Income Index Series. Discretionary Income is calculated by deducting from disposable personal income (a.) a computed historical level of outlays for food and clothing; (b.) all outlays for medical services, utilities, and public transportation; (c.) payment of fixed commitments, such as rent, home owner taxes, net insurance payments, and installment debt; (d.) homeowner taxes; and (e.) imputed income and income in kind.

**DISCRETIONARY INCOME**—That portion of personal income, in excess of the amount necessary to maintain a defined or historical standard of living, which may be saved with no immediate impairment of living standards or may be as a result of consumer decision relatively free of prior commitment or pressure of need.

**DISPOSABLE INCOME**—Personal income remaining after the deduction of taxes on personal income and compulsory payment, such as social security levies.

*Comment.* This is substantially the Department of Commerce concept.

**DISTRIBUTION**—The Committee recommends that the term Distribution be used as synonymous with Marketing.

*Comment.* The term Distribution is also sometimes used to refer to the extent of market coverage.

In using this term marketing men should clearly distinguish it from the sense in which it is employed in economic theory, that is, the process of dividing the fund of value produced by industry among the several factors engaged in economic production.

For these reasons marketing men may be wise to use the term sparingly.

**DISTRIBUTION COST ANALYSIS—See Marketing Cost Analysis.**

**DISTRIBUTOR**—In its general usage, this term is synonymous with "Wholesaler."

*Comment.* In some trades and by many firms it is used to designate an outlet having some sort of preferential relationship with the manufacturer. This meaning is not so widely used or so standardized as to justify inclusion in the definition.

The term is sometimes used to designate a manufacturer's agent or a sales representative in the employ of a manufacturer.

**DROP SHIPMENT WHOLESALER—See Wholesaler.**

# E

**EQUIPMENT**—Those industrial goods that do not become part of the physical product and which are exhausted only after repeated use, such as Machinery, Installed Equipment and Accessories, or Auxiliary Equipment.

Installed Equipment includes such items as boilers, linotype machines, power lathes, bank vaults. Accessories include such items as gauges, meters, and control devices.

Auxiliary Equipment includes such items as trucks, typewriters, filing cases, and industrial hoists.

**EXCLUSIVE OUTLET SELLING**—That form of selective selling whereby sales of an article or service or brand of an article to any one type of buyer are confined to one retailer or wholesaler in each area, usually on a contractual basis.

*Comment.* This definition does not include the practice of designating two or more wholesalers or retailers in an area as selected outlets. While this practice is a form of Selective Selling, it is not Exclusive Outlet Selling.

The term does not apply to the reverse contractual relationship in which a dealer must buy exclusively from a supplier.

# F

**FABRICATING MATERIALS**—Those industrial goods which become a part of the finished product and which have undergone processing beyond that required for raw materials but not as much as finished parts.

*Comment.* Examples are plastic moulding compounds.

**FACILITATING AGENCIES IN MARKETING**—Those agencies which perform or assist in the performance of one or a number of the marketing functions but which neither take title to goods nor negotiate purchases or sales.

Common types are banks, railroads, storage warehouses, commodity exchanges, stock yards, insurance companies, graders and inspectors, advertising agencies, firms engaged in marketing research, cattle loan companies, furniture marts, and packers and shippers.

**FACTOR**—(1.) A specialized financial institution engaged in factoring accounts receivable and lending on the security of inventory.

(2.) A type of commission house which often advances funds to the consigner, identified chiefly with the raw cotton and naval stores trades.

*Comment.* The type of factor described in (1) above operates extensively in the textile field but is expanding into other fields.

**FACTORING**—A specialized financial function whereby producers, wholesalers, and retailers sell their accounts receivable to financial institutions, including factors and banks, often on a non-recourse basis.

*Comment.* Commerical banks as well as factors and finance companies engage in this activity.

**FAIR TRADE**—Retail resale price maintenance imposed by suppliers of branded goods under authorization of state and federal laws.

*Comment.* This is a special usage of the term promulgated by the advocates of resale price maintenance and bears no relation to the fair practices concept of the Federal Trade Commission; nor is it the antithesis of unfair trading outlawed by the antitrust laws.

# G

**GENERAL STORE**—A small retailing business unit, not departmentized, usually located in a rural community and primarily engaged in selling a general assortment of merchandise of which the most important line is food, and the more important subsidiary lines are notions, apparel, farm supplies, and gasoline. These stores are often known as "country general stores."

*Comment.* This is roughly the Bureau of the Census usage.

**GRADING**—Assigning predetermined standards of quality classifications to individual units or lots of a commodity.

*Comment.* This process of assignment may be carried on by sorting.

This term is often defined so as to include the work of setting up classes or grades. This work is really a part of standardization.

# H

**HOUSE-TO-HOUSE SALESMAN**—A salesman who is primarily engaged in making sales direct to ultimate consumers in their homes.

*Comment.* The term Canvasser is often employed as synonymous with House-to-House Salesman. Due to its extensive use in fields other than marketing this usage is not recommended.

# I

**INDEPENDENT STORE**—A retailing business unit which is controlled by its own individual ownership or management rather than from without, except insofar as its management is limited by voluntary group arrangements.

*Comment.* This definition includes a member of a voluntary group organization. It is recognized that the voluntary group possesses many of the characteristics of and presents many of the same problems as the chain store system. In the final analysis, however, the members of the voluntary groups are independent stores, cooperating, perhaps temporarily, in the accomplishment of certain marketing purposes. Their collective action is entirely voluntary and the retailers engaging in it consider themselves to be independent.

**INDUSTRIAL GOODS**—Goods which are destined to be sold primarily for use in producing other goods or rendering services as contrasted with goods destined to be sold primarily to the ultimate consumer.

They include equipment (installed and accessory), component parts, maintenance, repair and operating supplies, raw materials, fabricating materials.

*Comment.* The distinguishing characteristics of these goods is the purpose for which they are primarily destined to be used, in carrying on business or industrial activities rather than for consumption by individual ultimate consumers or resale to them. The category also includes merchandise destined for use in carrying on various types of institutional enterprises.

Relatively few goods are exclusively industrial goods. The same article may, under one set of circumstances, be an industrial good, and under other conditions a consumers' good.

**INDUSTRIAL STORE**—A retail store owned and operated by a company or governmental unit to sell primarily to its employees.

Non-governmental establishments of this type are often referred to as "Company Stores" or "Commissary Stores." In certain trades the term "Company Store" is applied to a store through which a firm sells its own products, often together with those of other manufacturers, to the consumer market.

*Comment.* Many of these establishments are not operated for profit. The matter of the location of the control over and responsibility for these stores rather than the motive for their operation constitutes their distinguishing characteristic.

**INSTALLED EQUIPMENT—See Equipment.**

# J

**JOBBER**—This term is widely used as a synonym of "wholesaler" or "distributor."

*Comment.* The term is sometimes used in certain trades and localities to designate special types of wholesalers. This usage is especially common in the distribution of agricultural products. The characteristics of the wholesalers so designated vary from trade to trade and from locality to locality. Most of the schedules submitted to the Bureau of the Census by the members of the wholesale trades show no clear line of demarcation between those who call themselves jobbers and those who prefer to be known as wholesalers. Therefore, it does not seem wise to attempt to set up any general basis of distinction between the terms in those few trades or markets in which one exists. There are scattered examples of special distinctive usage of the term "Jobber." The precise nature of such usage must be sought in each trade or area in which it is employed.

# L

**LIMITED FUNCTION WHOLESALER—See Wholesaler.**

**LOSS LEADER**—A product of known or accepted quality priced at a loss or no profit for the purpose of attracting patronage to a store.

*Comment.* This term is peculiar to the retail trade—elsewhere the same item is called a "leader" or a "special."

# M

**MAIL ORDER HOUSE (retail)**—A retailing business that receives its orders primarily by mail or telephone and generally offers its goods and services for its sale from a catalogue or other printed material.

*Comment.* Other types of retail stores often conduct a mail order business, usually through departments set up for that purpose, although this fact does not make them mail order houses. On the other hand, some firms that originally confined themselves to the mail order business now also operate chain store systems. For example, Sears Roebuck and Company and Montgomery Ward and Company are both mail order houses and chain store systems.

**MAIL ORDER WHOLESALER—See Wholesaler.**

**MANUFACTURER'S AGENT**—An agent who generally operates on an extended contractual basis; often sells within an exclusive territory; handles non-competing but related lines of goods; and possesses limited authority with regard to prices and terms of sale. He may be authorized to sell a definite portion of his principal's output.

*Comment.* The manufacturer's agent has often been defined as a species of broker. In the majority of cases this seems to be substantially accurate. It is probably more accurate in seeking to define the entire group not to classify them as a specialized type of broker but to regard them as a special variety of agent since many of them carry stocks. The term "Manufacturer's Representative" is sometimes applied to this agent. Since this term is also used to designate a salesman in the employ of a manufacturer, its use as a synonym for "Manufacturer's Agent" is discouraged.

**MANUFACTURER'S STORE**—A retail store owned and operated by a manufacturer, sometimes as outlets for his goods, sometimes primarily for experimental or publicity purposes.

**MARKET**—(1.) The aggregate of forces or conditions within which buyers and sellers make decisions that result in the transfer of goods and services.

(2.) The aggregate demand of the potential buyers of a commodity or service.

*Comment.* The business man often uses the term to mean an opportunity to sell his goods. He also often attaches to it a connotation of a geographical area, such as the "New England market," or of a customer group, such as the "college market" or the "agricultural market." Retailers often use the term to mean the aggregate group of suppliers from whom a buyer purchases.

**MARKET ANALYSIS**—A sub-division of marketing research which involves the measurement of the extent of a market and the determination of its characteristics.

*Comment.* See also Marketing Research. The activity described above consists essentially in the process of exploring and evaluating the marketing possibilities of the aggregates described in (2.) of the definition of Market.

**MARKET POTENTIAL (also Market or Total Market)**—A calculation of maximum possible sales opportunities for all sellers of a good or service during a stated period.

**MARKET SHARE (or Sales Potential)**—The ratio of a company's sales to the total industry sales on either an actual or potential basis.

*Comment.* This term is often used to designate the part of total industry sales a company hopes or expects to get. Since this concept usually has in it a considerable element of "blue sky," this usage is not encouraged.

**MARKETING**—The performance of business activities that direct the flow of goods and services from producer to consumer or user.

*Comment.* The task of defining Marketing may be approached from at least three points of view.
(1.) The "legalistic" of which the following is a good example: "Marketing includes all activities having to do with effecting changes in the ownership and possession of goods and services." It seems obviously of doubtful desirability to adopt a definition which throws so much emphasis upon the legal phases of what is essentially a commercial subject.
(2.) The "economic" examples of which are: "That part of economics which deals with the creation of time, place, and possession utilities."
"That phase of business activity through which human wants are satisfied by the exchange of goods and services for some valuable consideration."
Such definitions are apt to assume somewhat more understanding of economic concepts than are ordinarily found in the market place.
(3.) The "factual or descriptive" of which the definition suggested by the Committee is an example. This type of definition merely seeks to describe its subject in terms likely to be understood by both professional economists and business men without reference to legal or economic implications.

This definition seeks to include such facilitating activities as marketing research, transportation, certain aspects of product and package planning, and the use of credit as a means of influencing patronage.

**MARKETING BUDGET**—A statement of the planned dollar sales and planned marketing costs for a specified future period.

*Comment.* The use of this term is sometimes confined to an estimate of future sales. This does not conform to the general use of the term "budget" which includes schedules of both receipts and expenditures. If the marketing budget is to be used as a device to facilitate marketing control and management, it should include the probable cost of getting the estimated volume of sales. The failure to allow proper weight to this item in their calculations is one of the most consistently persistent and fatal mistakes made by American business concerns. It has led to much of the striving after unprofitable volume that has been so costly.

A firm may prepare a marketing budget for each brand or product or for a group of brands or products it sells or for each group of customers to whom it markets. See also Sales Budget.

**MARKETING COOPERATIVE**—See **Producers' Cooperative Marketing.**

**MARKETING COST ACCOUNTING**—The branch of cost accounting which involves the allocation of marketing costs according to customers, marketing units, products, territories, or marketing activities.

**MARKETING COST ANALYSIS**—The study and evaluation of the relative profitability or costs of different marketing operations in terms of customers, marketing units, commodities, territories, or marketing activities.

*Comment.* Marketing Cost Accounting is one of the tools used in Marketing Cost Analysis.

**MARKETING FUNCTION**—A major specialized activity or group of related activities performed in marketing.

*Comment.* There is no generally accepted list of marketing functions, nor is there any generally accepted basis on which the lists compiled by various writers are chosen. The reason for these limitations is fairly apparent. Under this term students of marketing have sought to squeeze a heterogeneous and non-consistent group of activities. Some of them are broad business functions with special marketing implications; others are peculiar to the marketing process. The function of assembling is performed through buying, selling, and transportation. Assembling, storage, and transporting are general economic functions; selling and buying are more nearly individual in character. Most of the lists fail sadly to embrace all the activities a marketing manager worries about in the course of doing his job.

**MARKETING MANAGEMENT**—The planning, direction and control of the entire marketing activity of a firm or division of a firm, including the formulation of marketing objectives, policies, programs and strategy, and commonly embracing product development, organizing and staffing to carry out plans, supervising marketing operations, and controlling marketing performance.

*Comment.* In most firms the man who performs these functions is a member of top management in that he plays a part in determining company policy, in making product decisions, and in coordinating marketing operations with other functional activities to achieve the objectives of the company as a whole.

No definition of his position is included in this report because there is no uniformity in the titles applied to it. He is variously designated Marketing Manager, Director of Marketing, Vice President for Marketing, Director or Vice President of Marketing and Sales, General Sales Manager.

**MARKETING PLANNING**—The work of setting up objectives for marketing activity and of determining and scheduling the steps necessary to achieve such objectives.

*Comment.* This term includes not only the work of deciding upon the goals or results to be attained through marketing activity but also the determination in detail of exactly how they are to be accomplished.

**MARKETING POLICY**—A course of action established to obtain consistency of marketing decisions and operations under recurring and essentially similar circumstances.

**MARKETING RESEARCH**—The systematic gathering, recording, and analyzing of data about problems relating to the marketing of goods and services. Such research may be undertaken by impartial agencies or by business firms or their agents for the solution of their marketing problems.

*Comment.* Marketing Research is the inclusive term which embraces all research activities carried on in connection with the management of marketing work. It includes various subsidiary types of research, such as (1) Market Analysis, which is a study of the size, location, nature, and characteristics of markets, (2) Sales Analysis (or Research), which is largely an analysis of sales data, (3) Consumer Research, of which Motivation Research is a type, which is concerned chiefly with the discovery and analysis of consumer attitudes, reactions, and preferences, and (4) Advertising Research which is carried on chiefly as an aid to the management of advertising work. The techniques of Operations Research are often useful in Marketing Research.

The term Market Research is often loosely used as synonymous with Marketing Research.

**MERCHANDISING**—The planning and supervision involved in marketing the particular merchandise or service at the places, times, and prices and in the quantities which will best serve to realize the marketing objectives of the business.

*Comment.* This term has been used in a great variety of meanings, most of them confusing. The usage recommended by the Committee adheres closely to the essential meaning of the word. The term is most widely used in this sense in the wholesaling and retailing trades.
Many manufacturers designate this activity as Product Planning or Management and include in it such tasks as selecting the article to be produced or stocked and deciding such matters as the size, appearance, form, packaging, quantities to be bought or made, time of procurement, and price lines to be offered.

**MERCHANT**—A business unit that buys, takes title to, and resells merchandise.

*Comment.* The distinctive feature of this middleman lies in the fact that he takes title to the goods he handles. The extent to which he performs the marketing functions is incidental to the definition. Wholesalers and retailers are the chief types of merchants.

**MIDDLEMAN**—A business concern that specializes in performing operations or rendering services directly involved in the purchase and/or sale of goods in the process of their flow from producer to consumer.
Middlemen are of two types, MERCHANTS and AGENTS.

*Comment.* The essence of the middleman's operation lies in the fact that he plays an active and prominent part in the negotiations leading up to transactions of purchase and sale. This is what distinguishes him from a Marketing Facilitating Agent who, while he performs certain marketing functions, participates only incidentally in negotiations of purchase and sale.
This term is very general in its meaning. It also possesses an unfortunate emotional content. Therefore, the Committee recommends that whenever possible more specific terms be used, such as agent, merchant, retailer, wholesaler.

**MISSIONARY SALESMAN**—A salesman employed by a manufacturer to call on customers of his distributors, usually to develop good will and stimulate demand, to help or induce them to promote the sale of his employer's goods, to help them train their salesmen to do so, and, often, to take orders for delivery by such distributors.

**MOTIVATION RESEARCH**—A group of techniques developed by the behavioral scientists which are used by marketing researchers to discover factors influencing marketing behavior.

*Comment.* These techniques are widely used outside the marketing sphere, for example, to discover factors influencing the behavior of employees and voters. The Committee has confined its definition to the marketing uses of the tool.
Motivation Research is only one of several ways to study marketing behavior.

# N

**NATIONAL BRAND**—A manufacturer's or producer's brand, usually enjoying wide territorial distribution.

*Comment.* The usage of the terms National Brand and Private Brand in this report, while generally current and commonly accepted, is highly illogical and non-descriptive. But since it is widespread and persistent, the Committee embodies it in this report.

# P

**PERSONAL SELLING**—Oral presentation in a conversation with one or more prospective purchasers for the purpose of making sales.

*Comment.* This definition contemplates that the presentation may be either formal, (as a "canned" sales talk), or informal, although it is rather likely to be informal, either in the actual presence of the customer or by telephone although usually the former, either to an individual or to a small group, although usually the former.

**PHYSICAL DISTRIBUTION**—The management of the movement and handling of goods from the point of production to the point of consumption or use.

**PRICE CUTTING**—Offering merchandise or a service for sale at a price below that recognized as usual or appropriate by its buyers and sellers.

*Comment.* One obvious criticism of this definition is that it is indefinite. But that very indefiniteness also causes it to be more accurately descriptive of a concept which is characterized by a high degree of indefiniteness in the mind of the average person affected by price cutting.
Traders' ideas of what constitutes price cutting are so vague and indefinite that any precise or highly specific definition of the phenomenon is bound to fail to include all its manifestations. If you ask a group of traders in a specific commodity to define price cutting, you will get as many conflicting formulas as there are traders. But if you ask those same traders at any particular time whether selling at a certain price constitutes price cutting, you will probably get a considerable degree of uniformity of opinion. It is precisely this condition which the definition is designed to reflect.

**PRICE LEADER**—A firm whose pricing behavior is followed by other companies in the same industry.

*Comment.* The price leadership of a firm may be limited to a certain geographical area, as in the oil business, or to certain products or groups of products, as in the steel business.

**PRIVATE BRANDS**—Brands sponsored by merchants or agents as distinguished from those sponsored by manufacturers or producers.

*Comment.* This usage is thoroughly illogical, since no seller wants his brand to be private in the sense of being secret and all brands are private in the sense that they are special and not common or general in use. But the usage is common in marketing literature and among traders. Therefore the Committee presents it in this report.

**PRODUCERS' COOPERATIVE MARKETING**—That type of cooperative marketing which primarily involves the sale of goods or services of the associated producing membership. May perform only an assembly or brokerage function but in some cases, notably milk marketing, extends into processing and distribution of the members' production.

*Comment.* Many producers' cooperative marketing associations also buy for their members. This fact does not subtract from their status as producers' cooperatives; This is especially true of the farm cooperatives.
The term does not include those activities of trade associations that affect only indirectly the sales of the membership. Such activities are the maintenance of credit rating bureaus, design registration bureaus, and brand protection machinery.

**PRODUCT LINE**—A group of products that are closely related either because they satisfy a class of need, are used together, are sold to the same customer groups, are marketed through the same type of outlets or fall within given price ranges. Example, carpenters' tools.

*Comment.* Sub-lines of products may be distinguished, such as hammers or saws, within a Product Line.

**PRODUCT MANAGEMENT**—The planning, direction, and control of all phases of the life cycle of products, including the creation or discovery of ideas for new products, the screening of such ideas, the coordination of the work of research and physical development of products, their packaging and branding, their introduction on the market, their market development, their modification, the discovery of new uses for them, their repair and servicing, and their deletion.

*Comment.* It is not safe to think of Product Management as the work of the executive known as the Product Manager, because the dimensions of his job vary widely from company to company, sometimes embracing all the activities listed in the definition and sometimes being limited to the sales promotion of the products in his care.

**PRODUCT MIX**—The composite of products offered for sale by a firm or a business unit.

*Comment.* Tooth paste is a product. The 50 cent tube of Whosis ammoniated tooth paste is an item. Tooth pastes and powders, mouth washes, and other allied items compose an oral hygiene product line. Soaps, cosmetics, dentifrices, drug items, cake mixes, shortenings and other items may comprise a product mix if marketed by the same company.

**PUBLICITY**—Non-personal stimulation of demand for a product, service or business unit by planting commercially significant news about it in a published medium or obtaining favorable presentation of it upon radio, television, or stage that is not paid for by the sponsor.

*Comment.* Retailers use the term to denote the sum of the functions of advertising, display, and publicity as defined above.

**PURCHASING POWER (Buying Power)**—The capacity to purchase possessed by an individual buyer, a group of buyers, or the aggregate of the buyers in an area or a market.

# R

**RACK JOBBER**—A wholesaling business unit that markets specialized lines of merchandise to certain types of retail stores and provides the special services of selective brand and item merchandising and arrangement, maintenance, and stocking of display racks.

*Comment.* The Rack Jobber usually, but not always, puts his merchandise in the store of the retailer on consignment. Rack Jobbers are most prevalent in the food business.

**RESALE PRICE MAINTENANCE**—Control by a supplier of the selling prices of his branded goods at subsequent stages of distribution by means of contractual agreement under fair trade laws or other devices.

**RESIDENT BUYER**—An agent who specializes in buying, on a fee or commission basis, chiefly for retailers.

*Comment.* The term as defined above, is limited to agents residing in the market cities who charge their retail principals fees for buying assistance rendered, but there are resident buying offices that are owned by out-of-town stores and some that are owned cooperatively by a group of stores. The former are called *private* offices and the latter *associated* offices. Neither of them should be confused with the central buying office of the typical chain, where the buying function is performed by the office directly, not acting as a specialized assistant to store buyers. Resident Buyers should also be distinguished from apparel *merchandise brokers* who represent competing manufacturers in the garment trades and have as customers out-of-town smaller stores in search of fashion merchandise. These brokers are paid by the manufacturers to whom they bring additional business, on a percentage of sales basis.

**RETAILER**—A merchant, or occasionally an agent, whose main business is selling directly to the ultimate consumer.

*Comment.* The retailer is to be distinguished by the nature of his sales rather than by the way he procures the goods in which he deals. The size of the units in which he sells is an incidental rather than a primary element in his character. His essential distinguishing mark is the fact that his typical sale is made to the ultimate consumer.

**RETAILER COOPERATIVE**—A group of independent retailers organized to buy cooperatively either through a jointly owned warehouse or through a buying club.

*Comment.* Their cooperative activities may include operating under a group name, joint advertising and cooperative managerial supervision.

**RETAILING**—The activities involved in selling directly to the ultimate consumer.

*Comment.* This definition includes all forms of selling to the ultimate consumer. It embraces the direct-to-consumer sales activities of the producer whether through his own stores, by house-to-house canvass, or by mail order. It does not cover the sale by producers of industrial goods, by industrial supply houses, or by retailers to industrial, commercial, or institutional buyers for use in the conduct of their enterprises.

# S

**SALES AGENT—See Selling Agent.**
**SALES ANALYSIS**—A subdivision of Marketing Research which involves the systematic study and comparison of sales data.

*Comment.* The purpose of such analysis is usually to aid in marketing management by providing sales information along the lines of market areas, organizational units, products or product groups, customers or customer groups, or such other units as may be useful.

**SALES BUDGET**—The part of the marketing budget which is concerned with planned dollar sales and planned costs of personal selling during a specified future period.

**SALES FORECAST**—An estimate of sales, in dollars or physical units for a specified future period under a proposed marketing plan or program and under an assumed set of economic and other forces outside the unit for which the forecast is made. The forecast may be for a specified item of merchandise or for an entire line.

*Comment.* Two sets of factors are involved in making a Sales Forecast; (1) those forces outside the control of the firm for which the forecast is made that are likely to influence its sales, and (2) changes in the marketing methods or practices of the firm that are likely to affect its sales.
In the course of planning future activities, the management of a given firm may make several sales forecasts each consisting of an estimate of probable sales if a given marketing plan is adopted or a given set of outside forces prevails. The estimated effects that several marketing plans may have on Sales and Profits may be compared in the process of arriving at that marketing program which will, in the opinion of the officials of the company, be best designed to promote its welfare.

**SALES MANAGEMENT**—The planning, direction, and control of the personal selling activities of a business unit, including recruiting, selecting, training, equipping, assigning, routing, supervising, paying, and motivating as these tasks apply to the personal sales force.

*Comment.* These activities are sometimes but not generally designated Sales Administration or Sales Force Management.

**SALES MANAGER**—The executive who plans, directs, and controls the activities of salesmen.

*Comment.* This definition distinguishes sharply between the manager who conducts the personal selling activities of a business unit and his superior, the executive, variously called Marketing Manager, Director of Marketing, Vice President for Marketing, who has charge of all marketing activities. The usage of this form of organization has been growing rapidly during recent years.

**SALES PLANNING**—That part of the Marketing Planning work which is concerned with making sales forecasts, devising programs for reaching the sales target, and deriving a sales budget.

**SALES POTENTIAL—See Market Share.**

**SALES PROMOTION**—(1.) In a specific sense, those marketing activities, other than personal selling, advertising, and publicity, that stimulate consumer purchasing and dealer effectiveness, such as display, shows and exhibitions, demonstrations, and various non-recurrent selling efforts not in the ordinary routine.

(2.) In retailing, all methods of stimulating customer purchasing, including personal selling, advertising, and publicity.

*Comment.* This definition includes the two most logical and commonly accepted usages of this much abused term. It is the suggestion of the Committee that insofar as possible, the use of the term be confined to the first of the two definitions given above.

**SALES QUOTA**—A projected volume of sales assigned to a marketing unit for use in the management of sales efforts. It applies to a specified period and may be expressed in dollars or in physical units.

*Comment.* The quota may be used in checking the efficiency or stimulating the efforts of or in remunerating individual salesmen or other personnel engaged in sales work.

A quota may be for a salesman, a territory, a department, a branch house, a wholesaler or retailer, or for the company as a whole. It may be different from the sales figure set up in the sales budget. Since it is a managerial device, it is not an immutable figure inexorably arrived at by the application of absolutely exact statistical formulas.

**SALES RESEARCH—See Marketing Research and Sales Analysis.**

**SELECTIVE SELLING**—The policy of selling to a limited number of customers in a market.

**SELF SELECTION**—The method used in retailing by which the customer may choose the desired merchandise without direct assistance of store personnel.

**SELF SERVICE**—The method used in retailing whereby the customer selects his own merchandise, removes it from the shelves or bulk containers, carries it to a check-out stand to complete the transaction and transports it to the point of use.

**SELLING**—The personal or impersonal process of assisting and/or persuading a prospective customer to buy a commodity or a service or to act favorably upon an idea that has commercial significance to the seller.

*Comment.* This definition includes advertising, other forms of publicity, and sales promotion as well as personal selling.

**SELLING AGENT**—An agent who operates on an extended contractual basis; sells all of a specified line of merchandise or the entire output of his principal, and usually has full authority with regard to prices, terms, and other conditions of sale.

He occasionally renders financial aid to his principal.

*Comment.* This functionary is often called a Sales Agent.

**SERVICE WHOLESALER—See Wholesaler.**

**SERVICES**—Activities, benefits, or satisfactions which are offered for sale, or are provided in connection with the sale of goods.

Examples are amusements, hotel service, electric service, transportation, the services of barber shops and beauty shops, repair and maintenance service, the work of credit rating bureaus. This list is merely illustrative and no attempt has been made to make it complete. The term also applies to the various activities such as credit extension, advice and help of sales people, delivery, by which the seller serves the convenience of his customers.

**SHOPPING CENTER**—A geographical cluster of retail stores, collectively handling an assortment of goods varied enough to satisfy most of the merchandise wants of consumers within convenient travelling time, and, thereby, attracting a general shopping trade.

*Comment.* During recent years, the term has acquired a special usage in its application to the planned or integrated centers developed in suburban or semi-suburban areas usually along main highways and featuring ample parking spaces.

**SHOPPING GOODS**—Those consumers' goods which the customer in the process of selection and purchase characteristically compares on such bases as suitability, quality, price and style.

Examples of goods that most consumers probably buy as Shopping Goods are: millinery, furniture, dress goods, women's ready-to-wear and shoes, used automobiles, and major appliances.

*Comment.* It should be emphasized that a given article may be bought by one customer as a Shopping Good and by another as a Specialty or Convenience Good. The general classification depends upon the way in which the average or typical buyer purchases.

See Comment under Specialty Goods.

**SPECIALTY GOODS**—Those consumers' goods with unique characteristics and/or brand identification for which a significant group of buyers are habitually willing to make a special purchasing effort.

Examples of articles that are usually bought as Specialty Goods are: specific brands and types of fancy foods, hi-fi components, certain types of sporting equipment, photographic equipment, and men's suits.

*Comment.* Price is not usually the primary factor in consumer choice of specialty goods although their prices are often higher than those of other articles serving the same basic want but without their special characteristics.

**SPECIALTY STORE**—A retail store that makes its appeal on the basis of a restricted class of shopping goods.

**STANDARDIZATION**—The determination of basic limits or grade ranges in the form of uniform specifications to which particular manufactured goods may conform and uniform classes into which the products of agriculture and the extractive industries may or must be sorted or assigned.

*Comment.* This term does not include Grading which is the process of sorting or assigning units of a commodity to the grades or classes that have been established through the process of Standardization. Some systems of standardization and grading for agricultural products are compulsory by law.

**STOCK or INVENTORY CONTROL**—The use of a system or mechanism to maintain stocks of goods at desired levels.

*Comment.* Such control is usually exercised to maintain stocks that are (a) representative in that they include all the items the customer group served expects to be able to buy from the firm involved, (b) adequate in that a sufficient quantity of each item is included to satisfy all reasonably foreseeable demands for it, and (c) economical in that no funds of the firm are held in inventory beyond those needed to serve purposes (a) and (b) and in that it facilitates savings in costs of production.

**STORAGE**—The marketing function that involves holding goods between the time of their production and their final sale.

*Comment.* Some processing is often done while goods are in storage. It is probable that this should be regarded as a part of production rather than of marketing.

**SUPERETTE—See Supermarket.**

**SUPERMARKET**—A large retailing business unit selling mainly food and grocery items on the basis of the low margin appeal, wide variety and assortments, self-service, and heavy emphasis on merchandise appeal.

*Comment.* In its bid for patronage the Supermarket makes heavy use of the visual appeal of the merchandise itself.

The Committee realizes that it would be fool-hardy in this day of rapid change to try to indicate how large a store must be to be a Supermarket. At the time of this report the latest figures indicate that the average store recognized by the Supermarket Institute as belonging to the class has annual sales of somewhat under $2,010,000, and that about 45 percent of them sell more than that amount each

year. Both of these figures have been changing rapidly and may continue to do so. A Superette is a store, somewhat smaller than a Supermarket, and possessing most of the same characteristics.

## T

**TRADE-MARK**—A brand or part of a brand that is given legal protection because it is capable of exclusive appropriation; because it is used in a manner sufficiently fanciful, distinctive, and arbitrary, because it is affixed to the product when sold, or because it otherwise satisfies the requirements set up by law.

*Comment.* Trade-mark is essentially a legal term and includes only those brands or parts of brands which the law designates as trademarks. In the final analysis in any specific case a Trade-mark is what the court in that case decides to regard as a Trade-mark.

**TRADING AREA**—A district whose size is usually determined by the boundaries within which it is economical in terms of volume and cost for a marketing unit or group to sell and/or deliver a good or service.

*Comment.* A single business may have several trading areas; for example, the Trading Area of Marshall Field for its store business is different from that for its catalogue business.

**TRAFFIC MANAGEMENT**—The planning, selection, and direction of all means and methods of transportation involved in the movement of goods in the marketing process.

*Comment.* This definition is confined to those activities in connection with transportation that have to do particularly with marketing and form an inseparable part of any well-organized system of distribution. It includes control of the movement of goods in trucks owned by the marketing concern as well as by public carrier. It does not include the movement of goods within the warehouse of a producer or within the store of a retail concern.

**TRUCK WHOLESALER—See Wholesaler.**

## U

**ULTIMATE CONSUMER**—One who buys and/or uses goods or services to satisfy personal or household wants rather than for resale or for use in business, institutional, or industrial operations.

*Comment.* The definition distinguishes sharply between Industrial Users and Ultimate Consumers. A firm buying and using an office machine, a drum of lubricating oil, or a carload of steel billets is an Industrial User of those products, not an Ultimate Consumer of them. A vital difference exists between the purposes motivating the two types of purchases which in turn results in highly significant differences in buying methods, marketing organization, and selling practices.

# V

**VALUE ADDED BY MARKETING**—The part of the value of a product or a service to the consumer or user which results from marketing activities.

*Comment.* There is urgent need of a method or formula for computing Value Added by Marketing. Increased attention is being devoted to developing such a formula. At present none of those suggested have gained enough acceptance to justify inclusion in this definition or comment.

**VARIETY STORE**—A retailing business unit that handles a wide assortment of goods, usually in the low or popular segment of the price range.

*Comment.* While some foods are generally handled, the major emphasis is devoted to nonfood products.

**VOLUNTARY GROUP**—A group of retailers each of whom owns and operates his own store and is associated with a wholesale organization or manufacturer to carry on joint merchandising activities and who are characterized by some degree of group identity and uniformity of operation.
Such joint activities have been largely of two kinds; cooperative advertising and group control of store operation.

*Comment.* A Voluntary Group is usually sponsored by a wholesaler. Similar groups sponsored by retailers do not belong in this category. Groups of independent stores sponsored by a chain store system are usually called "Agency Stores."

# W

**WHOLESALER**—A business unit which buys and resells merchandise to retailers and other merchants and/or to industrial, institutional, and commercial users but which does not sell in significant amounts to ultimate consumers.
In the basic materials, semi-finished goods, and tool and machinery trades merchants of this type are commonly known as "distributors" or "supply houses."

*Comment.* Generally these merchants render a wide variety of services to their customers. Those who render all the services normally expected in the wholesale trade are known as Service Wholesalers; those who render only a few of the wholesale services are known as Limited Function Wholesalers. The latter group is composed mainly of Cash and Carry Wholesalers who do not render the credit or delivery service, Drop Shipment Wholesalers who sell for delivery by the producer direct to the buyer, Truck Wholesalers who combine selling, delivery, and collection in one operation, and Mail Order Wholesalers who perform the selling service entirely by mail.

This definition ignores or minimizes two bases upon which the term is often defined; first, the size of the lots in which wholesalers deal, and second, the fact that they habitually sell for resale. The figures show that many wholesalers operate on a very small scale and in small lots. Most of them make a significant portion of their sales to industrial users.

# REFERENCES

## CHAPTER 1

Reavis Cox, *Distribution in a High-Level Economy* (Englewood Cliffs, N.J.: Prentice-Hall, © 1965), p. 149. Reprinted by permission.

The Ohio State University Marketing Faculty, *Statement of the Philosophy of Marketing* (Columbus, Ohio: 1964).

Philip Kotler and Gerald Zaltman, "Social Marketing: An Approach to Planned Social Change," *Journal of Marketing*, Vol. 35 (July 1971), p. 5.

## CHAPTER 2

Dean P. Fite, Vice President-Corporate Affairs, The Procter & Gamble Company, in a presentation before the Financial Analysts of Philadelphia, March 26, 1970 (no copyright).

## CHAPTER 3

American Marketing Association, Committee on Definitions, *Marketing Definitions* (Chicago: American Marketing Association, 1960).

Paul D. Converse, Harvey W. Huegy, and Robert V. Mitchell, *Elements of Marketing* (Englewood Cliffs, N.J.: Prentice-Hall, © 1965), p. 7.

Lee E. Preston, *Markets and Marketing* (Glenview, Ill.: Scott, Foresman, 1970), p. 1.

Peter O. Steiner, "Markets and Industries," *International Encyclopedia of the Social Sciences* (New York: Crowell-Collier & Macmillan, 1968), p. 575.

U.S. Department of Commerce, Bureau of the Census, *1967 Census of Business, Selected Services, United States* (Washington, D.C.: GPO, 1967).

U.S. Department of Commerce, Bureau of the Census, *1967 Census of Business, Wholesale Trade, United States* (Washington, D.C.: GPO, 1967).

U.S. Department of Commerce, Bureau of the Census, *1967 Census of Business, Retail Trade, United States* (Washington, D.C.: GPO, 1967).

Roland S. Vaile, E. T. Grether, and Reavis Cox, *Marketing in the American Economy* (New York: Ronald Press, 1952), p. 150.

## CHAPTER 4

M. Argunov, "What Advertising Does," *Journal of Advertising Research*, Vol. 6 (December 1966), pp. 2–3. © Copyright by the Advertising Research Foundation.

Robert Bartels, "A Methodological Framework for Comparative Marketing Study," in Stephen A. Greyser (ed.), *Toward Scientific Marketing* (Chicago: American Marketing Association, 1964), p. 383.

Robert Bartels, *Comparative Marketing: Wholesaling in Fifteen Countries* (Homewood, Ill.: Richard D. Irwin, © 1963), pp. 299–308. Reproduced with permission.

J. Boddewyn, "A Construct for Comparative Marketing Research," *Journal of Marketing Research*, Vol. 3 (May 1966), pp. 149–153.

R. V. Call, "Wholesaling in Lebanon," The University of Arizona, 1965, unpublished.

Reavis Cox, "The Search for Universals in Comparative Studies of Domestic Marketing Systems," in Peter D. Bennett (ed.), *Marketing and Economic Development* (Chicago: American Marketing Association, 1965), p. 144.

Bernard Gwertzman, "Soviet Shoppers Spend Years in Line," *The New York Times*, © May 12, 1969.

C. William Skinner, "Marketing and Social Structure in Rural China," *The Journal of Asian Studies*, Vol. 24 (November 1964, February and May 1965), pp. 3, 399.

Montrose S. Sommers and Jerome B. Kernan (eds.), *Comparative Marketing Systems*. By permission of Appleton-Century-Crofts, Educational Division, Meredith Corporation, Copyright © 1968.

"Take-off, Catch-up, Satiety," *Business Week*, April 9, 1960, p. 100. Copyright held by McGraw-Hill Book Company, Inc.

Richard S. Thoman, *The Geography of Economic Activity* (New York: McGraw-Hill, © 1962), p. 31.

## CHAPTER 5

Gunnar Alexandersson, *Geography of Manufacturing* (Englewood Cliffs, N.J.: Prentice-Hall, © 1967), pp. 5–19.

Ruben L. Parson, *Conserving American Resources*, 2nd ed. (Englewood Cliffs, N.J.: Prentice-Hall, © 1964), p. 25.

*The Suburbanization of Retail Trade: A Study of Retail Trade Dispersion in Major U.S. Markets: 1958–1967*, pp. 3–12, 67–76. Published with the permission of Columbia Broadcasting System, Inc., © 1970. All rights reserved.

Stewart L. Udall, *The Quiet Crisis* (New York: Discus/Avon Books, 1963).

U.S. Department of Commerce, Bureau of Census, various series of *Population, Retail and Wholesale Trades*, and *Manufacturing*.

James E. Vance, *The Merchant's World: The Geography of Wholesaling* (Englewood Cliffs, N.J.: Prentice-Hall, © 1970), p. 11.

## CHAPTER 6

Jules Backman, *Price Practices and Policies* (New York: Ronald Press, 1953), p. 89.

Edward Hastings Chamberlin, *The Theory of Monopolistic Competition* (Cambridge: Harvard University Press, 1947), pp. 56–57.

Richard H. Leftwich, *The Price System and Resource Allocation* (New York: Holt, Rinehart and Winston, © 1966), p. 243. Reprinted by permission.

## CHAPTER 7

Edward S. Mason, "The Effectiveness of the Federal Antitrust Laws: A Symposium," *American Economic Review*, Vol. 39 (1949), p. 713.

Dudley F. Pegrum, *Public Regulation of Business* (Homewood, Ill.: Richard D. Irwin, © 1965), p. 286.

Richard Austin Smith, "The Incredible Electrical Conspiracy," *Fortune* (April and May 1961).

Simon N. Whitney, *Antitrust Policies* (New York: Twentieth Century Fund, 1958), Vol. 2, p. 429.

Clair Wilcox, *Public Policies toward Business* (Homewood, Ill.: Richard D. Irwin, © 1960), pp. 52–54.

## CHAPTER 8

Francis R. Allen, Hornell Hart, Delbert C. Miller, William F. Ogburn, and Meyer F. Nimkoff, *Technology and Social Change* (New York: Appleton-Century-Crofts, © 1957), Ch. 6.

Francis Bellow, in H. C. Barksdale, *Marketing: Change and Exchange, Readings from Fortune* (New York: Holt, Rinehart and Winston, © 1964), pp. 78–79, 93.

James R. Bright, in Floyd A. Bond, *Technological Change and Economic Growth*, Michigan Business Paper No. 41 (Ann Arbor, Mich.: Bureau of Business Research, Graduate School of Business, University of Michigan, 1965), p. 46. Copyright by the University of Michigan.

James R. Bright, "Evaluating Signals of Technological Change," *Harvard Business Review*, Vol. 48, No. 1 (January–February 1970), pp. 46, 64, 66.

Robert D. Bruce, in Floyd A. Bond, *Technological Change and Economic Growth*, Michigan Business Paper No. 41 (Ann Arbor, Mich.: Bureau of Business Research, Graduate School of Business, University of Michigan, 1965), p. 51. Copyright by the University of Michigan.

*Business Week*, March 14, 1970, p. 130. Copyright held by McGraw-Hill Book Company, Inc.

Robert L. Clewett, "Integrating Science, Technology, and Marketing: An Overview," in Raymond M. Haas (ed.), *Science, Technology, and Marketing* (Chicago: American Marketing Association, Fall 1966), pp. 3, 11.

Victor J. Danilov, "Bridging the R & D Marketing Gap," in M.S. Moyer and R. E. Vosburgh (eds.), *Marketing for Tomorrow . . . Today* (Chicago: American Marketing Association, June 1967), pp. S64–68.

Donald N. Frey, "Change in the Auto Industry," *Innovation* No. 6 (1969), pp. 7, 9.

Theodore J. Gordon, in Kurt Baier and Nicholas Rescher, *Values and the Future* (New York: Free Press, 1969), pp. 163, 181.

Herman Kahn and Anthony J. Wiener, *The Year 2000*, p. 116. © 1967 by the Hudson Institute, Inc. Reprinted with permission of the Macmillan Company.

Joseph W. Krutch, "Must Technology and Humanity Conflict?" *Bell Telephone Magazine*, Vol. 48, No. 2 (March–April 1969), p. 5.

Edwin H. Land, *The Polarized Headlight System*, Highway Research Board, National Research Council, June 1948, pp. 1–36.

Theodore Levitt, "Marketing Myopia," *Harvard Business Review*, Vol. 38 (July–August 1960), p. 45.

Theodore Levitt, "The New Markets—Think Before You Leap," *Harvard Business Review*, Vol. 47 (May–June 1969), p. 53.

Emmanuel G. Mesthene, "Technology, Society, and the Corporation," *The Corporation and Social Responsibility*, Symposium, University of Illinois, April 20, 1967, p. 33.

Roger M. Pegram and Earl L. Bailey, "The Marketing Executive Looks Ahead," (New York: National Industrial Conference Board, 1967), p. 17.

Alvin Pitcher, "The Importance of Being Human," *Harvard Business Review*, Vol. 39 (January–February 1961), p. 42.

James B. Quinn, "Technological Forecasting," *Harvard Business Review*, Vol. 45 (March–April 1967), pp. 91–99, 101–103.

W. B. Reynolds, "Research and the Marketing Concept," in Robert J. Holloway and Robert S. Hancock (eds.), *The Environment of Marketing Behavior* (New York: John Wiley, 1969), pp. 224, 229.

Jacob Schmookler, *Invention and Economic Growth* (Cambridge, Mass.: Harvard University Press, 1966), p. 213.

"The Seventies: Super but Seething," *Business Week*, December 6, 1969, p. 150. Copyright held by McGraw-Hill Book Company, Inc.

Harry R. Tosdal, *Selling in Our Economy* (Homewood, Ill.: Richard D. Irwin, © 1957), pp. 154, 161, 167, 171.

## CHAPTER 9

George Katona, *The Powerful Consumer* (New York: McGraw-Hill, © 1960), pp. 5–6.

## CHAPTER 10

Robert J. Keith, "The Marketing Revolution," *Journal of Marketing*, Vol. 24 (January 1960), p. 37.

William Lazer, "Changing Societal Norms and Marketing Implications," in Reed Moyer (ed.), *Changing Marketing Systems* (Chicago: American Marketing Association, December 1967), pp. 156–160.

Harold J. Leavitt, *Managerial Psychology* (Chicago: University of Chicago Press, © 1958), p. 296.

Dorothy Lee, in Perry Bliss (ed.), *Marketing and the Behavioral Sciences: Selected Readings*, 2nd ed. (Boston: Allyn & Bacon, 1967), p. 158.

Abraham H. Maslow, *Motivation and Personality*, 2nd ed. (New York: Harper & Row, 1970), pp. 35–37.

Adam Smith, *Wealth of Nations* (London: Methuen, 1904), p. 159.

W. T. Tucker, "Consumer Research: Status and Prospects," in Reed Moyer (ed.), *Changing Marketing Systems* (Chicago: American Marketing Association, December 1967), p. 267.

Walter A. Woods, "Psychological Dimensions of Consumer Decision," *Journal of Marketing*, Vol. 24, No. 3 (January 1960), pp. 15–19.

## CHAPTER 11

Lee Adler, "Cashing in on the Cop-Out," *Business Horizons*, Vol. 12 (February 1970), pp. 22, 28.

Alan R. Andreasen and Peter G. Durkson, "Market Learning of New Residents," *Journal of Marketing Research*, Vol. 5 (May 1968), pp. 166–176.

Seymour Banks, "The Relationships between Preference and Purchase of Brands," *Journal of Marketing*, Vol. 15 (October 1950), pp. 145–157.

Bolger Co., *Media Image Profiles* (Chicago, 1960).

Neil H. Borden, "The Concept of the Marketing Mix," *Journal of Advertising Research*, Vol. 4 (June 1964), pp. 2–7. Copyright by the Advertising Research Foundation.

Steuart Henderson Britt, "Four Hazards of Motivation Research: How To Avoid Them," *Printer's Ink*, Vol. 2 (June 1965), pp. 40, 45, 48.

R. L. Brown, "Wrapper Influence on the Perception of Freshness in Bread," *Journal of Applied Psychology*, Vol. 42 (August 1958), pp. 257–260.

Grady D. Bruce and William P. Dommermuth, "Social Class Differences in Shopping Activities," *Marquette Business Review*, Vol. 12 (Spring 1968), pp. 1–6.

Marguerite C. Burk, *Consumption Economics: A Multidisciplinary Approach* (New York: John Wiley, 1968), p. 61.

Franklin B. Evans, "Psychological and Objective Factors in the Prediction of Brand Choice—Ford Versus Chevrolet," *Journal of Business*, Vol. 32 (October 1959), pp. 340–369.

Sidney P. Feldman and Merlin C. Spencer, "The Effect of Personal Influence in the Selection of Consumer Services," in Peter D. Bennett (ed.), *Marketing and Economic Development* (Chicago: American Marketing Association, Fall 1965), pp. 440–452.

Harold Kassarjian, speech before the American Marketing Association, Boston, 1970.

J. M. Keynes, *The General Theory of Employment Interest and Money* (New York: Harcourt, Brace, 1936), p. 96.

Benjamin S. Loeb, "The Use of Engel's Laws as a Basis for Predicting Consumer Expenditures," *Journal of Marketing*, Vol. 20 (July 1955), pp. 20–27.

Market Facts, "The Made In . . . Image," (Chicago: Roc International, 1960).

Lee H. Mathews and John W. Slocum, "Social Class and Commercial Bank Credit Card Usage," *Journal of Marketing*, Vol. 33 (January 1969), pp. 71–78.

Peter J. McClure and John K. Ryans, Jr., "Differences between Retailers' and Consumers' Perceptions," *Journal of Marketing Research*, Vol. 5 (February 1968), pp. 35–40.

J. Douglas McConnell, "Effect of Pricing and Perception of Product Quality," *Journal of Applied Psychology*, Vol. 52 (August 1968), pp. 331–334.

Akira Nagashima, "A Comparison of Japanese and U.S. Attitudes toward Foreign Products," *Journal of Marketing*, Vol. 34 (January 1970), pp. 68–74.

James N. Porter, "Consumption Patterns of Professors and Businessmen: A Pilot Study of Conspicuous Consumption and Status," *Sociological Inquiry*, Vol. 37 (September 1967), pp. 255–265.

Louise G. Richards, "Consumer Practices of the Poor," in Lola M. Ireland (ed.), *Low-Income Life Styles* (Washington, D.C.: U.S. Department of Health, Education and Welfare, GPO, 1966), p. 82.

Vercors (Jean Bruller), *Quota* (New York: G. P. Putman, 1966).

## CHAPTER 12

Alan R. Andreasen, "Attitudes and Customer Behavior: A Decision Model," in Lee E. Preston (ed.), *New Research in Marketing* (Berkeley: Institute of Business and Economic Research, University of California, 1965), p. 16. By permission of the Regents of the University of California.

Lewis A. Berey and Richard W. Pollay, "The Influencing Role of the Child in Family Decision-Making," *Journal of Marketing Research*, Vol. 5, No. 1 (February 1968), p. 70.

Richard N. Cardozo, "An Experimental Study of Customer Effort, Expectation, and Satisfaction," *Journal of Marketing Research*, Vol. 2 (August 1965), pp. 246, 249.

James M. Carman, "Correlates of Brand Loyalty: Some Positive Results," *Journal of Marketing Research*, Vol. 7 (February 1970), pp. 67–76.

James M. Carman, "Some Insights into Reasonable Grocery Shopping Strategies," *Journal of Marketing*, Vol. 33 (October 1969), pp. 70–72.

"Consumer Dynamics in the Supermarket," *Progressive Grocer* (1965), p. K33.

Donald F. Cox and Stuart U. Rich, "Perceived Risk and Consumer Decision-Making—The Case of Telephone Shopping," *Journal of Marketing,* Vol. 1 (November 1964), pp. 37–38.

A. S. C. Ehrenberg and G. J. Goodhardt, "A Comparison of American and British Repeat-Buying Habits," *Journal of Marketing Research,* Vol. 5, No. 1 (February 1968), p. 30.

James F. Engel, David T. Kollat, and Roger D. Blackwell, *Consumer Behavior* (New York: Holt, Rinehart and Winston, Copyright © 1968), pp. 349, 350, 351, 365. Reprinted by permission of Holt, Rinehart and Winston, Inc.

John U. Farley, "Why Does 'Brand Loyalty' Vary over Products?" *Journal of Marketing Research,* Vol. 1 (November 1964), p. 14.

Lester Guest, "Brand Loyalty Revisited: A Twenty-Year Report," *Journal of Applied Psychology,* Vol. 48, No. 2 (April 1964), p. 97.

Reuben Hill, "Judgment and Consumership in the Management of Family Resources," *Sociology and Social Research,* Vol. 47 (July 1963), p. 460.

Robert J. Holloway, "An Experiment on Consumer Dissonance," *Journal of Marketing,* Vol. 30 (January 1967), p. 40.

John A. Howard and Jagdish N. Sheth, *The Theory of Buyer Behavior* (New York: John Wiley, 1969), p. 30.

David T. Kollat, "A Decision-Process Approach to Impulse Purchasing," in James F. Engel (ed.), *Consumer Behavior: Selected Readings* (Homewood, Ill.: Richard D. Irwin, © 1968), pp. 191, 195.

Frederick E. May, "Adaptive Behavior in Automobile Brand Choices," *Journal of Marketing Research,* Vol. 6 (February 1969), pp. 62–65.

J. Douglas McConnell, "The Development of Brand Loyalty: An Experimental Study," *Journal of Marketing Research,* Vol. 5 (February 1968), p. 18.

Joseph W. Newman (ed.), *On Knowing the Consumer* (New York: John Wiley, 1966), p. 64.

Francesco M. Nicosia, "Consumer Behavior and Computer Simulation," *Journal of Advertising Research,* Vol. 8 (March 1968), pp. 29–37. Copyright by the Advertising Research Foundation.

Allan L. Pennington, "Customer-Salesman Bargaining Behavior in Retail Transactions," *Journal of Marketing.* Vol. 5 (August 1968), p. 257.

Robert W. Pratt, Jr., "Consumer Buying Intentions as an Aid in Formulating Marketing Strategy," General Electric Co. (New York: 1967), p. 297.

R. Tanniro Rao, "Are Some Consumers More Prone To Purchase Private Brands?" *Journal of Marketing Research,* Vol. 6 (November 1969), p. 449.

James D. Shaffer, "The Influence of 'Impulse Buying' or 'In-the-Store' Decisions on Consumers' Food Purchases," *Journal of Farm Economics,* Vol. 42 (May 1960), pp. 317–324.

CHAPTER 13

Ralph S. Alexander, James S. Cross, and Ross M. Cunningham, *Industrial Marketing* (Homewood, Ill.: Richard D. Irwin, © 1961), Chs. 1 and 4.

Army Times Publishing Co., advertisement in *The New York Times,* © October 13, 1971.

Arthur Anderson & Co., "Reviewing Purchasing Performances," in Paul T. McElhiney and Robert I. Cook (eds.), *The Logistics of Materials Management: Readings in Modern Purchasing* (Boston: Houghton Mifflin, 1969), pp. 241–255. Reprinted by permission of the publisher.

Louis E. Boone and Robert E. Stevens, "Emotional Motives in the Purchase of Industrial Goods: Historically Considered," *Purchasing,* Vol. 6 (August 1970), p. 48.

James Durham, "Consumer's Point of View," in L. George Smith (ed.), Reflections on Progress in Marketing (Chicago: American Marketing Association, December 1964), p. 438.

Duncan S. Gregg, "Changes in Industrial Buying Habits," in Frederick E. Webster, Jr. (ed.), *New Directions in Marketing* (Chicago: American Marketing Association, 1965), pp. 629–630.

Richard H. Holton, "Consumer Behavior, Market Imperfections, and Public Policy," in Jesse W. Markham and Gustav F. Pananek (eds.), *Industrial Organization and Economic Development: In Honor of Edward S. Mason* (Boston: Houghton Mifflin, 1970).

Myron J. Hubler, "The Make or Buy Decision," in Paul T. McElhiney and Robert I. Cook (eds.), *The Logistics of Materials Management: Readings in Modern Purchasing* (Boston: Houghton-Mifflin, 1969), p. 175. Reprinted by permission of the publisher.

Hector Lazo, "Emotional Aspects of Industrial Buying," in Robert S. Hancock (ed.), *Dynamic Marketing for a Changing World* (Chicago: American Marketing Association, 1960), p. 265.

Victor H. Poole, "The Purchasing Man and His Job," from Paul T. McElhiney and Robert I. Cook (eds.), *The Logistics of Materials Management: Readings in Modern Purchasing* (Boston: Houghton Mifflin, 1969), p. 12. Reprinted by permission of the publisher.

William Rudelius, "Selling to the Government," in Victor P. Buell (ed.), *Marketing Handbook* (New York: McGraw-Hill, © 1970), Ch. 11.

Lloyd Stouffer, "Biggest Thing Since Mass Production," in Paul T. McElhiney and Robert I. Cook (eds.), *The Logistics of Materials Management: Readings in*

*Modern Purchasing* (Boston: Houghton Mifflin, 1969), pp. 225–227.

James C. Tanner, "Canny Buyers," *Wall Street Journal*, June 23, 1964.

Frederick E. Webster, Jr., "Industrial Buying Behavior: A State of the Arts Appraisal," in Bernard A. Morin (ed.), *Marketing in a Changing World* (Chicago: American Marketing Association Proceedings, June 1969), p. 256.

Murray L. Weidenbaum, "Concentration and Competition in the Military Market," *The Quarterly Review of Economics and Business*, Vol. 8 (Spring 1968), p. 16.

## CHAPTER 14

B. Charles Ames, "Trappings vs. Substance in Industrial Marketing," *Harvard Business Review*, Vol. 48 (July 1970), p. 94.

Hiram C. Barksdale and Bill Darden, "Marketers' Attitudes toward the Marketing Concept," *Journal of Marketing*, Vol. 35 (October 1971), p. 33.

Martin L. Bell and C. William Emory, "The Faltering Marketing Concept," *Journal of Marketing*, Vol. 35 (October 1971), p. 39.

Neil Borden, "The Concept of the Marketing Mix," *Journal of Advertising Research*, Vol. 4 (June 1964), pp. 2–7. Copyright by the Advertising Research Foundation.

Leslie M. Dawson, "The Human Concept: New Philosophy for Business," *Business Horizons*, Vol. 12 (December 1969), p. 32.

Peter Drucker, "The Shame of Marketing," *Marketing/Communications*, Vol. 297 (August 1969), p. 60.

Philip Kotler, *Marketing Management* (Englewood Cliffs, N.J.: Prentice-Hall, © 1967), Ch. 23.

Carlton P. McNamara, "The Present Status of the Marketing Concept," *Journal of Marketing*, Vol. 36 (January 1972), pp. 50–57.

Alfred Oxenfeldt, "The Marketing Audit: Its Nature, Purposes, and Problems," *Analyzing and Improving Marketing Performance, American Management Association Management Report*, No. 32 (New York: 1959), p. 11.

Lyndall F. Urwick, *The Pattern of Management* (Minneapolis: University of Minnesota Press, 1956), pp. 85–88.

Philip L. Wagner, *The Human Use of the Earth* (Glencoe, Ill.: Free Press, 1960), p. 6.

## CHAPTER 15

American Marketing Association, Committee on Definitions, *Marketing Definitions* (Chicago: American Marketing Association, 1960).

Conrad Berenson, "Marketing Information Systems," *Journal of Marketing*, Vol. 33 (October 1969), p. 17.

Richard H. Brien and James E. Stafford, "Marketing Information Systems: A New Dimension for Marketing Research," *Journal of Marketing*, Vol. 32 (July 1968), p. 21.

Lyndon O. Brown, *Marketing and Distribution Research* (New York: Ronald Press, 1955), pp. 10–11.

Ralph Cassady, Jr., "Market Measurement in a Free Society," *California Management Review*, Vol. 2 (Winter 1960), p. 57. © by the Regents of the University of California. Reprinted by permission.

Donald F. Cox and Robert E. Good, "How To Build a Marketing Information System," *Harvard Business Review*, Vol. 45 (May–June 1957), pp. 147, 149.

C. S. Duncan, *Commercial Research* (New York: Macmillan, 1921), p. v.

Robert J. Holloway, "Marketing Research and Market Planning for the Small Manufacturer," *Small Business Management Research Reports* (Minneapolis: University of Minnesota, 1961), p. 16.

James R. Krum, "Perceptions and Evaluation of the Role of the Corporate Marketing Research Department," *Journal of Marketing Research*, Vol. 6 (November 1969), p. 464.

Joseph W. Newman, "Put Research into Marketing Decisions," *Harvard Business Review*, Vol. 40 (March–April 1962), p. 180.

Arch W. Shaw, *Some Problems in Market Distribution* (Cambridge, Mass.: Harvard University Press, 1915), p. 16.

Donald L. Shawver, personal correspondence, 1971.

Dik Warren Twedt (ed.), *1968 Survey of Marketing Research* (Chicago: American Marketing Association, 1969), pp. 17, 21, 25, 27.

Percival White, *Market Analysis* (New York: McGraw-Hill, © 1925) p. 1.

## CHAPTER 16

C. Merle Crawford, "Attitudes of Marketing Executives toward Ethics in Marketing Research," *Journal of Marketing*, Vol. 34 (April 1970), pp. 46–52.

Lewis W. Forman and Earl L. Bailey, *The Role and Organization of Marketing Research* (New York: National Industrial Conference Board, 1969), pp. 23–24.

Willard M. Fox, *How To Use Market Research for Profit* (Englewood Cliffs, N.J.: Prentice-Hall, © 1950), p. 327.

Paul E. Green, "EDITORIAL: Where is the Research Generalist?" *Journal of Marketing Research*, Vol. 5 (November 1968), p. 442.

David K. Hardin, "EDITORIAL: Marketing Research—Is It Used or Abused?" *Journal of Marketing Research*, Vol. 6 (May 1969), p. 239.

Paul W. Stewart and Fred R. Haviland, Jr., "The Growth of Marketing Research as a Management Tool," in Hugh Wales (ed.), *Changing Perspectives in Market-*

*ing* (Urbana, Ill: University of Illinois Press, 1951), p. 279.

Eugene J. Webb, Donald T. Campbell, Richard D. Schwartz, and Lee Sechrest, *Unobtrusive Measures* ' (Chicago: Rand McNally, 1966), p. 2.

## CHAPTER 17

Lee Adler, "Time Lag in New Product Development," *Journal of Marketing*, Vol. 30 (January 1966), pp. 17–21.

R. S. Alexander, "The Death and Burial of 'Sick' Products," *Journal of Marketing*, Vol. 28 (April 1964), pp. 1–7.

American Marketing Association, Committee on Definitions, *Marketing Definitions* (Chicago: American Marketing Association, 1960).

Leo V. Aspinwall, "The Characteristics of Good Theory," in William Lazer and Eugene J. Kelley (eds.), *Managerial Marketing: Perspectives and Viewpoints* (Homewood, Ill.: Richard D. Irwin, © 1962), pp. 633–643.

Booz, Allen & Hamilton, *Management of New Products* (New York: Booz, Allen & Hamilton, 1965), p. 9.

Robert D. Buzzell, *The Role of Advertising in the Marketing Mix*, (Cambridge, Mass.: Marketing Science Institute, 1971), p. 14 and Exhibit 11.

Clare Elmer Griffin, "The Evolution of the Automobile Market," *Harvard Business Review*, Vol. 4 (July 1926), p. 416.

Harry L. Hansen, Marketing (Homewood, Ill.: Richard D. Irwin, © 1967), p. 437.

Samuel C. Johnson and Conrad Jones, "How To Organize for New Products," *Harvard Business Review*, Vol. 35 (May–June 1957), p. 52.

Theodore Levitt, "Exploit the Product Life Cycle," *Harvard Business Review* (November–December 1965), p. 88.

Theodore Levitt, *The Marketing Mode* (New York: McGraw-Hill, © 1969), pp. 28–29. Used with permission of the McGraw-Hill Book Company, Inc.

Gordon E. Miracle. "Product Characteristics and Marketing," *Journal of Marketing*, Vol. 29 (January 1965), pp. 18–24.

Jack Olsen, "Bad Show Out in the Cold Snow," *Sports Illustrated*, March 16, 1970, p. 28.

John T. O'Meara, Jr., "Selecting Profitable Products," *Harvard Business Review*, Vol. 39 (January–February 1961), pp. 84–85.

Victor Papanek, *Design for the Real World: Human Ecology and Social Change* (New York: Pantheon, 1972).

Thomas S. Robertson, "The New Product Diffusion Process," in Bernard A. Morin (ed.), *Marketing in a Changing World* (Chicago: American Marketing Association Proceedings, June 1969), pp. 80–86.

Eberhard E. Scheuing, "The Product Life Cycle as an Aid in Strategy Decisions, " *International Management Review*, Vol. 9 (April–May 1969), pp. 111–124.

"Sticking with Gum," *The Wall Street Journal*, August 16, 1967, p. 1.

"3M Co.—Little Drops of Water, Little Grains of Sand," *Marketing Insights*, May 4, 1970, p. 12.

Louis T. Wells, Jr., "A Product Life Cycle for International Trade?" *Journal of Marketing*, Vol. 32 (July 1968), pp. 1–16.

Daniel Yankelovich, "New Criteria for Market Segmentation," *Harvard Business Review*, Vol. 42 (March–April 1964), pp. 83–90.

## CHAPTER 18

T. W. Beckman and W. R. Davidson, *Marketing* (New York: Ronald Press, 1967), pp. 233, 396–397.

B. C. McCammon and R. W. Little, "Marketing Channels: Analytical Systems and Approaches," in G. Schwartz (ed.), *Science in Marketing* (New York: John Wiley, 1965), p. 349.

L. W. Stern, "Channel Control and Interorganization Management," in Peter D. Bennett (ed.), *Marketing and Economic Development* (Chicago: American Marketing Association, 1965), pp. 655–665.

W. G. Zikmund and W. J. Stanton, "Recycling Solid Wastes: A Channels-of-Distribution Problem," *Journal of Marketing* Vol. 35 (July 1971), pp. 34–39.

## CHAPTER 19

B. B. Barrick, "What 'Unimarket' Does for Raytheon, " *Industrial Marketing*, Vol. 48 (February 1963), pp. 84–89.

"The Case for 90% Satisfaction," *Business Week*, January 14, 1961, pp. 82–85. Copyright held by McGraw-Hill Book Company, Inc.

D. V. Harper, "Transportation: A Forgotten Function of Marketing" *Boston University Business Review* (Spring 1964), p. 46.

J. L. Heskett, R. M. Ivie, N. A. Glaskowsky, *Business Logistics* (New York: Ronald Press, 1964), pp. 8–9, 15–16, 452. Also see John Magee, *Physical Distribution Systems* (New York: McGraw-Hill, 1967), pp. 1–2.

John Magee, "The Logistics of Distribution," *Harvard Business Review*, Vol. 38 (July–August 1960), p. 93.

*Progressive Grocer*, 38th Annual Report (April 1971), p. 64.

Western Railroad Association, *Yearbook of Railroad Facts* (Chicago: Economics and Finance Department, Association of American Railroads, April 1970), p. 52.

## CHAPTER 20

Jules Backman, *Pricing: Policies and Practices* (New York: National Industrial Conference Board, 1961), p. 35.

Jules Backman, *Price Practices and Price Policies* (New York: Ronald Press, 1953), pp. 8, 9, 14, 123.

Joel Dean, *Managerial Economics* (Englewood Cliffs, N.J.: Prentice-Hall, © 1951), Chs. 7–9.

Joel Dean, "Pricing Policies for New Products," *Harvard Business Review,* Vol. 28 (November 1950), pp. 49–53.

Donald V. Harper, *Price Policy and Procedure* (New York: Harcourt Brace Jovanovich, 1966), p. 53.

A. D. H. Kaplan, Joel B. Dirlam, and Robert E. Lanzillotti, *Pricing in Big Business* (Washington, D.C.: The Brookings Institution, © 1958), especially pp. 127–219.

## CHAPTER 21

Jules Backman, *Pricing Practices and Price Policies* (New York: Ronald Press, 1953), pp. 174–175.

William Crissy and Robert Boewadt, "Pricing in Perspective," *Sales Management,* June 15, 1971, pp. 43–44.

Donald V. Harper, *Price Policy and Procedure* (New York: Harcourt Brace Jovanovich, 1966), pp. 53, 55–56.

Benson P. Shapiro, *The Pricing of Consumer Goods: Theory and Practice* (Cambridge, Mass.: Marketing Science Institute, 1972), pp. 3–5.

Milton H. Spencer, *Managerial Economics,* 3rd ed. (Homewood, Ill.: Richard D. Irwin, © 1968), pp. 289–292.

## CHAPTER 22

American Marketing Association, Committee on Definitions, *Marketing Definitions* (Chicago: American Marketing Association, 1960).

M. Argunov, "Sovetskaya Torgovlya" (February 1966), translated in "What Advertising Does," *Journal of Advertising Research,* Vol. 6 (December 1966), p. 5. © Copyright by the Advertising Research Foundation.

Ben H. Bagdikian, "How Much More Communication Can We Stand?" *The Futurist,* Vol. 5 (October 1971), p. 180.

Raymond A. Bauer and Mark G. Field, "Ironic Contrast: US and USSR Drug Industries," *Harvard Business Review,* Vol. 40 (September–October 1962), pp. 90, 97.

Miriam Beard, *A History of the Business Man* (New York: Macmillan, © 1938), p. 11.

Bernard Berelson and Gary A. Steiner, *Human Behavior* (New York: Harcourt Brace Jovanovich, 1964).

Neil H. Borden, "Findings of the Harvard Study on the Economic Effects of Advertising," *Journal of Marketing,* Vol. 6 (April 1942), pp. 89–99.

Robert D. Buzzell, *The Role of Advertising in the Marketing Mix,* remarks prepared for the Federal Trade Commission's Hearings (Cambridge, Mass.: Marketing Science Institute, 1971), Exhibits 2, 12, 13.

Russell H. Colley, *Defining Advertising Goals for Measured Advertising Results* (New York: Association of National Advertisers, 1961), p. 39.

"Federal Trade Commission Hearings—Behind the Scenes," *The 4A Newsletter,* Vol. 9 (December 2, 1971), p. 4.

Stephen A. Greyser and Bonnie B. Reece, "Businessmen Look Hard at Advertising," *Harvard Business Review,* Vol. 49 (May–June 1971), pp. 18–27.

Michael Halbert, *The Meaning and Sources of Marketing Theory* (New York: McGraw-Hill, 1965).

John Hobson, "The Influence and Techniques of Modern Advertising," Three Cantor Lectures from the *Journal of the Royal Society of Arts,* London (July 1964), p. 23.

Stanley C. Hollander, *Sales Devices Throughout the Ages* (New York: Joshua Meier Company, 1953), p. 6.

Carl I. Hovland, Irvin L. Janis, and Harold H. Kelly, *Communication and Persuasion* (New Haven: Yale University Press, 1953), pp. 11–14.

Dexter Masters, *The Intelligent Buyer's Guide to Sellers* (Mount Vernon, N.Y.: Consumers Union, 1965), p. 21.

David Ogilvy, "How To Create Advertising That Sells," *The New York Times,* © April 7, 1971.

John M. Rathmell, "The Salesman and Competition," in Taylor W. Meloan and Charles M. Whitlo (eds.), *Competition in Marketing* (Los Angeles: University of Southern California, 1964), p. 94.

Harry R. Tosdal, *Selling in Our Economy* (Homewood, Ill.: Richard D. Irwin, © 1957), pp. 4, 328.

Colston E. Warne, "Advertising—A Critic's View," *Journal of Marketing,* Vol. 26 (October 1962), pp. 11–12.

"What Use Is Advertising?" *Royal Bank of Canada Monthly Letter,* Vol. 49 (October 1968), p. 1.

James Playsted Wood, *The Story of Advertising* (New York: Ronald Press, 1958), p. 18.

## CHAPTER 23

Steuart Henderson Britt, "Advertising Research in Action," in Taylor W. Meloan and Charles M. Whitlo (eds.), *Competition in Marketing* (Los Angeles: University of Southern California, 1964), p. 73.

Robert D. Buzzell, *The Role of Advertising in the Marketing Mix,* remarks prepared for the Federal Trade Commission's Hearings (Cambridge, Mass.: Marketing Science Institute, 1971), Exhibits 2, 12, 13.

Alfred D. Chandler, Jr., *Giant Enterprise* (New York: Harcourt Brace Jovanovich, 1964), pp. 35, 37, 150, 160.

S. Watson Dunn, *Advertising: Its Role in Modern Marketing,* 2nd ed. (New York: Holt, Rinehart and Winston, © 1969), pp. 135–136.

Lawrence M. Hughes, "How is Hershey Doing—Without Advertising?" *Sales Management,* Vol. 84 (May 20, 1960), pp. 33–114.

Ralph Leezenbaum, "Coffee Makers Ignore Warning Signals," *Marketing/Communications* (May 1970), pp. 18–27.

Edwin H. Lewis, "The Changing Dimensions of Field Selling," mimeographed report, University of Minnesota, 1970.

Edwin H. Lewis, "Sales Promotion Decisions," *Business News Notes,* University of Minnesota, No. 18 (November 1954), p. 5.

Edmund D. McGarry, "The Propaganda Function in Marketing," *Journal of Marketing,* Vol. 23 (October 1958), pp. 131–139.

Robert S. McMurray, "Clearing the New Product for Commercialization," *Sales Management,* Vol. 93 (August 15, 1954), pp. 102–105.

John S. Radosta, "Auto Racing and the Market Place," *The New York Times,* © October 14, 1971.

John M. Rathmell, "The Salesman and Competition," in Taylor W. Meloan and Charles M. Whitlo (eds.), *Competition in Marketing* (Los Angeles: University of Southern California, 1964), p. 94.

"Setting Advertising Objectives," *Studies in Business Policy,* No. 118 (New York: National Industrial Conference Board, 1966), pp. 4–5.

James M. Wallace, "A Perfect Measure of Advertising's Contribution to Marketing," *Journal of Marketing,* Vol. 30 (July 1966), p. 16.

R. S. Wilson, "Salesmanship as a Profession," AMA Philadelphia Chapter, Charles Parlin Lectures, 1947.

## CHAPTER 24

J. Boddewyn, "The Top Management Job in International Business," *Temple University Economic and Business Bulletin,* Vol. 23 (Fall 1970), pp. 1–5.

David Carson and Lawrence H. Wortzel, "Soviets Challenge U.S. Marketing," *Business Horizons,* Vol. 13 (June 1970), p. 44.

George A. Elgass, "Marketing in Japan: An Expanding Economy," in William D. Stevens (ed.), *The Social Responsibilities of Marketing* (Chicago: American Marketing Association, 1961), p. 429.

Edward T. Hall, "The Silent Language in Overseas Business," *Harvard Business Review,* Vol. 38 (September–October 1960), p. 107.

Neil H. Jacoby, "The Multinational Corporation," *The Center Magazine,* Vol. 3 (May 1970), pp. 37–55.

Endel J. Kolde, "Business Enterprise in a Global Context," *California Management Review,* Vol. 9 (September 1966), pp. 31–48. © 1966 by the Regents of the University of California. Published by permission of the Regents.

David S. R. Leighton, "The Internationalization of American Business—The Third Industrial Revolution," *Journal of Marketing,* Vol. 34 (July 1970), pp. 3–6.

Arthur C. Nielsen, Jr., "Dos and Don'ts in Selling Abroad," *Journal of Marketing,* Vol. 23 (April 1959), pp. 405–411.

James R. Piper, Jr., "How U.S. Firms Evaluate Foreign Investment Opportunities," *MSU Business Topics,* Vol. 19 (Summer 1971), pp. 11–20.

John K. Ryans, Jr. and James H. Donnelly, Jr., "Standardized Global Advertising, A Call As Yet Unanswered," *Journal of Marketing,* Vol. 33 (April 1969), pp. 57–59.

Mihoril Skobe, "Marketing and Advertising in Yugoslavia," in Peter D. Bennett (ed.), *Marketing and Economic Development* (Chicago: American Marketing Association, 1965), p. 99.

Yoshi Tsurumi, "Myths That Mislead U.S. Managers in Japan," *Harvard Business Review,* Vol. 49 (July–August 1971), pp. 118–127.

U.S. Department of Commerce, *U.S. Foreign Trade: A Five-Year Outlook* (Washington, D.C.: GPO, 1969), pp. 32, 51.

M. Y. Yoshino, *The Japanese Marketing System* (Cambridge, Mass.: MIT Press, 1971), pp. 11–12, 109–111.

## CHAPTER 25

"Americans Put the Car in its Place," *Business Week,* September 18, 1971, pp. 66–68. Copyright held by McGraw-Hill Book Company, Inc.

Robert Bartels, "A Model for Ethics in Marketing," *Journal of Marketing,* Vol. 31 (January 1967), pp. 20–26.

Kenneth E. Boulding, *Beyond Economics* (Ann Arbor, Mich.: University of Michigan Press, 1969), pp. 227–238.

Howard R. Bowen, *Social Responsibilities of Businessmen* (New York: Harper & Row, 1953), pp. 214–215.

The Canadian Association of Broadcasters, *Broadcast Code for Advertising to Children,* mimeographed (Ottawa, Canada: October 1971).

Albert Z. Carr, "Is Business Bluffing Ethical?" *Harvard Business Review,* Vol. 46 (January–February 1968), pp. 143–153.

J. M. Clark, *Social Control of Business* (Chicago: University of Chicago Press, 1926), p. 47.

William J. Colihan, Jr., "The Consumer Issues of Advertising," speech, Washington, D.C., December 5, 1969.

"The Coming Conflict in Business Discipline," *Fortune* (September 1969), p. 95.

Fred J. Cook, "The Corrupt Society," *The Nation,* Vol. 196 (January 1–8, 1963), p. 458.

Peter Drucker, "Marketing and Economic Development," *Journal of Marketing,* Vol. 22 (January 1958), p. 259.

Economic Priorities Report, *Corporate Advertising and the Environment* (Washington, D.C.: Council on Economic Priorities, 1971).

Bert Elwert, "Social and Ethical Problems of Marketing Planning," in Robert L. King (ed.), *Marketing and the New Science of Planning* (Chicago: American Marketing Association, 1968), p. 133.

Richard N. Farmer, "Would You Want Your Daughter To Marry a Marketing Man?" *Journal of Marketing*, Vol. 31 (January 1967), p. 3.

Lawrence P. Feldman, "Societal Adaptation: A New Challenge for Marketing," *Journal of Marketing*, Vol. 35 (July 1971), p. 56.

John Kenneth Galbraith, *The Affluent Society* (Boston: Houghton Mifflin, 1958), pp. 199–200.

Stephen A. Greyser and Bonnie B. Reece, "Businessmen Look Hard at Advertising," *Harvard Business Review*, Vol. 49 (May–June 1971), pp. 18–27.

Nicholas Johnson, speech reported by Irv Letofsky, "Is TV Guilty of Child Abuse?" *Minneapolis Tribune*, November 7, 1971, p. 1.

Jack Kemp, "What's the Issue?" Speech released by *Chamber of Commerce* of the United States, November 5, 1971.

Aldo Leopold, *A Sand County Almanac* (New York: Sierra Club/Ballantine Books, 1970), pp. 237–261.

Albert William Levi, "Ethical Confusion and the Business community," in Joseph W. Towle (ed.), *Ethics and Standards in American Business* (Boston: Houghton Mifflin, 1964), pp. 20–29.

John D. Morris, "Cigarette Ads Found Doubled in 14 Magazines," *The New York Times*, © May 17, 1971.

Ralph Nader, as quoted in *Business Week*, September 18, 1971, p. 66. Copyright held by McGraw-Hill Book Company, Inc.

Vance Packard, "The Growing Power of Admen," *Atlantic*, Vol. 200 (September 1957), pp. 55, 59.

Donald E. Petersen, as quoted in *Business Week*, September 18, 1971, p. 66.

Henry O. Pruden, "Which Ethic for Marketers?" in John R. Wish and Stephen H. Gamble (eds.), *Marketing and Social Issues: An Action Reader* (New York: John Wiley, 1971), pp. 98–104.

Claude Robinson from Charles A. Perlitz, "A Look at Business Ethics," *Petroleum Today*, Vol. 4 (Summer 1963), p. 1.

Leo D. Stone, "The History of Ethics in American Business," in Robert Bartels (ed.) *Ethics in Business* (Columbus, Ohio: The Ohio State University, 1963), p. 20.

Eleanor Johnson Tracy, "Lush Times for the Pet-Food Producers," *Fortune* (December 1971), p. 110.

Lyndall F. Urwick, *The Elements of Administration* (New York: Harper & Row, 1943), p. 27.

J. Howard Westing, "Some Thoughts on the Nature of Ethics in Marketing," in Reed Moyer (ed.), *Changing Marketing Systems* (Chicago: American Marketing Association, December 1967), pp. 161–163.

Janet Whitney (ed.), *The Journal of John Woolman* (Chicago: Henry Regnery, 1950), pp. 36, 37, 39.

## CHAPTER 26

Paul Baran, "A Marxist View of Consumer Sovereignty," *The Political Economy of Growth* (New York: Monthly Review, Inc., 1957), p. xvii.

*Christian Advocate*, Vol. 138 (September 1, 1955).

"Consumerism in the U.S.," *Marketing Horizons* (October, 1969), p. 11.

David W. Cravens and Gerald E. Hills, "Consumerism: A Perspective for Business," *Business Horizons*, Vol. 13 (August 1970), p. 24.

Peter F. Drucker, "The Shame of Marketing," *Marketing/Communications* (August 1969), p. 61.

Robert Ferber, "Rising Consumerism Primary Concern to Market Managers," *The Marketing News*, Vol. 3 (June 1970), p. 4.

E. T. Grether, "Sharp Practice in Merchandising and Advertising," *Annals*, Vol. 363 (January 1966), p. 116.

Richard H. Holton, "A Management Response to the Consumer Furor," A.A.A.A. Western Region Annual Meeting, October 16–19, 1966.

National Commission on Product Safety, *Final Report to the President and Congress* (Washington, D.C.: GPO, June 1970).

Bernard Rosenberg, "A Dictionary for the Disenchanted," *Harper's* (November 1970), p. 94.

Aaron S. Yohalem, "The Challenge of Consumerism," *Sales/Marketing Today* (March 1970), pp. 9–10.

## CHAPTER 27

Roy Alexander, "The Marketer in the Ghetto," *Industrial Marketing*, Vol. 54 (October 1969), pp. 69–72.

Marcus Alexis, George H. Haines, Jr., and Leonard S. Simon, *Consumption Behavior of Prisoners: The Case of the Inner City Shopper* (Rochester, N.Y.: University of Rochester, 1970).

Raymond A. Bauer and Scott M. Cunningham, "The Negro Market," *Journal of Advertising Research*, Vol. 10 (April 1970), p. 10. © Copyright by the Advertising Research Foundation.

Gordon F. Bloom, "Black Capitalism in Ghetto Supermarkets: Problems and Prospects," *Industrial Management Review*, Vol. 11 (Spring 1970), p. 47.

Nathan S. Caplan and Jeffrey M. Paige, "A Study of Ghetto Rioters," *Scientific American*, Vol. 219 (© August 1968), p. 15.

David Caplovitz, *The Poor Pay More* (Glencoe, Ill.: Free Press, 1963).

Kenneth B. Clark, *Dark Ghetto* (New York: Harper Torchbooks, 1965), pp. 27–28.

"Consumer Dynamics in the Supermarket," *Progressive Grocer* (1965).

Keith Cox, James E. Stafford, and James B. Higginbotham, "Negro Retail Shopping and Credit Behavior," unpublished at time of writing.

William E. Cox, Jr., and Sue R. Siedman, "Cooperatives in the Ghetto," in Philip R. McDonald (ed.), *Marketing Involvement in Society and the Economy* (Chicago: American Marketing Association, 1969), p. 42.

Detroit Urban League, *A Survey of Attitudes of Detroit Negroes After the Riot of 1967*, coordinated by the *Detroit Free Press* (Detroit, 1967), p. 9. Reprinted with permission of the Detroit Free Press.

Donald F. Dixon and Daniel J. McLaughlin, Jr., "Do the Inner City Poor Pay More for Food?" *Temple University Economic and Business Bulletin*, Vol. 20 (Spring 1968), pp. 6–12.

Federal Trade Commission, *Economic Report on Installment Credit and Retail Sales Practices of District of Columbia Retailers* (Washington, D.C.: GPO, 1968).

Daniel R. Fusfeld, "Post-Post-Keynes: The Shattered Synthesis," *Saturday Review*, January 22, 1972, p. 39.

Charles S. Goodman, "Do The Poor Pay More?" *Journal of Marketing*, Vol. 32 (January 1968), pp. 6–12.

Bradley Greenberg and Brenda Dervin, "Mass Communication among the Poor," *Public Opinion Quarterly*, Vol. 34 (Summer 1970), p. 227.

Phyllis Groom, "Prices in Poor Neighborhoods," *Monthly Labor Review*, Vol. 89 (October 1966), pp. 1085–1090.

Robert J. Holloway and Richard N. Cardozo, *Consumer Problems and Marketing Patterns in Low-Income Neighborhoods: An Exploratory Study* (Minneapolis: University of Minnesota, 1969), pp. 40–41.

Robert L. King and Earl Robert DeManche, "Comparative Acceptance of Selected Private-Branded Food Products by Low-Income Negro and White Families," in Philip R. McDonald (ed.), *Marketing in Society and the Economy* (Chicago: American Marketing Association, 1969), pp. 63–69.

Carl M. Larson, "Racial Brand Usage and Media Exposure Differentials," in Keith Cox and Ben M. Enis (eds.), *A New Measure of Responsibility for Marketing* (Chicago: American Marketing Association, 1968), pp. 208–215.

Oscar Lewis, "The Culture of Poverty," *Scientific American*, Vol. 215 (© October 1966), p. 19.

Burton H. Marcus, "Similarity of Ghetto and Nonghetto Food Costs," *Journal of Marketing Research*, Vol. 6 (August 1969), p. 366.

Bruce W. Marion, Lois A. Simonds, and Dan E. Moore, *Food Marketing in Low-Income Areas* (Columbus, Ohio: The Ohio State University, 1969).

Walter F. Mondale, "The Challenge of the Ghetto to Marketing," in Keith Cox and Ben M. Enis (eds.), *A New Measure of Responsibility for Marketing* (Chi-

cago: American Marketing Association, 1968), p. 14.

Raymond O. Oladipupo, *How Distinct Is the Negro Market?* (New York: Ogilvy & Mather, Inc., 1970).

*Report of the National Advisory Committee on Civil Disorder* (Washington, D.C.: GPO, 1968), p. 83.

Louise G. Richards, "Consumer Practices of the Poor," in Lola M. Ireland (ed.), *Low-Income Life Styles* (Washington, D.C.: U.S. Department of Health, Education, and Welfare, GPO, 1966), p. 82.

Donald E. Sexton, Jr., "Comparing the Cost of Food to Blacks and to Whites—A Survey," *Journal of Marketing*, Vol. 35 (July 1971), pp. 40–46.

*Supplementary Studies for the National Advisory Commission on Civil Disorders* (Washington, D.C.: GPO, 1968), pp. 126–131.

Richard Teach, "Supermarket Pricing Practices in Various Areas of a Large City," in Philip R. McDonald (ed.), *Marketing Involvement in Society and the Economy* (Chicago: American Marketing Association, 1969), p. 62.

U.S. Department of Labor, *A Study of Prices Charged in Stores Located in Low and Higher-Income Areas of Six Large Cities for Non-Food Items* (Washington, D.C.: GPO, 1966), pp. 1–66.

Kelvin A. Wall, "Marketing to Low-Income Neighborhoods: A Systems Approach," *Business Review* (University of Washington), Vol. 24 (Autumn 1969), pp. 18–26.

John Wright, "Report on Business in Low-Income Districts," mimeographed report, University of Minnesota, 1970.

## CHAPTER 28

Wroe Alderson, "Ethics, Ideologies, and Sanction," in Robert J. Lavidge and Robert J. Holloway (eds.), *Marketing and Society: The Challenge* (Homewood, Ill.: Richard D. Irwin, © 1969), pp. 74–84.

Henry R. Bernstein, "End Slurs on Mexican Americans, Senators Urge Eight Advertisers," *Advertising Age*, February 9, 1970. Copyright by Crain Communications, Inc.

"The Booming World Trade in Arms," *Business Week*, May 23, 1970, pp. 114–118. Copyright held by McGraw-Hill Book Company, Inc.

Harrison Brown, *The Challenge of Man's Future* (New York: Viking, 1954).

Earl Cook, "Energy in the Transition to the Steady State," paper presented at American Association for Advancement of Science, Philadelphia, 1972.

Etienne Cracco and Jacques Rostenne, "The Socioecological Product," *MSU Business Topics*, Vol. 19 (Summer 1971), pp. 27–34.

Leslie M. Dawson, "Marketing Science in the Age of Aquarius," *Journal of Marketing*, Vol. 35 (July 1971), pp. 66–72.

Daniel V. DeSimone, "Moving to Metric makes Dollars and Sense," *Harvard Business Review*, Vol. 50 (January–February 1972), pp. 100–111.

Edwin G. Dolan, *TANSTAAFL: There ain't no such thing as a free lunch* (New York: Holt, Rinehart and Winston, © 1971), p. 4.

Henry Ford II, *The Human Environment and Business* (New York; Weybright and Talley, 1970), p. 60.

Daniel R. Fusfeld, "Post-Post-Keynes: The Shattered Synthesis," *Saturday Review*, January 22, 1972, pp. 36–39.

Betsy D. Gelb and Richard H. Brien, "Survival and Social Responsibility: Themes for Marketing Education and Management," *Journal of Marketing*, Vol. 35 (April 1971), pp. 3–9.

Samuel M. Gillespie, "Historical Perspective of the Ecological Problem," paper presented at Southern Marketing Association Meetings, Fall 1971.

Robert R. Grinstead, "No Deposit No Return," *Environment*, Vol. 11 (November 1969), pp. 17–23.

Walter W. Heller, "Coming to Terms with Growth and the Environment," paper presented for the Forum on Energy, Economic Growth, and the Environment, April 1971.

Philip Kotler and Sidney J. Levy, "Broadening the Concept of Marketing," *Journal of Marketing*, Vol. 33 (January 1969), pp. 10–15.

Philip Kotler and Sidney J. Levy, "Demarketing, yes, Demarketing," *Harvard Business Review*, Vol. 49 (November–December 1971) pp. 74–80.

William Lazer, "Marketing's Changing Social Relationships," *Journal of Marketing*, Vol. 33 (January 1969), p. 3.

Ralph Leezenbaum, "The New American Woman . . . and Marketing," *Marketing/Communications*, Vol. 298 (July 1970), pp. 22–28.

Robert Lekachman, "Phase II: Casting Light on Economic Power," *Saturday Review*, January 22, 1972, pp. 44–45.

Robert Lindsey, "Airlines Seeking To Balance Capacity and Demand," *The New York Times*, © January 9, 1972, p. 29.

Arthur Miller, "Lines from California," *Harper's* (May 1969), p. 97.

National Wildlife Federation, "1971 EQ Index," *National Wildlife Magazine* (October–November 1971).

Robert Rienow and Leona Train Rienow, *Moment in the Sun* (New York: Dial Press, 1967), p. 3.

David Rockefeller, "The Era of Growing Business Accountability," speech, December 1971.

Sierra Club, "The Trans-Alaska Pipeline: The Un-answered Questions," *Sierra Club Bulletin*, Vol. 57 (January 1972), pp. 4–9.

Paul Swatek, *The User's Guide to the Protection of the Environment* (New York: Friends of the Earth/Ballantine Books, 1970).

U.S. Department of Commerce, *U.S. Economic Growth* (Washington, D.C.: GPO, 1966), p. 42.

William G. Zikmund and William J. Stanton, "Recycling Solid Wastes: A Channels-of-Distribution Problem," *Journal of Marketing*, Vol. 35 (July 1971), pp. 34–39.

## CHAPTER 29

Theodore N. Beckman, "Criteria of Marketing Efficiency," *The Annals of the American Academy of Political and Social Science*, Vol. 209 (May 1940), p. 133.

Reavis Cox, *Distribution in a High-Level Economy* (Englewood Cliffs, N.J.: Prentice-Hall, © 1965), pp. 135, 165, 173.

Reavis Cox and Charles S. Goodman, "Marketing of Housebuilding Materials," *Journal of Marketing*, Vol. 21 (July 1956), pp. 41–43.

Robert G. Gardner, "Distribution Cost Analysis," in Bernard A. Morin (ed.), *Marketing in a Changing World* (Chicago: American Marketing Association Proceedings, June 1969), pp. 200–202.

Alfred Kuhn, *The Study of Society: A Unified Approach* (Homewood, Ill.: Richard D. Irwin and the Dorsey Press, © 1963), p. 585.

Karl Marx, *Capital* (Chicago: Clark H. Kerr & Co., 1907), Vol. 2, p. 169.

The Ohio State University Marketing Faculty, *Statement of the Philosophy of Marketing* (Columbus, Ohio; 1964).

Alfred R. Oxenfeldt, *Economic Systems in Action* (New York: Rinehart & Co., 1957), p. 8.

Otto Ruhle, *Karl Marx, His Life and Work* (New York: Viking, 1929), p. 353.

Paul W. Stewart and J. Frederick Dewhurst, *Does Distribution Cost Too Much?* (New York: The Twentieth Century Fund, 1939).

U.S. Department of Health, Education, and Welfare, *Toward a Social Report* (Washington, D.C.: GPO, 1969), p. xi.

E. B. Weiss, "Assaulting the High Costs of Marketing Drugs," *Marketing Insights*, January 13, 1969, pp. 15–17.

## CHAPTER 30

Theodore J. Gordon, Dennis L. Little, Harold L. Strudler, and Donna D. Lustgarten, *A Forecast of the Interaction between Business and Society in the Next Five Years* (Middletown, Conn.: Institute for the Future, 1971), pp. 4–5.

Franklin H. Graf, *Marketing Changes in the 70's* (Chicago: A. C. Nielsen Co., 1970).

Richard S. Lopata, "Faster Pace in Wholesaling," *Harvard Business Review,* Vol. 47 (July–August 1969), pp. 130–143.

Dennis L. Meadows, "The Predicament of Mankind," *The Futurist,* Vol. 5 (August 1971), pp. 143–144.

"The Seventies: Super but Seething," *Business Week,* December 6, 1969, p. 77. Copyright held by McGraw-Hill Book Company, Inc.

Daniel Yankelovich, "What New Life Styles Mean to Market Planners," *Marketing/Communications* (June 1971), pp. 38–45.

# NAME INDEX

# SUBJECT INDEX

Katona model, 248–249
Nicosia model, 252–254

Cargill Co., 479
Celler-Kefauver Act, 136–137
Channel of distribution, 47–48, 384–403 (see also Marketing channel)
  illustrated, 385
  in international marketing, 521–522
  for motor oil, illustrated, 410
Clayton Act, 133–134
Code for marketing researchers, 352–353
Cognitive dissonance, 246–248
Commission merchants, 52
Communications (see Marketing communications)
Comparative marketing, 64–79
  Boddewyn's framework, 69
  the nature of, 64–67
  and relationship of environment, 75–76
  Rostow's stages of development, 70–71
  the Rostow timetable, 71
  selected country comparisons, 76–78
  the study of, 67–68
    approaches to, 68–74
    limitations, 67–68
    an outline for, 71–74
    purpose, 67
Competition:
  administered prices, 107
  and differentiation, 110–112
  the hallmarks of, 117
  interchannel, 392
  and marketing research, 314–315
  monopolistic, 109–113
  nonprice, 117–118
  oligopoly, 113–116
  pure, 107–108
Consumer:
  buying motives, 194–196
  code for business relations, 577
  complaints, 564–565
  decision-making, 209, 239
  disadvantaged, 585–606

economic forces, 223–225
expectations, 184
and fashion, 198–199
importance of, 192–193
low-income, 589–599
  buying habits of, 592–596
  and guideline questions about, 603
  problems reported by, 596–599
mobility, 218–221
the mythical, 225
Negro versus white expenditures, 595
predisposition to buy, 237
tastes and preferences, 183
and trademarks, 213
Consumer behavior (see also Buyer behavior)
  structure of, 252
Consumer expenditures, 667
Consumer goods:
  classified, 198, 202, 362–363
  parallel systems theory, 362
  pricing relationships, 449
Consumerism, 559–582
  business view about, 569
  causes of, 564–568
  consumer view about, 569
  defined, 561–562
  development of movement, 560–561
  and Federal Trade Commission, 575
  government view about, 569
  meaning of, 561–562
  movement leaders, 562–563
  and National Commission on Product Safety, 574–575
  President Lyndon Johnson on, 571–572
  President John F. Kennedy on, 565–566, 570–571
  President Richard M. Nixon on, 572–573
  responses to movement, 568–579
    by business, 575–578
    by consumer, 568–570
    by government, 570–575
    other, 578–579
  right to be heard, 566
  right to be informed, 565

right to choose, 565–566
right to safety, 565
survey on, 564
the system illustrated, 563
Consumer panels, 339–340
Consumer price trends, 431
Consumer protection laws, 143–144
  demand for, 142–145
Consumption and innovation, 158
Consumption expenditures, 181, 666
Convenience goods, 202, 362
Cost of distribution, 639–645

Deceptive practices and the law, 141–145
Demand:
  consumer expectations, 184
  derived, 432, 502
  determinants of, 178–179
  discretionary income, 179–182
  disposable income, 179–182
  economics of, 177–189
  elasticity of, 185–186
  joint, 432–434
  manipulation of, 203
  and number of buyers, 185
  and price of related goods, 184–185
  and price of substitute goods, 184–185
  primary, 500–502
  selective, 501
  tastes and preferences of consumers, 183
  the willingness to buy, 182–185
Demarketing, 617–619
Delphi method, 166, 346
Differentiation:
  the basis of, 111–112
  the concept of, 110–111
Disadvantaged (see Marketing to the disadvantaged)
Discretionary income, 179–182
Disposable income, 179–182, 662
Distribution channel (see Marketing channel)
Distribution cost analysis, 645–647
Distribution systems, 383–423 (see also Logistics
  channels, 384–403
  logistics systems, 407–413

Profit analysis, 378–379
Psychological pricing, 458–459
Purchasing agents, 52
Pure competition, 107–108

Quality of life and marketing, 612–615
  ranking of states, 614

Reference groups, influence of, 221–222
Resale-price maintenance, 145–149
Research (*see also* Marketing research)
  technical, 169
Research and development, technology, 163–164
Retail sales in selected SMSAs, 97–99
Retail trade:
  and geographical structure, 95–99
  in SMSAs, 95–99
  and urbanization, 94–95
Retailers:
  attitudes toward, 588
  pricing by, 456
Retailing establishments, 53–54
  as component of marketing structure, 53–54
  nonstore retailing, 53
  number of, 54
  total sales of, 54
  types of, 53–54
Retailing in the United States, *1967,* 54
Return-on-investment pricing, 452–453
Robinson-Patman Act, 134–136
Rostow's stages of development, 70–71

Sales management, changing emphasis in, 488
Sales promotion, *defined,* 467
Selective distribution, 397
Selling agents, 52

Sherman Act, 128–130
Shopping goods, 202, 362
Social change and affluence, 672
Social evaluation of marketing, 639–645
Social marketing, 12–13
Specialization:
  regional, 6
  social and economic advantage of, 5–6
Specialty goods, 202, 362
Standard Metropolitan Statistical Areas, 95–99
Swissair's corporate objectives, 290

Tastemaker theory, 219
Technology:
  and consumerism, 566
  and consumption, 158
  feedback system, 160–162
  and firm's environment, 164–165
  forecasting of, 165–168
  and the future, 167
  impact on marketing, 157–160
  impact on society, 170–171
  and innovation, 155, 166
  and invention, 155
  the long view, 169–170
  management of, 162–163
  market development for, 171–172
  and marketing institutions, 160
  the marketplace, 160–162
  and media, 158
  in the *1960s,* 165
  and physical handling, 159
  and pricing, 158–159
  product impact, 170–171
  progress of, 157
  relationship to marketing, 168–169
  research and development, 163–164
  and selling, 158
  and society, 154–157
  visibility of, 155–156
Television Code, The, 552

3M Company, 371
Time utility, 13–14
Trade, barter, 5
Trademarks, 213, 367
Transportation, 413–415
Truth-in-Advertising Act, 471

Unethical business practices, 541 (*see also* Ethics)
United States Chamber of Commerce Code for Business-Consumer Relations, 577
Urbanization, 94–99
U.S. economy in 1980, 666

Value-added concept, 29, 639–645

Wheeler-Lea Act, 132, 471
Wholesale establishments (*see* Wholesale middlemen)
Wholesale middlemen:
  agents, 51–52
    auction companies, 51–52
    commission merchants, 52
    export agents, 52
    import agents, 52
    manufacturers' agents, 52
    merchandise brokers, 51–52
    purchasing agents, 52
    selling agents, 52
  *defined,* 49–52
  farm products assemblers, 50
  manufacturers' sales branches and offices, 50–52
  as marketing institutions, 46–53
  merchandise agents and brokers, 5
  merchant wholesalers, 50–51
  petroleum bulk stations, terminals LP gas facilities, 50
Wholesale price trends, 430
Wholesale shipments, *1967,* 29
Wholesale trade and geographical structure, 95–97
Wholesaling in the U.S., *1967,* 50
World 3, 668–669

# THE MARKETING SYSTEM

### FACILITATING AGENCIES

Advertising
Marketing research
Transportation
Credit
Storage

### WHOLESALERS

Merchant wholesalers
Merchandise agents and brokers
Manufacturers' sales branches
   and sales offices
Petroleum bulk stations,
   terminals, LP gas
Farm products assemblers

### RETAILERS

General merchandise
Building materials
Food stores
Automotive dealers
Gasoline service stations
Apparel shops
Furniture stores
Eating and drinking
Drug stores
Nonstore retailers